7

The Soviet Union in
the Third World

Also of Interest

The Soviet Union in World Politics, edited by Kurt London

The Domestic Context of Soviet Foreign Policy, edited by Seweryn Bialer

About the Book and Editor

The Soviet Union in the Third World:
Successes and Failures
edited by
Robert H. Donaldson

What are the Soviet objectives in the Third World? What instruments of foreign policy have been employed by the USSR toward the achievement of these objectives, and with what success? What are the implications of Soviet foreign policy in the Third World for the international system in general and for U.S. foreign and defense policies in particular? Twenty leading specialists address these and other questions in this analysis of Soviet involvement in Latin America, Africa, the Middle East, and Asia. Discussing the subject from both security and economic perspectives, they conclude that the influence of the USSR in the Third World remains limited and that U.S. policymakers should not overestimate the Soviet's appeal. They also emphasize the importance of economic, rather than military, measures in the U.S. approach to Third World countries.

Robert H. Donaldson is associate professor of political science and associate dean of the College of Arts and Sciences at Vanderbilt University. He has served as consultant to the Department of State on the Council on Foreign Relations, and in 1978–1979 was visiting research professor at the Strategic Studies Institute, U.S. Army War College.

The Soviet Union in the Third World: Successes and Failures

edited by
Robert H. Donaldson

Westview Press • Boulder, Colorado
Croom Helm • London, England

This volume is included in Westview's Special Studies on the Soviet Union and Eastern Europe.

Copyright © 1981 by Westview Press, Inc.

Published in 1981 in the United States of America by
    Westview Press, Inc.
    5500 Central Avenue
    Boulder, Colorado 80301
    Frederick A. Praeger, Publisher

Published in 1981 in Great Britain by
    Croom Helm Ltd.
    2-10 St John's Road
    London, SW 11

Library of Congress Catalog Card Number: 80-24261
ISBN (U.S.): 0-89158-974-0
ISBN (U.K.): 0-7099-0801-6

Composition for this book was provided by the editor.
Printed and bound in the United States of America.

CONTENTS

PART 1
THE SOVIET UNION IN LATIN AMERICA

PART 2
THE SOVIET UNION IN AFRICA AND THE MIDDLE EAST

PART 5
SUMMARY AND CONCLUSIONS

ix

TABLES

PREFACE

The chapters in this volume evolved from a conference held in September 1979 at the US Army War College, under the auspices of the Strategic Studies Institute. The conference participants, drawn from both the academic world and government, assembled in the wake of conflicts involving Soviet power and presence in Indochina and Africa, in the midst of the controversy surrounding the Carter Administration's "discovery" of a Soviet training brigade in Cuba, and just in advance of the Soviet invasion of Afghanistan.

Although the swirl of current events provided ample occasion for discussion of Soviet intentions and activities in several "hot spots" of the Third World, the conference agenda and the papers that have been collected in this volume deliberately chose a longer-range perspective. Precisely because the attention of the public and policy-makers has lately been so intensely focused on Soviet activity in Asia, Africa, the Middle East, and Latin America, with overtones of crisis and potential superpower confrontation in each region, this assessment in the larger context is so vitally needed.

In this volume twenty prominent specialists on Soviet and/or Third World politics have surveyed the record of the Soviet Union's involvement in the regions and leading countries of the Third World, with an eye toward analyzing the factors that have contributed to Soviet success or failure. In preparing their analyses, all authors focused on a set of common issues:

- What are the objectives that the Soviet Union is pursuing in Third World countries?
- What instruments of foreign policy have been employed by the USSR toward the achievement of these objectives, and with what success?
- What trends or patterns in Soviet policy have been highlighted by the history of the USSR's involvement, and how does Moscow itself assess the costs and benefits of its activities?

xiii

- What are the implications of Soviet policy in the Third World for the future stability of the international system, and in particular, for the foreign and defense policies of the United States?

A summary of the contributors' assessments of Soviet policy and of the emerging patterns of Soviet behavior is provided in Joseph Nogee's concluding chapter. By way of preview, let it be noted here that the evidence adduced in these studies is that Soviet influence in the Third World remains limited, in part by the strong impulses toward autonomy and national self-determination of the Third World countries themselves. Many of Moscow's biggest "victories" have resulted from events over which it had little or no control. Thus US policy-makers should not overestimate the appeal of the Soviet Union in the Third World or its prospects for success there. Moreover, the US, in its own choice of policy instruments in these regions, should give as much or more careful attention to the promotion of economic development and political institutionalization as to the military aspects of enhancing security.

Our grateful appreciation for hosting the conference and for assisting in preparing this volume is extended to the staff of the Strategic Studies Institute and its director, Colonel Andrew C. Remson, Jr. Special thanks are due to the Institute's publications editor, Mrs. Marianne Cowling, for directing the preparation of the manuscript, and to Cathleen Brannen and Debra Hance (of Vanderbilt University) for applying the finishing touches.

Robert H. Donaldson
Nashville, Tennessee

PART 1
THE SOVIET UNION IN LATIN AMERICA

1

SOVIET POWER IN LATIN AMERICA:
SUCCESS OR FAILURE?

W. Raymond Duncan

Soviet policy in Latin America, at least from American perspectives, is deceptively easy to analyze. Moscow's power appears increasingly to extend to previous North American spheres of influence—or threatens to do so. This apparent transition began with Cuba's turn to Marxism-Leninism in 1961, became less pronounced in the early 1970's, then spread anew with Moscow's Caribbean and Mexican ties from the mid-1970's onward. By the summer and fall of 1979—with the victory of Marxist-led pro-Cuban revolutionaries over Anastasio Somoza in Nicaragua, the ruckus over 3,000 Soviet troops in Cuba, and Fidel Castro's blatant attempt to move the sixth summit meeting of nonaligned countries toward open support of Moscow—Soviet presence in Latin America had reached crisis proportions in the minds of many influential observers, most notably in the US Congress.[1]

The 1979 perception of escalated Soviet power in the Caribbean and Latin America in turn shaped American foreign policy. It prompted Washington to demand a change in the *status quo* of Havana-based Soviet "combat" troops and produced the consequent image of a president not precisely in control of Caribbean foreign policy.[2] The threatening Soviet power image meanwhile adversely affected Strategic Arms Limitation Talks (SALT II), shaped growing negative moods about detente and the Russians in general, and added momentum toward increased military spending.[3] As a result of these events—locked into US media coverage, congressional politics, executive-congressional relations, and public opinion surrounding Soviet and Cuban policies during the summer and fall of 1979—how easy it is to assess Kremlin power in Latin America as distinctly on the rise.

Admittedly, the idea of expanding Soviet power in Latin America is a compelling image. Cuba's "surrogate" or "proxy" role under Soviet leadership is central to the case.[4] In the context of Soviet-Cuban military cooperation in Africa since 1975, any Cuban initiatives in the Caribbean or support for revolutionary leaders in Nicaragua and Central America naturally produce the assumption of Soviet conniving. Congressional responses to the Nicaraguan civil war in 1979 demonstrate this type of logic.[5] More overt Soviet influence appears in expanded diplomatic and economic ties in Latin America since the early 1960's, the sale of SU-22 fighter-bombers to Peru in 1977, and Caribbean-Mexican links with the Council for Mutual Economic Assistance (CEMA) in the late 1970's—all of which denote Moscow's keen attention to Washington's "strategic rear" in the Caribbean.[6] Meanwhile the Soviet Union continues to nourish its links with the Latin American Communist parties through multiple channels.[7] To all appearances, this record surely suggests increased Soviet power over Latin America's internal, regional and global affairs.

Looking at conditions and trends in the Caribbean and Latin America, one side of the current Soviet debate about the region argues that it is characterized by a "mounting anti-imperialist struggle for democracy and social justice," and a positive "present upsurge in the Latin American countries' struggle for economic independence."[8] The Caribbean is of special attention in this debate, with its proximity to revolutionary Cuba which has stirred "profound progressive changes in this region and raised the people's anti-imperialist struggle to a new level."[9] This "progressive" interpretation coincides with a wider belief frequently asserted by Soviet analysts that the world "correlation of forces" now is running in favor of socialism, and that the forces of capitalism, imperalism and neocolonialism, led by the United States, have entered a "protracted phase of profound difficulties."[10]

On the basis of this type of argument a number of Soviet writers naturally insist on the encouraging Latin America's economic nationalism and its regional organizations, such as the Economic System of Latin America (SELA, which includes Cuba), in an effort to weaken Washington's power. Other trends can be identified in Latin America that seem to support this interpretation that events there currently serve to strengthen the position of Moscow and the world socialist system. The quest for more control by Latin Americans over their natural resources and their territory, the expropriation of foreign multinational operations, and the spread of national liberation movements like the Sandinistas in Nicaragua or the Independistas of Puerto Rico are cases in point. From this specific Soviet point of view, then, Moscow's power is increasing in Latin America insofar as events weaken the United States and contribute to a positive correlation of socialist forces worldwide.

Easy conclusions can be drawn from this assumption of growing Soviet power in Latin America. One might conclude, for example, that a "Soviet threat" lurks behind indigenous revolutionary events or leftist civil disturbances, especially those close to home in the Caribbean and Central America where Moscow's "proxy," Cuba, operates. The conclusion naturally leads to the demand for military responses—as occurred in the Dominican Republic in 1965 and as was advocated in Nicaragua in 1979.[11] This type of military response argument rests upon the assumption that Soviet-backed Cuban action in Africa will likely be replicated in Latin America and the Caribbean, thus largely conditioning events there to the detriment of US interests, or at least that Soviet and Cuban military strength is *capable* of projection into Latin America and the Caribbean.

Aside from the possibility of a Soviet-backed Cuban military thrust, there is the prospect that Marxism-Leninism will spread through the Communist parties of the region, strengthened through continued Soviet and Cuban ties with these parties. Delegations of Latin American Communist parties continue to circulate through Moscow, and Havana convened major meetings of Latin American Communist parties in 1975 and in 1977. This type of analysis would stress, moreover, that despite the setback to continental

3

communism in Chile after 1973, Mexican Communist Party membership grew from 5,000 in 1973 to approximately 60,000 in 1977, with the Mexican Communist Party in 1978 becoming fully legal and capable of participating in elections.[12] Communist party membership also registered growth in Colombia, the Dominican Republic, Ecuador, Honduras, Nicaragua, Peru, and Venezuela from 1972 to 1977.[13] In the Caribbean it could be argued, the full impact of Soviet and Cuban ties has not yet been felt, but the 1977 return from Cuba of a Jamaican youth construction brigade, determined to organize itself into a movement along Marxist-Leninist lines, is ominous.[14]

Another possible conclusion from this prognosis of expanding Marxism-Leninism is that the underlying problem in Latin America is strictly economic, demanding more US economic aid. The conclusion rests upon the deterioration in many Latin American and Caribbean economies juxtaposed against the precipitous decline in US-Latin American relations during the 1970's caused by conflicts over international economic matters. The latter is mirrored in the sharpening identification of Latin American leaders with the Third World drive for a New International Economic Order, in Venezuela and Ecuadorian participation in oil increases through the Organization of Petroleum Exporting Countries (OPEC) since 1973, and in the post-1975 operation of SELA. These events, which Moscow cites as evidence of deteriorating US power in Latin America, drive home the Latin American focus on economic development and dissatisfaction with Washington's legendary treatment of the region as of secondary importance in global affairs except in times of violent crisis.[15]

These types of conclusions, resting upon the notion of expanded Soviet power in the Caribbean and Latin America, merit closer attention if we are to separate illusion from reality in the search for appropriate US policy responses. Is Soviet policy in Latin America as influential as it may at first appear? Is the record of Soviet diplomacy in the region one of unconditioned "success"? These questions are explored in this paper as we identify the discernible features of recent Soviet-Latin American relations, while suggesting some of the less perceptible underlying aspects of the relationship. The paper is divided into three sections: Soviet objectives; instruments of Soviet policy; and, implications for the United States.

SOVIET OBJECTIVES

Moscow's objectives in Latin America, as best we can determine from available data, are a product of the recent escalated importance of Third World affairs in Soviet perspective.[16] Especially since 1975, when Angola opened the path to increased Soviet involvement in Africa, the Third World has become a major setting of Soviet policy initiative.[17] Some of its regions are imperative to Soviet security (the periphery countries), while others offer Moscow the opportunity to play an interventionist superpower role in behalf of strengthening the world socialist system (Angola, Ethiopia, Vietnam). The Third World, in short, has come to play an enormous part in Soviet international relations perceptions, for as Soviet writers see it, "these countries have an ever-growing influence in world politics and economics" and "the identity of anti-imperalist aspirations within the national liberation struggle is the cornerstone of the Soviet Union's cooperation with the developing countries."[18]

But what of specific Soviet objectives in Latin America? Here we enter murky terrain. For Soviet analysts now seem engaged in a major debate over Latin American conditions and trends. One school of thought, as suggested above, adopts the line that "progressive forces" are on the ascendancy. A second line of argument, in contrast, depicts the area as essentially one of "dependent capitalism" where the growth of foreign control and US multinational corporate interests predominate.[19] The first view of Latin America is optimistic regarding Soviet ability to ride with the tide of economic nationalism and to help in a variety of ways to encourage the weakening of US economic power south of the Rio Grande. The second image is pessimistic about Moscow's ability to influence economic development along socialist lines in Latin America and about any short term emergence of economic independence within the region.

Measuring these two arguments against the recent pattern of Soviet diplomatic, economic, technical, and trade relations with Latin America, a portrait of traditional power politics emerges. It is one where the Soviets envision limited opportunities to erode US and Western influence, but where the region remains of a lower priority than Africa and Asia. The possibility of an imminent transition to socialism and communism through expanded state

5

sector economic development does not seem large in Soviet perspectives, and in this measure the era is distinctly different than the early days of the Cuban revolution and the exuberant optimism of Nikita Khruschev.

One key area of opportunity for the Soviet Union, if we examine the amount of Soviet writing on the subject, lies in the arena of raw materials.[20] Moscow analysts appear encouraged by nationalization of foreign concerns in the region, such as Kaiser Reynolds and Alcoa Aluminum in Jamaica, and by any moves toward formation of regional raw materials organizations, e.g. the International Bauxite Association that includes Guyana, Jamaica, and the Dominican Republic. While Latin American control over strategic raw materials by no means implies that the Soviet Union will somehow be able to encourage these countries to deny them to the United States, it does open the door for increased access on Moscow's part. Any redirection of raw materials trade of this type during the last quarter of the 20th century, in the context of shrinking global supplies of raw materials and increasing world demands, helps the Soviets in the game of power politics and great power status.[21] Here it should be noted that Latin America indeed possesses valuable raw materials—oil in Ecuador, Mexico, Trinidad/Tobago and Venezuela, with lesser quantities in other countries and potentially substantial quantities in the Caribbean; coal in Brazil; iron ore in Brazil, Mexico and Venezuela; uranium in Argentina, Brazil and Mexico.[22] Recent Soviet aid and trade patterns show a trend toward highlighting energy products in Latin America, especially hydroelectric projects—a trend which suggests that Moscow wants to keep its doors open to Latin American resources by aiding those countries in need of energy-producing assistance. This aim is underscored by the Soviet Union's courtship of countries which are military-ruled (Argentina, Brazil, and Peru for example), do not especially promote the lot of local Communist organizations, are permeated by the transnational corporations of western capitalism and "imperalism" (Peru excepted), but whose territories contain commodities and raw materials strategically important to the Soviet Union as well as to the United States.[23]

The Soviet Union, in another dimension of its pragmatic approach to Latin America, is keen on keeping its solid relationship with Cuba intact. So long as Cuba's foreign policy continued to sail in directions familiar on the Soviet charts—broad fronts of nonmilitary struggle in the Americas, support of nationalism in its

6

diverse anti-imperalist economic and political forms, care in continuing an anti-Chinese profile, adherence to recognized diplomatic state-to-state relations—Moscow's leverage in Latin America and the Caribbean can be strengthened.[24] For not only can Cuba conduct military policies in Africa that a Russian superpower cannot risk, Havana similarly can act as a leading edge in Soviet-supported projects in Latin America, such as diplomatic support for Puerto Rican independence, overthrow of the Somoza regime in Nicaragua, or strengthening the economic development of Caribbean states along expanded state-sector profiles, as in Guyana and especially (lately) Jamaica. This is due simply to Cuba's greater acceptance generally in that region as a legitimate member of the "Latin American family," defined in cultural, ethnic, historic, and national terms. Cuba is also a key maritime strategic piece on Moscow's global chessboard, as well as a port of call for merchant marine fishing fleet operations, trade activities, and oceanographic work. In this context should be noted Cuba's spectacular growth in merchant marine operations, as well as the Soviet Union's own merchant marine development since World War II, compared to that of the United States.[25] Not surprisingly, then, many a Soviet pronouncement on Latin American affairs cites Cuba's importance in the international relations of the region.

The Soviet Union appears to be acutely aware of the force of nationalism in Latin America. A composite of national entities, the USSR has survived internal national agitation for years and faces it daily in domestic political affairs, as well as externally in East European states. Any Latin American movement to regain national control over raw materials, economic life, or physical territory thus strikes a sensitive nerve in the Russian psyche. Among the nationalist forces now at work in Latin America are the vocal and persuasive economic nationalisms of energy-producing giants, Mexico and Venezuela, whose resources carry significant weight today in Latin American-US relations and potentially much more weight in the future as energy supplies diminish. And how attractive to Moscow must be the "national liberation movements" in Guatemala, El Salvador, Nicaragua, Puerto Rico, and Belize. The Caribbean, meanwhile is aflame with its own forms of leftist nationalism—in Guyana, Jamaica, and now, Grenada, where the New Jewel Movement led by Prime Minister Maurice Bishop staged a leftist coup in March 1979.[26] Nationalism is alive and kicking in

7

Latin America and the Caribbean. It takes distinct forms, but always carries the seed of independence from US domination—a point not missed by Soviet officials.

In its overall approach to Latin America, Moscow continues to promote the values of Marxism-Leninism, principally through the pro-Soviet "broad peaceful front" Communist parties of Latin America. These parties in some respects reflect favorable trends for Moscow, despite the setback in Chile for Communist party membership after September 1973, and it is not unusual to find continued Soviet emphasis on the role of Communist parties. Where only four Communist parties were legal in 1972 (Colombia, Cuba, Mexico, and Venezuela), ten were either legal or tolerated by 1977.[27] A number of parties boosted their membership substantially by late 1977, as in the cases of Cuba (125,000 in 1972 to 204,000 in 1977), Mexico (5,000 in 1972 to 60,000 in 1977), and Venezuela (8,000 in 1972 to 10,000 in 1977).

Yet it would be erroneous to identify direct promotion of communism in Latin America as extraordinarily high on the Soviet agenda—as high, say, as support of Latin American nationalism through legitimate state-to-state relations. Despite the Soviet willingness to welcome delegates from the pro-Soviet Latin American Communist parties to the capital, the Kremlin continues to pursue active diplomatic, trade, and technical assistance programs in countries where Communist parties are proscribed (Bolivia, Brazil, Uruguay), where the government makes life difficult for Marxists associated with guerrilla movements (as in Argentina in the mid 1970's), and where transnational corporations strongly link the Latin American countries with western capitalism. A distinct pragmatism, then, underscores Soviet objectives—an inclination to ride with Latin American nationalist aspirations rather than trying to force-feed doctrinaire Marxism-Leninism to unwilling subjects. Here it should be stressed that apart from Fidel Castro, Latin America simply has not produced the rash of new Communist leaders found in Africa and Asia, where seven pro-Soviet Communist parties have seized power or territory with armed force since 1975 (Vietnam, Laos, Angola, Ethiopia, Afghanistan, South Yemen, Cambodia).[28] Moscow faces a different set of realities and opportunities in the western hemisphere compared to those in Africa and the periphery countries.

8

The Soviets are conscious of a Chinese challenge to their Latin American presence, and they seek to check it when and where possible. As the Soviets interpret the situation, the Chinese thrust in Latin America is essentially "anti-Soviet" in nature and, moreover, helps to consolidate US "imperialism" in the region.[29] Moscow worries—at least in available published literature—about Peking's propaganda campaign against the Soviet Union in Latin America, which began to gather steam in the early 1970's.[30] Since then Peking's diplomatic, trade, economic, and military delegations to Latin America increased in what Soviet writers describe as the "intensive Chinese drive in Latin America."[31] Here it should be noted that the PRC established diplomatic relations in Chile in 1970, and it gave diplomatic recognition to the new conservative military government of Augusto Pinochet in 1973. This followed with diplomatic ties to Peru in 1971; Argentina, Guyana, Mexico, and Jamaica in 1972; Brazil, Venezuela, and Trinidad/Tobago in 1974; Surinam in 1976; and Barbados in 1977. And the Caribbean region began to receive special PRC attention in 1978, with a trade delegation travelling to Jamaica, Trinidad/Tobago, Guyana, and Mexico.[32]

These relations provided the Chinese with the opportunity to make life unpleasant for the Soviets. "Anti-Soviet" and "Anti-Cuban" statements were published during these forays, which accused the Soviet Union and Cuba of "jeopardizing the international balance of forces by their actions in Africa," and charged that Cubans were in effect the "Trojan horse of Soviet claims to hegemony in the Caribbean area."[33] China also began to make trade inroads in Latin America, as new trade ties with Brazil indicated. These links augmented previous trade relations with Argentina and Chile. Brazil's trade with mainland China in fact is expected to reach $200 million in 1979.[34] The Soviet Union, in short, clearly perceives the PRC as a diplomatic and trade challenge, not only with the strategically located and large Latin American countries, but also in the Caribbean.

SOVIET OBJECTIVES IN PERSPECTIVE

This overview of Soviet objectives establishes a point of departure for analyzing more deeply the nuances of Moscow's power in the Latin American setting. First, Moscow's policies in

9

the region strike one as essentially those of a great power in quest of traditional great power concerns. These include at minimum the search for influence to guarantee territorial security in the long run, access to markets and resources so necessary for economic prosperity—increasingly so as global demand and lesser supply pressures mount—and a generally cautious and pragmatic assessment of opportunities. Although Moscow's objectives turn in part upon ideological considerations, reflected in the continued support of Latin American Communist parties and of state-controlled economic enterprises rather than those in the private sector, Soviet national interests appear to be defined primarily in terms of economic and political power. This is not to say that Marxist-Leninist ideology does not condition Soviet conceptions of power; quite the contrary. But it does suggest that the direct promotion of communism in Latin America is overshadowed by the interests of Moscow as an evolving great power with traditional world requirements—particularly in terms of its ideologically and territorially perceived adversaries, the United States and mainland China.

Moscow's pragmatic approach to Latin American affairs is explained in part by dìffèrent types of data that can be found "between the lines" of the identifiable objectives spelled out above. The economic ledger reveals that Soviet and East European credits extended to Latin American countries concentrate on trading heavy industrial machinery and equipment for natural resources, e.g., alumina from Jamaica (the Soviets may be running out of alumina), sugar from Cuba, grain and meat from Argentina—plus an interest in Mexican and Venezuelan oil. The data also indicates that Moscow does not wish to become overburdened with aid programs in Latin America, undoubtedly due to the Soviet Union's own internal economic difficulties, the overt pessimism in some quarters over Moscow's ability to alter the "dependent capitalism" of Latin America, and already high cost of the Cuban game.[35] Moscow meanwhile is running a heavy trade imbalance with Latin American countries, who prefer traditional Western goods and who drew only $525 million of the $2.4 billion of Communist credits extended between 1959 and 1977.[36] It is perhaps no surprise that Soviet economic credits to Latin America appear to have fallen off sharply by 1977—a pattern consistent with general Soviet-Third World aid, where new commitments fell more than 50 percent from 1976, and 60 percent below the average for the 5 previous years.[37]

Political data equally suggest caution in Soviet-Latin American affairs. Moscow certainly continues to send its CPSU delegations to visit Latin American Communist leaders, and the latter are still welcomed in the Soviet Union.[38] And the Kremlin is not short on media support of "national liberation movements," such as in Nicaragua, where Soviet media coverage escalated sharply from January 1978 onwards.[39] The United Nations decision to declare Puerto Rico a "colony" of the United States—a position long advocated in the United Nations Decolonization Committee by Cuba—also received strong coverage from the USSR.[40] Yet on the whole, the political posture is one of formal state-to-state relations with established governments, trade and aid even with conservative military regimes (Argentina and Brazil), a low-key approach to certain crisis events in the backyard of the United States (Nicaragua and Panama), and even tacit support for a Cuban-US rapprochement.[41]

In the military sphere, the situation in Latin America contrasts sharply with Soviet policy in Africa, the Middle East, and Asia, where overt military support of Marxist movements is clear. The only military aid agreement in Latin America (outside of Cuba) is with Peru, while no direct military involvement with Nicaraguan Sandinistas or Puerto Rican Independistas can be identified. It must be said, however, that Cuba plays an indirect supportive role in these two cases.[42] The Soviet Union, then, is clearly unwilling to risk open confrontation in a geographical region where sensitive US interests abound.

STRATEGIC CONCERNS

In pursuing great power interests in Latin America, the Soviet Union is conscious of countries and regions that are strategically important to Moscow's own interests or to the United States. By the late 1970's, Soviet ties were markedly emphasized with Argentina (traditionally independent in US-Latin American affairs), Brazil (where President Jimmy Carter's statements on human rights and nuclear energy had strained US-Brazilian ties), Mexico (with clear problems over issues of natural gas sales and emigration to the United States), and Venezuela (under an oil-conscious Third World leader, Carlos Andres Perez). The

Caribbean area in particular rated increased Soviet attention, especially Guyana and Jamaica, which moved more closely to Moscow and Havana through diplomatic, economic, and trade relations from the mid-1970's onwards.

A number of key developments in the late 1970's bear out this observation. The Argentine government announced in November 1978 that Moscow had been awarded a 2-year contract to work on the Parana Medio hydroelectric project, which paved the way for more lucrative contracts for turbines and generators worth about $2.5 billion.[43] The visit to Moscow of the Mexican President, Jose Lopez Portillo, in May 1978 resulted in a new scientific and technical cooperation project for 1978-79, along with cultural, sports, educational, and social sciences agreements.[44] Prime Minister Forbes Burnham of Guyana visited the Soviet Union in April 1978, followed by Prime Minister Michael Manley of Jamaica in April 1979.[45] Guyana's efforts led to a Soviet agreement to expand its fishing fleet and to help expand alumina production, while the Jamaican trip led to new agreements in sports, broadcasting, cultural affairs, and air service. Moscow's ties with Cuba, meanwhile, remained stronger than ever. The Soviets thus appeared to be casting their nets in the most likely fishing spots, reaching toward key Caribbean and Latin American countries.

Soviet pragmatism, again, must be defined in terms of pronounced awareness of just how tenacious is private foreign capital, led by the United States, in the Latin American setting. One Soviet writer noted that:

> direct private investments, which, despite the rather wide measures to nationalize foreign property in a number of Latin American countries, continued to grow. At present they are assessed at approximately $40 billion.[46]

Later in the same article, he commented upon the new "joint companies" of Latin America that give host countries more control:

> As a rule, foreign capital...continues to control the joint companies where it has only minority participation...This has placed the Latin American countries in a position of extreme technological dependence on the imperalist states...Latin America has in fact become meshed in a neo-colonial system of financial dependence, according to figures for the end of 1977 fiscal year, its foreign debt exceeded $100 billion.[47]

12

This theme of American capital's strong position in Latin America indicates how Soviet theorists think in power categories, which in this case finds the United States in a still dominant position.

To the extent that Soviet objectives in Latin America operate around power concepts, conditioned by Marxist-Leninist ideological modes of thought, there appear complexities in analyzing Soviet foreign policy in this region of the world. The "Soviet threat," for example, appears somewhat less urgent than a superficial look at the record suggests. The Soviets appear careful about where and how they become involved and under what conditions. They seem to be aware of limitations and constraints to their power in Latin America. And the limits to Soviet power are there. Moscow's presence, moreover, does not result in a unilinear equation with influence—economic credits have been extended, but few are accepted. Trade imbalances with Latin American countries run against the USSR, and Latin American countries strongly prefer Western goods. Meanwhile, the Soviets must compete for Latin American markets and materials not only with the United States, but also with West European countries and with Japan. The objective of spreading communism is in fact seen to be of lesser priority than riding with nationalist aspirations—and this could become a useful lesson for American policymakers.

All of this is not to say that American policy can drift because the Soviet ship is caught in the doldrums, for it is not. Given Latin American history and traditional power structures, the Soviet Union has in fact remarkably expanded its relations in the area. And from the Soviets' view, this certainly opens up the number of options compared to pre-Castro days. Future opportunities can be created for Moscow by a variety of conditions, not least being an ineffective US policy toward the region.

INSTRUMENTS OF SOVIET POLICY

The Soviet Union, like the United States, has a number of policy instruments that can be orchestrated in pursuit of its objectives. Economic aid, trade, propaganda, diplomatic ties, cultural exchanges, and technical assistance are the typical instruments utilized by Moscow in its Latin American relations. Beyond these identifiable policy forms, the Soviet Union enjoys a special instrument of power in Latin America that is not available to the

United States—a client state whose domestic policies in many cases parallel the objectives of other modernizing political groups in the region. Here the role of Cuba, as well as of Latin America's local Communist parties, must be assessed in terms of Soviet instruments of power-seeking in the region.

When we move into the realm of evaluating the effectiveness of these instruments of power, however, a special set of questions must be addressed. For the degree to which these policy instruments in fact produce a Soviet influence over Latin American events does not turn upon the mere *presence* of an extended number of economic credits from Moscow, the signing of a scientific and technical cooperation agreement, or the distribution of Marxist-Leninist literature by a local Communist party. We need to probe to what extent Latin American events might have gone (or will go) in specific directions, whether or not the Soviets were present.[48] This essential proposition leads to seveal key questions.

These questions suggest just how difficult it is to make judgements about the impact of Moscow's activities in other countries. To what degree do the Soviets actually control political and economic outcomes in Latin America? How sensitive and vulnerable is a given Latin American country to Soviet influence-seeking? What capacity does Moscow have to deliver what a Latin American country may want? And how entangled has Moscow become in the globally interdependent system which limits *all* states in their pursuit of power?[49] Moscow, for example, is in domestic economic difficulty, relies upon external capital goods and food for continued development, and faces increasing energy demands internally and from its external clients (East European states) under an increasingly cloudy supply future. What effect do these trends have on Soviet policy?

It is not easy, then, to produce a simple assessment of Soviet "successes" or "failures" in terms of how effective its instruments of power operate to produce *influence* for Moscow over Latin American events. But it must be stressed that power increasingly is not a one-way direct route of one country over another. What appears to be Soviet influence may in fact be a reverse situation of a Latin American country gaining the leverage over outcomes favorable to its own self-perceived objectives, as illustrated by the imbalance in Soviet trade in favor of the Latin American countries. Cuba illustrates this too in its ability to receive over $9 million per

14

day in assistance from Moscow and support for an African policy favorable to its own foreign policy posture. The failure of Moscow to support strongly the Salvador Allende government between 1970-73, the substantial number of undrawn economic credits and continued favoring of Western over Soviet goods by the Latin American countries, and the economic drain on Moscow produced by Cuba—which limits aid programs elsewhere—all these events portray an image of less Soviet capacity to deliver what the Latin Americans want than at first meets the eye.[50]

We face also the difficulty of *defining* "success". If we do so in terms of direct Soviet influence in weakening the United States in Latin America, in strengthening the state sectors of Latin American economies, in forging Latin American nationalism, or in spawning communism, we run into various types of analytical problems. For where indeed is the correlation between what Moscow does with its policy instruments and what happens in Latin America? In fact, when we shift the kaleidoscope of analytic variables from Soviet-Latin American to US-Latin American relations, or to internal Latin American forces, we perceive different systematic relationships.

It can well be argued that Washington's weakened position is principally a consequence of US responses to Latin American demands. By this is meant essentially the absence of effective aid, diplomatic, and trade policies to deal with Latin America's growing economic nationalism, and growing grass roots rebellions against conservative ruling elites.[51] It is not that Washington had no policy—President Carter's human rights posture shows the contrary—but the *economic* options either were not effectively played, (as in the natural gas debate with Mexico only recently partly resolved), or were blocked by Congress, as is continually the case with favorable tariffs and higher aid. Latin America's economic nationalism is not produced by Moscow but from the unique internal conditions of each Latin American country, and one doubts seriously the ability of Moscow to control the winds of nationalism in Latin America once they begin to blow.[52] Latin American communism, meanwhile, beats with a distinct national impulse, a point certainly underscored by events in Cuba and Mexico, and by Allende when he became the first Communist elected to power. Just how much the Soviet Union can influence the nature and scope of Latin America's national Communists is a subject ripe for debate.

15

The special case of Cuba as an instrument of Soviet policy in Latin America bears examination. Certainly it is true that Cuba can advocate and pursue policies favorable to Moscow, such as strengthening "national liberation movements" (as in Nicaragua and Puerto Rico) while supporting left leaning governments (as in Guyana and Jamaica). Havana also serves as an outspoken Latin American critic of the United States—once a more or less lone voice in the region, but now joined by a number of other regional compatriots. Havana, moreover, is a visible regional supporter of pro-Soviet Communist parties, through its hosting of regional Communist party meetings. It also plays a vital role in the nonaligned movement, drawing Latin American countries into common alliances against the developed world, led by the United States, as in its role of host to the September 1979 meeting of nonaligned countries in Havana. And it must be said that as a small nonthreatening Caribbean island with unique experiments in economic, educational, and cultural modernization—poised against the North American Goliath—the island has a certain attraction (and hence influence) for other Caribbean leftists.[53] As a model to be emulated in certain respects, Cuba may carry more direct weight in the Caribbean than does the Soviet Union.

While the immediate influence of Cuba since the early 1970's cannot be discounted, its longer run effectiveness in support of pro-Soviet positions should be examined. Havana's dependence on Soviet aid reduces its capacity to extend enormous economic support in the Caribbean. This point is underlined by Havana's own acknowledged economic difficulties, which may be resolved partially through new trade relations with the United States at some future date. Cuba's African interventions also have raised problems in the nonaligned movement, which could spill over into Latin American and Caribbean politics.[54] Third, Cuba's national communism is acceptable to the USSR today, but what of tomorrow? The island has its own perceived role to play in Caribbean relations, and what will happen if and when Washington and Havana restore full diplomatic and economic ties?

This brief overview of Soviet instruments of power on the whole indicates that Moscow is substantially constrained in the actual influence that it exerts in Latin America. Limits arise in part from the multiple channels open to Latin American nationalists in pursuit of their development-oriented objectives, so pronounced since World War II. These channels reduce western hemispheric vulnerability and sensitivity to Soviet policies. Latin American governments now trade with and receive technical assistance from Western European countries, as well as from Japan and mainland China—and this diversified trade pattern includes Cuba. They also listen to Western and US radio broadcasts, see US movies, and read books and literature printed in the United States—as countervailing pressures to the Soviet radio broadcasts in Spanish, Soviet movies and local pro-Soviet Communist party literature.[55] Constraints to Moscow's influence arise, moreover, from the continued economic appeal and capacity of western capital, despite Moscow's attempts to discredit these channels, a point clearly recognized by those Soviet analysts stressing Moscow's "dependent capitalism" profile.[56]

Soviet instruments of power in Latin America are conditioned by Moscow's evolving global interdependence and consequent vulnerability to outside world pressures. Moscow faces future energy shortages measured against client state demands, raw materials depletion in light of Soviet domestic needs, and the economic costs at home and abroad of weapons production versus nonmilitary capital investment demands for sustaining economic development.[57] If Washington's leaders find Latin American issues difficult to comprehend after living in close proximity for all these years, the Soviet leaders may find them unfathomable, to the detriment of effective policy. This is due in part to their cultural and geographic distance from Latin America. In light of the costs and benefits of getting too deeply involved in Latin America, especially in the context of global interdependence and the geographical proximity of other Third World regions which offer greater opportunities for Soviet influence, the Kremlin undoubtedly is all the less inclined to go much beyond Cuba in large measure.

IMPLICATIONS FOR THE UNITED STATES

Soviet policy in Latin America, while of limited influence on regional events, provides a helpful analytic medium for development of appropriate US policy guidelines. It suggests, for example, that the region is going through a volatile period of change, where economic and political nationalism take distinct forms replete with opportunities and pitfalls for the United States.

It also highlights the nature of global interdependence, of which the United States is a part, whereby all states are becoming increasingly sensitive and vulnerable to each other's foreign policy actions.[58] This phenomenon is especially (but not exclusively) true of the areas of energy and raw materials supply and demand. Moscow's search for energy, raw materials and trade markets in Latin America illustrates the region's role in the interdependent great power game—a game from which the United States cannot isolate itself.

The nature of the Soviet threat is not indirect military action or expansionist Marxism-Leninism. It is more through the encouragement of other events detrimental to US interests: a decrease in available energy and natural resource exports through nationalization of US and other western private foreign holdings; the forging of alliances between Moscow and potentially important countries of the future—Puerto Rico (if it becomes independent), the Caribbean states (Jamaica and Guyana), Brazil, Mexico, and Venezuela. As a dynamic region in which Soviet policies accentuate the stakes of the game, Latin America more than ever requires effective US policy responses.

Advocating hasty military action, as occurred on the eve of the overthrow of General Anastasio Somoza Debayle in July 1979, does not seem warranted. Rather than attempting to stop nationalist movements by military efforts, the United States would be wiser to ride with them, as in fact Washington began to do in Nicaragua once the Sandinistas achieved power.[59] Increased economic aid to Latin America is called for, but not in isolation from an effective trade policy. This guideline means increased recognition of Latin American aspirations expressed through support of the New International Economic Order, and a willingness to ride with radical nationalist policies. So much of Soviet activity in Latin America is a result of deteriorating US-Latin American ties; to improve those relations in the economic realm is to weaken Soviet options.

In gearing US policy to the economic and political nationalism which guides much of the Soviet-Latin American patterns, certain countries are especially critical. Restoring economic and full diplomatic ties with *Cuba,* rather than using the promise of ties as leverage for an African retreat, makes sense for the United States. To strengthen Cuba's economic development program is to fortify internal historic nationalist roots, to improve Havana's negotiating strength with the USSR, and perhaps even to weaken Cuba's perception of North America as leader of the "imperialist camp." *Mexico* is another case in point. Without belaboring the obvious, US-Mexican interdependence is notorious—a mixture of US energy needs, Mexico's need for emigration and employment outlets into the United States, and other issues which bring the two countries close together.[60]

To leave these issues unattended in Cuba and Mexico—not to mention similar economic development issues in Central America in view of the Sandinista victory—is bad policy. Inattention also invites Cuban and Soviet overtures which in turn distort the realities of Soviet influence, setting the scene for inappropriate policy responses to a perceived "Soviet threat." Better to act in ways that minimize the Latin American attraction toward ties with the USSR in the first place, thus helping to keep the horizons clear for rational policy debates in the US Congress and public.[61] Would not more economic attention to Puerto Rico, for example, serve as a showplace for improved US-Latin American ties?

One final point merits consideration. All too frequently, the American executive branch, the legislature or the media describes events in Latin America in distorted broad terms, e.g., the "red tide," "Soviet threat," or "another Cuba" in the making—referring most recently to Central America since the Sandinista victory in Nicaragua.[62] The uniqueness of each political setting, the vastly complicated global arena of interdependence to which each Latin American state is linked, and the distinct elements of nationalism in each country are submerged in greatly oversimplified portraits of reality. This simplifying of the Latin American setting is to be seen in the degree to which Washington underestimated the likelihood of a Sandinista victory in Nicaragua (somewhat like the case of Iran earlier), overlooked the weakness of Communism in the Dominican Republic in April 1965, or underestimated the strength of Castro in Cuba in 1961. Nationalism, in short, remains to be fully understood in Latin America as it affects communism in Soviet and US policy.

CONCLUSION

Soviet policy in Latin America, as in other Third World regions, must be assessed in light of regional Latin American conditions.

Study of Moscow's objectives and policy instruments in isolation from the regional and global arena may impute more power to the USSR than in fact exists. Regional and world forces conditioning Soviet performance also help to explain not only the existing constraints on Soviet influence but also the nature of trends that will shape the pattern of future Soviet successes and failures. Finally, the regional and international contours of Soviet foreign policy suggest policy guidelines appropriate for America's foreign posture, provided that a consensus on American national interests emerges from US public, private, and governmental interest groups and bureaucratic agencies. Constraints on Soviet policy in Latin America are built into the global setting in which Moscow finds itself in the last quarter of the 20th century. Perhaps the concept of global "interdependence" best captures this situation. By this term is meant that Moscow is sensitive and vulnerable to outside pressures—as are all countries in the game of modern international politics. These external pressures increasingly include the need for access to energy, food, markets, raw materials, and technology. The politics and economics behind the need for these items, defined in terms of supply and demand, mean that Soviet policy is not a simple formula of calculated objectives and executed procedures which bring forth automatic and total success. The situation is rather a constant trade-off between desired and attained goals, between policies pursued and constraints that check. Interdependence forces us to evaluate the costs and benefits in Soviet policy toward Latin America and other regions, as well as the constraints on a one-way power flow from Moscow into the Latin American region.

Nationalism in Latin America forms a regional force working against Soviet policy as much or more than a current to be guided by external Soviet pressures. Its form and content varies from country to country in Latin America, just as it does in, say, Egypt or Somalia—countries where the Soviets were asked recently to pack their bags. The essential point here is that nationalism, rooted deep in indigenous traditions and ethnic conditions, is a constant barrier to Soviet penetration—the guardian of *sui generis* domestic conditions and foreign policies in the long run. This point applies to Cuba as well as to Mexico or Nicaragua, and it teaches a lesson that bears far more attention from Washington than has been the case during the recent era in US-Latin American affairs.

ENDNOTES

1. See the full page *New York Times* appeal by US Congressmen to President Carter, urging him to not allow "another Cuba" in Nicaragua. The appeal, with 125 signatures, depicts a Soviet arm (bearing the hammer and sickle) drawn across the island of Cuba, thrusting a large sickle into Nicaragua. *The New York Times,* June 18, 1979. The announcement of Soviet troops was made on August 30, 1979, simultaneous with the opening of the sixth summit conference of nonaligned countries in Havana. See *The New York Times, The Washington Post* and the *Christian Science Monitor* from August 30 onward.

2. *The New York Times,* September 6, 1979. Moscow categorically asserted that the Soviet military personnel were in Cuba strictly for training purposes. See *Pravda,* September 11, 1979. On the political effects of the administration's overreaction to the Soviet troop matter, see *The New York Times,* September 16, 1969, Section 4, p. 2.

3. US media coverage between August 30 and September 20, 1979 details these trends. The Senate approved a $3.2 billion increase in defense spending on September 18, 1979. Rochester, New York, *Democrat and Chronicle,* September 19, 1979.

4. For an argument that Cuba is a "surrogate" force of the USSR, which the Soviets can use to project power, see International Institute for Strategic Studies, *Strategic Survey 1978,* London, pp. 13-14. By mid-1978 Cuba had 17,000 troops in Ethiopia, 20,000 in Angola, and 3,000 elsewhere in Africa.

5. See the advertisement referred to in note 1.

6. V. Vasilyev, "The United States' 'New Approach' to Latin America," *International Affairs,* (Moscow), No. 6, June 1971, p. 43.

7. For a recent discussion of Latin America's Communist parties, see Richard F. Staar, ed., *Yearbook of International Communist Affairs 1978,* ed. *et. al.,* Stanford: Hoover Institution Press, 1978, pp. xxvii-xxviii; pp. 331-438.

8. L. Klochkovsky, "The Struggle for Economic Emancipation in Latin America," *International Affairs,* April 1979, pp. 39-47.

9. V. Yakubov, "Behind the Screen of the 'New Approach'," *Pravda,* March 2, 1978 in *Foreign Broadcast Information Service (FBIS),* March 7, 1978, USSR International Affairs.

10. *Pravda,* January 6, 1978, in *FBIS,* January 11, 1978.

11. Secretary of State Cyrus R. Vance called for the urgent consideration of an inter-American peace force to restore order and democracy in Nicaragua on June 21, 1979. *The New York Times,* June 22, 1979. See also the congressional appeal to President Carter cited in note 1.

12. The Mexican Communist Party made its first electoral appearance in the July 1979 congressional elections and won 10 to 15 percent in low-income areas of Mexico City. It received only 1 to 2 percent in each district outside the capital.

13. See *Yearbook of International Communist Affairs 1978,* p. xxiii.

14. *Christian Science Monitor,* November 30, 1977, quoting from the *Daily Gleaner,* Jamaica.

15. On Soviet perceptions of these trends see L. Klochkovsky, "The Struggle for Economic Emancipation in Latin America," *International Affairs,* April 1979, pp. 43-44. On the special importance Moscow attaches to Caribbean unity in the face of US "imperialism," see *Pravda,* March 2, 1978, in *FBIS,* March 7, 1978.

21

16. See *Strategic Survey 1978,* pp. 13-14.

17. See two illuminating essays on recent Soviet attention to the Third World: Donald Zagoria, "Into the Breach: New Soviet Alliances in the Third World," *Foreign Affairs,* Vol. 57, No. 4, Spring 1979, pp. 733-754; and Robert Legvold, "The Super Rivals: Conflict in the Third World," *Foreign Affairs, Ibid.,* pp. 755-778.

18. Professor K. Brutents, "The Soviet Union and the Newly-Independent Countries," *International Affairs,* April 1979, pp. 3-4.

19. See Victor Volsky, "Relative Maturity, Absolute Dependence," *World Marxist Review,* June 1979, pp. 40-45.

20. See L. Klochkovsky, pp. 39-47. Also V. Vasilyev, p. 43; and G. Kim, "The Successes of the National Liberation Movement and World Politics," *International Affairs,* February 1979, pp. 84-89; *Pravda,* March 2, 1978, in *FBIS,* March 7, 1978 (where the Caribbean is cited as a special region of "profound progressive changes"); and *Pravda,* April 5, 1978, in *FBIS,* April 12, 1978 (where the nature of the present epoch in Latin America is described as the "transition from capitalism to socialism," led by the "victory of the Cuban revolution.").

21. On the Soviet Union's general quest for great power status during the postwar period, see Robert Legvold's insightful essay, "The Nature of Soviet Power," in *Foreign Affairs,* Vol. 56, No. 1, October 1977, pp. 49-71. See also James Reston's interview with Zbigniew Brzezinski, "The World According to Brzezinski," *The New York Times Magazine,* December 31, 1978, pp. 9-12. The increasing importance of Soviet access to markets and raw materials in the last quarter of the 20th century—and for the United States—is sharply stressed in *Strategic Survey 1978,* pp. 1, 4-6, and in *Communist Aid to Less Developed Countries of the Free World, 1977,* US Central Intelligence Agency, National Foreign Assessment Center, November 1978.

22. Oil exploration is soon due to increase in Cuba and Puerto Rico. The Bahamas are optimistic about oil deposits there, and Jamaica is looking for offshore deposits. See *Latin America Economic Report,* Vol. VII, No. 24, June 22, 1979, p. 191.

23. Argentina produces valuable food products (wheat, corn, meat), as well as metals such as tungsten, zinc, lead, tin, and silver. Brazil's resources include manganese, diamonds, lumber, rubber, and foodstuffs.

24. Cuba is repeatedly cited by the USSR as the leading force in the Latin American transition from capitalism to socialism. See, for example, *Pravda,* April 5, 1978. See also S. Mishin, "Latin America: Two Trends of Development," *International Affairs,* June 1976, pp. 64-71.

25. See James D. Theberge, ed., *Soviet Seapower in the Caribbean: Political and Strategic Implications,* New York: Praeger Publishers, 1972.

26. See also my essay on "Caribbean Leftism," in *Problems of Communism,* Vol. XXVII, No. 3, May-June 1978, pp. 33-57.

27. *Yearbook of International Communist Affairs 1978,* p. xxiii.

28. D. Zagoria, pp. 733-754.

29. K. Khachaturov, "Maoism in Latin America," *International Affairs,* March 1979, pp. 55-63.

30. Cecil Johnson, "China and Latin America: New Ties and Tactics," *Problems of Communism,* Vol. XXI, No. 4, July-August 1972, pp. 53-66.

31. K. Khachaturov, p. 59.

32. See *Peking Review,* Vol. 21, August 4, 1978, p. 4.

33. K. Khachaturov, p. 60.

34. *Latin American Economic Report,* Vol. VII, No. 7, February 16, 1979, p. 55.

35. Estimates vary on Soviet aid to Cuba, but rough figures are around $9 million per day on top of the expenses in underwriting the Cuban military presence in Africa. The latter includes over 45 transport missions to Angola in 1975, plus some 50 flights in the first 60 days of airlifts to Ethiopia beginning in November 1977. *Strategic Survey 1978,* p. 13.

36. *Communist Aid to Less Developed Countries of the Free World,* pp. 24-28.

37. *Ibid.,* p. 4.

38. A substantial number of Latin American Communist party delegations travelled to Moscow in 1978, e.g. the Argentine delegation in September; the Uruguayan delegation in October (received by Boris Ponomarev, nonvoting member of the CPSU Central Committee Politburo and Secretary of CPSU Central Committee); the Bolivian CP delegation in December.

39. The Soviet Union's radio coverage of Nicaragua is intensive, beginning in January 1978. Broadcasts are in Russian, English, and Spanish, depending on the audience, and they generally link US imperialism with the Somoza region. See *FBIS,* January 14, 23, and 31, 1978.

40. It was the Cuban resolution to place Puerto Rico on the United Nation's list of colonies. The vote occurred on September 12, 1978, with 10 in favor (including the Soviet Union and China) and 12 abstentions (including Chile and Trinidad/Tobago). For Moscow coverage, see Radio Broadcast, Moscow *Tass* in English, September 5, 1978 in *FBIS,* September 7, 1978; *Pravda,* September 25, 1978 in *FBIS,* September 28, 1978.

41. *Izvestiia,* November 2, 1978 in *FBIS,* November 7, 1978.

42. On Cuban involvement in the *Sandinista* affair, see James Nelson Goodsell's articles in *Christian Science Monitor,* e.g. "Nicaragua: What's Behind the Struggle?" June 22, 1979. Cuba meanwhile has long pressed for the independence of Puerto Rico through Cuban radio broadcasts allowing Puerto Rican *independistas* to be interviewed in Cuba, and strong efforts in the United Nations Decolonization Committee.

43. *Latin American Economic Report,* Vol. VI, No. 45, November 17, 1978, p. 1.

44. *Izvestiia,* May 17, 1978, in *FBIS,* May 20, 1978.

45. *TASS* in English, April 26, 1978, in *FBIS,* April 27, 1978. See also Moscow Radio Domestic Service in Russian, April 10, 1979; *Pravda,* April 11, 1979; and *TASS* in English, April 11, 1979 in *FBIS,* April 9-11, 1979.

46. Klockkovsky, p. 39. The Soviets also stress US heavy investments and consequent power in the Caribbean, noting the over $4.5 billion invested there by 1978. *Pravda,* March 2, 1978 in *FBIS,* March 4, 1978.

47. *Ibid.,* p. 41.

48. The issue of limits to Soviet influence in Third World countries began to be raised in 1975 with the publicaton of Alvin Z. Rubinstein's incisive book, *Soviet and Chinese Influence in the Third World,* New York: Praeger Publishing Co., 1975. See especially chapters 8 and 9 by Andres Suarez and George Ginsbergs, as well as Rubinstein's own chapters 1 and 10.

49. Global interdependence theory is helpful in assessing Moscow's cost/benefit trade-offs in pursuance of a specific Latin American policy and trying to explore the Soviet Union's long-run capacity to be influential in Third World regions. On global

interdependence, see Robert Keohane and Joseph Nye, *Power and Interdependence,* Boston: Little, Brown, 1977; and Dennis Pirages, *The New Context for International Relations: Global Ecopolitics,* North Scituate, Massachusetts: Duxbury Press, 1978.

50. To put the Soviet aid program in global perspective, note that aid offered by Communist countries during the last 25 years totals less than the overall flow of Western aid in 1977 alone. The Non-Aligned Foreign Ministers noted at their July 1978 Belgrade meeting that aid from the developed Communist states had declined steadily from 1974 and that in 1976 it was less than 0.1 percent of their combined Gross National Product. The Group of 77 Ministerial Meeting in Arusha, February 1979, urged the Communist states to increase their development aid. Soviet aid allocations in 1977 were .03 percent of their GNP, compared with .31 percent for Western industrialized countries.

51. This point is well made by Alan Riding of *The New York Times* staff in an unpublished paper for the Council on Foreign Relations, "Political Trends in Central America," 1978. The absence of an effective policy seems highlighted in President Carter's visit to Venezuela and Brazil in March 1978, which produced no firm initiatives, and in the President's subsequent trip to Mexico in February 1979, which seemed monumentally short on preparation. See also *Latin American Political Report,* Vol. 12, No. 13, April 7, 1978. For the Soviet coverage which hit home the "failure" of these trips, see especially *TASS* in Russian, March 29, 1978, in *FBIS,* March 30, 1978; *TASS* in English, in *FBIS,* March 31, 1978, and other Moscow radio broadcasts on March 31 - April 7, 1978.

52. Observe here the historic roots of different Latin American national movements predating the 1917 Bolshevik Revolution, as in Cuba (1876) and Mexico (1910).

53. Duncan, "Caribbean Leftism," pp. 46-57.

54. At the Conference of Foreign Ministers of the Non-Aligned Countries, held in Belgrade on July 25-30, several leading members were displeased with Cuba's attempts to commit the movement to a tacit alliance with the "socialist countries," notably the Soviet bloc, with Cuba's military role in Africa. In fact a majority of the nonaligned countries opposed Cuba's intervention in Africa and by implication that of the USSR as well. See *Keesings Contemporary Archives,* October 27, 1978, pp. 29281-29562.

55. As a point of interest, the USSR was the second major Communist broadcasting country to Latin America by 1977, with a weekly total of 143 hours, preceded by Cuba with 253 hours weekly and followed by the PRC with 90 hours. The Soviets ceased broadcasting in Guarani (to Paraguay) that year. *Communist International Radio Broadcasting - 1977,* Washington: International Communication Agency, November 20, 1978, p. 8.

56. This point bears added commentary. The Inter-American Development Bank, to which the United States is the largest contributor, extended $792 million in loans to the Latin American countries in 1978, with $657 million going to the least developed and $135 million to the more developed states. This compares to a total Third World net economic aid flow from the Soviet Union of $260 million in 1977. Figures for 1978 are unavailable at the time of this writing. See *Inter-American Development Bank, Annual Report, 1978,* Washington, DC, p. 11. The World Bank is another multilateral lending institution for Latin America, again with the United States as a major contributor. As an indication of its financial capacity, it extended

a $105 million to $688 million to Brazil, and $416 million to Colombia in 1978—to identify only three of the Latin American World Bank loan recipients. See *International Bank for Reconstruction and Development* (IBRD), *Statement of Loans,* Washington, DC, March 31, 1979. The World Bank also approved $43.5 million in two loans to Jamaica in June 1979 and a $20 million loan for education in Trinidad and Tobago in that year. *World Bank News Releases,* No. 79/100, June 4, 1979, and No. 79/105, June 11, 1979. Moscow meanwhile claims that the IBRD ignores Third World needs, especially drawing attention to the mounting debts of Third World countries, the continued trade barriers, low prices for raw materials, and their balance of payments deficit. *TASS* in English, September 28, 1978.

57. This observation is designed to raise the question of tradeoffs in capital formation when so substantial a proportion of Soviet capital goes into military production rather than nonmilitary capital formation. At the same time, when Third World countries allocate major portions of scarce capital into military production, do they not decrease their potential for capital formation and economic development? To the extent that expanded state sector growth is prohibited by military expenditures, the Soviets may be losing one objective while possibly gaining another (potential influence through arms sales).

58. See Stanley Hoffman, "No Choice, No Illusions," *Foreign Policy,* No. 25, Winter 1976-77, pp. 97-104.

59. James Nelson Goodsell, "Nicaragua, U.S. Try to Wipe the Slate Clean," *Christian Science Monitor,* July 26, 1979, p. 1.

60. See George W. Grayson, "Mexico's Opportunity: The Oil Boom," *Foreign Policy,* No. 29, Winter 1977-78, pp. 65-89.

61. On the need for new assumptions about American foreign policy in Latin America, see Abraham F. Lowenthal, "The United States and Latin America: Ending the Hegemonic Presumptions," *Foreign Affairs,* Vol. 55, No. 1, October 1976, pp. 199-213.

62. For example, "After Somoza, Another Cuba in the Making," *U.S. News and World Report,* July 30, 1979, pp. 33-35.

2

THE USSR, CUBA, AND THE REVOLUTION IN CHILE

Paul E. Sigmund

The Soviet Union is both a major power and the center of a worldwide ideological movement that claims to possess a scientific insight into the process of history. Soviet foreign policy, therefore, must carry out two potentially complicating roles. It must not only defend the security of the USSR and extend its influence and power, but it must also be able to appeal to Marxism-Leninism to explain, prescribe, and predict the course of world events. The defense of the Soviet Union, therefore, involves as well the manipulation of the official ideology to analyze current world politics and to indicate what actions should be taken in the future. This appeal to universal laws gives Soviet policy additional support from those who are attracted by its ideology but it places upon it the additional burden of interpretation of the complex and unpredictable events of international politics in terms that relate it to Marxism-Leninism.

The task has become more formidable in the last two decades as other governments have disputed the Soviet regime's claim to be the sole correct interpreter of Marxism-Leninism. Soviet ideology has responded by attempting to situate itself in a central or orthodox position and describing the other positions as errors of

26

the right or left. In the 1960's those erroneous positions were represented by China and Yugoslavia, and the Soviet spokesmen had to answer explicit or implicit challenges from both directions as they interpreted world events.

A further problem created by the universalistic ideological claims of Soviet policy is the conflict that often arises between the requirements of the Soviet Union as a major power involved in government-to-government relations, and those which derive from its claim to hegemony over a world doctrinal movement with adherents within each country. The needs of power politics may be difficult to reconcile with the promotion of ideologically sympathetic movements, leaders, and even governments. To be successful, Soviet policy must both promote the Soviet Union's world power, and maintain its claim to represent the "correct" interpretation of world history. One of the areas where this claim was tested and its complex effects illustrated was Latin America in the 1960's and 1970's.

In two countries, in particular, the tensions and contradictions of Soviet ideology and practice were demonstrated: Chile and Cuba. Both had relatively large and long-standing Communist parties. In both, Communist influence expanded suddenly and rapidly in ways which tested the Soviet Union's ability to respond both as a government and as an ideological center. At least from the vantage of the late 1970's those responses met with varying degrees of success which this study will attempt to evaluate.

Ideological factors were involved in the alignment of Cuba with the Soviet Union in international politics, but initially they seem to have been subordinated to calculations of national interest on both sides. Before he took power Castro himself was not a member of the Cuban Communist Party (PSP), and until mid-1958 he was regarded with hostility by the Cuban Communists. Castro now argues that at heart he was a Communist at the time that he came to power: "Although our program was not Socialist as yet, I did myself have deep Socialist and Communist convictions."[1] Nevertheless, the evidence of his public and private statements as well as the testimony of those who were close to him at the time indicates that he did not decide to break with the United States and to align himself with the Soviet Union until some time between April and November 1959. In fact, there may have been two separate decisions—the first that a conflict with the United States was likely or even inevitable, made at the time of his trip to the

27

United States in the spring, and a later decision made in the fall to secure Soviet support by aligning Cuba politically with the USSR. From October 1959 Castro actively sought Soviet economic assistance, began to court the Cuban Communist Party, and stepped up the anti-American content of his public statements and actions. In mid-1960, in response to the US cut in the Cuban sugar quota, he intervened and then nationalized some and then all of US property in Cuba and secured Soviet military aid. In early 1961 he proclaimed the Cuban Revolution socialist, and by the end of the same year announced that he was a Marxist-Leninist and would be one until the last day of his life. Ideology therefore played an important role in Castro's effort to secure Soviet economic and military aid—although it seems initially to have been related in Castro's mind to a more important goal, the protection of Cuba from an American-sponsored invasion along the lines of the 1954 CIA intervention in Guatemala. In fact, of course, the measures he took to protect Cuba against such an invasion made his belief in imminent US intervention a self-fulfilling prophecy and led to a massive Soviet program of economic and military assistance to Cuba which continues to the present day.

What comes through clearly, however, in all the public statements of the Soviet leaders through this period is their caution about taking advantage of the opportunity that Castro offered. From an ideological point of view, they were aware that Castro had had no previous affiliation with international communism and was not subject to Soviet influence or control. From a pragmatic point of view, it seems that like Castro the Soviet policymakers were convinced that the United States would follow the Guatemalan scenario and intervene directly or indirectly to overthrow Castro if he continued his attacks on American interests. In addition, the beginnings of detente with the American government in the period from the Camp David meeting in September 1959 to the cancellation of the Paris Summit in May 1960 may have deterred the Soviets from taking steps in Cuba that would antagonize the United States. It is true that an economic agreement between Cuba and the USSR was signed in February 1960, and formal diplomatic relations were opened in May. However, it was only in July 1960 that the Soviets made a substantial commitment—Khrushchev's mention of Soviet rocket support "figuratively speaking," an agreement for military aid and a commitment to purchase the bulk

28

of the Cuban sugar crop. It was not until April 1962 that Cuba was recognized as Socialist in a Soviet publication, although Castro himself had so described Cuba's revolution a year earlier and in December 1961 had announced the beginnings of the formation of a Unified Party of the Socialist Revolution to be organized along Leninist lines. In March 1962 a new Soviet aid agreement was signed marking the firm decision by the Soviet Union to continue to support Cuba indefinitely by buying its sugar, providing it with oil, and extending military assistance free of the obligation of repayment.[2]

The decision to support Cuba against US pressures and then to recognize its government as ideologically aligned with the socialist camp is often described as an expensive one for the Soviet Union. The figure cited during the 1960's for Soviet aid to Cuba was $1 million a day, and present support is much higher. The cost of the Soviet subsidy to Cuba has varied from year to year and includes general balance of payments assistance, the financing of a trade deficit with the Soviet Union, free military aid, a price paid for sugar and nickel exports that is pegged well above the world sugar price, and—since 1974—a price charged for petroleum that is below the world price (although linked to it, because it is based on average prices over the preceding 3 years). In addition, since 1973, no interest repayments are required on Cuba's debt to the Soviet Union until 1986. If one includes the forgiven interest, military aid (estimated by Jorge Dominguez at $4.5 billion to 1975 and increased substantially since the involvement of Cuban troops in Africa), and the subsidized prices, Soviet aid to Cuba may be as high as $4 million a day, and total assistance to Cuba over the last 20 years in excess of $12 billion.[3]

The pattern of increasing Soviet support for and identification with Castro was set back in 1962 with the Cuban missile crisis. Here national interest considerations were predominant when the Soviets failed to include Castro in the negotiations with the United States over the withdrawal of Soviet missiles from the island. The fact that the Soviets had bypassed Castro in the missile crisis influenced him to adopt a more critical stance to the USSR for much of the rest of the decade. Along with Castro's efforts to establish the Cuban experience of a rural guerrilla-based revolution as a model for all of Latin America ("The Andes as the Sierra Maestra of Latin America"), it led to a period of tension in Soviet-Cuban relations that was not fully resolved until after 1970.

That tension was increased by Castro's attacks on the pro-Moscow Communist parties in other Latin American countries, his purge of the old Communists (former members of the PSP) from the Communist Party of Cuba, and his public criticisms of the USSR for extending credits to governments such as that of Colombia that were engaged in putting down Castro-oriented guerrilla movements. When he attempted to organize a Latin American revolutionary international, the Latin American Solidarity Organization (OLAS), the Russians decided to use economic pressure to bring Castro into line. Oil deliveries to Cuba were slowed down in early 1968, and the signing of a new aid agreement was delayed. While Castro did not immediately change his tune, in August 1968 he was one of the few Communist leaders in the West to defend the Soviet invasion of Czechoslovakia and thereafter he took a considerably less active role in promoting revolution in Latin America. In 1969 and 1970 the Cubans turned their energies inward in an unsuccessful attempt to achieve a 10 million ton sugar harvest by July 1970. When that effort failed, Castro was more amenable to Soviet advice on the domestic front, as well as internationally.[4]

Following the failure of the 1970 sugar harvest, Cuba became much more closely aligned with the Soviet Union than in the preceding decade. In 1972 Cuba joined the Council for Economic Mutual Assistance (CEMA) and Brezhnev pronounced it "a strong constituent part of the world system of socialism." In January 1973 five long-term economic assistance agreements were announced, and in 1974 Brezhnev himself visited Cuba. In 1975 and 1977 Cuba hosted meetings of the Latin American Communist Parties. Cuban courses in Marxism-Leninism in Cuba now no longer used Cuban writers such as Carlos Rafael Rodriguez and Che Guevara but translated Russian texts. The Cuban Communist Party held its first congress in December 1975, and a constitution that resembled the Soviet model was adopted in 1976. The only important institutional differences from the Soviet model were the continuing important role of the Committees for the Defense of the Revolution and the complicated system of indirect (and on the local level, competitive) elections to the Organs of Popular Power introduced in 1976.

By the mid-1970's it was apparent that the problems in the relations of the two countries had been resolved through the discreet manipulation of Soviet military and economic assistance and Cuba's continuing dependence upon them. The Soviet desire to reduce the burden of that assistance helps to explain the efforts made by Castro to improve relations with the United States beginning in 1974. These efforts met with a favorable US response in mid-1975 and again in early 1977, but in both cases the improvement of relations was halted by Cuban military activities in Africa.

The Cuban intervention in Africa, which clearly turned the tide in Angola and probably in Ethiopia as well, makes the Soviet expenditures of the last 20 years worthwhile. Two regimes that are oriented towards the Soviet Union are supported by Cuban armies that in turn receive substantial logistic and military equipment from the Soviet Union.

What little evidence there is on Cuban involvement in Angola seems to indicate that it was more a Cuban than a Soviet initiative. Cuba had ties with the Marxist-oriented Movimento Popular de Libertacao de Angola (MPLA) going back to 1965, and it had been far more consistent in its support for that movement than had the Soviet Union. It is possible that the Soviets suggested the initial involvement of Cuban instructors in training Angolans in the use of Soviet equipment, which began to be sent to the MPLA in late 1974. However, the Cuban decision to send 1,000 regular soldiers in late August 1975 followed a visit to Luanda by a Cuban military delegation after a reported rejection by Moscow of an MPLA request for further aid. Cuban involvement was sharply increased in early November following South African intervention. The Soviets themselves became more directly involved at the end of the year when Soviet planes began to ferry Cuban troops as part of the escalation, which quickly reached a level of 18,000 troops.

When the Cubans intervened in Ethiopia in 1977 and 1978, the coordination of policies with the Soviets was earlier and more evident. Soviet troop transports brought the Cuban troops, Soviet military advisors were active, and joint planning of military involvement took place. For geopolitical reasons the Soviet interest in the Horn is greater than it is in Southern Africa, while the ideological interest of Cuba in support of the MPLA is stronger than that of the Soviet Union. The net result of the joint Soviet-Cuban activities in Africa, however, has been to reinforce the close coordination of policy that began to develop in the early 1970's, and to give the Soviet Union a roving expeditionary force in Africa.[5]

Particularly in view of the recent developments in Africa, Soviet policy towards Cuba would have to be regarded as a success. Soviet support has enabled Cuba as a Communist state to withstand US hostility for nearly 20 years. The USSR has established economic and military links that have enabled it to temper Castro's earlier ideological excesses and to induce him to follow the Soviet model. It has been able to take advantage of Castro's own revolutionary pretensions in ways which strengthen Soviet power by weakening the influence of the West in Africa. The burden of assistance to Cuba has been an investment that has paid off.

The success of Soviet Cuban policy is attributable to a combination of caution in the initial involvement with Castro, willingness to take a good deal of abuse during the period of tension and ideological difference in the middle 1960's, the ability to act quickly when opportunity presented itself (as in July 1960 after the cut in the sugar quota and in late 1975 when Soviet planes transported thousands of Cuban troops to Angola in only a few weeks), and the use of economic incentives to maintain a continuing Cuban dependence on the USSR while allowing Castro considerable leeway to pursue his own policies in the Third World. In the final analysis, the decisive instrument of control over Castro is the economic one. Even with increased Cuban trade with the West, that instrument will remain, since Cuba's two basic problems—an economy which must export low-priced sugar and import oil at increasingly high prices, and a geopolitical location in which it needs a military defender and a reliable supplier of weapons other than the United States—are not likely to be resolved in any other way.

By a curious irony, the Soviet Union's success in Cuba made it more likely to fail elsewhere in Latin America. This has been true for a number of reasons. In the first place, the existence of a Communist state in the Western hemisphere prompted United States and Latin American policymakers to regard the spread of communism in the area as a greater threat and to take measures to respond to that threat—including the modernization of the military establishment, the reform efforts associated with the Alliance for Progress, and the coordination of Western Hemisphere policies in an anti-Cuban alliance in the period between 1962 and 1975. Secondly, the economic burden of supporting Cuba has made the Soviet Union reluctant to undertake a similar burden, thus lessening the possibility of the encouragement and support of Communist movements elsewhere in Latin America. Thirdly, at least until the foreign policies of the Soviet Union and Cuba became more closely coordinated in the 1970's, Cuban support of radical left and guerrilla movements in Latin America divided the Marxist movement and undermined the influence of the orthodox Communist parties that were loyal to Moscow. In a number of countries the radicalism espoused in theory and practice by the Castroite movements provoked the military to intervention and repression, and undermined the policy of gradualism and national democracy favored by Moscow and the parties aligned with it. The best although by no means the only example of this is Chile under Allende.

The Communist Party of Chile is one of the oldest and largest in Latin America. Its antecedent party, the Socialist Workers Party, was founded in 1912 and joined the Third International and changed its name to the Communist Party in 1921. At that time it already had elected two members in the lower house of the Chilean Congress and had strong influence—if not control—of the Chilean trade union movement. Following the change of the international Communist line in 1935, the Chilean Communists supported the Popular Front candidate for the presidency, Pedro Aguirre Cerda of the Radical Party in 1938. In 1946, they again supported a victorious candidate from the Radical Party, Gabriel Gonzalez Videla, and for the first time were represented by three cabinet ministers in his government. Government participation lasted only 5 months, and by 1948 the Communists, again following the international line, were organizing strikes and violence in the copper and coal mines. This led Gonzalez Videla to outlaw them and imprison their leadership in remote areas of the north.

By the time that the Party was legalized again in 1956, it had so improved its relations with the rival Socialist Party that an electoral alliance was formed, the FRAP or Population Action Front. This coalition narrowly missed electing Salvador Allende of the Socialist Party to the presidency in 1958. Allende made another strong bid for the presidency in 1964 but he was decisively defeated by a centrist candidate, Eduardo Frei of the Christian Democrats, chiefly because of the rightist parties threw their support to Frei for fear that Allende would be elected. (Cuba also played a role in the campaign since a major feature of the right wing propaganda was

33

the threat that if Allende were elected Chile would become "another Cuba.")

At least from the time of the Popular Front, and certainly after the Twentieth Party Congress of the Communist Party of the Soviet Union in 1956, the Chilean Communist Party consistently supported the *via pacifica* or peaceful road to socialism in Chile. That policy was both a reflection of the party's long history of participation in Chilean democratic institutions and of the international line of the Soviet Union. In this they frequently differed from the rival Socialist Party, first organized in 1933 and frequently split thereafter, which contained a sizeable group that regarded violent revolution as the only way to achieve power for the proletariat. In 1967 the Socialist Party rejected any alliance with "reformism," as represented by both the Christian Democratic and Radical Parties, and stated that "the Socialist Party does not reject the utilization of peaceful and legal methods, such as the struggle for just demands, ideological and mass activities and political processes, but it considers that those methods alone will not lead to the conquest of power."[6] At about the time that those words were uttered, a Castroite revolutionary group, the Movement of the Revolutionary Left (MIR), was beginning to be active, organizing strikes, seizures of factories and farms, and a series of bank robberies and bomb explosions that made the issue of political violence an important one in the 1970 presidential campaign. A number of the members of the MIR were also active in the Socialist Party, and the MIR was supported and publicized in the magazine, *Punto Final,* which was believed to receive financial assistance from Cuba.

Meanwhile, the Communist Party followed a different and more sophisticated policy. It encouraged the most likely Christian Democratic candidate for the 1970 elections, Radomiro Tomic, to believe that he might secure Communist support. The result was to persuade the right, already increasingly hostile to the Christian Democrats because of the adoption of an agrarian reform law and increased taxes, to promote their own candidate in 1970, thus ensuring a three-way race which would make it easier for the candidate of the left to win than if the right and center supported a single candidate as in 1964. The Communists also took a different position from the Socialists when a Chilean military regiment revolted over salary demands in October 1969. The Communists rallied to the support of the government, while the Socialists issued a declaration indicating that they hoped that the military would take over and carry out a revolutionary policy.

Yet despite the increasing differences between the two parties, a Popular Unity coalition was formed in late 1969 comprising not only the Communists and Socialists but the Radical Party as well and supporting a common program and the candidacy of a Socialist, Salvador Allende. This seeming political miracle was achieved largely through the efforts of the Chilean Communist Party—with the cooperation of the Soviet Union. During the 1960's the Soviets used the Chilean Party as their principal spokesman for Latin America in the international ideological battle, first against the Chinese, and then to criticize Castro's endorsement of guerrilla warfare. *Pravda,* for example, replied to Castro's 1967 attacks on the Soviet Union by printing an article by Luis Corvalan, the Secretary General of the Chilean Party, which—without mentioning Castro by name—criticized his followers as "inclined toward nationalism, adventurism, and terrorism," and accused them of attempting "to create a vanguard arbitrarily or artificially around a leader or people who individually occupy the most radical—at least in their opinions—positions and who are prepared to take one or another revolutionary action." Corvalan argued for cooperation of the left with the petty bourgeoisie through "the joint leadership of the liberation struggle of each people by (the Communist parties and other revolutionary forces) which in a certain sense share the function of the vanguard."[7]

This is the policy that the Communist Party successfully implemented in Chile in forging the Popular Unity Alliance. It worked together with the elements in the Socialist Party led by Salvador Allende that were close to the Communists, and with the left wing of the Radical Party which had captured control of that party in 1967. (The Radicals had been allied with the right in the early 1960's but the move to the left was a response to pressure by the party youth wing which had become more sympathetic to Marxism as a result of a campaign of international travel and assistance to its leadership by the Soviet Embassy in Chile.) In the fall of 1969, the Communists succeeded in getting all three parties as well as a left-wing splinter group from the Christian Democrats and two minor groups to appoint representatives to draw up a common Popular Unity program. When it was published in December it bore a striking resemblance, sometimes word for

35

word, to the program adopted by the Communist Party congress held in November. By brilliant maneuvering during an additional month of bitter negotiations, the Communists then succeeded in securing Allende's nomination in mid-January.[8]

What was the role of the Soviet Union in the nominatioin and election of Allende? The Frei government had reestablished relations with the USSR after the 1964 election and in 1967 the Soviets had extended a $40 million credit to his government which was never used. The 1975 US Senate Intelligence Committee report on Chile contained no figures on Soviet aid to the Allende campaign, although it mentioned, apparently relying on CIA sources, the figure of $350 thousand in Cuban aid to Allende. Soviet aid went to the Chilean Communist Party, probably through commercial channels, rather than to Allende, since although Allende's policy was close to that of the Communists, he was a member of a rival party, and was close personally to Fidel Castro. In addition, the Soviet embassy, like the Chilean left in general, probably believed that the rightist candidate, former president Jorge Alessandri, would win.[9]

Once Allende took office in November 1970 the Soviets were faced with the question of how much assistance should be given to a regime in which a pro-Moscow party had an important role, but which was headed by a Marxist who was not a party member. Reluctant to take on a substantial economic burden, the Soviets did not rush in with large amounts of aid to Chile. In May 1971 they renewed the earlier Frei credit at a lower interest rate and granted additional funds for the purchase of machinery and the construction of a prefabricated housing plant. Later in the year they agreed to help the Chilean fishing industry, and a Soviet expert team also assisted in the evaluation of the nationalized copper mines between July and September 1971. Brezhnev noted the coming to power of a Marxist regime in Chile in his speech to the Twenty-Fourth Party Congress in March 1971, but warned that Yankee imperialism sought to deprive the Chilean people of their gains. The Soviet press was favorable to the Chilean developments but careful to emphasize that the Allende headed a coalition, rather than a Communist government. Soviet commentators cited the Allende victory as a confirmation of the "peaceful road" policy of mobilization of the proletariat and a refutation of the Chinese proponents of violation as well as of unspecified, but clearly Castroite, claims for a vanguard role for students, the intelligentsia, and other groups.[10]

The Soviet commentators had good reason to be cautious since the Popular Unity coalition contained representatives of views that were at considerable variance from the Soviet official position. Many of the Socialists were sympathetic to or even members of the Castroite Movement of the Revolutionary Left (MIR) which rejected both bourgeois democracy and the Soviet model of development. The Radicals and ex-Christian Democrats, while increasingly influenced by Marxism, came from very different political traditions. In his inaugural address Allende himself promised a new model of socialism, the *via Chilena* ''in democracy, pluralism, and liberty'' and quoted Engels on the possibility of ''a peaceful transition from the old society to the new.'' Even the faithful Communist Party deemphasized—although out of deference to the Soviet Union never totally abandoned—its belief in the dictatorship of the proletariat, outlining in its party program a plan for the transition to socialism which involved a plebiscite on constitutional reforms to establish a unicameral legislature and continued respect for civil liberties, pluralism, and the role of law.

Sensitive to the opposition of the military to Communist control of the interior or defense ministries, Allende gave only the ministries of labor, finance, and public works to Communist representatives. However, the party had influence elsewhere as well, since the Popular Unity agreements had specified that, in order to avoid the creation of party fiefdoms, the deputies to each minister should come from a different party. Communists also headed the economics ministry after December 1972. The Popular Unity parties had also agreed that the interparty Political Command set up during the campaign would continue to meet to discuss and approve major policy decisions of the president. When a split developed fairly early in Allende's term between the Radicals, the Communists, and Allende himself on one side, and the Socialists and the ex-Christian Democratic MAPU on the other (MAPU itself later split into two along the same lines) over the pace and method of the changes to be carried out by the government, Allende allowed both sides, in effect, to exercise a veto power over his policies.

The differences between the two groups were focused first on the issue of violence. Shortly after his election Allende pardoned the members of the MIR who had been imprisoned for various acts of violence under the Frei regime. In the south the MIR and related groups led seizures of 1,458 farms in Allende's first year. A month after his election there were street battles between the Communists and the MIR in Concepcion and in January in interviews with the French pro-Castro philosopher, Regis Debray, Allende argued that he was observing legality "for the time being" and stated that his differences with revolutionaries like Che Guevara were only "tactical."[11] Like his government, Allende was himself divided between a belief that violence was necessary to effect genuine changes, and a commitment to the observance of "bourgeois legalism" as the only way to achieve change in Chile, given its democratic tradition, the provisions of the Statute of Democratic Guarantees that he had accepted as a condition of his election, and the fact that respect for the constitutional rules of the game was the only thing that prevented many of the leaders of the armed forces from staging a coup.

The Communists, recognizing that they would be the first to be suppressed in the event of military intervention, agreed with Allende in this analysis. In public commentaries by the international Communist press and in the Communist Chilean daily, *El Siglo,* there was little discussion of the possibility of military intervention. Allende's skill in handling the military, and in particular his apparent conversion of General Carlos Prats from opposition and suspicion to support, had allayed fears of such intervention once the crucial period before the congressional vote of later October 1970 had passed. Most of the criticism by the Communists was directed at the extreme left, the MIR and Socialist Party, now dominated by Senator Carlos Altamirano who made no secret of his belief in the inevitability and desirability of violence.

The Allende government reestablished relations with Cuba, broken off in 1964 as a result of a vote of the Organization of American States but Castro followed a low-profile policy. He did not come to Allende's inauguration as some believed he would, and he wrote Allende urging him to keep on good terms with the United States. Yet there was no doubt where the Cubans stood in the debate over the role of violence. They had supported the MIR from the beginning, they established a large embassy in Chile which included Allende's Cuban son-in-law and Cuban military experts gave instruction in the use of modern firearms to Allende's personal bodyguard—the so-called GAP or Group of Personal Friends, and to Allende himself.

The most spectacular example of Cuban actions that undermined Allende's claim to the strict observance of legality took place in March 1972, when 13 large wooden crates from Cuba bypassed customs examination and were taken from the airfield on orders of the interior ministry. A customs official reported this to the Congress, the government made contradictory statements about the contents of the crates, and the armed forces began, we now know, for the first time to give active consideration to the possibility of a coup. After September 1973 the Pinochet government published photostatic copies of a list of the contents found in the apartment of the Communist Director of *Investigaciones*. The crates had contained submachine guns, matching pistols, revolvers, and ammunition.[12]

By early 1972 a process of political polarization had set in—with the centrist Christian Democrats now working regularly with the rightist National Party in the Congress to oppose the Allende government. In January two by-elections in the south indicated increasing opposition to the government. In Allende's first year in office, the international reserves built up by the preceding government had been spent, and what had seemed initially to be a successful economic policy began in his second year as president to produce shortages and inflationary pressures which led to a runaway inflation later in the year.

The only ones in the Allende coalition to recognize the seriousness of the situation were the Communists. In a secret report prepared for a meeting of the Popular Unity parties in early February 1972, the Communists blamed the violence preached and practiced by the extreme left for the recent electoral losses, predicted that during 1972 there would be "strong inflationary pressures that could make our situations acute," and called for a dialogue with the Christian Democrats in order to prevent the consolidation of their emerging alliance with the right. (They also took credit for having pursued such a policy before the 1970 election, thus making Allende's election possible.)[13]

Partly as a result of Communist pressure within the Popular Unity coalition, negotiations were initiated between the Christian Democrats and moderate members of the Allende government. An initial agreement was reached in March, but the left wing of the Popular Unity Political Command vetoed the accord, leading the Left Radical group that had engineered the agreement to resign from the government, and in July to join the opposition. A second set of negotiations in June reached partial agreement, but they were broken off by the Christian Democrats in early July when the time limit they had set in anticipation of an impending by-election expired. In retrospect, this turns out to have been the last chance to prevent the polarization that eventually resulted in the 1973 coup. Here as earlier, the Communist Party was right in recognizing that an agreement with the Christian Democrats was necessary to save the constitutional order, and their own freedom to function in a democratic society. The Christian Democratic candidate in 1970, Radimiro Tomic, also recognized this, but by 1972 he was pessimistic about the possibilities of reaching agreements that could have been arrived at earlier.[14]

Yet at the same time that the Communists were attempting to keep the opposition divided, they were working to unite the Popular Unity coalition. They even proposed the creation of a single Popular Unity party, but their proposal received no support from the other parties which feared that such a party would be dominated by the Communists because of their superior organizing ability and substantial membership.

Besides the increasing political polarization between the two groups of parties, and between the president on one side and the opposition-dominated Congress on the other, the other major problem was the economy. In September 1972 the annual inflation rate reached 114 percent and industrial production began to drop. (It continued to do so until the September 1973 coup.) The seizures in the countryside had also cut into food production, and the declining price of copper as well as the difficulties of securing loans from New York banks created problems in securing foreign exchange necessary to pay for the estimated $500 million in food imports in 1972.

One might have expected Allende to turn to the Soviet Union for help in this situation, but he was remarkably slow to do so. In fact, most of the short-term credits for Chile came from countries like Canada, Australia, and Argentina for the importation of wheat and meat. A major effort to secure Soviet assistance was not made until Allende's trip to Moscow in December 1972. As a result of the trip, Allende received $30 million for the purchase of food and cotton, and a $20 million increase in earlier short-term loans. (Other reports indicated a figure of $100 million.) It was also announced in Santiago that the Soviet Union had granted $108 million for long-term projects, but some of these had been included in earlier announcements. The Moscow trip ended in a communique which also promised Soviet support for Chilean power production and the expansion of the fishing industry.[15]

What comes through clearly is that nothing like the general balance of payments support that Cuba enjoyed was ever considered by the Soviets for Allende. They were willing to approve some individual projects, and give some food aid, but not the massive assistance that Castro received. In actual fact, the Chilean debt to all the Communist countries, including China, increased from $14 million in 1970 to only $40 million in 1973, at the same time that its debt to other Latin American countries and Spain increased from $9 million to nearly $150 million.[16] The Soviet Union bought copper from Chile and exported machinery and food, chiefly condensed milk, wheat, and meat, but the total volume of trade with Chile did not expand to anything like the degree of the expansion of Soviet trade with Cuba in the early 1960's. Chile's basic trading partners were still in the West, including, despite all of Allende's talk of an "invisible blockade," the United States.[17]

The breach between the Communists, the Radicals, and Allende on one side, and the Socialists and other left groups on the other, widened in late 1972 as Popular Unity debated what to do with factories which had been taken over by the workers during the month-long truckers' strike in October 1972. In January 1973 the Communist economics minister, Orlando Millas, sent a bill to Congress to regularize the legal situation of the factories that had been taken over in the truckers' strike on a supposedly temporary basis. This provoked a furious debate among the Socialists over whether any of the factories should be handed back to the owners. The Communists, calling on the government to "consolidate" in order to advance," favored taking over only those on the original government list of firms to be expropriated, and setting up a commission to study what should be done with the others. This provoked one wing of the MAPU to issue a report accusing the Communists and Allende of adopting a "state capitalist" position which was not fundamentally different from that of the opposition. Calling on the workers to "advance without compromise" and claiming to have developed a new political form of "people's power," the Socialists and the MIR organized worker belts (*cordones*), commune commands, and camps which were outside of the regular governmental structure. Again, the Communists opposed this tactic, both because of its adverse economic effects (Corvalan described it as "suicidal" in an open letter to the Socialists in February) and because it meant that the transition to socialism was running out of control.

A revolt by the Second Armored Regiment at the end of June 1973 was put down by General Prats, but not before the Communist-dominated trade union federation had attempted to outflank the Socialists by ordering the occupation of more factories—leading to the rekindling of the controversy over the legal status of the worker takeovers. In July as political polarization intensified and the inflation rate reached 323 percent, the Communists reverted to support for Chilean constitutionalism and made a last attempt to stave off the coup which now seemed only a matter of time. Timing their campaign to coincide with an appeal by the Chilean bishops for a "political truce," the Party initiated a campaign with the slogan, "No, to civil war." The efforts of the Communists and the bishops produced a series of fruitless discussions between Allende and the head of the Christian Democrats at the end of July, and a secret meeting in August between the two at the residence of Cardinal Silva. Castro sent a letter to Allende supporting the dialogue but urging him to resist the pressure of the opposition, telling him: "Your decision to defend the (revolutionary) process with firmness and honor even at the cost of your own life will draw all forces capable of fighting to your side."[18]

By August, Chile was an armed camp. The military intelligence services had detected the beginning of arms training by the Popular Unity parties, and the armed forces began to carry out raids seeking arms caches—although without much success.[19] The MIR published a leaflet with the heading "Soldier, disobey your officers who are inciting a coup." The classic precipitant of the *coup d'etat,* the threat to the military monopoly of the use of force, was heading Chile directly to a military takeover.

When the coup took place on September 11, the MIR leadership went underground and Senator Altamirano slipped out of the country—to emerge later in Cuba. The top Communist leaders were arrested and detained on an island in the south, and the military attempted to destroy the infrastructure of the party, although their most intense efforts were aimed at the *violentistas* of the MIR.

After the coup, the military claimed to have saved the country from Communism and civil war. They were more persuasive on the latter point than on the former, since at least in the short run it is difficult to construct a scenario for a Communist takeover in Chile in 1973 as long as the Armed Forces remained unsympathetic to Marxism. (In the longer run, however, the Communists never denied that their ultimate objective was the dictatorship of the proletariat.)

Castro proclaimed that the coup demonstrated that there was no alternative but armed revolutionary struggle, while Radio Moscow and exiled members of the Chilean Communist Party stressed the coalition nature of the Allende regime and its internal divisions, as well as the lack of support for it by the middle class. Surprisingly little attention was given to the US role. As they had done during the Allende period, the Soviet writers emphasized that the Allende regime was not a socialist one but a national democratic revolution which was preparing the transition to socialism. They also noted that a further problem of the Allende regime was that the Communist Party was not able to play a "vanguard" role.[20]

Volodia Teitelboim, a Communist senator who was out of Chile at the time of the coup, became the Chilean Communist spokesman in exile. Writing from Moscow, his verdict on the coup directly contradicted that of Castro. He denied that the coup refuted the Chilean Communist position that "a people can come to power without recourse to arms." Declaring that "Marxism-Leninism envisages both the armed and nonarmed path to power," with the later defined as "a process of aggravated class struggle but without civil war," he blamed the failure of Popular Unity on "the existence of two opposite trends within the Popular Unity government." One of them "guided by Leninist theory" and acting in accordance with the "objective laws of social development . . . envisaged uniting the people around the working class, the mainstay of the revolution" while the other "took a sectarian attitude" producing "endless futile discussions," which paralyzed the government, and "isolated the working class from its allies."[21]

What should be the verdict on the success or failure of Soviet policy towards Chile? It is clear that the USSR was always somewhat dubious about the chances of success of the Allende experiment and unwilling to make a major economic commitment to it. That doubt was justified in the event, since Allende and the heterogeneous coalition that he headed were not responsive to Soviet policies and did not, in the Soviet view, offer enough in the way of a political return to compensate for the economic and political risks involved in a major commitment. Military guarantees made no sense, given the attitude of the United States and the Chilean military, and economic support would have required massive quantities of wheat, oil, and meat that the Soviet Union did not have, or hard currency that it could not spare. It is true that a successful Chilean experiment in Marxist pluralism would have had a major impact on Western Europe, but the Soviets had never favored such a system except as a transitional stage, with a preponderant influence by the Communist Party, towards the dictatorship of the proletariat. What appeared at the time to be a movement to the left in surrounding countries such as Bolivia, Peru, and Argentina turned out to be evanescent, and there was little geopolitical advantage to a Marxist government located about as far from Moscow as any government could be. Combined with the domestic correlation of forces—Allende's status as a minority president, opposition control of the congress and courts, the influence of the opposition media, and strong US pressure—there was little to attract the Soviets to a major commitment. The policy that the Soviets and the Communist Party of Chile pursued, avoidance of violence and attempts to compromise with the centrist Christian Democrats,[22] was in retrospect the only possible one, but it was sabotaged from the outset by the extreme left. (The leading senatorial spokesman for the extreme left, Carlos Altamirano, has now recognized that his policy was erroneous, and has announced his commitment to democratic socialism.)

After the coup, the Soviet Union and orthodox Communist Parties around the world were able to extract major political benefits from it since it spurred the formation of anti-facist solidarity committees and rallies for Chilean democracy all over the world, as Chile became "the Spain of the 1970's." It put the Communists in the role of defenders of democracy, and seemed to confirm the argument that capitalism and "facist" repression were inevitably connected.

If we compare the policies that the Soviet Union followed in Cuba and Chile—two very different situations—we find some interesting common elements. In both cases, a large and homegrown Communist Party played an important role in increasing Soviet influence, although the relationships between the PSP and Castro and the Chilean Communist Party and Allende were very different. In both cases, Soviet policy makers at the outset were cautious and unwilling to make major commitments, regarding Latin America as located within the American sphere of influence and fearful that other goals in Moscow's relationship with the United States would be jeopardized. There is evidence in both cases of the tension that has always existed in Marxist-Leninist doctrine between a belief in violent revolution as the principal method of historical change and a willingness to adjust one's methods to historical circumstances—in particular to the possibilities of expansion of influence through "bourgeois" democratic methods. In both cases too, policy makers judged the future by the past—with Guatemala playing a major role in the thinking of those involved with Cuba, and Cuba playing such a role in Chile.

There are important differences as well. The Soviet policy instrument of economic and military assistance was able to produce over the long run a relatively smooth relationship between the Soviet Union and Cuba, while there was not much hope that either could be effective in Chile. Cuba was a strategic success at least after the settlement of the missile crisis, but it was a source of ideological difficulty until the 1970's. The Allende experience in Chile, on the other hand, confirmed the Soviet ideological approach, but marked a substantial strategic setback in Latin America. However, it took 15 years for the Cuban relationship to sort itself out, and in the Chilean case, the long-term impact of the 1973 coup on Soviet power and influence is still to be measured.

This essay began with the observation that Soviet policy towards Cuba and Chile could be evaluated in two ways. It can be discussed in the conventional manner, assessing how it served to advance or impede Soviet security and national interests and how these related to the perceived interests of other governments or Communist parties. It can also be used to evaluate the Soviet claim that Marxism-Leninism provides a scientific insight into historical processes, enabling those who espouse it to explain, prescribe, and predict the course of national and international politics.

Taking the two points in reverse order, we can say that Soviet ideology was quite inadequate as a guide to the future in Cuba and Chile. Soviet policymakers did not expect the sudden turn to the left in the two countries, and they were initially very cautious in the policies which they adopted towards them. Yet in both cases, they were aided by a domestic Communist party which assisted them in evaluating events and deciding on policy. The policies which they

45

ultimately adopted were confirmed by subsequent events—in the Cuban case in ways that decisively advanced Soviet strategic interests in the Western Hemisphere and Africa, and in the Chilean case in ways that confirmed the wisdom of Moscow's original cautious assessment of the Allende experiment and that will provide grist for the Soviet propaganda and organizational mill for years to come.

On the other hand, it is also evident from the two cases that when Soviet national interests and those of other countries or parties are seen to conflict, the Soviet interest is immediately preferred. Thus, Castro was ignored in the 1962 missile crisis, the Latin American Communist parties received very little assistance during their polemic with Castro, and the Chilean Communists and their fellow-traveler, Allende, received hardly more than token economic aid. While there were instances of Soviet initiatives that involved risk—the commitments to Castro in 1960, the missile emplacements in 1962, and the African adventures of the mid-1970's, the overall Soviet pattern has been one of conservatism, caution, and preference for gradual change. Whether that pattern is now beginning to change is a question still to be answered.

ENDNOTES

1. Barbara Walters, "An Interview with Fidel Castro," *Foreign Policy*, No. 28, Fall 1977, p. 34.

2. On the complex interplay between the Soviet Union, Castro, and the Cuban Communist Party (PSP) in this period, see Edward Gonzalez, "Castro's Revolution, Cuban Communist Appeals, and the Soviet Response," *World Politics*, Vol. XXI, October 1968, pp. 39-68; as well as his "Relationship with the Soviet Union" in *Revolutionary Change in Cuba*, ed. by Carmelo Mesa-Lago, Pittsburgh: University of Pittsburgh Press, 1971, pp. 81-105. Hugh Thomas, *Cuba, The Pursuit of Freedom*, New York: Harper and Row, 1971, chs. 105-106 provide the best history of the period. On the Soviet preference for a gradual transition to communism in Latin America through "an extended period of national democracy" see Herbert Dinerstein, "Soviet Policy in Latin America," *American Political Science Review*, Vol. LXI, No. 1, April 1967, p. 80.

3. On Soviet economic and military aid to Cuba, see the articles by Jorge Perez-Lopez, Jorge Dominguez, and Carmelo Mesa-Lago in *Cuba in the World*, ed. by Cole Blasier and Carmelo Mesa-Lago, Pittsburgh: University of Pittsburgh Press, 1979. Overpricing of Soviet exports may reduce the size of the subsidiary somewhat—but it is still very large—and growing much larger as a result of support for Cuban troops in Africa.

4. On Soviet Cuban-relations in the mid-1960's see D. Bruce Jackson, *Castro, the Kremlin, and Communism in Latin America*, Baltimore: Johns Hopkins Press, 1969; Jacques Levesque, *The USSR and the Cuban Revolution*, New York: Praeger, 1978; the documents in *Models of Political Change in Latin America*, ed. by Paul E. Sigmund, New York: Praeger, 1970, pp. 101-111; and in *Marxism in Latin America*, (revised edition), ed. by Luis E. Aguilar, Philadelphia: Temple University Press, 1978, pp. 252-258. Castro's August 1968 speech was not the unqualified endorsement of Soviet policy that was widely reported. In it he said that "the violation (of Czech sovereignty) was, in fact, of a flagrant nature" although "a bitter necessity," and he once again criticized the necessity," and he once again criticized the Soviet Union for "drawing closer economically, culturally, and politically to the oligarchic governments of Latin America which are not merely reactionary governments and exploiters of their people but also shameless accomplices in the imperialist aggressions against Cuba." The evidence on Soviet pressure on Castgro through a slowdown in oil deliveries appears in *Granma Weekly Review*, January 5, 1968, p. 3; *Granma*, Feb. ll, 1968, p. 9; and in Jorge Dominguez, *Cuba, Order and Revolution*, Cambridge, Massachusetts: Harvard University Press, 1978, pp. 162-163.

5. On Cuba and the Soviet Union in Africa, see Abraham Lowenthal, "Cuba's African Adventure," *International Security*, Vol. 2, No. l, Summer 1977, pp. 3-10; Gerald Bender, "Angola, the Cubans and American Anxieties," *Foreign Policy*, No. 31, Summer, 1978, pp. 3-30; Jorge Dominguez, "Cuban Foreign Policy," *Foreign Affairs*, Vol. 57, No. 1, Fall l980, pp. 83-108; John A. Marcum, *The Angolan Revolution*, Vol. II, Cambridge, Massachusetts: MIT Press, 1978, pp. 225-229, 272-281. Castro himself argued in the Barbara Walters' interview (note 1) that Cuba did not decide to send in military units until November 5, 1975, because of the South African invasion that began on October 23. As noted above, however, 1,000 regular troops had arrived in Angola in late September. For a chronology and an

47

analysis that relates the initial Cuban involvement to the need for assistance to the Angolans in the use of Soviet weaponry, see Richard Henry Weiss, "Cuban Involvement in Angola: A Study in the Foreign Policy of a Revolutionary State," Senior Thesis, Princeton University, 1979.

6. "The Socialist Party against Reformism," translated by the editor in *Models of Political Change in Latin America,* ed. by Paul E. Sigmund, New York: Praeger Publishers, 1970, p. 327. On the earlier history of the Chilean Communist Party, see Robert Alexander, *Communism in Latin America,* New Brunswick: Rutgers University Press, 1957, and Ernst Halperin, *Nationalism and Communism in Chile,* Cambridge, Massachusetts: MIT Press, 1965, ch. 3.

7. Luis Corvalan, "The Alliance of Revolutionary Anti-imperialist Forces in Latin America" in Sigmund, *Models,* p. 110. Note that Corvalan seems to compromise on the classic Marxist-Leninist doctrine that the Communist Party alone is the vanguard of the proletariat.

8. Allende was named the Socialist candidate for the negotiations by one vote— his own. For an account of the Popular Unity negotiations, and a comparison of its program with that of the Communist Party, see Paul E. Sigmund, *The Overthrow of Allende and the Politics of Chile, 1964-1976,* Pittsburgh: University of Pittsburgh Press, 1977, pp. 88-91, 302-303. The Communist role is analyzed in Eduardo Labarca Goddard, *Chile at Rojo,* Santiago: Universidad Tecnica del Estado, 1971. See also Luis Corvalan, *El Camino de Victoria,* Santiago: Impresova Horizonte, 1971, pp. 295ff. It is probably not a coincidence that in his inaugural address Allende quoted a passage from Engels on the possibility of a peaceful evolution to socialism that was central to the argument made by a leading Uruguayan Communist, Rodney Arismendi, in his recent book, *Lenin La Revolucion y America Latina,* Montevideo: Pueblos Unidos, 1970.

9. In an effort to influence the election in Alessandri's direction, *El Mercurio,* a widely-read and respected conservative newspaper in Santiago, printed in serial form the papers of Vladimir Kunakov, a Chilean citizen who had acted as a spy for the Soviet Embassy from 1968 until his death in March 1970. See *El Mercurio,* August 23-29, 1970. They mention the commercial firms through which the Communist Party was supported, but reveal a good deal of tension between the Embassy and the Party over Czechoslovakia despite the fact that the Chilean Party supported the Soviet intervention. One of Kunakov's principal duties was reporting to the Embassy on the attitudes of the Party leaders towards the Soviet Union. For the figure on Cuban aid to Allende, see US Senate, Select Committee on Intelligence Activities, *Intelligence Activities, Covert Action,* December 4-5, 1975, Washington, DC: US Government Printing Office, 1976, p. 167. The report estimates that the US Government spent $800 thousand to $1 million against Allende (including the attempt to promote a military coup in October) and that US businesses spent another $700 thousand.

10. See reviews of Soviet reactions in Roger Hamburg, "The Soviet Union and Latin America," in *The Soviet Union and the Developing Nations,* ed. by Roger Kanet, Baltimore: Johns Hopkins Press, 1974, at pages 190-195, and Leon Goure and Morris Rothenberg, *Soviet Penetration of Latin America,* Miami: University of Miami Monographs in International Affairs, 1975, ch. IV.

11. Regis Debray, *Conversations with Allende,* New York: Pantheon, 1971, pp. 97 and 77.

12. *Libro Blanco del Cambio de Gobierno en Chile,* Santiago: Editorial Lord

48

Cochrane, 1973, pp. 103-108. See also page 8 for a photograph of Allende receiving machine gun training from a Cuban instructor at his personal retreat.

13. "Los communistas analizan la situacion politica," *El Siglo,* February 3, 1972, p. 4, reported in INDAL, *Partido Communista de Chile,* Dossier No. 9, October 1974, pp. 131-138.

14. See Radomiro Tomic, "One View of Chile's Present Political and Economic Sutuation," in *The Chilean Road to Socialism,* ed. by J. Ann Zammit, Austin, Texas: University of Texas Press, pp. 31-40. For a chillingly accurate forecast made by Tomic in October 1972 of the results of the breakdown of the constitutional order, see Sigmund, *The Overthrow of Allende,* p. 187.

15. Sigmund, *Overthrow of Allende,* p. 194; Goure and Rothenberg, *Soviet Penetration,* pp. 142-143; *The New York Times,* December 2, 1972.

16. CIAP Subcommittee on Chile, Interamerican Economic and Social Council, Organization of American States, *El Esfuerzo Interno y las Necesidades de Financamento Externo para el Desarrollo de Chile,* January 28, 1974, p. V-9.

17. New aid loans from the United States declined to $5.5 million under Allende and short-term credits from US banks dropped from $219 million to $27 million but Chile still received $10 million worth of food under the Food for Peace Program from the United States and replaced US loans with credits from Western Europe, Argentina, Brazil, and Mexico. Allende claimed that it was impossible to get spare parts from the US copper companies, but secured them from Canada and Japan. See Paul E. Sigmund, "The Invisible Blockade and the Overthrow of Allende." *Foreign Affairs,* Vol. 52, No. 2, January 1974, pp. 322-340. On Soviet food exports to Chile, see Goure and Rothenberg, *Soviet Penetration,* p. 144.

18. The letter in Castro's handwriting is published in the *Libro Blanco,* p. 101-102. In the UN debates after the coup, it was recognized as genuine by the Cuban representative. For the Communist position on people's power *(poder popular)* see Genaro Arriagada, *De la Via Chilena a la Via Insurreccional,* Santiago: Editorial del Pacifico, 1974, pp. 296ff.

19. *Libro Blanco* includes (pp. 192 and 197) what appear to be authentic documents that indicate the beginnings of arms training by MAPU in December 1972 and the Radicals in July 1973. More questionable is a document dated June 30, 1973, instructing all Communist Party members in Santiago to secure arms and to evacuate the upper class *barrio alto* in case of conflict, and gratuitously stating that "a specialized team of the Communist Party will physically eliminate the leaders of the opposition— which the membership should keep strictly secret" (p. 48). Also included in the *Libro Blanco* are excerpts from a Plan Z of unidentified origin calling for the assassination of the leaders of the armed forces on September 19th (pp. 53-65).

20. See reviews of Soviet reactions by Goure and Rothenberg, pp. 107-125, and Roger Hamburg, "The Lessons of Allende," *Problems of Communism,* Vol. XXVII, January-February 1978, pp. 71-76. (Hamburg is preparing a monograph on the subject.) For a comparison of the interpretation of the Allende experience by the Italian and Soviet Communist Parties, see Joan Barth Urban, "Socialist Pluralism in Soviet and Italian Communist Perspective: The Chilean Catalyst," *Orbis,* Vol. XVIII, No. 2, Summer 1974, pp. 482-509.

21. Velodia Teitelboim, "The Failure in Chile and the Future of a Strategy," *Political Affairs,* August 1974, excerpted in *Marxism in Latin America* (revised edition), ed. by Luis Aguilar, pp. 329-333. See also summaries of other articles by Teitelboim in Goure and Rothenberg, pp. 109 and 119.

22. The only evidence for pursuit of a different policy is the Chilean Communist Party support for the factory seizures of June 1973, the assertion by Chilean naval intelligence after the coup that Russian advisors at the prefabricated housing plant near Valparaiso were giving guerrilla training to some of the workers (*Ercilla,* October 10-16, 1973), and the somewhat questionable Communist document published in the *Libro Blanco* (note 19).

3

THE SOVIET-CUBAN RELATIONSHIP: SYMBIOTIC OR PARASITIC?

Gabriel Marcella and Daniel S. Papp

The Soviet Union has traditionally relegated Latin America to a subsidiary position in its foreign policy. It has conceded the remote region as an area of US political, economic, and military dominance, neither important to its vital interests nor a promising environment for socialist revolution. Generally speaking Latin America has not been viewed by the Soviets as worth large expenditures in attention, resources, or risks.

These characteristics of Soviet policy towards Latin America did not discourage efforts to promote the growth of Communist movements loyal to the Soviet Union. The parties that emerged were usually small and often were encouraged to maintain a relatively low profile, to propose and adjust to popular front strategies by taking advantage of tactical alliances with "progressive" forces, and to support the Soviet position in international affairs while calling attention to the dangers of American imperialism.

Indigenous revolutionary movements and situations that emerged in the 1950's, 1960's, and 1970's—most notably the

51

Chilean and Cuban—modified considerably the Soviet calculus of opportunities in Latin America. Whereas Salvador Allende's "peaceful road to socialism" foundered on its internal contradictions, thus depriving the Soviets of possibilities on the west coast of South America,[1] Fidel Castro's earlier nationalist revolution in Cuba provided the basis for forging an enduring and successful relationship based on convergent national interests. The balance of this paper discusses the political, economic, and military components of the relationship, examines from the perspectives of both Moscow and Havana the dynamics of the quasi-alliance, analyzes the role of the United States in that context, and speculates on the future course of Soviet-Cuban relations.

AN OVERVIEW OF SOVIET-CUBAN COOPERATION

Soviet relations with Cuba since Fidel Castro took power in 1959 have at times been tumultuous. In some instances, the level of Soviet-Cuban agreement has been striking: as examples, the agreement to permit Soviet intermediate ballistic missiles on Cuban soil in 1962; the qualified Cuban support for the Soviet invasion of Czechoslovakia as unfortunate but nevertheless necessary to protect socialism; the recent jointly coordinated military deployments into Africa (Angola 1975, Ethiopia 1978); Cuba's activist role in supporting the rejectionist bloc against the Egyptian-Israeli peace treaty of 1978; Cuba's outbursts against China's "dogmatists" and "hegamonists"; and the January 14, 1980 qualified support in the United Nations' General Assembly for the Soviet move into Afghanistan.

In other cases, disagreement between the two has been just as formidable: the latter stages of the missile crisis where the Soviets dismantled and withdrew the missiles without Castro's concurrence; Cuba's criticism that the Soviets did not go far enough in assisting the North Vietnamese against the Americans and the Saigon government; Soviet disapproval of Cuban efforts to export revolution to Latin America in the 1960's, the partial result of serious idealogical disputes over the correct revolutionary techniques for Lation America;[2] plus differences in respective approaches to African problems, most notably on policy towards the Eritrean question and the internal politics of Angola.[3]

These are examples of the shifting trends in the history of Soviet-Cuban relations and are not intended as portents of future policy convergence or divergence. In fact the current level of political-military cooperation in Africa, the Middle East, Asia, and Latin America, as well as Cuba's emphatic efforts to orient the movement of nonaligned nations towards a pro-socialist bloc position—supports the thesis of convergent policies. Thus the two nations may be minimizing their policy differences, and there is little on the horizon that threatens the convergence of national interests.

Soviet-Cuban relations can best be viewed as a convenient parallel of national interests and foreign policies involving a level of cooperation that may either be extended indefinitely or peak relatively soon. Regardless of which direction these interests may go, both nations evidently derive considerable benefit from the current state of their relationship.

From the Soviet vantage, a close relationship with Cuba offers numerous benefits. The Caribbean island represents a Communist outpost in a Western Hemisphere once conceded to the hegemony of the United States. Cuba has also in recent years become a rare political phenomenon that the Soviets could cite in attempting to improve their international image—a noncontiguous socialist state amenable to pro-Soviet orientation without gross coercion. In recent years Cuba, which is not a Warsaw Pact member, has provided through its military forces and civilian technical assistance personnel a method to further Soviet global objectives.[4] Finally, Cuba offers potential utility as a military facility and listening post well within the defense perimeter of the United States.

From the Cuban standpoint, close relations with Moscow are similarly beneficial. The Soviet Union provides the Castro government critical economic subsidies. Additionally, Soviet military and technical assistance has lessened traditional weaknesses in in both areas. Thirdly, the Soviet Union serves Cuba as a political sponsor willing to promote and support Cuba's aspirations of leadership in the nonaligned movement. Finally, the Kremlin acts as protector though not as guarantor of Cuban independence from the United States. The extensive levels of Soviet political, economic, and military support provide the Cubans sufficient margin of flexibility to conduct an activist foreign policy all out of proportion with Cuba's physical size.

Thus from the viewpoint of both Havana and Moscow a close relationship provides certain benefits which would not otherwise be available. Viewed in this manner, a *quid pro quo* relationship—simultaneously symbiotic and parasitic—clearly exists. Given the historical record of troubled Soviet-Cuban relations, it will be useful to turn to the perspective of each party, examine each aspect of the *quid pro quo,* and see how potentially enduring the convergence of national interests may be.

MOSCOW'S VIEW OF RELATIONS WITH CUBA

Revolutionary Cuba has presented Moscow with fascinating and perplexing foreign policy problems. Ever since Castro's accession to power, Soviet policy toward Cuba has reflected the Kremlin's quandary of how best to take advantage of a self-proclaimed Marxist-Leninist outpost in the Western Hemisphere.[5] From the Kremlin's perspective, at least through most of the post-1959 period, too much or too little Soviet support and interest in the Caribbean nation could lead to adverse results for Soviet foreign policy objectives. Either extreme may have resulted either in American intervention in Cuba, thereby highlighting Soviet impotence in the Caribbean region, or in Cuban alienation, thereby depriving the Soviet Union of the reflected glory found in an alliance with one of the few Marxist-Leninist regimes to gain power without the benefit of the Red Army.[6] To be sure, the Kremlin on occasion fell prey to the urge to pursue more adventurous policy lines in its relations with Cuba—such as the 1962 missiles gamble and the alleged meddling in Cuban affairs that led to the expulsion of the pro-Soviet "micro faction" from the party in 1968. Yet for the most part, Soviet leaders have been cognizant of the constraints within which their policy toward the island must operate.

Nonetheless it is evident that as far as the Kremlin is concerned Cuba has value as the sole Communist outpost in the otherwise inhospitable Western Hemisphere. Cuba consequently serves the Soviet Union as a "showcase of Communism," a showcase which must succeed both from an ideological and a pragmatic viewpoint. The Caribbean island may therefore be viewed as the most successful instance to which the Kremlin may point as proof that Soviet Marxism-Leninism and economic aid has relevance to the economic and social growth of developing nations.

Beyond this, the Cuban revolutionary experience marks the only instance of an indigenous national movement which gained power through its own efforts, adapted Marxism-Leninism to its own needs and circumstances, and adopted a predominantly pro-Soviet foreign policy orientation. While these facts are often overlooked in the West, Kremlin leaders are certainly aware of them as they consider their own claims to political legitimacy and universal appeal.

Yet another benefit the Soviet Union obtains from close relations with Cuba is support for Soviet foreign policy. The most spectacular instances of this have been in Angola and Ethiopia, where Soviet-equipped (and in the Somalia-Ethiopia war, Soviet-led) Cuban troops have fought for Soviet-supported political movements. Despite evidence that the Cubans may have dragged the Soviets into the Angolan commitment and that the two disagree on the proper policy toward Eritrea, the point to be emphasized is that Cuban forces clearly rendered a service which furthered Soviet and Cuban foreign policy objectives in both African nations. Together with the Bulgarians, the Cubans are probably the most ardent supporters of the Soviet Unions's foreign and domestic policies.

Finally, the Soviet Union benefits from close relations with Cuba in a purely military sense through its use of base facilities on the island. These facilities permit the Soviet Union to periodically test the limits of US tolerance for Soviet air and naval deployments in the Caribbean, provide tropical training for its military, give tangible evidence and reassurance to the Cuban leadership of Soviet support, and assist in the large security assistance program to Cuba.[7] The Soviets are, however, mindful of observing the post-missile crisis US-Soviet understandings about refraining from granting the Cubans offensive military capabilities. Additionally, the Soviet military presence in the Caribbean enhances the political impact of the apparent Soviet ability to project power into the Western Hemisphere. As evidenced by debate on the Soviet "brigade" in late summer 1979, that presence may also be counterproductive to both Cuban and Soviet interests.

Obviously the Soviet Union has some impelling reasons to maintain close ties with Cuba. Still the question needs to be asked, what costs exist in a close relationship, as seen from Moscow? Perhaps the most obvious disadvantage is the necessity for long-term, large-scale economic subsidy. Given the Soviet Union's own economic problems, the size of that subsidy—reported at $1.2 billion in 1976 and probably in excess of $3 billion in 1979—indicates the importance that the Kremlin attaches to close Soviet-

Cuban ties.

A second disadvantage of close ties is the continued risk, even though minimal, of Soviet-American confrontation arising from any of a number of disagreements between Cuba and the United States. Cuba's activist foreign policy, though currently congruent with Soviet policy objectives, has historically been determined by Havana's perceptions of its own interests. Thus if Soviet policy objectives and Cuban activism diverge in the future as they have done in the past, the close identity between the two nations may involve the Kremlin in Cuban initiatives which the Soviet Union deems not in its interest.

What is the sum total of these Soviet calculations? While a definitive answer is of course impossible, it is evident that the Kremlin currently believes the advantages of close relations with Cuba far outweigh the disadvantages. But this trend need not necessarily continue. Seeds of discord do exist, even though they are currently not consequential. Soviet client states have in the past proved less than totally compliant to Soviet desires, and the Soviet leadership has shown little hesitancy to reduce its support for regimes in disfavor or to deny economic aid to enforce compliance.

Nonetheless this remains only a possibility, not a probability. All things remaining equal, there is nothing on the present political-military horizon which suggests that the Soviet Union will downgrade its relations with the Cuban leadership. Setting aside the perspective from Moscow, it is now appropriate to consider the view from Havana.

THE PERSPECTIVE FROM HAVANA

The relationship with the Soviet Union has been useful to Cuban leadership in a number of ways. In the face of an economic embargo and the posture of hostility maintained by the United States, that linkage provides critical political, economic, and military support of an ideologically sympathetic superpower to a militarily vulnerable and geographically and politically isolated island. Thus the search for national security has been a major force driving Cuba to seek closer ties with the Soviet Union. Despite past disagreements on matters of foreign and defense policy, on the proper political and economic structure of Cuba's socialist system, on ideological issues, and on the role of the Cuban Communist Party, there exists sufficient convergence of national interests for

56

Cuba and the Soviet Union to forge a formidable political-military alliance for the pursuit of common objectives in international affairs. The development of such an alliance is a new phenomenon in Cuba's history, giving that country a bargaining position in world affairs far in excess of its own power capabilities and out of character with its traditional dependency—as a colony of Spain until 1898 and thereafter for all practical purposes as one of the United States.

Relations with the Soviet Union in the 1960's were marked by the tension surrounding the need to maintain the autonomy of the revolution itself and the need to acquire and retain Soviet economic and military assistance at the very same time. Much to the disappointment of the Cubans, the Soviets provided a decidedly conservative response to Cuba's efforts to spearhead guerrilla warfare and national liberation in Latin America during the 1960's. Concurrently, the ongoing revolution of Cuban society disrupted the economy as the result of deemphasis (and later reemphasis) of sugar production, forced industrialization, loss of the US market for sugar, capital and technology, and loss of skilled manpower to emigration. Given continued American hostility toward Cuba, the defeat of the strategy of guerrilla warfare, signalled by the death of Che Guevara in the Bolivian mountains, increased diplomatic isolation within Latin America, and severe economic pressures imposed by Moscow (such as the reduction of petroleum shipments), Havana was forced to draw closer to Moscow. Cuba thus saw the wisdom of relinquishing its ideological misgivings about Soviet pragmatism and conservatism and opted to accept greater Soviet assistance and progressively greater guidance in its own affairs. The Cubans are reluctant to permit this relationship to evolve into a third phase of colonial dependency. However the euphemism is couched in the terminology of relations among socialist countries—be it "socialist solidarity" or "proletarian internationalism"—the fear of neocolonial exploitation must be a genuine one within the Cuban leadership.

Premier Castro recognized the necessity of rapprochement with the Soviet benefactors in 1968 in his celebrated but nonetheless qualified approval of the Brezhnev doctrine of "limited sovereignty" exercised in the invasion of Czechoslovakia. Relations solidified further with the July and December 1972 agreements that made Cuba a member of the Council for Mutual Economic Assistance (CMEA), and that secured a stable market for Cuban sugar and nickel through long-term trading agreements and subsequent technical assistance programs. It was further agreed that repayment on the accumulated Cuban debt of $4.6 billion would be suspended until 1985 and spread over a period of 25 years—tantamount to cancellation. Currently the Soviet Union maintains the price of Cuba's principal export, sugar, at above 30 cents per pound, close to 20 cents above the prevailing international market price. Moreover the Soviets assist in numerous tasks of economic reorganization and development (such as nickel mining and deep sea fishing), provide petroleum, and in sum account for nearly 60 percent of Cuban trade.[8] The Soviet subsidy and trade are crucial to Cuba, permitting Havana the luxury of buying time for further reorganization and diversification of an economy which gives every indication of continuing to be monoculturist—heavily dependent upon sugar and to an increasing degree upon nickel (of which Cuba has the world's fourth largest ore reserves).

The concept of subsidy also applies to the Cuban military establishment, for which the Soviet Union provides equipment, training, and personnel. Without the price supports and outright grants, Cuba would be hard put to free sufficient manpower resources for its extensive overseas technical assistance, security assistance, and its large combat deployments to Angola and Ethiopia, now estimated to be 19-20 thousand and 12-18 thousand, respectively.[9]

Of Cuba's total trade, 70 percent is with Communist countries, including China. In 1976, Cuban exports to the Council for Mutual Economic Assistance (CMEA) reached $2.2 billion and imports $2.1 billion. Soviet trade accounts for 80 percent of Cuba's intra-CMEA trade. In 1976, Cuban exports to the USSR were estimated at slightly over $2 billion versus $1.8 billion in imports. Sugar comprised about 90 percent of Cuba's exports to CMEA, with the USSR importing 85 percent of the total.

Cuba will continue to be an important source of sugar for CMEA. The Soviet Union also purchases three-fourths of the island's nickel production at $6,050 per ton compared to the 1977 international market price of $5,400 per ton. Citrus, a growing component of Cuban export agriculture, is also intended for the CMEA market, but here also the Soviet Union is increasing its own production.[10]

In the area of imports, the Soviet Union in 1977 provided 95 percent of Cuba's petroleum requirements at $7.00 per ton, a considerable savings over the world price of $14.00 per ton, and the $8.00 per ton that the Soviet Union charges East European consumers. The Soviet Union, in view of anticipated decreases in domestic energy production, concluded an agreement with Venezuela in 1976 to exchange petroleum markets for a volume of 20,000 barrels a day. Under the agreement, Venezuela would ship crude oil to Cuba and the Soviet Union would take over some of Venezuela's West European markets. In 1974, Cuba received 155,000 barrels of oil a day from the Soviet Union.[11] A similar agreement was concluded between Mexico and the Soviet Union in May 1978 by which Mexico would supply oil to Cuba in exchange for Soviet deliveries to Mexican oil customers in Greece, Turkey, and Eastern Europe.[12]

While Cuba conducts the bulk of its trade with CMEA, it is keenly interested in expanding trade with and securing capital from the West. Because of long-term trading agreements with CMEA and the vagaries of sugar production and pricing, trade with the West will in the foreseeable future be in the area of 30 to 40 percent of total Cuban trade. With the improved prices that sugar commanded in 1974, trade with the West reached 41 percent, whereas it averaged 30 percent in the early 1970's. The volume of sugar production, its price, and its ability to gain access to alternative markets in a period of rising world production and stocks, will thus go a long way toward determining the extent and composition of Cuba's trade with CMEA, the Soviet Union, and the West. At the same time, the degree of convergence of Soviet and Cuban policies will be reflected in the extent and duration of the Soviet subsidy of the Cuban economy. A recently announced Soviet-Cuban commerical agreement for the period 1981-85 appears to buttress the convergence. In his December 27, 1979 speech to the National Assembly, Fidel Castro referred to an economic aid agreement worth approximately $10 million per day for that period. During those 5 years, the Soviet Union will deliver 61 million tons of oil, or 12.2 million tons per year. Cuba's current annual consumption is 11 million tons. Cuba is scheduled to buy the oil at $105 per ton (while the international market price for early 1980 was $250). Cuba will sell 3.5 million tons of sugar per year during the period, for which the Soviets will pay the preferential rate of $880 per ton, a figure that can be adjusted to any increase in the Soviet oil price.

The $10 million economic aid per day amount is based on a calculation of $2.1 billion for sugar combined with a savings of $1.77 billion on the oil bill.[13]

Future US participation in Cuban trade, optimistically projected at $600-700 million, is not likely to make an appreciable dent in the Soviet subsidy cost, because the Cuban market promises to be one of limited access for US products and capital. These facts underline the disadvantages that ensue for Cuba in being locked into CMEA trade arrangements, for Cuba sorely needs Western technology and capital to increase the productivity of its dominant sugar industry and the development of the nickel industry.

CUBAN FOREIGN POLICY AND THE SOVIET UNION

The foregoing discussion on the advantages and disadvantages of Cuba's relationship with the Soviet Union does not sufficiently explain certain aspects of Cuba's contemporary foreign policy behavior. Economic and military dependence upon the Soviet Union does not explain the apparent contradictions of this behavior—for example, deployments in African wars juxtaposed with the inclination to normalize relations with the United States and the desire to acquire Western capital and technology. Of course in Marxist-Leninist terms these are not at all contradictory aspects.

Edward Gonzales, a leading scholar on Cuban affairs, has proposed some approaches for explaining Cuba's activist foreign policy. In his view, the assumption that Cuba is dependent on the Soviet Union should not imply that Cuba is a surrogate or proxy for the Soviet Union, essentially doing the Soviet bidding whenever and wherever the Soviet Union calls the shots or going where the Soviets themselves are reluctant to go. Gonzales challenges the surrogate theory for its failure to account for Cuba's own foreign policy interests in its capacity as an autonomous actor.[14] Moreover, he argues that it clearly overlooks cases where Cuba has not acceded to Soviet policy preferences and has acted independently of the Soviet Union and without its logistical support, such as in Africa and Latin America in the 1960's and early 1970's.

The second thesis, that ideology is the force pushing Cuba to spearhead the Third World revolution, is also insufficient by itself since it does not explain certain pragmatic aspects of Cuban policy behavior or Havana's urge for normalization with its ideological enemy, the United States. Gonzales places emphasis on internal

60

determinants—economic necessity and the role of pragmatic technocrats—as important modifiers of Cuban behavior. Institutional factors, interests of the Cuban military, encourage overseas deployments at the very same time that Cuba seeks to extend its diplomatic relations in the world and to normalize its relations with the United States.[15] Castro's personality and his infatuation with his historical destiny to lead the Third World revolution are also important factors spurring Cuban involvement overseas.

In its relations with Moscow, Cuba sees itself providing considerable benefits in return for the Kremlin's support. As far as the Cuban leadership is concerned, the Kremlin's close ties with Havana confer a considerable respectability and international prestige upon the Soviet Union. Moreover, they constitute ongoing evidence for the validity of Moscow's claim of socialist solidarity. Cuba thus generally views itself as a state freely associated with the Soviets and of course Cuba's geographic situation precludes Moscow's use of force against Havana. The absence of brute coercion indicates that close ties with the Soviets are, in view of Cuba's geopolitical situation, possibly more acceptable to the Cuban leadership than to Eastern European counterparts. Does it also suggest that Cuba can unbind itself from the Soviet link more easily? Certainly, but only if and when that link is no longer necessary for the survival of socialist Cuba.

Thus the Cubans enjoy the friendship of the socialist superpower that brings its economic and military presence virtually within the shadow of the United States and helps create the image of an alliance with which to promote joint objectives in the Third World—an arena which Cuba (as a self-styled Afro-Latin nation) considers its legitimate domain of activity. Indeed, there is hardly a question in international affairs on which Cuba and the Soviet Union do not agree. They both support East-West detente and extol each other's socialist achievements. They work in tandem to undermine the US international position by attacking the shortcomings of American society and by coordinating policies designed to diminish US influence in Africa, the Middle East, and lately with renewed vigor in Latin America.

Cuba, moreover, articulates a world view that sees the "correlation of forces" becoming increasingly favorable to the socialist bloc. For some years the Cubans have actively participated in the nonaligned movement, and recently they have been reprimanded by other members of that movement—notably Yugoslavia—for their efforts to push the movement into a pro-Soviet stance on world affairs. Havana hosted the 1979 summit of nonaligned and will head the movement's coordinating bureau for the next 3 years. Indeed, President Castro will be the movement's senior statesman upon Tito's death. More recently, Cuba's support for the Soviet Union has earned it considerable costs within the nonaligned movement. In the wake of the Soviet move into Afghanistan on December 25, 1979, Cuba lost its bid to achieve the coveted United Nations Security Council seat. President Castro staked Cuba's prestige on this effort, vowing not to accept defeat.[16] Predictably, the General Assembly debate on Afghanistan presented the Cubans with a "dilemma"—to use their term—as they were forced to vote against the general condemnation (by a vote of 104 to 18) of the Soviet invasion.

Cuba's activist foreign policy thus enhances its relatively limited power and increases its bargaining position vis-a-vis the United States and the Soviet Union. It does so by interposing itself in issues of international and regional concern as an actor with distinctive needs and with leverage that must be reckoned with by other powers. Ultimately it seeks to establish as irrefutable the legitimacy of its socialist revolution and the inviolability of its sovereignty. As socialist values become more internalized in Cuban society, these twin objectives become inseparable from the notion of national security. In a sense, Cuba has externalized the revolution in overseas enterprises in order to defend it at home, from both its internal and external enemies. Externalizing the revolution has the additional effect of rationalizing to its own people the economic shortcomings of Cuban socialism, which the Cuban media attributes to the economic warfare waged against the nation by the United States.

However it rationalizes its linkage with the Soviet Union, there are definite costs and contradictions that Cuba must endure. Cuba's economic and military dependency upon the Soviet Union is well known and not admired in the Third World—the very arena where Cuba seeks to project itself as an independent actor. Moreover, its military diplomacy is feared in many sectors of the world. Cuba is hardly seen as a disinterested revolutionary in Africa, and in the immediate Caribbean area it is only slowly making friends—Grenada, Jamaica, Guyana, Nicaragua. Ties with the Soviet Union, its internal totalitarianism, and its proximity to the United States will continue to constrain Cuba's efforts to expand its influence in Latin America.

If Cuba's close association with the Soviet Union is resented by many countries, it also may help promote more fractures in international communism. The association earns it the opprobrium of China and Yugoslavia. It also puts it out of touch with Eurocommunism—a movement which asserts ideological independence from the Soviet Union and speaks on behalf of national roads to socialism and the un-Leninist notion of respecting pluralistic structures.[17] The ultimate cost for Cuba may be a mortgage of its image of sovereignty. If it is so evidently dependent upon the Soviet Union, then it is not independent in the eyes of the world. There is, moreover, the remote possibility that the Soviet Union may weaken its support of Cuba in order to concentrate on internal needs or to pursue its own political objectives elsewhere. To render this possibility even more remote and protect its national security, Cuba must make itself indispensable to the Soviet Union while maintaining the seemingly contradictory appearance of an independent and sovereign state. Therein lies the grave risk that such behavior may ultimately involve a compromise of those attributes, since Cuba is relatively powerless by itself.

Other disadvantages ensue for Cuba from the linkage with the Soviet Union. The long-term trading agreements with CMEA complicate Cuba's efforts to diversify trade and acquire sorely needed Western capital and technology. Trade with CMEA is done mostly on a barter basis whereby Cuba does not receive hard currency for the transactions. In recent years, Cuban trade has generated a positive balance with non-Communist countries only once, in 1974, when the price of sugar reached 68 cents per pound. When sugar prices fell and limited quantities were available for export to non-CMEA economies, large negative trade balances followed. The hardships imposed by Cuba's artificial economic relations are not likely to dispose the leadership to compromise the idealogical content of its foreign policy nor drive Cuba to alter its relations with the socialist bloc in a major way.

To sum up, Cuba believes that the advantages of close ties with Moscow are more than sufficient to outweigh the disadvantages. Cuba is involved in a very sophisticated political game of asserting its autonomy within a relationship of dependency. The apparent contradictions of Cuba's foreign policy make sense only within the context of Cuba's perceptions of its relations with both superpower friend and superpower enemy—the Soviet Union and the United States.

SOVIET-CUBAN RELATIONS AND THE UNITED STATES

When all is said and done, what conclusions can be derived from the evolution of Soviet-Cuban relations? On the basis of the preceding analysis, it appears that the relationship will remain close for the foreseeable future. Despite certain strains in the relationship—expressed in policy differences in Africa and the escalating costs of the Soviet economic subsidy—the preponderant evidence indicates that numerous instances of mutual advantage will continue to bind the two socialist states into an intimate relationship. Possible setbacks on the African continent and within the nonaligned movement may intensify some of these strains but not necessarily sever the relationship.

Such an assessment is further strengthened when one analyzes the leadership of both nations. In the Soviet Union, geriatric decisionmakers have long argued for international socialist solidarity, support for the Cuban revolution, and the provision of necessary assistance to friendly socialist states. Given the other benefits the Kremlin accrues from its Cuban connection, and the unlikelihood of a sharp attitudinal change in either the present or emerging leadership group, it is highly unlikely that Moscow will alter its current Cuban policy.

The same argument may be made for the current Cuban leadership, most particularly Castro. Castro retains a siege mentality and his revolutionary fervor combined with his willingness aggressively to exploit opportunities in the Third World and most recently closer to home in the Caribbean have undoubtedly heightened his perception of a hardening US position towards Cuba. Without even considering Soviet economic subsidies, it is evident that Castro's Cuba benefits from close Soviet-Cuban relations. Thus, from the Cuban leader's perspective, there appears little likelihood of change in that relationship, since there is little likelihood of change in the US posture toward Cuba, as Castro has frequently stated.

What impact may the United States hope to have on this relationship? Given the many congruencies of Soviet and Cuban national interests now and in the near future, as well as the political inclinations of both leaderships, it is almost impossible to foresee

64

that US actions can have more than a negligible impact on Soviet-Cuban relations. Even with an extreme turn in policy—on the one hand, toward a further tightening of economic sanctions in response to Cuba's foreign adventurism, and on the other hand, toward "normalization" of Cuban-American relations to the point of resuming trade relations—the evolution of the Soviet-Cuban relationship would doubtless be dominated by factors beyond Washington's influence. If a "hard-line" US policy option were adopted, current Soviet-Cuban solidarity would inevitably be perpetuated. If a "soft-line" US policy approach were adopted, it would certainly enable the Kremlin to reduce marginally its economic subsidy to Cuba, but there is nothing to suggest that this reduction would be significant in diluting the quality of the Soviet-Cuban relationship.

The preceding analysis addresses the short-term impact of US policy on Soviet-Cuban relations. The longer-term prospects are somewhat different, however. Under a hard-line US policy scenario, the Cuban leadership would still be faced with a menacing superpower to the north, with few policy options from which to choose. In essence, the Cubans would be forced to minimize their differences with the Soviet Union and accentuate their policy congruencies, as they currently appear to be doing. Since policy advantages which the Kremlin presently reaps from its close ties with Havana appear not to be time sensitive, it is reasonable to assume that the post-Brezhnev Soviet leadership would continue to bear the Cuban economic burden. Thus, given the assumption of a hard-line US policy toward Cuba, a continuation of the status quo appears likely.

It is the long-term impact of a soft-line US policy which presents a different prospect. In the next one to two decades a large proportion of the leaderships of the two nations will change, and it is after these leadership changes that the benefits of the hypothetical soft-line US policy might accrue. Put simply, a soft-line policy would increase the options available to the newly emerging Cuban leadership—a leadership probably seeking to solidify its hold on Cuban power (with or without Castro), and therefore willing and able to choose policy options not now available to Castro. These options are not available to him both because of his own political-ideological attitudes and because these options have been precluded by the hardening of American policy toward normalization of relations. The danger of such an

American policy, of course, is that the Cuban leadership—Castro or others—may view it as indicative of American weak will and equivocation and hence conducive to additional Cuban foreign policy activism and risk taking.

CONCLUSION

In conclusion then, it would appear that Soviet-Cuban relations will remain intimate throughout the near-term future. The problems that exist in that relationship are likely to have significance only in the long term, and even then, only if a number of factors coincide: if the Soviets are compelled by their national interests to reduce or eliminate the economic subsidy and if they decide to abandon Cuba and pursue their interests elsewhere. It appears that if the United States were to adopt a "soft-line" policy, the probability of reduced Soviet-Cuban intimacy in the long-term future would be maximized. However, such a policy decision would also increase the risk of Soviet-Cuban adventurism in the short- and mid-term since a soft-line US policy could be construed by the two socialist countries as indicative of weak American resolve. That perception has been a factor in Soviet-Cuban-US relations since 1975 and may now be heightened by the recent setbacks to US foreign policy.

US policy makers are thus faced with a complex choice. Their decision must be based on the answers to a series of other questions which are somewhat beyond the scope of this paper. Nonetheless, if a comprehensive improvement in Cuban-American relations is in the American interest, and if continued Soviet and Cuban political and military adventurism is seen as compromising American security interests, than a new policy is appropriate. The United States should adopt a policy that diminishes the targets of opportunity for the Cubans in the troubled Third World, that also involves the Soviets in exerting a moderating influence over Cuban behavior (mindful at the same time of Moscow's own leverage problems with the Cubans), and that preserves for both the US and Cuban leaderships the option of developing normalized relations to their mutual advantage.

ENDNOTES

1. For an analysis of the problems of Chilean-Soviet relations in the period 1970-73, see Joseph L. Nogee and John W. Sloan, "Allende's Chile and the Soviet Union: A Policy Lesson for Latin American Nations Seeking Autonomy," unpublished paper, University of Houston, 1979. Useful appraisals of Soviet policy in Latin America are: D. Bruce Jackson, *Castro, the Kremlin, and Communism in Latin America*, Baltimore: Johns Hopkins Press, 1969; Leon Goure and Morris Rothenberg, *Soviet Penetration of Latin America*, Miami: University of Miami Press, 1975; J.G. Oswald and A.J. Strover, eds., *The Soviet Union and Latin America*, New York: Praeger, 1970.

2. On this point see Edward Gonzalez, "A Comparison of Soviet and Cuban Approaches to Latin America," *Studies in Comparative Communism*, Vol. V, No. 1, Spring 1972, pp. 21-35; and Herbert S. Dinerstein, "Soviet and Cuban Conceptions of Revolution," *Studies in Comparative Communism*, Vol. IV, No. 1, January 1972, pp. 3-22. Dinerstein observed: "Castro through the mouth of (Regis) Debray challenged the Soviet doctrine of revolution and implied that many opportunities for the establishment of communism had been missed because of the conservatism of the Soviet Union and of Communist parties that followed in its lead." (p. 12)

3. On the Eritrea question the Cubans are reluctant to assume a direct combat role in support of Addis Ababa and Soviet policy. See Daniel S. Papp, *Eritrea and the Soviet-Cuban Connection*, Military Issues Research Memorandum, Carlisle Barracks, Pennsylvania: Strategic Studies Institute, July 31, 1978. On Angola, the Cubans have apparently balanced off Soviet influence among the contending factions within the governing Movement for the Liberation of Angola. On this point, see Charles K. Ebinger, "External Intervention in Internal War: The Politics and Diplomacy of the Angolan Civil War," *Orbis*, Vol. 20, No. 3, Fall 1976, pp. 697-698, and William M. LeoGrande, paper presented at the annual meeting of the International Studies Association, Toronto, Canada, March 22-26, 1979, pp. 26-27.

4. By August 1979 there were approximately 39,000 Cuban military personnel performing combat and security assistance roles along with 12,000 non-diplomatic civilian personnel in the following countries: Angola, Benin, Cape Verde, Congo, Equatorial Guinea, Ethiopia, Guinea, Guinea-Bissau, Mozambique, Sao Tome and Principe, Tanzania, Zambia, Algeria, Iraq, Libya, People's Republic of Yemen, Western Sahara (Polisario movement), Laos, Vietnam, Grenada, Guyana, Jamaica, and Nicaragua. Sources: Various editions of *Granma, Granma Weekly Review, Foreign Broadcast Information Service* (Latin America, Middle East, Sub-Saharan Africa), *Juventud Rebelde, The Washington Post, The New York Times*.

5. Although Castro proclaimed his revolution socialist during an oration following the initial Bay of Pigs bombardments in April 1961, and avowed himself a Marxist-Leninist in a December 1, 1961 speech, the Soviet Union made no reference to socialism in Cuba until April 11, 1962, when *Pravda* finally acknowledged that the Caribbean island was moving on a socialist road.

6. The Cuban Communist Party did not participate in and was originally skeptical of the revolutionary potential of Castro's movement. Castro came to rely more on the party in the mid-1960's, and it was eventually integrated into the government. For an excellent review of the history of strategic and ideological misgivings, see Jacques Levesque, *The USSR and the Cuban Revolution: Soviet Ideological and Strategical Perspectives, 1959-77*, New York: Praeger, 1978.

7. According to various authorities, the Soviet air and naval deployments are intended more for political than for military reasons. See Cole Blasier, "The Soviet Union in the Cuban-American Conflict," and Jorge I. Dominguez, "The Armed Forces and Foreign Relations," in *Cuba in the World*, ed. by Blasier and Carmelo Mesa-Lago, Pittsburgh: University of Pittsburgh Press, 1979, pp. 37-51, 53-86.

8. There are indications that the Soviet Union through CMEA gives Cuba preferential treatment in petroleum prices over its East European customers by bracketing Cuba with Mongolia, North Korea, and North Vietnam as developing socialist countries. For additional discussion on Cuba trade relations and prospects for economic development see Carmelo Mesa-Lago, "The Economy and International Economic Relations;" Cole Blasier, "COMECON in Cuban Development;" Theodore H. Moran, "Cuban Nickel Development;" Jorge F. Perez-Lopez, "Sugar and Petroleum in Cuban-Soviet Terms of Trade," in Blasier and Mesa-Lago, *Cuba in the World*.

9. For speculation on the negative economic impact of Cuba's extensive overseas commitments see Mesa-Lago, *Present and Future of Cuba's Economy and International Economic Relations*, unpublished manuscript, University of Pittsburgh, 1977, pp. 9, 13, and footnote 16.

10. The accompanying analysis of Cuba's trade relations is derived from Lawrence Theriot, *Cuba in CMEA*, US Department of Commerce, 1977, pp. 3-5.

11. David Binder, "Venezuela and Soviet Union Reach an Agreement on Oil," *The New York Times*, December 10, 1976, p. D3.

12. Marian Leighton, "Mexico, Cuba, and the Soviet Union: Ferment in the US's Back Yard," *Radio Free Liberty Research*, December 27, 1979, p. 9.

13. "Castro Speech Underscores Close Ties With USSR," Agence France Press, (February 6, 1980) as transcribed in Foreign Broadcast Information Service, *Daily Report: Latin America*, February 8, 1980, p. Q1.

14. Don Bohning and Tom Fiedler, "Cuba's Prestige is a Casualty of Afghanistan Invasion," *Philadelphia Inquirer*, January 10, 1980, p. 5-A; "Mexico Wins a U.N. Council Seat in Vote Viewed as Defeat for Cuba," *The New York Times*, January 8, 1980, p. A-2.

15. Gonzalez, *Problems of Communism*, Vol. 36, No. 6, November-December 1977, pp. 1-15.

16. *Ibid.*, pp. 9-10.

17. In their theoretical writings the Cubans refer to Eurocommunist parties as serious movements that speak about the possibility of achieving socialism through a nonviolent revolutionary process. "We should not preclude the possibility that with a world balance of forces decidedly in favor of the socialist system, the coming to power and establishment of a proletarian state in a given country could take place without use of force." Gaspar Jorge Garcia Gallo, "Focus on Marxism," *Granma Weekly Review*, June 3, 1979, p. 2.

PART 2
THE SOVIET UNION IN AFRICA
AND THE MIDDLE EAST

4

THE SOVIET UNION AND SOUTHERN AFRICA

Daniel S. Papp

The collapse of the Portuguese colonial empire and the ac-
celeration of the struggle for black majority rule have combined to
make Southern Africa one of the major centers of contemporary
international conflict.[1] These two factors alone would have been
sufficient to guarantee years of turmoil in Southern Africa. Unfortunately, however, although not unexpectedly, Soviet-American
rivalry has also been interjected into Southern African affairs,
adding additional tension and danger to an already volatile
situation.

This rivalry to a great extent has been an outgrowth of large-scale
Soviet and Cuban involvement in the Angolan Civil War, which
began in 1975. That involvement and its motivation have been
analyzed elsewhere,[2] and will not be examined here. However, very
little study has been undertaken of Soviet policy toward the
Southern African region as a whole. What objectives does the
USSR seek to achieve in the region? What instruments of policy
does the Soviet Union employ? How successful have the men in the
Kremlin been in achieving their objectives, and what is the
prognosis for future Soviet policy? What implications may be
drawn for the United States? These and other questions will be
analyzed in this study.

SOVIET OBJECTIVES

Soviet objectives in Southern Africa fall into three broadly defined categories.[3] The first category is composed of objectives which have been explicitly *declared* by the Soviet government. These objectives include establishing and improving relations with the front-line states of Angola, Botswana, Mozambique, Tanzania, and Zambia; strengthening and supporting national liberation movements in South Africa, Namibia, and Zimbabwe; opposing and removing remaining vestiges of colonialism and racism; and supporting and aiding what the Soviet Union identifies as national independence and social progress.

The second category of Soviet objectives in Southern Africa may be viewed as a corollary of the first and includes two clear though *undeclared* aims of Soviet policy. These are the reduction of American and/or Western European influence in the area and the reduction of Communist Chinese influence in the area.

The final category of Soviet objectives is the subject of much debate in the West and includes at least three pragmatic though hypothetical Soviet goals, each of which has been specifically *denied* by the Soviet Union. This category of objectives includes obtaining military base rights and reconnaissance rights in the area; reducing American and Western European access to the rich mineral resources of the region; and threatening the oil supply lines of the United States and Western Europe, thereby accelerating the so-called "Finlandization" of Western Europe in particular.

Each of these categories will be individually examined, although it should be noted that the objectives within one category are often directly related to objectives in other categories.

Objectives Specified By the Soviet Government

Perhaps the clearest recent official Soviet government statement on its objectives in Southern Africa was the USSR's "Statement on African Policy," released on June 23, 1978. In this statement the Soviet government argued that it sought to strengthen and expand its "peaceful relations" with all legitimately-ruling African governments; to aid national liberation movements throughout Africa in their struggles against outside domination; to oppose colonialism, neocolonialism, and racism; and to support progressive programs adopted by African governments which had embarked on the noncapitalist path of development. This

70

statement, originally released as an apparent reaction to American charges of ''Soviet expansionism'' in Africa, has since been repeated by Soviet leaders and media in numerous forms and forums.[4]

The public declaration of such objectives produces certain specific dividends for the USSR. Soviet protestations calling for improved and expanded relations with legitimately ruling Africa governments provide the logical basis for expanded political, economic, military, and cultural relations with the front-line states in Southern Africa. Indeed, when former Soviet President Podgorny journeyed to Tanzania, Zambia, and Mozambique in March 1977, he often called for closer Soviet-African contacts. Soviet desire for improved relations with the front-line states is directly abetted by Soviet support for national liberation movements in South Africa, Namibia, and Zimbabwe. The front-line states have been exceedingly vocal in their support for the African People's Organization (SWAPO) in Southwest Africa and the Patriotic Front, composed of Joshua Nkomo's Zimbabwe African People's Union (ZAPU) and Robert Mugabe's Zimbabwe African National Union (ZANU), in Zimbabwe. It is therefore not surprising that the Soviet Union supports these movements as well, although with varying degrees of moral and material backing. This is not to argue that Soviet support for these national liberation movements emanates solely from a Soviet attempt to improve its relations with the front-line nations; it is to point out that the Soviet objectives of strengthening relations with the front-line nations and of aiding national liberation movements are in many instances complementary from both the Soviet and front-line perspectives.

Much the same argument may be made for Soviet opposition to colonialism, neocolonialism, and racism. Without exception, leaders of the front-line nations and the national liberation movements in Southern Africa have verbally assaulted these vestiges of European presence in the region. Soviet leaders have followed suit. This is again comprehensible from both policy and ideological perspectives. Equally notable are Soviet attitudes toward the rather restrained position on white rule in the region adopted by President Seretse Khama of Botswana. Soviet reaction to Khama's position has paralleled the attitudes adopted by the four other front-line states. All recognize that Botswana's restraint is determined ''more by geography than preference.''[5] Thus, once again, self-proclaimed Soviet objectives are complementary, and coincide with those of the front-line states and national liberation movements.

Finally, the declarative Soviet objective of supporting progressive governments embarked on noncapitalist paths of development theoretically coincides with the objectives of at least four of the front-line governments. Two of the ruling parties, the Movimento Popular de Libertacao de Angola (MPLA) and the Frente de Libertacao de Mocambique (Frelimo), have adopted "scientific socialism" as part of their party programs. The Soviet Union, of course, loudly supports this effort. Additionally, since 1974 the Soviet Union has even been willing to adopt lenient attitudes toward the "African socialism" of Tanzanian President Julius Nyerere and Zambian President Kenneth Kaunda.

This evident similarity between the policy objectives which the USSR itself claims it seeks in Southern Africa and those which most front-line states and national liberation movements seek presents the Soviet Union with certain opportunites in its Southern African policies. Nevertheless, at times policy problems also develop. However, skillful manipulation of ideological precepts enables the Soviet Union to fashion its policies to minimize these difficulties.[6] For example, with Robert Mugabe's ZANU being predominantly pro-Maoist, Soviet opposition to ZANU might have been expected. Nevertheless even though until 1978 the Soviet Union gave only small amounts of material aid to ZANU, the USSR still recognized Mugabe's faction of the Patriotic Front as a national liberation movement. Was this recognition ideologically induced, pragmatically oriented in the hope of improving reactions with ZANU in the future, or produced by a Soviet desire to once again have its objectives and policies appear congruent with those of the front-line states? While the answer to this question may never be known, it is clear that ideological differences have been conveniently overlooked.

Clear Though Unspecified Objectives

Soviet declarative objectives in Southern Africa carry with them a hidden agenda of reducing and potentially eliminating US and Chinese influence in the region. Given Soviet identification of American influences as "imperialistic" and of Chinese influence as "expansionistic," and given the existence of the real and tangible rivalry which exists between and among the three nations, it is

72

understandable that the USSR would seek at the very least to reduce US and Chinese influence in Southern Africa.

Soviet warnings about the danger of American imperialism in Southern Africa appear in the Soviet media on almost a daily basis. Often these warnings are coupled with admonishments that the changes in US policy toward Southern Africa which followed former Secretary of State Henry Kissinger's 1976 Lusaka speech simply presaged new and more insidious methods to maintain and extend American positions in the region.[7] Recent US and British efforts to achieve a peaceful transition to black rule have been similarly interpreted.[8] Warnings about the dangers of imperialism and admonishments about the insidiousness of US policy may thus be viewed as two sides of the same coin—an effort to reduce US influence in the area.

Parallel to these efforts are Soviet desires to reduce Chinese influence in the region. Sino-Soviet rivalry in Southern Africa has long been a divisive force within the front-line nations and national liberation movements of Southern Africa. Much to Soviet chagrin, Mozambique, Tanzania, and Zambia during their early stages of independence adopted pro-Chinese attitudes.[9] Soviet efforts to arrange a high-level visit to these nations were repeatedly rejected until December 1976, when it was announced that Podgorny would visit the three nations in the following March. Since then the front-line states as a whole have for the most part adopted what may be termed "even-handed" policies in the Sino-Soviet struggle for influence.

The Sino-Soviet struggle for influence had impact upon the national liberation movements as well. As has already been noted, Robert Mugabe has declared that ZANU's policies are dictated by "Marxism-Leninism of Maoist thought," while ZAPU's Joshua Nkomo prefers a more orthodox Soviet model of socialism. In a more striking characterization of alleged Chinese influence in Zimbabwe TASS even accused the Chinese of extending military aid to Ian Smith's government. These accusations (April and May 1979) began even as the USSR apparently began to accelerate its aid to ZANU.[10]

Sino-Soviet rivalry has been well documented in the Angolan national liberation movement as well. Soviet support for the MPLA was in marked contrast to Chinese support for the Frente Nacional de Libertacao de Angola (FNLA) and Uniao Nacional para a Independencia Total de Angola (UNITA). Indeed, civil war

73

in that unhappy country still rages as the two socialist powers continue to give aid to their own preferred segments of the former national liberation movement. The Soviets have labelled the FNLA and UNITA "splittists" since the MPLA established control of Luanda, and have accused these movements, China, and of course the United States, of collaborating with South Africa in an effort to establish neocolonialism in Angola.[11]

It is rather evident then that the USSR seeks to reduce and perhaps eliminate US and Chinese influence in Southern Africa. Whether the Soviet Union conversely seeks directly to increase its own influence and long-term physical presence in the region is a more debatable issue. It is this type of putative goal which comprises the third category of Soviet objectives.

Possible Although Hypothetical Objectives

Three possible Soviet objectives in South Africa include obtaining military base and reconnaissance rights in the area; reducing American and Western European access to the mineral resources of the area; and threatening the oil supply lines of the US and Western Europe. While Soviet spokesmen have regularly denied that the Soviet Union has any of these objectives,[12] doubts continue to linger about the veracity of Soviet denials.

Some of these doubts stem directly from Soviet behavior. Soviet military presence in Southern Africa has indeed been growing remarkably. Soviet reconnaissance flights do fly out of Luanda, and naval squadrons have called in Angola, Mozambique, and Tanzania, the only front-line states with ports. Although reports in 1977 and 1978 of Soviet basing rights on Bazaruto Island off Mozambique and in the Seychelles Islands have proven false, it is clear that Soviet naval interest in Southern Africa has picked up. Indeed, as the Angolan Civil War heated up in early 1976, a Kotlin class destroyer, Kresta class cruiser, and an amphibious vessel with 100 to 150 troops on board cruised off Angola.

Other doubts, particularly concerning mineral resources and oil, stem directly from Southern Africa's resource wealth and strategic location. As recently as 1969, Southern Africa (including, in this case, Zaire) accounted for 69 percent of the world's gold production, 64 percent of the world's gem and industrial diamond production, 32 percent of its chromite production, 22 percent of its copper, and 28 percent of its antimony and platinum. Additionally,

74

57 percent of the world's known cobalt resources and 17 percent known uranium resources were in this one region.[14] Given this incredible wealth and the regular Soviet condemnation of US and Western European efforts to "plunder the wealth" of the region,[15] it is not surprising that some analysts reject Soviet denials and argue that the USSR has opted for a "strategy of mineral denial."[16] At the same time, with Southern Africa astride the tanker route from the Persian Gulf to the United States and Western Europe, the Soviet presence in Southern Africa evokes fears that the western states, in the event of an East-West crisis, may be vulnerable to Soviet pressure.

INSTRUMENTS OF SOVIET POLICY

Instruments of Soviet policy toward Southern Africa may be broadly classified as diplomacy, military support, and trade and aid. It should once again be recognized that these delineations are in many instances artificial, and that the categories do in fact impact each other.

Diplomacy

Until recently, Soviet diplomatic contacts with Southern Africa have been rather limited. Soviet efforts to send a high level delegation to the independent states in the area did not succeed until 1977. While the different variations of African socialism which developed throughout Africa and particularly Tanzania and Zambia were viewed with varying degrees of hesitant support from Moscow,[17] it was not really until the Portuguese colonial empire in Southern Africa collapsed and the struggle for black rule accelerated that diplomatic contacts between Moscow and the region proliferated. Table 1 illustrates this proliferation.

In addition to the increased number of recent contacts between the Soviet Union and Southern Africa, it should also be noted that these contacts took place on a higher level. Thus, two Soviet Politburo members travelled to the front-line states in 1977. Additionally, in July 1976 Vassily Solodovnikov, former Director of the African Institute of the Academy of Sciences and the Soviet Union's leading Africanist, was appointed Ambassador to Zambia. Earlier in 1976 the Soviet Union had appointed a new Ambassador to Mozambique who reportedly enjoyed easy access to President

TABLE 1

Major Soviet-Southern African Visits Since 1975[a]

Year	Angola	Mozambique	Namibia	S. Africa	Tanzania	Zambia	Zimbabwe
1976	Jan: FM→SU May: PM→SU Oct: Pres→SU	Apr: DM→SU May: Pres→SU	Aug: SWAPO Hd→ SU	Apr: ANC GS→ SU			Apr: ZAPU Hd→ SU
1977	Sep: Pres→SU Dec: Kirilenko → A	Feb: SU Del→ M Mar: Podgorny→ M	Mar: SWAPO Hd Meets Podgorny	Mar: ANC Hd Meets Podgorny	Mar: Podgorny → T	Mar: Podgorny → Za	Feb: ZAPU Hd → SU
1978	Apr: Pres→SU Nov: Pres→SU	Nov: M Del→ SU					
1979	Sep: Pres→SU dies in SU Dec: A Del→SU	Feb: Dep FM→ M			Feb: Dep FM→ T	Feb: Dep FM→Z	Jan: ZAPU Hd→ SU

Key: Del = Delegation; FM = Foreign Minister; PM = Prime Minister; Pres = President; DM = Defense Minister
Dep = Deputy; GS = General Secretary; Hd = Head; ANC = African National Council

[a]No visits have been reported between the Soviet Union and Botswana.

Source: Numerous Soviet sources were used to compile this chart.

Machel.[18] Finally, in August 1978 TASS reported the formation and meeting of the "Alliance of Communist and Workers' Parties of Tropical and Southern Africa."

There can be little doubt then, that diplomacy plays a key role in Soviet-southern African relations, both in state-to-state and in party-to-party relations. There can similarly be little doubt that the two most prominent events in those relations were the signing of Treaties of Friendship and Cooperation with Angola and Mozambique in October 1976 and February 1977 respectively, and Podgorny's March 1977 trip to the front-line states. While the treaties were notable since they were the first of their kind signed between the Soviet Union and Southern African states, Podgorny's trip marked the first occasion that a Soviet Politburo member had travelled to the region.[19]

The Soviet President's trip coincided with Fidel Castro's month-long tour of Africa, and on at least one occasion the Cuban leader changed his itinerary because it might have "conflicted" with the Soviet president's visit.[20] However, there may well have been another cause for the change in Castro's itinerary. When Castro visited Tanzania, he received lavish praise and a warm reception; when Podgorny visited Tanzania shortly after Castro left, the Soviet President received a subdued welcome despite the fact that the USSR had recently provided MIGs, tanks, and air defense components.[21] Castro's changed itinerary may have been an effort to avoid further comparison of African attitudes toward the USSR and Cuba.

Podgorny also met with ZAPU leader Nkomo, SWAPO head Sam Nujoma and African National Council (ANC) leader Oliver Tambo. Podgorny promised all of them "permanent support" in their respective struggles.[22]

Since Podgorny's trip, Soviet relations with the front-line states have remained friendly and cordial although there are clear indications of African hesitancy to become too intimate with the USSR. Soviet relations with the national liberation movements have followed suit. Indeed, an interesting twist to recent Soviet diplomatic relations with the Patriotic Front in Zimbabwe is the apparent willingness of the USSR to improve its relations with ZANU and the emergence of Colonel Haile Mengistu, head of the ruling pro-Soviet Dergue in Ethiopia, as a mediator between ZAPU and ZANU.

77

Military Support

Soviet military support to front-line states and national liberation movements is the most visible instrument of Soviet policy in Southern Africa. It is this element of Soviet policy which has raised American, Chinese, Western European, and some African concern that the USSR has embarked on a policy of African expansion.

Until the outbreak of the Angolan Civil War, Soviet military presence in Southern Africa was minimal. In the decade 1965-74, the Soviet Union transferred only $3 million worth of arms into all of Southern Africa. During 1975 alone, Soviet arms transfers rose to $6 million. In 1976, the figure climbed to an astonishing $236 million. Table 2 illustrates this growth, and contrasts it to American and Chinese arms transfers to the area.

TABLE 2

Arms Transfers to Ruling Governments[a]

(In Millions of Dollars)

Recipient/Source	1965-74			1975			1976		
	US	USSR	PRC	US	USSR	PRC	US	USSR	PRC
Angola[b]	-	-	-	-	-	-	-	190	-
Mozambique[b]	-	-	-	-	-	-	-	15	-
Tanzania	2	2	62	-	3	-	-	25	75
Zambia	6	1	1	1	3	1	-	6	3

[a]ACDA cautions that these figures are not exact; no arms transfers to Botswana were reported.

[b]Angola and Mozambique did not receive their independence until 1975.

Source: US Arms Control and Disarmament Agency, World Military Exports and Arms Transfers 1965-74, Washington: US Government Printing Office, 1976. Also the same volume for 1966-75 (published 1977), and 1967-76 (published 1978).

78

It should be noted that Soviet arms transfers to Zambia increased in 1976 despite the fact that Zambian President Kaunda was highly critical of Soviet involvement in the Angolan Civil War. Also, in July 1979, the Zambian defense minister travelled to East Germany in an effort to secure additional arms for his country. East Germany reportedly agreed to increase military cooperation, although the specific terms of agreement are not known.

While this chart does not include arms transfers to nonruling movements such as SWAPO, ZANU, UNITA, and FNLA, it nonetheless does illustrate the growth of Soviet military support to the ruling governments in the area. Soviet support to SWAPO, ZANU, and ZAPU has also grown since 1975, although dollar figures are not available. Western news sources have regularly carried reports of Soviet military equipment being shipped to the front-line states for transmittal to particularly ZAPU, and to lesser degrees ZANU and SWAPO.[23] This aid included T-34 and T-54 tanks, 122 millimeter rocket launchers, personnel carriers, and large quantities of small arms.[24] Much of the equipment was landed in Dar es Salaam, Tanzania, and Maputo and Beira, Mozambique. This aid has been transmitted to some extent through the Soviet Ministry of Defense; General S.L. Sokolov, the First Deputy Minister of Defense and a key link in Soviet arms distribution to national liberation movements, accompanied Podgorny on his 1977 trip to Africa, and reportedly met with Nujoma, Nkomo, and Tambo.

The Soviet Union, along with Cuba and certain Eastern European countries, particularly East Germany, also engages in training and advisory activities. Soviet advisors are currently in all the front-line countries except Botswana, and rumors have circulated that they have assumed some combat role in Angola and Mozambique.[25] It has also been reported that ZAPU and SWAPO guerrillas have trained in the Soviet Union and Cuba and returned to Zimbabwe and Namibia to fight, while South Africa has charged that Soviet-Cuban advisors have trained guerrillas in Angola to fight in both Namibia and South Africa itself. Zaire made similar charges of Soviet-Cuban complicity following guerrilla attacks into Shaba province in 1977 and 1978.[26] Table 3 shows the size and depth of the Soviet advisor commitment to Africa in general and Southern Africa in particular.

79

TABLE 3

Pro-Soviet Military Technicians in Less Developed Countries, 1976

Location	USSR/Eastern European	Cuban
Mozambique	50	350
Angola	500	10,000
All Africa	3,900	11,150
All LDC's	9,080	11,656

Source: Central Intelligence Agency, Communist Aid to the Less Developed Countries of the Free World 1976, Washington: US Government Printing Office, 1977, p. 4.

There is little doubt that Soviet policy objectives in Southern Africa have been furthered by so-called "surrogate forces" in Southern Africa, particularly Cubans in Angola. While it is generally accepted that surrogate forces operate in Southern Africa on the volition of both the host government and the donor government, with considerable Soviet encouragement and financial support, there is little agreement on how widespread the activities of these surrogate forces currently are or will become. Potential surrogate involvement in Namibia and Zimbabwe is of particular concern to the West. However, Castro himself has said on repeated occasions that Cuban forces would give "material support" to the Patriotic Front, SWAPO, and ANC, but would never fight their battles since "independence is never delivered from abroad. The people concerned must fight for their independence."[27]

None of the foregoing should be interpreted to imply that the Soviet exercise in "military diplomacy," if it may be termed that, has been totally successful or problem free. When the Soviet Union first expanded its military involvement in Angola, Kenneth Kaunda lambasted the Russians, warning his African compatriots that "a plundering tiger with its deadly cubs (was) now coming in through the back door." Soviet-Zambian relations froze, not to be improved until a year later when Podgorny visited Zambia.

Botswana has also apparently had doubts about Soviet intentions in Africa. Although Botswana has had fewer contacts with the USSR than any other front-line state, a curious episode in late 1976 nonetheless illustrated this point. A senior government official in Gaborone declared that his nation "would consider" Soviet military aid to help repulse Rhodesian border attacks; the Soviet Union quickly responded that it would consider an "official request" for such aid.[28] To date, Botswana has not made an official request. (In late 1977, Botswana formed a 2,000-man "army" to protect its borders from Rhodesian attacks on refugee camps within its territory. The "army" was armed primarily with British weapons).

Even the Treaties of Friendship and Cooperation signed with Angola and Mozambique have apparently been the source of some contention in Soviet-front-line-nation military relations. The Soviet-Mozambique pact, for example, declares that "in the case of situations tending to threaten or disturb the peace," the two nations would "enter into immediate contact with the aim of coordinating their position in the interest of eliminating the threat or reestablishing peace." In the years since the treaty was signed, Rhodesia has launched punitive air strikes and ground operations into Mozambique primarily against ZANU guerrilla bases. These attacks have been carried out with impunity. Until recently, the only air defense capabilities the USSR provided the Maputo government were a few MIG-17's. It may well have been because of this apparent Soviet hesitancy to provide the military aid Mozambique expected under the terms of the treaty that Machel showed a new willingness to turn to the United States. The Mozambiquean President described his October 1977 meeting with Jimmy Carter as the start of a "new era" in US-Mozambique relations. Subsequent Soviet deliveries of SAM-7 air defense missiles and warnings to Rhodesia that Mozambique was "not alone" in facing Salisbury's attacks[29] somewhat assuaged Machel's disenchantment, but Brezhnev's recent comments that the Soviet-Mozambique treaty was nonmilitary in nature undoubtedly increased it once again, even though the Soviet leader's statement was probably directed at a Western audience.[30]

Soviet military relations with national liberation movements, particularly those of Zimbabwe, have been no less complicated. We have already viewed Moscow's putative support for the Patriotic

81

Front, even though in actuality the USSR funnelled most of its military support to only ZAPU. Robert Mugabe commented on this reality in an October 2, 1978 *Newsweek* interview declaring that his segment of the Patriotic Front had not received much support from either the Soviet Union or Cuba. (He also commented that he did not understand why this was true. This hardly seems believable, given the fact that he declared ZANU's philosophy "Marxism-Leninism of Maoist thought." Obviously, this does not sell in Moscow). Even so, again as already observed, the USSR has moved to a more even-handed position *vis-a-vis* ZAPU and ZANU. This does not mean, however, that Moscow's problems within the Patriotic Front are solved, even if the Mengistu mediation proves successful. As recently as 1976, ZANU trainees with their Chinese advisors attacked ZAPU recruits in Tanzanis.[31] Such animosity, grounded in ideology, tribalism, ego, and the drive for power, may not be easy to overcome.

There is yet another problem that Soviet military diplomacy must overcome: mounting casualties. While the Soviet Union itself has suffered few personnel losses, the same is not true of its Cuban surrogate. Although no large-scale opposition to Cuba's involvement in Africa has as yet surfaced in the Caribbean island, the fact remains that over 1,500 Cubans have died on that continent, over 1,000 in Angola alone. Reports from Angola indicate that Cuban forces have been reluctant to move along the critical Benguela rail line in central Angola because of the high casualties exacted by UNITA forces in the area.[32]

One remaining point should be analyzed in our discussion of Soviet military support for front-line nations and the national liberation movements. Does this considerable Soviet emphasis on military relations in the area indicate that the USSR opposes a peaceful and/or negotiated transition to black majority rule in Namibia, Zimbabwe, and eventually South Africa? While the men in the Kremlin have rarely, if ever, declared that a nonmilitary solution to the transition problem was impossible, it is exceedingly clear that they believe it is improbable on terms which they view as acceptable. US and British efforts to arrange peaceful transitions of power in Zimbabwe and Namibia have been regularly decried as efforts to maintain white domination and neocolonial control. This was also true of the original "all parties" conference proposal, the frustrated UN Namibian election solution, the various "internal" solutions, and the compromise conference solution reached at the

British Commonwealth Conference in Lusaka in August, 1979.[33] Bishop Abel Muzorewa and Reverend Ndabaningi Sithole were even categorized as the "local African puppets" of the United States and Great Britain.[34] To the Soviets, a peaceful solution to the situation was simple: transfer political power to the Patriotic Front in Zimbabwe and SWAPO in Namibia.[35] Both, in Soviet eyes, were the only legitimate representatives of their respective people.

Given these Soviet attitudes toward a peaceful settlement of the Zimbabwe situation, it is not too surprising that the Soviet media and government were rather reticent in their commentary on the results of the fall 1979 London Conference. The Soviet media regularly attributed the successes of the conference to the "flexible and realistic" attitudes of the United Patriotic Front, and the difficulties of the conference to the "self-serving" policies of the Muzorewa government and the British government. *Pravda* and *Izvestiia* both warned that despite the appearance of progress, numerous difficulties remained, imposed by the Muzorewa-British effort to retain privileges for whites and by the possibility of introducing mercenaries from the West to the conflict. The distinct impression created (and it should be stressed, this is only an impression) was that the Soviet leadership was taken aback by the settlement, and believed that its influence in the area had been further reduced.

Trade and Aid

Soviet trade and aid in Southern Africa has shown no growth since 1975. The only major exception to this rule is Soviet trade with Angola. Table 4 shows Soviet trade figures for 1975 through 1978 with the front-line states, while Table 5 illustrates the pattern of aid Southern Africa states have received from the Soviet Union, Eastern European states, and the PRC.

Given the economic hardships brought about by Southern African conflicts, and given the relatively underdeveloped status of Southern African economies, it is somewhat surprising that the USSR has not chosen to direct more trade and aid to Southern Africa. Soviet authorities maintain that trade and aid are instruments for "strengthening national and economic independence" and are therefore "useful weapons" against imperialism,[36] but, at least through 1979, have employed neither extensively in pursuit of their policy objectives in southern Africa.

TABLE 4

Soviet Trade with the Front-Line States[a]

(In Millions of Rubles)

Country	1975		1976		1977		1978	
	Soviet Exports	Soviet Imports	Soviet Exports	Soviet Imports	Soviet Exports	Soviet Imports	Soviet Exports	Soviet Imports
Angola	-	-	5.3	14.4	69.2	10.4	47.8	9.6
Mozambique	-	-	-	-	5.9	-	17.4	.8
Tanzania	2.6	5.9	1.2	2.8	1.2	3.5	6.2	3.4
Zambia	-	7.5	2.3	-	1.4	.4	.6	.8
ALL LDC's	3310.0	2998.8	3740.1	2827.0	5336.7	2997.2	5726.4	2831.2

[a]No trade figures were reported for Botswana

Source: Foreign Trade (Moscow), Number 3 (March, 1977), supplement; Foreign Trade (Moscow), Number 12 (December, 1978), supplement; and Foreign Trade (Moscow), Number 3 (March, 1979), supplement.

84

TABLE 5

Communist Economic Credits and Grants

(In Millions of Dollars)

Recipient[a]/Source	1954-74			1975			1976		
	USSR	E. Europe	PRC	USSR	E. Europe	PRC	USSR	E. Europe	PRC
Angola[b]	-	-	-	-	-	-	10	10	-
Mozambique[b]	-	-	-	-	-	59	3	1	-
Tanzania	20	13	331	-	-	-	-	-	28
Zambia	6	50	279	-	-	-	-	-	28

[a]No credits or grants were reported for Botswana.

[b]Angola and Mozambique did not receive their independence until 1975.

Source: Central Intelligence Agency, Communist Aid to the Less Developed Countries of the Free World 1976, Washington: US Government Printing Office, 1977, pp. 11-12.

85

There are several reasons for this. First, speaking in pragmatic historical terms, trade and aid have not proven overly effective in providing long-term reductions of the influence of potential opponents, nor in providing long-term increases in one's own influence. The Soviet Union, the United States, and China have all discovered this. Second, the Soviet Union itself is concentrating on internal development, and thus extends limited credit and offers little aid. Third, Soviet trade authorities apparently seek to have a surplus in trade balance with the developing countries, perhaps to offset the trade deficit the USSR has with developed countries. For example in 1975 the Soviet Union exported 3,310 million rubles worth of goods to developing countries, and imported 2,998.8 million rubles worth of goods from them. Three years later Soviet exports to these same countries had climbed to 5,726.4 million rubles, while imports had actually *dropped* to 2,831.2 million rubles.

Finally, Southern African states themselves may be somewhat hesitant to become too closely tied in an economic sense to the USSR. The West has capital to invest; the USSR does not. Thus, the presidents of Angola, Botswana, Mozambique, and Zambia have all recently called for increased Western investments in their respective countries during the very period when Soviet interest in Southern Africa has been increasing.[37] Even in the one exception to the prevalent Soviet trade pattern in Southern Africa, Angola, trade has dropped off considerably since 1977. Most significantly, almost all of the drop has been in Angolan imports of Soviet goods. It may well be that Angolan and other Southern African leaders concur with an upper level official from Mozambique who declared, "We don't intend to become another Bulgaria here, and we certainly do not want to get involved in bloc politics."[38]

In sum, then, while the USSR argues that trade and aid are significant instruments of policy, the men in the Kremlin employ neither extensively in their efforts to attain their Southern African objective. Soviet policy toward Southern Africa continues to be dominated by diplomatic and military factors, with no change of emphasis in sight.

EXTRANEOUS IMPACTS ON SOVIET POLICY

Regardless of what objectives the USSR seeks in Southern Africa, and regardless of what instruments of policy it chooses to employ, certain local, regional, and international factors obviously contribute to the success or failure of Soviet policy in the region. In general terms, these extraneous factors include but are not limited to nationalist sentiments, disagreements between various segments of national liberation movements, pragmatic economic con- siderations, and countermoves adopted by other non-African nations.

Nationalism

Nationalist sentiment in the front-line states appears both to aid the Soviet Union in its efforts to reduce US and Chinese influence in the region and to hinder the Soviet Union in its attempts to expand its own influence in the area. This nationalism has often manifested itself in an unwillingness to become or remain dependent on non-African actors. Rather, in their brief histories of independence, Southern African states have in most cases been willing to accept economic, military, and technical assistance from any nation willing to extend it. This has led to continual frustrations for non-African states involved in the area.

In Angola, Agostinho Neto regularly declared his government's intention to repay all aid it received from the Soviet Union. Despite the decisive importance of Soviet and Cuban military support to the MPLA, as early as July 1976 reports began surfacing of disagreements between the Soviets and Neto about the nonaligned stance Neto reportedly preferred.[39] Less than a year later, an abortive coup against Neto, led by pro-Soviet elements of the MPLA, was put down by Neto loyalists and Cuban troops.[40] In November 1978, amid reports that the Angolan government was seeking to strengthen its ties to the West, Neto appeared on Moscow television and declared that his country was grateful to the Soviet Union for its support, but at the same time wanted peaceful relations with all countries and intended to remain nonaligned.[41] A month later, Neto removed yet another pro-Soviet MPLA member from power (Premier Lopo de Nascimento), and again affirmed that it was necessary at all times to defend national independence.

Following Neto's death in September 1979, Angolan sources revealed additional specifics about Soviet-Angolan disagreement during Neto's presidency. The more striking revelations included Neto's 1977 request to the Portuguese government for 20,000 troops to replace the Cubans (Portugal declined the request); Neto's refusal to grant Soviet base rights; and at least three

87

assassination attempts by pro-Soviet segments of the MPLA.

Since Neto's death, there has been no noticeable change in Soviet-Angolan relations. The new president, Jose Eduardo dos Santos, pledged to continue Neto's policies, including seeking Western investment and remaining nonaligned. While Brezhnev and dos Santos exchanged messages on the third anniversary of their nations' Treaty of Friendship and Cooperation, there was nothing of moment in the exchange.[42]

The Soviet Union's policy toward Mozambique immediately following the African country's 1975 independence succeeded in substantially increasing Soviet influence in Maputo. This increased Soviet influence was at the expense of the PRC, which temporarily decreased its involvement in African affairs following its futile support for the FNLA and UNITA in Angola. Samora Machel regularly described his country's relations with the USSR as "exemplary" throughout 1976 and early 1977, but as Soviet economic and military aid to Mozambique remained inconsequential, the Mozambiquean president began to look to the West for assistance, particularly as Rhodesian raids into his country against ZANU guerrilla bases located there increased in frequency and ferocity.[43] Machel has both called for Western investment in Mozambique, and proclaimed a "new era" in relations with the United States. Perhaps most telling, in February 1979 L.F. Ilichev, a Soviet Deputy Foreign Minister, visited Mozambique for discussions of "comradely frankness" with Machel. As analysts of Soviet politics know, "comradely frankness" implies that serious disagreements exist.

Soviet-Tanzanian relations have also followed a varied path, although they have never been truly warm. Tanzanian president Julius Nyerere has been highly critical of the West for its apparent lack of support for majority rule in Southern Africa, and at the same time has been highly supportive of the Soviet-Cuban presence in Africa. This, he explained, was because the threat of Southern African independence was greater from the West than from the East. Nonetheless, there has been little Soviet military or economic support to the Nyerere government. Nyerere himself appears quite cognizant that Soviet objectives in the region may not be identical to Southern African objectives. As the Tanzanian president observed, "Why countries gave arms to the MPLA is a matter which they know and others can only conjecture. What is certain is that the arms were obtained, and used. They were used by nationalists for nationalistic purposes.[44] Even more pointedly, Nyerere has declared, "Tanzania does not want anyone from outside Africa to govern Africa."[45]

Zambian relations with the Soviet Union, although never close, became extremely cold following Kaunda's "plundering tiger with cubs" statement concerning Soviet-Cuban presence in Angola. Kaunda's praise of Chinese support for national liberation movements further alienated the Russians.[46] Although Soviet support for ZAPU, the segment of the Zimbabwe Patriotic Front operating primarily out of Zambia, has succeeded in somewhat closing the Soviet-Zambian gap, it is still evident that the two governments are far from close. During 1979, however, the Muzorewa government launched air strikes against ZAPU in Zambia. In response to these strikes, Zambia unsuccessfully sought Western military aid. Kaunda's government then turned to East Germany, and has apparently received at least some unspecified military aid.

On the whole then, the front-line states have been unwilling to maintain extremely close ties with the USSR. To be sure, when the USSR has offered military aid, the African states have taken it. Rhodesian attacks on Patriotic Front bases in the front-line states, and South African attacks on SWAPO bases in Angola and Zambia may influence the front-line states to seek even more military aid from the USSR if negotiated settlements fail, but if their history of avoiding dependence is any indication, such steps need not necessarily be advantageous to the USSR. Nationalism in Southern Africa is without doubt a force with which the USSR must contend.

National Liberation Rivalry

Rivalry within the various national liberation movements is a second major factor which complicates Soviet policy toward Southern Africa. In Angola, of course, civil war still rages between the MPLA, which currently controls the government, and the FNLA and UNITA. Because of their erstwhile support from the United States, China, and Southern Africa, the latter two segments of the one-time national liberation movement have been labelled "splittists" by the Kremlin. While a non-Marxist would probably term the split between the three movements as tribal or regional in origin, the USSR terms it ideological, and caused by Western neocolonial intrigues. It has been clear for some time, however, that in this intramovement rivalry, the Soviets have opted for the MPLA.

The MPLA itself, however, has shown signs of fracture. The May 27, 1977 coup attempt against Neto was carried out by the pro-Soviet wing of the MPLA. Thus, even within the MPLA, the USSR may in the future be forced to make difficult decisions about which wing to support.

In Namibia, SWAPO appears to be the only major political force which actively seeks independence and black majority rule. The Soviet Union—and indeed, much of the world—is firmly behind SWAPO in its efforts. The Turnhalle Alliance, a white-dominated political organization in Namibia, is generally viewed as a surrogate for continued white control. The Soviet Union concurs.

In South Africa, Soviet support is tendered to both the ANC and the South African Communist Party. Currently, neither organization is particularly influential, although it may be expected that particularly the ANC's strength will increase.

It is in Zimbabwe that the USSR faces difficult choices. While the "internal solution" advocated by Smith, Muzorewa, Sithole, and Chirau was vehemently condemned by the Soviet Union, and while the USSR ardently supports the Patriotic Front of ZANU and ZAPU, until recently almost all Soviet aid and support was directed to Joshua Nkomo's ZAPU. However, unfortunately for the Soviets, Robert Mugabe's ZANU has become the stronger military force, receiving aid from a variety of sources. Since mid-1978, as previously noted, the USSR has shown a pronounced increase in support of ZANU. The unified front adopted by ZANU and ZAPU for the London Conference reduced the problem of intra-national liberation movement rivalry for the Soviets, but raised an even more disquieting prospect: a solution to the Zimbabwe situation which prescribed Soviet influence in the country. Obviously, from the Soviet perspective, such a solution is not preferred.

Economics

The internecine warfare of the last half-decade has seriously degraded the national economies of all states in the region. In Angola, the civil war has closed the Benuela rail line and destroyed what little industry the country had. White flight following independence had an adverse impact on both Angola and Mozambique, and the latter's 1976 closure of its border with Rhodesia has undermined Mozambique's economy as much as Rhodesia's. In 1977, Zambia closed its border with Rhodesia as well, but in later 1978 reopened the railway in order to receive much needed imports landed in South Africa. Zambia's one other rail link to the sea, the Tazara (Tanzam) railroad, is operating considerably under its peak efficiency.[47] Zambia and Angola, in short, are facing bankruptcy, and Mozambique's economy is sustained to a great extent by Mozambiquean workers in South African mines. To an extent, the same is true of Botswana. In the white-dominated areas of the regions, white flight and civil war is eroding Zimbabwe's economy, and Namibia relies primarily on mining. Only South Africa remains economically strong.

The implications for Soviet policy are obvious: the entire region, regardless of the outcomes of the Namibia and Zimbabwe situations, is in dire need of economic assistance, and the Soviet Union has extended very little. While it may be that Soviet policy will change once those situations are resolved, there is nothing to indicate that it will. Indeed, it may be that economic exigencies forced the front-line states to apply pressure to the national liberation movements to accept gradual transition to black rule. The need for military equipment, if these transitions are successful, will obviously be reduced, thereby depriving the USSR of one of its two effective instruments of policy in Southern Africa.

Non-African Countermoves

Increased Soviet activity in Southern Africa has directly precipitated increased Western activity in the region, primarily on the part of Great Britain and the United States. Indeed, it may safely be argued that the entire face of US policy toward Southern Africa has been altered by the Soviet presence there. In his 1976 Lusaka speech, former US Secretary of State Kissinger promised American support for black majority rule. Since that time, the United States has diplomatically supported the front-line states and the national liberation movements, and in conjunction with Great Britain has continually sought to arrange an acceptable peaceful transition to black rule. The acceptance of the various proposals put forward by the British at the London Conference by both the "internal" and "external" forces has lent additional weight to Julius Nyerere's observation that a political change has occurred in Zimbabwe.[48] Perhaps even more strikingly, both the United States

91

and Great Britain have taken steps to increase their economic aid to the region. Thus, on July 31, 1979, perhaps in "preparation" for the Commonwealth Conference held in Lusaka in early August, Great Britain cancelled the debt on $1.74 billion in loans it had previously made to Commonwealth nations, including Botswana and Tanzania; and in mid-November 1979 Great Britain ended its economic sanctions against Zimbabwe. The United States followed the British lead in December.

China, meanwhile, has slowed its economic support to the front-line states since Mao's death and since the MPLA victory in Angola. China's major economic impact in the region was the construction of the Tanzam railroad, which was turned over to the African states in 1976. Even with its reduced interest in the area, however, the PRC saw fit to donate a squadron of MIG-19's to Zambia for air defense in 1978.[49]

The Soviet Union, of course, argues that these policies of other non-African states are neocolonial in nature. The Soviet media is particularly fond of accusing the United States, China, and to a lesser degree Great Britain of cooperating to establish regional hegemony.[50] In any event, the USSR recognizes that these nations retain considerable influence throughout Southern Africa, and that their success or failure in extending economic and military aid and arranging a peaceful transition to black majority rule will go a long way toward determining the success or failure of Soviet policy in the region.

CONCLUSION

All things considered, it cannot be argued that Soviet policy has been especially successful in achieving its objectives in Southern Africa. To be sure, Western and Chinese influence in Southern Africa has perceptively decreased, while Soviet influence has increased. However, it is difficult to conclude that this is the result of Soviet policy. Harold Macmillan, in his 1960 Capetown speech, observed that "winds of change" were sweeping Southern Africa; by today, those winds have reached hurricane force, and Soviet policy by itself adds very little to them.

Nonetheless, large-scale Soviet interest in Southern Africa necessitates careful policy responses on the part of the United States. As we have seen neither the front-line states or the national liberation movements appear inclined to adopt a blindly pro-Soviet or anti-American stance in the long term. To some extent, the Soviet Union is relying on hope of a lack of political sophistication on the part of the black African states in its efforts to persuade them that the United States is trying to maintain white minority governments and establish neocolonial control. So far, the African states appear too sophisticated to accept the Soviet line.

Hopefully the United States itself will be sophisticated enough not to overreact to this Soviet gambit in Southern Africa. President Carter in his June 1978 Annapolis speech and US Ambassador to the Soviet Union Malcolm Toon in his October 1978 Atlanta speech both gave indications of such sophistication. Carter observed that even some Marxist-Leninist groups no longer look on the Soviet Union as a role model. Toon maintained that in the long run he did not expect any substantial Soviet presence in Africa because of the factors discussed above.

If there is danger of over-reacting, however, there is also danger of under-reacting. As Donald Zagoria has pointed out, seven pro-Communist movements have seized power with armed force in Africa or Asia since 1975.[51] In the crudest global context, such a fact inevitably creates in the minds of many people the image that ''winds of change'' are blowing not only in Southern Africa against white-minority rule, but also throughout the world against the United States. To do nothing would be to create the appearance that the United States has in effect conceded the field to the USSR.

In the final analysis, the future of Southern Africa will be determined by the people of the region itself. But it must be remembered that the future which they choose will be influenced by forces both internal and external to the region, and it is this fact which makes Soviet policy toward the region of continuing vital interest for both the United States and the governments of Southern Africa themselves.

ENDNOTES

1. For the purpose of this paper, Southern Africa has been somewhat arbitrarily defined as the white-dominated states of South Africa, Rhodesia, and Southwest Africa (the last two of which hereafter will be identified by their respective African names of Zimbabwe and Namibia): and the black-ruled front-line states of Angola, Botswana, Mozambique, Tanzania, and Zambia.

2. For just a few of these discussions, see John Marcum, *The Angolan Revolution*, Cambridge: The MIT Press, 1978; Peter Vanneman and Martin James, "The Soviet Intervention in Angola: Intentions and Implications," *Strategic Review*, Summer, 1976; Jiri Valenta, "The Soviet-Cuban Intervention in Angola, 1975," *Studies in Comparative Communism*, Spring-Summer, 1978, pp. 3-34; and Daniel S. Papp, "Angola, National Liberation, and the Soviet Union," *Parameters*, March 1978, pp. 26-39.

3. For other analyses of Soviet objectives in Southen Africa, see US Library of Congress, *The Soviet Union and the Third World: A Watershed in Great Power Politics*, Washington: US Government Printing Office, May 1977; and "Communist Penetration in Africa," *Africa Institute Bulletin*, Vol. 16, No. 2, 1978, pp. 62-69.

4. See, for example, L.I. Brezhnev, "In the Name of the Happiness of Soviet People," *Vital Speeches*, Vol. XLV, No. 12, April 1979, p. 371; V. Vorobyev, "Colonialist Policies in Africa," *International Affairs*, No. 9, September 1978, pp. 47-48; D. Volsky, "Southern Africa: Protracted Convulsion," *New Times*, No. 22, May 1979, p. 7; G. Roshchin, "International Monopoly Expansion in Africa," *International Affairs*, No. 7, July 1979, pp. 68-69; and *Izvestiia*, January 31, 1979.

5. For a discussion of this Soviet attitude, see Charles B. McLane, *Soviet-African Relations*, London: Central Asian Research Center, 1974, p. 16.

6. For a detailed development of this argument, see Daniel S. Papp, *Toward an Estimate of the Soviet Worldview*, Military Issues Research Memorandum, Carlisle Barracks, Pennsylvania: Strategic Studies Institute, March 15, 1979. For the application of this argument specifically to the national liberation movement, see Daniel S. Papp, "National Liberation During Detente: The Soviet Outlook," *International Journal*, Vol. XXXII, No. 1, Winter 1976-77, pp. 82-99.

7. See, for example, Roshchin, p. 5; and *Izvestiia*, January 12, 1979. In his April 1976 Lusaka speech, Kissinger declared American support for black majority rule throughout Southern Africa.

8. See *Pravda*, December 11, 1978; Radio Moscow, August 6, 1979, in Foreign Broadcast Information Service, Daily Report: *Soviet Union*, (hereafter *FBIS: Soviet Union*) August 8, 1979.

9. Mozambique attained independence in 1975, Tanzania in 1961, and Zambia in 1964.

10. According to one report, Soviet bloc arms comprised roughly 30 percent of ZANU's armaments in the summer of 1978, and 80 percent in the summer of 1979. See "Can It Last," *African Confidential*, Vol. 20, No. 12, June 6, 1979, p. 2; and "Nkomo's Isolation," *African Confidential*, Vol. 20, No. 13, June 20, 1979, p. 1.

11. V. Sofinsky and A. Khazanov, "Angolan Chronicle of the Peking Betrayal," *International Affairs*, No. 7, July 1978, pp. 60-69.

12. Brezhnev and Gromyko in particular have denied such objectives. See also Vorobyov, pp. 47-48, and V. Kudryavtsev, "Africa Fights for its Future," *International Affairs*, No. 5, May 1978, p. 38.

13. *The Washington Post*, January 27, 1976.

14. William Minter, *Portuguese Africa and the West*, New York: Monthly Review Press, 1972, p. 166.

15. See *Pravda*, October 24, 1978; *Izvestiia*, October 3, 1978, December 5, 1978, and January 12, 1978; and M. Alexandrov, "Southern Africa-The Struggle Continues," *Soviet Military Review*, No. 5, May 1979, pp. 53-54.

16. Peter Janke, "The Soviet Strategy of Mineral Denial," *Soviet Analyst*, Vol. 7, No. 22, November 1978, pp. 5-6.

17. See Arthur Jay Klinghoffer, "The Soviet View of African Socialism" in *On the Road to Communism*, ed. by Roger Kanet, Lawrence: University Press of Kansas, 1972; and McLane, pp. 145-154, and pp. 174-178.

18. *The Washington Post*, April 16, 1976.

19. Three measures of the importance the Kremlin attached to Podgorny's trip was the size of his delegation (120 members); his mode of arrival (Tu-144, the Soviet equivilant of the Concorde); and the timing of his visit (during Cyrus Vance's abortive trip to Moscow for SALT negotiations).

20. This was in Zambia. See *The Washington Post*, March 29, 1977.

21. *Ibid.*, March 24, 1977. Another indication of some degree of Soviet-Tanzanian disagreement was the final communique issued by the Soviet and Tanzanian governments, which noted merely that the formation of the Patriotic Front in Zimbabwe the previous fall was an "important step" in the stuggle to achieve majority rule in Zimbabwe. The Soviets had hoped to convince Tanzanian President Nyerere to endorse the Front as the sole legitimate representative of the Zimbabwe people.

22. *Ibid.*, March 29, 1977. Podgorny returned to the Soviet Union on April 3, and on May 24 was removed from the Politburo. There is no apparent linkage between his African trip and his removal.

23. For references in *The New York Times* during 1976 alone, see March 10, June 21, November 18, and November 30.

24. *The Washington Post*, March 28, 1977.

25. See, for example, *The Atlanta Constitution*, August 30, 1979, where it was reported that five Soviet advisors participating in an action against anti-Frelimo forces in Mozambique had been killed.

26 *The New York Times*, April 24, 1977; and *The Washington Post*, April 26, 1977, June 22, 1977; and May 22, 1979.

27. *The Washington Post*, March 23, 1977. See also *The Washington Post*, April 2, 1977; and *Facts on File* 1977, p. 456.

28. *The Washington Post*, December 22, 1976.

29. *Izvestiia,* December 15, 1978.

30. Brezhnev, p. 371.

31. *The Washington Post*, August 23, 1976.

32. "The UNITA Thorn," *Africa Confidential*, Vol. 20, No. 11, May 23, 1979, p. 1.

33. For Soviet reaction to these proposals, ideas, and steps, see for example *Izvestiia*, December 15, 1978; January 15, 1978; January 24, 1979; and August 8, 1979; and *Pravda*, January 31, 1979; and February 1, 1979.

34. *Izvestiia*, December 15, 1978.

35. *Pravda*, November 5, 1978; and V. Sidenko, "The 'International Settlement' Farce" *New Times*, No. 20, May 1979, pp. 10-11.

36. B. Kozintsev and P. Kashelov, "Economic Cooperations of the USSR with the Countries of Tropical Africa," *Foreign Trade* (Moscow), No. 2, February 1978, p. 30.

37. *The Washington Post*, December 13, 1977; and December 15, 1977; and *Africa Report*, No. 2, March-April, 1979, p. 32.

38. *The Washington Post*, February 16, 1977.

39. *Ibid.*, July 16, 1976.

40. See *Ibid.*, June 28, 1977; *The New York Times*, June 20, 1977; and David Birmingham, "The Twenty Seventh of May," *African Affairs*, Vol. 77, No. 309, October 1978.

41. Moscow Television, as reported in *FBIS: Soviet Union*, November 15, 1978, p. 112.

42. *Pravda*, October 8, 1979; and October 9, 1979.

43. For a interesting discussion on Mozambiquean affairs, see Thomas H. Heniksen, "Marxism and Mozambique," *African Affairs*, Vol. 77, No. 309, October 1978, pp. 441-462.

44. Julius Nyerere, "The Conflict is Not a Fight between Communists and Anti-Communists," *The Washington Post*, January 12, 1976.

45. Julius Nyerere, "Foreign Troops in Africa," *African Report*, Vol. 23, No. 4, July-August 1978, pp. 10-14.

46. Colin Legum, "The End of Cloud-Cuckoo Land," *The New York Times Magazine*, March 28, 1976, p. 60.

47. *Los Angeles Times*, October 1, 1978.

48. *The Washington Post*, August 4, 1979.

49. *The Washington Post*, May 23, 1979.

50. See *Izvestiia*, October 26, 1978; Radio Moscow, October 29, 1978, in *FBIS: Soviet Union*, October 31, 1978, p. H2; Radio Moscow, December 20, 1978, in *FBIS: Soviet Union*, December 22, 1978; and *Izvestiia*, January 17, 1979.

51. Donald Zagoria, "Into the Breach: New Soviet Alliances in the Third World," *Foreign Affairs*, Vol. 57, No. 4, Spring 1979, p. 733.

5

THE SOVIET UNION AND ANGOLA

Arthur Jay Klinghoffer

The Soviet Union, assisted by Cuba, was instrumental in effecting the victory of the MPLA (Movimento Popular de Libertacao de Angola) in the Angolan war of 1975-76. Subsequently, in October 1976, it concluded a treaty of friendship and cooperation with Angola, its first pact of this type with a sub-Saharan African state. Policies toward Angola have been consistent with the development of the Soviet Union's overall approach to Africa and should not be viewed as anomalous. The degree of Soviet involvement in Angola only accentuated a trend already evident. It is now apparent that the Soviet role in Ethiopia in 1977-78 was a further extension of policies already implemented in Angola.

Soviet behavior in Angola was illustrative of eight basic policy parameters that may be applied to the overall evolution of Soviet policy toward Africa:[1]

• The Soviet Union has generally adopted the Organization of African Unity's position that the territorial integrity of African states must be preserved. The concept of national self-determination for ethnic minorities is downplayed and secession is denounced. The Soviet Union opposed the efforts of Katanga and

97

Biafra to establish separate states and it recently supported Ethiopia against the Eritrean secessionists. In Angola the Soviet Union consistently condemned Cabindan separatism and any efforts to partition Angolan territory.

• The Soviet Union has become increasingly concerned about logistic rights in Africa. The extensive presence in Egypt until 1972, which was facilitated by port and airfield rights, provides the most striking example and the Soviet naval and air presence in Somalia until 1977 is another case in point. The growing Soviet naval role around the periphery of Africa requires access to ports for the purpose of repairs and refueling and the Soviets have managed to secure the right to use facilities in Algeria, Guinea, Nigeria, Congo, and other states. Surveillance aircraft have operated out of Conakry, Guinea and Berbera, Somalia, but Soviet operations have now been terminated at both locations by the host states. However, the Soviets do fly surveillance aircraft out of Luanda, Angola and their naval vessels may call at the Angolan ports of Luanda, Lobito, and Mocamedes. In April 1979 the newest Soviet aircraft carrier, the *Minsk*, visited Luanda.

• The Soviet military has become more directly involved in African conflicts. Military technicians assisted Nigeria in 1967 during its war with Biafra and Soviet pilots participated in combat operations during the 1969-70 Egyptian-Israeli "War of Attrition." The presence of 200 military advisers in Angola was not an isolated instance but part of a progression leading to the field command of Ethiopian troops by Soviet generals in 1978.

• The Soviet Union has been forging informal alliances with Afro-Asian states through treaties of friendship and cooperation. The Soviet-Angolan treaty of 1976 was preceded by similar pacts with Egypt in May 1971, India in August 1971, Iraq in April 1972, and Somalia in July 1974. It was followed by agreements with Mozambique in March 1977, Vietnam and Ethiopia in November 1978, and Afghanistan in December 1978. The treaties with Egypt and Somalia have subsequently been abrogated by those states.

• The Cubans have become a significant ally of the Soviets in Africa. Cuban soldiers fought with the Algerians against the Moroccans in 1963 and with the PAIGC (Partido Africano da Independencia da Guine e Cabo Verde) against the Portuguese during the early 1970's in what is now Guinea-Bissau. The Cuban military role in Angola far exceeded earlier forays in Africa in

98

terms of both personnel (17,000 by the end of the war in March 1976) and armaments. Cuban successes there led to even greater military involvement in Ethiopia in 1978-79.

• Soviet policies toward sub-Saharan Africa have come to be influenced substantially by the China factor. China was closely aligned with Zaire during the Angolan war, and it assisted the FNLA (Frente Nacional de Libertacao de Angola) and UNITA (Uniao Nacional para a Independencia Total de Angola) against the Soviet-supported MPLA. Sino-Soviet competition was also evident in Mozambique, Tanzania, and Zambia. The victory of the MPLA has weakened the Chinese position in southern Africa and has led guerrilla organizations in Zimbabwe-Rhodesia, Namibia, and South Africa to turn increasingly toward the Soviet Union for material and financial support. Independent black governments have generally taken the same course of action.

• The problems of southern Africa have been of growing concern to the Soviet Union. The Angolan war escalated Soviet involvement in the region and was followed in July 1976 by the appointment of Vassily Solodovnikov, Director of the African Institute of the Academy of Sciences, as Ambassador to Zambia. Solodovnikov was to act as overseer of Soviet interests throughout southern Africa. His position in Moscow was filled by Anatoly Gromyko, son of the Soviet foreign minister. In March 1977, Chairman of the Presidium of the Supreme Soviet Nikolai Podgorny led a huge delegation of 108 members on a tour of Mozambique, Tanzania, and Zambia. He was the most senior Soviet official ever to visit the region. Soviet assistance to liberation movements such as SWAPO (South-West Africa People's Organization) in Namibia, ZAPU (Zimbabwe African People's Union) in Zimbabwe-Rhodesia, and the ANC (African National Congress) in South Africa, and strong Soviet verbal endorsement of black majority rule, obviously strike responsive chords in most African states.

• The pragmatic phase in Soviet relations with African states, exhibited over the past 15 years, now appears to be giving way to a neo-ideological approach. The Soviets had been willing to work closely with any cooperative African leader, irrespective of his ideological persuasion, and this led to cordial ties with Amin, Qaddafi, and other non-Marxists. The expulsion of Soviet advisers and the termination of logistic rights by Egypt, Somalia, and Sudan may have convinced the Soviet Union that long-lasting political bonds must be based on a common ideological perspective. The MPLA was clearly the most Marxist of the competing Angolan movements and Soviet relations with Angola, Mozambique, and Ethiopia have a strong ideological component. Outside of Africa, South Yemen and Afghanistan conform to the same pattern.

The Soviet Union portrayed its assistance to the MPLA as an example of continued support for African national liberation movements and as a contribution to the struggle against neo-colonialist, mercenary, and South African forces. But what were the Soviet Union's actual motivations? Perhaps an assessment of the Soviet role in Angola in terms of seven different aspects of the conflict can help us reconstruct the most important considerations influencing the Soviet decision-making elite.

SOVIET MOTIVATIONS: THE INTERNAL ANGOLAN SITUATION

Looking at the internal dynamics of Angolan politics, it is apparent that the Soviet Union always favored the Marxist MPLA over its rivals, the FNLA and UNITA.[2] MPLA leader Agostinho Neto visited Moscow in 1964, and the Soviets agreed to supply arms and to provide military training in the USSR. Neto attended the Twenty-Third Congress of the Communist Party of the Soviet Union in 1966, the Twenty-Fourth Congress in 1971, and celebrations in 1967 marking the 50th anniversary of the Bolshevik Revolution and in 1970 marking the 100th anniversary of Lenin's birth. Neto was also a member of the presidium of the pro-Soviet World Peace Council.

Soviet weapons deliveries to the MPLA were suspended in 1973-74 when the MPLA experienced factional difficulties but were renewed in October 1974 after Neto had reasserted his dominance. In December at least 200 MPLA members arrived in the Soviet Union for military training. By the end of 1974 the Soviet Union had given approximately $54 million in aid to the MPLA.[3] It could be argued that the resumption of assistance to the MPLA in late 1974 was interfering with the decolonization process in Angola, since the Portuguese revolution of April 1974 had already effected a policy change recognizing Angola's right to independence. The Soviets, however, maintained that they had consistently supported the MPLA against the Portuguese and were just continuing their previous course of action. They pointed out that the United States and China, which had generally remained aloof from the anti-Portuguese struggle, had started to aid rival Angolan nationalist movements once the decolonization process was underway.[4]

The Soviet Union endorsed the Alvor Agreement of January 1975, which provided for a transitional government in which all three nationalist movements would participate equally. However, it was deeply concerned about the actions of Daniel Chipenda, who had lost out in his challenge to Neto and had been expelled from the MPLA in December 1974. Chipenda did not play a role in formulating the Alvor Agreement and his army of 2-3,000 men was not recognized in the stipulation calling for equalization of the military strengths of all three movements at 8,000 men each. Chipenda had opened an office in Kinshasa, Zaire in October 1974 and had developed close ties to the FNLA. Despite his lack of official standing under the Alvor Agreement, he opened an office in Luanda as well. But it was raided by MPLA militants on two occasions in February 1975, and Chipenda was unable to operate from the Angolan capital. Soviet fears were realized in April 1975 when Chipanda officially joined the FNLA and added his troops to the FNLA's ranks. The FNLA already had a military advantage over the MPLA so the addition of Chipenda's "illegal" men alarmed the Soviet Union. Serious FNLA violations of the Alvor Agreement were frequent in March and April 1975, as an offensive was undertaken against members of the MPLA. The Soviets thus saw their extensive provision of arms to the MPLA in the spring of 1975 as a necessary response to the undermining of the Alvor Agreement by Chipenda and the FNLA.

Soviet arms deliveries continued even after the MPLA had gained the military advantage in July, as the Soviets sought to counter American assistance to the FNLA and UNITA, as well as direct intervention by South African and Zairian troops. The Soviets feared that the anti-MPLA forces would seize the capital city of Luanda prior to the scheduled independence date of November 11, or that Portugal would postpone its exit from Angola due to the serious internecine strife. Consequently, the Soviet Union acted to buttress the MPLA's military position so that it would be able to proclaim its control of an independent government in Luanda on November 11. The Soviets actively collaborated with the Cubans toward this end.

Once the MPLA declared the establishment of the People's Republic of Angola (PRA), the Soviets extended immediate recognition and began to portray their assistance as overt support for a legitimate sovereign state. They contrasted this with the continued covert assistance provided by the United States to anti-government forces. The FNLA and UNITA had actually instituted a rival government in the city of Nova Lisboa (Huambo), but not one state extended official recognition. The Soviets therefore claimed, with some justification, that the PRA was the only legitimate Angolan government, since it was recognized by approximately 30 states within a month of its formation.

The Soviet Union adhered to the Organization of African Unity's position on the maintenance of the territorial integrity of African states because this helped the MPLA in its struggle against "splittist" forces. Soviet assistance was also viewed in Moscow as coming to the defense of a state subjected to external aggression. *Pravda* declared: "One can say with full justification that what is happening in Angola is not a civil war but a full-scale intervention against the Angolan people" and another commentary averred: "It is no secret now that, under the guise of a 'civil war,' intervention by imperialist and neocolonialist forces has begun in Angola."[5] Soviet spokesmen also pointed out that the Organization of African Unity and the United Nations had requested assistance for southern African liberation forces, thus aid to the MPLA was seen as consistent with resolutions of these organizations. Furthermore, the MPLA was fighting against movements supported by "racist" South Africa.[6] From the Soviet perspective, a victory for the FNLA or UNITA would further the capitalist development of Angola, extend imperialist influence and investments, and retard the movement toward black majority rule in other southern African states as a result of such a regime's ties to South Africa.

THE LUSITANIAN MATRIX

Soviet reactions to the Portuguese revolution and to Portugal's decolonization process in other African states affected Soviet motivations in Angola. The evolution of events in Angola was clearly part of a broader Lusitanian political process. The Soviet leadership had a rather realistic understanding of the attendant linkages.

The disaffection of Portuguese troops, bogged down in a seemingly endless antinationalist struggle in Angola, helped provide the impetus for the April 1974 seizure of power in Portugal by the Armed Forces Movement (MFA). General Antonio Sebastiao Ribeiro de Spinola, a major figure in the prosecution of Portugal's African wars, provided the trigger for the April revolution when his book, *Portugal and The Future*, called for "political-social solutions" for the African wars and deemed "an exclusively military victory as untenable."[7] Spinola was named provisional president by the new MFA regime.

Spinola advocated a federal Lusitanian community and a referendum in each African territory on the issue of independence. Foreign minister Mario Soares and a majority of the MFA wanted rapid transitions to independence without any referenda. By late July, Spinola accepted this latter position, and Portugal began to decolonize. Spinola was removed from power on September 28, but this did not obstruct the MFA's African independence process. Gradually, independence was granted to Guinea-Bissau (September 10, 1974), Mozambique (June 25, 1975), Cape Verde (July 5, 1975), and Sao Tome e Principe (July 12, 1975). Angola lugged behind the other African territories as a result of the internecine nationalist strife which complicated any negotiated political devolution.

Angola was governed by a Portuguese military council, and a high commissioner served as the symbol of Portuguese authority throughout the rule of the post-Alvor, Angolan transitional government. All Portuguese troops withdrew from Angola by independence day, November 11, 1975, even though the Alvor Agreement had permitted a Portuguese military presence until February 29, 1976. As the Portuguese left Angola, they turned over sovereignty to the people of Angola rather than to any specific nationalist movement. Portugal did not recognize the People's Republic of Angola until February 1976, when an MPLA military victory was already assured.

The MPLA had close ties to the Portuguese Communist and socialist parties, and it also was aligned with the dominant nationalist movements in other Portuguese African territories through CONCP (Conferencia das Organizacoes Nacionalistas das Colonias Portuguesas). CONCP members favored the MPLA over its rivals and later, during the 1975-76 war, the PAIGC in Guinea-Bissau provided some troops and logistic support and FRELIMO

(Frente de Libertacao de Mocambique) in Mozambique contributed funds. Based on these conditions, the Soviet leadership, as of mid-1974, apparently believed that the left-leaning MFA, in conjunction with the CONCP parties being placed in power in other African territories, could install an MPLA government in Angola. Gradually, the Soviets came to place less stock in such a possibility and increased their commitment to an MPLA-imposed military solution.

General Spinola was wary of Neto's MPLA and its ties to the Soviet Union and the Portuguese Communists, and he tried to prevent its rise to power.[8] He voiced his concern to Richard Nixon when the two leaders met at Lajes in the Azores on June 19, 1974. This consultation led to a conference at Sal in the Cape Verde islands on September 14. Spinola, FNLA leader Roberto, representatives of Chipenda, and Zairian president Mobutu Sese Seko attended, and their aim was to work toward a coalition government in Angola that would exclude the Neto faction of the MPLA. Mobutu agreed to the opening of a Chipenda headquarters in Kinshasa, and FNLA troops started to enter Angola from Zairian territory. To the advantage of the Soviet Union, Spinola was removed from power on September 28. Thus his anti-Neto efforts were nipped in the bud.

However, the Soviets were deeply concerned about a potential white rightist conspiracy in Angola which could have produced a unilateral declaration of independence a la Rhodesia or an alliance between Angolan whites and UNITA. The Soviets probably exaggerated white political strength, but it was true that UNITA was seeking support from the white community. The Soviets called upon the whites to back the MPLA, portraying it rather accurately as the only multiracial movement in Angola.[9] Soviet analysts presented a conspiracy theory in which a white rightist coup in Angola could be expected in light of the perceived linkages between the unsuccessful white rightist revolt in Mozambique on September 7-10, 1974 and the pro-Spinola "silent majority" demonstrations in Portugal on September 28.[10]

The Soviet delivery of arms to Neto in October 1974 may be interpreted as a response to the Sal conference, intrigues by white rightists, and a growing alliance of Zaire, the United States, the FNLA, and Chipenda against what the Soviets viewed as the authentic, MPLA-assisted, revolutionary process. The January

1975 removal of the pro-MPLA Antonio Alba Rosa Coutinho as head of the military council in Angola was further evidence of the growing strength of counter-revolutionary forces. Likewise, the attempted coup in Portugal by pro-Spinola forces on March 11 was seen as linked to the FNLA offensive of that month.[11] Furthermore, the failure of Spinola's supporters led to greater American involvement in domestic Portuguese politics in an attempt to block Communist advances. As revealed later, the Forty Committee (responsible for approving all funds for CIA undercover operations) in April 1975 voted to provide money for CIA use in Portugal. The Soviets also believed that the United States was fomenting separatism in the Azores so that American bases could be retained.[12]

The Communists received less than 13 percent of the vote in the April 1975 Portuguese legislative elections. Communist fortunes were again set back when the leftist Vasco dos Santos Goncalves was removed as prime minister at the end of August. He was replaced by the more centrist Jose Baptista Pinheiro de Azevedo. Contributing to Portugal's movement to the right was the influx of half a million white Angolan refugees. The Soviets feared their potential rightist proclivities in domestic Portuguese politics and had earlier advocated that they remain in Angola.[13] On November 25-26, 1975, Portuguese Communists participated in an unsuccessful leftist uprising against the Azevedo government.

Throughout the spring, summer, and fall of 1975, Communist strength in the Portuguese government was declining. The Soviet Union had counted on Communist influence being sufficient to steer the MFA on a pro-MPLA course, but the reality was that the MFA generally acted as a neutral force in Angola and was not prepared to turn power over to the MPLA. As the Soviets came to recognize this situation, they accelerated their military deliveries to the MPLA and sought a solution on the battlefield. The fall of the Goncalves government was a key turning point as it led to extensive involvement of Cuban troops on the side of the MPLA.

THE REGIONAL DIMENSION

In a regional context the Soviets saw Angola as a test case that would determine the future of black majority rule throughout southern Africa. They believed that Western states were trying to retard the liberation process and that they had secured the support of South Africa, Zaire, and Zambia in their effort to combat the MPLA. The United States was seen as collaborating closely with South Africa on an anti-Marxist platform. It was noted in Moscow that Zaire and Zambia were adherents of the "dialogue" or "detente" policy of fostering ties between black African states and South Africa. Soviet spokesmen maintained that an MPLA triumph in Angola would pave the way for the elimination of white minority rule in Zimbabwe-Rhodesia, Namibia, and South Africa. They later described the MPLA victory as a "stimulus" to southern African liberation movements and as a major contribution to the positive change in the region's military balance of forces. "All-round support" for the MPLA by Communist-ruled states was held largely responsible for these developments.[14]

South African troops had entered Angola numerous times in "hot pursuit" of SWAPO forces operating on the Angolan side of the border with Namibia. They also occupied part of the Cunene district in August 1975 to protect economic projects (basically hydroelectric and irrigation) in which South Africa was a major participant. Thereafter, the South African role was clearly aimed at thwarting the MPLA, as close military collaboration with the FNLA and UNITA was developed. Chipenda, Roberto, and UNITA leader Savimbi all had meetings with South African officials during the period May to August 1975, and South Africa directly entered the Angolan war in September.[15] Troops advanced northward from Namibia, and advisers aided UNITA. A large South African offensive took place in two stages in October, in collaboration with white mercenaries and forces loyal to Chipenda. Their march north toward Luanda was stopped in early November, just 150 miles short of the capital. At the same time, South African advisers were serving with FNLA units that were able to reach the outskirts of Luanda from the north. Additional South African troops entered the war in November and December. The total reached at least 5,000 and perhaps as high as 6,000. South Africa also introduced fighter-bombers into the conflict.

The Soviet provision of arms to the MPLA and the extensive participation of Cuban troops during the fall of 1975 were influenced by the South African factor. In particular, the major Soviet arms airlift to Luanda after independence was aimed at shoring up the MPLA defenses against the South Africans, who still posed a threat to Luanda from the south. The Soviets believed that South Africa was acting with American approval, a viewpoint supported by the fact that American officials condemned "extracontinental powers" for their involvement in the Angolan war but did not publicly admonish South Africa for her role until late December.[16]

Zaire provided arms, funds, and bases for the FNLA, and Zaire assisted the CIA in channeling American support to the FNLA. Zaire had traditionally denied the MPLA land access through its territory so its troops could pass from the Congo to Angola. Furthermore, Mobutu, at the Sal conference, had tried to freeze Neto out of a negotiated solution for the Angolan crisis. To the Soviets, Zaire was the backbone of the FNLA and was acting as an American proxy. Zaire's role in the Angolan war was viewed very seriously, especially after Zaire began to intervene directly. Zairian officers served with FNLA units in Angola as early as February 1975, and regular Zairian units first entered the fray in July. Zambia too was viewed warily by the Soviets. It had aided Chipenda and UNITA, encouraged South African involvement, and President Kaunda had asked for a more comprehensive American commitment when he met President Ford in Washington in April 1975. After Angola became independent, Zambia was a strong vocal critic of the Soviet and Cuban roles in support of the MPLA.

In addition to countering the Americans, South Africans, Zairians, and Zambians, the Soviet Union also had its own regional ambitions. Influence in an MPLA-ruled Angola would tend to give the Soviet Union some leverage over several southern African liberation movements (notably SWAPO, ZAPU, and the ANC). Angola could possibly be used as a forward base of military operations for these movements. Defeating the FNLA and UNITA would also serve to set back the "dialogue" process being evolved by South Africa, Zaire, and Zambia, and the latter two states could be subjected to pressure due to their great dependence on rail transport through Angola for their copper exports. Their pro-Western orientations and collaboration with South Africa could therefore be transformed. Perhaps a string of Marxist states from Congo to Mozambique could be established, giving the Soviets excellent strategic position in any ensuing struggle in southern Africa. Congo was already a major logistic center for the Soviets, providing training facilities for MPLA troops, transshipping Soviet arms to Angola, and serving as a staging area for Cuban troops.

South Africa's involvement in the Angolan war was counter-productive, as it helped legitimize the Soviet and Cuban roles. The FNLA and UNITA lost credibility among black African states because they were aligned with South Africa, as the diplomatic momentum swung toward the MPLA. States such as Nigeria which had been wary of Soviet actions rallied to the MPLA side, since South Africa was clearly the *beta noire* of black Africa and its intervention was deemed a greater evil than that of the Soviet Union and Cuba.

THE AFRICAN CONTEXT

The Soviet Union endorsed the Organization of African Unity's position on upholding the Alvor Agreement and reconciling the three Angolan movements, but it violated the OAU's strictures on noninterference by delivering arms to the MPLA. By July 1975 the MPLA had gained the military advantage. This made the Soviets less amenable to any coalition solution negotiated by the OAU. Also instrumental to the Soviet Union's growing estrangement from the OAU was the election late that month of Idi Amin as OAU chairman for the coming year. The choice of Amin, although controversial within the organization, was in accordance with the tradition that the host of an OAU summit serve as the next chairman. The July summit had long ago been scheduled for Kampala, Uganda. The Soviet Union was therefore concerned that Amin would use his chairmanship in a pro-Zairian and anti-MPLA manner.

Amin had meetings with Mobutu in April and July, and a deal was made whereby Amin agreed to support Mobutu on the Angola issue. In return, Mobutu promised to attend the Kampala summit (which was being boycotted by some anti-Amin African leaders) and to back Amin for the chairmanship of the OAU.[17] While in Kinshasa in early July, Amin met with Luis Ranque Franque, a leader of the Cabindan separatist movement with close ties to Mobutu. Amin endorsed the Cabindan right to independence, and Ranque Franque was invited to attend the Kampala summit later that month. Amin's action ran counter to the interests of the MPLA, since that movement militarily controlled most of Cabinda and was opposed to Cabindan separatism.

108

On September 23 Amin and Mobutu conferred with FNLA and UNITA representatives in Kinshasa. The MPLA was not invited.[18] Another meeting was arranged in Kampala on September 30 so that the Angolan movements could present their positions to a conciliation commission being instituted by the OAU. The FNLA and UNITA were given advance notice, but the MPLA was not informed until the night of September 29, when Amin phoned Neto. The MPLA felt slighted and sent observers rather than an official delegation.[19] In early November, Zairian foreign minister Mandungu Bula Nyati said "that President Mobutu is happy about President Amin's handling of the Angolan issue." Amin then sent a message to Mobutu thanking him for his support.[20] He also praised the positions on Angola taken by the United States, Great Britain. and China.[21]

Differences on the Angola issue brought about a deterioration in Soviet-Ugandan relations. Amin condemned the Soviet Union for providing arms to the MPLA and for indicating, prior to Angolan independence day, its intention to recognize the MPLA-controlled People's Republic of Angola. Amin and the OAU had hoped to work out some compromise solution prior to November 11. When the Soviets tried to pressure Amin on Angola, he reacted by expelling the Soviet ambassador on November 10. The Soviets broke diplomatic relations the next day, but ties were restored on November 17.

Amin also irked the Soviets by procrastinating on the convening of an emergency OAU summit to deal with Angola. The pro-MPLA states felt that they had majority support within the organizations, but the anti-MPLA states were able to delay the summit until January 1976. By the time that the Addis Ababa meeting took place, the United States had effectively lobbied many African states, particularly those which were Francophone. The vote at the summit was a 22-22 deadlock, with half the members favoring recognition of the People's Republic of Angola and half advocating a government of national unity including representatives of all three movements. Uganda abstained on the ground that it should not take sides while Amin was chairman of the session, but Amin indicated after the vote that he was on the anti-MPLA side of the issue.

The Soviets acted in Angola irrespective of the positions taken by the OAU, since they did not believe that this fragmented organization could have a decisive impact on the course of the war. They also felt that Amin was trying to steer the OAU against the MPLA, but the extent of his partisanship was probably exaggerated. Amin did not advocate recognition of the FNLA-UNITA government in Nova Lisboa (Huambo), and he abstained at the Addis Ababa summit. He also did not try to translate his support for Cabindan separatism into OAU policy.

The Soviet Union risked antagonizing many OAU members by its introduction of arms and its assistance to Cuban troops, but it correctly perceived the weakness of the OAU. This organization proved incapable of reconciling the movements and it did not send a peacekeeping force to Angola. It also was divided on the issues of recognizing the PRA and accepting Soviet and Cuban actions as legitimate. As South African involvement in the war increased and as the MPLA moved toward victory, the majority viewpoint in the OAU became consistent with the policy interests of the Soviet Union. Opposition to South African troops and white mercenaries, recognition of the PRA, maintenance of the territorial unity of Angola, and the strengthening of MPLA ties to SWAPO, ZAPU, and the ANC formed part of a common perspective. Less than a month after the Addis Ababa summit, the OAU officially recognized the PRA and so did Uganda.

THE INTERNATIONAL FRAMEWORK

Viewed in a global setting, Angola was a major focus of Soviet-American competition even though it was not intrinsically vital to either superpower. The Portuguese revolution had caught both states by surprise, and each reacted to the rapid decolonization process engendered in Angola by moving to counter the perceived threat from the other. Superpower concerns about a world strategic balance were superimposed on an indigenously African problem, and Angola also became a testing ground for an anticipated struggle for influence in South Africa. In addition, the Soviet Union and United States each wanted in Angola to prove its resolve to help reverse recent setbacks that had wounded its political psyche. The Soviet Union had witnessed the American and Japanese rapprochements with China in 1971-72, the explusion of its military advisers from Egypt in 1972, and the overthrow of Salvador Allende of Chile in 1973. After the 1973 Arab-Israeli war, the United States had seized the diplomatic initiative in the Middle

110

East and had generally frozen the Soviet Union out of the process. In Portugal, the Communists were not very successful in steering the MFA leftward. The United States was trying to recover from the domestic trauma of Watergate and from the victories of Communist forces in Vietnam, Laos, and Cambodia in the spring of 1975.

The Soviet Union saw an American effort to incorporate Angola into its economic orbit. The United States was the largest importer of Angolan goods and Gulf Oil was the most prominent enterprise in Angola, its tax and royalty payments accounting for at least 60 percent of the Angolan budget. Angola was endowed with significant quantities of oil and diamonds and it was also a major producer of coffee. The Soviet interpretation of American economic intentions followed naturally from the theories of imperialism and neocolonialism but, in the Angolan case, this perception of the situation was rather distorted. A dichotomy actually existed between the state and corporate interests in terms of the activities of Gulf Oil as tax and royalty payments were made to the MPLA during the fall of 1975. US government pressure on Gulf led to a policy change in late December, as payments started to be placed in an escrow account.

The Soviets were also concerned that the United States wanted to retain Angola as an extension of NATO, as it had been while under Portuguese control, and it was feared that NATO operations would be further extended in the South Atlantic.[22] The Soviets obviously wanted to deny to the United States the strategic rights which previously existed in Angola such as access to ports and aircraft overflight and landing privileges. At the same time, the Soviet Union sought strategic *entree*. It had actively developed a network of installations in African coastal states during the 1970's. Once the MPLA won the war, Moscow was able to gain the rights earlier possessed by the now replaced United States. Air reconnaissance flights out of Luanda also turned out to be an important asset. The Soviet Union's "power-projection" into Angola may be more significant strategically than any capacity it may possess to influence the MPLA government, if one takes into account its prepositioning of forces (Cuban) and equipment, naval support capability, extent of air reconnaissance operations, and communications network development.[23]

The Soviet Union's "power projection" into Angola may

111

become instrumental if major conflicts develop in Zimbabwe-Rhodesia and South Africa in the coming years. It is already clear that Angola has become a logistic base of operations for several southern African liberation groups which are armed by the Soviet Union. On the other hand, it is unlikely that the Soviets will take advantage of their port rights in Angola to interfere with tankers plying the Cape oil route. Slow, unarmed tankers can be interdicted anywhere between the Persian Gulf and the Western oil-importing states so any Soviet naval presence in Angolan waters would prove redundant. Furthermore, such action would constitute an act tantamount to war and would most likely evoke a Western military response.[24] It is very unlikely that the Soviet Union got involved in the Angolan war primarily in order to be in a better position to cut off the flow of oil to the West.

THE AMERICAN CONNECTION

The Soviet Union had to consider the potential effects of its Angolan actions on detente with the United States. The possibility of a direct American military response or assistance to Angolan movements or neighboring states also had to be taken into account. On the whole, however, the American factor did not greatly affect Soviet motivations during the Angolan war, although the Soviet factor certainly influenced American policymakers.

American clandestine activities in Angola during the last half of 1974 may have had some effect on the Soviet delivery of arms to the MPLA in October 1974, but the Soviets were probably more concerned about the collaboration of the FNLA, Zaire, and China.[25] More consequential were American actions in 1975. On January 22, 1975, one week after the signing of the Alvor Agreement, the Forty Committee decided that the CIA could provide $300 thousand for the FNLA, but this money was not to be used for arms. On July 17, an additional $30 million, which included arms, was committed to the FNLA and UNITA and channeled into the war through Zaire and Zambia. Another $10.7 million followed on August 20 and $7 million in late November. Overall, $32 million had been allocated in cash and $16 million in arms. The total was actually higher, as funds approved for Zaire were actually used to help the FNLA, the arms supplied were undervalued, and some of the cash was multiplied when converted into local currencies through the Zairian black market. Going beyond the provision of arms and funds, American military advisers were sent to Angola, the CIA participated in the training of Angolan troops, the CIA hired mercenaries, and five American spotter planes, operating out of Zairian bases, surveyed Angola.[26]

Although the United States had become enmeshed in the Angolan war, the roles of the Soviet Union and United States were disproportionate, since the Soviets were trying to cope with much more than the Americans. The Soviets spent at least $300 million on the MPLA, provided 200 advisers and assisted the Cubans in introducing an armed force of 17,000 men. The United States did try to augment its role, but Kissinger's request to Congress for an additional $28 million was turned down. On December 19, 1975, the Senate voted 54-22 to attach the Tunney amendment to the Defense Appropriations Bill, thus preventing the allocation of any more funds for covert actions in Angola. The House concurred on January 27, 1976 by a vote of 323-99, and President Ford signed the Defense Appropriations Act on February 9.

Soviet and Cuban support for the MPLA escalated once the Senate's action made clear that the United States would not get more deeply involved in the war, but causality is hard to prove. In any case, the $28 million would not have altered the course of the war. The MPLA had already seized the military initiative, and the funds would have arrived too late to reverse the course of events. Furthermore, the funds could not be effectively converted into military strength, since the FNLA and UNITA were incapable of handling the sophisticated armaments necessary to prevent their defeat. The MPLA too had its technological deficiencies but it also had the assistance of Cuban troops trained in the use of advanced Soviet weapons. At this stage, ony a massive South African intervention could have proved effective, and therefore the United States was in a no-win situation. Even a South African-aided triumph would have been a diplomatic defeat in terms of overall American policy toward Africa since the South African connection would have tarnished American credibility in the eyes of most black Africans.

In January 1976, the Soviet press alluded to the possibility of finding a political solution for the Angolan conflict.[27] The MPLA already had a decisive military advantage and a negotiated settlement would surely have favored its interests. The Soviets may have been amendable to an MPLA-dominated government of national unity since it would have had some prospect of preventing continued harassment of the MPLA by UNITA. However, the Soviets must have realized that the MPLA was opposed to negotiations, so its peace feelers seem to have been aimed primarily at misleading the United States.[28] The Soviets wanted to make sure that the Defense Appropriations Bill, with its Tunney amendment, was passed by the House and signed by President Ford, and they did not want the United States to develop linkages between its trade with the Soviet Union and its consternation over Soviet actions in Angola. The Soviets also wanted to make sure that Kissinger would not cancel his scheduled trip to Moscow in late January to negotiate a SALT agreement.

Beginning in the fall of 1975, US officials persistently attacked the Soviet Union for its interference in Angola and they warned the Soviets that detente could be seriously undermined. The Soviets were able to act boldly nevertheless, because they realized that American verbiage was not accompanied by any retaliatory actions. The United States did not exert economic pressure, and President Ford indicated publicly on January 5, 1976 that grain would not be withheld to protest Soviet actions in Angola. Secretary Kissinger went to Moscow later that month to continue the SALT process and the Soviet leaders, rejecting the linkage concept, refused to discuss Angola with him at all.

The Soviets must have been aware that much of the American rhetoric on Angola was conditioned by internal political considerations. Congress, in a continuing extension of its reaction to Watergate and Vietnam, was trying to assert its powers in the area of foreign policy by challenging the executive branch. Conversely, the Republican Administration wanted to make the Democrat-controlled Congress look weak and defeatist due to its unwillingness to counter the Soviet Union in Angola. At the same time, President Ford was engaged in a struggle with Ronald Reagan for the Republican presidential nomination, and he had to strengthen his ties to the conservative wing of the party by taking a verbal hard line on Soviet involvement in Angola. Taking these factors into account, as well as the American predilection to avoid "another Vietnam," the Soviet leadership probably came to the conclusion that its massive commitment to the MPLA would not be matched by American support for the FNLA and UNITA and that its detente relationship with the United States could withstand the strains engendered by the Angolan conflict.

114

THE CHINESE ENTANGLEMENT

Chinese actions greatly influenced Soviet behavior in Angola in late 1974 and early 1975, but not thereafter. It must be emphasized that China's position in southern and south-central Africa was very strong prior to the Angolan war. Close bonds had been developed with Zaire, Zambia, and Tanzania, and China later gained the inside track on the Soviet Union in Mozambique once it became independent in June 1975. China also enjoyed cordial relations with ZANU and SWAPO, and it was aiding the FNLA and UNITA in Angola. China was actually far surpassing the Soviet Union in the amount of assistance given to African states. In 1974 Chinese aid totaled $237 million, while the Soviets provided only $17 million. In fact, the Chinese had outdistanced the Soviets in terms of total aid to Africa over the previous 20 years and had concentrated their largesse in the southern half of the continent. Chinese aid to Tanzania, Zambia, Zaire, and even Congo far exceeded that provided by the Soviets.[29]

After Jonas Savimbi split with the FNLA in 1964, he traveled to China and was received by both Mao Tse-tung and Chou En-lai.[30] After UNITA was formed under his leadership in 1966, some of its top military commanders were trained in China, and the Chinese provided a small amount of military and financial assistance. Later, when Daniel Chipenda became a rival to Agostinho Neto within the MPLA, the Chinese gave him arms as well.[31] UNITA and Chipenda had close ties to the Zambian govenment of Kenneth Kaunda, which in turn had good relations with China.

China's most significant involvement in Angola was through its collaboration with the FNLA, and Zaire was instrumental in arranging this connection. Zaire followed the American lead in effecting a diplomatic opening to China, and Mobutu visited Peking in January 1973 and December 1974. Zaire was clearly a patron of the FNLA and its new relationship to China led to FNLA-Chinese ties as well. FNLA leader Holden Roberto journeyed to Peking in December 1973, and the Chinese agreed to provide military instructors to train his troops in Zaire. They started to arrive on May 29, 1974, and their number reached at least 120 and possibly as high as 200. In August and early September Chinese arms were delivered to the FNLA, and the Soviet provision of arms to the MPLA in October was probably affected by Chinese actions.

Though China's support for the FNLA was an important factor in motivating the Soviet Union, it should be pointed out that China to some extent was trying to implement an evenhanded policy in Angola. It sent arms to the Neto faction of the MPLA through 1974 and also assisted Chipenda and UNITA. Nevertheless, its assistance to the FNLA was greater than that provided to other movements. China praised the Alvor Agreement and hosted delegations from UNITA, MPLA, and the FNLA during the period March-July 1975. China endorsed the OAU's position of favoring a negotiated solution, and it did not recognize either the Luanda or Nova Lisboa (Huambo) government upon Angolan independence. It also phased out its aid to Angolan movements and withdrew its advisers to the FNLA on October 27. China could not effectively compete with the Soviet Union in terms of arms or the logistics for introducing them into the conflict, and it was certainly unprepared to match the involvement of Cuban troops. It also did not want to be tarnished by collaboration with South Africa. China hoped that the United States would play a greater role in opposing the MPLA.

China was not an important factor in the war during the last half of 1975 or in 1976 but, from a Soviet perspective, it was still a dangerous competitor. Zairian troops were fighting in Angola and they were supplied with Chinese arms. In addition, North Korea provided arms and advisers to the FNLA in Zaire. Rumania was arming all three movements.

The Soviet Union was especially wary of any Sino-American collusion. China and the United States were supporters of the FNLA, and both played major roles in Zaire. It appears that some coordination on Angolan policy had been worked out between the two states in Zaire beginning in mid-1974. The Soviets claimed that US liaison officer George Bush had contacts with Chinese officials in Peking on the Angolan issue.[32] Henry Kissinger visited China during October 19-23, 1975, just before Angola became independent, and he was there again with President Ford during December 1-5. When testifying before a Senate subcommittee, Kissinger was asked by Senator Charles Percy about discussions he may have had in Peking on the Angolan conflict. Kissinger said that he could not respond in public session.[33]

THE POSTWAR MOMENTUM

The Soviet-Angolan relationship has been solidified by the 1976 friendship treaty, extensive Soviet economic assistance, a Moscow-Luanda air route, and the education of Angolan students in the Soviet Union. Agostinho Neto was awarded a Lenin Peace Prize in 1977. There are other, more subtle signs of the strength of Soviet-Angolan ties. Angola was the only African state mentioned in the Soviet Union's May Day slogans for 1976. In November 1976, Neto's message to Brezhnev on the occasion of the 59th anniversary of the Bolshevik Revolution appeared in *Pravda* ahead of those from other African leaders. On the following revolutionary anniversary, the text of the speech by Angolan prime minister Lopo do Nascimento was printed in *Pravda* the same day as Brezhnev's. Of the 15 speeches delivered by foreigners, it was the only one by a non-Communist.[34]

The Angolan government has not become subservient to Soviet interests nor economically enmeshed with Communist-ruled states. There are no permanent Soviet military bases and Angola has developed diplomatic and economic ties with many Western states. Foreign investment in Angola has increased, despite the avowed dedication of the government to a socialist economy, and Gulf Oil is still operating in Cabinda. The Soviet Union may actually approve such policies since it does not want Angola to become a drain on its financial resources.

Certain political actions of the Angolan government represented setbacks for the Soviet Union. Late in 1976, following the signing of the Friendship Treaty, the Ministry of Internal Administration was abolished. This effectively removed Nito Alves, a strong supporter of ties to the Soviet Union, from the Cabinet. Jose Eduardo dos Santos, another pro-Soviet figure, was replaced as foreign minister. He became the first deputy prime minister but lost that post in another reshuffle in December 1978. Also significant was Soviet behavior during the attempted seizure of power by Nito Alves in May 1977. The Soviet media were very slow in condemning the Nitists and rallying to the support of Neto.[35] Available evidence seems to indicate that the Soviet Union was aware of Alves' plot, looked upon it favorably, and did not forewarn Neto.

The MPLA has been organized as a Marxist-Leninist party and it held its first party congress in December 1977. The party is

117

dedicated to "scientific socialism" and "proletarian internationalism" and defines itself as the vanguard movement of the working class.[36] In October 1976, a party-to-party agreement was reached between the MPLA and the Communist Party of the Soviet Union (CPSU). This was an unusual step, since the MPLA had not yet been transformed from a movement into a party and the party-to-party agreement was only the sixth entered into by the CPSU with a non-Communist partner. The others had been with the ruling parties in Egypt, Algeria, Iraq, Syria, and Mali.

Since the Angolan war, Cuban troops provisioned with Soviet arms have turned increasingly toward the use of military force to resolve African disputes, as in the Ogaden and Eritrean conflicts. At the same time the Cubans have been instrumental in maintaining the MPLA in power, and the number of Cuban troops in Angola has actually increased since the war ended in 1976. The MPLA is concerned about the military threats of South Africa, UNITA, and the Cabindan separatists. The mesticos and whites in the Angolan administration welcome the Cuban presence as a shield against black militants who want them removed from their posts. The departure of the Cubans could abet the rise of black consciousness forces which favor closer relations with the Soviet Union. Thus the Soviet and Cuban roles, though certainly allied, must not be viewed as completely complementary. When Nito Alves and his black power supporters tried to overthrow Neto, Cuban troops helped put down the insurrection, but the Soviet Union probably would have preferred a victory by Nito Alves.

Southern African liberation groups have strongly gravitated toward the Soviet Union for assistance and have greatly limited their contacts with China. China has largely disengaged from the revolutionary process, and even ZANU is now seeking Soviet arms. Southern African states which previously had close ties to China are now abandoning a sinking ship. Zambia and Tanzania have turned to the Soviet Union as an arms supplier, and Mozambique has even signed a friendship pact with the Soviets.

The Angolan war forced the United States to reassess its African policies and to pay much greater attention to southern African problems. Henry Kissinger, who had not visited southern Africa during his previous 7 years in the Nixon and Ford administrations, made an extensive tour in April and May 1976 that included stops in Tanzania, Zambia, and Zaire. In September he journeyed to

Tanzania, Zambia, and South Africa. Kissinger basically wanted to work toward negotiated solutions for southern African problems so that the Soviet Union and Cuba could not press their military advantage in the area. The United States started to work toward black majority rule and to foster contacts with liberation movements, with the aim of backing black moderate forces which could assume power without causing an exodus of the white minority from Namibia, Zimbabwe-Rhodesia, and South Africa. Kissinger's new approach to Africa was continued by the Carter administration, since it became obvious that the days of white rule were numbered. The United States therefore became deeply involved in negotiations on the Namibian and Zimbabwe-Rhodesian issues and tried to dissociate itself from former links to the South African government.

SOME ANALYTIC CONSIDERATIONS

The Soviet Union clearly sided with the MPLA, and it was faced with several policy options in 1974-76 as it considered its reaction to the MPLA's fortunes:

• To stay uninvolved in the Angolan conflict and therefore place itself in a position to chastise other states for their interference. Such an option must have been rejected rather easily, since it would have permitted the United States and China to act freely and help install an FNLA or an FNLA-UNITA government. The Soviet Union would also have lost credibility as a supporter of southern African liberation movements, and many of them may have turned increasingly toward China as their patron.

• To intervene directly with Soviet armed forces. Again, such an option must have been dismissed as unviable because of logistic factors and the possibility of American counteraction. Furthermore, such an intervention would have been highly inconsistent with previous Soviet behavior outside of Eastern Europe. The Soviets did not send troops to assist the North Koreans or the North Vietnamese, so coming to the aid of the MPLA was most unlikely.

• To work with the OAU to institute a government of national unity. This appears to have been the fallback position in case the MPLA was unable to win militarily. Another variation would have been to encourage the OAU to arm and finance the MPLA, but this

119

was unrealistic since the OAU was too divided on the Angolan issue to effect such a policy.

 • To work toward an agreement with the United States on noninterference by either superpower in Angolan affairs. Detente would have been promoted, and an African and Portuguese solution for the Angolan conflict would have been explored. However, the Soviets would not have any assurance that South Africa, Zaire, and China would not get involved on the side of the FNLA and UNITA.

 • To arm the MPLA, provide Soviet advisers, facilitate the intervention of Cuban troops, but keep the Soviet profile low enough so that there would not be a major American military response. Soviet assistance to the MPLA would be sufficient to ensure an MPLA victory while the United States, still obsessed with its defeat in Vietnam, would greatly limit its support for the FNLA and UNITA. The Soviets would risk some deterioration in relations with the United States but would seek to preserve the rudiments of detente. This was the option chosen by the Soviet leadership, and it produced most advantageous results.

The Soviet Union's foreign policy objectives in Angola were to cement ties to southern African liberation movements, to develop a base of operations in Angola for use in future conflicts in southern Africa, and to project Soviet power into Angola through the acquisition of logistic rights. The Soviets also sought to prevent the establishment of a Zairian-American sphere of influence in Angola, or a Chinese one, and to isolate Zaire politically and geographically, with the downfall of the Mobutu government an eventual consequence. Perhaps there was also a desire to limit the access of Western states to Angolan natural resources.

The major battlefield objective was to help the MPLA gain control of Angola, including the enclave of Cabinda. The emphasis was on securing Luanda, the Capital, and other major ports. Such tactics were consistent with logistic needs as well as the MPLA's pattern of geographical and ethnic influence. The political objectives were to portray the Soviet Union as an anti-colonial, anti-imperialist power and to link the United States and China to counterrevolutionary and racist forces. The Soviets also wanted to display their reliability as an ally of Third World liberation movements and as a defender of the territorial integrity of African states. They tried to depict the MPLA as a multiracial, detribalized movement and contrasted it with the FNLA and UNITA, which

120

were labeled as racist and ethnically exclusive. The Soviets additionally wanted to emphasize that detente would not be permitted to inhibit their behavior in those parts of the Third World where neither the Soviet Union nor the United States had a vital interest at stake.[37]

Soviet strategy was seemingly based on the proposition that the MPLA could not win an election nor gain dominance within a coalition government so its military strength had to be built up. It was hoped that a combination of MPLA battlefield prowess and Armed Forces Movement (MFA) partisanship in its favor would lead to ultimate victory. The Soviet leadership was surprised by the Portuguese revolution, and it was not prepared with any grand design that it could apply to the Angolan situation. Policy therefore evolved incrementally in reaction to the internal dynamics of the conflict as well as to the courses charted by other external actors. Soviet tactics were conditioned primarily by the military circumstances and the MFA's attitude toward the MPLA. Periods during which the MPLA had an inferior military position or the MFA was acting neutrally rather than in a pro-MPLA manner tended to coincide with the extent of Soviet arms supplies. Also significant was Soviet reluctance to provide combat aircraft. Their entry in support of the MPLA would have encouraged Zaire and South Africa to expand the air war, and the United States may have intervened as well. Furthermore, the MPLA would have been at a disadvantage in an air war, since it could more easily have been targeted in its fixed urban locations than could the FNLA and UNITA in their more mobile bases in the countryside.

Soviet policy toward Angola must, at least temporarily, be viewed as successful. A political ally has been gained and, as a side effect of the Soviet role in Angola, contacts with states and liberation movements in the southern African region have been extended significantly. Soviet Angolan relations have developed on a firm economic, military, and ideological basis, and no major change should be engendered by the death in September 1979 of Agostinho Neto. His successor as president, Jose Eduardo dos Santos, is committed to the maintenance of close ties to the Soviet Union, and thus a short-term dividend for the Soviets may gradually evolve into a long-term asset.

ENDNOTES

1. For previous analyses by this author of Soviet policies toward Africa, see *Soviet Perspectives on African Socialism*, Cranbury, New Jersey: Associated University Presses, 1969; "The Soviet View of African Socialism" in *On The Road to Communism*, ed. by Roger Kanet and Ivan Volgyes, Lawrence, Kansas: University Press of Kansas, 1972; "The Soviet Union and Africa" in *The Soviet Union and the Developing Nations*, ed. by Roger Kanet, Baltimore: Johns Hopkins University Press, 1974; "The USSR and Nigeria: Why the Soviets Chose Sides," *Africa Report*, February 1968; and *Soviet Policy Toward Southern Africa: An Angolan Case Study*, Boulder, Colorado: Westview Press, 1980.

2. The MPLA was founded in December 1956, the FNLA in March 1962, and UNITA in March 1966.

3. Peter Vanneman and Martin James, "The Soviet Intervention in Angola: Intentions and Implications," *Strategic Review*, Summer 1976, p. 94, and Fred Bridgland, *The Washington Post*, November 23, 1975.

4. Soviet interaction with American and Chinese interests will be discussed below.

5. Oleg Ignatyev, *Pravda*, October 30, 1975, in *USSR and Third World*, Vol. V, Nos. 6-8, July 7-December 31, 1975, p. 406; *Pravda*, November 8, 1975, p. 5 in *Current Digest of The Soviet Press*, Vol. XXVII, No. 45, December 3, 1975, p. 16.

6. See editorial, "The Cause of People's Angola," *New Times*, No. 48, December 1975, p. 1 and K. Uralov, "New Advances in Angola," *International Affairs*, (Moscow), No. 8, August 1976, p. 78.

7. Translated in *Africa Report*, Vol. 19, No. 2, March-April 1974, p. 38. In addition to Angola, the Portuguese were engaged in antinationalist struggles in Guinea-Bissau and Mozambique.

8. See *Diario de Noticias*, April 21, 1975, in *Facts and Reports*, Vol. 5, No. 10, May 17, 1975, p. 22, and Jonathan Story, "Portugal's Revolution of Carnations: Patterns of Change and Continuity," *International Affairs* (London), Vol. 52, No. 3, July 1976, pp. 422-423.

9. See Radio Peace and Progress in English to Africa, November 27, 1974, in Foreign Broadcast Information Service, *Daily Report: Soviet Union*, December 5, 1974, p. 235 and Radio Moscow in Portuguese to Africa, December 11, 1974, *Ibid.*, December 12, 1974, p. 240.

10. Oleg Ignatyev, *Secret Weapon in Africa*, Moscow: Izdatelstvo "Progress," 1977, p. 103. See also James Mittleman, "State Power in Mozambique,"*Issue*, Vol. VIII, No. 1 Spring 1978, p.7.

11. Fyodor Tarasov, *Pravda*, April 24, 1975, p. 5 and Radio Moscow in Portuguese to Africa, March 14, 1975, in BBC, *Summary of World Broadcasts*, Vol. 1, March 18, 1975, p. A5/2.

12. Tad Szulc, "Lisbon and Washington: Behind Portugal's Revolution," *Foreign Policy*, No. 21, Winter 1975-76, pp. 36-37 and 42-43, and V. Kuznetsov, *Izvestiia*, September 23, 1975, p. 4.

13. Boris Pilyatskin, *Izvestiia*, July 19, 1975, p. 4.

14. *Pravda*, November 8, 1975, p. 5.; *Pravda*, February 11, 1976, p. 4; Alexander Ignatov, "Clouds Over Luanda," *New Times*, No. 23, June 1975, p. 13; and Yurii Gavrilov, Radio Moscow in English to Africa, March 27, 1976, in *USSR and Third World*, Vol. VI, No. 1, January 1-March 31, 1976, p. 50.

15. For information on these meetings, see *Daily News* (Tanzania), July 29, 1975, in *Facts and Reports*, Vol. 5, Nos. 17-18, September 6, 1975, p. 5; *Star Weekly*

(South Africa), December 13, 1975, in *Facts and Reports*, Vol. 5, December 27, 1975, p. 7; Ignatyev, *Secret Weapon*, pp. 137-38; John Marcum, *The Angolan Revolution*, Volume II, Cambridge: MIT Press, 1978, p. 269; Moscow Domestic Service, August 7, 1975, in Foreign Broadcast Information Service, *Daily Report: Soviet Union*, August 8, 1975, p. 154; and Radio Moscow in English to Africa, January 10, 1976, in Foreign Broadcast Information Service, *Daily Report: Soviet Union*, January 12, 1976, p. H9.

16. On the issue of South African-American collaboration, see testimony of Edward Mulcahy, Subcommittee on African Affairs, Senate Committee on Foreign Relations, Angola Hearings, Washington: US Government Printing Office, 1976, p. 187; Bernard Nossiter, *The Washington Post*, February 4, 1976; John Kane-Berman, *The Guardian*, April 21, 1978; John Stockwell, *In Search of Enemies*, New York: Norton, 1978, p. 187; Johannesburg radio in English for abroad, January 19, 1976 in BBC, *Summary of World Broadcasts*, Vol. 4, January 21, 1976, p. B/2; and Arnaud de Borchgrave interview with John Vorster, *Newsweek*, May 17, 1976, p. 53.

17. See *Africa Contemporary Record, 1975-76*, New York: Africana, 1976, p. B362.

18. Luanda radio, September 30, 1975, in BBC, *Summary of World Broadcasts*, Vol. 4, October 2, 1975, p. B/7.

19. Luanda radio, October 1, 1975, in *Ibid.*, October 3, 1975, pp. B/3-5.

20. Kampala home service in English, November 7, 1975, in *Facts and Reports*, Vol. 5, No. 24, November 29, 1975, p. 13, and AZAP in French, November 8, 1975, in *Ibid.*, p. 13.

21. *Africa Contemporary Record, 1975-76*, p. B366.

22. K. Uralov, "Angola: The Triumph of the Right Cause," *International Affairs* (Moscow), No. 5, May 1976, p. 56.

23. See W. Scott Thompson, "The Projection of Soviet Power," RAND/WN-9822-DNA, Santa Monica: RAND Corporation, October 1977, p. 1.

24. See Robert Price, *U.S. Foreign Policy in Sub-Saharan Africa: National Interests and Global Strategy*, No. 8, Policy Papers in International Affairs, Berkeley: Institute of International Studies, 1978, pp. 10-13.

25. See Viktor Sidenko, "The Nakuru Agreement," *New Times*, No. 26, June 1975, p. 16; Sidenko, "The Intrigues of Angola's Enemies," *New Times*, No. 30, July 1975, p. 14; Stockwell, p. 258; and Per Wastberg, *Dagens Nyheter* (Sweden), March 11, 1975 in *Facts and Reports*, Vol. 5, No. 7, April 5, 1975, p. 3.

26. Stockwell, pp. 55, 208-209, 267-68 and chapters 7 and 8; Seymour Hersh, *The New York Times*, July 16, 1978, p. 12; David Binder, *The New York Times*, December 12, 1975, and "CIA's Secret War in Angola," *Intelligence Report*, Center for National Security Studies, Vol. 1, No. 1, December 1975, p. 4.

27. For examples of Soviet press commentaries on the prospects for a negotiated settlement, see *Pravda*, January 3, 1976, p. 4 and *Izvestiia*, January 30, 1976, p. 2.

28. The US Government did appear to be misled by Soviet pronouncements in support of a political solution. See Philip Shabecoff, *The New York Times*, January 6, 1976, p. 1; George Wilson, *The Washington Post*, January 5, 1976, and Jeremiah O'Leary, *The Washington Star*, January 31, 1976.

29. US Central Intelligence Agency, *Communist Aid to Less Developed Countries of the Free World*, ER 76-10372U, July 1976, p. 32-33.

30. Marcum, p. 160.

31. Charles Ebinger, "External Intervention in Internal War: The Politics and Diplomacy of the Angolan Civil War," *Orbis*, Vol. 20, No. 3, Fall 1976, p. 686-88.

32. Ignatyev, *Secret Weapon*, pp. 120-21.

33. *Angola Hearings*, p. 49.

34. *Pravda*, April 15, 1976, p. 1; November 9, 1976, p. 4; and November 3, 1977, p. 7.

35. *Pravda*, May 28, 1977, p. 5; May 29, p. 5; May 30, p. 3; May 31, p. 5; June 1, p.5; June 4, p. 5; and June 5, p. 5. See also *Jornal de Angola*, June 24, 1977, in *Facts and Reports*, Vol. 7, No. 14, July 13, 1977, p. 19.

36. See *The New York Times*, December 5, 1977, p. 11; *Pravda*, December 6, 1977, p. 4; *TASS* in English, December 4, 1977, in Foreign Broadcast Information Service, *Daily Report: Soviet Union*, December 5, 1977, p. H4; Luanda radio, December 10, 1977 in *Facts and Reports*, Vol. 7, No. 26, December 28, 1977, pp. 8-9; and *Daily News* (Tanzania), December 23, 1977, *Ibid.*, Vol. 8, No. 1, January 11, 1978, p. 8.

37. For a discussion of foreign policy, battlefield, and political-effects objectives, see Morton Halperin, *Limited War in The Nuclear Age*, New York: John Wiley, 1963, pp. 3-4.

SOVIET POLICY IN THE HORN OF AFRICA:
THE DECISION TO INTERVENE

Richard B. Remnek

This essay attempts to evaluate recent Soviet policy on the Horn of Africa.[1] Its temporal focus is the period immediately preceding and during the Somali-Ethiopian conflict in the Ogaden, roughly from 1976 to late 1977. It was then that the Soviet Union made critical commitments to support the Dergue, Ethiopia's radical military government. These decisions ultimately brought about a major diplomatic realignment in the Horn. This period can therefore be considered a major turning point in Soviet policy on the Horn.

The intent of this study is not to provide a comprehensive historical narrative documenting the major events during this period. Nevertheless, a summary of the major events marking the stages of escalating Soviet military support for Ethiopia is useful for later reference.

The first Soviet military aid agreement, a limited one worth roughly $100 million for second-line equipment such as T-34 tanks, was signed in December 1976.[2] This was about the time that the outgoing Ford Administration cancelled its military grants assistance program.³ In February 1977, just a few weeks after the abortive coup from which the pro-Soviet Lieutenant Colonel Mengistu Haile Mariam emerged as the preeminent leader of the Provisional Military Administrative Committee (or Dergue), the incoming Carter Administration announced that military aid to Ethiopia had been suspended on the grounds of human rights violations. In April, the Dergue retaliated by expelling the US military assistance advisory group and closing down other US military installations, including the once-important Kagnew communications station. The Soviets soon stepped in to fill the void. A large military aid agreement of approximately $500 million for more modern weapons was signed after Mengistu's trip to Moscow in May.⁴ In July Somalia challenged this new Soviet-Ethiopian military connection by invading the Ogaden—an initiative that eventually forced the Soviets to increase their support for Ethiopia. On November 13, 1977 Mogadiscio boldly responded by abrogating its 1974 Friendship Treaty with Moscow, terminating Soviet access to all naval support facilities, expelling Soviet advisers, and severing diplomatic relations with Cuba. In late November the Soviets initiated a major air and sealift to Ethiopia. And during the next month, the first of approximately 16,000 Cuban ground combat troops arrived to take part in the fighting. In February 1978 the Ethiopian counteroffensive in the Ogaden began, and by March Somali armed forces were withdrawn from the Ogaden.

The main intent of this study is to elucidate the factors that appear to have influenced Soviet decisions to support Ethiopia during three stages of escalating involvement: prior to the Somali invasion in July; in the aftermath of the invasion; and, following the Somali expulsion of the Soviets in November. We shall also try to analyze the priorities and preferences that were reflected in the policy choices made in Moscow during these periods. Understanding these decisions is essential to any further evaluation of Soviet policy.

In few other cases of Soviet involvement in the Third World have Soviet actions had such an immediate and clear-cut impact on events. Had the Soviets and their allies (Cubans, South Yemenis, Libyans, etc.) not come to the Dergue's assistance, at best, anarchy would have prevailed in Ethiopia and, at worst, the map of the Horn might have been redrawn. That their actions did have such clear consequences affords an unusual opportunity to evaluate Soviet policy and to assess the extent to which the Soviets achieved their objectives. We also can consider the reasons for Soviet success or failure: was their policy realistic or unrealistic, effective or ineffective, or were they simply lucky or unlucky?

In international affairs, as in sports, it is not just what you win or lose, it's how you play the game. Thus, questions pertaining to the conduct of Soviet foreign policy, such as whether the Soviets acted recklessly or cautiously, timidly or boldly, obtusely or prudently, offer additional criteria by which to evaluate their behavior.

PART I

One concrete indication of the Soviet Union's interest in the Horn of Africa has been the continuous deployment of a naval squadron of approximately 18 ships (about one-third of which are combatants) in adjacent waters.[5] But this observation, of course, only begs the more important question of why the Soviets are there.

As has often been noted, the Horn of Africa is situated at the junction of the Red Sea and Indian Ocean, astride two of the world's most important shipping lanes. It has frequently been assumed that because of their presence in the area, Soviet warships pose a serious threat to the Persian Gulf oil lifeline. In a general war one would of course assume that oil tankers would be targeted by any Soviet combatants remaining in the area, but such activity would pale in significance compared to hostilities elsewhere. In the peacetime context Soviet interdiction of oil tankers might constitute an improbable *casus belli*. (Surely, there are better ways to start a general war.) Not even those in the business of insuring oil tankers, such as Lloyd's of London, think that the Soviets would act so recklessly. They recently raised rates on tankers transiting the Strait of Hormuz not because of the Soviet naval presence, but on account of an increased possibility of terrorist attacks.

An alternative explanation for the Soviet naval presence in the Indian Ocean is the strategic threat that would be posed to Soviet territory if US SSBN's were deployed.[6] Hypothetically, stationing submarines of the pre-TRIDENT generation in the Arabian Sea offers certain advantages: military objectives ranging from deep inside the Soviet European heartland to Western China could be

127

targeted from one location; and if only on account of its physical characteristics, the Indian Ocean affords submarines better protection against Soviet ASW than, for example, the Eastern Mediterranean. But these are offset by very long transit times between the nearest submarine base, in Guam, and the Arabian Sea.[7] The consequent reduction in total on-station time of US strategic submarine forces would have seriously weakened our overall defense capability. It is not surprising, therefore, that US SSBN's have not patrolled these waters, nor were they ever likely to. To be sure, the Soviets have often expressed fears about a possible US strategic threat from the Indian Ocean. But they have not seen fit to upgrade significantly the very limited ASW capabilities of the forces they maintain in the area,[8] nor have any large-scale Soviet ASW exercises been reported to have taken place there. The Soviets thus appear to have acted as though a US strategic submarine threat from the Indian Ocean did not exist. This, however, does not rule out an interest on their part in receiving formal guarantees regarding the deployment of US strategic forces there. And, as we shall discuss below, this became a real possibility precisely during the period under review.

Rather than a specific wartime mission, such as sea interdiction or strategic defense, it is its peacetime role that best explains the Soviet naval presence in the Indian Ocean. This is a region in which the Soviets have acquired important state interests. The shortest sea route open year-round between the USSR's European and Pacific ports runs through these waters. A continuous Soviet naval presence at one of the two points of entry into the Indian Ocean signals their interest in keeping these sea lanes open. Indeed, their sensitivity on this point was transparent in their sharp negative reaction toward the so-called "Arab Lake" Red Sea security plan that surfaced in early 1977—a matter to which we shall later return.

The Soviet Union also has greatly expanded its ties with the states of this region of enormous human and critically important material resources. During the past decade, Soviet naval forces have been employed in numerous ways to strengthen those ties. Examples of Soviet naval diplomacy in the Indian Ocean include official port calls (for example, a prolonged diplomatic visit to Mogadiscio in April 1970, apparently to support the Somali regime against an alleged coup attempt); mine and harbor-clearing operations in the Gulf of Suez and Bangladesh, respectively; crisis deployments to

128

counter Western naval forces during the 1971 Indo-Pakistani War and in the aftermath of the October 1973 Middle East War,[9] and, most recently, in support of Ethiopia at the height of the Ogaden War.[10] The Soviet naval presence in the Indian Ocean has thus been a valuable instrument of their foreign policy in the region. But the needs of the Soviet Indian Ocean squadron for shore-based support also have been an important object of Soviet foreign policy.

In assessing the Indian Ocean squadron's needs for shore-based support, it should be kept in mind that its operating area is a very long way from Vladivostok, the port from which most units deploy. It takes approximately 3 weeks with normal transit speeds of 10 to 12 knots to sail to the Gulf of Aden (a distance of 6,700 nm).[11] Prior to obtaining in 1972 extensive access to the Somali port of Berbera, the mean length of Soviet combatant deployments in the Indian Ocean was roughly 5 months. Their warships thus wasted a high proportion of their total deployment time in transit. By lengthening those deployments, the Soviets could reduce the pool of ships needed to keep the same number of units continuously on-station.[12]

But the longer ships are deployed, the greater are their needs for logistic support and maintenance. And with the great distances involved in the Indian Ocean, it is important to have access to local ports, where supplies can be obtained and repairs made that cannot be done satisfactorily at sea. One indication of the value that the Soviets place on access to local ports is the degree to which they make use of them. Whereas, prior to 1972, Soviet warships had made occasional business calls to Indian Ocean ports, in that year they gained unrestricted access to Berbera; and after the arrival in the fall of that year of a barracks and repair ship, which significantly improved the Indian Ocean squadron's ability to supply and repair its units and rest their crews on-station, the frequency of Soviet operational visits increased sharply (see Table 1)—a trend that coincided with the lengthening of deployments.

But the value of local shore-based support is not limited to port access. In 1972 Somalia became the second Third World country, after Egypt, to grant the USSR access to extensive facilities ashore. Soviet access privileges included the exclusive use of a long-range communications station and the rights to stage periodic maritime reconnaissance flights from Somali airfields. Although the Soviets also built (for their own though not necessarily exclusive use) a missile-handling and storage facility and an airfield at Berbera,

129

TABLE 1

Soviet Naval Operational Ship Visits
in the Indian Ocean, 1967-76[a]

Country	1967	1968	1969	1970	1971	1972	1973	1974	1975	1976	1967-1976
Somalia	–	–	2	7	22	20	42	61	54	75	283
S. Yemen	–	–	4	5	15	7	14	37	34	18	134
Iraq	–	–	4	1	2	8	15	17	8	12	67
Sri Lanka	–	1	2	1	–	6	2	5	6	6	29
Mauritius	–	–	1	7	1	9	1	2	2	1	24
India	–	–	1	6	2	–	3	2	4	2	20
Kenya	–	–	1	4	–	–	2	4	1	–	12
N. Yemen	–	–	1	2	–	–	–	1	2	3	9
Pakistan	–	–	5	2	–	–	–	–	1	–	8
Maldives	–	–	–	–	3	–	–	–	1	1	5
Iran	–	–	2	–	–	–	–	–	–	1	3
Tanzania	–	–	–	2	–	–	–	–	–	–	2
Ethiopia	–	–	1	–	–	–	–	–	–	–	1
Kuwait	–	–	1	–	–	–	–	–	–	–	1
Madagascar	–	–	1	–	–	–	–	–	–	–	1
Seychelles[b]	1	–	–	–	–	–	–	–	–	–	1
Sudan	–	–	–	1	–	–	–	–	–	–	1
TOTALS	1	1	26	38	45	50	79	129	113	119	601

[a]Excluding visits by oceanographic research ships and space support ships.

[b]U.K. colony until June 1976.

Source: Adapted from Dismukes and McConnell, eds., Soviet Naval Diplomacy,
         Table 2.7.

they apparently did not actually use them. What access privileges they did enjoy were nevertheless quite important. The periodic staging from Somali airfields of Il-38 May ASW and (on one occasion) Tu-95 Bear D maritime reconnaissance aircraft gave the Soviets ASW coverage and greatly expanded and improved their aerial reconnaissance of the Indian Ocean.

It should be emphasized that the acquisition of extensive facilities ashore is no easy matter. Access privileges tend to compromise the sovereignty of the host nation and subject it to negative publicity over Soviet "bases." As an illustrative example, we may note that Somalia's sovereign control over these facilities was called into question when the team of experts led by Senator Dewey F. Bartlett was barred from entering the Berbera communications station in July 1975. Even though a high-ranking Somali officer (Colonel Suleiman, the head of the Somali secret police and President Siad Barre's son-in-law) had requested the Somali guards to allow the Bartlett delegation to enter the installation, the request was evidently overruled by a Soviet officer inside the facility.[13]

It is understandable then why even those countries inclined to support the Soviet Navy have limited their support to the water's edge. And had it not been for Somalia's strong desire for arms, which only the Soviets saw fit to satisfy, it is highly unlikely that the Soviets would have obtained shore-based facilities even there.[14]

In the period under consideration, moreover, access to the Somali facilities had become more important with the initiation of the Indian Ocean naval arms limitations talks (NALT) in the spring of 1977, some 6 years after a proposal to curb naval activity of nonlittoral states in the Indian Ocean had been raised in a speech by Brezhnev.[15] The dismantling of what the Soviets called the US "base" on Diego Garcia had long been a major Soviet objective in the Indian Ocean. Although the Soviets have never in form or in substance equated their facilities in Berbera with the US "base" at Diego Garcia, they nevertheless could easily have realized that they would have little left with which to bargain should they lose access to Berbera.

In fact, the prospect that the Somali facilities could be replaced readily must have appeared rather dim to the Soviets on the eve of the NALT discussions. In return for their support, the Soviets could have counted on eventual access to Ethiopian ports of Assab and Massawa, but even in normal times these Red Sea ports are congested in comparison to Berbera.[16] And by the spring of 1977, if not earlier, it was clear that these ports might soon be put under siege by Eritrean guerrillas.[17] Nor did the prospects appear much better for Soviet naval access to Aden, which with its large bunkering facilities, repair yards, and cooler temperatures, is a far better harbor than Berbera. Soviet warships had never enjoyed the same degree of access to Aden as to Berbera. And with the improvement in 1976 of South Yemen's relations with Saudi Arabia, which has persistently sought to reduce the Soviet presence in the area, the prospects for access may have seemed even worse.[18]

Thus if only to preserve their bargaining power during the NALT negotiations, from which they had much to gain, the Soviets had a major stake in maintaining access to the Somali facilities. But why

131

then did they jeopardize their access by supporting Ethiopia? Obviously, access to naval support facilities was not the only factor driving Soviet policy on the Horn at the time. And it is to the consideration of the reasons for Soviet support for Ethiopia that we should now turn.

Two years after the overthrow of Haile Selassie, the Ethiopian revolution was entering a critical stage of instability. Nationalization, land reforms and other measures ostensibly designed to uproot the old imperial order had produced a backlash of resistance and unrest in the cities and countryside alike. Despite its nine-point plan for autonomy in Eritrea, the Dergue appeared still to be pursuing a military solution to the problem but with disastrous results. A 40,000-man peasant "militia" was easily routed by Eritrean guerrillas in the summer of 1976. Further, the victories of the Eritrean insurgents—by the spring of the following year, they controlled virtually all of Eritrea except the major towns—were severely sapping the morale of the Ethiopian Army, the mainstay of the regime. By late 1976, the Ethiopian state was drifting toward disintegration and anarchy.

External forces were also speeding this process along. The Sudanese Government, whose rapidly worsening relations with Moscow culminated in its expulsion of the Soviet military mission in May 1977, was actively supporting the Eritrean guerrillas as well as other Ethiopian opposition groups, such as the liberal Ethiopian Democratic Union. Not surprisingly, tensions mounted along the Sudanese-Ethiopia border in the spring.[19]

During the previous year, border tensions also had arisen on the Ethiopian-Somali border, but in connection with Somalia's political maneuvering over Djibouti.[20] By this time as well, the recruitment and training of Ogaden guerrillas were already well advanced, but insurgency in the Ogaden was not activated until early 1977. Thus during the last part of 1976 and the first few months of 1977 when the important initial Soviet security commitments to Ethiopia were made, the immediate danger to the military regime in Addis Ababa lay not in the Ogaden—a point to which we shall later return.

Not only, from the Soviet perspective, was a classic "confrontation between the forces of progress and reaction" emerging on the Horn, but Soviet state interests were also being challenged on another issue, the plan to turn the Red Sea into an "Arab Lake." Though very little, if anything, concrete regarding

132

Red Sea security emerged from meetings of Arab states in early 1977 (Sudan, Egypt, and Syria at Khartoum in February; Sudan, YAR, PDRY, and Somalia at Ta'izz, YAR in March), the Soviets saw these talks as a Saudi-inspired effort to forge a pro-imperialist military bloc in the area, with the aims of obstructing both Israeli and Soviet shipping through the Red Sea, and of eventually eliminating Soviet influence in the area as well. Increased Arab support for the Eritreans and other opposition forces was thus seen as part of this broader plan to establish an unbroken chain of Arab states on the Red Sea. While Soviet influence in Somalia and to a lesser extent in South Yemen was still strong, Moscow may well have feared that its position would quickly erode with the breakup of the Ethiopian state.

Besides these perceptible negative consequences of Soviet inaction, there were positive inducements for the Soviets to act in support of Ethiopia. To the "world socialist community," Soviet support would provide confirmation that the USSR was not only willing but increasingly able to perform its "proletarian internationalist duty" to the world revolutionary movement. To the Third World and to Africa in particular, such support would demonstrate Soviet ability to stabilize regimes and in the process to defend their territorial integrity. And with the US military role in the Third World receding, unstable regimes there might look increasingly to the USSR as a "visiting fireman."

It has also been widely noted that Ethiopia offers certain intrinsic benefits to the USSR as a "client state." With the second largest population in Black Africa (ten times larger than that of Somalia), with resources sufficient to justify good prospects for long-run economic development, and with its capital the headquarters of the OAU (thanks largely to its independent historical tradition), Ethiopia is both an important African country and the key state in the African Horn. Clearly, involvement in Ethiopia offered the Soviets an opportunity to expand their influence in Africa.

But Moscow's realization of this opportunity remains problematic. An unstable Ethiopia, one highly dependent upon Soviet support, was likely to be far less influential in African affairs than a stable Ethiopia. But with increasing security and stability, Ethiopia was likely to be more independent of the USSR. If there is one thing that Moscow should have learned by this point from its involvement in the Third World, it is not to expect gratitude for past favors. All of this of course is not to deny the likelihood that a leftist, stable and independent Ethiopian government would share Moscow's views on matters of international importance. An independent Ethiopia after all need not automatically be anti-Soviet.

While there were ample positive and negative reasons for the Soviets to support Ethiopia, such support also entailed risks. Indeed, at the outset of their involvement it was not clear that the Soviets would be able to reverse the process of anarchy and disintegration in Ethiopia.

Nevertheless, they may have had reason to believe that Ethiopia would not become another quagmire like Vietnam. In the first place, they may well have been confident that they could tip the military balance in the Horn in Ethiopia's favor. Unlike Vietnam, the amount of arms available to the insurgents was likely to be limited. Though Arab petrodollars could buy light arms on the open market, they could not buy major weapons that would greatly improve the insurgents' chances of holding key cities in the periphery—a prerequisite for international recognition.

As matters turned out, Somalia did, of course, support the insurgents in the Ogaden, as well as in other regions of Ethiopia, with most of the resources available to its large, modern, Soviet-equipped army[21]—an action that probably caught the Soviets by surprise. But even the Somali "exception" tends to prove the point. No Western government would allow even third parties to transfer weapons to a state engaged in blatant aggression in contravention of the OAU's principle of the inviolability of African borders. Though Somalia was able to find alternative sources of POL, military technicians, light arms, and even spare parts for major weapons, it could not make up its losses of major weapons.[22] Thus, the Somali offensive seemed doomed from the start.

A second factor was the morale of the Ethiopian Army. By early 1977, there were reports of large-scale troop defections and rumors of mutiny in the Second Division based in Asmara.[23] In fact, some of the defeats that the Ethiopians suffered in the summer of 1977 seem largely related to disaffection among the troops. In July the fortified city of Keren, which took the British 3 months to wrest from the Italians in 1941, fell to the Eritreans after a 3-day battle.[24] In September, the Somalis captured the important tank base of Jigjiga after Ethiopian units had mutinied.[25]

Whatever concern the Soviets may have had for the morale problem in the Ethiopian Army, it does not seem to have affected

134

their behavior. Well before the 25-year-old US-Ethiopian military relationship was terminated in April 1977, the Soviets had reportedly willfully sought to replace the United States as Ethiopia's principal armorer.[26] But this honor also entailed a responsibility for the defense of Ethiopia's borders that went well beyond verbal support.[27] And in July 1977, when Somalia employed *Soviet*-made weapons to invade the Ogaden, the Soviet duty to respond was even greater. It seems reasonable to assume therefore that the Soviets would have done something more than simply stage an evacuation of foreign advisers had the Ethiopian Army wholly collapsed under the pressure of the Somali and Eritrean offensives in the summer of 1977. In point of fact, the one action that made the issue of Ethiopian morale largely irrelevant, i.e., the commitment of large numbers of Cuban troops in direct combat, was not taken until December 1977—well after the battle lines had stabilized and the morale of Ethiopia's armed forces had improved, thanks largely to the large-scale influx of Soviet weapons and to the patriotic response to the Somali invasion. The introduction of Cuban troops was thus not a matter of necessity.

The one major danger that the Soviets appear to have underestimated was Somalia's sharp nationalistic response to their support for Ethiopia. They knew of course that this decision would not be welcome in Mogadiscio. They may also have anticipated increased Somali support for guerrillas inside the Ogaden and other parts of Ethiopia. But they apparently did not think that Somalia would take advantage of Ethiopia's disintegration and of the Dergue's military vulnerability (to which the conversion from US to Soviet arms contributed) by mounting a large-scale invasion. In the spring, the main threats to Ethiopia's security were in Eritrea and along the Sudanese border, not in the Ogaden. In April, Moscow apparently gave Addis Ababa assurances that Mogadiscio would not attack the Ogaden.[28] Although this information was disclosed by Ethiopian government sources after the Somali attack, it nevertheless seems to reflect fairly accurately Soviet thinking at a time when they were promoting a *pax Sovietica* in the region. If the Soviets did misjudge Somali intentions, then what prompted this miscalculation?

It is possible that, having regarded Somalia's leaders as "revolutionary democrats" in good standing, the Soviets underestimated the force of Somali nationalism, as both Ethiopian

135

and Somali sources allege.[29] But it is perhaps more likely that the Soviets overestimated their own leverage over the Somalis. Soviet confidence derived not simply from Somali reliance upon Soviet arms, oil, technicians, and aid.[30] Rather, Moscow may have felt that Mogadiscio had little choice but to acquiesce to the Soviet decision to support Ethiopia. The Soviets, as we have already noted, probably reasoned correctly that no Western state would underwrite militarily a Somali gamble to achieve by force of arms their ambitions for a "greater Somalia." Moreover, to avert a major Somali invasion with the weapons on hand, the Soviets might even have intimated to Mogadiscio that they would do what was necessary to help Ethiopia repel such an attack.[31]

While we do not know that the Soviets threatened to apply the stick to Somalia to avoid a war, we do know that they were offering a carrot to promote what would have become a *pax Sovietica* on the Horn. In what appears to have been a counter initiative to Saudi/Sudanese efforts to forge an Arab bloc of Red Sea states, the Soviets, following close on the heels of the Cubans, proposed in April that Ethiopia and Somalia join South Yemen and independent Djibouti in a federation of Marxist states, in which Eritrea and the Ogaden would receive substantial autonomy. Regardless of whether the Soviets thought that the Somalis would readily accept the plan, they seem nevertheless to have hoped that Mogadiscio would realize that its ambitions could be accommodated best through Moscow's mediation.[32] The Soviets might have been prepared to offer Somalia anything short of hoisting a Somali flag over the Ogaden (e.g., unhindered rights of passage for Somali herdsmen, and restrictions upon the Ethiopian military presence in the region). However, the Soviets appear to have consistently abided by the principle of the inviolability of sovereign borders, even during the critical period after the Somali assault when the battlefield situation was in doubt.

As matters turned out, of course, the Somalis rejected the Soviet/Cuban federation scheme and opted for a military solution to Somalia's "national problem." This gamble probably was based upon the beliefs that there would be no better time than the present to employ force (certainly not after Ethiopia's transition to Soviet weapons systems was completed) and that Ethiopia was "too far gone" for the Soviets to save anyway.[33]

The available evidence then suggests that the Soviets

136

miscalculated in expecting the Somalis to exercise greater prudence. As a Soviet commentary explains:

> The Soviet Union, for its part, did everything possible to avert an armed conflict between Ethiopia and Somalia. However, when the leaders of the latter country despite common sense and the efforts of the true friends of the Somali people began in the summer of 1977 military operations against Ethiopia and Somali troops invaded its territory, the Soviet Union, as always in such situations, came out on the side of the victim of aggression: at the request of the Ethiopian government the Soviet Union rendered Ethiopia material aid to repulse the attack. Our country did so proceeding from the principled purposes of its foreign policy, despite the fact that because of this there could have (and did in fact) ensue unfriendly acts by the Somali leadership against the Soviet Union.[34]

The "basic principles" of Soviet foreign policy aside, after July 1977 their options were constrained. They had little choice but to support Ethiopia, particularly against an act of aggression committed with Soviet-made weapons. The Somali attack also represented an open challenge to Soviet policy on the Horn, which, if unanswered, would tarnish the USSR's image as a *bona fide* superpower.

However, the Soviets came to Ethiopia's aid slowly, in a manner indicative of their increasing difficulty in straddling both camels on the Horn. For several weeks following the Somali assault, Soviet weapons deliveries to Ethiopia were reportedly slow and limited.[35] At the same time, though Soviet deliveries of major weapons systems to Somalia had ceased, shipments of light arms and spare parts reportedly continued, though on a reduced scale and with delays.[36] There were other indications of Soviet interest in preserving the Somali connection, the most important aspect of which—after the Somali regime had lost much of its "revolutionary democratic" allure,[37]—had become the naval access privileges. Even after Soviet weapons deliveries to Somalia had finally stopped, probably by mid-October at the latest, Moscow evidently sought to preserve some semblance of its military assistance program in Mogadiscio. Though Soviet military advisers who finished their tours of duty were not replaced and those who remained were in effect quarantined in compounds for security reasons by the Somali authorities, there were still surprisingly large numbers left when they were ordered to leave in November. (According to official Somali sources, 1,678 military advisers and their families were evacuated at that time.)[38] In addition, Moscow signed two economic aid protocols with Mogadiscio after the Somali attack,[39] undoubtedly to remind Somalia not only of its pressing needs for economic development, but also of the enduring value of Soviet assistance for this purpose. Further, though the Soviets made known their sympathies for Ethiopia by emphasizing respect for the principle of territorial integrity as the basis for a negotiated settlement of the conflict,[40] they avoided antagonizing Somalia unnecessarily by not directly accusing it of aggression against Ethiopia until after Mogadiscio's unilateral abrogation of the friendship treaty and termination of Soviet naval facilities in November. (In the interim, "reactionary" Arab and "imperialist" states were accused of setting Somalia against Ethiopia and of seeking to undermine both the revolutionary gains of the Somali regime and Soviet-Somali relations.)[41]

But while the Soviets clearly sought to preserve their ties to Somalia, pressures mounted for them to step up their support for Ethiopia. After weeks of intensive diplomatic efforts, a negotiated, peaceful resolution of the conflict was nowhere in sight. The Soviets and Somalis remained so far apart that when Siad Barre finally made his long-delayed visit to Moscow in late August, Brezhnev did not even grant him an audience.[42] Perhaps in recognition of the bleak peace prospects in the near term, Moscow reportedly agreed to commit an additional $385 million of modern weapons to Ethiopia at this time.[43] The level of Soviet weapons deliveries to Ethiopia increased soon thereafter.[44] Coming at a time when Ethiopia was rather desperately seeking to renew its military ties to the United States,[45] this increased Soviet commitment may have removed some Ethiopian anxieties regarding Moscow's fence-sitting. But Addis Ababa was still upset with the continuation of Soviet arms deliveries to Somalia. In fact, Mengistu angrily remarked during a September 18th press conference: "If socialist countries are still supplying arms to Somalia, then this is not only violating one's principles, but also tantamount to complicity with the reactionary Mogadiscio regime."[46] This embarrassing public rebuke may have contributed to the Soviet decision, evidently taken soon thereafter, to terminate all arms deliveries to Somalia. By mid-October, the Soviet Ambassador to Ethiopia announced publicly that Soviet weapons deliveries to Somalia had stopped.[47] Ethiopia's socialist benefactors also seemed responsive to Mengistu's requests for additional support during the latter's secret visit to Havana and Moscow at the end of October,[48] for the number of Cuban military advisers in Ethiopia sharply increased during the next two weeks from 150 to 400.[49]

Though the Soviets were clearly "tilting" increasingly toward Ethiopia, on the eve of the Somali decision to expel them Moscow's support for Ethiopia was still not open-ended. Somali allegations to the contrary,[50] the evidence available does not indicate that Cuban combat units were directly involved in the fighting as yet. Neither the massive air and sealifts of Soviet material nor the influx of Cuban soldiers began until *after* the Somali expulsion.

By holding in reserve considerable power to punish Somalia and by preserving, more in form than in substance, its remaining ties to Somalia, the Soviet Union may have hoped that this final step would not be taken. Indeed, the first official Soviet response to the Somali decision adjudged that "chauvinist moods had prevailed over common sense in the Somali government."[51]

There are grounds to share this Soviet view that the Somali decision, taken after a marathon 10-hour session of the Central Committee of Somalia's ruling Revolutionary Socialist Party,[52] was ill-conceived. At best, it represented something of a desperate gamble that Western aid would be forthcoming in return for the eviction of the Soviets. The Somalis certainly seemed to be building a "case" for such support by alleging that a Soviet-Cuban-Ethiopian invasion of Somalia was imminent.[53] But other than the possible release of some reported $300 million that Saudi Arabia had put up as a bounty for the eviction of the Soviets,[54] the Somalis received little tangible reward for their deed.

Having undoubtedly forewarned Mogadiscio about the possible consequences of such anti-Soviet actions, Moscow was virtually obliged to respond in kind to Somalia's *lese majeste.* Hence, Moscow and Havana decided to upgrade dramatically the level of their support for Addis Ababa. The first sign of this shift was the arrival, a few days after the Somali eviction notice, of General V.I. Petrov, Deputy Commander-in-Chief of Soviet Ground Forces, to direct the war against the Somalis.[55] A far more obvious signal came toward the end of the month when the major Soviet airlifts commenced. And by the following month, Cuban troop units began arriving in Ethiopia to assume a direct role in the fighting.

Other factors in addition to Somalia's open challenge contributed to this Soviet-Cuban decision to intervene directly and massively in the Ogaden war. With Mogadiscio having played its "last ace," there was now nothing to prevent the Soviets from speeding up the timetable for the prosecution of the war. With the United States and other Western powers firmly opposed to the transmission of weapons to the Somalis from even third parties as long as Somali armed forces remained in the Ogaden, the Soviets could well have predicted that a military confrontation with the West was highly unlikely as long as no Soviet combat forces participated in the fighting and Soviet objectives remained limited to the expulsion of Somali forces from the Ogaden. In fact, direct involvement gave the Soviets and Cubans greater control over the outcome of the war and made it easier for them to restrain the Ethiopians from invading Somalia.[56] Moreover, the Soviets may have felt that a large-scale Cuban military presence remaining in the Ogaden after the inevitable defeat of Somali armed forces would not only discourage another Somali attack, but also inhibit Ethiopian reprisals against Ogadeni tribesmen. Indeed, the 15,000 Cuban troops manning garrisons in the Ogaden afford Moscow and Havana significant potential leverage in future dealings with Mogadiscio.

Broader political considerations also may have affected Moscow's decision to intervene in the Ogaden. Just a few days prior to Mogadiscio's abrogation of the Friendship Treaty, Egyptian President Sadat made his dramatic announcement that he would visit Jerusalem—a move that unhinged plans for reconvening multilateral talks at Geneva and suddenly removed the Soviets from playing a direct role in the Arab-Israeli peace negotiations. Moscow may have hoped that a graphic demonstration of Soviet intervention capabilities would convey the message that the USSR could still play a major role in obstructing, if not in promoting, peace in the Middle East and would be neither ignored nor slighted.

It should also be added that Moscow's reasons for intervening on a large scale in the Ogaden war seem largely independent of conditions on the battlefield. It is true that Mogadiscio's abrogation of the Soviet Friendship Treaty coincided with the last major Somali offensive of the war. But the drive against the Ethiopian positions in the Ogaden had just about peaked by the time that the first Soviet airlifts began.[57] While the situation on the battlefield remained serious, it is doubtful that the Ethiopians needed much more than an incremental increase in Soviet/Cuban support to blunt the Somali offensive. Of course, they received

140

much more than this. By contrast, it is worth recalling that during the period in which the Ethiopian forces may have needed Soviet assistance the most, that is, in the weeks immediately following the Somali attack, very little of it was to be had. It was only *after* Ethiopian defense lines had stabilized outside of Harar in late September that Soviet arms began to pour into Ethiopia.

The joint Soviet-Cuban decision to intervene in the Ogaden War also entailed problems and costs in its implementation. Staging a large-scale air and sealift was quite demanding, probably more for political than for technical reasons. Most of the states that Soviet transport planes overflew either directly supported (with supplies and advisers) or were sympathetic to the Somalis during the conflict. In order to airlift materiel to Ethiopia, the Soviets found it necessary to employ a wide variety of flight routes, to abuse the Montreux Convention's provisions for overflights through Turkish air corridors,[58] to engage widely in such subterfuges as listing false final destinations (usually Aden, which served as a major transshipment point for materiel to Ethiopia)[59] and, on one occasion, to substitute military transports for the civilian aircraft for which overflight permission had been granted.[60]

The Soviets also had to surmount certain technical problems connected with the sealift. With the railroad connection to Djibouti cut, Addis Ababa had to rely on the road to Assab, which ran through Afar and Eritrean territory subject to guerrilla attack. Because of both congestion at the port of Assab and the adaptability of Aden's Khormaksar airport to amphibious transport operations, the Soviets made extensive use of tank landing ships in the sealift.[61] In large part to protect this sealift, the Soviets also increased the number of their naval units to the highest level ever maintained in the Indian Ocean.[62] Moreover, they did so *after* they had lost their access to Berbera—a feat that suggests that the Soviet Navy has not found extensive access to shore-based facilities necessary in the performance of even some of its more demanding peacetime missions.

Even before the first Soviet airlifts, Moscow had already committed nearly $1 billion in military aid to Ethiopia, but at least some of this cost will eventually be repaid. However, the intervention itself entailed substantial additional costs, including those directly connected with staging the air and sealift, as well as those related to the replacement by Soviet air defense pilots of Cuban pilots on assignment in Ethiopia.[63]

141

In comparison to the intervention's economic costs, its political costs have appeared to be inconsequential. The US Government, claiming that the Soviet naval buildup at the height of the war cast doubt upon their sincerity and interest in Indian Ocean naval limitations, suspended the talks after the fourth round in February 1978.[64] But the Soviets probably saw this simply as a convenient pretext. The negotiations had been effectively derailed anyway by their loss of Berbera.

Further, the Soviets might have anticipated that ill feelings among Arab supporters of Somalia aroused by their intervention were likely to be transient at best. In view of the fact that effective measures were not taken to obstruct the Soviet air and sealift, the Arab reaction does not appear to have been very severe. Their support for Somalia was undoubtedly tempered by the knowledge that Mogadiscio was engaged in thinly-disguised aggression against a sovereign state.[65]

PART II

If the ultimate objective of Soviet policy in the Horn was to establish a *pax Sovietica,* in which all states in the region would be linked in a federation that would resolve age-old hostilities, and with each country making sure progress under Soviet tutelage towards socialism, then obviously Moscow has not succeeded. What the Soviets have clearly accomplished has been to bring an appreciable degree of stability to Ethiopia and in so doing they may have cut short any remote plans to establish a conservative military bloc of Arab states in the region. With Somali armed forces (but not guerrillas) expelled from the Ogaden and insurgency in Eritrea and in other regions in a state of remission, the radical leftist military leaders of Ethiopia are far more secure today than even before. But the Dergue's dependence upon Soviet support does not appear to have given Moscow great influence in shaping the subsequent course of the Ethiopian revolution. In fact, the availability of Soviet weapons may have emboldened Mengistu to seek military solutions to Ethiopia's political problems. With Ethiopian forces on the offensive in Eritrea, the Dergue's earlier proposals for regional autonomy there appear to be something of a dead letter for the time being. Whether the Dergue will be any more successful than its predecessor in imposing its authority in Eritrea by sheer force of arms remains to be seen. At the present time, it appears that the Dergue's policies are sowing the seeds of future instability.

Where Soviet efforts do seem to have met with some belated success is in the organization of a ruling political party, the Ethiopian Workers' Party.[66] But whether this "vanguard" party will institutionalize the Ethiopian revolution, as Moscow would like or will merely strengthen Mengistu's power still further, is uncertain. It is instructive to note that the Somali military regime also formed in 1976 what the Soviets termed at the time a vanguard party—only to join the "forces of reaction" during the following year. It is quite possible that despite their best efforts, the Soviets may have accomplished little more to engineer revolutionary change in Ethiopia than to strengthen Mengistu's power base.

Whereas Soviet gains in Ethiopia may turn out to be less impressive than at first glance, their losses in Somalia may also not be as irretrievable as they initially seemed. In the first place, the Soviets now appear to have more or less made up for what they lost in Somalia with combined access to support facilities in Ethiopia and South Yemen. (Though, as has been noted above, the Soviets had little reason to expect such a fortuitous outcome.)

Secondly, despite the termination of the Soviet presence in Somalia, they had not lost all their influence in that country. While the former basis of their relationship (i.e., "arms for access") no longer can be reconstructed, some limited rapprochement cannot be ruled out in the future.[67] In fact, should the Somalis ever seek a negotiated settlement on the Ogaden, the Soviets and Cubans would be the logical mediators. Thus, however remote prospects for a *pax Sovietica* on the Horn may presently appear, they exist nonetheless.

The one major loss the Soviets suffered that may well be irretrievable is an Indian Ocean treaty. Although the Soviet Union seems now to have regained its "bargaining chips" after the loss of Berbera, the United States may have, for various reasons (including the events in Iran), lost interest in the talks in the interim. If talks are not resumed, then Moscow will have lost an excellent opportunity to obtain some important legal guarantees satisfying a major Soviet security concern.

Soviet losses in Somalia and more significantly in the suspension of the Indian Ocean talks should be weighed against their gains in Ethiopia. The possibility cannot be ruled out that the Soviets would have acted differently had they foreseen the outcomes of their support for Ethiopia. At the outset of their involvement, the Soviets apparently thought they could have their cake and eat it too. The reasons for the Soviets to come to Ethiopia's assistance were evidently sufficiently strong for them to take a calculated risk that they would not alienate Somalia to the point of eventually forfeiting their access to naval support facilities there. To be sure this risk, which was based upon the assumption that Somalia would pursue its rational self-interests, may have appeared quite small at the time. But the point is that they took it nonetheless. Had they not wanted to take any chances of jeopardizing their access, they would never have supported Ethiopia in the first place. Thus, although the Soviets did not get what they had hoped for on the Horn, the results of their actions, on balance, bear an imprint of the choices they made.

Furthermore, there is reason to believe that the Soviets would have acted much the same even had they predicted Somalia's response. It is worth noting that in the case of Egypt, whose naval support facilities were more important operationally, but not politically (NALT), than those of Somalia, concern for the loss of naval access did not alter the fundamental thrust of Soviet foreign policy, which was inimical to Egypt's interests. In the Horn the Soviets tried to accommodate Somali sensitivities, but they never gave in to Mogadiscio's demand that they not support Ethiopia. They may have recognized that submitting to Somali blackmail over access would establish an extremely dangerous precedent entailing greater long-term dilemmas than losing access and thereby jeopardizing the strong prospects for an Indian Ocean treaty.

From the Soviet perspective, therefore, it seems that Moscow gained more than it lost on the Horn. The Soviets also can claim that in supporting Ethiopia, they were doing the right thing. Through the course of their involvement, they did indeed pursue (more than less) a "principled policy." By performing their "proletarian internationalist" duty toward a revolutionary regime in extremis, by defending the inviolability of sovereign borders, by assuming responsibility for past decisions (e.g., to arm first Somalia and later Ethiopia), and finally, by acting boldly but not rashly when openly challenged, the Soviets "walked on the side of the angels" in the Horn.

144

ENDNOTES

1. I would like to acknowledge the valuable assistance in the preparation of this paper of my colleague, Kenneth G. Weiss.

2. *The Washington Post,* May 7, 1977, p. A1 and March 5, 1978, p. A1.

3. *The Washington Post,* March 5, 1978, p. A10. It is worth adding that during the previous two years, the Ford Administration had increased significantly the level of US weapons deliveries to Ethiopia. Consult US Arms Control and Disarmament Agency. *World Military Expenditures and Arms Transfers, 1967-76,* Washington, DC: US Government Printing Office, 1978, p. 129.

4. *The Washington Post,* March 5, 1978, p. A10.

5. The Soviet Indian Ocean squadron, in fact, has historically spent most of its time in the Gulf of Aden.

6. This argument was first presented in Geoffrey Jukes, *The Indian Ocean in Soviet Naval Policy,* Adelphi Papers, No. 87, May 1972.

7. This point was made in James M. McConnell "The Soviet Navy in the Indian Ocean" in *Soviet Naval Developments,* ed. by Michael MccGwire, New York: Praeger Publishers, 1973, pp. 389-406.

8. Lt. Cmdr. William F. Hickman, "Soviet Naval Policy in the Indian Ocean," *US Naval Institute Proceedings,* August 1979, p. 44.

9. Soviet naval diplomacy in the Indian Ocean has been comprehensively discussed in *Soviet Naval Diplomacy,* ed. by Bradford Dismukes and James M. McConnell, New York: Pergamon Press, 1979.

10. Soviet naval units directly participated in the sealift of materiel via Aden to Ethiopia and provided protection for that sealift. See *The Times* (London), February 12, 1978, p. 9.

11. The Gulf of Aden not only is where most of "the action is" in the Indian Ocean (or close to it), but also contains sheltered waters offering protection from swells during the monsoon seasons. Information on Soviet naval operations in the Indian Ocean may be found in Charles C. Petersen, "Trends in Soviet Naval Operations," in *Soviet Naval Diplomacy*, Chapter 2.

12. In fact, after the Soviets gained unrestricted access to Berbera, they increased the number of units in the squadron as well as lengthening their deployment times significantly.

13. US Congress. *Soviet Military Capability in Berbera, Somalia.* Report of Senator Bartlett to the Committee on Armed Services, Washington, DC: US Government Printing Office, 1975.

14. The Soviets have been Somalia's main source of weapons since the early 1960's. But, as a *quid pro quo* for naval access, they began to modernize Somalia's armed forces in 1972. The nature of the bargaining over Soviet access to Somali facilities is discussed in the author's "The Soviet-Somali Influence Relationship," a paper delivered at the Second World Congress of Soviet and East European Studies, Garmisch-Partenkirchen, West Germany, September 1979.

15. *Pravda*, June 12, 1971, p. 2.

16. After June 1977, when insurgents cut the railroad line between Addis Ababa and Djibouti, which had handled over 60 percent of Ethiopia's trade overseas, congestion at Assab became much worse.

17. What the Soviet Indian Ocean squadron eventually got to use as its main support base in the Red Sea was an island in the Dahlac Archipelago—a poor substitute indeed for Berbera. See *Detroit News*, July 9, 1978, p. 19.

18. To be sure, the Soviet Union later obtained important access privileges in the PDRY, apparently including staging rights for maritime reconnaissance aircraft. See *San Diego Union,* December 1, 1978, p. 1. But these gains were largely unrelated to events on the Horn. Certainly during the period under review, the Soviets had little reason to be confident that they could replace the Somali facilities so easily. It should be remembered that years after the Soviets lost their airfield privileges in Egypt, they still have not been able to fly maritime reconnaissance flights from local airfields

19. Colin Legum and Bill Lee, *Conflict in the Horn of Africa,* New York and London: Africana Publishing Co., 1977.

20. In December 1975, the French Government announced plans for the independence of the French Territory of the Afars and Issas—a decision that initiated a power struggle over the fate of a territory claimed by Somalia but, due to the railroad connection, was economically important only to Ethiopia. However, as much as Somalia wanted to annex the territory, it had to settle for a Republic of Djibouti, whose independence (in June 1977) was guaranteed by the continuation of a French military presence. Parenthetically, a Soviet article welcoming Djibouti's independence failed to mention the French military connection—an omission that undoubtedly signifies Soviet approval for the French security guarantee. See A. Nikanorov, "In the Land of the Afars and the Issas," *New Times,* No. 26, June 1977, pp. 29-30.

21. Prior to the Somali invasion, the USSR was Somalia's principal armorer and exclusive supplier of POL. Though military supplies, spare parts, and presumably military-related POL were kept in short supply, this obviously did not afford the Soviets sufficient leverage to prevent the Somali attack. Even though the Somali army was large and modern by African standards, it was small enough to make the Soviet "short leash" ineffectual. See Tom J. Farer, *War Clouds on the Horn of Africa,* Second Revised Edition, New York: Carnegie Endowment for International Peace, 1979, p. 116.

22. *Newsweek,* February 20, 1978, p. 40 and *The Economist,* January 7, 1978, p. 50.

23. See Legum and Lee, p. 48.

24. *Le Monde,* November 16, 1977, p. 3.

25. *Le Monde,* November 6-7, 1977, p. 6.

26. Legum and Lee, p. 13.

27. By 1976, the Soviets had come around to endorsing explicitly Ethiopia's sovereignty in Eritrea and had withdrawn their earlier support for Eritrean guerrillas. See in particular Radio Moscow in Amharic to Ethiopia, June 14, 1976; in *Foreign Broadcast Information Service, Daily Report: Soviet Union (hereafter, FBIS: Soviet Union,* June 16, 1976, p. H-15. By subscribing to the 1964 OAU declaration upholding the inviolability of existing African borders, the Soviets had implicitly aligned themselves with Ethiopia on the Ogaden issue. (For a pre-1964 statement sympathetic to Somali irredentism, see the article by V. Kudriavtsev in *Izvestiia,* March 29, 1963.) The closest that the Soviets ever came to encouraging Somali territorial ambitions was in the wording of the 1974 Soviet-Somali Friendship Treaty. Article 7 of the Treaty's Russian text calls upon the signatories to combat "colonialism in all its forms and manifestations." The Somalis translated this phrase as "colonialism whatever its color"—a codeword for Somali irredentism. (The Russian text may be found in *Izvestiia,* October 30, 1974, p.2; the Somali text is summarized in *October Star* (Mogadiscio), October 29, 1975.) It is

worth noting that the Russian phrasing is not typical, for it appeared only once before, in the 1971 treaty with Egypt, and not since. Perhaps, it was partly to avoid any embarrassment resultant from the comparison of the Russian and Somali texts that the publication of the treaty was delayed for several months.

28. *The Washington Post*, September 27, 1977, p. A14.

29. In July, an Ethiopian radio broadcast commented:

> Faced with all this revolutionary activity next door a truly revolutionary Somalia should have been filled with joy and should have joined its class allies in Ethiopia to strike at the enemies of reaction and international imperalism. To those observers who had entertained ideas about the socialist leadership in Somalia, the reaction came as a shock. But for those keen observers who had known the Somali leaders for the ethnocentric, petit bourgeois chauvinists that they are there was no surprise.

(Addis Ababa Voice of Revolutionary Ethiopia in English, July 18, 1977; transcribed in *Foreign Broadcast Information Service, Daily Report: Sub-Saharan Africa (hereafter, FBIS: Sub-Saharan Africa),* July 20, 1977, p. B2. In October, a Somali official noted:

> The Russians knew at the outset that we aspired to reunite the Somali nation...When they helped build up our army, what did they think our intentions were? They knew and approved or at least they used our aspirations and manipulated us...

(Baltimore Sun, October 28, 1977, p. 6).

30. Besides serving as Somalia's principal supplier of arms and POL, the Soviets had by 1976 provided some 2,500 military and civilian technicians, attached to virtually all government ministries, Soviet-aided projects and military units, and had trained most of the Somali military and civilian elite as well. Although the Somalis had received economic aid from other sources, the Soviets had extended large amounts of credit on generous terms for a variety of important projects. It seems interesting to add that by 1976 there were actually more Chinese than Soviet economic technicians in Somalia. See Central Intelligence Agency, *Communist Aid to Less Developed Countries of the Free World,* 1976. However, because virtually all the Chinese technicians were working on one project. the 600-mile road running parallel to the Ethiopian border from Beledwein to Burao, the Chinese presence was far less obtrusive (and odious) than the Soviet one in Somalia.

31. They undoubtedly also told Mogadiscio that the arms they were furnishing Ethiopia posed no threat to Somalia's security.

32. Legum and Lee, p. 13.

33. The Somalis claimed, after the fact, that the US Government had encouraged their offensive. Washington did indeed announce in late July, at the moment that the Somali offensive was underway, that it agreed "in principle" to meet Somalia's "legitimate defense requirements." About a month earlier, Dr. Kevin Cahill, Siad Barre's personal physician and American friend, was reportedly told by a State Department official that the US Government was "not averse to further guerrilla pressure in the Ogaden." But as the US Assistant Secretary for African Affairs, Richard Morse, aptly noted '...our assurances were not of such a nature that a prudent man would have mounted an offensive on the basis of them.' See *Newsweek,* September 26, 1977, pp. 42-43.

34. V. Vorobyov, "Colonialist Policies in Africa," *International Affairs,* No. 9, 1978, p. 42.

35. *The Washington Post*, August 12, 1977, p. 21.

36. *The New York Times,* September 16, 1977, p. A3.

37. By early October, the Soviets were drawing comparisons between the Ethiopian and Somali regimes unfavorable to the latter. See *Moscow Radio* in French to Africa, October 1, 1977; translated in *FBIS: Soviet Union*, October 3, 1977, p. H2.

38. *Newsweek,* February 13, 1978, p. 48.

39. One agreement, which included continuation of work on the Fanole Dam project, was signed in August; and another, for a water exploration project, was signed in October. See *Marches Tropicaux et Mediterraneens,* August 26, 1977, p. 2294; and *Mogadishu Domestic Service* in Somalia, October 5, 1977; translated in *FBIS: Sub-Saharan Africa*, October 6, 1977, p. B3.

40. See, for example, *Moscow TASS* in English, October 11, 1977; transcribed in *FBIS: Soviet Union,* November 15, 1977, p. H1.

41. *Moscow Radio Peace and Progress* in English to Africa, October 28, 1977; transcribed in *FBIS: Soviet Union,* October 31, 1977, p. H4.

42. *Moscow TASS* in English, August 31, 1977; translated in *FBIS: Soviet Union,* September 1, 1977, p. H1.

43. See *The New York Times,* September 25, 1977, p. 2. It was also about this time that the USSR ceased deliveries of POL to Somalia. See *October* (Cairo), September 11, 1977.

44. *Baltimore Sun,* September 23, 1977, p. 2.

45. *Baltimore Sun,* September 18, 1977, p. 2 and *The Washington Post,* September 29, 1977, p. 1.

46. *The Washington Post,* September 27, 1977, p. A14.

47. *Addis Ababa Voice of Revolutionary Ethiopia* in English, October 19, 1977; transcribed in *FBIS: Sub-Saharan Africa,* October 20, 1977, p. B4.

48. *The New York Times,* November 27, 1977, p. E3.

49. *The New York Times,* November 15, 1977, p. 1.

50. As early as October, the Somalis claimed that Cuban troops in large numbers were fighting in the Ogaden. See *Mogadishu Domestic Service* in Somali, October 21, 1977; translated in *FBIS: Sub-Saharan Africa,* October 25, 1977, p. B6.

51. *Moscow TASS* in English, November 15, 1977; transcribed in *FBIS: Soviet Union,* November 15, 1977, p. H1.

52. *Mogadishu Domestic Service* in Somali, November 13, 1977; translated in *FBIS: Sub-Saharan Africa,* November 14, 1977, p. B2.

53. *Mogadishu Domestic Service* in English, November 14, 1977; transcribed in *FBIS: Sub-Saharan Africa,* November 14, 1977, p. B3. It also may be recalled that in October the Somalis had permitted the West Germans to liberate at Mogadiscio airport a Lufthansa jet that had been hijacked by Palestinians—a gesture undoubtedly designed to improve Somalia's image in the West.

54. *Doha QNA* in Arabic, November 24, 1977; translated in *FBIS: Sub-Saharan Africa,* November 25, 1977, p. B7.

55. *Washington Star,* January 17, 1978, p. 2.

56. Some members of the Dergue apparently wanted to seize northern Somalia in order to exchange it for the Ogaden in future negotiations. See *Africa,* No. 79, March 1978, p. 19.

57. *Manchester Guardian,* November 28, 1977.

58. *Istanbul Milliyet,* January 27, 1978; translated in *FBIS: Western Europe,* January 30, 1978, pp. T2-T3.

59. *Newsweek,* January 23, 1978, p. 35; and July 17, 1978, p. 54.

60. The An-22 military transports in question were detained in Karachi when Pakistani authorities demanded to inspect their cargo, but released after the personal intervention of the Soviet ambassador. See *Foreign Report,* January 11, 1978, pp. 5-6.

61. *Times* (London), February 12, 1978, p. 9.

62. *Statement of Rear Admiral S. Shapiro, Director of Naval Intelligence Before the Seapower Subcommittee of the House Armed Services Committee,* p. 12.

63. *The New York Times,* February 14, 1978, p. 1.

64. *The New York Times,* February 22, 1978, p. 2.

65. Eritrea, however, was a different matter. Not only have Moscow's Arab friends (e.g., Syria and Iraq) taken a far stronger stand in support of the Eritreans, but the Cubans themselves were reluctant to participate directly in the suppression of local insurgents, many of whom were recent recipients of Cuban support and training. See *The Economist,* June 3, 1978, p. 68. It is not surprising, therefore, that the Soviets sought a negotiated political solution to the Eritrean problem far more earnestly than the Dergue. (In the brief history of the Dergue's deadly internecine conflicts, those leaders who have favored accommodation with the Eritreans have not survived very long.) Moscow has, nevertheless, provided logistic support for Ethiopian forces in their efforts to crush the Eritreans who have now been dislodged from most of their formerly-held positions.

66. *Africa Confidential,* August 22, 1979, pp. 6-7.

67. For indications of recent Somali interest in improving relations with the USSR, see the transcription of Siad Barre's January 1979 speech at an extraordinary congress of the Somali Revolutionary Socialist Party. (*Mogadishu Domestic Service* in Somali, January 20, 1979; translated in *FBIS: Sub-Saharan Africa,* January 23, 1979, p. B4.) It also may be noted that however slight prospects for a future Soviet-Somali rapprochement may be, they remain better with Siad Barre in than out of power. Siad Barre was after all the architect of Soviet-Somali friendship; any successor in order to strengthen his position might remove from the closet "skeletons" that might impede an improvement in Soviet-Somali relations. As one of the few Third World leaders strong enough to have survived such turbulent events of recent years, Siad Barre is probably also capable of orchestrating a rapprochement with Moscow.

149

7

SOVIET POLICY IN THE MIDDLE EAST:
PERSPECTIVES FROM THREE CAPITALS

Alvin Z. Rubinstein

Just as "beauty is in the eyes of the beholder," so, too, is the attribution of success or failure to Soviet Third World policy very much a function of the individual scholar, unless and until we devise some workable criteria, based on empirically and experientially rooted research, that can muster a consensus of experts capable of attracting the attention of US decisionmakers. The essays presented here contribute toward this objective. They are solid assessments of what Soviet policy has been, a record we need to know in as much detail as possible.

When assessing Soviet policy in the Third World, it is important not to impute to Soviet leaders yardsticks of success and failure that seem reasonable or compelling to us. For in diplomacy the success or failure of a policy inheres not only in palpable increments but also in the broader strategic value that the involved party attributes to the overall consequences of its policy, and of the latter we know precious little. Ideally, the Soviets should be judged in terms of success or failure in the objectives which they themselves have set up. But there is no way of knowing what ex-

150

pectations Soviet leaders have for a particular policy, though "guesstimates" abound. Soviet leaders do not tell us what they are after; certainly they are less than candid about the considerations that prompt specific policies. Given Moscow's far-ranging and increasingly determined pursuit of a number of simultaneous objectives in the Third World—from strengthening anti-West governments to acquiring military facilities, from exploiting US policy dilemmas and initiatives to aspiring to the former British role of arbiter of regional conflicts, from encouraging radical movements to undermining pro-Western governments and attempts by the United States to fashion its Pax Americana in the Third World—the task of singling out successes and failures becomes increasingly complex.

What is the appropriate level of analysis at which to evaluate Soviet policy? Should the focus be on the CPSU's relations with a Third World Communist party or radical movement? For example, is "success" the very close ties Moscow has forged with the self-proclaimed Marxist-Leninist leadership in the People's Democratic Republic of Yemen (PDRY)? Is "failure" to be seen in Ethiopia's strongman Mengistu's reluctance to establish a Soviet-style vanguard party and to staff it with pro-Soviet cadres? Or is the crucial level of analysis the government-to-government relationship? And if so, what considerations does one use in evaluating the nature or quality of Moscow's ties with Iraq, Cuba, Syria, Vietnam, and Libya? Or ought the level of analysis on which our evaluations of success and failure are based be the impact of Soviet policy on regional alignments and affairs? Perhaps strategic context transcends the importance of influence in this or that country or on this or that issue in the Kremlin's net assessment of how well its policy is faring.

Strategic context merits greater attention from Western analysts, because of all the levels of analysis it is the least ephemeral. Even if Soviet relations with, let us say, Egypt, Yemen, Somalia, Indonesia, or Nigeria did not live up to Moscow's expectations because of unanticipated and unforeseeable complications over which Moscow had little or no control—and Soviet analysts are wont to refer to the "complexity" (*slozhnost*) of developments—that is not reason enough to fault the policy that had been followed. Even in setbacks there is advantage to be derived, witness the Soviet position in the Arab world in the aftermath of Camp David and the Egyptian-Israeli treaty of March 1979. Seldom are

151

reverses decisive. Viewed from the perspective of the 1950's, net Soviet gains in the 1960's increased, and viewed from the 1960's, Soviet gains in the 1970's were even more evident. Quite simply, the criteria for success that I use for evaluating Soviet policy are, in order of importance, first, the changed configuration of regional alignments that emerge as a consequence of Soviet behavior; second, the extent to which US policy or interests are undermined; and third, the increments in Moscow's influence in specific countries or movements.

How one is doing depends, as noted earlier, on who is making the assessment. For example, in February 1979, as the Iranian revolution reached its climax, National Security Council Adviser Zbigniew Brzezinski and Secretary of Defense Harold Brown made a hurried trip to Saudi Arabia, Egypt, and Israel. Their purpose was variously described as an attempt (1) to demonstrate US determination to stand by our (remaining) friends; (2) to deter the Soviets from intervening on the Arabian Peninsula; (3) to explore with these three countries the possibilities of de facto military cooperation to stop the spread of Soviet influence (shades of John Foster Dulles' visit to the Middle East in June 1953!); and, (4) to mount a forceful response to the outbreak of fighting between the two Yemens. Washington, dismayed by its failure to save the Shah, obsessed by the ubiquitous Russians, and worried that our friends worried about America's "will," sought to affirm its resolute commitment to the defense of these pro-Western governments.

Washington deployed an aircraft carrier and airlifted several hundred million dollars worth of military equipment to Yemen, presumably intent on demonstrating that it was making a commitment, not a contribution. The US press lauded the administration's forceful actions, and no doubt this was tallied in Washington as a "success." But a few weeks later, I came away from a visit to Egypt and Israel with the impression that neither the Egyptians nor the Israelis were impressed by the US moves, or by the unmistakable signal that they were supposed to convey to the Soviet and PDRY governments. Indeed, in both countries there were those who thought the US response reflected panic not disciplined pressure, an egregious failure to understand the dynamics of the region's politics, and an inability to distinguish image from impact. Both believed the US response was not an effective counter to the long-term Soviet challenge, which is more ambiguous and political. Both had the sense that America's credibility was not particularly enhanced; and both expressed concern at the US propensity toward showing muscle rather than engaging in diplomatic maneuver. Egyptian officials stressed that Iraq had taken steps to stop the Yemeni fighting by requesting an emergency meeting of the Arab League, which had already set a mediation effort in motion, since none of the Arab states, least of all Iraq, wanted an escalation of the Yemeni war with a superpower involvement. Moreover, both the Egyptians and Israelis wondered about the effectiveness of a sudden massive infusion of arms that supplied weapons the client was not capable of using and that were of questionable military utility in the Yemeni terrain. Washington may have been pleased with the exercise, because, as I have been told, it showed that "we could airlift substantial quantities of arms to a client in 48 to 72 hours." But what of the client, and what of those who have to depend on the American commitment? One is reminded of the story of the pig and the chicken who were walking along a road and came to a sign "ham and eggs." The pig looked at it and said, "for you it's a contribution, for me it's a commitment."

Talking with officials, journalists, and scholars in Egypt, Israel, and the Soviet Union over a two month period gave me a somewhat different perspective on Soviet policy from studying the phenomenon on this side. My purpose was to meet with knowledgeable people to learn how Soviet policy in the Middle East and Horn of Africa looked from Cairo, Jerusalem (and Tel Aviv, which has fine institutes on the Middle East and the Soviet Union), and Moscow. This tale of three cities has many dangling ends, but permit me to share a few observations.

Back-to-back visits to Egypt and then Israel sharpened my impressions of each country's policy outlook. There were a number of important similarities. In both Egypt and Israel, the Ministry of Foreign Affairs plays an unimportant role in analyzing Soviet policy in the area or in directly servicing the policy process of the top leadership. Strong leaders make policy toward the Soviet Union with little recourse to the analyses of subordinates or the concerns of pressure groups. In Egypt the Ministry of Foreign Affairs (MFA) has a very limited research capability; in Israel, it is much stronger. To the extent that Sadat seeks ideas he looks to the staff attached to the Presidency; Prime Minister Begin looks to Weizman, a few loyalists, and military intelligence. The military in both countries have excellent capabilities for keeping tabs on Soviet activities. One Egyptian journalist said that when he wants some information on what the Soviets are up to in the area he goes not to the MFA but to the Gezira Club to have a drink with a friend in military intelligence. Neither Cairo nor Jerusalem wants the Soviet Union brought into the Arab-Israeli negotiations: both mistrust Moscow, regard Soviet diplomats as utterly incapable of unbending enough to establish the close personal relationships with their opposite numbers that are essential for sensitive talks, and believe that Moscow does not want a genuine settlement, since it stands to be the principal loser. Moreover, Sadat is convinced that Moscow is out to get him. Both capitals believe that regional developments are more apt to be affected by domestic politics and upheavals than by anything the Soviet Union can do; they see Moscow's capacity for initiative or innovation as severely limited for the time being and believe that Washington tends to see the Soviet hand as far more prominent in muddying Middle East waters than it actually is. Finally, neither country studies the United States in any systematic way—a neglect top leaders do not see as harmful.

Among the observable differences two are noteworthy: first, whereas Egypt lacks any academic superstructure conducting research on Soviet policy in the Middle East, Israel has outstanding programs attached to universities and institutes. Second, in Israel most of the academics have very close ties with military intelligence, since they do annual military reserve duty; in Egypt there is no link between academic research, such as it is, and the military-political leadership.

I was in Cairo the two weeks before the Egyptian-Israeli treaty was signed, and those whom I interviewed—primarily middle-range officials in the Ministry of Foreign Affairs (heads of departments, members of the policy planning staff, etc.)—invariably wanted to talk about the treaty and what was happening in Israel, on which they had limited information. The openness with which they expressed their lack of enthusiasm for the treaty was surprising: "The only official in Egypt who is wholeheartedly for the treaty," they said, "is the President."

Egyptian assessments of Soviet policy looked something like this. First, there was no concern over any direct Soviet threat to Egypt's vital interests in the Arab world. To the extent that there is a long-

154

term threat, such as Soviet intervention in another Arab-Israeli or Yemeni war, the threat was one that would inevitably enmesh the United States. The task of diplomacy was to prevent a war. Short of actual involvement by Soviet forces, the local actors had the ball and they should be encouraged by the United States to run with it more openly. The Egyptians thought Soviet influence was greatest in the PDRY. But no one thought the PDRY or any Arab country was about to fall under Soviet control, though one analyst hypothesized that Fateh Ismail had started a disturbance in Yemen to help Moscow signal Washington not to back the Chinese against Vietnam!

Second, notwithstanding this restrained evaluation of present Soviet threats in the Middle East as a whole, all concurred that Sadat is deeply anti-Soviet. (Husni Mubarak, the Vice-President, shares his antipathy toward the USSR for its supposedly limited air assistance in October 1973). Since Egypt's policy is Sadat's policy, "Egypt" officially sees the Soviet Union behind every problem. Sadat is shrewd enough to realize that this "perception" is a plus for him in his relations with the US Congress. Sadat's opposition to Soviet involvement in Ethiopia is rooted in his anxiety over the future of the Sudan. Further, Soviet courtship and encouragement to Libya is a factor seriously aggravating Soviet-Egyptian relations. The Soviet threat in Libya stems from the implicit encouragement Moscow gives to Qadaffi's intrigues and provocations, which are undertaken in the surety of Soviet protection from serious retaliation.

Third, the Egyptians stated openly that each Arab state wants to constrain Soviet activity in the Middle East but at the same time wants to use the Soviet Union for its own purposes. Moscow cannot sabotage the Egyptian-Israeli treaty, but it can provide the arms to keep the military option alive and thereby thwart US aims, and undermine Sadat's regime. All thought that the USSR wants to be part of the peace process, something it had seemingly achieved with the October 1977 joint statement. Moscow is angry because a settlement without Soviet participation would leave the Soviets odd men out.

Fourth, Cairo sees the USSR's task of establishing influence in the Arab world as more difficult now than in the 1950's and 1960's, when Arab attitudes toward Moscow were shaped in important ways by Egypt's policy, in part because of Nasser's prestige and in part because of Egypt's intensive experience in dealing with the Russians. However, in the 1980's each Arab leadership is likely to rely on its own experience and use its own litmus test for dealing with Moscow. Additionally, each will be more active in maneuvering within the Arab world against perceived threats, with the result that coalition building and diplomatic activity will be affected by many more considerations than heretofore. In this there are both promises and pitfalls for Moscow.

Fifth, Egyptian officials found Brzezinski's notion of "an arc of crisis" wanting, because it assumed greater Soviet control over events than was warranted. American fumbling was of more concern than Soviet manipulation. Moscow intervened in response to opportunity. Judging by Egypt's experience, they thought the USSR would find it difficult to create a secure political base (epitomized by establishment of a Marxist-Leninist party) in Arab or African countries. One high ranking official noted that even in the PDRY, where life in Aden is being shaped by a Marxist-Leninist party, the bulk of the country goes on pretty much as always. The Soviets have tangible strategic advantages—landing rights, a dry dock and port facilities, storage and repair installations—but their strategic advantages do not automatically transfer to control over the internal political system or the policies pursued by Fatah Ismail. Nor are these current signposts of success any more permanent than were those Moscow once had in Egypt.

Finally, Egyptians in and out of office emphasized that the West's policy of helping Egypt improve its economic condition and prospects would have telling effect on Soviet prospects for making trouble. Meaningful support for Egypt and the Sudan now would be the best guarantee against the spread of Soviet influence in the area. The military side is important, but so is timely, effectively administered, high impact economic assistance.

My discussions with Israeli officials and scholars on Soviet policy in the Middle East yielded a rich harvest, and these brief observations cannot do justice to their perceptive assessments.

First, the Israeli military is deeply concerned about the sustained flow of Soviet arms to the confrontation states. The sheer quantity of weaponry—and Israelis say that US arms to Saudi Arabia must also be included—in the hands of avowed enemies is staggering. None of the military analysts thought the Soviet Union wanted another war, but they stressed that this was as little relevant now as it had been in 1967 or 1973. By giving Iraq and Syria a military option and the assurance of support in the event of difficulty, Moscow is priming the trigger. The USSR is not a niggardly supplier. In general, it gives arms up to the absorptive limit of the client. The military groups disagreed on the Syrian situation—some contending that Moscow had not given Syria all that it could absorb, others insisting that it had. In the PDRY, Soviet, Cuban, and East German advisers are absolutely necessary to ensure that the weapons are used properly; in Syria and Iraq, they are not.

The different policies on arms transfers can be explained by differences in motives. Thus, the USSR has sold Qadaffi more then three times as much weaponry as Libya can absorb. There is little danger of Qadaffi's starting a war with Egypt. By selling massive amounts of arms, Moscow obtains hard currency, encourages Libyan dependency on Soviet expertise, and positions itself for the future. This sitution is quite different from the buildup of Syria, whose critical mass of arms could trigger serious fighting and embroil the USSR; hence the attempt to calibrate the military demands with the political risks.

Second, Israeli analysts are as divided as their American counterparts over the supposed aims of Soviet policy and the question of whether Moscow wants a settlement of the Arab-Israeli conflict. Unlike the situation in the United States, in Israel there is a marked asymmetry between the military's views and the academic community's relatively benign views of what the Soviet Union is up to in the Middle East, what it has accomplished, and what motivates its policy. Scholars were apt to urge the necessity of bringing the USSR into the next round of the Arab-Israeli talks. Military analysts tended to be opposed, arguing (1) that the USSR, as a partisan of the Arab confrontation states, could not be expected to adopt a balanced position on any crucial issue; (2) that as long as the Soviet Union pressed imperial aims elsewhere in the Middle East, as part of its overall rivalry with the United States, it could not be expected to play a constructive role in fashioning an Arab-Israeli settlement, the consequence of which would assuredly be a diminution of Soviet prospects everywhere in the region; and (3) that there is no evidence that Moscow would be constructive. The debate on this key issue is, of course, being conducted in the US Government as well.

Third, Israeli analysts expressed concern over Washington's growing vulnerability to Arab oil pressure. They felt that this could

157

prompt "refinements" of vital strategic interests in ways that would be detrimental to Israeli security and to the future of the Egyptian-Israeli treaty, and that might lead the United States to misperceive Middle East realities. They did not think that the US Government's record of understanding the dynamics and complexities of Middle East currents and crises was very good.

Finally, the Israelis were skeptical of prospects for Iraqi-Syrian unity. They discounted Moscow's public declarations of support as so much propaganda, noting that Moscow has always preferred to deal with each Arab government separately. Their sense of what the Soviets are doing in each Arab country is highly developed. (Soviet Jews in Israel have not had any effect on the Establishment's perception of Soviet activities in the Middle East; few of them had experience in the foreign policy field).

The visit to Moscow served as a useful reminder that Soviet specialists are very well informed on the Middle East, with the possible exception of Israel; that they are every bit as capable as their Western counterparts; and that their published writings, on which we tend to rely so much, do not reflect the depth of their analytical competence. They are a tough-minded, highly-trained breed of professionals. Indeed, in many ways, Soviet specialists are better equipped than we to follow the day-by-day developments in most areas of the Middle East. They have an army of researchers, trained in local languages, to service the research activities of key institutes. Soviet embassies have the manpower to keep close tabs on the local press, and they are rarely staffed by political appointees. I do not know any Soviet instance comparable to the US experience in Iran, in which the Soviet establishment bungled a strong hand, in part because of the absence of adequate information. Moscow has made mistakes, but from deficient judgment, not sparse information.

The Soviet research establishment on the Middle East is informed and capable. If there are "isolationists" or "doves," I did not meet them. As is to be expected, discussions in official surroundings have limited utility, for one reason because Soviet specialists would not deviate one iota from official policy. On a number of occasions, I suggested that Soviet opposition to the Camp David peace process and the Egyptian-Israeli treaty might be interpreted as evidence of Soviet opposition to peace and detente in the Middle East and might prompt a few Senators to vote against the SALT treaty, on the ground that Moscow was not interested in really improving US-Soviet relations. This elicited a fierce response from one leading specialist, who pointed a warning finger three times in the course of a two-hour discussion, saying, "The Soviet Union will not be pushed around. We will not allow the United States to dictate to us." This assertiveness reflected acceptance of the essential correctness of Soviet policy in the Middle East.

In private and relaxed settings, Soviet assessments were richer in detail and analytical insight. I was given a view of the "contradictions" that beset the Egyptian-Israeli treaty and attempts to fashion a comprehensive settlement that were sophisticated and subtle as the best I have heard in this country. If the Soviets come out at a different end of the spectrum in their analyses of the Middle East, it is not from want of data but from a different ascription of weights to that data and to different political preferences and objectives.

Soviet analysts may have a tougher time making sense out of US policy in the Third World than we have understanding Soviet policy there. Time and again, I was asked, "If the United States is interested in improving relations with the Soviet Union, why did it sign and then renege on the joint statement of October 1, 1977? Why did it summarily disrupt the Indian Ocean talks? Why does it persist in overreacting to Soviet support for legitimate governments, seeking to protect themselves from outside attacks, as in the cases of Angola and Ethiopia? Why does it 'threaten' the USSR with rejection of the SALT II treaty? Is the treaty not in the interests of both countries?"

Soviet specialists seemed more informed on Arab than American politics. None had ever heard of Senator Robert Byrd or Representative "Tip" O'Neill. I suspect they believe that US policy is made by a process akin to the one in the Kremlin. There are deep misconceptions concerning the relationship between Congress and public opinion, the nature of the US-Israeli relationship, and the powers of the President.

Moscow accepts the contradictions of Arab politics as a norm. Patient with dilemmas, reconciled to the permanence of regional conflicts it cannot solve, ever ready to commit resources in situations whose preferred outcomes are not always assured, and resigned to the vagaries of Arab political infighting, it seeks local advantages, more to offset its superpower adversary than to entrench Soviet or local Communist influence.

159

In contrast to their American counterparts, Soviet leaders are wedded to a tactical approach whose essence is a belief in the long-term efficacy of incremental gains in the region rather than a conceptual view that permits global considerations to shape regional responses. Where American policymakers are mesmerized by the goal of stability in superpower relationships, the Soviets posit differentiation and the compartmentalization of competition. Perhaps because they face no domestic pressures, they see no need for linkage: for them, tension and rivalry in the Middle East milieu are not inconsistent with peaceful coexistence or detente in Western Europe, the Far East, or SALT.

Egyptians and Israelis criticized the US administration for naivete in believing that the problems of peace and safeguarding vital strategic interests in the Middle East can be assured by felicitous combinations of activism, goodwill, and aid. Washington's propensity toward mounting initiatives was contrasted unfavorably with Moscow's doggedly inertial approach, a reflection no doubt of the former's aspirations and the latter's ambitions.

Though it has been relatively passive since Sadat's visit to Jerusalem in November 1977, the USSR is hardly in trouble in the Middle East, as many Western analysts allege. Soviet aims over the past generation have been remarkably consistent: to weaken the US position in the Middle East; to encourage *de facto* nonalignment along its southern tier; to establish a presence in the Arab world and a role for the Soviet Union in the management of regional affairs; to invest for the future. Moscow views the Middle East as a growth stock—it really doesn't need much in the way of dividends for the time being, although it has already reaped a good deal. By these criteria, the Soviet quotient of success seems greater than its quotient of failure.

8

SOVIET POLICY TOWARD BA'ATHIST IRAQ, 1968-1979

Robert O. Freedman

In order to assess the success or failure of Soviet policy toward Iraq it is first necessary to examine Soviet policy toward the entire Middle East, since Soviet policy toward Iraq is very much a component of its overall policy toward the region. In addition, it is necessary to examine the nature of the Ba'athist regime in Iraq, since many of the successes achieved and problems encountered by the USSR in its dealings with the Iraqis stem from the rather singular nature of the Iraqi regime which has been beset by serious domestic and foreign problems since it came to power. After these two topics are discussed, this study will examine the evolution of the Soviet-Iraqi relationship from the *coup d'etat* which brought the Ba'athists back to power in July 1968 until the present.

SOVIET GOALS AND TACTICS IN THE MIDDLE EAST

In order to understand Soviet policy toward Iraq, it is necessary to deal first with the problem of determining Moscow's goals in the Middle East. Observers of Soviet policy in this oil-rich and strategically located region are generally divided into two schools of thought on this question.[1] While both agree that the Soviet Union wants to be considered a major factor in Middle Eastern affairs, if only because of the USSR's propinquity to the region, they differ on the ultimate Soviet goal in the Middle East. One school of thought sees Soviet Middle Eastern policy as being primarily defensive in nature; that is, as directed toward preventing the region from being used as a base for military attack or political subversion against the USSR. The other school of thought sees Soviet policy as primarily offensive in nature, as aimed at the limitation and ultimate exclusion of Western influence from the region and its replacement by Soviet influence.[2] It is the opinion of the author that Soviet goals in the Middle East, at least since the mid-1960's, have been primarily offensive in nature, and in the Arab segment of the Middle East, the Soviet Union appears to have been engaged in a zero-sum game competition for influence with the United States.

In its efforts to weaken and ultimately eliminate Western influence from the Middle East and particularly from the Arab world while promoting Soviet influence, the Soviet leadership has employed a number of tactics. First and foremost has been the supply of military aid to its regional clients.[3] Next in importance comes economic aid; the Aswan dam in Egypt and the Euphrates dam in Syria are prominent examples of Soviet economic assistance, although each project has had serious problems. In recent years Moscow has also sought to solidify its influence through the conclusion of long-term Friendship and Cooperation Treaties such as the ones concluded with Egypt (1971), Iraq (1972), Somalia (1974), Ethiopia (1978) and Afghanistan (1978). However, the repudiation of the treaties by Egypt (1976) and Somalia (1977) indicate that this has not been too successful a tactic. Moscow has also attempted to exploit both the lingering memories of Western colonialism and Western threats against Arab oil producers. In addition, the Russians have offered the Arabs diplomatic support at such international forums as the United Nations and the Geneva Conference on an Arab-Israeli peace settlement. However, both its diplomatic and military aid to the Arabs against Israel has been limited in scope by the Soviet Union. Moscow continues to support Israel's right to exist, both for fear of unduly alienating the United States at a time when the Russians desire additional SALT agreements and improved trade relations, and also because Israel serves as a convenient rallying point for potentially anti-Western forces in the Arab world.[4]

While the USSR has used all these tactics, it has also run into serious problems in its quest for influence in the Middle East. The numerous inter-Arab and regional conflicts (Syria-Iraq, North Yemen-South Yemen, Ethiopia-Somalia, Algeria-Morocco) have usually meant that when the USSR has favored one party, it has alienated the other, often driving it toward the West. Secondly, the existence of Arab Communist parties has proven to be a handicap for the Russians, as Communist activities have, on occasion, caused a sharp deterioration in relations between the USSR and the country in which the Arab Communist party has operated. The Communist-supported *coup d'etat* in the Sudan in 1971, and Communist efforts to organize cells in the Iraqi Army in the mid and late 1970's are recent examples of this problem.[5] Third, the wealth which flowed to the Arab world (or at least to its major oil producers) since the quadrupling of oil prices in late 1973 has enabled the Arabs to buy quality technology from the West and Japan, and this has helped weaken the economic bond between the USSR and a number of Arab states such as Iraq and Syria. Fourth, since 1967 and particularly since the 1973 Arab-Israeli war, Islam has been resurgent throughout the Arab world, and the USSR, identified in the Arab world with atheism, has been hampered as a result. Finally, the United States and to a lesser extent France and China have actively opposed Soviet efforts to achieve predominant influence in the region and this has frequently enabled Middle Eastern states to play the extra-regional powers off against each other and thereby prevent any one of them from securing predominant influence.

Given the problems that the USSR has faced, the Russians have adopted one overall strategy to seek to maximize their influence while weakening that of the West. The strategy had been to try to unite the Arab states (irrespective of their mutual conflicts) together with "progressive" Arab political organizations, such as the Arab Communist parties and the PLO, into a large "anti-imperialist" Arab front directed against what the USSR has termed the linchpin of Western imperialism—Israel—and its Western supporters. Given the heterogeneous composition of the front, the USSR has not had too much success with this strategy, although it appeared to bear fruit during the 1973 war when the Arabs united against Israel and placed an oil embargo on the West. Unfortunately for Moscow, however, the astute diplomacy of Henry Kissinger and policy changes by Egyptian President Anwar Sadat led to a splintering of this "anti-imperialist Arab unity" and the emergence of a core of pro-Western Arab states in the aftermath of of the 1973 war left the USSR in a weak position in the Arab world at the time of the Carter Administration's accession to power in January 1977.[6] Moscow's position was to improve, however, by the time of the Carter-Sadat-Begin summit at Camp David in September 1978, and it improved still further following the two anti-Egyptian conferences organized by Iraq in Baghdad in November 1978 and March 1979, as it appeared that the pro-Western grouping of Arab states had disintegrated. Nonetheless, the USSR was unable to capitalize on this situation to create its long-sought bloc of pro-Soviet Arab states—a development due at least in part to opposition from its erstwhile ally, Iraq.

THE NATURE OF THE IRAQI BA'ATHIST REGIME

The recent abortive *coup d'etat* in Iraq and the subsequent execution of a large number of high-ranking Ba'athist officials underlines the tenuous hold on power of the elite which has ruled Iraq since July 1968.[7] Major coup attempts against the regime have occurred in 1970, 1973, and 1979, and the regime has also been faced with an endemic conflict with the autonomy-seeking Kurds who inhabit the northern mountains of Iraq, as well as resentment from the Shiite majority in Iraq over domination by the Sunni Moslem minority regime, most of whose top leaders come from the town of Takrit. Even among the Takriti elite itself there has been conflict as evidenced by the ouster of Hardan al-Takriti from his position as vice-president in 1970, and his subsequent murder (most probably by an Iraqi "hit team") in 1971.

During its period of rule the Iraqi Ba'athists have also been faced with a number of foreign problems. One, a conflict with their fellow Ba'athists who rule in neighboring Syria, appears to have been at least temporarily resolved by the Camp David-induced rapprochement of October 1978, although the abortive July 1979 coup again soured relations. A second major problem concerns the border with Iran, whose population is predominately Shiite Moslem, and which until the fall of the Shah received extensive military support from the United States. While the 1975 treaty

164

between Iraq and Iran seemed to reduce the tensions between the two countries, the rise to power of Ayatollah Khomeini precipitated a new round of conflict. Foreign problems of a less severe nature facing the Iraqi Ba'ath include a continuing border dispute with Kuwait, strained relations with neighboring Saudi Arabia, and poor relations with Egypt, with whom Iraq has long been competing for leadership in the Arab world.

Given these domestic and foreign difficulties, it is perhaps not surprising that the minority dictatorship which currently rules Iraq has been rather paranoid about threats to its control over the country, whether real or only potential. Out of this situation has arisen a dependency on the USSR, on whom the Iraqis have relied heavily (although not exclusively) for weaponry. At the same time it has fostered a deep suspicion in the minds of the Iraqi leaders about the goals of the Iraqi Communist Party (ICP), which they see as actual or potential competitors for power. This, in turn, has created occasional conflict in Iraqi-Soviet relations, since the Iraqis see the USSR as a strong supporter of the ICP. This perception persists despite periodic Soviet statements that each Communist party has to achieve power by its own efforts.

The chronically suspicious nature of the Iraqi leadership has also been reflected in its efforts not to become too dependent on any one outside power for assistance. Thus in its early years when the nationalization and development of Iraqi oil were highest priorities of the Ba'athist regime, Iraq called upon France as well as the USSR for assistance. Following the quadrupling of oil prices, when general economic development became a major national priority, Iraq awarded major contracts not only to the USSR but also to firms in France, Japan and even the United States (with whom diplomatic relations remained broken because of Iraq's position on the Arab-Israeli conflict). The Soviet Union thus found itself obtaining a decreasing share of Iraqi trade. Even in the realm of military assistance, the Iraqis have been careful to seek aid from France so as to avoid too great a dependency on the USSR.

Interestingly enough, however, while the Iraqi leadership has sought to avoid too close a dependence on the USSR, it seems to have adopted several aspects of what might be termed the "Soviet model" to enhance its control over Iraqi society. Thus, there is a quasi-commissar system in the Iraqi armed forces both to help prevent a military coup and also to indoctrinate the officers in Ba'athist ideology. In addition the Iraqi leaders have sought to

165

keep the party and state separate, with the Ba'ath party in a position where it can control government activities by means of a unit of Ba'ath party members in each government department. Similarly the Ba'athists have organized a network of such cells in many factories, trade unions, and other official and unofficial organizations throughout the country.[8] While this system has not prevented societal disturbances or attempted coups, it has helped, at least so far, to keep the ruling elite in power. Needless to say, however, adoption of such a system, modeled as it may be on the CPSU, does not mean that the Iraqi leadership is any more dependent on the USSR. Indeed, as the next section of this study will seek to demonstrate, the Iraqi leadership reached its high point of dependency on the USSR in the 1973-74 period and has been moving away from its position of dependency ever since.

THE EVOLUTION OF SOVIET-IRAQI RELATIONS, 1968-79 .

July 1968 - July 1973: The Growth of Dependency
The return of the Ba'ath to power in Iraq in July 1968 may have been greeted with mixed feelings by Moscow. On the one hand, only 5 years before the Ba'athists had slaughtered a large number of Iraqi Communists in their brief 10 month rule over the country. This reign had followed the overthrow of Abdul Qassim, with whom the Russians had established close ties. As a result, Soviet-Iraqi relations had deteriorated sharply. On the other hand, the al-Bakr led Ba'athists were at least professed socialists, albeit moderate ones, which was more than could be said for the regime of Abdul Rahman Aref which they overthrew. Even more important, however, the new regime's internal and external difficulties and the changing situation in the Persian Gulf made it opportune for Moscow to welcome the Iraqi Ba'athist quest for improved relations.

Soon after taking power the al-Bakr regime found itself caught up in an escalating conflict with Iran. On April 19, 1969, Teheran denounced the 1937 Iraqi-Iranian treaty fixing their frontier on the eastern (Iranian) side of the Shaat al-Arab River.[9] In addition, by professing hostility to Western-oriented Turkey and the monarchies of the Persian Gulf, the Iraqis soon found themselves distrusted by virtually all of their neighbors. To make matters worse they were also beset by internal problems such as the con-

166

tinuing conflict with the Kurds, extensive overt and covert opposition to their regime, and an abortive *coup d'etat* attempt in January 1970. Thus beset by internal strife and external threats, the new Iraqi regime was in need of assistance.

From the point of view of the USSR, the possibility of exploiting such a situation must have appeared to be most timely indeed. On January 16, 1968, British Prime Minister Harold Wilson had announced that England would maintain its forces in the Persian Gulf only until the end of 1971, and Moscow may have seen the possibility of filling the vacuum of political/military power that would result. Iraq, with its public opposition to the Western-oriented monarchies in the Gulf and to American efforts to forge a Persian Gulf security pact to fill the void left by the departing British, seemed to be an excellent candidate for Soviet assistance.[10]

Soviet aid to Iraq was to be both military and economic in nature. Arms sale negotiations began in Baghdad early in 1969 and an agreement was reached when Iraqi military delegates journeyed to Moscow in May of that year.[11] (See Table 1 for a description of the subsequent rise in Iraqi military power.) Perhaps almost as important to the Iraqi Ba'athists as Soviet military aid was the Soviet willingness to help Iraq develop its oil industry. The Iraqis had long been locked in conflict with the Western-owned oil companies over such issues as the price Iraq would receive for its oil, and the quantity of oil the Western companies would be willing to pump.[12] Thus Iraq could only welcome the agreement signed between its state oil company, INOC, and the USSR in June 1969 for a $72 million loan for drilling rigs, survey teams, and other oil field equipment; the loan the following month of an additional $70 million to help develop Iraq's northern Rumelia oil fields; and a major $222 million loan in April 1971—the latter two loans to be repaid in oil, a commodity which the USSR was beginning to find in tight supply.[13]   While the USSR and Iraq were able to agree on oil development (although the Iraqis were not always happy with the quality of Soviet equipment), and the Soviet government hailed the autonomy agreement reached on March 11, 1970, between the Iraqi government and the Kurds, differences remained on policy toward the Arab-Israeli conflict. Iraq opposed both UN Resolution 242 (which the USSR and Egypt had accepted) and the Israeli-Egyptian ceasefire agreement of August 1970. Indeed, *Pravda* on August 1, 1970, called Iraqi opposition to the latter agreement "incomprehensible." Iraqi opposition to these Soviet-backed

167

TABLE 1

The Rise in Iraqi Military Power, 1969-79

	1969-70	1975-76	1977-78
Army			
Total Strength	70,000	120,000	160,000
Armored divisions	1	3	4
Mechanized divisions	-	-	2
Infantry divisions	3	4	4
Republican guard mechanized			
brigade	-	1	1
Special forces brigade	-	-	1
Independent infantry brigade	-	-	2
Independent armored brigade	-	-	1
Tanks			
T-62, T-54/55, T-34, Centurion			
Mark Five, AMX	300	1,290	1,420
Light tanks	40	-	100
Armored fighting vehicles	NA	1,300	1,850
Artillery			
Howitzers	NA	700	700
Self-propelled guns	-	90	90
Surface-to-surface missiles			
(frog, scud)	-	NA	20
Anti-aircraft guns	-	800	800
Navy			
Fast torpedo boats	-	8	12
Torpedo boats	-	13	12
Minesweepers	-	2	2
Small patrol boats	-	3	4
Air Force			
Total combat aircraft	213	247	420*
Bombers	18	7	14
Fighter/ground attack	135	140	235*
Interceptors	60	100	171
Transport	40	30	59*
Helicopters	20	101	185*

*estimated

Sources: The Military Balance 1969-1970, London: Institute for Strategic Studies, 1969, p. 34.
The Military Balance 1975-76, Boulder, Col.: Westview Press, 1975, p. 34.
The Military Balance 1977-78, London: Institute for Strategic Studies, 1978, p. 36.
SIPRI Yearbook 1979, London: Taylor & Francis Ltd., 1979, pp. 218-220.

agreements helped to undermine the "anti-imperalist" Arab unity the USSR had been endeavoring to achieve. Nevertheless, the Soviet leaders not only did not exert any pressure on the Iraqi leadership (such as limiting economic or military aid), but they went ahead and signed a protocol on trade and economic cooperation with the Iraqis on August 13, 1970, which called for an increase in trade and Soviet assistance, and then granted the Iraqis a $34 million loan on August 30, 1970.[14] These events indicated not only the limited degree of Soviet influence in Iraq, but also a clear desire by the Russians to maintain good relations with the oil-rich and strategically located nation which, as in the days of Nuri Said and Abdul Qassim, had become Egypt's chief rival in the Arab world.

Moscow's efforts to establish a positive relationship with Iraq took on an added significance as Soviet-Egyptian relations began to cool with the death of Nasser and the advent of Anwar Sadat to Egypt's Presidency. Disagreements over Soviet military assistance to Egypt and Soviet policy toward the Communist-supported *coup d'etat* in the Sudan in July 1971, together with Egyptian gestures toward the United States, led to the deterioration of the Soviet position in Egypt.[15] By contrast, Soviet-Iraqi relations began to improve rapidly. In a major article on July 14, 1971, *Pravda* hailed "positive changes" in Iraq, citing especially the Ba'athists willingness to consider including the ICP in a national front.

Soviet-Iraqi relations grew still warmer following the abortive coup in the Sudan several days later. Faced by a hostile Saudi Arabia and Iran to her south and east, and with her western neighbor Syria having joined an Arab Federation led by Egypt, Iraq was isolated both in the Arab world and in the Middle East as a whole. The Iraqis had probably hoped that, by supporting the military *coup d'etat* against Sudanese President Jaafar Nimeri, they might wean the Sudan away from its ties with Egypt and into a close relationship with Iraq. When the coup failed and Nimeri returned to power, the Soviet Union was the only country that surpassed Iraq in its condemnation of Nimeri's activities—albeit for different reasons.[16]

Iraq's isolation grew stronger during the Indo-Pakistani war in December 1971 when its Persian Gulf rival Iran seized control of three strategically placed islands in the Persian Gulf and all Iraqi appeals for assistance went unheeded by her fellow Arab states. At the same time, the truce between the Iraqi government and the

Kurds had broken down, with Kurdish leader Mullah Mustafa Barzani accusing the Iraqi government of not fulfilling the agreement of March 11, 1970, and of trying to assassinate him. The Iraqi government then began arresting a large number of Kurds, while other Kurds returned to Barzani's mountain fortresses to prepare for war. To make matters worse for the narrowly based Ba'athist government, Iranian Foreign Minister Abbas Khalatbari stated in early December 1971 that Iran would aid the Iraqi Kurds should civil war between the Kurds and the Iraqi government break out again.[17] Meanwhile the Iraqi government continued to have difficulties in negotiations with the Western oil companies as it sought increased control over its oil and increased output by the oil companies. Frustrated and isolated, Iraq turned again to the USSR.

In February 1972 Saddam Hussein, the second most powerful member and heir apparent in the Iraqi regime, journeyed to Moscow in quest of a treaty. For reasons of its own, the Soviet Union was also interested in a treaty arrangement. In the first place it would give the Russians another strong point in the Arab world and make the USSR less dependent on its position in Egypt. Perhaps even more important, a treaty with Iraq would strengthen the Soviet Union's position in the Persian Gulf at a time when politics in the oil-rich region were in a great state of flux. Consequently, less than two months later the Iraqis obtained their treaty during Kosygin's visit to Iraq to inaugurate the Northern Rumelia oil fields.

The treaty bore a number of similarities to the Soviet-Egyptian treaty that had been signed 11 months earlier. Lasting for 15 years, the treaty provided that Iraq and the USSR would contact each other "in the event of the development of situations spelling a danger to the peace of either party or creating a danger to peace." In addition, the two sides agreed not to enter into any alliance aimed against the other. The Soviet commitment on military aid, however, was even more vague than in the case of the Egyptian treaty, stating merely that the two sides "will continue to develop cooperation in the strengthening of their defense capacities."[18]

Backed by the treaty, the Iraqi government took a harder position in its negotiations with the Western oil companies. As the confrontation became more intense the Iraqi regime made a gesture to the USSR by taking two ICP members into the cabinet as "a necessary political requirement for the confrontation."[19] Then, on June 1, 1972, less than two months after the signing of the treaty, the major Western oil company, the Iraq Petroleum Company, was nationalized. There appears to be little doubt that the USSR actively encouraged the Iraqi nationalization decision. The USSR had long urged the Arab states to nationalize their oil holdings and thus strike a blow at "Western imperialism," and by February 1972 Soviet spokesmen had begun to point out that unlike the situation at the time of the Arab oil boycott after the June 1967 war, both Western Europe and the United States were now vulnerable to Arab oil pressure.[20]

Meanwhile, the Western oil companies were steadily retreating in the face of price demands from the Organization of Petroleum Exporting Countries (OPEC), and the oil-producing nations were now also demanding an increasing percentage of the companies' oil for their own use. Accordingly, the Soviet leaders may have seen the IPC nationalization as another major blow to the whole structure of Western oil holdings in the Middle East and a reinforcement of the trend toward full nationalization of Arab oil and the consequent weakening of the Western alliance system headed by the United States. In the meantime, the increasing Soviet involvement in the development of Iraq's oil industry, highlighted by the Northern Rumelia agreement, was a demonstration to the Arabs that if cut off by the West, they could turn to the USSR as an alternative source of oil development assistance.[21]

Nonetheless, despite their enthusiastic acceptance and encouragement of the Iraqi government's nationalization decision, this action was not without cost to the Soviet leaders. The day after the nationalization Iraqi Foreign Minister M.S.A. Baki flew to Moscow in quest of economic and technical assistance to help compensate for the expected losses and difficulties resulting from nationalizaion. Lacking a tanker fleet of its own, and possessing only a limited refining capacity, Iraq was hard put to market its oil. To make matters worse, the regime had also lost about $780 million in hard-currency revenue as a result of the nationalization. While the Russians may have welcomed the increased dependency of the Iraqi regime, a situation that could lead to closer cooperation in exploiting the unstable situation in the Persian Gulf (assuming such cooperation could be achieved without unduly alarming Iran), nevertheless, the Russians would have to pay for this dependency. Thus, 5 days after Baki's arrival, an agreement was signed stipulating that the Soviet Union would help Iraq transport is oil, build a refinery in Mosul (near the Kirkuk field) with an annual capacity of 1.5 million tons, and help prospect for oil in southern Iraq. The Russians also agreed to give further assistance to the Baghdad-Basra oil pipeline. This agreement, like previous Soviet-Iraqi ones, stipulated that the USSR would be paid for its assistance by Iraqi oil exports.[22] Indeed, the sharp increase in Iraqi exports to the USSR in 1973 (see Table 2), composed almost entirely of oil,[23] demonstrates that this commodity had become an important factor in Soviet-Iraqi trade.

TABLE 2

Soviet-Iraqi Trade, 1969-77 (in millions of rubles)

Year	Soviet exports	Soviet imports	Total trade
1969	60.9	4.2	65.1
1970	59.4	4.1	63.5
1971	99.1	5.5	104.6
1972	90.1	61.6	151.7
1973	141.5	190.6	332.1
1974	182.3	270.8	453.1
1975	274.1	325.4	599.5
1976	341.6	372.9	714.5
1977	281.0	321.0	602.0

Sources: Vneshniaia torgovlia SSSR statisticheskii sbornik, 1970, 1972, 1974, 1976, 1977.

Interestingly enough, even at this period of great dependence on the USSR the Iraqi Ba'athists were careful not to become too closely linked to Moscow. Thus less than a week after Baki's visit to the Soviet Union, Saddam Hussein made an official visit to Paris and on June 18 a 10-year agreement was signed whereby the French oil firm CFP would buy 23.75 percent of the production of the nationalized oil fields.[24] To emphasize still further the Iraqi desire to balance the USSR and France, Saddam Hussein stated in an interview in *Le Monde* that he wished to see Iraq's relations with France raised to the level of those with the USSR.[25] Iraqi efforts to avoid too great a dependence on the USSR were not limited to France, however. In August 1972 the Iraqis agreed to the opening of a US Interests Section in the Belgian Embassy in Baghdad, and in 1973 major oil agreements were signed with Italy and Japan.

172

Although the Iraqi government was careful to keep its distance from the USSR, Moscow after its enforced exodus from Egypt in July 1972 sought to counter this blow to its Middle East position by emphasizing its greatly improved relations with Iraq, which it hailed for taking the lead in combating "anti-Sovietism" in the Arab world.[26] Another tactic utilized by the USSR during this period was to encourage the establishment of national fronts in Arab countries where Communist parties could function as junior partners and thereby hopefully influence the Arab national leaders to take more pro-Soviet positions. While the Iraqi regime had given lip service to the establishment of a national front that the ICP had long been advocating, the Ba'athists did not seriously entertain the idea until a *coup d'etat* attempt on June 30, 1973, almost succeeded in assassinating al-Bakr and overthrowing the regime. In reporting this development, the Soviet foreign affairs weekly *New Times* urged the al-Bakr regime to learn from this experience and finally implement the long-promised "progressive national front" of the Iraqi Ba'ath Party, the ICP, and the Kurdish National Party.[27] Perhaps because it was severely shaken by the abortive *coup d'etat* or because its conflict with Iran had escalated to the brink of open warfare, the al-Bakr regime consented to the formation of the National Front, although on terms that insured the absolute dominance of the Ba'ath party. While the ICP, which was legalized, agreed to the terms of the Front, the Kurds refused and Kurdish-Iraqi relations degenerated to the point of virtual full-scale warfare.

In addition to the establishment of the National Front and the inclusion of two Communists in the Iraqi cabinet, Soviet assistance was playing a key role in Iraqi efforts to develop its oil industry, and Soviet military aid was helping to protect Iraq against its hostile neighbors (and perhaps encouraging Iraq to take a more aggressive stance in its border conflict with Kuwait.) In light of these developments, Soviet influence in Iraq, highlighted by the visits of the Soviet navy to the Iraqi part of Umm Qasr,[28] may be said to have reached a high point in July 1973. However, Moscow's influence remained clearly limited, and events of the following 2 years were to lead to a diminution of even this limited position.

July 1973 - March 1975: Dependency Diminished
The two major difficulties facing the Iraqi regime during this

173

period, once it had recovered from the effects of the abortive *coup d'etat*, were its conflicts with Iran and with the Kurds who were receiving military aid from Iran. While Soviet military assistance was needed both to deter Iran from an overt attack and to oust the Kurds from their mountain fortresses, Iraq was to receive an unexpected bonus during this period. As a result of the quadrupling of oil prices, the regime found itself able to shop in the world market for capital goods to aid in its economic development and for military equipment as well. It was also now able to end its barter deals with socialist countries, including the USSR, and to demand direct payment for its oil. This new situation was to lead to a diminished Iraqi dependence on the USSR, a phenomenon that was to make itself increasingly felt in the post-1975 period.

From the Soviet viewpoint, aid to Iraq against the Kurds was perhaps distasteful. Previous Soviet policy toward the Kurds had fluctuated between assistance during periods when relations were strained between Baghdad and Moscow and calls for Kurdish-Arab cooperation when Soviet-Iraqi relations were good. But in the spring of 1974 when the Iraqi government began preparations for an all-out attack against the Kurds, the USSR may have seen aid to Baghdad as a necessity. After a temporary improvement in its Middle East position during the 1973 Arab-Israeli war, the Soviet Union's fortunes had turned downwards again as Egypt, once the primary Soviet ally in the Arab world, began to move into the American camp and the United States, long dormant in Middle East diplomacy, took the lead in the postwar efforts to achieve Arab-Israeli disengagement and settlement. During this process a pro-Western Egyptian-Saudi Arabian axis emerged which appeared capable of attracting other Arab states to its ranks. Given this development, the USSR faced the danger of isolation in the Arab world. Good relations with Iraq, one of the few remaining Arab countries in which the USSR could claim influence and an opponent of American diplomatic efforts, became a necessity.

Thus, following a Moscow visit by Saddam Hussein in February 1974, the USSR came out in full support of the Iraqi government against the Kurds. The Soviet media now claimed that the Kurds had been infiltrated and influenced by "imperialist and reactionary" elements.[29] The USSR also stepped up its military aid as Soviet Defense Minister Grechko paid a visit to Iraq in March 1974, most probably to inspect Iraqi preparations for their offensive against the Kurds.[30] In return for the Soviet diplomatic and military

174

support, the Ba'athist regime signed a joint communique with the USSR which advocated the solidarity of the Arab states "on an anti-imperialist basis" and the "consolidation" of their cooperation with the USSR. This declaration seemed a small price to pay for extensive Soviet aid.

Although Moscow was prepared to aid the Iraqis against the Kurds, it was more reluctant to get involved in the conflict between Iran and Iraq. While the USSR clearly did not like the way in which Iran was becoming the American policeman of the Persian Gulf, Teheran's role in the region was certainly preferable to a direct American one. In addition the USSR had not abandoned the hope of ultimately neutralizing Iran, and Moscow had begun to develop extensive trade relations with Iran, as it now imported Iranian natural gas and even sold some military equipment to the Shah's regime. Indeed at the high point of the Iran-Iraq conflict in 1974, Soviet trade with Iran exceeded that with Iraq, 495.7 million rubles to 453.1 million rubles.[31]

As a result, the USSR sought to play an even-handed role in the Iranian-Iraqi conflict, frequently urging the leaders of both countries to improve relations. The USSR warmly welcomed, therefore, the agreement of March 1975 between Iran and Iraq in which the two nations signed an agreement delineating their long-disputed border and agreeing to cease assistance to dissident groups within each other's territory. This meant a termination of Iranian aid to the Kurds, who were then in the midst of a life-and-death struggle with the advancing Iraqi army. With the end of the Iran-Iraq conflict and the inevitable end of the Kurdish struggle for autonomy, the Soviet position in the Persian Gulf seemed to be greatly enhanced. The long-feared possibility that the USSR would be drawn into a war between Iran and Iraq was now eliminated. The USSR could continue to improve its relations with Iran as well as Iraq while also assuring itself a continued flow of oil from Iraq and natural gas from Iran.

The Iranian-Iraqi agreement was to have another effect on Soviet policy, however. By removing the two main threats to the Iraqi government, the agreement made the Ba'athists far less dependent for military aid on the USSR. In addition, with the quadrupling of oil prices in December 1973, the Iraqi government was at the end of its economic dependence on the USSR. Baghdad then embarked on a major economic development plan and increasingly placed its

175

orders for factories and other goods with Western European, Japanese, and even American firms rather than with the USSR and East Europe. Although Soviet-Iraqi trade sharply increased during this period (see Table 2), Iraqi exports were already outstripping Soviet exports, as the Iraqis began to repay previous Soviet loans (see Table 3). To be sure, the USSR remained actively involved in the Iraqi economy, training Iraqi workers, building factories, canals, and power stations, and Iraq did sign a cooperation agreement with the Council for Mutual Economic Assistance in July 1975.[32] Nonetheless, the thrust of Iraqi economic relations was clearly in a Western direction, a development which was to become even more evident in the 1975-78 period.

TABLE 3

Iraqi Trade, 1969-77 (in millions of US dollars)

Year	Iraqi Imports	Iraqi Exports	Total trade
1969	440	1,042	1,482
1970	509	1,100	1,609
1971	694	1,530	3,334
1972	713	1,370	2,083
1973	906	2,190	3,096
1974	2,365	6,942	9,307
1975	4,204	8,276	12,480
1976	3,470	8,841	12,311
1977	3,898	9,664	13,562

Sources: UN Statistical Yearbook, 1977, New York: United Nations, 1978, pp. 472-277; and, Foreign Trade (Moscow), No. 7, 1979, p. 45.

July 1975 - September 1978: Adopting an Independent Line

In the period following the signing of its treaty with Iran, Iraq embarked on a policy of improving relations with its other neighbors in the Gulf, particularly Saudi Arabia and the United Arab Emirates. Increased conflict with Syria and the PLO, however, clouded Iraq's efforts to assume a position of leadership of the Arab world and contributed to its continuing isolation there. Meanwhile, Iraq's economic ties to the West continued to develop. Of even more serious concern to Moscow during this period was Iraq's continued opposition to Soviet peace initiatives in the Middle East, and its persecution of the Iraqi Communist party which had openly opposed a number of Iraqi government policies.

The Iraqi government made a definite effort to improve relations with its once hostile Persian Gulf neighbors in the aftermath of the Iran-Iraq Treaty. Thus in July 1975, an agreement between Iraq and Saudi Arabia was signed, dividing the neutral zone which lay along their common border.[33] In addition, several Iraqi officials made tours of Gulf states in an effort to develop cooperation and enhance the Iraqi role in the Gulf. Iraq also began to extend economic assistance to Jordan during this period, and a road between the Jordanian port of Aquaba and Iraq was planned.

From the Soviet viewpoint the new Iraqi initiatives held both advantages and disadvantages. Should Iraq draw closer to Saudi Arabia, it could conceivably influence the Saudi government to adopt a less pro-Western policy and erode the Saudi Arabian-Egyptian axis which by 1976 had attracted a number of other Arab states including the Sudan and North Yemen.[34] On the other hand, by drawing closer to Saudi Arabia, Iraq might itself come under Saudi influence and draw further away from the USSR. This was a development the USSR could ill afford at a time when its Middle East position was continuing to deteriorate in the face of American diplomatic success. However, the issue was at least temporarily mooted by Iraqi assistance to leftist forces during the Lebanese civil war of 1965-76, a development which blunted Baghdad's diplomatic initiative in the Persian Gulf by once again raising suspicions of Iraqi intentions among the pro-Western monarchies of the region.[35]

The primary Iraqi foreign problem, once its conflict with Iran was settled, was Syria, and this was one conflict in which the Iraqis could not call upon Moscow for assistance. Indeed, in his speech to the Twenty-Fifth Party Congress in February 1976, Brezhnev publicly ranked Syria over Iraq in its list of Arab allies, something the Iraqi leadership may not have appreciated.[36] In any case, there were a number of issues dividing the rival Ba'athist regimes including Syria's cutting off Euphrates River water to Iraq, Iraq's cutting off oil supplies to Syria, and attempts by each government to assassinate the leaders of the other. The USSR, still seeking to forge an "anti-imperialist" alignment in the Arab world, was clearly concerned about the Syrian-Iraqi conflict and sought to overcome it through public admonishments and a mediation effort by Soviet Prime Minister Aleksei Kosygin. At the height of the Lebanese civil war, he journeyed to both Baghdad and Damascus which were backing opposing sides in the conflict. But Kosygin's efforts were to no avail.[37] Even when Syria and Iraq joined a number of other Arab states in forming the Front of Steadfastness and Confrontation to protest Sadat's visit to Jerusalem in November 1977, this unity did not last. Iraq pulled out of the meeting, claiming that Syria wanted a deal with Israel.[38] Indeed, not only was Iraq in conflict with Syria over this point, it also became involved in the summer of 1978 in an assassination campaign against PLO leaders whom it claimed were seeking an agreement with Israel.[39]

By this time Iraqi opposition even to Soviet-endorsed peace plans, such as the October 1977 joint statement with the United States, was becoming a problem for the USSR, which was trying to rebuild its Middle East position by co-sponsoring with the United States the renewal of the Geneva Conference. Even more aggravating to the USSR during this period, however, was the continued westward turn of the Iraqi economy. Indeed by 1977 as Soviet-Iraqi trade began to drop (see Table 2), Iraqi-American trade had sharply increased to the point that it almost equalled Iraqi-Soviet trade.[40] The Soviet leadership, which has long emphasized the connection between economics and politics, could have drawn small comfort from Iraq's frequent protestations that its economic ties in no way influenced its political relationships.[41]

Several additional problems clouded Soviet-Iraqi relations in 1978. Soviet aid to the Mengistu regime in Ethiopia in its war against the independence-seeking Eritreans, one faction of whom were backed by Iraq, clearly antagonized Baghdad.[42] On the other hand, in the spring of 1978 the Iraqi government announced the execution of a number of Iraqi Communists, which could only anger Moscow.

Conflict between the ICP and the Iraqi Ba'athists had long been brewing. By 1976, the ICP had become increasingly unhappy with its virtually powerless position in the Iraqi government and had begun to advocate openly an increased role for itself in the National Front. In addition the ICP began to advocate genuine autonomy for the Kurds and openly opposed the Ba'athist policy of resettling Kurds outside of Kurdistan. Clearly unhappy with the westward drift of the Iraqi economy, the ICP also condemned the growing power of "private capital" and Iraq's "continuing dependence on the capitalist world market."[43]

In addition to making these open criticisms of Ba'athist policy, the Communists reportedly sought to form secret cells in the Iraqi armed forces and carried on antigovernment propaganda among Iraq's Kurds and Shiites—the groups most disaffected with the Sunni Ba'athist rule in Iraq.[44] Indeed the Ba'athists may well have suspected Communist involvement in the February 1977 Shiite religious protest demonstrations. Given the Iraqi regime's readiness to liquidate any of its outspoken opponents whether or not they resided in Iraq, it appeared only a matter of time until the crackdowns occurred.[45] Persecution of the ICP became increasingly open in 1977, but in the spring of 1978 the Iraqi government decided to execute a number of Communists. Possibly reacting to the pro-Soviet coup in nearby Afghanistan, the Ba'athist regime evidently decided that the crackdown took precedence over its relations with the USSR. Indeed as Naim Haddad, one of the leaders of Iraq's ruling Revolutionary Command Council, bluntly stated: "All Comunist parties all over the world are always trying to get power. We chop off any weed that pops up."[46]

The executions cast a pall over Soviet-Iraqi relations, despite the protestations of Iraqi leaders that they wanted good relations with the USSR. Significantly, however, Haddad stated "the Soviet Union is a friend with whom we can cooperate as long as there is no interference in our internal affairs."[47] But in the midst of Moscow's growing concern about trends in Iraqi foreign and domestic policy, the Camp David agreements gave the USSR another opportunity to rebuild its position in the Middle East.

September 1978 - July 1979: The Aftermath of Camp David

While the Soviet leadership was undoubtedly unhappy with the results of Camp David, Moscow could only have been pleased with a number of developments in the Arab world that the Egyptian-Israeli-American summit precipitated. These included the reconciliations between Iraq and Syria, Jordan and the PLO, and Iraq and the PLO, culminating in the Baghdad Conference of November 1978, which appeared to align almost the entire Arab world against Sadat. In addition, several months later Moscow received an unexpected bonus when the Shah of Iran was ousted and the Islamic government which replaced his regime left CENTO, proclaimed Iranian neutrality, and offered full support to the Palestinian cause. Unfortunately for the USSR, however,

179

just as its long-sought anti-imperialist bloc in the Arab world appeared to be forming (and had the possibility of expanding to include Iran), actions by Iraq served not only to divide the nascent bloc but also to run counter to Soviet policies in a number of areas.

While the Camp David summit was in progress, the USSR seemed particularly concerned that the United States would obtain a military base in either Egypt or Israel.[48] Although the outcome of Camp David did not provide for such a military base, it was clear that the United States, buy virtue of its mediating efforts and its promises of economic and military aid, was becoming even more involved in Egypt and Israel. The USSR may well have feared that a more formal military arrangement was not far off and that the Camp David system might expand to include such states as Syria and Jordan and possibly even the PLO.

Not unexpectedly, therefore, the USSR greeted the agreements with hostility. In a major speech at Baku on September 22, Brezhnev denounced what he termed the US attempt to ''split the Arab ranks'' and force the Arabs to accept Israeli peace terms. In addition he returned to the old four part Soviet peace plan, emphasizing that Israel had to withdraw totally from all territory captured in the 1967 war and agree to the establishment of a Palestinian state in the West Bank and Gaza. Brezhnev also repeated the Soviet call for a return to the Geneva Conference, with full participation of the PLO. Interestingly enough, perhaps to balance the American success at Camp David, Brezhnev hailed events in Afghanistan in his Baku speech, emphasizing that the new left-wing government which had seized power in that country in April had embarked on the road to socialism.[49]

If the Soviet reaction to Camp David was hostile, the reaction of most of the Arab states was not much warmer. While President Carter dispatched a series of administrative representatives to try to sell the agreement to such key Arab states as Saudi Arabia, Jordan, and Syria, they met with little success. Indeed, only three days after the announcement of the Camp David agreements, the Front of Steadfastness and Confrontation met in Damascus. Not only did it condemn Camp David, which it termed ''illegal,'' and reaffirm the role of the PLO as the sole representative of the Palestinian people, it also decided on the need to ''develop and strengthen friendly relations with the Socialist community led by the USSR.''[50] Reinforcing Soviet satisfaction with this development, PLO

Moscow representative Mohammed Shaer stated that the Front for Steadfastness and Confrontation was "the core of a future broad pan-Arab anti-imperialist front."[51]

The Soviet Union for its part moved once again to reinforce its ties with key members of the rejectionist front as first Assad of Syria, then Boumedienne of Algeria, and finally Arafat of the PLO visited Moscow in October. The Soviet media hailed the visiting Assad as a representative of the Steadfastness Front. One result of the meeting, besides the joint denunciation of Camp David and of attempts to "undermine Soviet-Arab friendship," was a Soviet decision to "further strengthen Syria's defense potential."[52]

While the the visit of Assad to Moscow could be considered a success for the USSR in its efforts to prevent the Camp David agreement from acquiring further Arab support, the Syrian leader's subsequent move toward a reconciliation with Iraq was even more warmly endorsed by the USSR. As discussed above, the Syrian-Iraqi conflict had long bedeviled Soviet attempts to create a unified "anti-imperialist" bloc of Arab states. Therefore when Assad announced that he had accepted an invitation to visit Iraq, the Soviet leadership must have seen this as a major step toward creating the long-sought "anti-imperialist" Arab bloc. While many observers saw Assad's visit as a tactical ploy to strengthen Syria's position in the face of the projected Israeli-Egyptian treaty, the USSR was effusive in its praise. Moscow Radio called it "an event of truly enormous importance which had considerably strengthened the position of those forces that decisively reject the capitulatory plans for a settlement drawn up at Camp David."[53]

While the Syrian-Iraqi reconciliation could be considered by Moscow as the most positive result of Camp David, the limited rapprochement between the PLO and Jordan was also deemed a favorable development, since it further reduced the chances of Jordanian participation in the Camp David accords and brought Jordan closer to an alignment with the anti-Sadat forces in the Arab world. The two rapprochements helped set the stage for the Baghdad Conference which appeared to further consolidate the bloc of Arab states opposing Sadat—a development warmly greeted by Moscow. At Baghdad, not only were the Camp David agreements condemned, with even Saudi Arabia participating (the Saudis may have been influenced, if not intimidated by the Syrian-Iraqi rapprochement), but a joint PLO-Jordanian commission was established, foreshadowing further cooperation between these two erstwhile enemies. In addition, another reconciliation took place as the PLO and Iraq, which had been involved in an assassination campaign against each other in the summer, also appeared to end their conflict. Besides these reconciliations, specific anti-Egyptian measures were decided upon at Baghdad. Thus, the Arab League headquarters was to be removed from Cairo and economic sanctions taken against Egypt should Sadat go ahead with the signing of the treaty.

Finally the USSR must have been pleased by the Baghdad Conference's formula for a "just peace" in the Middle East: Israeli withdrawal from the territories captured in 1967 and the recognition of the "right of the Palestinian people to establish an independent state on their national soil."[54] While the latter phase was open to differing interpretations, the juxtapositon of the two statements seemed to indicate that even such radical states as Iraq and Libya might, for the first time, be willing to grudgingly accept Israel's existence. Although the Baghdad statement on peace was far from the trade, tourism, and normal diplomatic relations wanted by the Israelis, it was very close to the peace formula which had been advocated by the USSR since 1974. In sum, the Soviet leadership was undoubtedly pleased with the results of the Baghdad summit, with one Soviet commentator deeming it "a final blow to imperialist intentions aimed at dissolving Arab unity and pressuring other Arabs to join Camp David."[55]

Given the key role of Iraq in orchestrating the anti-Sadat forces at Baghdad and helping to form what the USSR hoped might become the nucleus of the long-sought anti-imperialist Arab bloc, it is not surprising that Soviet-Iraqi relations improved in the aftermath of the conference. Indeed, one month later, Saddam Hussein himself was invited to Moscow. While the main purpose of his visit was probably to coordinate the Soviet and Iraqi positions opposing Camp David, it appears that other issues occupied the discussions as well. These included Soviet-Iraqi trade relations, problems pertaining to Iraq's Communist party, and the Soviet supply of arms to Iraq following Camp David. In this regard there were a number of reports in the Western press that both Syria and Iraq were asking for sharp increases in Soviet weapons supplies to compensate the Arabs for Egypt's departure from the Arab camp.[56] The USSR, however, reportedly told Syria and Iraq that since they were now cooperating they could pool their weapons.[57]

182

In resisting the Syrian and Iraqi demands (if this, indeed, is what happened), the USSR may have been concerned that if the Syrians and Iraqis were too well armed they might provoke a war against Israel at a time inconvenient for the USSR,[58] or it may have simply been one more case where an arms supplier was unwilling to met all the demands of its clients.

At any rate, while there appeared to have been progress on the question of economic relations during the talks, the outcome of the military aid question was not clear. The final communique stipulated only that "the sides reiterated their readiness to keep cooperating in strengthening the defense capacity of the Iraqi Republic."[59] Even less was said on the subject of the Iraqi Communist party. The only public reference (and a veiled one at that) to this area of conflict in Soviet-Iraqi relations was made in a dinner speech by Kosygin who stated:

> Friendly relations with the Republic of Iraq are highly valued in the Soviet Union and we are doing everything to make them more durable. This is our firm course and it is not affected by circumstantial considerations.[60]

If the Soviet leadership sought to use the Brezhnev-Hussein meeting to secure improved treatment for the Iraqi Communists, it was not successful. Less than a month later, on January 10, *Pravda* published an editorial from the Iraqi Communist paper *Tariq Ash-Shab* deploring "the widespread persecution of Commuinists in Iraq and repression against the Communist party's organization and press." *Pravda* followed the editorial 3 days later by publishing the statement of the December 1978 Conference of Arab Communist parties which similarly condemned Iraq for its treatment of the ICP.[61]

The anti-Iraq campaign in the Soviet press is of particular interest. In the past the USSR had grudgingly tolerated attacks on local Communist parties so long as the regime responsible adopted a proper "anti-imperialist" stance. Indeed, the USSR has even gone so far as to urge the dissolution of Arab Communist parties or their restriction to the role of teachers of "scientific socialism" in Third World countries to avoid such conflicts.[62]

It may well be, therefore, that Moscow saw more than just a domestic problem in Iraq's persecution of the ICP, which continued through the first half of 1979. Iraq, in leading the opposition to the Egyptian-Israeli treaty, was seeking to project itself as the leader of the Arab world. In order to accomplish this task, however, Iraq had not only to arrange a rapprochement with Syria and the PLO, but it had as well to establish a working relationship with Saudi Arabia, the Arab world's leading financier and a growing Persian Gulf military power. The Soviet leadership may have suspected, therefore, that the overt anti-Communist campaign in Iraq was designed to signal to the Saudis that Iraq was no longer a close ally of the USSR. When Iraqi strongman Saddam Hussein went so far as to state that ''we reject the wide expansion by the Soviet Union in the Arab homeland'' and that ''the Arabs should fight anyone—even friends like the Soviets who try to occupy the Saudi land,'' this may have confirmed Soviet suspicions.[63]

Yet another factor which may have tarnished somewhat Iraq's usefulness to the USSR as a leader of the anti-Sadat and anti-American forces in the Arab world was the eruption of a serious quarrel beween Iraq and South Yemen (the PDRY), the most Marxist of the Soviet Union's Arab allies. There appear to have been two major causes for the quarrel. In the first place, when the PDRY invaded pro-American North Yemen in late February 1979, Iraq led an Arab mediation mission which, against the background of a major American military build-up of North Yemen, pressured the South Yemenis to withdraw before any of their major objectives were achieved. Given the apparent Soviet support for the invasion, this would appear to have been a case where Soviet and Iraqi objectives were in conflict.[64] Secondly, several months later, an Iraqi Communist party member, Taufiq Rushdi, who had been lecturing in the PDRY, was murdered—apparently by a ''hit team'' of Iraqi security men attached to Iraq's Aden Embassy. In reprisal, a PDRY force stormed the Iraqi embassy and seized the gunmen, an action which provoked a storm of protest from Baghdad.[65]

If the unity of the anti-Sadat forces in the Arab world was threatened by the Iraq-PDRY conflict, it was also endangered by the growing strife between Iraq and the Moslem fundamentalist government led by the Ayatollah Khomeini in Iran. The problem originated in Iranian Kurdistan where the Kurds, seizing the opportunity provided by the disintegration of the Shah's regime and of the Iranian army, demanded autonomy.[66] This in turn led to bloody clashes between the central authorities and Iran's Kurds. As the Iranian Kurds agitated for independence, this inevitably affected the Kurds living in Iraq who, after receiving arms from their brethren in Iran, rekindled their war against the Ba'athist regime in Iraq. This in turn led to Iraqi bombing of Kurdish border villages in Iran and a sharp deterioration in Iranian-Iraqi relations.[67] Relations between the two states deteriorated further with charges by the Iranian Governor General of Khuzistan that Iraq had smuggled weapons into the region in which most of Iran's ethnic Arabs live. This was followed by an Iraqi crackdown on Shiite religious leaders in Iraq who had maintained close relations with Khomeini,[68] a development which may have precipitated the abortive *coup d'etat* in July 1979. Iran's clash with Iraq also affected its relations with other Arab states. In response to Iraqi demands that Iran return the three Arab islands in the Straits of Hormuz seized by the Shah in 1971, a religious leader close to Khomeini reasserted Iran's claim to Bahrein which the Shah had renounced in 1970.[69]

The rise in Iranian-Iraqi tensions served to split further the camp of the anti-Sadat Arabs, with Kuwait and Bahrein lining up behind Iraq while Libya and the PLO, which had been early supporters of Khomeini, continued to back the Iranians.[70] It also negatively affected Iranian-Soviet relations, already strained by growing anti-Communist sentiment in Iran and by Soviet support for what was perceived in Iran as the anti-Islamic Taraki regime of Afghanistan. Thus a front page editorial in a government-supported Iranian newspaper, the *Islamic Republic*, claimed that "the ruling clique in Iraq" was plotting against Iran both to "prevent the spread of Iran's Islamic revolution into Iraq" and to "open the road to the warm waters of the Persian Gulf to their big master"—a clear reference to the Soviet Union.[71]

In spite of these events, however, Iraqi-Soviet relations did not reach the breaking point. Iraq still proved able to play a role in Soviet strategy when Iraqi objectives coincided with those of the USSR, as in the case of the second Baghdad Conference of late March 1979, which voted sanctions against Egypt for signing the peace treaty with Israel and also condemned the United States for its role in the peace settlement. Nonetheless by June 1979 it was clear that Iraq was no longer a client of the USSR. It could not be counted on for pro-Soviet statements in return for Soviet economic and military aid. While the USSR continued to sell military equipment to Iraq, the Iraqis were also receiving an increasing amount of military equipment from France. (The French sold Iraq

18 Mirage F-1 interceptors and 30 helicopters in 1978[72] and were negotiating a major $2 billion arms deal for aircraft, tanks and other weapons in the summer of 1979.)[73] In addition, Iraq continued to depend heavily on the West for its economic development as it sought to play an increasing role in Arab, regional and world affairs.

The abortive *coup d'etat* of July 1979 in which Syria may have been implicated, served to cool Syrian-Iraqi relations and slow Iraq's quest for leadership in the Arab world. This event, which once again underlines the precarious nature of the ruling elite's hold over the Iraqi government, serves as a useful point to review Soviet-Iraqi relations since the Ba'athists returned to power in 1968.

CONCLUSIONS

In evaluating Soviet policy towards Ba'athist Iraq in the 1968-79 period, one can make several general comments about the success—or the lack thereof—of Soviet policy. In the first place, Soviet influence with the elite ruling Iraq has been shown to be very limited indeed. If one measures influence in terms of the Soviet ability to modify the behavior of a ruling elite, the USSR has been singularly ineffective with the Iraqis on matters of significance to Iraq. Thus the USSR has not been able to alter Iraqi opposition to Soviet-endorsed plans for ending the Arab-Israeli conflict; nor has it been able to prevent mistreatment of the Iraqi Community party. Indeed, only in the period from 1972 to 1975 when Iraq was in greatest need of Soviet help were the Ba'athists willing to make concessions *vis-a-vis* the Communists. Even the concessions that were made, the inclusion of two Communists in cabinet posts and the establishment of a national front with Communist participation, were relatively insignificant ones, since the Ba'athists kept the reins of power firmly in their own hands. In any case, the crackdown on the ICP which began in 1977 effectively eliminated any hopes the USSR might have had that the ICP would have any influence in the Iraqi regime.

In the area of behavior reinforcement, a much lower indicator of intrastate influence, the USSR has had more success. Thus Soviet oil development assistance strengthened the Iraqis in their opposition to the Western-owned oil companies and was a factor in

Iraq's June 1972 decision to nationalize the Iraq Petroleum Company. Similarly, Soviet military aid to Iraq helped it to defeat the Kurds, deter an attack from pro-Western Iran, and build up Iraqi military strength so that it might serve as rival leader of the Arab world to Egypt. Indeed, by aiding the Iraqis in areas where Iraqi interests coincided with those of the USSR, as in the oil nationalization and in Iraq's opposition to Sadat's peace initiative, Moscow has sought to utilize Iraq as a major "anti-imperialist" force in the Middle East in the overall Soviet strategy of weakening and ultimately excluding Western influence from the region.

Unfortunately for Moscow, however, Iraqi and Soviet objectives have not always coincided. Divergences in the approaches of the two countries became increasingly apparent in the period following the Iranian-Iraqi Treaty of 1975 when Iraqi dependence on the USSR diminished. Thus while the USSR had looked to Iraq to be a center of anti-Western activity in the Arab world, Iraq began to develop very close and military ties to France, and reoriented its economy toward the West. In addition, as Iraq began to project itself as the leader of the Arab world, its anti-Communist domestic policy began to take on overtones of an anti-Soviet foreign policy. Finally Iraq's quarrels with the PDRY and Iran and its continued strained relations with the PLO served to weaken what Moscow had hoped would emerge as a solid "anti-imperialist" bloc of Middle Eastern states following the Camp David agreements and the revolution in Iran.

In sum, therefore, the Soviet Union's record of success in its dealings with Iraq is a mixed one. Its economic and military aid have proved useful in establishing ties with the regime, but the value of both instruments of Soviet policy have tended to diminish as Iraq deepened its relationship with France and other Western countries. At the same time the Iraqi Communist party has proven to be a major obstacle in the path of establishing a close relationship between Moscow and Baghdad, since the Iraqi regime tends to see the hand of Moscow behind the activities of the ICP. All in all the course of Iraqi-Soviet relations in the 1968-79 period indicates the low level of Soviet influence over a "client state" that has given relatively little in the way of political obedience in return for a large amount of Soviet economic and military assistance.

ENDNOTES

1. For recent studies of Soviet policy in the Middle East, see Robert O. Freedman, *Soviet Policy Toward the Middle East Since 1970*, second edition, New York: Praeger, 1978; Jon D. Glassman, *Arms for the Arabs: The Soviet Union and War in the Middle East*, Baltimore: Johns Hopkins, 1975; Galia Golan, *Yom Kippur and After: The Soviet Union and the Middle East Crisis*, London: Cambridge University Press, 1977 and Yaacov Ro'i, *From Encroachment to Involvement: A Documentary Study of Soviet Policy in the Middle East*, Jerusalem: Israel Universities Press, 1974. For a general study of possible Soviet objectives in the Middle East, see A.S. Becker and A.L. Horelick, *Soviet Policy in the Middle East*, Santa Monica, California: Rand Publication R-504-FF, 1970. For an Arab viewpoint, see Mohamed Helkal, *The Sphinx and the Commissar*, New York: Harper and Row, 1978.

2. Political science models dealing with the exertion of influence in Soviet foreign policy in general and Soviet foreign policy toward the Middle East in particular are still relatively rare. For a general study of influence, the interested reader is advised to consult J. David Singer's article, "Inter-Nation Influence: A Formal Model," in the influence theory section of *International Politics and Foreign Policy,* ed. by James N. Rosenau, New York: MacMillan, 1969. Singer makes the useful distinction between influence leading to behavior modification in a target state and influence leading to behavior reinforcement. Another useful study, which examines the phenomenon of influence from the perspective of the target state, is Marshall R. Singer, *Weak States in a World of Powers*, New York: Free Press, 1972, especially chapters 6, 7, 8. See also Richard W. Cottam, *Competitive Interference and Twentieth Century Diplomacy*, Pittsburgh: University of Pittsburgh Press, 1967. For an attempt to analyze Soviet influence in the Third World, see *Soviet and Chinese Influence in the Third World,* ed. by Alvin Z. Rubinstein, New York: Praeger, 1975. For an effort to measure Soviet influence In Egypt, see Alvin Z. Rubinstein, *Red Star on the Nile: The Soviet-Egyptian Influence Relationship Since the June War,* Princeton: Princeton University Press, 1977.

3. For studies of Soviet military aid, see Glassman, and George Lenczowski, *Soviet Advances in the Middle East*, Washington: American Enterprise Institute, 1972.

4. For a view of the role of Israel in Soviet Middle East strategy, see Freedman, chapter 8.

5. For a study of Soviet policy toward the Communist parties of the Arab world, see Robert O. Freedman, "The Soviet Union and the Communist Parties of the Arab World: An Uncertain Relationship" in *Soviet Economic and Political Relations with the Developing World,* ed. by Roger E. Kanet and Donna Bahry, New York: Praeger, 1975, pp. 100-134, and John K. Cooley, "The Shifting Sands of Arab Communism," *Problems of Communism*, Vol. 24, No. 2, 1975, pp. 22-42.

6. For an analysis of the Soviet diplomatic difficulties during the Lebanese civil war of 1975-76, see Freedman, chapter 7.

7. For two books which treat the Iraqi Ba'athist regime from very different perspectives, see Edith and E.F. Penrose, *Iraq: International Relations and National Development,* Boulder: Westview Press, 1978 and Majid Khadduri, *Socialist Iraq: A Study in Iraqi Politics,* Washington, DC: Middle East Institute, 1978. The study by the Penroses is highly critical of the Ba'athist regime, while Khadduri's book is so favorable in its treatment as to be almost a panegyric. For a background history on the Ba'ath, see John Devlin, *The Ba'ath Party: A History*

From Its Origins to 1966, Stanford: Hoover Institution, 1976. The role of Iraq's Communist party is extensively treated in Hanna Batatu, *The Old Social Classes and the Revolutionary Movements of Iraq,* Princeton: Princeton University Press, 1978.

8. See Khadduri, pp. 36-38 for a description of the Ba'athist efforts to keep party and state separate.

9. *Ibid.,* p. 7.

10. For an analysis of Soviet policy toward the Persian Gulf at this time, see A. Yodfat and M. Abir, *In the Direction of the Persian Gulf,* London: Frank Cass & Co., 1977, ch. 6.

11. Khadduri, p. 144.

12. See Penrose, chs. 10 and 16.

13. *Ibid.,* pp. 427-428. See also Arthur Klinghoffer, *The Soviet Union and International Oil Politics,* New York: Columbia University Press, 1977.

14. See Freedman, *Soviet Policy Toward the Middle East Since 1970,* p. 34.

15. For a description of these events, see *Ibid.,* pp. 54-60.

16. For an examination of the Iraqi role in the Sudanese events, see Haim Shaked, *et al.,* "The Communist Party in the Sudan 1946-1971," in *The USSR and the Middle East,* ed. by Michael Confino and Shimon Shamir, Jerusalem: Israel Universities Press, 1973, p. 362.

17. Cited in *Middle East Monitor,* Vol. 2, No. 1, January 1, 1972, pp. 2-3.

18. The text of the treaty is in Khadduri, pp. 241-243.

19. Cited in Penrose, p. 409.

20. See I. Bronin, "Arabskaia Neft-Ssha-Zapadnaia Europa," *Mirovaia economika i mezhdunarodyne otnosheniia,* No. 2, February 1972, pp. 31-42.

21. For an analysis of Soviet policy toward the Arab oil weapon, see Robert O. Freedman, "The Soviet Union and the Politics of Middle Eastern Oil," in *Arab Oil: Impact on the Arab Countries and Global Implications,* ed. by Mark Tessler and Naiem Sherbiny, New York: Praeger, 1976, pp. 305-327.

22. *Izvestiia,* July 22, 1972.

23. *Vneshniaia torgovliia SSR za 1974 god,* Moscow: International Relations, 1975, p. 238.

24. Penrose, p. 434.

25. *Ibid.,* p. 435.

26. See Freedman, *Soviet Policy Toward the Middle East Since 1970,* p. 100.

27. *New Times,* No. 28, 1973, p. 17.

28. For an analysis of the impact of Soviet port visits of this type, see Anne M. Kelly, "Port Visits and the Internationalist Mission of the Soviet Navy," *Soviet Naval Influence: Domestic and Foreign Dimensions,* ed. by Michael MccGwire and John McDonnell, New York: Praeger, 1977, pp. 510-529.

29. See *Pravda,* March 14, 1974; April 26, 1974.

30. *Pravda,* on March 27, 1974, stated that Grechko had come for "a detailed discussion of questions relating to the present state and future development of Soviet-Iraqi cooperation in the military and other spheres."

31. *Vneshniaia torgovliia SSR za 1974 god,* p. 14.

32. See *Foreign Trade* (Moscow), No. 10, 1975, pp. 8-14 for a Soviet view of Soviet economic cooperation with Iraq.

33. Khadduri, p. 160.

34. For a study of intra-Arab diplomacy during this period, see Freedman, *Soviet Policy Toward the Middle East Since 1970,* ch. 7.

189

35. *Ibid.*, Khadduri, p. 168.

36. Freedman, *Soviet Policy Toward the Middle East Since 1970*, p. 230.

37. *Ibid.*, pp. 242-245.

38. *Ibid.*, p. 318.

39. See Fulvio Grimaldi, "The PLO-Iraq Conflict," *Middle East*, No. 47, September 1978, pp. 38-39.

40. *Middle East*, July 1978, p. 63; total Iraqi-American trade in 1977 was $592,400,000.

41. See comments by Iraqi Trade Secretary Mahdi al-Ubaidi, *Middle East*, No. 41, March 1978, p. 101.

42. On this point, see David Albright, "The War in the Horn of Africa and the Arab-Israeli Conflict," in *World Politics and the Arab-Israeli Conflict*, ed. by Robert O. Freedman, New York: Pergamon, 1979.

43. See Baqir Ibrahim, "The Masses, The Party and the National Front," *World Marxist Review*, Vol. 19, No. 8, August 1976, pp. 49-56 and Aziz Mohammed, "Tasks of the Revolutionary Forces of Iraq," *World Marxist Review,* Vol. 19, No. 9, September 1976, pp. 10-18.

44. Tewfiq Mishlawi, "Crackdown on Communists in Iraq," *Middle East,* No. 45, July 1978, pp. 29-30.

45. For a list of Iraqi actions against enemies of the regime, see the article by J.P. Smith, *The Washington Post*, August 6, 1978.

46. Cited in *Ibid.*

47. Cited in Mishlawi, p. 30.

48. See *Pravda,* September 10, 1979.

49. *Pravda*, September 23, 1978.

50. Leonid Medvenko, "Middle East: Fictions and Realities," *New Times*, No. 40, 1978, p. 6.

51. A. Stepanov, "Hour of Trial for the Palestinians," *New Times*, No. 41, 1978, p. 7.

52. *Pravda,* October 7, 1978.

53. Radio Moscow (Domestic Service), October 28, 1978 (International Diary Program).

54. For a report on the results of the Baghdad Conference, see Baghdad I.N.A. November 5, 1978, in *Foreign Broadcast Information Service, Daily Report: Middle East and North Africa*, November 6, 1978, pp. A-13 - A-15. See also Amman Ar-Ra'y, in Arabic, November 6, 1978, in *Ibid.*, pp. A-19 - A-20.

55. Radio Moscow (in Arabic to the Arab World), November 6, 1978. Iraq, however, later backed away from the apparent concession of Israel's right to exist.

56. See Reuters report in *Jerusalem Post*, November 24, 1978; AP report in *The New York Times*, November 24, 1978; and the article by Ned Temko, *Christian Science Monitor*, November 30, 1978. See also the broadcast by Radio Kuwait (KUNA) on December 13, 1978 of an *Ar-Ra'y Ai-'am* article challenging the USSR to give more military assistance to Iraq and Syria.

57. AP report from Moscow, *Jerusalem Post*, January 5, 1979.

58. If so, the incident is reminiscent of Moscow's unwillingness to provide Egypt with the weaponry Sadat wanted in 1971 and 1972. There were also reports that following Camp David, the USSR felt it had greater leverage over Iraq and Syria and it could exercise that leverage to obtain improved treatment of the ICP from Iraq and the long-sought friendship and cooperation treaty from Syria. (See the

Western sources mentioned in footnote 56 above).

59. *Pravda*, December 14, 1978.

60. *Tass* in English, December 12, 1978. (*Foreign Broadcast Information Service, Daily Report: Soviet Union*, Vol. III, December 13, 1978, p. F-3).

61. *Pravda*, January 13, 1979.

62. On this point, see Freedman, "The USSR and the Communist Parties of the Arab World."

63. Cited in report by Ned Temko, *Christian Science Monitor*, April 11, 1979.

64. For an analysis of the Soviet role in the PDRY invasion of North Yemen, see Robert O. Freedman, "Soviet Middle East Policy in the Aftermath of Camp David," a paper delivered to the 1979 Annual Meeting of the American Political Science Association, Washington, 1979, pp. 33-36.

65. This incident is discussed in Tewfiq Mishlawi, "Iraq's Foreign Policy Headaches," *The Middle East,* No. 57, July 1979, p. 10.

66. For a discussion of the events in Iran, see Robert O. Freedman, "Iran's Revolution and the Mideast Balance of Power," *Jewish Frontier*, Vol. 46, No. 6, June-July 1979, pp. 4-5; 30.

67. See report in *The Washington Post*, June 15, 1979.

68. Cited in AP report from Teheran, *Baltimore Evening Sun*, June 6, 1979.

69. Cited in report by William Branigin, *The Washington Post*, June 16, 1979.

70. See report by Ned Temko, *Christian Science Monitor,* June 18, 1979.

71. Cited in AP report from Teheran, *The Baltimore Evening Sun*, June 6, 1979.

72. *SIPRI Yearbook, 1979*, London: Taylor & Francis Ltd., 1979, pp. 218-220.

73. See report in *The New York Times*, July 28, 1979 and UPI report in *Jerusalem Post*, August 5, 1979.

191

9

CHANGES IN SOVIET POLICY TOWARD IRAN

Robert G. Irani

The evolution of Soviet foreign policy toward Iran during the reign of Mohammad Reza Shah Pahlavi (1941-78) reflected the changes in the international system, as the Soviet Union and the United States rose from the ashes of World War II to become the two principal centers of power. Before World War II Iran's relations with the USSR reflected British-Soviet rivalry in that country; after the war they were increasingly influenced by American-Soviet rivalry, as the United States began to replace Britain as the principal anchor of Western influence in the Middle East.

Mohammad Reza Pahlavi, following in the footsteps of other Persian monarchs, pursued a cautious, calculated, tactful policy in Iran's relations with the United States and the Soviet Union, in order to ensure Iran's independence and territorial integrity and to maintain himself on the Peacock Throne. Despite the Shah's preference for the United States he sought to pursue a relationship with the two rival superpowers that would provide both the United States and the Soviet Union with a stake in the maintenance of an independent Iran. This effort remained an underlying theme of Iran's foreign policy throughout the rule of the last member of the Pahlavi dynasty.

The purpose of this essay is to interpret the changing dimensions of Soviet foreign policy toward Iran since the outset of the Second World War. Several premises undergird the argument. First, from the perspective of a small nation located contiguous to a superpower, Soviet objectives toward Iran should be viewed in historical context, ranging from the traditional Tsarist and Stalinist policy of aggrandizement at Iran's expense to contemporary detente and good-neighborliness. Second, the inequitable relationship between Moscow and Tehran, reflecting the immense disparity of power between an unpredictable giant and its relatively small neighbor, leads Iran to seek to ensure its survival by aligning itself with another giant, the United States—which at times appears equally unpredictable—in order to try to balance superpower interests. In sum, Iran's location directly below the Soviet Union is a geopolitical reality which has left a deep, permanent impression on Iranian leaders in their efforts to stabilize Tehran's precarious position between Moscow and Washington.

In a global context there are two major interpretations of the ultimate direction of Soviet policy toward Iran and the Persian Gulf area. The first holds that the Soviet Union essentially pursues a defensive objective in this part of the world, aimed at preventing Iran from being used as a base against the Soviet Union. The second interpretation portrays Soviet objectives in an offensive context aimed at weakening Western influence and increasing that of the Soviet Union in the area, in order to dominate or neutralize the countries located directly adjacent to the Soviet Union on the Eurasian landmass and to achieve the historic Tsarist drive for a warm-water port. These two divergent interpretations of Soviet policy are based upon two different sets of value-laden assumptions, difficult to validate or deny. At bottom, however, it is difficult to deny that Soviet leaders probably view Iran and the Persian gulf area as essential elements of their "backyard," and that the Soviets are committed to increase their influence and reduce the influence of their adversaries in this "backyard." In order to accomplish such a long-range goal, the Soviet Union has shifted its tactics from direct, offensive, military, and ideological methods of the Stalinist period to a more subtle posture based on the use of expanded commercial and economic ties in an essentially nonideological, defensive-oriented context.

193

IRAN'S STRATEGIC LOCATION

Iran has been a strategic target for both Tsarist and Soviet Russia, as shown by the occupation of northern Iran during both World War I and World War II.[1] Indeed, during the 19th and 20th centuries, Iran had on several occasions served as a sphere of competitive rivalry and intervention between Great Britain and the Tsarist and later Soviet regimes.

During World War II Iran served as a bridge for Allied victory against Nazi Germany—a critical land-route for the Western Allies, particularly the United States, to supply the Soviet Union with war materiel. Because of Iran's location, Soviet leaders continue to maintain a critical national security interest in preventing it from being used as a bridge to invade the Soviet heartland in any future conflict. Iran has had no choice in selecting the Soviet Union as its powerful, northern neighbor, but it has had to deal with this geographic *fait accompli* as both a beneficiary and a victim of changing Soviet policies and of diverging US-USSR interests in the Middle East. Iran's foreign policy, as a result, tends to reflect the changing international system and the dynamics of US-USSR policies toward Iran and the Persian Gulf area. Iran serves a pawn on the chessboard of superpower rivalry on the periphery of the Eurasian landmass, despite its efforts to pursue an independent foreign policy based on "equidistance" between Moscow and Washington.

Iran's propinquity to the Soviet Union will continue to require the calculated, diligent, and methodical pursuit of a balanced foreign policy by the leaders of the Islamic Republic. It would be naive for such a small nation to assume that the Soviet Union has permanently revised its traditional long-range objective of expanding its influence in the direction of the Persian Gulf, since closed societies and authoritarian, centralized systems such as the Soviet Union tend to maintain their long-range objectives, while allowing for flexible tactics adaptable to the needs of a given situation.

If the US/Allied reliance on Persian Gulf oil continues to expand, so will their interests in defense against potential Soviet actions to deny the West access to this vital, nonreplenishable resource. The Soviet Union and the Warsaw Pact nations will probably also become dependent upon Persian Gulf oil in the

194

1980's, a situation which will further expand Soviet interests in Iran and the Persian Gulf area. In short, Iran's contiguity to the Soviet Union, Soviet ambitions to gain access to the warm waters of the Persian Gulf in order to project Soviet power directly into the Indian Ocean area, and the rising global demand for oil are crucial strategic factors that will continue to ensure Iran's significance in the East-West global equilibrium. Under these circumstances it will be difficult for Iranian leaders to secure their future from potential external intervention, rivalry, and intrigue.

EVOLUTION OF SOVIET POLICY TOWARD IRAN

Soviet policy under Stalin had "a remarkable trait of continuity with that of the old policy of the Tsars."[2] The Tsarist Russian interest to expand southward in the direction of the Persian Gulf was an historic objective of imperial Russia and a continued objective of Soviet Russia during the reign of Stalin. In the contemporary international environment, however, it would be unrealistic to expect the Soviet Union to activate a grand design to march southward to Iran, toward the warm waters of the Persian Gulf and the Arabian Sea as long as relative peace, prosperity, and detente characterize the international environment. In such an international milieu, the Soviet Union can best maximize its gain through commercial, economic ties and military sales with the nations of this area at the expense of the West. However, in a resurging cold war environment—one which may be viewed by Moscow as the precursor of a world war—Soviet military intervention could again occur.

Articles VI and XIII of the Soviet-Iranian Treaty of 1921 were used as an excuse for Soviet military intervention at the onset of the Second World War. Article VI states that:

If a third party should attempt to carry out a policy of usurpation by means of armed intervention in Persia, or if such Power should desire to use Persian territory as a base of operations against Russia, or if a foreign Power should threaten the frontiers of Federal Russia or those of its allies, and if the Perian Government should not be able to put a stop to such menace after having been once called upon to do so by Russia, Russia shall have the right to advance her troops into the Persian interior for the purpose of carrying out the military operations necessary for its defense. Russia undertakes, however, to withdraw her troops from Persian territory as soon as the danger has been removed.[3]

195

Article XIII of this Treaty stipulates that "the Persian Government, for its part, promises not to cede to a third power, or to its subjects, the concessions and property restored to Persia by virtue of the present Treaty, and to maintain those rights for the Persian Nation."[4]

The occupation of northern Iran by the Soviet Union during World War II coupled with Soviet political intrigues, Soviet military interventions, and the Soviet role in the establishment of the Democratic Republic of Azerbaijan and the Republic of Mahabad in northern Iran were the most vivid violations of the spirit of the wartime Allied promises to support Iran's independence and territorial integrity. The ultimate withdrawal of Soviet forces from northern Iran took place because of the tactful diplomacy of Ahmad Ghavam-es-Saltaneh, Iran's Premier, the existence of the newly established United Nations, and the firm, forceful support of Harry S. Truman.

US support was indeed critical in the withdrawal of Soviet troops from northern Iran, and Iranian leaders recognized and appreciated the significance of this support, and they maintained a clearly pro-American foreign policy posture after the Second World War. Thus the Stalinist attempt to incorporate northern Iran into the Soviet orbit and neutralize the rest of Iran failed. The new US policy of containment of the Soviet Union, while it succeeded in stifling Soviet expansion of Iran, marked the dawn of the cold war and a new and dangerous era in the international system.

During the early 1950's, the people of Iran struggled against British domination of Iran's oil industry. The Mossadegh era is the forerunner of rising nationalism which reached its zenith in Iranian history during the Iranian Revolution of 1978-79. In the 1950's the United States misunderstood and underestimated the significance of the nationalist movement in Iran. The Soviets supported the movement insofar as it aimed at reducing American and British influence, but their main instrument was support of the Tudeh (Communist) Party in its attempt to gain control of Iran.

The main organ of the nationalist movement, the National Coalition Front (NCF), was formed in 1950 as a result of the union of four political parties represented in the Parliament. It was led by Dr. Mohammad Mossadegh, designated by the Shah as Iran's Prime Minister. During his premiership the Tudeh Party was the

196

most active political mechanism in Iran, playing a leading role in demonstrations, strikes, and other activities in trade unions and in the oilfields. The alienated, urban youth identified with the Tudeh Party.

The Tudeh Party disguised its pro-Soviet goals under the banner of Iranian nationalism. As a result, Tudeh members successfully penetrated the NCF during the Mossadegh era, tainting the NCF and its image in the West. The pro-Shah elements quickly emphasized this aspect of the NCF and the Mossadegh period, presenting the NCF as a misguided, pro-Communist element—a myth propagated systematically by the pro-Shah factions. This prevented the Shah from recognizing the growing long-range power and potential of the NCF, which would develop into a vital, legitimate, popular, and highly influential segment of the Iranian society in the 1970's. This self-deception and false myth ultimately led to the Shah's ouster from power in 1979.

The Shah left Iran in 1953 but was returned to power within a few days, reportedly with the assistance of the Central Intelligence Agency. After his return to power he suppressed the NCF and jailed or exiled its prominent leaders. The Tudeh Party was outlawed, and with US and Israeli assistance Iran's national secret service (SAVAK) was established in the 1950's.

One of the failures of the Soviet Union in the Middle East has been its inability to build strong Communist parties in the region. The opposition by Middle Eastern leaders to communism as an ideology has been exemplified by the determination of Egypt, Iran, Iraq, and to some extent Syria to maintain a certain distance from the Kremlin. These Mideastern nations opposed the Kremlin's attempts to establish, maintain, and support Communist parties in their countries because, in their view, Communist parties sought to gain power as instruments of Moscow. The inability of the Tudeh Party to gain and retain power in Iran reflects Moscow's larger failure to develop a successful Communist party in the Middle East.

A Tudeh Party conspiracy in Iran's army and air force in 1954, directed by a Soviet military attache, increased the Shah's suspicion of Soviet objectives. Despite this occurrence, however, the Shah was not unreceptive toward a rapprochement with the Soviet Union. The Shah's official visit to Moscow in 1956 led to the signing of a 3-year commercial agreement which made the Soviet

Union, once again, one of Iran's major customers. By 1957, twenty-one percent of Iran's exports were destined for the Soviet Union.[5]

Nevertheless, Iran was in a precarious security position vis-a-vis the Soviet Union, and the Shah chose to align Iran closely with the United States. As a result, the Shah, without hesitation, joined the Western-sponsored alliance known a the Baghdad Pact, later renamed the Central Treaty Organization (CENTO). Thereafter, US-Iranian ties expanded substantially. CENTO was considered a bulwark against international communism in this part of the Middle East. Comprised of Iran, Pakistan, Turkey, and the United Kingdom with active US participation, CENTO served as a major component in the implementation of the Western policy of containment of the Soviet Union. In 1959 the United States and Iran signed a bilateral executive defense agreement to cooperate in promoting the security and defense of CENTO members.[6] By its association with each member of CENTO through separate bilateral executive defense agreements, the United States was successful in building a "chain of friendship" between Iran, Pakistan, and Turkey. US participation in CENTO expanded significantly.[7]

Prior to signing the 1959 bilateral defense agreement with the United States, the Shah had rejected a Soviet proposal to sign a treaty of friendship and nonaggression. By signing the defense agreement with the principal adversary of the Soviet Union, the Shah provoked bitter Soviet attacks. He was depicted as a US puppet, a lackey of Western imperialism, and a traitor to Islam. Iranian Communists in exile in East Germany broadcasted inflammatory criticism of the Shah.[8]

As a close friend of Moscow's, Egypt's Nasser also launched a campaign against the Shah which in 1960 resulted in the rupture of diplomatic relations between Egypt and Iran. But this psychological war waged by Moscow and Egypt against the Shah proved to be short-lived. It ended in late 1960 in the exchange of a series of notes between the Shah and Khrushchev in which the Shah expressed his desire to maintain friendly relations with the Soviet Union, provided that such relations were based on mutual respect. The Shah, however, turned aside Soviet objections to Iran's defense ties with the United States. Finally Khrushchev realized that such objections were futile. The Soviet Union relented and a rapprochement was eventually reached that respected the Shah's perceived needs for Iran's defense ties with the United States.

The turning point in Soviet-Iranian relations came in September 1962, when the Shah gave Moscow assurance that his government would not permit the establishment of any foreign military base in Iran. As one author points out "even before the Cuban missile crisis, Iran had already moved to improve relations with the Soviet Union. In fact, the Iranian negotiating team was in Moscow during the crisis."[9] For the Soviets, these assurances from the Shah removed the last barriers toward good relations with Iran. Soviet commentators began to praise the Shah's land reforms which they had previously criticized.[10]

During Soviet President Brezhnev's official visit to Tehran in November 1963, several agreements were signed covering transit, economic and technical assistance, and the joint utilization of the resources adjacent to the rivers bordering Iran and the Soviet Union (Atrak and Aras). A joint cultural society was also established in both Moscow and Tehran. Moreover, several East European nations extended credit to Iran, which eventually resulted in a huge trade flow among Iran, the Soviet Union, and Eastern Europe.[11]

Perception of the vulnerability of his throne, major domestic economic problems in Iran, and Soviet pressure were the principal factors which in the early 1960's forced the Shah to improve Iran's ties with the Soviet Union. The Shah had introduced a land reform program, and his so-called "White Revolution" amounted to authoritarian, subjective changes dictated by him. He had suspended the Parliament, and the Iranian government faced a severe financial crisis which required drastic economic cuts. While the Soviet Union pressured the Shah against allowing the use of Iran as a US base, the United States pressed the Shah to improve Iran's standard of living and improve the lot of its people. The Shah of Iran stood on shaky ground. The arbitrary implementation of his land reform ended with the alienation of Shia Islamic leaders and the exile from Iran in 1963 of Ayatollah Rouhallah Khomeini, one of the staunch anti-land reform, anti-Shah leaders. This was the political phenomenon which germinated the seed of the destruction of the Pahlavi dynasty.

Domestic pressures and the opposition to the Shah and his programs from Iran's religious factions, the traditional landed

199

aristocracy, the rising middle class, the students, and the merchants were enormous internal pressures on the Shah in the 1960's. Instead of meeting these domestic needs the Shah focused his attention on external affairs such as seeking to improve Iran's relations with the Soviet Union, which had criticized the Shah and his program. The Shah wanted to reduce external pressures on his throne, because he perceived that satisfying the United States and the Soviet Union were of greater significance in insuring the survival of the Pahlavi dynasty than domestic consensus and support. This was a misperception which was to haunt him in 1978.

The "thaw" between the United States and the Soviet Union in the 1960's signaled changes in relations between the Soviet Union and its neighbors such as Iran, in the broader framework of the end of the cold war and the demise of the myth of a monolithic international communism centered in Moscow. The schism between Moscow and Peking surfaced and shattered the perceived monolithic threat which served as the basis for Western threat perception consensus.

These drastic changes in the global environment served the mutual advantage of Tehran and Moscow in expanding their commercial and economic ties. The Shah's visit to the Soviet Union in 1965 was a clear indicator of improved Iran-Soviet relations and the "thaw" in the international system. Soviet leaders expressed to the Shah their interest in the maintenance of world peace, reduction of tension, and expansion of cooperation. The joint communique issued by the Soviet and Iranian governments in Moscow after the Shah's visit expressed their mutual interest in expanding economic and commercial ties.[12]

The Shah also visited Bulgaria, Hungary, Poland, Rumania, and Yugoslavia. He was praised throughout Eastern Europe. For example, according to the Sofia Communique, the people of Bulgaria had the "highest praise for the initiatives of His Imperial Majesty the Shah in his campaign against illiteracy." The Poles praised the Shah for his "progressive foreign policy" and expressed their recognition of Iran's "progress." Meanwhile, the Tudeh Party members in exile in Eastern Europe criticized the Eastern European governments for such "excesses" in praising a ruler whom they considered "a reactionary monarch hated by his people."[13]

During the 1960's the Soviet Union, in return for a long-term sale of Iranian natural gas at extremely favorable terms, assisted Iran in its industrialization drive by building its first steel mill and by constructing its first machine tool industries. The Soviets expanded Iran's railroads, developed some of its coal mines, constructed two hydroelectric projects on the Aras River, built the Mugham Dam and a hydroelectric complex, and laid its first natural gas pipeline across the rugged Iranian plateau to the Soviet Union. The Iranian natural gas pipeline began in the borough of Bid-e-Boland in the oil-rich, southwestern province of Khuzestan and connected almost 700 miles to the north with the city of Astara, USSR. A second Iranian natural gas pipeline to the Soviet Union, planned during the Shah's regime, would traverse over 840 miles, and could have provided the Soviet Union with 2.26 billion cubic feet of gas daily;[14] however, disagreements over the price of natural gas may result in its permanent cancellation. According to the agreement pertaining to the construction of the second gas pipeline, the Soviet Union would supply Austria, Czechoslovakia, France, and West Germany the same amount of gas Iran supplied to the Soviet Union. Iran would, however, be reimbursed directly for its natural gas in hard currency by the Europeans, and the Soviets would collect transit fees for gas delivered to Europe.[15] The price of gas set under the second pipeline agreement is $1.25 per cubic foot, which is higher than the price the Soviets pay Iran under the first pipeline,[16] but it is still much lower than the relative rise in cost of other sources of energy.

Trade between Iran and the Soviet Union grew substantially in the late 1960's, more than doubling between 1965 and 1969. In July 1966 Tehran announced that it was considering the purchase of surface-to-air missiles from the Soviet Union because Iran's oil installations at the northern mouth of the Persian Gulf, particularly at Kharg Island, were vulnerable to Iraqi forces equipped with Soviet weapons. The Soviet Union failed to express any enthusiasm regarding Iran's announcement, and Tehran turned to Washington for such weapons.[17]

The Shah, during the remaining period of his rule, concentrated his attention on ambitious, extravagant plans to make Iran the self-proclaimed policeman of the Persian Gulf area, particularly after the British announced their plan to withdraw the bulk of their forces from the Persian Gulf in 1969. US-Iranian foreign policy objectives converged on most major bilateral, regional, and international issues. For its part, the Soviet Union essentially viewed the Shah in positive and pragmatic terms, and the Shah tried hard to keep both superpowers content in their relations with Iran. In return, both Moscow and Washington supported the Shah and paid tributes to him for his leadership in modernizing Iran.

The Shah neglected the basic needs of the Iranian people and focused his attention on grand military projects aimed at fulfilling his personal vision of Persia's role in history. Thus it is ironic that the Soviet leadership praised the Shah, ignoring the fact that he was a Western-oriented, pro-American dictator who had outlawed the only Communist party in Iran, and who continued to exile and jail Communists and their sympathizers in Iran. Yet by the early 1970's the Soviets referred to their borders with Iran as "the frontiers of peace and good neighborliness."[18]

From the mid-1960's to the mid-1970's, the Soviet Union managed to become one of Iran's top trading partners. Soviet investments in Iran became one of "the largest undertakings by that country anywhere in the world."[19] By assisting Iran in its industrialization the Soviet Union improved Iranian-Soviet relations to a considerable extent. The Soviets pursued a responsible, pragmatic, nonideological policy toward Iran—a policy aimed at improved relations with a neighboring country.

In October 1972 a long-term economic agreement, expected to quadruple Soviet-Iranian trade within 5 years, was signed by the Shah during his visit to Moscow. In early 1973 Kosygin visited the Shah in Tehran and the two leaders announced their "firm conviction" that questions pertaining to the Persian Gulf area should be resolved without interference by external powers.[20]

Increasingly, however, the Shah's extravagant arms purchases annoyed Iraq and its Soviet patron. More frequent expressions of displeasure emanated from the Soviet Union after the October 1973 War. Kosygin's statement during his 1974 visit to Tehran, warning the Shah that "the policy of dealing from a position of strength and its associated arms race have been a heavy burden on the peoples that began to pursue such a policy but that have not become stronger as a result,"[21] was probably intended as support for Iraq. Meanwhile the Congress and the academic community in the United States was expressing a deep concern over the Shah's arms buildup and his failure to deal with serious socioeconomic problems in Iran.[22]

The Soviet effort to create a collective security system in South Asia failed to receive the support of the Shah, despite some nodding acquiescence by Iran's Premier Amir Abbas Hoveyda, as an indication of possible support for the Soviet efforts. For the most part, the Shah continued to perceive Soviet objectives in South Asia in expansionist terms, and he welcomed the inclusion of the PRC in South Asian affairs as a constructive, stabilizing force.

THE IRANIAN REVOLUTION OF 1978-79
AND THE SOVIET UNION

The full extent of the actual Soviet involvement in Iran, covert or overt, during the 1978-79 upheavals, remains unclear. At the present time there is little evidence available to indicate an overt, direct Soviet involvement in instigating the upheavals in Iran, despite assertions to the contrary by pro-Shah elements inside and outside Iran. However, the Soviet Union has contributed and will continue to contribute to the upheavals in Iran, and it will be prepared to lend assistance if and when the opportunity arises for the creation of a revolutionary, anti-Western, pro-Soviet regime in Iran.

During the first phase of the revolution, prior to the designation of Shahpour Bakhtiar as Iran's Premier, official Soviet pronouncements were supportive of the Shah. According to CIA Director Stansfield Turner, Soviet intelligence services felt that Iran's "bubbles of discontent would be kept under control."[23] As Mr. Turner points out, the Soviet Union took a public anti-Shah stance only after it was clear that the Shah would lose the battle against Iran's fervent nationalists. Furthermore, Soviet leaders carefully watched US responses toward the Shah and were probably uncertain of the extent of US support for the Shah. This uncertainty may have triggered Brezhnev's November 1978 statement in which he clearly depicted the arrival of foreign troops in Iran as "menacing Soviet security" in accordance with Article VI of the 1921 Soviet-Iranian Treaty.[24] In response to Brezhnev's statement, President Carter asserted that the United States had "no intention of interfering in the internal affairs of Iran," and that it had "no intention of permitting others to interfere in the internal affairs of Iran."[25] He added that Iran's upheavals had been "exacerbated by uncontrolled statements made from foreign nations that encourage bloodbaths and violence,''[26] a statement which was aimed at clandestine propaganda beamed into Iran against both the Shah and the United States from the Soviet Union. One station, known as "The National Voice of Iran," reportedly located in Baku, stated in January 1979 that: "Now that the Shah has gone, it is the turn of the Americans. US imperialism should be kicked out of the country and to hell."[27]

In late January 1979, *Pravda* itself stated that the Shah's fate should be a warning to other countries which cooperate with the United States. By this time *Pravda* was supporting Ayatollah Khomeini because, it said, the ayatollahs were opposed to the Shah's tyranny.[28] Pro-Soviet groups in Iran were by now very active in the effort to sweep away the remnants of the Shah's regime. Iran's Communists supported Khomeini's victory, as *Pravda* indicated, as "only the first step on the road to final popular victory."[29] In late January 1979 a group of 5,000 to 10,000 Marxists and other leftists marched through Tehran. One Marxist group, in a letter to Ayatollah Khomeini, warned Iran's leader and his followers against any "attempt to monopolize the revolution as a pretext to revive the Inquisition," and opposed the institution of a single party system in Iran.[30]

The Tudeh Party and other radical groups were highly influential in Iran's oilfields. According to the Department of State, the Tudeh Party itself had about 2,000 members in Iran, nearly half of whom worked in the oilfields. Marxist groups in general, however, were estimated to have up to 20,000 members and "sympathizers" in Iran. In addition to the Tudeh, the Iranian oilfields were also infiltrated by two other Marxist groups: the "People's Sacrifice Guerrillas" and the "People's Strugglers." They were, according to US intelligence analysts, "very small, but well-disciplined and well-organized."

The Fedayeen Khalgh, another small, highly effective, extremely well-organized, and armed group of Communists actively participated in the Iranian Revolution in 1978-1979. However, unlike the Tudeh Party, the Fedayeen Khalgh continues to retain its independence from the Soviet Union and aspires to institute a national version of communism in Iran.

The Soviet Union recognized Ayatollah Khomeini's Islamic Republic on February 12, 1979, expressing Soviet readiness to develop a relationship based on "equality, good neighborliness,

204

and respect for national sovereignty and noninterference in each other's internal affairs."[31] Prior to the Soviet Union's recognition of the new regime, Yasir Arafat had reportedly conveyed to the Soviet leaders Ayatollah Khomeini's assurances that the Islamic Republic of Iran would expand its commercial and economic ties with the Soviet Union.[32] The validity of this report, however, remains to be seen, because the leadership of the Islamic Republic has systematically criticized the Shah for "knuckling under the pressures of the big powers and sacrificing the country's interests."[33] In July 1979 these charges against the Shah were reiterated after the Islamic Republic cancelled the rest of the second gas pipeline project which would have exported Iranian natural gas to the Soviet Union in place of Soviet gas destined for some of the European countries.[34] The Islamic Republic appeared to be interested in expanding its economic ties with the Soviet Union only so long as such expansion was equitable and in Iran's national interests.

The Islamic Republic of Iran appears to be committed to reduce the potential for exploitation of Iran by any external power, and to a policy of "equidistance" between both Moscow and Washington. The withdrawal of Iran from the Central Treaty Organization and Iran's unilateral pronouncements to revoke both its 1959 defense agreement with the United States, and Article VI of the 1921 Soviet-Iranian Treaty simultaneously, indicate the Islamic Republic's dedication to this policy. The leaders of the Islamic Republic are quite aware of Iran's strategic location in a zone of potential superpower conflict, and that is precisely why they prefer to follow a "nonaligned" foreign policy posture.

The ouster of the Shah has ensured Iran's withdrawal from the Western orbit, a development which must please Moscow. The severance of Iran's ties with Israel and South Africa, the stoppage of Iran's oil shipments to those two countries, and the Islamic Republic's explicit announcement of support for the Palestine Liberation Organization also probably pleased Moscow— particularly since these moves were coupled with substantial increases in the price of oil and with the closure of US intelligence networks in northern Iran that closely watched Soviet military activities.[35] In this broad context, the establishment of a revolutionary Islamic republic in Iran could be interpreted as a benefit to the Soviet Union, because it upsets the pro-Western balance in the Persian Gulf and the Arabian Peninsula.

In the long run, however, the Islamic Republic of Iran essentially faces the same foreign policy and defense challenges which were faced by the Pahlavi regime. Iran—located in a zone of potential superpower conflict, between two severe regional conflicts (Arab-Israeli and the Indo-Pakistani), and torn by various separatist movements (Kurds and Arabs on its Western front, Baluch and Turkomans on its northern and eastern frontiers)—can ill afford to neglect its foreign, defense, and military sectors.

In the immediate period ahead, while the Islamic Republic is attempting to consolidate its rule, both the United States and the Soviet Union will probably avoid any direct activities in Iran. Both superpowers would be well advised to keep a low profile in Iran until the sandstorms of the Iranian Revolution settle down. Both the United States and the Soviet Union probably realize that such interference could have negative repercussions in their long-range relations with Iran.

CONCLUDING REMARKS

Soviet successes and failures in Iran during the reign of, Mohammad Reza Pahlavi illustrate broader changes in Soviet policy from overt expansionism to more subtle efforts at domination under the guise of ''good neighborly relations.''

The Soviet Union, despite several attempts since 1921, failed to establish by external force a permanent Soviet-style republic inside Iran. Although these attempts resulted in the creation of several short-lived republics in northern Iran, in each case Moscow retreated under pressure from other external powers interested in Iran.

A designed, aggressive, offensive Soviet policy in the Persian Gulf area has probably been shelved for the present time. However, rising Soviet demands for oil coupled with growing East European dependence on the Soviet Union and the Middle East for oil probably will tempt the Soviet Union to take more direct measures to expand its influence in the Persian Gulf area. Nevertheless, the complex, tangled regional political dynamics of the Persian Gulf area will likely prevent either the Soviet Union or the United States from achieving a successful prolonged domination of this area to the exclusion of the other. The level of Soviet or American

206

influence in individual countries of the Persian Gulf area will continue to vary, reflecting the changes in the international and regional system and the dynamics of US-Soviet relations. In this context, for example, Saudi Arabia may establish diplomatic relations with the Soviet Union in the 1980's, and Iran will probably pursue a "nonaligned" policy in its dealings with both Moscow and Washington, while Iraq may pull further away from Moscow.

In any event, Soviet prospects for dismembering or dominating Iran appear dim. Any direct offensive attempt by the Soviet Union against Iran could lead to the resurgence of a high tension between the United States and the Soviet Union and perhaps even to another world war. Should such a war come, Iran once again, would likely become a crossroad or battleground for opposing superpowers and a bridge for defeat or victory of the Soviet Union. In both war and peace, Iran is a geostrategic reality of considerable importance to both Moscow and Washington, and an object of superpower rivalry which may yet again bring deep suffering upon the people of Iran.

ENDNOTES

1. See Ivar Spector, *The Soviet Union and the Muslim World, 1917-1958*, Seattle: University of Washington Press, 1959, p. 85.

2. *Ibid*.

3. *Ibid*, p. 94.

4. *Ibid*.

5. Walter Laqueur, *The Struggle for the Middle East: The Soviet Union in the Mediterranean, 1958-1968*, New York: Macmillan, 1969, p. 45.

6. Department of State, *American Foreign Policy, Current Documents, 1959*, Washington: US Government Printing Office, 1963, p. 1060.

7. *Ibid*. For an anaylsis of the US policy toward Iran, see Robert Ghobad Irani, "US Strategic Interests in Iran and Saudi Arabia," *Parameters,* Fall 1977, republished in *DoD Current Digest*, 1978.

8. Laqueur, p. 46.

9. Abbas Amirie, "Iran's Foreign Policy Posture Toward the Persian Gulf and the Indian Ocean," paper presented at the Second New Zealand Conference on Asian Studies at Christchurch, New Zealand, May 14, 1977, p. 1.

10. Laqueur, p. 49.

11. *Ibid*., pp. 46-47.

12. Department of State, *American Foreign Policy, Current Documents, 1965*, Washington: US Government Printing Office, 1968, p. 611.

13. Laqueur, p. 52.

14. "Iran Lifts Gas Export to Soviet: 12 Other Buyers Sign Oil Pact," *The New York Times*, April 26, 1979, p. 4.

15. "Gas Pipeline is Cancelled by Iran: Project Was to Supply Soviet and 4 Other Lands," *The New York Times*, July 19, 1979, pp. 1 and 5.

16. *Ibid*. The Soviet Union is the major purchaser of Iran's natural gas; however, Iran's natural gas is not of critical significance to the Soviet Union, as was proven during the 1978-79 upheavals in Iran, when the flow of Iranian gas to the Soviet Union was interrupted.

17. Laqueur, p. 58.

18. Amirie, p. 3.

19. *Ibid*.

20. Quoted from *Izvestiia*, November 29, 1974, by Robert H. Donaldson, "Soviet Policy in South Asia: Aspirations and Limitations," in *Soviet Economic and Political Relations with the Developing World*, ed. by Roger E. Kanet and Donna Bahry, New York: Praeger, 1965, pp. 222-23.

21. Robert H. Donaldson, "Soviet Policy in South Asia: Aspirations and Limitations," in *Soviet Economic and Political Relations with the Developing World*, ed. by Roger E. Kanet and Donna Bahry, p.223.

22. Dale R. Tahtinen, *Arms in the Persian Gulf*, Washington, DC: American Enterprise Institute, 1974; Shahram Chubin, "Iran's Foreign Policy and Defense Perspective," paper delivered at the Institute for International Political and Economic Studies and Stanford Research Institute (IIPES/SRI) Symposium on "Iran in 1980's" in Washington, DC, October 4-6, 1977.

23. Warren Brown, "CIA Didn't Forsee National Revolt in Iran, Chief Says," *The Washington Post*, February 5, 1979, p. A5.

24. "Iran: A Protracted Struggle Ahead," *An-Nahar: Arab Report & Memo,* Vol. 2, December 11, 1978, p. 5.

25. Richard Burt, "200 American Workers Departing; U.S. Weighs Sending Ships to Area: Many Contingency Plans," *The New York Times*, December 29, 1978, pp. 1 and 4.

26. *Ibid*.

27. "Iranian Aides Believe That Soviet Is Root of Anti-U.S. Broadcasts," *The New York Times*, January 31, 1979, p. 4.

28. "Pravda Says Iran Proves U.S. Cannot Be Trusted," *The New York Times*, January 22, 1979, p. 9.

29. Craig R. Whitney, "Superpowers Getting Testier," *The New York Times*, February 22, 1979, p. 7.

30. R.W. Apple, Jr., "New Anti-American Wave Spreads in Iran," *The New York Times*, January 22, 1979, p. 8.

31. Craig R. Whitney, "Russians Recognize New Regime in Iran," *The New York Times*, February 13, 1979, p. 9.

32. Quoted in "Ayatollah and The Soviet Union," *The New York Times*, February 20, 1979, p. 4.

33. "Gas Pipeline Is Cancelled By Iran; Project Was to Supply Soviet and 4 Other Lands," *The New York Times*, July 19, 1979, pp. 1 and 5.

34. *Ibid*.

35. For an analysis of the Iranian upheavals, see Robert Ghobad Irani, "The Iranian Revolution of 1978-79: Potential Implications for Major Countries in the Area," paper delivered at the annual Security Issues Symposium, US Army War College, 1979.

10

GAUGING SOVIET SUCCESS
IN AFRICA AND THE MIDDLE EAST:
A COMMENTARY

David E. Albright

The purpose of this commentary is to offer a brief synthetic overview of Soviet successes and failures in Africa and the Middle East. At the outset, I should note that such an undertaking is complicated by two factors. First, we are dealing in this section with two specific areas, rather than one. Although the USSR's experiences in the two areas have many commonalities, they are not totally identical. Perhaps most important, heavy Soviet involvement began far earlier in the Middle East than it did in Africa. As a consequence, there has been a much longer time frame in which Moscow has had a chance to suffer major setbacks in the former than in the latter. Second, as the contributions to this symposium amply illustrate, criteria for evaluation of the success or failure of Soviet ventures can vary widely. Some observers, for example, see the growth of Soviet presence as the key gauge of the USSR's success; others hold that presence does not equate with influence and that any effort to assess Soviet successes and failures ought to focus on influence.

To cope with these problems, I have opted to structure my remarks in a particular way. Since Moscow has had relatively fewer opportunities to encounter severe reverses in Africa, this area

210

tends to reflect the upper limits of Soviet accomplishments to date; therefore, I will concentrate on Africa and use the Middle East as a comparative referent. I hasten to add, however, that the broad thrust of my observations applies to both regions. As for criteria for appraising Soviet success or failure, I propose to advance a set of my own. It seems to me that the criteria implicit or explicit in the papers covering Africa and the Middle East are not totally adequate to probe the topic in all its complexity. Others may, of course, disagree with this judgment, but at least the basis for my own analysis will be clear.

With these points in mind, let us turn, then, to the fundamental topic at hand. I would submit that any attempt to weigh the success or failure of the USSR in Africa and the Middle East must consider two distinct dimensions of the question. For convenience's sake, one might label these the subjective and objective dimensions. The first takes Moscow's perspective as its central concern. That is, it views success or failure in terms of essentially Soviet standards. The second adopts third-party standards as measures of success or failure. Such standards may not be wholly free of adversary overtones, but they are "objective" in the sense that they are not tied to the outlooks of either the USSR or the states of Africa and the Middle East.

In approaching the subjective aspect of the issue, it is essential to remember that the key to the Soviet leadership's conclusions about success or failure lies in the degree to which the USSR has achieved its goals. But since Moscow rarely, if ever, states its ends openly, its purposes by and large have to be inferred from the USSR's behavior, and arriving at such inferences is far from a simple, straightforward job. Indeed, Soviet policy at any given time or in any given instance may prove an inadequate guide to Soviet objectives, for some crucial variables stand between these objectives and actual policy outcomes.

Whatever Moscow's goals may be, for example, it must pursue these in the context of the opportunities available. Out of the interaction between goals and opportunities emerges a policy that the Soviet leadership wants to carry out. The policy outcomes that one can see, however, also depend upon how effectively the USSR implements the chosen policy. Selection of inappropriate means or poor follow-through can result in policy outcomes quite different from the intended ones.

211

Despite this analytical difficulty, I believe that it is possible to discern four ends to which the USSR has had long-standing commitment in Africa. These include establishing a lasting presence on the continent; gaining a voice in African affairs; undermining Western influence on the continent; and, preventing China from expanding its influence in Africa and reducing that influence whenever possible.

During the 1970's, the USSR has made significant strides toward the attainment of these goals, and Moscow has clearly recognized that fact. At the same time, its feelings of success have been tempered by a combination of factors. To begin with, it looks at its recent advances against the backdrop of its rather consistent pattern of failure in the past. Perhaps the best indication of its acute awareness of this pattern of failure has been the shifting Soviet emphasis with regard to means over the last three decades. [1]

From the earliest days of Soviet interest in Africa in the 1920's until the mid-1950's, Moscow sought to build up ties with the continent and conversely to diminish the roles of other outside powers there through ideological means. That is, it attempted to identify the USSR with the rising tide of African nationalism and to convince Africans that they and the Soviets were engaged in a common struggle against Western imperialism. It also encouraged Africans to establish organizations patterned on the Soviet party to wage this struggle.

By the mid-1950's, when the floodgates of African independence began to open, however, Moscow had remarkably few links to the continent to show for these efforts. As a consequence, it adopted during the period from the mid-1950's to the mid-1960's a new approach to furthering its purposes in Africa. While Soviet commentators continued to talk a lot about ideology, they did so largely in a "relativistic" sense, endeavoring to adapt their ideological perspectives to fit reality. The main basis upon which the USSR tried to find common ground with African states was a combination of aid (chiefly economic, although there was often a military component as well) and the Soviet model of development. Moscow argued that the only way that African countries could achieve genuine independence lay in freeing themselves from the economic fetters that still bound them to the imperialist world, and it claimed that embrace of the Soviet model of development and acceptance of the "disinterested" aid of the Soviet bloc (which by the early 1960's, in the Soviet leadership's eyes, no longer included

212

China) offered the sole viable method of accomplishing this end.

For a time, the USSR did register some gains in states like Ghana, Mali, Guinea, Algeria, and the United Arab Republic, but by the mid-1960's military coups, local conservative trends, or Soviet diplomatic clumsiness had wiped out many of these gains. Moreover, with the mounting signs of troubles in the Soviet economy, the Soviet model of development had decreasing appeal for Africans. Therefore, Moscow again felt compelled to alter the primary means it employed for pursuing its objectives. From the mid-1960's into the early 1970's, the USSR attempted to insulate itself from the buffeting of rapid political change in Africa by creating an international division of labor with at least some nations on the continent. Such a mutually beneficial relationship, Soviet leaders believed, would provide an incentive for long-term cooperation and thus prevent the USSR from suffering adversities whenever a friendly government fell or whenever a capricious ruler decided to shift either his domestic or his international course.

Yet, by the mid-1970's this method of promoting Soviet goals had lost a good deal of its original merit from Moscow's standpoint, for it had become increasingly apparent that the creation of a meaningful division of labor with most African countries would probably require decades, in light of the nature of their existing economies. Hence, the West was likely to retain a predominant economic position on the continent for some time to come. Confronted with this reality, the Soviet leadership came to look with high favor on military means for advancing its ends— especially since the rising level of conflict on the continent was sending African forces of all hues in search of military support. While Moscow has in the intervening years stressed military assistance rather than direct military involvement, it has not precluded the latter, as its behavior in the 1975-76 Angolan civil war and the 1977-78 Ethiopian crisis demonstrated.

In addition to being conscious of its past failures, Moscow appears to entertain the possibility that its recent advances in Africa may turn out to be fleeting in character. Soviet analysts, for instance, maintain that "even in the progressive states, the working class is but a rather small proportion of the population and their national leadership has to be formed of representatives of the revolutionary-minded petty bourgeoisie, which is typical of predominantly peasant countries." They go on to argue that while the "bourgeois nationalism" of such leaders can have a "positive

213

role," it can also lose its "democratic ambitions" and "play into the hands of imperialism." By way of illustration, they cite the case of Somalia.[2] From their commentaries, however, it is also clear that they have not forgotten the reverses that they encountered in the 1960's in African countries such as Ghana and Mali. Nor are they unmindful of the ups and downs in their position in the Middle East over the last quarter century. Indeed, they rail particularly at developments in Egypt since the death of Gamal Abdel Nassar in 1970.

In short, then, the Soviets tend to look at their record in Africa with quite mixed judgments. While they view their gains on the continent in the 1970's with satisfaction and hope, they know that they have experienced losses in the past, and they seem to fear that the same thing could happen again. Indeed, as long as the continent remains in the state of flux which has prevailed in the two decades of independence, that uneasiness is likely to endure.

When we come to the "objective" aspects of the question, it appears that there are two defensible measures that one can employ, but these two lead to somewhat different judgments about Soviet successes or failures. The first measure is influence. Using this yardstick, one would have to say that while Moscow has managed to reinforce the willingness of African states and liberation movements to do things that they were already inclined to do, it has been singularly ineffective in persuading them to do things which they have had no disposition to do. Somalia affords a classic case in point. The Mogadiscio government was perfectly prepared to grant the USSR access to naval facilities at Berbera and to air facilities at several places in the country in return for Soviet arms and military advisors, but it balked completely when Moscow tried to get it to abandon its claims to the Ogaden and form a Marxist federation with Ethiopia.

The second standard is the effectiveness of coalition building. This yardstick assumes two things: (1) there is rarely, if ever, a complete identity of interests and outlooks among states; and, (2) the name of the game is to identify convergences of interest and to form alliances, however temporary, based on these interests in order to further one's own ends. If we look at Soviet activities in Africa in such a light, these activities seem fairly successful. Although the USSR's relations with individual countries have waxed and waned as interests have converged and diverged, the Soviet role on the continent has by and large increased over the years. Perhaps even more significant, Moscow has managed to find substantial support for a wide range of its own foreign policy positions. This backing has proved of some consequence in forums such as the UN General Assembly and has added to Soviet confidence in the global arena.

The merits of these two criteria vary, I would contend, depending upon the overall context of world politics. "Influence" may be more relevant when a high degree of bipolarity characterizes global politics, for an examination of influence can provide insights into the extent to which the USSR has managed to make other states dependent upon itself. "Coalition building," in contrast, may be more meaningful in periods when multipolarity prevails in world politics. In such cases, the major powers may sometimes seek to create forms of dependency, but the dominant fashion in which they advance their causes is by pinpointing common interests with other nations and working out alliances, however fleeting, to pursue these mutual interests. Hence, the degree to which the USSR has been able to build coalitions of some sort with other states may constitute the most important gauge of its success or failure.

What I have attempted to suggest, in sum, is that any serious effort to evaluate the USSR's success or failure in Africa and the Middle East is, perforce, a complex undertaking. It does not yield simple, either/or conclusions. Moreover, the precise mix of success and failure may differ according to the particular perspective from which one approaches the assessment.

ENDNOTES

1. For more detailed discussion, see my "The Soviet Role in Africa from Moscow's Perspective," in *The Communist State and Africa,* ed. by David E. Albright and Jiri Valenta, Bloomington, Indiana: Indiana University Press, forthcoming.

2. The quotations come specifically from V. Kudryavtsev, "Africa Fights for Its Future," *International Affairs* (Moscow), No. 5, May 1978, p. 30.

PART 3
THE SOVIET UNION IN ASIA

11

THE SOVIET UNION IN AFGHANISTAN: BENEFITS AND COSTS

Shirin Tahir-Kheli

Russian interest in Afghanistan goes back to the Tsarist times. The small landlocked and backward country was then a buffer zone between two empires and it was keenly aware of its powerful northern neighbor. By virtue of its size and common border, the USSR has held an important place in Afghan foreign policy, even though the intensity of Moscow's relations with Kabul has varied. This essay will examine Soviet objectives in Afghanistan and gauge Soviet success in achieving these objectives and the cost that is involved.

SOVIET OBJECTIVES

Afghanistan did not in the 1950's become a party to the anti-Soviet alliances which were joined by its neighbors, Iran and Pakistan. One of the main objectives has been to continue to keep Afghanistan out of the western orbit. As expressed by the then President Podgorny at the conclusion of a visit to Afghanistan in June 1967, the Soviet Union had "high evaluation of Afghanistan's foreign policy, which is based on principles of positive neutrality, nonparticipation in blocs and military groupings. . ."[1]

A second objective of Soviet policy has been to use its relationship with Afghanistan to create difficulties for Pakistan, a US ally and one-time base for spying operations against the Soviet Union. Tacit support from the USSR was important in Afghanistan's decision in December 1953 to repudiate the 1921 treaty in which Afghanistan had recognized the Durand Line as the international boundary between Afghanistan and what was then British India. The same year, the Afghan premier declared that American military aid to Pakistan constituted a threat, a view that was shared in Moscow. And when Kabul articulated its support for Pakhtoonistan,[2] Moscow announced and repeatedly confirmed its support of the Afghan moves.[3]

The anti-Pakistan policies of Afghanistan elicited strong Soviet support in the diplomatic crises which on two occasions led to diplomatic breaks between Pakistan and Afghanistan. Nor has the Soviet objective in playing up the nuisance value of Afghanistan for Pakistan always been subtle. To this day, Moscow presses on Islamabad the need for strong Soviet-Pakistani relations as the only real guarantor of improved Pakistan-Afghan relations and of a peaceful northern border for Pakistan.

The third Soviet objective in Afghanistan is to demonstrate its "good neighborly" policies. The Soviets have repeatedly emphasized a policy termed by Khrushchev in 1960 as never having "a friendly neighbor alone in her needs."[4] Soviet aid to Afghanistan was part of this policy and Soviet cultivation of good relations with Muslim Afghanistan kept their common border peaceful and did not provoke the ethnically-related Soviet Muslims. The USSR's objective here was to demonstrate in Afghanistan the advantages that accrue to a Third World country that remains outside the American orbit.

The fourth Soviet objective can be characterized as an outgrowth of the Soviet Union's perceptions of its role. The USSR is an Asian as well as a European power and it projects its image in the Third World more as an Asian power which identifies with the concerns of the less-developed countries. Despite the challenge from the People's Republic of China in this quarter, Moscow has persisted. Soviet involvement with Afghanistan helps to legitimize the Soviet Union's Asian concerns. It also offers a foothold for Soviet

218

operations in a region that has seen rivalry between the three superpowers. The Soviet objective is to neutralize and if possible to exclude other powers from the region, and Afghanistan is an important part of this regional strategy.

INSTRUMENTS OF SOVIET POLICY

The USSR as a superpower has several means at its disposal which it can utilize in pursuit of its foreign policy objectives. The Soviets offered Afghanistan military aid as well as training for the Afghan armed forces, much needed economic aid to help develop their backward neighbor, trade which helped to offset the foreign aid debt and to offset the geographic disadvantages of diplomatic support for Afghan causes—in particular the Pakhtoonistan quarrel with Pakistan. Each of these will be analyzed below.

Initially, the Soviet Union gave military aid to Afghanistan to counter US aid to Pakistan and Iran. Considerations of *realpolitik* necessitated this Soviet attention to Afghanistan in the interests of denying that bordering country to the rapidly growing American alliance system. Between 1955 and 1972 Afghanistan, formally nonaligned, was given $455 million in military aid.[5] To date, Soviet military aid deliveries to Afghanistan are in excess of $600 million.[6] Since 1956 the USSR has supplied 95 percent of Afghan military equipment. In addition, as of 1979 there were some 4,500 Soviet military advisers in Afghanistan helping to maintain military equipment and to direct the fighting against insurgents. As Afghanistan moved closer to Moscow, its military dependence increased. With the Soviet invasion of Afghanistan, the Soviet military has essentially taken over all of the functions previously performed by the Afghan army.

Soviet military instructors accompanied modern Soviet weapons. In fact, Soviet instructors replaced the Turkish and German officers who were the traditional instructors of the Afghan army. Both at the military academy in Kabul and in the field Soviet instructors became closely involved with the development of the Afghan military, helping with the assembly and maintenance of military equipment, training local personnel in the use and maintenance of military equipment and advising staff and military officers. Furthermore, Soviet instructors have trained a substantial number of Afghan pilots and crewmen to operate the modern jets

219

delivered by the USSR. The closeness of this relationship has developed strong pro-Soviet elements within the officer corps in the Afghan military, and it is this group which executed the *coup d'etat* against King Zahir Shah in 1973 and played a key role in the 1978 coup against President Daud which brought the Communists to power in Afghanistan.

Military aid to Afghanistan has been a part of the overall pattern of Soviet relations. It was initially given to enhance Soviet power and prestige. In order to continue the pursuit of that power and prestige, Moscow has had to undertake a greater military commitment to the Afghan regime than it may at first have foreseen.

Economic aid has also been an important component in the Soviet-Afghan relationship. Between 1954 and 1975 the Soviet Union gave $1.263 billion in aid to Afghanistan, making it one of the largest recipients of Soviet assistance.[7] Grants comprise a larger share of Soviet aid to Afghanistan than to any other Third World country. Approximately 1,500 Soviet economic advisors and technicians are assisting Afghanistan in a multitude of projects.[8]

Afghan dependence on the USSR for economic aid has been pronounced since the fall of Daud. Indeed, the offer of $2 billion made by the Shah of Iran to help counteract this dependence was a factor in the overthrow of Daud, who was perceived by the pro-Soviet factions in Afghanistan as moving to the right and also as weakening the growing ties to Moscow. Economic aid from the United States reached $500 million by 1977 but was cut off in February 1979 after the murder of the American Ambassador Dubs. Thus Kabul is no longer able to exploit the competition between Washington and Moscow, as previously it had done so successfully.

The Soviet Union is Afghanistan's largest trading partner. Afghan trade with Eastern Europe is also shipped through the USSR, whereas trade with the West and with India is handled through Pakistan. Pakistan continues to allow transit facilities, but because of the poor state of its relations with Afghanistan, the latter's dependence on trade with and through the Soviet Union has increased.

Soviet diplomatic support has been instrumental in strengthening Afghan claims against Pakistan. Afghan calls for Pakhtoonistan have been credible because of Soviet backing, and it is for this reason that they have been taken seriously by Pakistan. Soviet diplomatic support is used as an instrument for rewarding the "correctness" of Afghan policy toward the USSR.

TABLE 1

Soviet Trade With Afghanistan

(In Millions of US Dollars)

Year	Exports	Imports
1970	40.0	34.3
1971	50.3	38.4
1972	46.1	37.3
1973	45.5	48.3
1974	81.6	80.0[a]
1975	93.7[b]	88.7
1976	116.4	88.8
1977	154.5	104.0

[a]The two-fold increase occurred following the 1973 pro-Soviet coup in Afghanistan. Imports increased due to Afghan sale of gas to the USSR.

[b]The jump in exports was tied to Moscow's $425 million credit, extended in 1975 for Afghanistan's current seven year plan (March 1976-March 1983). This represents the largest single commitment by the Soviet Union to Afghanistan.

Source: US Central Intelligence Agency, Changing Patterns in Soviet-LDC Trade, 1976-77, ER 78-10326, May 1978, pp. 10-11.

ASSESSMENT OF BENEFITS AND COSTS

The period of Zahir Shah's rule was the most trouble-free time in Soviet-Afghan relations. In retrospect, it is ironic that Moscow's tacit support was instrumental in the King's overthrow and the subsequent declaration of the Republic by his pro-Soviet cousin—Mohammed Daud, who took over as President—and the pro-Soviet elements in the Afghan military. For a time after taking over, Daud followed a classic pro-Soviet and anti-Pakistan stand, thereby pleasing the "activists" in the military who felt that Soviet backing was essential for a solution to Afghanistan's "only problem"—the Pakhtoonistan issue.[9]

221

Moscow greeted the Daud coup with enthusiasm and hailed the new regime's determination to pursue a policy of nonalignment and "nonadherence to military blocs."[10] Reaffirming the classic Soviet approach to South Asian politics, *Pravda* stated:

> Naturally the people of the Soviet Union cannot be indifferent to the political changes taking place in Afghanistan. The question is not merely concerned with the fact that our southern neighbour, Afghanistan, and the Soviet Union have a common border more than 2,000 km. long, but that Afghanistan is a friend and its people are our friends.[11]

There were other competitors for Soviet goodwill, apart from Daud himself and the Soviet-trained Afghan military personnel. The Marxist-Leninist Khalq (Masses) party (led by Taraki and Hafizullah Amin) went beyond Daud's program by calling for a policy which would alleviate "the boundless agonies of the oppressed peoples of Afghanistan," through a victory of international socialism over international capitalism, supremacy of public over private sector, and land reform to overhaul the feudal system dominating Afghan society. The Parcham (Flag) party (led by Babrak Karmal) was an offshoot of the Khalq party from which it had split in 1966, as a result more of tactics than philosophy. Parchamis were more in favor of working within the system and were even accused after the 1978 coup of collaboration with Daud, even though they had become disillusioned with the weakening of the "progressive" side of his regime and had largely withdrawn their support. Even though they had helped in the 1978 coup against Daud, Parcham leaders were either sent abroad or liquidated when the Khalq party took control.

The 1973 coup was expected to further Moscow's objectives in Afghanistan, and for a while it did. Daud at first allowed greater participation for the pro-Moscow left in Afghan politics and reaffirmed Afghan gratitude for Moscow's support and largesse. He not only moved closer to the Soviet Union in public support, but he also expressed support of Moscow's Asian "Collective Security" plan and became hostile to Iran and Pakistan. But soon Daud began to run into difficulty, losing the support of pro-Soviet elements who considered his modernization programs and reforms a farce. Expectations that Daud would broaden the decision making base to include those who helped him to power proved false, and the narrow base of power remained essentially in Mohammadzai hands. Furthermore, the traditional conservative elements in Afghan society were suspicious of Daud for his known flirtation with Moscow and his reliance on the latter in his 1973 takeover.[12]

The cost to the Soviet Union of Daud's takeover came in increased aid support in the economic and military sectors. While half of the $1.3 billion aid committed by Moscow to Kabul has been delivered, the pace of delivery was stepped up after 1973. The Soviet Union committed itself to 20 major projects in agriculture, irrigation, electric power, oil and gas exploration, mineral and metal processing and transportation.[13]

Moscow's honeymoon with Daud began to sour after the Shah of Iran successfully wooed the Afghan President away from exclusive dependence on Moscow. Daud, who was in trouble with domestic factions of both the left and the right, responded by settling his differences with Pakistan. He blamed domestic difficulties for the delay in signing an agreement recognizing the Durand Line as the legal boundary between Afghanistan and Pakistan. When Daud, during a visit to Sadat's Egypt in 1978, chastised Cuba for its non-neutral stand in the nonaligned movement, the Soviet Union saw that the success of its objectives in Afghanistan, achieved over decades of diplomacy, was in danger of turning to failure.

THE TARAKI COUP: ALLIANCE FOR MOSCOW

Although Daud's overthrow came at a time when Moscow was increasingly unhappy with his policies, there is little evidence to suggest direct Soviet interference in the April 1978 coup. In it Daud was killed along with 29 other members of his family and an estimated 3,000 others who were either Mohammadzais or simply guilty by association with the ruling family. There is, however, the possibility that Moscow's unhappiness with Daud's policies was a crucial factor in encouraging the Parcham and Khalq factions to unite.

The new Soviet leverage in Afghanistan is best understood in historical perspective. While successive Afghan rulers had been able in the 19th and 20th centuries to play off Russian interests against those of the British and later the Americans, their ability to perform this balancing act has now been complicated by the presence of domestic forces trained or influenced by Moscow. In other words, Moscow has acquired local allies who can press for reforms and policies that could be favorable for the USSR, but which it could not press for directly. Pro-Soviet elements in the military, a crucial source of support and power in the Afghan system, have proved particularly useful to Moscow in executing this strategy.[14]

The 1978 coup has been referred to as the "accidental coup" by an observer of the Afghan scene who witnessed it from close quarters.[15] It resulted from the frustrations caused by Daud and came as a direct consequence of the murder on April 17, 1978, of Akbar Khyber, the ideologue of the Parcham faction. Although the Khalq faction was suspected of involvement, anger was vented against Daud, and he ordered a crackdown against leftist leaders. Hafizullah Amin, the Khalq co-leader who later became president of Afghanistan, was able immediately before his arrest to contact three military officers (two majors in the army and a colonel in the air force), who launched the coup because of a feeling of "now or never." The 2,000 bodyguards of Daud were finally subdued by air force bombing. Air force squadrons loyal to Daud could not retaliate because of a communications breakdown. Thus the Democratic Republic of Afghanistan was born espousing nonalignment, the welfare of peasants and workers, and land reforms.

Once again the shift towards Moscow came immediately; Soviet recognition was extended to the new regime, and Moscow showed its delight at the Afghan tilt in its favor. Soviet objectives of a pro-Soviet Afghan regime, serving as an example for neighboring countries and assisting in denying the region to great-power competitors, was being fulfilled. Afghanistan had become yet another "success" in a series that encompassed Angola, Ethiopia, and South Yemen. It demonstrated the aggressive thrust (pursued actively or by default) of growing Soviet power. The United States, by contrast, seemed in the eyes of regional countries to be on the defensive and condemned to inaction.

The 1978 coup was followed by stepped up Soviet economic and military aid. The cost of alliance could be seen in this increased support. Seventy-five new economic assistance agreements were signed by Moscow between April 1978 and March 1979, and these were accompanied by an influx of almost 4,500 Soviet advisers. As the Taraki regime fought for legitimacy and control, it maneuvered the Soviet Union (by virtue of its self-declared alliance with Moscow) into giving greater support.

The careful balance in Afghan policy under Daud, who had sought economic assistance from both East and West, was once again dropped in favor of total reliance on Soviet aid. Because the Taraki regime turned against all technically trained or political Afghans, most of whom were linked to the previous regime, it desperately needed Soviet advisers to fill in the gap in each ministry of the government. In addition, Soviet advisers were posted in the office of the president. The culmination of the tilt came in the Treaty of Friendship signed by Taraki in Moscow on December 5, 1978. This pact institutionalized Afghan dependence on the USSR.

Taraki was unable to get a majority of Afghans to back his vision of a new Afghanistan. His reforms in education, land ownership, and social policy ran into difficulty as a revolt by a few tribesmen grew into large scale opposition in a majority of the 28 Afghan provinces. A trickle of refugees entered Pakistan after May 1978, and by August 1979 their number had increased to 100,000. They talked about the movement against the Communist regime in Kabul as a religious as well as a nationalistic revolt, since Taraki had turned against Islam and "sold Afghanistan to the Soviet Union."

Pakistan was the first country to recognize the Taraki government and had offered full cooperation in transit and trade facilities. The Pakistani president, General Zia, visited Kabul without an invitation in September 1978. However, as popular resistance to the Taraki regime spread, Pak-Afghan relations deteriorated. Pakistan counted 56 violations of its air and ground space (penetratioins of up to three miles above the 1,200 mile Pak-Afghan border) and Afghanistan charged Pakistani (as well as Chinese, Iranian, and American) collusion in the growing revolt within the country. These charges were supported by the Soviet Union, as Afghanistan's neighbors were made scapegoats on a campaign to persuade Afghans that the revolt was not internally based.

The Soviet Union continues to put pressure on Pakistan to send back the 450,000 Afghan refugees because their presence is seen as constituting an embarrassment to the success of a socialist regime. Pakistan has responded that it cannot force them back for humanitarian reasons. Furthermore, these refugees have relatives in Pakistan with whom many are staying. The border is a porous one and Pakistan is unable to stop them from crossing over.

However, according to the Pakistan government, it is up to the Afghan government to stop them, if that could somehow be managed. Moscow has subsequently put pressure on India to persuade Pakistan to return the refugees. The Indian response under Desai was to advise the Afghans to create internal conditions which would facilitate their return.

As the fighting increased, the Soviets were drawn in with increased military aid, and soon there were reports of Soviet pilots flying combat missions against rebel strongholds. In addition, an East German embassy was opened, and the Cuban mission enlarged to eighty persons. In contrast Kabul asked the missions of the United States, China, Iran and Pakistan to decrease their staffs.

While the Soviet Union benefitted in that Afghanistan began to follow Moscow's line slavishly after April 1978, the costs were increasing as Moscow became more heavily committed. It could be seen as a case of the tail wagging the dog and Moscow, for the first time, faced a dilemma in Afghanistan. It had a duty to support a self declared socialist regime, but the cost in material and diplomatic terms was increasingly high. Not to support the regime meant the collapse of Afghanistan's socialist experiment and a victory for "reactionary elements" there as well as in Iran, Pakistan, China and the United States, since Soviet propaganda has repeatedly linked these countries as conspirators seeking the overthrow of the Communist regime. There appeared to be no easy answers, and Moscow's search for a solution was complicated once more by yet another coup.

THE AMIN COUP: A CLIENT STATE FOR MOSCOW?

Soviet advisers cautioned Taraki and Amin to act more slowly in implementing reforms, in order not to alienate so many so rapidly. Reports of Soviet contacts with Afghan supporters of King Zahir Shah, who lives in Rome, sparked rumors of the King's return under a Soviet aegis. This may have contributed to the September 1979 coup in Kabul.

Hafizullah Amin was the strongman and ideologue of the Khalq party. He perceived that Taraki was succumbing to pressures to moderate. For example, at the Havana Summit of Nonaligned Nations, Taraki moved away from the direct confrontation with neighbors that he had previously threatened. That this moderation was not distasteful to the Soviets is suggested by the fact that Taraki stopped in Moscow on his journey home from Havana and was given a warm welcome. However, reports circulated that Moscow was less than satisfied with the prime minister, Hafizullah Amin, and would seek to replace him in a move to win support from the rebels. Instead, Amin moved first, and a week after Taraki returned from Havana he was overthrown in a coup and was killed. Amin declared that Taraki was alive but sick and almost a month later admitted he was dead as a result of a "long illness"!

Amin declared that his September 16, 1979, coup marked the "beginning of a better socialist order" in which the enemies of the people had been "eliminated."[16] He moved harshly against the opposition, dropping napalm on rebel villages, removing political opponents, organizing the secret police under his personal control, appointing his brother as Governor of four provinces and other friends and relatives to key posts. He had not previously listened to Soviet advice to go slowly, and there was little to indicate that he would do so after he assumed power.

Soviet stakes in Afghanistan are high, and Moscow was put in a position where it had to support Amin at least for a limited time or face the prospect of a backlash (similar to the anti-US feelings in post-Iran) if the rebels won. But Moscow was looking for an alternative leader even as President Brezhnev sent Amin a letter congratulating him on his "election" shortly after the coup.[17] Amin was committed to ensuring that reforms launched after 1978 were not set back. The coup was a desperate attempt to prevent a change in policies. To win Moscow's concurrence, Amin acted as a client of Moscow's—but a client that told its patrol that it cannot be forced off its chosen path to socialism. It was a new version of the patron-client relationship, and it turned out that Moscow did not like its new equation with Amin.

SOVIET INTERVENTION AND KARMAL—A PUPPET?

On December 27, 1979, the Soviets moved with 50,000 troops[18] into Afghanistan and established control. In the process, they killed Hafizullah Amin and brought in—three days after the "coup"—Babrak Karmal, the leader of the Parcham party, to be the new president of Afghanistan. This move, characterized as "the most serious challenge since World War II" by President Carter,

227

destroyed detente and put Southwest Asia directly in the path of a possible US-Soviet confrontation.

The timing of the Soviet move was curious. As early as June 1979 there had been reports in Pakistan of a Soviet division within Afghanistan's borders waiting to interject direct Soviet force. It is surprising that US intelligence reports did not pick up this information. Contrary to many reports, the rebel movement was inflicting no more damage against the Kabul government in December than it had been in the months past. In fact, there was some indication that the Soviet-backed Afghan army would make a successful bid against the insurgents before the winter snows deepened. So why did the Soviets invade Afghanistan now?

There are a number of plausible reasons for the Soviet move. First, Moscow perceived US policy in Southwest Asia to be essentially bankrupt and US responses limited by an inability to project American power beyond a temporary naval presence. The 100,000 man Rapid Deployment Force is operationally years away, and the lesson learned in projecting US forces even 90 miles from American shores in Cuba (in the exercise ordered by President Carter after the discovery of the Soviet brigade) could not have been lost on Moscow. The exercise, hopelessly delayed by foul weather and bogged down in bureaucratic and logistic problems, demonstrated the inadequacy of any US response in a critical situation half a world away.

Second, the Soviet Union took advantage of the American preoccupation with Iran. The spectacle of a United States condemned and held hostage in a country where only in January 1978 President Carter had proclaimed the Shah to be "an island of stability in an unstable area of the world" permitted a unique chance for Moscow to move to project its own power in a region where the United States had only recently been dominant.

Third, in the invasion of Afghanistan the USSR took advantage of a golden opportunity to move towards the final play of the "Great Game," i.e., fulfilling its ambitions to secure a warm water port on the Indian Ocean—now only 300 miles from Soviet army positions through troubled Baluchistan. The temporary collapse of detente seemed a price worth paying for the achievement of such a major and concrete objective. While the United States may threaten future action against further Soviet moves, for now the Soviet Union has dramatically changed the political map of areas

228

under its domination and control. One has to understand the larger objectives of this invasion—Afghanistan in and of itself is not a sufficient prize. The Soviet invasion has destroyed what remained of the "regional" leaders, a concept put forward by Dr. Brzezinski and endorsed in the Carter visit to New Delhi and Teheran. With the collapse of the Shah and his role as the policeman of the Persian Gulf, the return of a Moscow-oriented Mrs. Gandhi, and the Soviet takeover of Afghanistan, Washington can no longer count on any of its regional powers in Southwest Asia to guard its interests in a game where the stakes are high.

Fourth, the Soviet Union did not wish to see a "reactionary" Islamic revivalist area encompassing Iran, Afghanistan and Pakistan which might encourage its own Muslim population—a goal it probably shares with India. This could not have been a goal uppermost in the minds of the Soviet planners, but in combination with the other factors it undoubtedly influenced the decision to intervene.

Finally, the prospect of a failing Socialist experiment invited a Soviet response to move—with force sufficient to get the job done. While socialist honor had to be defended, Moscow must have recognized that the negative publicity of the move would not redound to its propaganda advantage, as seen in the condemnations of the Soviet move in the General Assembly and Islamic Nations Conference.

Babrak Karmal has, in the words of one Afghan, been brought to power "perched on Soviet tanks." Despite his attempts to discredit Amin as a "stooge of the CIA" and his promises to wipe out the brutal excesses of the Amin regime through gestures such as the release of Afghan political prisoners, there are few indications that he is perceived as being more benevolent—or more independent. While the Soviets are carrying out policies to "soften" the antireligion and antitradition perceptions of the Communist regime in power,[19] the presence of Soviet troops everywhere feeds the opposite belief, i.e., that Karmal is not the master in his own house.

CONCLUSION

Soviet policy in Afghanistan has so far been a success. Soviet objectives—to keep Afghanistan out of the Western orbit, to use the country to legitimize Soviet concern with Asia, to demonstrate to Pakistan the need for Soviet friendship—have now largely been realized. While the virtues of Soviet friendship are suspect in light of the strong embrace of Afghanistan, there is grudging respect for the extent of the support that a Soviet commitment brings.

The primary position of Moscow is ensured in Afghanistan by virtue of its size and common border and because it is Afghanistan's foremost trading partner. Soviet diplomacy has cultivated Afghan good-will over decades. In the last 5 years, it had become more heavily committed to the course of events unfolding in Kabul. Post-1973 success for Soviet policy in Afghanistan came as Moscow reaped the benefits of domestic discontent and pro-Soviet Afghan groups sought to initiate "progressive" changes. They have operated, at times, with direct Soviet approval, but have always had Moscow's tacit support in aiming Afghan policy towards a clearly Soviet orientation. These groups were encouraged by their perception of American unwillingness to get involved in regional problems driven by a desire to settle scores with their neighbors—Pakistan foremost among them.

The USSR is now heavily involved in Afghanistan. The cost of that involvement is rising. While Moscow may wish a reconciliation between the Afghan government and the rebels who disagree with "the socialist path," and may even look for a compromise, there is little indication that the regime will be able to get the support of the population. But they have military control and while Soviet power is dominant, their control is ensured. The Soviets may even succeed in "pacifying" the rebels with their vastly superior force and the use of nerve gas. They will run a puppet regime in Kabul knowing that otherwise the conservative Muslim rebel forces could win, thereby changing the Southwest Asian scene to a "mullah" controlled one—with possible adverse implications for Soviet control of the USSR's Muslim population.

The Soviet invasion may have been the last card that Moscow chose to play, but there is no doubt that it prefered to play the card rather than to lose its long cultivated and hard won place in Afghanistan. Moscow could not have wished for the souring of the Afghan revolution, but faced with its demise again "the Soviets will protect the Revolution."[20]

ENDNOTES

1. *Pravda,* June 4, l967, *Current Digest of the Soviet Press,* (hereafter referred to as *CDSP*), Vol XIX, No. 17, 1967.

2. Defined variously from an autonomous region for Pushtu speaking people, to a measure of freedom for them within a united Pakistan.

3. For example, Moscow stated that it could not remain indifferent as the Soviet Union bordered directly on this region. The Soviet Government therefore supported a "just" settlement of the problem, by which it means—"respect for the interest of the people inhabiting Pushtunistan." *Pravda,* March 21, 1961, *CDSP,* Vol. XIV, No. 13, 1961.

4. *Dawn,* Karachi, September 30, 1960.

5. US Department of State, *Communist States and Developing Countries: Aid and Trade in 1972,* Washington, DC: US Government Printing Office, August 1973.

6. US Central Intelligence Agency, *Communist Aid to Less Developed Countries of the Free World, 1977,* ER 78-10478 U, November 1978, p. 35.

7. Joint Economic Committee, Congress of the United States, *Soviet Economy in a New Perspective,* Washington, DC: US Government Printing Office, 1976, p. 194.

8. Central Intelligence Agency, p. 35.

9. Statement by Daud after 1973 take-over, quoted in *The New York Times,* July 29, 1973.

10. *Pravda,* July 18, 1973, quoted in *USSR and the Third World,* Vol. III, No. 6, September 2, 1973, London: Central Asian Research Center, p. 380.

11. *Ibid.,* July 22, 1973.

12. Hannah Negaran, "The Afghan Coup of April 1978: Revolution and International Security," *Orbis,* Vol. 23, No. l, Spring 1979, pp. 93-113.

13. The Soviets have developed Afghanistan's natural gas production facilities and built pipelines to transport gas to the USSR. In 1975 sale of natural gas amounted to 1/3 of Kabul's total exports to the USSR covering the debt service by Afghanistan. US Central Intelligence Agency, *Communist Aid to Less Developed Countries of the Free World, 1975,* ER 76-10372 U, July 1976.

14. Shirin Tahir-Kheli, "The Southern Flank of the USSR: Afghanistan, Iran, and Pakistan," *Naval War College Review,* Winter 1979, p. 36.

15. Louis Dupree, "Inside Afghanistan: Yesterday and Today—A Strategic Appraisal," *Strategic Studies,* Institute of Strategic Studies, Islamabad, Vol. II, No. 3, Spring 1979.

16. *The New York Times,* September 19, 1979.

17. *Philadelphia Inquirer,* September 19, 1979.

18. Now estimated to be in the range of 85,000.

19. *The New York Times,* January 28, 1980.

20. Declared, ironically, by Hafizullah Amin at the 61st anniversary of the Soviet revolution.

12

THE MILITARY AND SECURITY DIMENSIONS
OF SOVIET-INDIAN RELATIONS

M. Rajan Menon

Where it is concerned with the instruments of policy, the existing literature on Soviet-Indian relations is skewed by the large number of studies dealing with Soviet economic aid. Relatively few attempts have been made to examine the military and security dimension of Indo-Soviet interaction and to assess its significance as a means for attaining Soviet objectives.[1] This neglect is hardly warranted. From the mid-1960's, Indian repayments have exceeded incoming Soviet economic aid, while about $460 million in previously extended development credits are yet to be utilized. Further, the $340 million provided in May 1977 was the first commitment of development aid since 1966.[2] On the other hand, while economic aid has tended to taper off, since 1965 the USSR has emerged as India's largest supplier of military hardware and a central factor in Indian conceptions of security.

This study is concerned with an understanding of the military and security aspect of Soviet-Indian relations and an assessment of the extent to which it has brought gains to the USSR. While the precise determination of Soviet goals in any particular country or region is problematic, this analysis posits three probable Soviet objectives in India: (1) providing the basis for a stable and predictable bilateral relationship capable of enduring regime changes and periods of uncertainty in India; (2) evoking a responsive attitude to Soviet interests from the Indian leadership; and, (3) enlisting India as an asset in Soviet strategy against China. In the case of the last of these three goals, it is not clear what Soviet aims are, although they include the attainment of Indian support in the ongoing competition between Moscow and Peking as well as the building up of India as a military counterweight to China.[3]

THE USSR AND INDIA'S SECURITY

The linkage between Indo-Soviet relations and India's security needs is best examined in the context of the interaction of China, India, Pakistan, and the USSR. It is necessary to understand both the extent to which India's relations with Pakistan and China have improved over time, and the ways in which India's security concerns with respect to these two countries are served by its ties with the Soviet Union.

The India-Pakistan relationship has been a troubled one, and the issues dividing the two countries have resulted in four wars. Yet efforts have been made to resolve bilateral problems. Recent examples are the 1972 Simla talks following the Bangladesh war and the discussion held in February 1978 between Indian Foreign Minister Atal Bihari Vajpayee and Zia ul Haq, the head of Pakistan's military government. The Simla negotiations sought to achieve a detente between the two countries by paving the way for reaching an understanding on the major problems remaining in the wake of the Bangladesh war and by producing a commitment to restore bilateral ties. Since then communications and trade links have been restored, and in 1976 diplomatic ties were reestablished. The Vajpayee-Zia talks indicated a willingness on the part of both sides to consolidate and extend this trend.

However, though the Indo-Pakistan relationship has been drawn out of the doldrums into which it was cast by the 1971 war, several factors operate to limit the extent to which normalization has progressed. While with passage of time the Kashmir dispute has ceased to be the emotion-laden source of friction that it once was, as recently as March 1979 Zia identified it as the only hindrance to

233

a rapprochement between the two countries.[4] In addition, Pakistan continues to be wary of India's ties with the USSR. Several factors have caused the Pakistanis to respond by looking to China for support. The feeling—gaining ground since the mid-1960's—that Pakistan's past membership in military alliances sponsored by the West has failed to bring expected benefits, such as the required level of arms supplies and unambiguous support during Indo-Pakistan crises, has culminated in a withdrawal from SEATO and CENTO in the 1970's. In addition, the unwillingness of President Carter to sanction the supply of the A-7 aircraft offered under the Ford administration, the April 1979 US decision to withhold new economic aid in response to reports that Pakistan was attempting to acquire a plutonium separation facility, and Zia's belief that US behavior during the deposal of the Shah of Iran and its policy toward the Taraki government in Afghanistan indicates a lack of resolve to counter the Soviet Union have combined to generate within Pakistan a lack of confidence in the United States and a tendency to regard China as the most reliable source of support in present conditions.[5] In turn, India continues to regard its ties with the Soviet Union as an appropriate response to the Sino-Pakistani alignment.

In addition to the perceived value of a close relationship with the USSR in offsetting Pakistan's ties with China, New Delhi values the contribution that Soviet arms supplies to India can make to India's future efforts to maintain a sufficient military capability against Pakistan. This consideration will continue to be important since, despite the improvement of Indo-Pakistani relations since 1971, the two countries have not ceased to regard each other as an external threat. For the foreseeable future, defense planning and weapons procurement in each country will be conducted with an eye on the perceived capabilities of the other.[6]

Though the Soviet Union has been India's most important source of arms since 1965, there is evidence to indicate that the major Soviet motivations have been a general quest for influence in India and a desire to complicate China's security planning rather than an explicit desire to put Pakistan at a disadvantage. This is suggested by the fact that Moscow's increasing arms transfers to India from the mid-1960's were combined with a more balanced posture on Indo-Pakistani disputes, a concerted effort to counter Pakistan's increasing identification with China through aid commitments, and even a limited supply of arms to Pakistan in 1968.[7] Even after the signing of the Indo-Soviet treaty in August 1971, Moscow continued to urge restraint on India and Pakistan and avoided endorsing a political solution incompatible with a united Pakistan until full-scale war broke out between India and Pakistan in December.[8] Nonetheless, whatever the motives underlying Soviet arms supplies to India, from an Indian standpoint they will continue to be important to India's military requirements *vis-a-vis* Pakistan.

The course of Sino-Indian relations resembles India's relationship with Pakistan. Though the Sino-Indian relationship has been a troubled one since the 1962 border war, recent developments indicate mutual efforts to improve the situation. After a 15-year lapse, ambassadorial links were reestablished in 1976. In the following year, China broke a similar 15-year impasse by concluding an import agreement, while Indian representatives took part in the Canton trade fair. Following a number of Chinese statements denoting an interest in an improved relationship, it was announced in the summer of 1978 that Foreign Minister Vajpayee would visit Peking. Though the trip was deferred on one occasion, Vajpayee arrived in China in February 1979.

However, two decades of animosity, coupled with the existence of a number of unresolved issues separating the two countries, makes any rapid and fundamental change in Sino-Indian relations unlikely. Aside from the border dispute, which involves some 50,000 square miles of territory, the Chinese have long been suspicious of what they view as an alliance between India and the USSR. For its part, New Delhi appears unwilling to test the theory which holds that a loosening of Indo-Soviet ties would inexorably lead to greater harmony with China.[9]

Another controversy between India and China[10] concerns the presence in India of several Tibetan refugees and their leader, the Dalai Lama.[11] From the Indian side there has been concern that China is arming and training Mizo and Naga tribal insurgents in India's politically sensitive northeastern border region. New Delhi has also voiced its opposition to China's construction of the Karakoram Highway (inaugurated formally in June 1978) which links China and Pakistan through Pakistan-controlled Kashmir. Another problem area is India's concern about China's support of Pakistan. In recent years, Pakistan has become the largest recipient of Chinese economic and military aid. Further, mutual concern over increased Soviet presence and influence in Afghanistan has led

235

to increased contacts between China and Pakistan and reiteration of China's support for Pakistan's stand on the Kashmir dispute.[12] In December 1979 a massive Soviet military intervention into Afghanistan led to the ouster of Hafizullah Amin—who had toppled Taraki in a September coup— and the installation of a more compliant government led by Babrak Karmal. The speed with which the United States and China moved toward supplying arms to Pakistan caused major misgivings in India where as a result of the January 1980 elections Indira Gandhi made a comeback as Prime Minister. Although she called for a withdrawal of Soviet troops from Afghanistan, Mrs. Gandhi is likely to view the continuance of close ties with the USSR as a viable counterweight to the Sino-American effort to bolster Pakistan's military capability.

As for the impact of Vajpayee's negotiations in Peking on the future of Sino-Indian relations, Indian news reports indicated that the Chinese leaders were unwilling to moderate their support for the Pakistani position on Kashmir, despite the Indian foreign minister's contention that Peking's stand had been a major irritant in Sino-Indian relations.[13] Though Vajpayee was informed that China was no longer involved in supporting the Mizo and Naga rebels, no significant progress was made on the border dispute. Vajpayee would go no further than saying that the issue had been "unfrozen." But in references to the problem following his mission to China, both he and Desai maintained that the dispute was a continuing obstacle to a Sino-Indian rapproachement, and they reiterated India's unwillingness to concede any disputed territory to China in order to facilitate a settlement.[14] The gist of Vajpayee's report to Parliament on his exploratory mission—which was concluded ahead of schedule to protest Peking's decision to initiate its campaign against Vietnam while the Indian foreign minister was still in China—was that, while Sino-Indian differences on various issues had been discussed, substantial progress remained to be made prior to any fundamental change in the nature of bilateral relations.[15]

In the absence of a marked improvement in Sino-Indian relations, India will continue to regard its close ties with the USSR as a viable strategy to meet its security requirements. Similarly, China's continued support of Pakistan will be a major consideration precluding a loosening of India's ties with the USSR. In sum, therefore, a firm basis for Indo-Soviet relations will remain as long as India continues to perceive its relationship with the USSR and its security needs *vis-a-vis* Pakistan and China as being intertwined. From the Soviet point of view, such a situation is beneficial inasmuch as it lends an element of stability and predictability to the Indo-Soviet relationship.

SOVIET ARMS TRANSFERS TO INDIA

The linkage betwen Indo-Soviet relations and Indian security explains one facet of Soviet-Indian military relations. The other aspect involves the role that the USSR plays as a supplier of military hardware for the Indian armed forces. An analysis of Soviet military supplies to India reveals a marked increase in the importance of the USSR as a weapons source and a decrease in the importance of western countries in this respect.

Prior to the 1962 Sino-Indian war, India eschewed the acceptance of military aid from any quarter, and all imports of arms were purchased with cash. The vast majority of the arms bought in the 1950's came from Britain, and major acquisitions from either superpower were avoided.[16] Partly in response to emerging strains in the Sino-Indian relationship, procurement policy shifted in 1960 with the purchase of 24 Ilyushin IL-21 transport aircraft. With the outbreak of the Sino-Indian war, major arms deliveries were made to India by the United States, the Soviet Union, Britain, Canada, France, and Australia. For a variety of reasons, however, from 1965 India began to depend primarily on the USSR.[17]

The extent of this shift in policy is well depicted by the data presented in Table 1. As the table denotes, in contrast to India's reliance primarily on Britain in the 1950's, over the 1967-77 period the Soviet Union accounted for 81.2 percent of the monetary value of arms transferred to India. By contrast, acquisitions from Britain amounted to only 4.5 percent, while the United States and France each provided 2.4 percent. On the other hand, Czechoslovakia and Poland together supplied 6 percent. Thus in this period, of the states most extensively involved in the worldwide transfer of arms, the USSR has played the most important role in India.

Following the purchase of the 24 IL-21s in 1960, an agreement was reached between India and the USSR providing for the purchase by India of 12 MiG-21s and the provision of Soviet aid for the manufacture of these aircraft under license in India. Initial Soviet ambivalence on the Sino-Indian dispute delayed the implementation of the deal. But the open split between Moscow and

237

TABLE 1

Arms Transferred to India: 1967-76

Country	Millions of Current Dollars	Percent of Total[a]
United States	40	2.4
Soviet Union	1365	81.2
France	41	2.4
United Kingdom	75	4.5
Federal Republic of Germany	10	.6
Czechoslovakia	55	3.3
Poland	45	2.7
All Other	50	3.0
Total	1681	

[a]Percentages have been rounded. The total value was reported as $1680 million in the source.

Source: US Arms Control and Disarmament Agency, World Military Expenditures and Arms Transfers, Washington, DC: US Government Printing Office, 1978, Table VII, p. 158.

Peking removed this obstacle and the agreement was acted upon in late 1964.[18] Following that year Soviet arms transfers gained momentum, and in the ensuing period the USSR has provided India with the following types of hardware: MiG-21 interceptors; Sukhoi SU-7 and SU-7B attack fighters; Antonov AN-12, Ilyushin IL-14 and Tupolev TU-124 transport aircraft; Mi-4 and Mi-8 helicopters; Petya-class frigates; Polnocny-class landing craft; Poluchat-class coastal patrol vessels; Nanuchka-class missile corvettes; Osa-class patrol boats; an Ugra-class submarine tender; Atoll air-to-air missiles; SA-2 surface-to-air missiles; Styx surface-to-surface missiles; and T-54, T-55 and PT-76 tanks.[19]

Quite naturally, the large-scale delivery of Soviet arms has had an impact on the composition of India's armed forces. As Table 2 denotes, of the three service branches, the air force and navy have been most affected by the inflow of Soviet equipment and the army the least. As far as weapon types are concerned, equipment of Soviet origin is especially prominent in the case of frigates, submarines, patrol and missile boats, fighter-ground attack aircraft, interceptors, helicopters, tanks, and armored personnel carriers.

238

TABLE 2

The Soviet Component in Major Categories
of Indian Military Equipment as of 1977

	Number of Soviet Origin	Number of Western Origin or Produced Indigenously
Navy		
Aircraft Carriers	--	1
Cruisers	--	2[a]
Destroyers	--	3
Frigates	10	15
Submarines	8	--
Missile Boats and Patrol Craft	13	3[b]
Amphibious Forces	6	1
Minesweepers	--	8
Survey Ships	--	2
Service Forces	2	12
Naval Air Wing	3	102
Air Force		
Bombers	--	50
Fighter, Ground Attack Aircraft	100	115
Interceptors	270	130
Reconnaissance Aircraft	--	6
Transport Aircraft	45	141
Helicopters	135	188
Trainers		
Army		
Tanks	1,050	880
Armored Personnel Carriers	700[c]	--

[a] One of the cruisers has since been decommissioned.
[b] Includes one of Yugoslav origin.
[c] Includes an unspecified number of Czechoslovak OT 62 and OT 64 (2A) APCs.

Sources: International Institute for Strategic Studies, The Military
Balance, 1977-78, p. 58; Jane's Fighting Ships, 1976-77,
pp. 224-232; industry sources.

239

Despite the importance of the Soviet Union as an arms supplier, there has not been a tendency on India's part to turn solely to Moscow to fill emerging needs. For some years now, a major priority has been the acquisition of a deep penetration strike aircraft (DPSA) to replace the aging subsonic Canberras and Hunters that have served as a mainstay of India's bomber force.[20] In October 1978 it was officially announced that the Anglo-French Jaguar had been selected to meet the DPSA requirement in favor of its two major competitors, the French mirage F-1 and the Swedish Viggen.[21] Although it was reported that the Soviets had offered the MiG-23, SU-20, and SU-22 at favorable prices and with provisions for licensed production in India, technical considerations—such as the failure of the Soviet aircraft to meet the minimum range requirement of 300 nautical miles—led India to decline the offer.[22] Similarly, negotations between India and Britain have also been held for the acquisition of Harrier V/STOL aircraft to replace the outdated Sea Hawks currently operating from India's only aircraft carrier, *Vikrant*.[23]

While the prominence of the USSR as a source of arms has not inhibited India from seeking to diversify its sources of supply, certain factors point to the continued importance of the Soviet Union as a supplier. The high cost of modern military equipment inevitably raises the question of credit terms, especially for a developing country such as India. Since Indian arms procurements will have to be made with both cost and quality in mind, the Soviet Union's willingness to accept repayments in exports rather than convertible currency will continue to hold attraction. Further, given the importance attached to India by the Soviets as a counterweight to China and their long-standing interest in close and stable Indo-Soviet relations, Moscow is likely to be receptive to India's future military needs. By contrast, the politico-strategic basis for major arms transfers to India remains less salient in the case of the other major participants in the international arms trade.

Any discussion of the importance of external suppliers for India's defense needs must take into account the progress made by the country's armament industry, since the dependence on foreign sources will attenuate with the development of a viable indigenous capacity. As part of India's long-standing goal of achieving self-sufficiency in arms, a variety of weapons are being produced under license from Britain, Czechoslovakia, France, and the USSR.[24] The details concerning such production are provided in Table 3. In

TABLE 3

Weapons Produced Under License in India

Licensor	Designation, description	Powerplant	Armament	Date of License	Entered Production	Indigenous percent
Czecho-Slovakia	OT-62/64(2A) APC	--	--	1970	--	--
France	HAL SA-315 Cheetah high altitude helicopter (Aero-Spatiale SA-315 Lama)	TS (I:Fr)	SS.11 ATM (L:Fr)	1970	1972	--
	HAL SA-316 B Chetak general-purpose helicopter (Aero-Spatiale Aloutte III)	TS (I:Fr)	--	1962	1965	--
	Bharat SS-11 ATM	S	Warhead:HE	1970	1971	100
	Type A69 Avisos	D(I:Fr)	Exocet SSM (I:Fr);ASW	1974	1975	--
UK	HAL Ajeet Light weight fighter(Gnat Mark II)	TJ (L:UK)	Aden Cannon (I:UK)	1973	1976	90 (Indian R&D)
	HAL HS-748 transport	TP (L:UK)	--	--	1959	Assembled from imported kits
	Ajeet trainer verion	TJ (L:UK)	--	1973	1978	
	Vijayanta medium battle tank	D (L:UK)	105 mm guns	1965	1967	95
	Leander class ASW frigate	T (L:UK)	1 Wasp helicopter (I:UK); 2 seacat SAM launchers (I:UK); ASW	1965	1973	First = 53%

TABLE 3 (continued)

Licensor	Designation, description	Powerplant	Armament	Date of License	Entered Production	Indigenous percent
USSR	HAL MiG-21M fighter	TJ (L:USSR)	Atoll AAM (L:USSR)	1970 (License for an earlier version was in 1964)	1973	90
	Bharat K-13A Atoll AAM (Infrared Missile for Mi GI 21)	S	Warhead:HE	1964	1969	--
Switzerland	Electronics			1975	--	--

Abbreviations:

AAM = Air to Air Missile
APC = Armored Personnel Carrier
ASW = Anti Submarine Warfare
ATM = Anti Tank Missile
D = Diesel
HAL = Hindustan Aeronautics Ltd.
HE = High explosive
I = Imported
L = License
S = Solid Propellant
SAM = Ship to Air Missile
SSM = Ship to Ship Missile
TJ = Turbojet
TS = Turboshaft

242

Source: Stockholm International Peace Research Institute, World Armaments and Disarmaments: Yearbook 1977, Stockholm: Almquist and Wiksell, 1978, Appendix 7D, pp. 298-299.

addition several categories of indigenously designed arms are in development or production and the requirements for small arms, bombs, and explosives are now fully met by domestic production.[25]

Such progress notwithstanding, India is not likely to be able to meet all her defense needs through indigenous production in the near future. In the case of weapons produced under foreign license, despite a steady increase in the indigenous content, a reliance on the licenser exists for designs, critical components, and major maintenance. Furthermore, both in the case of such weapons, as well as in the case of indigenously developed systems, production delays have at times necessitated a reliance on imports.[26] Finally, if one considers that India's average annual expenditure on military research and development (R&D) has been less than 2 percent of the yearly defense budget over the 1969-70 to 1977-78 period, it would appear that India's defense industry will be hard pressed to keep pace with the rapid qualitative changes that are being made in modern weapons technology.[27]

SECURITY DEPENDENCE, ARMS TRANSFERS, AND SOVIET POLICY

A realization on the part of the Indian leadership of the importance of the USSR as a source of arms and a factor in Indian security has benefitted the Soviet Union by providing the basis for stable bilateral relations. An illustration of the value of such a situation for the Soviets is provided by a recent development in Indo-Soviet relations.

After Mrs. Gandhi's defeat in the March 1977 general election led to the formation of a government drawn from the victorious Janata party, Moscow was justifiably uncertain about the future direction of Indo-Soviet relations.[28] The Soviet media had enthusiastically supported Mrs. Gandhi's declaration of a State of Emergency on June 26, 1975. During the ensuing period of nearly two years, civil liberties were curtailed and many members of the Janata government had been arrested. Further, not only had prominent members of the new government been depicted in past years in the Soviet media as right-wing elements, but in addition, the new Prime Minister Morarji Desai had criticized Mrs. Gandhi for showing excessive deference for Soviet interests.[29]

Despite Soviet fears and Western predictions of a changed Indo-Soviet relationship, during its term in office the Desai government

243

continued the policy of maintaining the close ties with the USSR which successive Congress governments had adhered to since the mid-1950's. During the 27 months of the Desai government,[30] five top-level visits took place, and new trade and aid agreements were signed. Given the absence of any extensions of economic development credits between 1966 and May 1977, it is evident that the importance of the military and security dimension of Indo-Soviet relations played a major role in determining the Desai government's posture toward the USSR.

In addition to having provided New Delhi with an incentive for avoiding sharp discontinuities in its relationship with Moscow, the military and security dimension of Indo-Soviet relations has also evoked an Indian responsiveness to Soviet foreign policy interests. An example of this is provided by the Indian government's response to the Soviet invasion of Czechoslovakia in August 1968. Despite the condemnation of the invasion by the major Indian newspapers and non-ruling political parties, the parliamentary statement made by Mrs. Gandi, while calling for the early withdrawal of foreign troops from Czechoslovakia, was clearly drafted with Soviet sensibilities in mind.[31] A similar low-key posture was adopted by the Indian representative in the United Nations. On August 23, India abstained from a Western-sponsored resolution on the ground that its tone was too condemnatory. Following a Soviet veto, another resolution was tabled calling upon the Secretary General to appoint a representative to ascertain the safety of the Czechoslovak leadership. While the Indian representative praised the heroism of the Czechs, in defining India's stand on the proposal he opposed any interference in Czechoslovakia's internal affairs.[32] In a final move, indicative of India's guarded posture, prior to his departure for the October session of the UN General Assembly, the Indian Minister of State for External Affairs indicated his opposition to the inclusion of the Czechoslovak issue on the agenda of the session.[33]

While the Indian stand on the Czechoslovak episode was at least partly shaped by an awareness of Soviet interests, it should be noted that the costs attached to India's cautious behavior were essentially minor in that no sacrifice on key Indian interests was entailed.

Quite a different picture of India's behavior emerges if one considers instances in which acting in accord with Soviet

244

preferences would have been at variance with major Indian goals. Despite the importance envisaged for India in Moscow's strategy against Peking, India has steered clear of becoming an instrument of Soviet policy. Although the Soviets have made a concerted effort to win India's approval for the Asian Collective Security scheme which was first proposed by Brezhnev in June 1969, New Delhi has been unwilling to endorse the project. There has been a clear awareness in India that Peking views the proposal as a Soviet effort to construct a coalition of states to contain China. Similarly, though the Indo-Soviet treaty denoted to many observers a new and closer phase of Soviet-Indian interaction, by 1976 Mrs. Gandhi was embarked on an effort to normalize Sino-Indian relations. The Vajpayee mission indicated similar resolve on the part of the Desai government to conduct an independent China policy. In addition, despite the fact that a major objective underlying Kosygin's March 1979 visit to India was to win India's support for the Soviet position on the Sino-Vietnamese war, the results were unimpressive. New Delhi refused to join in Kosygin's repeated criticism of China and refused to be hurried into recognizing the Vietnamese-backed Heng Samrin government of Kampuchea. The joint statement avoided referring to Kampuchea and included only a terse call for the withdrawal of Chinese troops from Vietnam.[34]

India's stand on the nuclear Non-Proliferation Treaty (NPT) shows a similar unwillingness to make major sacrifices in order to facilitate Soviet objectives. In the negotiations leading up to the treaty and in the years since, New Delhi has refused to support it on the grounds that it contains an imbalance of obligations weighted against non-nuclear states. Moscow's approval of NPT as a regulatory regime and its reported efforts to get India to subscribe to it did not succeed in altering the Indian position.[35]

The USSR also failed to gain India's support for the embattled Taraki government in Afghanistan during Desai's June 1979 visit to the Soviet Union. Following the April 1978 coup which brought Taraki to power, there was an increase in the number of Soviet advisers in Afghanistan and a security-oriented treaty was signed between the two countries in December 1978. As the regime began to face mounting pressure from armed opponents, the Soviet media coupled increasing statements of support with allegations of Chinese, Pakistani and American interference on the side of the insurgents. Against this background, during Desai's visit, Kosygin stated that India could use its influence to help the Taraki

245

government acquire stability and to dissuade Pakistan from involving itself on the side of the opposition.[36] Despite the efforts to enlist India's support, Desai reportedly told the Soviet leaders that Taraki should enter into a dialogue with the opposition and broaden the basis of the regime's support in Afghanistan.[37] The joint statement signed at the close of his visit included only an elliptical reference to the rights of the "people" of Afghanistan to decide their future free of external interference, a sufficiently ambiguous choice of words in view of the increased Soviet presence in that country.[38]

On balance, therefore, the military and security dimension of Indo-Soviet relations has not provided Moscow with an assured basis for influencing Indian behavior. Clearly, focusing solely on the importance of the USSR for Indian security and a preoccupation with the data pertaining to Soviet arms transfers poses the danger of equating dependence and presence with influence. The need to put in perspective the data relating to Soviet arms supplies and training programs is especially important. Though the Soviet Union has provided $1.365 billion in arms to India from 1967 to 1976, it should be noted that the Indian defense budget in 1977-78 alone amounted to $3.45 billion.[39] Further, though the data included in Table 1 is the most recent available, it does not include the value of the Jaguar deal recently arrived at between India and Britain, which amounts to $1.5 billion-$2.0 billion—the largest arms agreement ever concluded by India.[40]

While 2,175 Indian military personnel have been trained in the USSR between 1956 and 1977, this figure should be viewed in relation to India's military manpower of 1,096,000. There are a larger number of Soviet-trained personnel (both in absolute terms and as a proportion of the size of the armed forces) in countries such as Afghanistan, Indonesia, Egypt, Iraq, Somalia, and Syria.[41] Nor has there been any evidence that personnel trained in the USSR constitute a pro-Soviet enclave in the armed forces. The number of Soviet military personnel in India has been relatively low and static. It stood at 200 in 1972, rose to 300 in 1973 and 1974, and dropped to 150 in 1977. Here again, countries that are much smaller than India—such as Afghanistan, Algeria, Iraq, Egypt, Somalia, and Syria—have hosted a larger number of Soviet military technicians.[42] Given the existence in India of a vast network of training establishments for armed services personnel, Soviet

246

personnel have never exercised the kind of impact that they have had on military strategy and training in countries such as Egypt.[43]

CONCLUSION: SUCCESS AND FAILURE

In the absence of a marked improvement in its relations with China and Pakistan, India will in the future adhere to the policy of maintaining close ties with the USSR. The importance of the Soviet Union as a source of arms will also continue, though for both political and technical reasons efforts will be made to pursue a diversified procurement policy. Thus for the foreseeable future the military and security dimension of Indo-Soviet relations will continue to be substantial and provide Moscow with the basis for a stable bilateral relationship. This observation should be qualified by taking into account that the Soviet relationship with Egypt and Somalia has deteriorated sharply in recent years despite the fact that the military and security aspect of the relationship with both countries was important.

The Soviet Union's success in utilizing arms supplies and security dependence to influence Indian behavior has, on the whole, been rather modest. India has been unwilling to align its conduct with Soviet preferences where doing so would have involved a sacrifice of major interests. New Delhi has not in any direct sense served as an instrument of Soviet diplomatic strategy against China and has kept open the option of normalizing ties with Peking. Further, unlike other major recepients of Soviet arms, India has been unwilling to provide the USSR with any naval facilities that can in any strict sense be regarded as military bases of support.[44] In sum, while the military and security dimension of Indo-Soviet relations provides for a durable bilateral relationship and enables the Soviets to establish a presence in India, they have been unable to translate this into a pattern of influence that is both predictable and substantial.

ENDNOTES

1. Two recent analyses of Soviet-Indian military relations are P. R. Chari, "Indo-Soviet Military Cooperation: A Review," *Asian Survey,* Vol. XIX, No. 3, March 1979, pp. 230-244; and Ashok Kapur, "Indo-Soviet Military Relations: Dependency, Interdependency and Uncertainties," *India Quarterly,* Vol. XXXIII, No. 3, July-September 1977, pp. 263-280.

2. US Central Intelligence Agency, National Foreign Assessment Center, *Communist Aid to Less Developed Countries of the Free World, 1977,* ER 77-10296, November 1978, pp. 7, 37.

3. While the possibility is remote that India would be willing to involve itself in a Sino-Soviet confrontation, the Soviets would benefit if the distribution of Chinese forces were affected by an uncertainty concerning India.

4. *Pakistan Times* (Lahore), March 20, 1979.

5. For a Pakistani analysis embodying some of the perceptions noted above, see Brigadier Abdul Rahman Siddiqi (Ret.), "Pakistan and its Neighbors," *Defence Journal* (Karachi), Vol. IV, No. 8, 1978, pp. 6-ll.

6. For an Indian assessment of Pakistan's current military capability, see Ravi Rikhye, "Proposal to Limit Arms: Difficulties with China and Pakistan," *Times of India* (New Delhi), June 26, 1978.

7. See Vijay Sen Budhraj, "The Evolution of Russia's Pakistan Policy," *Australian Journal of Politics and History,* Vol. XVI, No. 3, December 1979, pp. 343-360.

8. *Idem,* "Moscow and the Birth of Bangladesh," *Asian Survey,* Vol. XIII, No. 3, May 1973, pp. 482-495.

9. A prominent Indian defense analyst has observed: "The Chinese are believed to be inhibited by Indo-Soviet ties. But such tested links can hardly be sacrificed by India for gaining a larger relationship with China." P. R. Chari, "External Threats," *Seminar* (New Delhi), No. 225, May 1978, p. 14.

10. The major sources of friction in Sino-Indian relations are noted in US Congress, House of Representatives, Committee on International Relations, *The United States, India, and South Asia: Interests, Trends, and Issues for Congressional Concern.* Prepared by the Congressional Research Service. Washington, DC: US Government Printing Office, 1978, pp. 23-24.

11. Despite the recent encouraging developments in Sino-Indian relations, Prime Minister Morarji Desai met with the Dalai Lama in April 1977, and Peking responded with an official note of protest.

12. *The New York Times,* January 19, 1979; *Pakistan Times* (Lahore), March 26, 1979; Girilal Jain, "Fresh Look at China Policy," *Times of India* (Bombay), March 14, 1979.

13. For Indian press reports on the Vajpayee mission, see *Statesman* (Calcutta), February 22, 1979; *Times of India* (Bombay), March 15, 1979. It is significant that a Pakistani military delegation was in China during Vajpayee's visit. See Girilal Jain, "Fresh Look at China Policy."

14. *Times of India* (Bombay), March 15, 1979.

15. For the text of the report, see *Overseas Hindustan Times* (New Delhi), March 8, 1979.

16. For a listing of the weapons acquired from the United States and the Soviet Union prior to 1962, see Stockholm International Peace Research Institute (SIPRI), *Arms Trade with the Third World,* Stockholm: Almqvist and Wiksell, 1971, Register 8, pp. 833-836.

17. The factors explaining India's increasing dependence on the USSR include the cutback in US arms sales to South Asia, the intersection of Soviet and Indian interests owing to a shared concern regarding China, and the Soviet willingness to accept repayments for arms purchases in the form of exports by India.

18. For details on the MiG deal, see Ian C. C. Graham, "The Indo-Soviet MiG Deal and its International Repercussions," *Asian Survey,* Vol. IV, No. 5, May 1964, pp. 823-830.

19. SIPRI, *Arms Trade Register: The Arms Trade with the Third World,* Stockholm: Almqvist and Wiksell, 1975, Register 17, pp. 33-37. International Institute for Strategic Studies, *The Military Balance* (annual issues, 1969-70 through 1976-77); *Janes Fighting Ships* (London), 1976-77, pp. 226-232; Wing Commander Maharaj K. Chopra (Ret.), "To Russia with Love," *Organiser* (New Delhi), October 31, 1977; and industry sources. For a listing of the arms ordered from the USSR in 1977, see International Institute of Strategic Studies, *The Military Balance, 1978-79,* p. 106.

20. See "Quantity or Quality? The Indian Dilemma," *Air International,* October 1975, pp. 174-176.

21. *Times* (London), October 7, 1978.

22. On the Soviet offer, see *Times of India* (Bombay), February 10, 1978; *Hindu* (Madras), February 10, 1978; and *Economic and Political Weekly* (Bombay), April 8, 1978, p. 596.

23. *Hindu* (Madras), October 21, 1978; *Aviation Week and Space Technology,* October 23, 1978, p. 26.

24. The Soviet-licensed MiGs are produced at three factories located at Hyderabad, Koraput and Nasik, which manufacture electronic equipment, aeroengines, and air frames respectively. The three factories were set up with Soviet assistance under the 1962 agreement.

25. For details on the indigenously designed weapons under production or development, see SIPRI, *World Armaments and Disarmament: Yearbook 1976,* Stockholm: Almqvist and Wiksell, 1976, Appendix GE, p. 24. Also see *Janes All the World's Aircraft* (London), 1974-75, pp. 101-106.

26. A delay in the production of Vijayantas led to an order of 75 T-55 tanks from the USSR in the mid-1960's. SIPRI, *The Arms Trade with the Third World.* Later, owing to a similar delay in the production of the Indian-made HJT-16 Kiran trainer, Polish WSC-Mielec TS-11 Iskra jet trainers were purchased. SIPRI, *World Armaments and Disarmaments Yearbook 1975,* p. 230; *Ibid.,* 1976, p. 264.

27. For data on India's expenditure on military R&D, see Lieutenant Colonel Gautam Sharma (Ret.). "Defence Production in India," *Institute for Defence Studies and Analyses Journal* (New Delhi), Vol. X, No. 4, April-June 1978, Table 7, p. 242.

28. The following discussion of Indo-Soviet relations after the March 1977 elections is based upon Rajan Menon, "India and the Soviet Union: A New Stage of Relations?," *Asian Survey,* Vol. XVIII, No. 7, July 1978, pp. 731-750.

29. In a July 1975 interview with Oriana Fallaci, Desai remarked that, "She [Mrs. Gandhi] never loses an opportunity to please the Soviets." Oriana Fallaci, "Mrs. Gandhi's Opposition: Morarji Desai," *New Republic,* August 2 and 9, 1975, p. 155.

30. Following widespread defections from his party, Morarji Desai resigned in July 1979. A new government, headed by Charan Singh, was sworn in but Mrs. Gandhi became Prime Minister following the January 1980 elections.

31. The statement also noted India's long-standing friendship with the USSR. See *Amrita Bazar Patrika* (Calcutta), August 22, 1968.

32. *Ibid.,* August 24, 1968.

33. *Sunday Statesman* (Calcutta), September 29, 1968. A few days prior to the minister's statement, the Soviet and Czech ambassadors had called on him to express their concern of the critical attitudes adopted toward the Soviet invasion of Czechoslovakia by the Indian press. *Hindustan Times* (New Delhi), September 24, 1968.

34. For details on Kosygin's efforts and the Indian response, see *Times of India* (Bombay), March 14, 1979; March 15, 1979; March 17, 1979. For an advanced analysis of the visit, see Robert Rand, "Soviet Premier Kosygin Visits India," *Radio Liberty Research Bulletin,* RL 78/79, March 8, 1979, pp. 1-3. Following Kosygin's visit two former Indian officials—T. N. Kaul and Dinesh Singh—visited the capitals of the members of the Association of South East Asian Nations (ASEAN) in a reported effort to lobby for the recognition of the Heng Samrin government. These attempts follow from New Delhi's distrust of Peking and its traditionally good relationship with Hanoi, rather than from Kosygin's visit. See Rodney Tasker, "Short Shrift from Hanoi's Friend," *Far Eastern Economic Review* (Hong Kong), August 10, 1979, pp. 9-10.

35. According to one scholar, "In the new international division of labor, it had obviously fallen to the Soviet Union's lot to tackle India, whereas the United States was prompting West Germany to sign on the dotted line." Dietmar Rothermund, "India and the Soviet Union," *The Annals of the American Academy of Political and Social Science,* Vol. 386, November 1969, p. 87.

36. *Hindustan Times* (New Delhi), June 13, 1979.

37. *Ibid.*

38. Text in *Pravda.* June 15, 1979.

39. International Institute for Strategic Studies, *The Military Balance, 1977-78,* p. 58.

40. Chari, "Indo-Soviet Military Relations, p. 238.

41. US Central Intelligence Agency, *Communist Aid to Less Developed Countries of the Free World,* 1977, Table 3, p. 4.

42. *Ibid.,* Table 2, p. 3; US Department of State, Bureau of Intelligence and Research, *Communist States and Developing Countries: Aid and Trade in 1973,* INR RS-20, October 1974; US Department of State, Bureau of Public Services, *Communist States and Developing Countries: Aid and Trade in 1974,* Special Report, No. 23, February 1976, p. 14.

43. For details on Indian military training facilities, see Government of India, Ministry of Information and Broadcasting, *India: A Reference Annual, 1975,* New Delhi: Publications Division, 1975, pp. 40-43.

13

THE USSR AND VIETNAM

Douglas Pike

The USSR in Asia is seen by the Vietnamese as a *status-quo* power and as a European nation. Moscow has had weak party-to-party relations in Asia and its influence at the government-to-government level has been less than elsewhere in the world. It has not been thought to have much interest in leftist regimes, because their advent to power would serve China more than the USSR. For the same reason, its historical experience has been that it gains little from regional conflicts. Because of these factors, the USSR perenially has been at a strategic and tactical disadvantage in Asia. Vietnam represents a recent and—at least for the moment—striking exception to this experience.

Several other characteristics mark the USSR in Asia and Vietnam:

• USSR efforts to control events and influence decisions in the countries and within the Communist parties of Asia continually are thwarted or ruined by the local spirit of nationalism. A major test of this thesis will come in future Vietnamese-Soviet relations.

• The central thrust of the Soviet Union into Vietnam as into all of Asia always was (and remains today) essentially ideological. Its major concern in influencing policy and behavior was and probably will remain China. China's challenge is a mix of ideology and geopolitics, now more of the latter.

• USSR objectives in Vietnam are chiefly the desire to influence if not dominate, both ideologically and geopolitically, countries bordering on China—part of its broader anti-Chinese objective—and to lessen Chinese influence over all Asian Communist parties and countries, including Japan and the ASEAN nations.

• The USSR's basic technique in Vietnam (as in Asia) is to search for soft spot opportunities and then exploit them. The rule has been: push when softness develops and keep pushing until resistance hardens.

• However, almost every major move by the USSR in Vietnam in the past 50 years has been not an action but a reaction. Rather than pursuing a clearly defined predetermined course, the USSR chiefly has moved according to unfolding events. Nor has it been particularly skillful in dealing with Vietnam (or with Asia) but rather has often been ham-handed, its own worst enemy. This has tended to reduce its activity and limit its success. It also has meant being victimized by opportunism and adventurism.

• The USSR's reactive approach to events in Vietnam and Asia has consistently resulted in a considerable Soviet investment yielding only modest Soviet return. Nothing seems to work very well for the USSR in Asia, and despite considerable input and energy over the years it has surprisingly little to show for its efforts. Vietnam at the moment is the promising exception to this historical experience and that probably is the reason why it counts for so much in current Moscow thinking.

Communist Vietnam is now a major force in Asia. It has one of the largest and most effective military forces anywhere in the world. The long-range goal of the party and the new Socialist Republic of Vietnam probably is creation of a Federation of Indochina, composed of Vietnam, Laos, and Cambodia. In the shorter run, the next decade or so, it will seek to shape these three countries into a loosely structured, confederated arrangement—one in which there is mutual advantage to all three and in which Vietnam is the first among equals. Gradually, the Vietnamese would hope, this structure would become institutionalized and eventually would come full federation. To achieve this goal, the Vietnamese must overcome two major forces, historical fear and dislike by the non-Vietnamese involved and opposition from China and other nations. Vietnam and the USSR appear to be in harmony on the federation idea even though it is probable that ultimately Hanoi would seek to reduce to a minimum all foreign presence in Indochina, including Soviet presence.

SOVIET-VIETNAMESE RELATIONS

There never has been much warmth or empathy between Vietnamese and Soviet Communists, not even in the earliest years. Ho Chi Minh saw utility in a Moscow connection in terms of local influence but considered Soviet communism, save for some valuable organizational techniques, as irrelevant and even counterproductive for his use in Indochina. Early Vietnamese Communist theoreticians found the Soviet brand of communism of little use in solving Vietnam's problems, although its emotive content was regarded as valuable icon. Lenin scarcely thought about Indochina, and Stalin's continental mentality kept him from ever developing much interest. The Vietnamese Communists plunged into their revolution (the Viet Minh War) with the expectation of considerable Communist world support. They discovered that the USSR was willing to sacrifice what for them were life and death interests for only marginal advantage to Moscow. This left among the ruling Vietnamese Communists—most of whom are still in power—a lasting heritage of bitterness and distrust.

During the Vietnam War the USSR, as a leader of the international Communist movement, represented one of the three major sources of support for the Vietnamese Communist cause (the other two being true believers in Indochina and pacifistic and anti-American forces scattered around the world.) USSR support, material and psychological, made it possible for the Vietnamese Communists to persevere until victory—something they could not otherwise have done. USSR policy towards the war was an equal mixture of pragmatic international politics and judicious commitment. Soviet behavior was highly opportunistic, wary of confrontation and entrapment, conservative in taking risks, and continually plagued by ideological dilemmas. It is now clear that throughout the war USSR behavior was characterized by much less of a sense of certitude than was apparent at the time. The USSR managed to support the war fully—indeed the USSR made it possible for the war to continue—without this devolving into a confrontation with the United States. This was an almost ideal arrangement: the USSR funded a war against the United States yet remained only an adversary, not an enemy.

Never was a political settlement (in the sense of a truly shared power arrangement) acceptable to the Vietnamese Communists. Thus a true political settlement based on compromise never was actually possible. This was because of the nature of the basic Vietnamese Communist objective—unification of Vietnam under a Hanoi banner. Some objectives are given to negotiated compromise. For instance, the objective of political power, theoretically at least, can be divided and shared. Others are not so given. Because unification happens to be an indivisible objective, like death and pregnancy, it is not given to degrees. While a negotiated end to the war in which Hanoi would forego unification might have been forced on it by sheer military weight, it never would have accepted this outcome willingly. Probably the USSR recognized the impossibility of getting the Vietnamese Communists to accept an ending to the war short of unification. At times it attempted to pressure Hanoi into a political settlement because such was regarded as being in Soviet interests. But these attempts failed.

The Sino-Soviet dispute has long conditioned relations between Moscow and Hanoi. During the war and later the Vietnamese believed, correctly, that Vietnam's importance in the calculations of either Peking or Moscow was largely perceived in terms of what the other was up to. Therefore, reasoned the Vietnamese, both Moscow and Peking supported the Vietnamese cause for the wrong reasons. Influenced by the convolutions of the dispute, the respective positions of the USSR and China on various Vietnam War issues were often reversed, in some cases several times. Throughout the war the Vietnamese Communists were able to exploit the Sino-Soviet dispute to their advantage, something no one else was able to do so well.

Soviet aid for Vietnam was generous from the earliest days, first economic (circa 1960), later military and economic (after 1965). The USSR obfuscated its aid program with clouds of rationalizing rhetoric, extensive use of psychological warfare, and a good deal of dissembling. Somehow most Americans never understood that the USSR made the war possible, allowed it to continue, and could have stopped it at any time. Particularly after the advent of the Vietnamese Communist strategy of high-technology big-unit

254

warfare, continued combat would have been impossible without a continuous flow of Soviet war materiel. Despite this total Vietnamese dependence, the USSR did not enjoy much influence on Vietnamese war policy—this because of the Sino-Soviet dispute. Thus, the USSR could have halted the war, but it never could direct it. This may or may not be considered a Soviet policy failure.

There is less appreciation by the Vietnamese for Soviet aid than might be supposed. Rather the focus of the Vietnamese attitude is what was not given (anti-ship rockets, for instance), its general paucity, and the motives of the USSR (anti-Chinese rather than pro-Vietnamese). Soviet leaders are aware of this attitude and tend to regard the Vietnamese as ingrates.

The USSR and Vietnam today are intimately linked, by circumstance more than design, at least from the Vietnamese view. The relationship rests on an extraordinary Vietnamese dependence (both military and economic) and on Soviet opportunism at work as the USSR seeks to fill a political and diplomatic vacuum in Indochina. There is in the association an implied or potential blackmail by the USSR. At the moment, some 20 percent (possibly as much as 30 percent) of the rice eaten in Vietnam must be supplied by the USSR, the alternative to which is rice riots. There are no arms factories in Vietnam. Hence, all war materiel must be supplied from the outside, chiefly by the USSR. Without this military aid, the Vietnamese would be virtually helpless against China. The point has been reached, for the moment, where anything the USSR asks for, the Vietnamese will grant. If there is restraint in this it will be on the part of Moscow. Probably the USSR will not be unreasonable in its demands. It means to pull Vietnam into the Soviet orbit as deeply and as quickly as possible. It hopes first to lock the Vietnamese in economically, then strategically. There can and probably will be pressure in this, but not outright coercion. The USSR certainly must be aware that a close long-term relationship must rest on voluntary action by the Vietnamese, with Hanoi pursuing what it perceives as its own best interests.

Vietnam is obliged to go along with all this because—at the moment—it has no alternative. Its relationship with Moscow is held by steel bands of necessity. However, the arrangement is not a durable one. There are many natural centrifugal forces at work that press Vietnam away from the Soviet center. But the present relationship will continue until Vietnam is in better economic condition and able to feed itself, and until the threat of China subsides.

A PARADOX

A great paradox operates at the subliminal level of Soviet-Vietnamese relations. If ever there were two alien cultures, they are Vietnamese and Russian. Yet the personalities thrown up by each culture have similar dark sides. Both are marked by devious mentality, the result in both cases of a conspiratorial and brutalizing history. Both have paranoid tendencies, manifested by unremitting suspicion of strangers and a general inability to trust. Both exhibit the phenomenon of the tortured soul, abundantly illustrated by a literature of despair. Both also have the ability to throw up an exclusive sort of flaming creative genius, in art and music.[1] But these qualities of similarity, by their very nature, make the two cultures alien—hence the paradox.

Race and Reason

Vietnamese view foreigners through a special prism, one which both distances and stereotypes. What counts is the quality of the association, not what is inherent in it (such as mutuality) or its physical or material manifestations. As a result the individual Vietnamese Communist's perception of the Russian is almost entirely affective. It is idealized, both officially and individually, and almost always expressed in abstract terms. For instance, although the actual relationship over the past decades has been essentially material, there is virtually no sense of this in the Vietnamese consciousness. This attitude was captured in an article on the USSR by Hanoi intellectual, Nguyen Van Kinh. He writes:

> The fraternal peoples of Vietnam and the USSR have always been closely bound by relations of friendship and militant solidarity. Upholding their spirit of proletarian internationalism, the Soviet people have warmly supported and assisted the Vietnamese revolutionary movement right in its embryonic stage. The great victory of the USSR in World War II created favourable objective conditions for the Vietnamese people to successfully wage the August revolution and set up the Democratic Republic of Viet Nam. In Viet Nam's resistance to French colonialism in the past as well as in her present anti-US struggle, for national salvation and socialist building, through many rich and lively forms such as meetings, demonstrations, etc.,

256

the Soviet people have always deeply sympathized with, and vigorously supported the Vietnamese people's just cause. Solidarity with Viet Nam has become a mass movement throughout the USSR. "Weeks" and "Months of solidarity" with Viet Nam have become a tradition for the Soviet people to support and assist the Vietnamese people against the US imperialist aggressors.[2]

One notes the affective quality of Kinh's sense of the relationship. It is entirely immaterial and intellectualized. In dealing with Soviet support he does not speak of surface-to-air missiles or rice shipments or underwriting Hanoi's petroleum needs. Instead he writes of militant solidarity, of rich and lively demonstrations of sympathy such as blood donations. The USSR is not a fellow player in the revolutionary game but a spiritual cheering section. Moscow is seen not as an important ally, but only as a source of symbolic support.

The reason for this is not, as one might suppose, that selfish Vietnamese are unwilling to give credit where it is due and are determined to keep secret from the world the fact of Soviet assistance.[3] Rather it is a function of the fundamental concept which all Vietnamese hold about the proper relationship of Vietnamese to foreigner. It is a singular view, as we shall see below.

Most Vietnamese have a fairly strong emotive sense of the individual Russian. It is in no way as intricate or as psychologically complex as their attitude toward the average Chinese. The Russian is a strange foreigner from a distant country with alien customs. Culturally the Vietnamese considers himself far closer to other nations, to France, to Japan, even to the United States. In part, of course, this is a result of education. A majority of the Hanoi rulers received French education. None was schooled in the USSR.

The Vietnamese consider Soviet citizens to be extremely racist, more so than citizens of other white societies. In part this is due to tales told by Vietnamese returning from the USSR of racial prejudice which they experienced. Non-Russian visitors to Vietnam in the past several years reported frequent personal incidents with racial overtones in the streets of Hanoi and Ho Chi Minh City, in which they were insulted by Vietnamese taking them to be Soviet citizens. When a Belgian International Postal Union official was stabbed to death in Da Nang in 1977, the Belgians were told privately that his attacker thought him to be a Russian.

Within the ruling Vietnamese Communist Party, where such attitudes have greater political importance, the USSR long has been

257

stigmatized as having a barbarian mentality largely incapable of grasping the Vietnamese world view. Privately, in Party circles, this is labeled Soviet cultural chauvinism. Party historians may laud the USSR in terms of historic revolutionary accomplishments, but never for having made any specific contribution to the Vietnamese revolution. At best, the USSR serves as a vague model of ideological inspiration. From what little has been written in Moscow on the matter, it is clear that Soviet theoreticians tend to hold Vietnamese communism in low esteem, presumably because it departs so greatly from the Soviet brand. And indeed it does.

Marxism for the Vietnamese true believer is not a guide but an icon. The idea that Marxism is a body of knowledge to be absorbed hardly ever occurs to the average Vietnamese Communist. The notion that if one masters this body of knowledge, he becomes infallible in interpreting social phenomena and in predicting social change seems absurd to those few Vietnamese Communists who might think about it. Marxism may be something worth dying for, but it does not require understanding.

This long-standing disparity in Marxist thought has always conferred on the Vietnamese Communist-Soviet Communist relationship the overtone of tenuousness, of being delimited and hedged on both sides, and above all of being transitory. Never has Vietnamese communism had an aura of true proletarian kinship with the USSR. Hence there never has been any particular allegiance. The men of Moscow, to the Vietnamese, are distant from the Vietnamese cause, not because of lack of sympathy but because of ingrained inability to understand either the cause or the Vietnamese themselves. There is in this, of course, a reverse racism on the part of the Vietnamese.

Coupled to Hanoi's sense of superiority is a more finite memory of Kremlin indifference to Vietnam's fate and the Soviet record of frequent untrustworthiness in day-to-day dealings. Hanoi suspicion about Soviet motives is understandable even without a paranoid Vietnamese leadership. It is a suspicion rooted in a Vietnamese proverb: the wolf watches from the mountain top as the tigers battle in the valley.

This attitude has understandably had a backlash effect in Moscow. Soviet officials are not so insensitive to as to be unaware of Vietnamese disdain and distrust, even when it is carefully hidden. In discussing Vietnam privately with Americans and others, these officials commonly label the Vietnamese as unappreciative ingrates and double-dealing opportunists.

Power and Prestige

A second dimension of the subliminal Soviet-Vietnamese perception has to do with various concepts of authority and the meaning of these in terms of political and diplomatic influence. It involves the links among power, prestige, and success.

The Vietnamese respect power. Old guard officials in Hanoi still unabashedly admire Joseph Stalin, not because of his warm personality but because of the unique power he was able to command.[4] Their tributes to the USSR, in anniversary messages and similar vehicles, are always cast in the rhetoric of Soviet strength, iron determination, irresistible force.[5]

Those Vietnamese who think about the matter are extremely hard-nosed about the USSR. They regard it as a nation with immense military capability for intruding where it sees an opportunity for advancing what it considers to be progressive or revolutionary movements. That drive is not seen as ideological, as many in the West would view it, but as the proper use of raw power. The common-sense Vietnamese view is simply: if you have power, use it. The USSR is admired for its toughness in dealing with other countries, the United States and China particularly. Conversely, China and the United States are held in contempt to the extent that weakness is perceived.

The Kremlin leaders also venerate power and try to project the power image in Vietnam. The USSR's strength in Vietnam always has been regarded as material and its only perceived nonmaterial power as psychological. Certainly it is not a moral force. The USSR has operated in Vietnam using the Marxist myth of invincibility, with communism as the wave of the future. In terms of influencing Vietnamese thinking this is probably the weakest kind of evidence that can be offered for the existence of power. Historical determinism may prove to the Western mind that the future belongs to communism, but to the Vietnamese almost any device— even geomancy—is more persuasive than such dialectical reasoning.

In Vietnam, as in Asia, the other side of this power coin is status or prestige—in Vietnamese terms, face. Moscow, because of other forces at work there, long has recognized that nothing is more important to the Vietnamese than status. Soviet behavior often

259

strikes the outsider as pompous, but it is the use of pomp to engender prestige. For the USSR in Vietnam this means that it is difficult (even dangerous) to accept any sort of defeat, or even retreat. To do so reduces prestige, which undermines power.

Soviet status is measured by the Vietnamese with the test of success or failure. In Vietnamese thinking success counts for everything. Writing elsewhere the author has described this phenomenon as his Second Law of Asian Politics: nothing succeeds like success, nothing fails like failure. Success equals status. The only true hold Moscow has on Vietnam is in demonstrating its ability to apply power successfully. In dealing with Moscow (or Peking or Washington), the question the Vietnamese put is: are we dealing with a winner? The question may be simply stated, but determining the answer is never easy or certain, particularly if the estimate must calculate a complex multilateral relationship. Thus Hanoi, facing problems and issues which simultaneously involve Moscow, Peking, Tokyo, Washington, and others—and which also involve a good deal of dissembling, intrigue and ambiguity—must seek to determine who among these are winners, who merely appear to be winners, and who are losers.

In the future the USSR in Vietnam will continue to be locked into a position: its hold based on power which rests on prestige which is rooted in its invincibility. To the extent the Vietnamese perceive that Soviet power is in the ascendancy they will to that extent (and only to that extent) adjust their behavior accordingly. Thus Soviet ventures in Vietnam, indeed Moscow's entire future there, will stand or fall on the idea—the fable—of invincible power.

Doc Lap

The famed Vietnamese spirit of *doc lap* (independence)[6] is no simple impulse to throw off an alien yoke—that spirit is found in all societies—but rather is a highly complex attitude compounded of fear, racial memory, insecurity, ethnic pride, xenophobia, and desire for communion. As with children leaving their parents at maturity, it is an independence both to be desired and regretted, one which separates but hopefully does not isolate. Among Vietnamese the *doc lap* heritage manifests a singular view of the world.

Traditionally, Vietnamese view the world as a highly hostile place. Folk psychology has it that the individual cannot cope with aliens. Strangers are dangerous and clever; one should avoid them if possible, and one is permitted to lie, cheat, and secretly make fun of them. To make it through life one must develop a protective mechanism, a network of special relationships. Success consists in building such a network of contractual relations with those judged reliable. The relationships must be carefully defined (although usually not articulated), reciprocal, and not exploitative. It levies on both parties certain imperatives of behavior, because compliance and meeting demands are part of the arrangement. This is not friendship. It is an arrangement of personal power and status with nonfamily individuals. Its very heart, of course, is face.

When transferred to the broader scene, the international arena for instance, this traditional world calls for three separate behavioral patterns: maintaining minimal relations (but not avoidance of relations) wherever possible; being constantly suspicious of the actions and motives of other nations; and, establishing one reliable special relationship.

The genesis of *doc lap* unquestionably is the initial Vietnamese experience with China. In the beginning (about 500 B.C.), Vietnamese believe, there lived in what is now South China the Hundred Yeuh (Tribes), including one tribe called the Viets. Came the Chinese (i.e., the Han) and slowly all tribes were assimilated in *han-hwa* (sinoization)—all except the Viets, who fled from their home along the Yangtze southward to the delta of the Red River. The Chinese pursued them, occupying Vietnam (about the time of Christ). For 900 years they continued the *han-hwa* effort but to no avail, and finally they were forced out. They returned again in the 13th and 15th centuries and made war on the Vietnamese in campaigns of conquest. The dream of conquest resurfaced briefly in 1945, when the Chinese occupied northern Vietnam. A hint of it came once again in the winter of 1979. In the deep recesses of his mind the Vietnamese believes China still dreams of *han-hwa*.

Political Umbilical Cord

Doc lap then carried dual characteristics, the spirit of independence being balanced by special need for intimate external relations, often ironically, those regarded as threats to *doc lap*. Vietnamese relations with the Chinese and the French became not simply a matter of necessary outside support, but mandatory psychic sustenance from a mother figure abroad, without which survival was impossible.

261

In modern political terms this has meant an association best described as a political umbilical cord. Every major Vietnamese political movement of the 20th century has had a political umbilical cord to an outside source which the respective Vietnamese involved regarded as essential for survival. The Nationalists had such ties with Japan, China, and the United States; the Viet Nam Quoc Dan Dang, with the Kuomintang in China; the Dai Viets, with the Japanese; the Communists (Stalinists), with the USSR, the Chinese Communist Party, the French Communist Party and the worldwide Communist movement; the early reformist groups, both Catholic and non-Catholic, with elements in France; the Buddhists, with counterpart organizations in Ceylon, Japan, and elsewhere. Indeed the history of the early nationalist and Communist movements in Vietnam largely can be written in terms of leaders wandering in search of some mystic foreign connection. Ho Chi Minh, for example, for nearly 30 years never set foot in his homeland.

All revolutionary and anticolonial movements in Asian colonial countries had relations with left-wing groups in the mother country. But these ties elsewhere were never considered to be life-and-death associations, as they were by the Vietnamese. For example, the Indian Congress Party in its early days maintained liaison with supportive groups in London. But it was a nominal relationship. Congress Party leaders always thought of themselves as being on their own, and that their cause would succeed or fail depending on its merits and on Congress Party strategy. Victory would not be delivered by outsiders.

The Vietnamese equivalents of the Congress Party—in the Communist and Nationalist movements—never could embrace this attitude of self-reliance. Their leaders and emissaries went abroad not in search of political and financial support, but to find a sponsor who would provide permanent and total commitment. The Communists were luckier than the Nationalists in this respect, although the Comintern apparently thought the Vietnamese Communists expected too much and frequently made excessive demands. Mao Tse-tung supposedly muttered to an aide, as the plane carrying Ho Chi Minh, Le Duan, and Phan Van Dong landed at Peking airport for a "goodwill visit": "Here comes the three monks with their begging bowls." Vietnamese Nationalists were even more shameless in their demands—to Japanese, Chinese and the French—that they expel the French colonialists and deliver up

262

Vietnam. Vietnamese anticolonial figures spent decades abroad trying to engineer what in effect was a bilateral Vietnamese revolution.

The history of the Vietnamese Communists' relations with China and the USSR is filled with refusals of Vietnamese demands, regarded by the Vietnamese as acts of betrayal.[7] For the Vietnamese Communists this involved an involuted approach to proletarian solidarity. Even when the movement was totally dependent on outside economic assistance, the Party continued to act on the implicit assumption that, in the spirit of *doc lap*, all foreigners were betrayers. While asserting that Vietnamese independence meant depending on no one and trusting no one, they levied extraordinary aid requirements on their socialist allies.

Subliminal Heritage

Clearly a subliminal influence exerts itself today on Vietnamese attitudes toward foreigners, toward the USSR, and toward all other countries. It is a contradictory if not schizoid fear of emasculation, which requires that Vietnam escape from foreign influence even while demanding extraordinary commitment by outsiders. The heritage in sum is manifold and dichotomous, manifesting itself as enormous ambivalence towards friend and foe alike in the outside world. On the one hand is the desperate psychological need for ties of sustenance, born of past failure and never-ending gestures of defiance, which for all their magnificence came to nothing— leaving as the only hope the outsider who could put things right. On the other hand, also reinforced by experience, is an enormous distrust of outsiders who ultimately betray or abandon.

The heritage involves several internal behavioral patterns. There is an ingrained indecisiveness, the tendency forever to temporize. There also is great reluctance to assume leadership of attempted change. Responsibility in the past rested somewhere else—in the court, in the village council, with French liberals, among anti-imperalist friends in China or Moscow. Most of all there is this heritage: the Vietnamese, burdened by fear of failure, betrayal and impotency, too often lapse into imposing unreasonable demands on others. They become mean in spirit, hate-ridden—in Vietnamese it is known as *cam thu, cam hon*. It is the spirit of hate: hate the enemy, hate the traitor, hate the exploiter, hate even those who do change the hated condition, or those who come to help.

These then are the subliminal forces from the past. They remain present and operative in Vietnam today. They are difficult to chart or measure. And they are mutations, constantly being translated into new modes, appearing as new responses.

CONCLUSIONS AND FINAL THOUGHTS

Present-day Vietnamese-Soviet relations can be thought of in terms of superstructure and foundation, the first finite and material and the second psychological and abstract.

The superstructure of the relationship is composed of imperative dependency on Hanoi's part and perceived national interest and opportunism as far as the USSR is concerned. As long as Vietnam remains dependent on the USSR for 20 percent or more of the grain it consumes (and at the same time remains isolated and virtually friendless in the world), and as long as it needs massive arms flows for its Kampuchean War and to defend itself against China, and as long as the USSR's interests are served by feeding and arming Vietnam, then the present close relationship will continue.

It is in Vietnam's interest, and it is its intention, that it be able to feed itself. Eventually the China threat will subside and Kampuchea will be pacified. Then the steel bands of necessity which have bound Vietnam to the USSR will be loosened and the Vietnamese will seek to distance themselves from Moscow. There is virtually no possibility that Vietnam will ever become a satellite of the USSR, in the manner of East Europe.

The foundation of the relationship is subliminal. This is an abstraction and it may be an irrational one, but it is a most powerful force. It is a product of the Vietnamese psyche.

Because of their history, as well perhaps for other reasons, the Vietnamese have always had an extraordinarily singular relationship with peoples around them. Probably Vietnam is unique among all nations in this. In any event, it is a demonstrable historical fact that no neighbor (no nation for that matter) has ever had what could be called a successful long-term relationship with Vietnam. Not the Chinese for a millenium, not the now extinct Cham, not the Khmer of once-vast empire, not the Siamese (Thais) or Burmese since the 15th century, not the Montagnards of a dozen tribes, not the French, not the Americans. Each had moments of amicability and mutual interest, but each relationship carried the seed of its own destruction.

264

Thus there appears to be a great paradoxical law at work in associating oneself with the Vietnamese: any successful relationship is an eventual catastrophe. It is this law which Moscow now is testing. It may succeed where all others have failed, but more likely it too eventually will become a victim of Vietnam.

ENDNOTES

1. Vietnamese creative genius largely has gone unappreciated in the West. Vietnamese music, with its half-tone scale, is so vastly different from western music that years of special training are required for appreciation. There is an equally formidable barrier in literature. Vietnamese language is so subtle that it defies literal translation, while poetic translation is virtually a creative act in its own. Vietnamese poetry particularly must be read and appreciated in its original or untranslated form.

2. Nguyen Van Kinh, "Welcome to the 50th Founding Anniversary of the USSR," *Vietnam Magazine* (Hanoi), December 1972.

3. US experience with the South Vietnamese was similar. There were few gestures or genuine expressions of gratitude, either official or personal, experienced by Americans in assisting the South Vietnamese.

4. This is particularly evident from the tone of Hanoi press editorials on the various anniversaries of Stalin's death.

5. Typical of this is Foreign Minister Nguyen Duy Trinh's October 1977 speech, "Inexhaustible Source of Strength and Inspiration," published in *International Affairs* (Moscow), December 1977.

6. The term *doc lap* virtually defies accurate translation. Its literal meaning is independence, but as such it obscures more than it reveals. In English, independence means not dependent, which is not connoted by *doc lap*; it also implies not subject to the control of others, while the meaning in Vietnamese is of an intimate sort of obligatory control or reciprocal behavior. In English independence is bound up with freedom, with no corresponding relevance in Vietnamese usage. The full meaning of *doc lap* is best understood in its usage.

7. Because of space limitations Vietnamese resistance to the French in *doc lap* terms is not considered here. Resistance was one of the three responses which an individual Vietnamese could make (the other two being collaboration or deliberate "island in the lake" disassociation). The *doc lap* concept of course contributed to the Vietnamese response and was in turn conditioned by the experience of French colonialism.

266

14

THE SOVIET UNION AND ASEAN

Thomas L. Wilborn

As the 1970's draw to a close, with the Sino-Vietnamese confrontation continuing and the status of the Soviet-backed People's Republic of Kampuchea still unsettled, Soviet policy makers were directing increased attention to the Association of Southeast Asian Nations (ASEAN) and the states which compose it: Indonesia, Malaysia, Philippines, Singapore, and Thailand. Their proximity to Vietnam, Kampuchea, and Laos—now allies, if not clients, of the Soviet Union—and China's open conflict with Vietnam over Kampuchea and the treatment of ethnic Chinese make the region another battlefield in the cold war between Moscow and Beijing. Indeed, the continuing conflict between Pol Pot's guerrillas and other anti-Vietnam forces, supported by the People's Republic of China (PRC), and the Soviet and Vietnamese-sponsored Heng Samrin regime could cause part of one ASEAN country, Thailand, to become a hot war battlefield as well.

For ASEAN states to recognize the Kampuchean government imposed by Vietnam would not only imply their retroactive acceptance of Vietnam's invasion, but it would also dramatically deny legitimacy to China's armed assault against Vietnam and thus

267

be a stunning defeat for the PRC. But for ASEAN to continue to recognize Pol Pot's Democratic Kampuchea, even though the regime was the object of universal condemnation when it was in power, and to accept China's linkage of its attack on Vietnam to the continued presence of Vietnamese troops in Kampuchea, must be considered a Soviet diplomatic defeat, a barrier to the spread of Vietnamese and Soviet influence in the region, and a sign of the growing influence of the PRC. The positions of ASEAN governments are thus of major importance in the struggle of the Soviet Union with its Communist adversary, the People's Republic of China.

This relatively high concern is very recent, however. From 1965, when the unsuccessful coup in Jakarta temporarily ended its already declining ability to influence Indonesian policy, until 1978, when the Soviet-Vietnamese treaty of friendship and cooperation was signed, the Soviet Union placed greater emphasis on relations (or lack of them) with the United States, China, Western developed nations, and other Socialist states, and also seemed to have imputed more significance to other Third World areas such as South Asia, the Middle East, and Africa. Within Southeast Asia, Vietnam and the other states of Indochina received more of the Kremlin's attention than either ASEAN as an organization or its member governments.[1] An examination of the reasons for involvement in Indonesia before 1965, the failure of that policy, and the relative neglect from then until very recently should help in understanding and evaluating present Soviet policy towards the region.

SOVIET INVOLVEMENT AND FAILURE IN INDONESIA

Post-Stalin Soviet policy first recognized the Third World as an arena through which the influence of the West, particularly the United States, might be limited by encouraging neutralism. Then, as Khrushchev began to impose his personal stamp on Soviet foreign policy, an offensive was launched to expand Soviet influence and obtain allies among a few selected former colonies.

Indonesia was designated as one of the emerging nations forming what Khrushchev called a "zone of peace" with the Socialist countries. These countries were thought to be particularly open to Soviet assistance and Soviet interpretations of the international environment.[2]

Indonesia had a popular, anti-Western, charismatic leader in President Sukarno; a national elite that seemed largely committed to eradicating Western economic control and willing to make common cause with domestic Communists; a large and dynamic Communist party (by 1965, the largest in any non-Communist state); a leadership role among former colonies as a result of being the host of the first Afro-Asian summit (the Bandung Conference); and the potential to dominate the politics of Southeast Asia. Furthermore, because of its dispute with the Netherlands over the status of West Irian, Indonesia needed weapons and political support which the United States and its allies were unlikely to provide. Supporting Indonesia then seemed to Moscow a particularly useful way to promote tensions in an area of the world with important Western interests. To do so would present the Soviet Union as both an alternative source of foreign assistance and a consistent supporter of still weak former colonies against the exploitation of imperialists and colonialists.[3]

The expectations of Khrushchev and his colleagues, which must at least have included the calculation that Indonesia would not side with the enemies of the Soviet Union, were to be in large part unfulfilled. With Soviet support, Indonesia did cause tension and conflict in the region and present serious problems to the United States and its allies, but Soviet influence in Jakarta was always limited. The USSR offered Indonesia something over $1 billion in economic and military aid (but actually spent much less)[4] and gave Indonesia complete political support during its West Irian campaign and effective (albeit less enthusiastic) support against Malaysia. Nevertheless, President Sukarno and the Partai Komunis Indonesia (PKI) led Indonesia firmly into an alliance with the PRC, by then in open confrontation with the Soviet Union, and directly opposed Moscow's efforts to increase its influence with Third World nations. Thus the Soviet Union's diplomatic failure with Indonesia occurred before the abortive coup in 1965, partly as a result of relying too much on the response of one man, Sukarno, and partly as a consequence of the failure of the Soviet leadership to attend to the needs of the PKI as diligently as it did those of Indonesia's armed forces.[5]

Whatever the lessons which Khrushchev's successors learned from this "hare-brained" scheme,[6] it seems clear that their predisposition for a more cautious foreign policy style was affirmed. In the future they would intervene massively in the Third World only when significant Soviet interests were at stake and when favorable results were reasonably certain.

ASEAN'S LOW PRIORITY IN SOVIET POLICY

The low priority which Soviet policy makers had accorded the ASEAN area until recently grew out of ideology, the nature of foreign policy objectives, economic interests, and strategic considerations.

The ideological framework in which Soviet policy toward the Third World is articulated and rationalized has been described and analyzed by others,[7] and need not be reexamined here. Suffice it to say that current orthodox interpretations of Marxism-Leninism still confidently assert the inevitability of the victory of socialism, but at the same time urge caution and tactical flexibility. Capitalism is still considered very strong and the leading capitalist state, the United States, still has the capability to destroy much of the world—and many of the gains of socialism—in nuclear war. Moreover, nuclear war would leave agrarian societies relatively less damaged than industrialized societies, "thus eliminating most of the industrial working classes and leaving the future to the peasant-based Maoist 'model'."[8] As explained by Geoffrey Jukes of Australian National University,

> . . . basically the [ideological] framework, which is more a Beatitudes than a Ten Commandments, reflects the historical conditioning of a regime which has found (a) that the world does not change as fast as it might like, but (b) it has nevertheless, and contrary to the expectations of its founders, not merely managed to hold on to power for almost two generations, but has advanced the country which it controls to the status of one of the world's two superpowers. History, in short, appears to be on its side, and may safely be nudged now and then but not to the point of cataclysm; and maximization of the Soviet position within the existing system not merely does not contradict the revolutionary imperative to replace it with something else, it is a necessary precondition if the eventual inevitable change is to be of a welcome variety.[9]

In other words, the doctrine which provides the framework for perceptions and interpretations of the international environment for Soviet decisionmakers not only does not require that the USSR be heavily involved in the Third World, but it also provides the assurance of ultimate success, in spite of temporary setbacks and diversions, without intervention. Marxism-Leninism, then, would

270

not appear to counsel a more radical policy for the USSR than *realpolitik* considerations alone might dictate. To the contrary, as currently interpreted in the Soviet Union, it contains a conservative bias when applied to the Third World.

In the recent past, "maximization of the Soviet position within the existing system" apparently did not require Soviet leaders to be particularly concerned with the states which make up ASEAN, and certainly not with ASEAN itself. The principal Soviet political objectives in Asia (limiting the influence of China, the United States, and, to a lesser extent, Japan) have been negative,[10] and were not seriously threatened since these three rivals did not significantly increase the levels of their activities in such a way as to adversely affect the Soviet Union's strategic position. Indeed, since the defeat of South Vietnam in 1975, the US presence —specifically its military presence— in ASEAN has been measurably reduced. The United States removed 25,000 men and equipment for them, including 350 aircraft,[11] from Thailand at the request of the Thai government. Also, the number of personnel assigned to the military assistance advisory groups in Indonesia, the Philippines, and Thailand has significantly decreased. There are probably less than half as many US military personnel in all three countries as once were assigned for military assistance to Thailand alone.[12] While Japanese economic penetration of ASEAN nations and Chinese diplomatic efforts to gain support for its "anti-hegemony" campaign continue, the former has not seriously threatened Moscow's larger political or strategic interests there and the PRC has not been successful in its efforts.

In terms of volume, trade between the countries of ASEAN and the Soviet Union has been almost insignificant, and while it increased from $134.1 million in 1971 to $432.2 million in 1977, it represented a smaller share of total ASEAN trade in 1977 (0.7 percent) than it did in 1971 (0.9 percent). The figures for the Soviet Union's Socialist adversary, the PRC, included for comparison, suggest that Soviet trade is of little value in the overall competition. China maintained its share of ASEAN trade throughout the period at about twice the volume of the USSR's commerce. As shown in Table 2, thirty percent of this small volume represents trade with one ASEAN state, Malaysia, but this represented only 1.2 percent of Malaysia's total trade in 1977.

The small volume notwithstanding, Soviet trade with ASEAN

TABLE 1

Aggregate of ASEAN Trade With the USSR, China, and the World, 1971-77

(In Millions of Dollars)

	1971	1972	1973	1974	1975	1976	1977
EXPORTS							
USSR	103.8	83.8	192.0	335.0	202.1	309.6	366.0
China	33.4	50.2	140.8	152.0	135.3	183.2	390.4
World	6,579.2	7,842.8	13,371.1	18,594.2	20,764.5	29,991.0	31,826.2
IMPORTS							
USSR	30.3	21.8	21.8	54.7	59.6	61.2	66.3
China	226.6	251.6	456.8	605.4	706.3	661.2	719.2
World	7,993.0	9,403.3	14,217.9	22,956.8	23,412.4	26,230.8	30,131.8
TOTAL							
USSR	134.1	105.6	213.8	389.7	261.7	370.8	432.3
China	260.0	301.8	597.6	757.4	841.6	844.4	1,109.6
World	14,572.2	17,246.1	27,589.0	41,551.0	44,176.9	56,221.8	61,958.0

Source: Direction of Trade, Annual 1971-1977, Washington: International Monetary Fund, 1978, pp. 154-155, 186-187, 224-225, 239-240, 254-255.

TABLE 2

Malaysian Trade With the USSR, China, and the World, 1971-77

(In Millions of Dollars)

	1971	1972	1973	1974	1975	1976	1977
EXPORTS							
USSR	49.8	36.4	102.7	175.0	102.9	119.0	119.5
China	18.2	27.1	80.7	87.1	52.4	44.8	119.9
World	1,639.0	1,718.3	3,045.8	4,235.9	3,805.6	5,296.6	6,083.8
IMPORTS							
USSR	3.6	4.0	6.8	4.2	5.5	10.1	10.8
China	66.1	69.0	147.6	195.4	148.9	134.4	140.5
World	1,444.7	1,600.6	2,503.8	4,156.2	3,526.1	3,963.4	4,546.7
TOTAL							
USSR	53.4	40.4	109.5	179.2	107.5	129.1	130.3
China	84.3	96.1	228.3	282.5	201.3	179.2	260.4
World	3,083.7	3,318.9	5,549.6	8,392.1	7,331.7	9,260.0	10,630.5

Source: Direction of Trade, Annual 1971-1977, Washington: International Monetary Fund, 1978, pp. 224-225.

and especially with Malaysia is of some economic significance to the Soviet Union. This is because 97 percent of the natural rubber and latex it purchases comes from there. These purchases represent 12 to 15 percent of the total exports of these commodities from Malaysia, and 7 to 8 percent of the total export of them from Indonesia.[13] The supply of natural rubber and latex is important enough for the USSR to endure a very unfavorable trade balance to obtain it (see Table 2), but it is not vital to Soviet economic or national security. At any rate, natural rubber and latex are available through normal commercial avenues which are likely to remain open unless there is a major conflict in the area.

The ASEAN area is typically described as of great strategic importance to the West because it contains the Straits of Malacca, Sunda, and Lombak, which connect the Indian and Pacific Oceans, and through which pass at least 85 percent of Japan's crude oil imports, as well as other important commodities. These straits and the entire ASEAN area are not of comparable strategic significance to the Soviet Union, however.[14]

The Soviets are not in any serious way dependent on trade which passes through these waterways, although the Pacific Ocean Fleet of the Soviet Navy does transit waters which belong to ASEAN nations. Most Soviet ships in the Indian Ocean, including the antisubmarine craft which monitor US SLBM's, are from the Pacific Fleet, and must pass through straits claimed by Indonesia and/or Malaysia to get there.[15] A threat to free passage through the straits during a crisis might be inconvenient to the Soviet Union, to say the least, but such a development is highly improbable in the foreseeable future, since the littoral states are self-consciously nonaligned and unlikely to directly confront either superpower.

The straits of the area would be of limited significance to the Soviet Navy in the event of a general war. Soviet naval doctrine assumes a brief conflict,[16] and, in any case, the Pacific Ocean Fleet, the weakest of the four Soviet fleets,[17] does not have the capacity to engage American naval forces so far away from its bases and ground-based air cover in Vladivostok and Petropavalovsk.[18] In a crisis or conflict involving Japan, the Soviet Union might attempt to interfere with Japanese sea lanes of communications, but, as Jukes points out very strongly, there are easier ways for the Soviets to disrupt Japanese trade than launching a military operation against the Strait of Malacca.[19] Should the speculation that a Soviet

274

naval base will be established at Cam Rahn Bay prove correct, it is possible that the mission of the Pacific Ocean fleet in the Southwest Pacific will be changed and the strategic significance of the ASEAN region enhanced in Soviet naval strategy, although the logistical problems for the Soviets of sustaining a military installation in the South China Sea would limit its utility in wartime.

SOVIET POLICY TOWARD ASEAN

When ASEAN was founded in 1967, Moscow had diplomatic relations with only two of its members, Indonesia and Thailand, and these ties were not cordial. The Suharto regime in Indonesia had allowed (if it did not conduct) the massive vendetta against Communists and Communist sympathizers and was suspicious of the Soviet Union as a Communist government which harbored and protected some of the leaders of the PKI (even though it distrusted the PRC more).

The Thai Government, the United States' most faithful SEATO ally, whose territory was being used to conduct the war against the "patriotic forces of Vietnam," was characterized by Soviet propaganda as a clique of reactionary traitors who served the cause of imperialism, and obviously were not entitled to friendly relations with the Soviet Union.[20] In fact, Soviet interactions with Singapore and Malaysia, with whom there was no formal diplomatic representation until 1968, were more responsive and profitable than those with the states which housed Soviet embassies, for mutually beneficial trade was developing. But even these former British colonies were aligned with the enemies of the Soviet Union, since they both accepted the protection of their former colonial masters. They soon would enter into a defense agreement with Britain, Australia, and New Zealand, all participants in US-dominated anti-Soviet military blocs.

Given the nature of Soviet relations with the members of ASEAN, Soviet endorsement of the new organization was not anticipated and was not forthcoming. Instead, Soviet propaganda condemned it as a transparent effort of the United States and its followers to involve more Asian states in anti-Communist military alliances.

275

Today, the United States is taking particular interest in ASEAN, for besides the countries that are already tied to the West by military agreements, the organization includes Indonesia, one of the largest states in Southeast Asia. As pointed out in the *Christian Science Monitor,* Indonesia's membership immediately lent the new organization a "special character." Thailand, the Philippines, Malaysia and Singapore have even agreed to include in the ASEAN declaration a clause on the temporary nature of the foreign military bases on their territories. According to Reuter's News Agency, however, this was merely designed to "attract Indonesia."

The backstage initiators of ASEAN also hope to draw nonaligned states into the alliance . . . It is significant that after Indonesia joined ASEAN, Jakarta began to develop relations with the Chiang Kai-shek government and the South Vietnam puppet regime, and negative features began to appear in its foreign policy.[21]

Ultimately, after inducing other nonaligned states to join, the US imperialists hoped to merge ASEAN and the Asian and Pacific Council into one great military bloc, the Soviets contended. Moreover, they asserted that there was no possibility for ASEAN to achieve the goals of economic cooperation which were the formal basis for its existence.

Experience has shown that the success of regional alliances depends largely on the extent to which the countries involved are unified on an anti-imperialist basis, resist the pressure of foreign monopolies and on the extent to which their struggle for economic independence is supported by Socialist countries.[22]

Obviously, ASEAN would not have a chance.

The first positions of Soviet commentaries on ASEAN were thus highly critical and focused on the reprehensible relationship of the United States with the regional organization. This was a regular theme through the rest of the decade. The evaluations of ASEAN were anything but constant during the 12 years, however. By early 1972, Soviet publicists were preparing for the signing of the first SALT agreements and the Soviet-American statement on Basic Principles of Relations,[23] which, among other things, constituted formal US recognition of the superpower status of the Soviet Union and the supplanting of the Cold War by peaceful coexistence or detente. And in the spirit of detente, the Soviets were now discovering active progressive forces in many parts of the world, including Malaysia and Singapore, which had seemed before to be totally dominated by the agents of monopoly capitalism. In the

276

Philippines, they reported the existence of a president (Marcos) who had campaigned on positions which were "in the national interest," a phrase always reserved for commendation, even though he had accepted American guidance by joining ASEAN and allowing US bases to remain on Philippine territory.[24]

Descriptions of internal Indonesian politics in Soviet publications still failed to suggest any redeeming social value,[25] but they now did note that Suharto and his generals had refused to endorse American aggression in Vietnam and that Indonesia had resisted the transformation of ASEAN into a military bloc—both positions that allegedly enraged the Pentagon and thus pleased the Kremlin. The condemnatory tones of the first evaluations of ASEAN as an organization were also softened and then were replaced for a time by praise.

In a January 1972 commentary on the signing of the declaration by ASEAN foreign ministers supporting the establishment of a zone of peace, freedom, and neutrality in Southeast Asia (before the new line was clearly established), *Izvestiia* Political Observer V. Kudryavtsev reasoned that this support for neutralization resulted from the fear in "certain circles" that the Vietnamization policy being pursued by the United States at the time was a prelude to greater Chinese influence or perhaps greater Japanese influence—conditions that these groups did not want to develop. Kudryavtsev thought that the tendency to seek neutralization of the area was a positive one "since it demonstrates the downfall of the illusion that it is possible to find among the imperialist powers an unselfish protector that will help to strengthen the independence of one Asian country or another." However, the other side of the coin was that all of the ASEAN states except Indonesia had some kind of military arrangement with imperialist states. Peace, freedom, and neutrality could not come to Southeast Asia until all American troops and bases were thrown out, the military alliances dissolved, and the Nixon doctrine rejected.[27] The absence of these conditions was regrettable,he thought, for neutralization was an idea which was based in the "existing situation in Southeast Asia," and therefore presumedly in conformation with Soviet interests, which would also be based in the existing situation. "/P/ossibly neutralization would be conducive to the creation of a system of collective security in Asia; the proposal for creating such a system is cherished by all those who seek the normalization of the situation in Asia and the ensuring of peace and security in that region."[28]

Six months later (after the friendly line toward ASEAN was established), the same observer wrote an upbeat analysis which deemphasized the conditions which were unfavorable from a Soviet perspective. Although the advocates of neutralization in Southeast Asia were not always consistent, he said the idea was gradually asserting itself. One had to be wary that neocolonialism was not camouflaging some devious scheme, but:

> It would be wrong to ignore the frame of mind in the political circles of many Asian countries that is beginning to understand the pernicious effect of blocks, which prevent them from making full use of all their potential opportunities for economic and cultural development in conditions of national independence.[29]

The only evidence of this beneficial trend cited was President Marcos' verbal attacks on the agreements which allowed US military bases on Philippine soil.

Apparently, Soviet policy makers considered that positive trends continued to dominate developments within ASEAN and its members until late 1976. During this period, when the governments of ASEAN were attempting to come to grips with the Nixon doctrine, the fall of South Vietnam, and the expulsion of US forces from Thailand, Soviet commentaries on the individual states were generally benign. They virtually always noted that in the spirit of detente and in recognition of the victories of the patriotic forces of Indochina, the ASEAN states were seeking to broaden relations with the Socialist states and achieve more independent foreign policies. The principal theme applied to ASEAN itself was that the declaration to transform Southeast Asia into a zone of peace, freedom, and neutrality might be consistent with the Soviet proposal for Asian collective security, and that the declaration was evidence that the peoples of the area really desired true independence and the removal of foreign military forces.[30]

The theme that US imperialists wanted to convert ASEAN into a military pact was revived during 1976, especially after an agreement was reached to dismantle SEATO. This was very possibly a reflection of the general deterioration of US-Soviet relations at the time. Unlike the commentaries of 1968-70, the new versions always noted, until 1977, that ASEAN leaders rejected the devious scheme of American militarists, and they also made positive reference to the neutralization proposal. In a July 1976 broadcast in Indonesia,

278

Radio Moscow listeners were told that "sources close to the Pentagon" had confirmed that Indonesia had been offered an increase in annual aid of from $100 million to $700 million in exchange for approval of the development of a "so-called training base" for ASEAN which was to double as a harbor for part of the Seventh Fleet.[31] That Indonesian leaders refused such offers suggested that they were men of integrity committed to genuine peace.

During the same time (1967-76), Soviet activity among ASEAN nations was more consistent than the themes of its media. There was a continuous effort to expand trade, increase the volume of ASEAN nationals visiting the Soviet Union, and expand cultural contracts. When formal diplomatic relations were finally established with the Philippines in 1976, the Soviet Union had achieved full representation with all ASEAN nations, filling its embassies, according to some observers,[32] with many more people than the volume of trade or other interactions justified. This attention, which only involved routine relations except for a major initiative with Indonesia in 1975, still represented a much greater degree of Soviet activity than ASEAN governments were accustomed to. Foreign Minister Romulo of the Philippines described the situation this way in 1971:

> We in Asia are beginning to feel the impact of a Soviet Russian offensive, something we have never experienced before. The Soviets have sent mission after mission to almost all countries of the region except mainland China; she has put up trade fairs in Singapore and Malaysia and has in turn received missions from these countries. There is no denying the growth of Soviet presence.[33]

The major initiative toward the area was the extension of $100 million credit to Indonesia for the construction of two hydroelectric plants in 1975 and an offer of $360 million to build an alumina plant on Bintan Island.[34] Whether the latter represented a major attempt to regain a position of influence in Indonesia or primarily reflected the Soviet Union's resource needs is uncertain.[35] At any rate, the offer was rejected in 1977, presumedly because the Suharto regime objected to the influx of Soviet technicians which would accompany such a project.

In late 1976, the allegations that the United States, supported by the Maoists, planned to convert ASEAN into another SEATO became more numerous and began to dominate commentary on ASEAN. Unlike the comments of early 1976, these broadcasts and articles noted that some official ASEAN leaders, such as the militarists who had overthrown the short-lived democratic government of Thailand and the Indonesian minister of defense, supported the American generals.[36] Indeed, it was pointed out that there were already a number of bilateral military cooperation agreements, and that, if the practice were expanded, ASEAN would become a military bloc in fact even though it was not one in law.[37] As before, the intense American pressure on ASEAN leaders was emphasized, but with the new twist alleging that some of the military leaders of ASEAN countries, the special target of militaristic imperialism, had been won over.

> Attaching great role to the ASEAN in its Asian strategy, the Pentagon devotes special attention to the military circles of that organization. By bribery, flattery, paid trips to resort areas of the United States, by different receptions and promises, the Pentagon and the CIA are trying to make the military circles of the ASEAN countries take a pro-American stand in respect to the future of the association.

> It is mainly with the help of the military of the ASEAN that the Pentagon managed not only to strengthen its positions in Thailand but to a great degree to preserve its positions in Indonesia, in the Philippines and to penetrate other countries.[38]

The charge that the United States was attempting to make ASEAN into an anti-Communist military alliance was almost the only theme of greatly increased media coverage for about a year. American imperialists and military industrialists applied all manner of pressure, apparently with unlimited resources, by providing economic assistance to obtain political levers over military policy of ASEAN states, and by "imposing its own weapons and ammunition on them."[39] US militarists also enrolled the assistance of Australia, Japan, and New Zealand in the campaign to replace SEATO with ASEAN.[40] The Soviet media in this period avoided any commendation for the governments of ASEAN. Only "the people" or "progressive people" who opposed the dangerous trends received praise.[41]

Several developments apparently were unusually distressing to the Soviet media. One was a three-day symposium on military problems in Jakarta attended by representatives of ASEAN states, a gathering which was said to be inconsistent with the purpose of ASEAN. General Surono, identified as deputy commander of the Indonesian armed forces, addressed the symposium and called on

ASEAN countries "to sacrifice certain national interests for the defense of the region,"[42] presumedly against communism. Another was the alleged conspiracy between imperialism and Chinese hegemonism which was tied more directly to ASEAN militarization than before.[43] Chinese support for US forces in Southeast Asia was roundly condemned, and typically linked with the charge that Beijing manipulated the ethnic Chinese communities of ASEAN nations for use as spies and "fifth columns." A third dangerous development was the continuing proliferation of bilateral military agreements among ASEAN members. Long lists of such agreements were included in several commentaries, giving special attention and condemnation to a proposal for joint production of ammunition "with the support of US military industrialists," Indonesian Defense Minister Panggabean's plan for all ASEAN air forces to standardize with the F-5, the various joint maneuver proposals, and the agreement between Thailand and Malaysia to cooperate in opposing the "so-called Communist rebels" operating along their common border.[44] A practice which was held particularly incompatible with the cause of peace was the alleged use of the Seventh Fleet to influence the decisions of the Bali Summit in 1976 and the foreign ministers' meeting in 1977.[45] During both meetings, Soviet media reported that the United States deployed warships into the Indian Ocean for the purpose of putting pressure on ASEAN. Finally, outrage was repeatedly expressed against the slanderous, false, and malicious accusations of Beijing and the imperialists that the peaceloving outpost of socialism in Asia, the Socialist Republic of Vietnam (SRV), was a threat to any of its neighbors.[46]

Moscow's line changed abruptly in November 1977. All of the developments which had disturbed the Soviet media as recently as the previous month were still present and in fact tended to become more extensive and visible in the following months. The bilateral military cooperation agreements which, they had repeatedly complained, would automatically transform ASEAN into a military alliance at some point continued to proliferate. ASEAN weapons standardization, the practice which was supposed to lead to the dependence of the member nations on the military-industrial complex in the United States, was still discussed, being partially implemented by some ASEAN members. None of these matters were any longer mentioned as significant factors which should influence the relations of the Soviet Union and the five members of

281

ASEAN, however. According to the Soviet publicists, the reason for the positive appraisal was that members of ASEAN had finally "demonstrated a realistic and sober understanding of the situation "[47] that developed in Southeast Asia after the victory of the Vietnamese patriots over the American aggressors. As a result:

> In the past three years the developing countries of Southeast Asia have acquired great political weight in the international arena. This is explained above all by the fact that in the search for ways to resolve the urgent problems of development, an understanding of the need to establish and reinforce neighborliness is prevailing in the region. When the socialist countries of Indochina launched peace-loving initiatives, they did not fall on barren ground but met with a positive response among ASEAN countries.[48]

Additionally, the journal of the Institute for the Study of the USA and Canada concluded that ASEAN was founded, as the ASEAN members claimed, to develop cooperation in economic, social, and cultural questions, and that it was an outgrowth of "the objective trend toward economic integration in this area" which was manifest in 1967.[49] ASEAN must be congruent with the laws of historical development, then, and not a conspiracy created for the purpose of enmeshing Indonesia into an anti-Communist alliance, as it had been described in *International Affairs* in 1969.

The explanation for the shift back to positive media treatment can only partially be explained by changes within the member-states of ASEAN or in conditions of the region. It is true that Vietnam and the nations of ASEAN were expanding diplomatic, cultural, and economic relations, and the doctrinaire anti-Communist Thanin regime in Thailand had been replaced by a much more pragmatic one headed by General Kriangsak. But this might not have been adequate justification to ignore the developments which had previously been criticized. Except for improved ties with Thailand, the Soviet Union's diplomatic and economic relations with the members of ASEAN were generally unchanged, in spite of propaganda shifts. Media treatment of the individual countries also was generally unchanged, except that some atypical attacks were made against Indonesia,[50] and the Marcos regime received brief censure after signing the amendments to the base agreements with the United States in early 1979.[51] There were no reports of offers of Soviet economic aid to any ASEAN state other than Indonesia, although East Germany did extend $30 million to the Philippines.[52]

The principal reasons for the Soviet shift must have been the emerging conflict in Indochina and China's demands on Vietnam, which made it necessary to compete with Beijing for favorable relations with the states of ASEAN. As that conflict intensified, with Vietnam's invasion of Kampuchea and, later, China's attack on Vietnam, the strategic importance of ASEAN for the Soviet Union increased geometrically. If the neighbors of Indochina would accept the new regime in Kampuchea and condemn the Chinese attack against Vietnam, their action would tend to legitimize the domination of Indochina by the Soviet Union's ally, the SRV. Without their acceptance and condemnation, international recognition of Vietnamese hegemony of Indochina would be difficult to achieve.

Within the new approach, the Soviets continued to expose the devious schemes of the imperialists to turn ASEAN into a military alliance and the even more reprehensible plans of the hegemonists in Beijing to subdue Southeast Asia through the extensive overseas Chinese fifth columns. An extremely heavy barrage of anti-Beijing propaganda, especially stringent in the Mandarin language broadcasts to Southeast Asia, was unleashed about the same time that the new line toward ASEAN was adopted. Now, however, listeners and readers were assured that "responsible representatives" of ASEAN,[53] realistic enough to know that economic progress required stability and neighborly relations in Southeast Asia,[54]—that is good relations with Vietnam—had not been seduced. Public assurances that ASEAN would never be allowed to become a military pact, questioned only a year before because of the many bilateral military cooperation agreements, were now accepted at face value.

Following the positive line, Soviet writers began to find successes where a short time before contradictions or inconsistencies had always been present. ASEAN's economic achievements, which most Western observers think are rather modest, were described as extremely important accomplishments of economic cooperation. ASEAN states were even excused for accepting capital from foreign monopolists, because their poverty, resulting from years of exploitation by colonialists and neocolonialists, gave them no other choice. They were praised because they were trying "to limit manifestations of the exploitative essence of imperialist capital."[55] ASEAN's international policy was described as "constructive,"[56] and the members' foreign policies were said to contain principles that were almost the same as those of Vietnam.[57]

Four ASEAN positions apparently accounted for these commendations. The advocacy of friendly relations among all states of the region and the refusal to allow ASEAN to become a military pact have already been cited. In addition, ASEAN's proposal for the establishment of a zone of peace, freedom, and neutrality for Southeast Asia was also praised, sometimes very profusely, as being consistent with Soviet foreign policy.[58] (The Soviet Asian collective security proposal, always before the framework for discussing Southeast Asia neutrality, was no longer mentioned.) Soviet writers had some difficulty with semantics, however, since Vietnam had surfaced its own proposal for a zone of "peace, *independence,* and neutrality," and the difference between ASEAN's "freedom" and Vietnam's "independence"— the latter implying repudiation of existing security arrangements with the West— became the subject of some controversy.[59] At least once Vietnam's formula was identified with the original ASEAN proposal,[60] but finally the solution of leaving out the disputed words altogether and speaking of a "zone of peace and neutrality" was adopted for Southeast Asian audiences.[61] The contrasting solution of using both words—a zone of peace, freedom, independence, and neutrality—and ascribing authorship to Hanoi became the most favored mode of reference in the Russian language press.[62]

A final reason for the laudatory Soviet comments about the foreign policies of the ASEAN states related to their rejection of China's efforts to incorporate ASEAN into its anti-Soviet strategy, and otherwise frustrate Beijing's aggressive designs. China's threat to ASEAN was one of the major themes of Moscow's propaganda effort, reminding listeners and readers that the great-Han-nationalist hegemonists were conspiring with the imperialists to make ASEAN a military pact;[63] that the Hau/Deng clique supported antigovernment terrorists in Malaysia, the Philippines, and Thailand;[64] that their spies were all over Southeast Asia;[65] and that the overseas Chinese communities were potential fifth columns.[66] The spectre of Beijing manipulating 20 million overseas Chinese for its own purposes was particularly emphasized after the Chinese invasion of Vietnam.[67] The Soviets' determination not to criticize ASEAN governments was most obvious during the

Vietnamese attack on Kampuchea and the Chinese invasion of Vietnam. In all of the coverage of those two wars in the Soviet Union section of the *Foreign Broadcast Information Service Daily Report* there is no reference to the failure of the ASEAN states to adopt pro-Vietnam positions. For instance, there was no acknowledgement that the resolution before the Security Council linking Vietnam's actions in Kampuchea with the Chinese attack on Vietnam, which Vietnam and the Soviet Union adamantly opposed, was drafted by the ASEAN members. Although the Pol Pot regime which Vietnam deposed was characterized as bloodthirsty and tyrannical and the People's Republic of Kampuchea was called a true peoples' democracy,[68] Soviet media did not demand that ASEAN governments withdraw their recognition from Pol Pot and confer it on the government imposed by Vietnam. On the contrary, Soviet publicists implied some satisfaction that Southeast Asian "personages" and periodicals supported the Heng Samrin regime, and they simply failed to report the absence of support from political leaders and governments.

> More and more signs have shown that personages in ASEAN are increasingly fond of Kampuchea's new leadership and are planning the establishment of neighborly ties. . .
>
> Newspapers and magazines in this area say that ASEAN countries are likely to recognize Kampuchea's new leadership. This shows that the five ASEAN countries are taking an increasingly greater liking to the real democratic leadership of Kampuchea . . . ASEAN countries are taking a sober and patient attitude toward the SRV's policy in this area. . . .
>
> The ASEAN countries are taking a friendly and neutral stand toward the democratic forces in Indochina. They have rejected Beijing's anti-Vietnam and anti-Kampuchea appeal, and it is possible they will engage in constructive cooperation with Vietnam and Kampuchea in the future.[69]

The first significantly critical commentaries about ASEAN in almost two years appeared only in July 1979 in the context of the refugee question. The final communique of the ASEAN foreign ministers meeting considering the massive influx of "boat" and "land" people into the ASEAN countries called for the withdrawal of Vietamese forces from Kampuchea and placed the blame for the refugee problem on the SRV.[70] It was obligatory, therefore, for the Soviet Union to protest, since its position was that the whole refugee problem had been instigated by the United States and China, and that Vietnam was blameless. It was a muffled criticism, however, apparently distributed only within the Soviet Union:[71]

> attitudes were reflected which are hardly likely to lead to cooperation being established among the countries of the region...Responsibility for creating the so-called refugee problem is placed on Vietnam; and this is done despite facts known to all which testify that the departure of Chinese nationals from Vietnam was provoked by the Beijing leaders. Such positions are similar to Western appraisals of the situation in Indochina. This is connected, observers believe, with the desire of the countries of the association to obtain wider economic aid from the developed capitalist countries during the talks which begin today between ASEAN representatives and the US Secretary of State Vance and the Japanese, Australian, and New Zealand foreign ministers.[72]

In the next several days, the Soviet commentary on ASEAN directed to Southeast Asia questioned whether ASEAN's existence was endangered because of the tension being whipped up by Beijing. But these sources failed to mention the refugee question and they ended with positive appraisals.[73]

SUCCESS OR FAILURE?

Has Soviet foreign policy in ASEAN been a success or failure? Evaluation of a nation's foreign policy is always difficult, even in a general way, because the causes of international events and conditions are always complex. For instance, a goal of Soviet foreign policy toward the ASEAN states is to reduce the influence of the United States, but the possibility that US influence is less now (and almost certainly was less in 1976) than it was in 1967 does not necessarily imply that Soviet policy after 1967 was effective. A more plausible explanation would be that any reduction in US influence was a result of the outcome of the Vietnam War, at most only partially accounted for by Soviet policy, and the decision of the American government to concentrate on other areas of the world—Europe and the Middle East-rather than Southeast Asia. Thus, a condition desired by Soviet policy makers may have been partially achieved, at least temporarily, but more as a result of good fortune than of conscious design.

In contrast, the significantly improved official standing of the Soviet Union in the ASEAN region today compared to 1967 while no doubt facilitated by favorable (from the Soviet viewpoint) regional and international conditions which the Soviets did not themselves create, was directly the result of deliberate efforts by the USSR to take advantage of the opportunity provided by changes in US policy and to expand its diplomatic and trade relations with the five ASEAN members. This accomplishment should not be scored as an extremely important achievement, since most ASEAN elites were disposed to favor improved relations with the Soviet Union anyway. But it did represent a modest success. Uncertain about US intentions in the aftermath of the Vietnam debacle, the elites of ASEAN were probably more inclined to be responsive to Soviet policy needs (although they were suspicious at the same time) from 1975 until 1978 than at any other time.

In the case of the Soviet Union's policy toward ASEAN, evaluation is also complicated by the low priority which the region apparently was assigned by the Soviet policy makers until very recently. Given the low priority, it probably was (and would be) considered acceptable to try to limit Chinese influence only by propaganda, diplomatic reresentation, and other relatively low cost tactics. It may have been enough for Moscow that ASEAN formally abjured any kind of military role; Soviet publicists could claim that this was a victory achieved in spite of intense imperialist pressure. They undoubtedly would have preferred for governments of the area to be friendly to the Soviet Union, and for ASEAN to serve as an institutional framework through which its members could reduce their economic dependence on the West. Given the limited resources that the USSR committed to the region, however, the conditions that prevailed in 1977 were probably pleasing to the Soviets, particularly when compared to the late 1960's.

If (as has been argued here), ASEAN is no longer a low priority region, present Soviet policy must be judged by different criteria. At the least, a successful Soviet policy would have to strengthen the position of Vietnam in Southeast Asia and serve to reduce Chinese influence. Instead ASEAN governments have developed policies concerning the Vietnam-Kampuchea, Vietnam-China, and Indochinese refugee disputes which have been partially coordinated with the United States, and which are closer to Beijing's positions than those of Moscow. Moreover, the Soviets appear to have been excluded from participating in what they consider the most important regional decisions since the end of the second Vietnam war. The limited deference and responsiveness which ASEAN displayed toward the USSR for a brief time was completely negated by Soviet support for Vietnam's invasion of Kampuchea and for Hanoi's expulsion of hundreds of thousands of refugees.

The Soviets must be especially displeased that all ASEAN governments still recognized the Pol Pot regime as the legitimate government of Kampuchea at the end of 1979, that they drafted the resolution debated by the Security Council which linked the presence of Vietnamese troops in Kampuchea with the Chinese invasion of Vietnam, and that they have levied the blame for the refugee problem primarily on Vietnam, rather than on the targets of Soviet propaganda—the United States and China.

In fact, in the relatively short time since ASEAN has become dramatically more saliant in the Soviet perspective, there has probably been nothing which the Soviets could have done to improve their position. Presently there are no Moscow or Hanoi-associated Communist parties of any significance in any ASEAN country which could have been manipulated to put pressure on the regimes of the region. Soviet trade with ASEAN was very small and could not have been used to influence any of the governments in the current regional conflicts. Promises of foreign aid may become a factor in future Soviet strategy to obtain more favorable decisions from ASEAN governments, but given the swift pace of developments in Indochina and the sensitivities raised by the refugee problem, it could not have been an effective short-term instrument of Soviet policy. Demonstrations of military force might not have been as impressive as those the United States could have deployed, and, in any case, probably would have proven counterproductive by playing into the hands of factions which supported the presence of US forces in the area.

Appropriate opportunities and usable capabilities simply were not available to the USSR. The failure to obtain short-term objectives was part of the price for acquiring its relationship with Vietnam, and Soviet leaders may have been more than willing to pay it in the short run. In the longer term, however, the relative advantage *vis-a-vis* China that has been gained through pro-Moscow governments in Indochina will lose much of its value to the Soviet Union if ASEAN governments become more responsive to Chinese and/or US desires. At the least, the Soviet Union needs to induce ASEAN governments to accept the Heng Samrin government in Kampuchea and to support the SRV against China, possibly using assets (e.g., insurgent groups and military bases) acquired as a result of SRV victories in Indochina. Soviet efforts to achieve these ends should be expected to intensify and probably become more varied.

Thus the answer to the question of the success or failure of Soviet policy toward ASEAN at this time must be that there is as yet no evidence of success. However, the final judgment cannot be rendered until a degree of stability in Indochina has been achieved, and this may take a long time indeed.

ENDNOTES

1. See Robert C. Horn, "The USSR and Southeast Asia: The Limits of Influence," in *Soviet Economic and Political Relations with the Developing World,* ed. by Roger E. Kanet and Donna Bahry, New York: Praeger Publishers, 1975, pp. 156-178, and Geoffrey Jukes, "The Soviet Union and Southeast Asia," *Australian Outlook,* Vol. 31, April 1977, pp. 174-184.

2. See Elizabeth Kridl Valkenier, "The Soviet Union and the Third World: From Khrushchev's 'Zone of Peace' to Brezhnev's Peace Program," in Kanet and Bahry, p. 4.

3. Indonesia's relations with the Soviet Union are briefly discussed in most accounts of the abortive coup in 1965 and in analyses of Soviet policy toward Southeast Asia. See, for instance, Antonie C. A. Dake, *In the Spirit of the Red Benteng: Indonesia Communists between Moscow and Peking, 1959-1965,* The Hague: Mouton, 1973, *passim;* Horn; Jukes; Guy Pauker, "The Soviet Union and Southeast Asia," Rand Paper Series, P-5080, July 1973, and Uri Ra'anan, *The USSR Arms the Third World: Case Studies in Soviet Foreign Policy,* Cambridge: The M.I.T. Press, 1969, pp. 175-245.

4. Pauker, p. 8, computes the total grants of credits at more than $1 billion. Except for the sports coliseum in Jakarta and a hospital which was a gift to the people of Indonesia, no Soviet economic projects were completed. Horn, p. 164.

5. Horn, p. 164; Jukes, p. 176; and Justus M. van der Kroef, "The Soviet Union and Southeast Asia," in *The Soviet Union and the Developing Nations,* ed. by Roger E. Kanet, Baltimore: The Johns Hopkins University Press, 1974, p. 103, emphasize that the basic cause for the Soviet diplomatic defeat was overdependence on President Sukarno personally. On the other hand, Ra'anan, p. 235, tends to stress the fact that the PKI was not discouraged from supporting Chinese positions by the USSR.

6. Valkenier, p. 4.

7. See Horn; Jukes; Roger E. Kanet, "Soviet Attitudes Toward Developing Nations Since Stalin," in Kanet, pp. 27-50; Bhabani Sen Gupta, *Soviet-Asian Relations in the 1970's and Beyond: An Interperceptual Study,* New York: Praeger Publishers, 1976, especially Chapter 1, and "An Approach to the Study of Soviet Policies for the Third World," in Kanet and Bahry, pp. 20-32; and Valkenier, pp. 3-9.

8. Jukes, p. 1.

9. *Ibid.,* p. 2.

10. See Horn; Sen Gupta; *Soviet-Asian Relations in the 1970's and Beyond;* and Pauker for discussions of Soviet objectives in Southeast Asia.

11. These were the figures used by *The New York Times,* March 18, 1975, p. 1.

12. The Security Assistance Program proposed for FY 1980 authorized 98 personnel in the three countries. US Defense Security Assistance Agency, *Security Assistance Program: Congressional Presentation, FY 1980,* p. 40.

13. Joint Publication Research Service (JPRS), No. 72385, p. 37, translated from *DDR Aussenwirtschaft* (Berlin), January 31, 1979, p. 3.

14. Jukes, pp. 181-183, for elaboration.

15. Donald C. Daniel, "The Soviet Navy in the Pacific," *Asia Pacific Community,* Spring/Early Summer 1979, p. 73.

16. In sustained naval conflict, the Pacific Ocean Fleet would have to be resupplied through the straits of the area. With their present capabilities, however, the Soviets could not protect these routes, especially from air attacks. This may be the major reason—it is certainly a sufficient reason—why Soviet doctrine only provides for a short naval campaign.

17. *Asia Yearbook,* 1979, p. 39.

18. Daniel, p. 73, and *Understanding Soviet Naval Developments,* Third Edition, Washington: Office of the Chief of Naval Operations, January 1978, p. 14.

19. Jukes, p. 183.

20. For example, see Y. Kusnetsov, "Thailand: People and Bases," *New Times,* No. 12, October 1967.

21. V. Pavlovsky, "Problems of Regionalism in Asia," *International Affairs* (Moscow), April 1969, p.50.

22. *Ibid.,* p.46.

23. The Statement on Basic Principles of Relations was signed at the Moscow summit in conjunction with the first SALT agreements. Basically, these principles affirmed that the United States and the Soviet Union should practice peaceful coexistence or detente.

24. William Pomeroy, "New Trends in the Philippines," *New Times,* No. 5, February 1970, p. 20, and V. Spandaryan, "In the Land of Rubber," *New Times,* No. 22, May 1967, pp. 21-24.

25. B. Vetin, "The Situation in Indonesia," *New Times,* No. 8, February 1973, pp. 26-27.

26. For example, *Ibid.,* and N. Volghin, "The Options Before Indonesia," *International Affairs,* December 1971, pp. 65-68.

27. Current Digest of the Soviet Press (CDSP), Vol. XXIV, No. 1, p. 11, translated from *Izvestiia,* January 7, 1972, p. 2.

28. *Ibid.,* p. 12.

29. *Ibid.,* Vol. XXIV, No. 25, p. 9, translated from *Izvestiia,* June 22, 1972, p. 3.

30. Dimitry Volsky, "Common Cause of the Asian Peoples," *New Times,* No. 50, December 1974, pp. 18-19.

31. Foreign Broadcast Information Service (FBIS), *Soviet Union Daily Report,* July 13, 1976, p. K2, translated from Radio Moscow broadcast in Indonesian to Indonesia, July 7, 1976. (All subsequent reference to FBIS will be from the *Soviet Union Daily Report.*)

32. Rodney Tasker, "ASEAN: Stopping Any Shade of Red," *Far Eastern Economic Review,* August 24, 1979, pp. 24, 26.

33. Sen Gupta, *Soviet-Asian Relations in the 1970's and Beyond,* p. 234, reprinted from the *Manila Bulletin,* February 17, 1971.

34. US Central Intelligence Agency, p. 24.

35. The Soviet Union is dependent on imported bauxite and aluminum.

36. Alexander Usuatov, "Where ASEAN is Being Pushed," *New Times,* No. 3, January 1977, pp. 8-9.

37. *Ibid.,* p. 8.

38. FBIS, January 7, 1977, p. K1, transcribed from a Radio Peace and Progress broadcast in English to Asia, July 5, 1977.

39. FBIS, April 6, 1977, translated from *Krasnaia Zvezda,* April 2, 1977.

40. FBIS, March 2, 1977, K1, translated from Moscow Radio broadcast in Indonesian to Indonesia, February 21, 1977.

41. *Ibid.,* p. K2, and FBIS, June 23, 1977, p. C1, translated from Radio Moscow in Indonesian to Indonesia, June 20, 1977.

42. FBIS, February 7, 1977, p. K1, translated from TASS International Service, February 3, 1977.

43. For example, see A Chernyshov, "The Pacific: Problems of International Security and Cooperation," *International Affairs* (Moscow), November 1977.

44. FBIS, September 19, 1977, pp. K1-K2, translated from *Sotsialisticheskaya Industriya,* September 13, 1977, p. 3, and October 7, 1977, p. K1, translated from *Krasnaia Zvezda,* October 2, 1977, p. 3.

45. FBIS, March 2, 1979, p. K1, translated from Radio Moscow in Indonesian to Indonesia, February 21, 1977.

46. Chernyshor, p. 82.

47. FBIS, July 18, 1978, p. K1, translated from *Izvestiia,* July 12, 1978, morning editorial, p. 5.

48. FBIS, November 1, 1978.

49. JPRS No. 72348, p. 78, translated from *SSHA: Ekonomika, Politika Ideologiia,* No. 10, October 1978, pp. 61-65.

50. FBIS, May 8, 1978, p. K1, translated from Radio Peace and Progress in Indonesian, May 3, 1978; and January 3, 1979, p. K2, transcribed from TASS in English, December 25, 1978.

51. FBIS, January 8, 1979, pp. K1-K2, translated from Radio Moscow in Japanese to Japan, January 5, 1979.

52. US Central Intelligence Agency, National Foreign Assessment Center, *Communist Aid to Less Developed Countries of the Free World, 1978,* March 15, 1979, p. 28.

53. JPRS, No. 72348, p. 78.

54. FBIS, June 19, 1978, p. K1, transcribed from TASS in English, June 16, 1978.

55. FBIS, October 10, 1978, p. K1, translation from V. Kalinin, *Pravda,* October 4, 1978, p. 4.

56. FBIS, August 16, 1978, p. K1, translated from Radio Peace and Progress in Mandarin to Southeast Asia, August 8, 1978.

57. Yuri Nikolayev, "Soviet Writer Looks at ASEAN Indochina Relations," *Business Times* (Kuala Lumpur), April 15, 1978, p. 6.

58. For instance, FBIS, September 13, 1978, p. K1, translated from Radio Peace and Progress in Mandarin to Southeast Asia, September 9, 1978.

59. See Justus M. van der Kroef, "The USSR and Indonesia," pp. 6-7, for a discussion of the controversy.

60. FBIS, March 19, 1979.

61. See note 53.

62. CDSP, Vol. XXX, No. 42, p. 10, translated from *Pravda,* October 21, 1978, p. 5, and No. 43, p. 9, translated from *Pravda,* October 29, 1978, p. 4.

63. FBIS, January 12, 1979, p. K1, translated from Radio Peace and Progress in Mandarin to Southeast Asia, January 10, 1979.

64. CDSP, Vol. XXX, No. 43, p. 9, translated from *Pravda,* October 26, 1978, p. 5.

65. FBIS, February 14, 1979, p. K4, translated from Radio Moscow in Indonesian to Indonesia, February 9, 1979.

66. FBIS, September 12, 1978, p. C2, translated from TASS International Service, September 8, 1978.

67. FBIS, June 20, 1979, pp. E1-E2, translated from TASS International Service, June 19, 1978.

68. FBIS, June 21, 1979, p. E1, transcribed from TASS in English, June 19, 1979.

69. FBIS, January 18, 1979, p. L9, translated from Radio Peace and Progress in Mandarin to Southeast Asia, January 16, 1979.

70. FBIS, July 3, 1979, p. E3, translated from Moscow Domestic Service, July 2, 1979.

71. FBIS contained no criticisms beamed at foreign audiences.

72. FBIS, July 3, 1979, p. E3.

73. FBIS, July 10, 1979, pp. E4-E5, transcribed from TASS in English, July 2, 1979.

15

ON SOVIET ASIAN POLICY:
A COMMENTARY

Thomas W. Robinson

By way of introduction, it may be helpful to note four generalities that are commonly observed about Soviet Asian policy. First, Soviet policy has sought to accommodate to Asia's very size. Moscow cannot simultaneously play a role—much less a major one—in each Asian region and with regard to each issue, merely because Asia is so big. Distance and geography are stern barriers to the Soviets in Asian policy. Second, we must consider Soviet policy as it is applied to each of Asia's four subregions—Northeast Asia, East Asia, Southeast Asia, and South Asia—and treat each region, for policy purposes, as an autonomous entity. Indeed, the history of Soviet Asian policy indicated Moscow has tended to develop separate regional policies according to its perceptions of regional requirements and its differential ability to apply instruments of policy at a distance. Third, it is necessary to treat certain aspects of Soviet Asian policy as derivative from its global policy. Thus, Soviet actions with regard to the other global actors involved in Asia—notably Japan, China, and the United States—reflect Soviet global strategy and relations more than Moscow's regional Asian policy. Since the Soviet Union is a global power, it conducts its Asian policies with one eye to how they affect, and are affected by, its global objectives.

Fourth, and in contrast to the previous point, the argument has long been made that Asia as a political arena should be treated *sui generis*. This view maintains that every Asian region has special characteristics, separated for analytical purposes each from the other. Thus, Soviet Asian policy need not be viewed in the context of its—or America's or China's—"global" strategy. This view is elaborated on in Douglas Pike's paper, and is shared by many. It is also one which the Soviets have found, much to their dismay, to be increasingly true. This view is in some respects the contrary of the global strategy orientation, but it is possible to strike some sort of balance between them. Soviet Asian policy does indeed fall within the framework of its global strategy, but Moscow has also been forced to recognize distinctive characteristics of Asia that necessarily set its policy toward that region apart from its global orientation.

Any coherent view of Soviet Asian policy must integrate all four of these aspects. The papers under discussion for the most part address only certain aspects of Soviet Asian policy, mostly as concerns Southeast Asia, and tend to exclude reference to global Soviet strategy and the differential influence of characteristics of Moscow's overall Asian policy. If one remains only within their context, it is difficult to extrapolate to the general scene, to analyze Soviet Asian policy in light of their—and our—global interests and comparative approaches to international relations. Douglas Pike's paper, on the other hand, is an excellent microcosm of the whole.

FIVE SPECIFICS OF SOVIET ASIAN POLICY

We need to look further, then, to certain other aspects of Soviet Asian policy from which it may be possible to draw conclusions for Soviet foreign policy as a whole. The remainder of these comments examine five specifics of Soviet Asian policy in an effort to understand more fully the meaning of recent Soviet policy initiatives in Asia.

• We begin by noting that, in general, Asia has been a "tough nut to crack" for the Soviet Union, and is becoming more so. This is true for many reasons. Most important is the fact that all Asian states, with the exception of Burma and perhaps Bangladesh, are for the first time strong as well as independent. Everywhere in Asia are found strong central governments, rapidly growing economies, and activist foreign policies. Moreover, many Asian states are overtly anti-Soviet, several are outright allies of the United States, and a "special relationship" is being forged between the United States and China, Moscow's principal global and regional opponents. So Moscow finds Asia a difficult place to make gains merely because of the growth of indigenous regional power.

• Added to this fact of strength and the configuration of power that follows from it, a further dimension is that the area is not a single region or a collection of subregions. There are, for example, actually two different East Asias, geopolitically and ideologically distinct from one another. On the one hand, there is "island East Asia," the off-shore or near off-shore nations (or city-states) of Japan, the Philippines, South Korea, Hong Kong, Singapore, and Taiwan. To varying degrees, these states are non-Communist, pro-Western, rapidly industrializing, economically capitalist, base their modernization effort on the foreign-trade development model, and are democratic or democratizing. On the other hand, there is "continental East Asia," consisting of China, Vietnam and its Indo-China satraps, North Korea, and Mongolia. These countries are Communist, anti-Western, have socialist economies, are not foreign-trade oriented, and are essentially autarkic and nondemocratic. Here again, even among the anti-Western states of continental Asia, the Soviet Union has found itself kept out of the larger Asian picture. Neither island East Asia nor continental East Asia (with the exceptions of Vietnam and Mongolia) look to Moscow for leadership. Continental and island East Asian states are concerned either with their own internal order or, in the case of island Asia, with their relations with the broader Western world.

Most every Asian state looks away from, or beyond, Moscow and would disregard the Soviet Union entirely were it not for the newly developed Russian ability to project raw military power into the area.

The Soviet Union is strikingly out of place in Asia, as both sets of nations grow in different directions from that toward which Moscow moves. It follows that, to best achieve their global foreign policy objectives, the Soviets would be well to seek success in some other region. Indeed, this is what we already see to some extent with Soviet activism in the Middle East, the Persian Gulf, and Africa, regions where they may expect gains through use of force or as a result of internal division.

Other, more basic aspects of the Soviet foreign and domestic environment tend to place Asia well down the list of Soviet policy priorities. On the domestic side, several well-known factors account for the predominance of Europe in Soviet policy concerns and help make Moscow disinclined to play a major role in Asia. The majority of the Soviet population is concentrated in European Russia and not in Siberia, along the border with China, or the Pacific. Thus, the immediacy of a threat from Western Europe as well as potential opportunities in that area compel more European, less Asian-centered policy priorities. Similarly, because the bulk of Soviet industry is located in European Russia, economic security interests are not focused in the Soviet East. The forbidding Siberian climate also plays a part in the subordination of Moscow's Asian interest to others, making the entire Trans-Urals area less attractive to the Soviet population and not conducive to active interest in direct relations with Asia.

Internationally, the Soviets must place greater importance on the threats and/or opportunities of Europe and the Middle East. To a large extent, they must concentrate their efforts in those areas, as well as against the United States strategically. These Soviet interests have dominated, and will continue to dominate, those in Asia. If Moscow is an "imperalist" power in Asia, she is so only "defensively."

• Indeed, it is tempting to argue that the Soviet Union is defensively drawn into Asia merely because of the need to compete with China there and not because of any real or perceived opportunities there. To the extent that they have involved themselves in Asia in recent years, the Soviets have done so in order to address directly the threat of perceived Chinese aggression, imperialism, and ideological competition. Much of Soviet Asian policy and activity toward states, Communist and non-Communist alike, and relating to such wide-area issues as development and foreign aid, is linked directly to the China factor.

• "Defensive imperialism" is only a part of Soviet Asian policy. Another is a combination of:

—global competition, particularly military, with the United States, exemplified in Asia by Soviet naval deployments in the North Pacific;

—the innate need to seek out opportunities in other nations, as in Indonesia in the early 1960's;

297

—geopolitical great-power pretensions, evident in the general build-up of Soviet naval presence in the Pacific and Indian Oceans as well as the military-economic movement into Indochina;

—the defense of socialism against attack by perceived Western imperalism, as in Soviet support of North Vietnam against America in the 1960's and 1970's; and,

—trade interests, most importantly with Japan as a means to obtain capital to assist in developing Siberia.

Moscow's Asian policy thus has defensive and offensive components, both of which serve to increase the degree of her interest there. The upshot ought to be that the Russians should be heavily involved everywhere in Asia. Yet they are not. In fact, as we noted above, most Asian states either resist Russian pressures, or allow the Soviets in only as a temporary makeweight for their own foreign policy purposes, or attempt to push them out. Moscow has no genuine, long-term friends in Asia. She has only temporary collaborators, satellites (Mongolia and Afghanistan), suspicious allies, or opponents, with the result that the Kremlin's success in Asia is minimal. This outcome is considerably different from Soviet experience in the Middle East and Africa.

A major reason for Soviet difficulties in Asia is to be found in the very nature of the instruments available to support Soviet foreign policy. Moscow finds the going hard in Asia merely because it lacks the usual panoply of policy instruments with which to influence Asian developments and thus to advance Soviet interests. A successful cultural diplomacy, an important means of policy, is virtually nonexistent in the Soviet case. Moreover, Soviet economic policy toward Asia is highly unsuccessful. With the exception of Vietnam, the Soviets have maintained an inordinately small economic assistance program in Asia, and have not succeeded in building strong and enduring trade ties with Asian states, except in the case of India. Most Asian states find Soviet goods unattractive, Soviet terms of assistance objectionable, Soviet technology second-rate. With the exception of certain primary products of interest to Japan, the Soviet Union has not been able to trade her surplus of natural resources in Siberia for Asian consumer goods—an exchange that ought to be beneficial to both sides.

In terms of diplomatic style, Moscow's motives have been patently transparent, its manner heavy-handed and manipulative, and its appeal generally unsuccessful. Soviet relations with ASEAN are a good example. The ideology which the Soviets seek to project to Asian countries, i.e., simple anti-imperialism and Communist party-led economic development, no longer falls on such receptive ears in Asia as previously, or as compared with other regions. This is true for reasons of recent history—Soviet perfidy has come to be well known in Asia—and because of the general decline in the appeal of the Soviet domestic example.

Effective Soviet policy instruments have been reduced to the military/conspiratorial tool, the only one in which the USSR excels and to which it continues to devote most of its energies. Moscow has deployed an enormous air/land force against China; developed an air/sea threat to Japan; sent forth missile-carrying submarines into the Pacific against the United States; and recently based in Soviet Asian waters an aircraft carrier capable of attacking American and other states' bases in Asia. Soviet attack submarines threaten American access to such allies as South Korea. The Soviets have undertaken militarily to assist their only close Asian ally, Vietnam, in its own course of regional imperialism, despite the great distance involved. Finally, the Soviets have the ability to pose a sea and airborne military threat to all-important Japanese trade links to the Middle East through the Sea of Japan, the East and South China Seas, the Straits of Malacca, and the Indian Ocean.

Yet so long as China remains as firmly anti-Soviet as it has been in recent years, and now appears to be, and so long as the United States continues to maintain a reasonably strong diplomatic/military posture in Asia, the military instrument cannot be very effective for the Soviets. This is true for several reasons. First, the continued expenditures necessary to maintain the required effectiveness of the Soviet military, particularly with regard to China, poses a substantial domestic drain for the Soviets. Second, reliance on military force to achieve policy objectives, or to maintain the *status quo*, drives Asian states in the opposite direction. This has happened, for example, with Japan over the northern islands issue and the severe air threat to the Japanese islands. Finally, and perhaps most importantly, reduction of Soviet foreign policy to military threat tends to polarize Asian subregions, as in Southeast Asia. Ultimately it serves to coalesce the opposition more rapidly and more firmly, e.g., the United States and China, and South Asia after Afghanistan.

It should follow that the future for the Soviet Union in Asia looks rather bleak. The Soviets appear bereft of the necessary mix of policy instruments with which they might exercise superpower prerogatives effectively. The only useable instrument they do possess is by itself and by its nature only marginally useful and in the end self-defeating. Indeed, as we have noted, the Kremlin has already redirected its main foreign (i.e., military) policy effort elsewhere. Afghanistan is the obvious but by no means solitary illustration of this trend.

• But clearly the situation in Asia is changing in ways that may yet permit the Soviets to attain much of their ends in the region. For one thing, the United States is neither as steadfast as the situation demands nor as purposeful as its Asian allies, including China, desire. Second, until the Soviet invasion of Afghanistan in late 1979, it was evident that China had been more than toying with the idea of making major changes toward moderating its anti-Soviet policy. Afghanistan notwithstanding, it may well proceed along that path. As such, continued American reliance on Sino-Soviet enmity as the cornerstone of American-Chinese relations, and on the constancy of China's interest in good relations with its "enemy's enemy," represents a precarious course.

Third, Vietnamese military involvement in Cambodia and Laos—and perhaps elsewhere in Southeast Asia—will most likely continue for a long time, thereby guaranteeing a firm and perhaps increasing Soviet military presence in that region. Coupled with this are internal threats to stability of Indonesia and the Philippines that threaten to weaken the American presence in the region, thus giving Moscow renewed hopes for establishing itself further in the area. Fourth, it cannot be presumed that Sino-American relations will remain forever positive. Already the first beginnings of public differences over the future of Taiwan are apparent and voices are heard publicly in China criticizing the very fact of the American connection, to say nothing of its closeness.

Fifth, the Soviets for the first time can look forward to possessing an indigenous Asian base of power as a result of the slow strengthening of Soviet Siberia. This has the obvious positive implications for enhanced Sino-Soviet and Soviet-Japanese trade. Finally, we can see most clearly the rapid spread of the "island Asia" mode of modernization to Southeast Asia and even inland to China itself. This causes irrevocable changes in the Asian *status quo* and implies the limited adequacy of any continuously static policy, Soviet or American, toward the region.

300

CONCLUSION: FOUR CRITERIA OF SOVIET POLICY SUCCESS OR FAILURE

What do all of these changes and policy characterizations imply for Soviet "success" or "failure" in Asia? Obviously failure thus far has outweighed success for the Soviets. Indeed, the USSR's policy itself is largely responsible for the fact that the majority of the important Asian states (including China and Japan) have lined up against it, for the wariness of many of the rest (e.g., ASEAN) and for the crudely utilitarian nature of relations that states such as India, Vietnam, and North Korea have with Moscow. The upshot has been that the Soviets have been frozen out of the first group, pushed around by the second, and taken advantage of by the third.

This trend is likely to continue so long as the China and American factors described previously remain reasonably constant and thus diminish Soviet appeal and viability in the region. It will be augmented by the Kremlin's own shortcomings: a conspicuous lack of nonmilitary policy instruments; a deficient diplomatic style; and an over-reliance on threat of force, necessarily the most alienating policy. The Soviets have two hopes for their future in Asia: an increase in the number of "trouble spots," permitting Moscow to use the military instrument to greatest effect; and learning from their own and others' experience and mistakes.

What lessons can be drawn from Soviet Asian policy for determining general success or failure in foreign policy? Success or failure in the broader sense can be assessed only over a longer term than is considered here and only as measured against some agreed criteria. If, for example, we inspect the entire 60-odd years of Soviet Asian policy, the Soviets have had numerous policy failures in each short term.

Nevertheless, each "failure" contributed something to longer term overall "success," if we understand "success" according to four criteria: Soviet participation in and thus influence over the area; comparison of domestic costs to foreign policy benefits; the general trend of Asian history; and, the degree to which Asia has figured in Moscow's global competition with Washington and, more recently, Peking.

On these criteria, if one computes an approximate weighted average, Soviet policy in Asia over the last 50 years has been marginally successful, while over the last 20, it has been mostly a

301

failure. Over the longer term, Soviet influence in Asia has grown—although not greatly as compared with the 1920's; the domestic cost has not been overly high; the trend of Asian history has generally been favorable to Leninist communism—although not necessarily to Soviet leadership of Asian Communist parties; and Asia has at least not been a hinderance to Soviet competition elsewhere with the United States.

In the last 20 years, however, the story has been somewhat different. The Soviet Union today is probably no more influential in all of Asia than it was in 1960, and probably less; domestic costs in support of its Asian military outreach have risen perceptively; the general trend of history has turned against Moscow, when one considers strong local nationalism, the rise of "island Asia," and the loss of China and North Korea to Moscow; and Asia has turned out to be a net drain on Russian energies, drawing attention and resources away from the more important global competition with Washington and forcing Moscow to change the nature of its investment in Africa and the Middle East just to compete with Peking there.

What the future will hold is, naturally, difficult to say. But these same criteria, and the generalities and specifics of Soviet Asian policy, would seem to indicate that Asia will not be the place of great forward movement for the Soviet Union over the next decade or two.

PART 4
THE CONTEXT AND INSTRUMENTS
OF SOVIET POLICY

16

SOVIET MUSLIM POLICY:
DOMESTIC AND FOREIGN POLICY LINKAGES

Edward A. Corcoran

   Islam is a potent influence in the modern world, providing some 700 million Muslims[1] a code of social organization whose adherents live in constant awareness of their allegiance. Although split into two major divisions—the majority Sunnis and the generally more fundamentalist Shiites—it forms a strong cultural bond between the Islamic nations.[2] In the last decade, with the growing political power of oil and then spurred by Iran's revolution, the belt of Islamic nations, stretching from Morocco to Indonesia, has become a major force on the international scene.[3] It is also the portion of the international environment most directly connected with the Muslim population of the Soviet Union.
   This paper will focus on the linkages between the Islamic nations and the Soviet Muslims, and how those linkages affect the relations between the Soviet Muslims and their own government, and between the Soviet government and the total international environment. These linkages will be discussed in terms of the actors involved—individuals, unofficial groups and government organizations or institutions—and the outputs which specific actors

make in various settings and which, in turn, serve as inputs for other actors. The outputs will be identified as direct if they are intended to bring about a response from another specific actor, as when an individual sends a request to an official organization. Indirect outputs, on the other hand, occur when activities of one actor elicit an unintentional response, as when the cultural activities of one group inspire another group to produce its own artistic creations.[4]

THE SOVIET MUSLIMS

Ethnic groups with a Muslim cultural heritage constitute the largest non-Slavic element in Soviet history.[5] As discussed below, they are a cohesive and dynamic segment of this society and their continued social and political development poses a number of fundamental dilemmas for the Soviet leadership, dilemmas which have wide implications for the Soviet political structure and for its foreign policy.

Internally, the Muslims are the most rapidly expanding segment of the Soviet population. They will provide a significant proportion of Soviet manpower by the close of this century.[6] It is unclear whether this will result in increased industrialization of Central Asia or increased pressures on Muslims to relocate outside their traditional homelands, nor is it clear whether the resolution of this problem will increase or decrease Muslim commitment to the Soviet system. At the same time, the growing educational qualifications of the Muslim population threatens to bring them into direct competition with Slavic settlers in Central Asia for a limited number of desirable jobs.[7] Whether this can be resolved without exacerbating ethnic tensions is questionable. What is clear is that Soviet Muslim policy will have profound effects on the entire Soviet system.

Externally, the Soviet appeal, particularly to the Third World, is heavily based on its claim to provide a developmental model for the emerging nations. Central Asia is the showplace of this model because of its many similarities with the Third World and its shared heritage with the Islamic nations of the Middle East and South Asia. Third World delegations to the Soviet Union are constantly being given tours of this region, and Central Asians are prominent in Soviet delegations to emerging nations. As a result of these direct and officially sponsored linkages, developments in Soviet Central

304

Asia are directly relevant to Soviet relations with the Third World. Conversely, as contacts with the Third World increase, Soviet Muslims become increasingly aware of alternative methods of handling some of the same problems which they face, so Third World policies have an indirect linkage with Soviet Central Asia.

EARLY SOVIET MUSLIM POLICY

The Soviet Muslims are basically of Turkic and Iranian stock, with some admixtures from the Mongol hordes of the 12th and 13th centuries. Linguistically and ethnically they are related to the indigenous populations of Xinjiang (Sinkiang), Afghanistan, Iran and Turkey. Their Muslim heritage derives from Persian and Arabic sources; consequently their written languages generally used Arabic script prior to the Soviet period. Among some of the ethnic groups the Muslim influence dates from as early as the 7th century and is strongly ingrained in the traditional culture. Among other groups, it is of more recent origin and more superficial impact.[8]

The Soviet domination of Central Asia derives from the Tsarist eastward expansion which began in the 17th century. The main thrust of this expansion was into Siberia, and so it first brought the Tatars and Bashkirs, straddling the southern Urals, under Russian domination and subsequently the northern lowland areas of Central Asia. By the time of the 1917 revolution, Tsarist imperalism had established domination over the entire region from the Transcaucasus to the Pamirs, eventually colliding with British interests in Afghanistan and Chinese interests in Xinjiang.[9]

While the final defeat of the White forces in July 1919 established Soviet domination of Central Asia, gaining control was no easy task. The Red Army insured the absorption of the nominally independent People's Republics of Khiva and Bukhara into the Soviet Union and the suppression of their national Communist elements, but armed conflict in the area did not end until the early 1930's when the Basmachi opposition, representing the traditional Muslim leadership, was finally crushed.[10]

Although Soviet policy of the 1920's and 1930's included the suppression of private industry, the establishment of firm Communist Party control over local political, economic and social life, and the forced collectivization of farmers, it also included some significant concessions to Muslim sensitivities, including the establishment of nominally autonomous territorial ethnic republics and the toleration of many aspects of the Muslim culture. Political control was established by co-opting native elements into the local party and government posts, while retaining key posts in the hands of ethnic Slavs. By a series of alternating recruitment campaigns and purges, the Soviets were able to offer social mobility to ambitious elements of the local population. From them, they developed a local elite which not only had strong vested interests in the maintenance of the system, but also was entirely beholden to Moscow for their position. Furthermore, by assuming the positions of earlier purged elites, the new local elites were implicated as beneficiaries of the earlier purges.[11]

Culturally, the Soviets moved to cut the ties of Soviet Muslims with their ethnic brothers outside the Soviet Union. Borders were sealed and heavily patrolled, physically cutting off linkages with neighboring Muslim countries. The traditional Arabic script was replaced, first by Latin script and then by Cyrillic. Major achievements of earlier Turkic and Iranic cultures were claimed for the predecessors of the Soviet ethnic groups, emphasizing their cultural heritage as decidedly superior to that of the neighboring areas and thus undermining any grounds for establishing external cultural linkages. Muslim religious practices were suppressed, eliminating much of the influence of the Muslim clergy and stopping pilgrimages of Soviet Muslims to shrines outside the Soviet Union. The slightest expressions of pan-Muslim or pan-Turkic sentiments were ruthlessly exterminated.[12]

Soviet basic nationality policy envisioned the temporary flowering of major nationalities as they absorbed minor nationalities and carried out the economic and political development of their territories in preparation for an eventual merging into a single (largely Russian) "multi-national Soviet people." One visible manifestation of this policy was the formation of nominally independent republics for the Uzbeks, Tadzhiks, Kazakhs, Turkmens and Azerbaidzhanis with local autonomous entities set up for some of the larger remaining groups, such as the Tatars, Bashkirs and Karakalpaks. To some extent this produced an artificial fragmentation of the region, insuring against the development of a single cohesive national group while simultaneously undermining the viability of many smaller cultural units. Adopting the Russian language and culture became a prerequisite for advancement. Typically, members of the titular nationality held the leading positions in the local party and government, but they would invariably have Russian (or occasionally Belorussian or Ukrainian) deputies closely watching them and also filling lesser key posts, such as the local Minister of the Interior in charge of police operations. Slavs dominated the organizations with actual political power (such as the bureaus of the local central committees).[13]

Economically, there was a heavy investment in regional development and industrialization, with Central Asians generally supplying unskilled and semi-skilled labor, while Russians and Ukrainians provided the skilled labor and management expertise. This brought about a significant influx of Slavic elements who were heavily concentrated in the cities. Simultaneously, a massive educational program was set in motion, producing a steady stream of native technicians who were readily absorbed into the expanding industrial establishment. Industrial development of the area received a further impetus during World War II, when many industries were relocated from European portions of the Soviet Union.[14]

CURRENT AND PROSPECTIVE SOVIET MUSLIM POLICY

The basic Muslim policies established in the 1930's have been followed into the 1970's. However, there have been tremendous changes in Central Asia and in Soviet society as a whole during this period. Some very fundamental problems in Central Asia are acquiring an increasing urgency; significant changes appear inevitable during the coming decades.

Probably the most fundamental change is the growing pressure for participation within the Soviet system. The relative backwardness of the Muslim nationalities has been largely eliminated and can no longer serve as a primary justification for Slavic domination of local political and economic life nor for practical exclusion of Muslim elites from the actual power centers in Moscow. Furthermore, the developing Muslim elite is no longer as dependent upon Moscow as its predecessors of the 1940's and 1950's were, nor is it implicated as the direct heir of the purges of the 1930's. As such, it is more inclined to assert its own interests and press for a larger voice in the system. The results are apparent throughout Central Asia. In 1976, for example, Uzbeks actually

307

gained a majority in their Central Committee Bureau (holding 6 of 11 posts, compared to only 5 of 14 posts in 1949).[15] Similar change is evident on a broad statistical scale in Communist Party membership and membership of party bodies at all levels.[16] At the center, too, such shifts are visible; the Politburo itself now contains three Central Asians.

With Russians constituting barely 50 percent of the total Soviet population, the trend toward wider participation of other ethnic groups in the political process could change the basic political forces in the Soviet system. But actions to reverse this trend and reassert Russian or Slavic ethnic discrimination could alienate minority groups, particularly the cohesive Muslim minority, and produce strong tensions in Soviet society.

Economically the development of Central Asia has been impressive. Not only has there been a tremendous increase in agricultural production (cotton output has increased tenfold over prerevolutionary levels), but there has been widespread industrialization, with capital input far exceeding profits or goods extracted from the area. Education levels have improved dramatically; cultural, housing and sanitary development is widespread, and extensive medical services are free.[17]

The figures look all the more impressive when compared with neighboring countries. Measures of economic growth (say, electricity production or per capita income) unquestionably favor the Soviet republics, as do gross measures of social services (such as student enrollments, literacy rates, infant mortality, or the numbers of doctors or hospital beds per thousand inhabitants.)[18]

The costs associated with this development are much harder to measure. Much of the traditional Muslim way of life has changed, but to some extent this is necessary for modernization and hardly unique to the Soviet Union. More pervasive is Moscow's control of the local life. Whatever the benefits of this rule, it has taken freedom of political choice from the indigenous population.[19]

Furthermore, the comparisons with the past, although undeniably impressive, are somewhat inflated—they usually use the very poor years around 1913 as the base for comparison. And of course, while comparisons with some relatively underdeveloped nations are favorable, comparisons with other regions (e.g., Japan, Korea) and with the industrial countries are not so favorable. More importantly, comparisons with most other sections of the Soviet Union are also unfavorable. Despite all the advances, Central Asia

308

remains basically a supplier of raw material to the rest of the Soviet Union. Local industrialization is heavily centered on textile production; there is very little heavy industry, and electrification lags noticeably behind other areas. Education levels also lag, particularly when one considers that Russians and other settlers account for a disproportionate share of the overall student population and of the number of Central Asian residents with higher education.[20]

Population dynamics seem bound to exacerbate these problems. During the 1980's, the increases in the local Soviet labor pool will come from the Muslim ethnic groups of Central Asia. They will provide far more labor than the projected level of Central Asian industrialization will be able to absorb. Nevertheless, there is still a continuing influx of Russians, Ukranians and Belorussians.[21] There are two serious implications of these trends. First, competition for local jobs, especially for the better paid ones requiring skilled labor, can be expected to increase significantly. The very visible disproportion of Slavs in these positions may well fuel a growing resentment.[22] Secondly, many other areas of the Soviet Union have projected labor shortages, and there are already indications of pressures to move the excess Central Asian labor to these areas. However, the Muslim ethnic groups have been very reluctant to move outside their traditional homeland areas, increasing the potential for aggravated tensions.[23]

Overall then, by comparison with neighboring countries or with its own past, Central Asia has shown a very impressive development; the Soviet authorities work hard not to let the indigenous population forget that. Nevertheless, there are costs to this development and latent dissatisfaction over the relatively privileged position of Slavic settlers. Demographic trends indicate that there will be strong pressures for change in the 1980's. If the Soviet government is able to convince large numbers of Central Asian workers to move to the other areas of the Soviet Union, while allowing a continued influx of Slavic workers into this area, there could be a significant mixing of the Soviet population and a strong push to the development of the multinational Soviet people which is sought by official nationality policy. On the other hand, if a more modest out-migration from Central Asia is not balanced by significant increases in local industrialization, this could exacerbate latent anti-Russian feelings and result in a dramatic increase of ethnic tension.

Culturally, there has been a steady growth in the use of Russian as a second language by the Muslim ethnic groups. Recent Soviet conferences indicate even more emphasis is to be expected in this area, raising possibilities that linguistic Russification will undermine local languages.[24] However, in many cases linguistic Russification is at best superficial; it does not necessarily undermine one's ethnic consciousness, as clearly shown by a number of Central Asian authors who write in Russian but with a high regard for their own cultural antecedents.[25] In general Soviet Muslims are now showing a broad interest in their cultural heritage, as seen in such phenomena as the increase of historical literature in Uzbekistan,[26] appeals for the wider publicaton of the Kirghiz epic *Manas*,[27] and the humanist emphasis in Central Asian cinema.[28] Indeed, native language development seems to have gained a momentum of its own and has become a vehicle of cultural revival throughout the Soviet Union.[29]

The Soviet Muslims have generally shown a strong sense of ethnic identity and a dogged resistance to cultural assimilation.[30] Even small ethnic communities which are no longer officially recognized (as the Khorezm Turks) have retained their distinctiveness.[31] At the same time, there is a growing recognition of the common cultural heritage of the Central Asian nationalities and their ties with Muslim elements abroad.[32]

This cultural tenacity also extends to the religious elements of the Muslim heritage. While formal religious organization has been largely suppressed, Muslim religious practices remain strong and the Soviet press still mounts regular attacks on Islam as a support of reactionary social elements.[33]

One further complication is the growth of political dissent in the Soviet Union, dating from the Sinyavsky-Daniel trial of 1966. Since then a wide range of dissident groupings have been established, many inspired by nationalist and religious sentiments, with Ukrainians, Lithuanians, Armenians and Georgians prominent among them. Although the authorities have taken stern measures against the dissidents, they have been unable to eliminate the protests. On the contrary, they have seen the individual and initially isolated groups amalgamate into an informal network centered on Moscow intellectuals but loosely coordinating dissident groups from Leningrad to Yerevan. This has encouraged a degree of mutual support and initiated an unprecedented rise in publicity with hundreds of appeals to foreign organizations and governments and a phenomenal growth of uncensored typescript manuscripts usually referred to as samizdat ("self-published," in imitation of typical Soviet publishing house acronyms).[34] With two exceptions, this dissent has barely touched the Muslim population, there being only infrequent references to individual protests. The two exceptions, though, are significant ones, involving the Crimean Tatars and Meskhetian Turks.

The Crimean Tatars are one of the nationalities suppressed *en masse* by Stalin. On the night of May 18, 1944, the entire Tatar population on the Crimea (approximately 200,000 persons) was herded into collection stations and forcibly deported to a Central Asian exile. As a result of this deportation, 46 percent of the entire Crimean Tatar population perished.[35] After Stalin's death, the Crimean Tatars began a campaign for exoneration and received a formal rehabilitation in a decree of September 5, 1967; they were not, however, permitted to return to their traditional homeland, even though the Crimea (now a part of the Ukraine) is a labor deficit area. Practically the entire Crimean Tatar population has been mobilized in support of this objective, with individual petitions signed by tens of thousands. The authorities have responded with long prison terms for their leaders, forcible expulsion of those families who do return to the Crimea, dispersal of gatherings of Crimean Tatars, and official de-nationalization (census counts now lump the Crimean Tatars with the Volga Tatars, even though there is no common origin for these two widely separated peoples.)[36] Being concentrated in Central Asia, the movement of the Crimean Tatars has relatively high visibility among wide segments of other Muslim elements and presents a clear picture of ethnic discrimination. Although there have been few indications of support from the other Muslims, there is a definite potential for the Crimean Tatar example to spark dissent among larger Central Asian ethnic groups.

The second exception is the Meskhetian Turks. They are likewise a deported ethnic group, originally native to the Georgian-Turkish border area and forcibly deplaced to Central Asia on November 15, 1944. Their campaign parallels that of the Crimean Tatars, though on a smaller scale. One noteworthy aspect of the Meskhetian situation is that they were never accused of anti-Soviet activities, but moved presumably because of potential ties with the Turks.

Indeed, they have shown an apparent readiness to seek assistance from the Turkish government; at least one of these appeals reportedly resulted in some Soviet concessions.[37]

Overall, Soviet Muslim policy has had very mixed results. On the one hand, it has had impressive success in mobilizing a hostile and heterogeneous population in a very undeveloped area, bringing about a tremendous improvement in education levels, an impressive degree of industrialization and a standard of living visibly higher than in neighboring countries. It has generally eliminated a number of degrading discriminatory social practices, particularly in regard to the status of women. On the other hand, the growth of a common Soviet patriotism is now threatened by a dynamic interest in local culture. Pressures for full economic and political quality could threaten the Russian hegemony of the entire Soviet system. Two dissident Muslim groups have set examples of determined quest for recognition which would be decidedly destabilizing if they spread to larger ethnic groups. These conflicting tendencies make it appear likely that there will be significant changes in Central Asia in the coming decades, but the direction of these changes is not yet set.

EXTERNAL IMPACT OF SOVIET MUSLIM POLICY

Understandably stressing the positive aspects of Central Asian development, the Soviets tout the superiority of their model of development. To many in the Third World, the impressive change in Central Asia speaks for itself as proof of these Soviet claims, even though the Soviets themselves have been unable to express the tangled, chaotic and often improvisational development of Central Asia in anything resembling a coherent model. Furthermore, several aspects of Central Asian development which can be considered as negative (such as the suppression of independent political opinion) are probably seen as positive by revolutionary leaders seeking to solidify their own power base. Nevertheless, Third World leaders are often hesitant to adopt many Soviet practices, and try to develop alternate approaches to problems of development.

The net result is that Soviet relations with Third World countries often have their reflection in Central Asia. A review of specific aspects of Soviet relations with individual countries and regions will make these implications more concrete.

China

Soviet relations with China have deteriorated significantly since the early 1960's, bringing tension and conflict to their inner Asian border, stretching from Mongolia to the Pamirs. This is one of the most remote areas in the world and unbiased information on conditions there is very scarce. Nevertheless, the general situation can be outlined. The Chinese side of this border is the Xinjiang Uighur Autonomous Region, whose indigenous population is largely Uighurs, Kazakhs, Kirghiz and Uzbeks, ethnically identical with their Soviet brothers. For centuries, these nomadic peoples roamed this entire region, which became an area of Russian-Chinese confrontation in the 19th century. The present border was established in 1884.[38] During the repressive years of the 1930's, as many as half a million Central Asians fled the Soviet Union into Xinjiang.[39]

In the post-war era, the Soviets developed a strong base of influence in Xinjiang, with an active consulate in Kuldja and broad contacts among the largely autonomous Xinjiang rulers. As Sino-Soviet relations deteriorated, the Soviets apparently used their position to try to subvert Chinese control. The Kuldja consulate issued thousands of Soviet passports to Chinese Kazakhs and Uighurs. The Chinese responded by closing the consulate and greatly increasing the influx of Chinese into the region, with over a million resettling there in the late 1950's. This influx of Chinese and repressive measures against the indigenous population spurred another mass migration, this time from Xinjiang into the Soviet Union and involving perhaps 50,000 Kazakhs. The Chinese purged pro-Soviet officials and laid claim to thousands of square miles of Soviet territory.[40]

Since then, the border has been closed, effectively cutting direct linkages by mass population movement. There have, though, been continuous reports of skirmishes and intrusions,[41] so some direct personal linkages apparently still exist. Additionally, there has been a thriving propaganda war, with each side accusing the other of suppressing its Muslim minorities while asserting that is own minority population enjoys wide privileges.[42] These form direct outputs from each side, though it is an open question what attention their intended recipients give to them. But even without a direct response, these broadcasts certainly give each side an impetus to avoid minority dissatisfactions which the other side could exploit. In fact, the treatment of the minorities serves as an indirect output by each side, an output which the propaganda broadcasts insure will not be ignored. The Soviets have even reportedly formed a Uighur National Liberation Council in Exile,[43] and Uighur literature has undergone a modest resurgence.[44] Additionally, there is a widespread practice of unofficial Islam among the Soviet Uighurs, particularly those who have most recently come from Xinjiang.[45] Overall, then, there is quite a variety of cross-border linkages between Soviet Central Asia and Xinjiang. Any widespread dissatisfaction among the Soviet Muslims would certainly be used by the Chinese for propaganda purposes both to Soviet Muslims and to the Muslim world.[46] More disturbing to the Soviets though is undoubtedly the potential for Chinese instigation or support of unrest or even active insurgency. These considerations give the Soviets a strong incentive to avoid any growth of Muslim unrest in Central Asia.

Afghanistan

Afghanistan was long an isolated and fiercely independent buffer state on the Soviet border. During the 1920's a number of the anti-Soviet guerrilla movements in Central Asia operated from Afghanistan, and when they were finally suppressed in 1926, remnants returned there.[47] For 40 years, the border remained reasonably well sealed and the Soviets appeared content to have modest ties with an Afghanistan largely isolated from Western influence. This changed in April 1978, when a violent coup established a pro-Communist government under Nur Mohammed Taraki, who quickly turned to the Soviets for support. Since then it appears that the Soviets had a hand in the preparation of the coup. They became a major force in the country, with up to 6,000 military advisors and high level visitors, including Army General A.A. Yepishev, Chief of the Main Political Directorate and a key figure in the 1968 Czechoslovak invasion. The Taraki government proceeded ruthlessly against traditional elements, with widespread arrests and thousands of executions reported.[48] What this succeeded in doing was alienating large sections of the population and spawning a widespread insurgency among traditionalist Muslim elements whose anti-Russian anger reportedly resulted in hundreds of deaths among Soviet advisors. When the Soviets apparently attempted to form a more moderate Afghan government, the result instead was the seizure of power by an uncompromising Marxist, Hafizullah Amin. The crescendo of

314

resistance rose to the point where there was a serious threat of the government actually falling to an anti-Soviet, fundamentalist Muslim grouping.[49]

The Soviets reacted by a massive invasion of the country in December 1979, resulting in the death of Amin, installing Babrak Karmal as the new Afghan President and using Soviet ground forces to help the disintegrating Afghan Army reestablish order in the countryside. While the reasons for the Soviet intervention are speculative, concern over rising Muslim unrest on the border appears to have been an important consideration.[50] At the risk of a strong Western reaction—which they apparently underestimated— the Soviets have become involved in a military operation which has brought them overwhelming censure by both the United Nations[51] and the Islamic Conference, whose condemnation included a call for other Islamic states "to affirm their solidarity with the Afghan people in their just struggle to safeguard their faith, national independence and territorial integrity and to recover their right to determine their destiny."[52]

These events are closely linked to the Soviet Muslims. There is, first of all, the indirect linkage of the example of Afghan Muslim insurgents fighting a Soviet sponsored Marxist government and of the UN and Islamic Conference condemnations of Soviet actions against Muslim insurgents. Additionally, a number of the Soviet troops involved are Soviet Muslims, particularly since some of the units involved were reportedly from Central Asia and used local reservists to fill their ranks prior to the invasion.[53] By Soviet law, these reservists can be held on active duty only for a restricted period of time. Thus any protracted conflict will require the rotation of troops and the direct involvement of more Soviet Muslims not only participating in the actual events, but talking with the Afghans in their own language and being able, on their return home, to spread first hand accounts throughout Soviet Central Asia. Furthermore, many Soviet casualties are being returned to Central Asia. Judging by casualty reports from Afghanistan, they include several hundred dead and perhaps two thousand wounded.[54] These casualties provide another direct input from Afghanistan to Central Asia. Furthermore these inputs are being intensified by indirect inputs through increased Cental Asia broadcasting by the Voice of America and Radio Liberty[55] and undoubtedly also by Chinese radio propaganda.

On the other side of the ledger, a sizable number of Soviet civilians have accompanied the invasion forces into Afghanistan and are supervising civil government operations. These Soviet civilians include officials who have had long experience in overseeing Soviet Muslims and channeling their energies into productive activities. But how effective they will be in Afghanistan is open to question. There is a potential for protracted anti-Soviet guerrilla warfare and for Afghan disaffection to spread into the Soviet forces, bringing possible desertions of Soviet troops or friction between Muslim and Slavic elements.[56] While it is too early to judge the long-term effects of the intervention, there will certainly be an increased awareness by Soviet Muslims of conditions in the Muslim world beyond their border. The intervention marks the first time since the closing of the Soviet-Xinjiang border that there have been large scale, direct linkages between Soviet Muslims and neighboring Muslim regions. And Afghanistan, although remote, is not nearly so remote as Xinjiang; it does have contacts through both Pakistan and Iran with the outside world.

Iran

Direct Russian involvement in Iran dates from the early 19th century when Czarist troops forced Iran to cede Georgia and portions of Armenia to Russian control. This historic interest in Iran was rekindled in a 1907 agreement between Russia and Great Britain dividing Iran into spheres of influence. Both these countries stationed troops in Iran during World War I. Although most of the Russian forces were withdrawn during the 1917 Russian Revolution, postwar anarchy in Iran allowed Bolshevik troops to set up a short-lived Soviet Socialist Republic of Gilan, including much of the Iranian Caspian Sea coast. But in 1921, the Soviet Union signed a Treaty of Friendship with Iran and withdrew its troops. This treaty allowed the Soviets to reinsert troops into Iran if it were used as a base of activities against the Soviet government.

During World War II, Iran was again unable to maintain a neutral stance and was simultaneously invaded by Great Britain and the Soviet Union on August 26, 1941. For the remainder of the war Iran was a key route for Allied assistance to the Soviet Union. Under these wartime conditions, a strongly leftist Tudeh Party was established with Soviet backing. In December 1945 the Soviets backed leftist declarations of an autonomous state of Azarbaijan and a neighboring Kurdish Republic of Mahabad. Soviet military and political influence in support of Tudeh Party agitations threatened to bring the whole of Iran under Soviet domination. However, with British and American backing the Shah suppressed the Tudeh Party and Iranian troops reoccupied the secessionist areas in December 1946. Nevertheless, a strong leftist influence on the government remained until the military ousted Premier Mohammed Mossadegh and placed the Shah in firm control of the country on August 19, 1953. Relations between the Soviet Union and Iran after the fall of Mossadegh were correct but not cordial, with gradually increasing commercial and political contacts in the 1970's.[57] In particular, Iran began supplying most of the natural gas requirements of Soviet Azerbaidzhan, with Soviet gas in turn diverted to East European customers.

The Iranian revolution of 1979 practically neutralized the extensive Western influence in Iran and met with strong Soviet approbation. While it was clearly the religious supporters of Ayatollah Khomeini who were the driving force behind this revolution, other forces combined with the "Khomeini phenomenon" to bring down the Shah and transform the old order. Specifically dedicated urban Marxist guerrillas turned the tide against the Iranian armed forces in the final days of street fighting.[58] The extent of direct Soviet involvement in the revolution is unclear. Soviet intelligence services have long operated in Iran and an anti-Western Radio of National Liberation has broadcast from Baku for a number of years. In the year preceding the Shah's downfall, a weekly Tudeh Party bulletin, *Navid*, made its appearance, apparently produced on presses in the Soviet Embassy. But while the Soviets worked to destabliize the situation in Iran, there is no direct evidence of actual involvement in the revolutionary events.[59]

Two particular aspects of the Iranian Revolution which have broad implications for the Soviet Union are Muslims and minorities. The Soviets have downplayed the religious elements of the revolution, referring blandly to its "religious coloration" and asserting that the basic reasons for the disturbances are the corruption and abuses of power.[60] They have also stressed the alleged compatibility of Marxism with Islam.[61] Nevertheless, the Shiite Muslim doctrines of the Iranian Revolution pose awkward

317

problems for the Soviet Union. They are far removed from any portrayal of Islam as a conservative force; rather they fuse opposition to tyrannical government with resistance to foreign domination. This certainly feeds Soviet misgivings about the impact of such beliefs on Soviet Muslims, particularly the predominately Shiite Azerbaidzhanis.[62] This is further complicated by Khomeini's own statements that the Islamic Republic knows no boundaries, and the calls of some of his supporters for sending Islamic preachers into the Soviet Union.[63] Not only has Iran set an example of Islamic revolt against an oppressive government, it has also continued to speak out for the religious rights of Soviet and Afghan Muslims.[64] Under these conditions, the Soviet Union can expect to have great difficulty maintaining cordial relations with Iran while actively suppressing Muslim dissent in Afghanistan, particularly if it spreads to Soviet Central Asia. It is also unclear as to what extent the Afghan rebel Muslims can draw support from Iran.

The ethnic minorities of Iran further complicate the question of Soviet relations. While the population of Iran's central plateau is remarkably homogeneous and comprises the majority of the total population of some 33 million, there is a great ethnic admixture in the frontier regions, including Azarbaijanis, Kurds, Turkomans, Baluchi and Arabs.[65]

The Azarbaijanis number about 5 million. They are the largest minority in Iran and are concentrated in the border area directly below Soviet Azerbaidzhan. Both the abortive 1920 Soviet Socialist Republic of Gilan and the 1945 autonomous state of Azarbaijan were located in this area. While there is undoubtedly a reservoir of Soviet influence in the area, there is also a reservoir of separatist sentiment. One of the most crucial splits to develop early in Iran's Islamic Republic was the boycott of national elections by the Ayatollah Shariat-Madari, one of Iran's five Grand Ayatollahs and the unquestioned religious leader of Iranian Azarbaijan. Since then there has been frequent rioting in Azarbaijan and continuing pressure for autonomy.[66] While the Soviets have a potential to stir up unrest on the Iranian side of the border, this would certainly alienate the Teheran government. On the other hand, if an autonomous Iranian Azarbaijan develops, it would provide an obvious contrast to adjacent Soviet Azerbaidzhan and could easily raise pressures for Soviet concessions to their Muslims.

A similar situation exists in northeastern Iran, where some half a million seminomadic Turkomans share an ethnic heritage with the indigenous population of Soviet Turkemistan and the tribes of western Afghanistan. The Turkomans have been actively battling Iranian revolutionary forces for their own autonomous region.[67] An autonomous state in this region would not only contrast with its Soviet counterpart, but could also be a direct source of support for Muslim rebels in Afghanistan.

The Kurds in Iran number over 2 million and pose an even more difficult problem than either the Azarbaijanis or Turkomans. They are one of the largest minority groups in the Middle East, but have little recognized official status. Total population estimates are very rough, ranging around 10 million most of whom live in Jurdistan, a roughly defined area in the Soviet-Turkish-Iranian-Syrian-Iraqi border region. Almost half are in Turkey, which refuses to even recognize them as a separate ethnic group, bans the use of their language, and generally refers to them simply as "mountain Turks" or "Easterners." There are over 3 million in northwest Iran, and probably a slightly lower number in eastern Iraq. Smaller groups live in Syria (400,000) and the Soviet Union (89,000).[68] The Kurds have been persistent fighters for autonomy. In Iraq they have carried on a campaign for over two decades, initially (when Iraq was a pro-Western member of the Baghdad Pact) drawing support from the Soviet bloc.[69] Later Soviet equipment spearheaded Iraqi drives which cost thousands of lives while the Kurds drew support from Iran. Now within Iran's Islamic Republic, the Kurds were the first to fight for autonomy. Their religious leader, Sheik Ezzedin Hosseini also boycotted the Iranian elections. By heavy fighting the Kurds have apparently gained a good measure of de facto autonomy within the Islamic Republic.[70] An autonomous Iranian Kurdistan could be very destabilizing for both Turkey and Iraq, as well as having a potential for reflection within the Soviet Union.

The Baluchi live in the tri-border area of eastern Iran, western Pakistan and southern Afghanistan. As with the Kurds, they have long agitated for an independent homeland. Many Baluchi leaders have strong leftist orientations and have drawn support from the Soviet Union. Now, with the Soviet occupation of Afghanistan, only Baluchistan separates the Soviets from warm water ports on the Arabian Sea. The possibility of eventually moving to secure this

319

area was probably one consideration behind the Soviet move into Afghanistan and has prompted much nervousness both in Pakistan and in Iran where armed clashes were reported in December 1979.[71]

Iran's Arab population of at least a half million is centered in Khuzhistan at the head of the Persian Gulf and Iran's oil production area. Strikes by the Arab workers were one of the critical elements in the downfall of the Shah, and the Arabs have continued their activism with demands for autonomy on the new Islamic Republic. Their religious leader, Ayatollah al-Shobel Khangani, also boycotted the national elections and there has been sporadic fighting and leftist agitation by the Arabs.[72]

Overall, the situation in Iran is certainly complex. Its Islamic Republic projects an image of Islam which could easily spur an increased cultural awareness among the Soviet Muslims. On the other hand, the long-term stability of the Islamic Republic is questionable, especially in the presence of radical Marxist groups and with the unsettling activities of the country's minorities. These minorities include four sizable groups (Azarbaijanis, Turkomans, Kurds and Baluchi) with strong separatist movements. In the past, the Soviets have often given support to these movements and could do so again to undermine the stability of the Teheran government, or even as a pretext for intervention under the terms of the 1921 Soviet-Iranian Treaty, which the Soviets have openly referred to in recent months.[73] On the other hand, if the Islamic Republic is successful in defining spheres of autonomy for its minority groups, this would not only remove a basis for Soviet political or military intervention, but would also provide visible contrasts with the Soviet Muslim areas and could act to increase further the internal demands of Soviet Muslims. At this point, the only direct linkages across the Iranian-Soviet border are the Soviet radio broadcasts plus whatever clandestine support the Soviets are giving to leftist elements in Iran. But, as in Afghanistan, any direct Soviet involvement in Iran would greatly increase the direct linkages between Soviet and local Muslims.

Turkey

Turkey has a long history of conflict with Russian governments seeking an outlet to the Mediterranean. Additionally, a number of pan-Turkic movements have presented attractions for the Turkic peoples of the Soviet Union—attractions strongly denounced since the 1920's but still not squelched.[74] Recently this staunchly anti-

Soviet country and strong member of NATO has undergone noticeable change, particularly following the Cyprus crisis and the subsequent deterioration of relations with the United States. The Soviets have taken advantage of this new mood in Turkey to build a modest rapprochement with the government.[75] At the same time, there has been a renewed leftist militancy among the Turkish Kurds.[76] Even in the past the Turkish government was reluctant to become involved in the question of Soviet political dissent, grudgingly giving minimal attention to Meskhetian appeals. Now in a climate of Soviet-Turkish rapprochement and against a Soviet potential for instigating unrest among Turkey's minority Kurds, the Turkish government is unlikely to provide any direct support for Soviet Muslim dissidents. However, growing cultural exchange programs provide a basis for open Turkish support of the increasing interest among Soviet Turkic peoples in their own cultural heritage. And certainly any harsh repression of Soviet Muslims would undermine the fragile Turkish-Soviet rapprochement which Moscow apparently views as an important vehicle for weakening the cohesiveness of NATO's southern flank.

The Third World

Although few Soviet Muslims share a common ethnic basis with the Arab world, this area was the basic source of their Muslim heritage. Indeed some use of the traditional Arabic script apparently still survives within religious portions of the Soviet Muslim community,[77] and the Soviets send carefully controlled and selected groups on pilgrimages to Muslim shrines and to various Muslim conferences.[78] While the Soviets have close relations with a number of modernizing Arab states, several of these governments (particularly Iraq and Libya) are strongly Muslim and have denounced the Soviet intervention in Afghanistan. As such, Soviet Muslim policy is particularly relevant for Soviet relations with Arab states, providing a strong incentive not to further alienate them by obvious repression of Central Asian Muslims.

Overall, relations with the Third World significantly restrain the adoption of certain options for handling internal problems of Muslim assertiveness.[79] Curtailing Muslim access to key positions, dispersing Muslim workers throughout the Soviet Union, or suppressing the growing interest in the Soviet Muslim heritage would invite denunciations from neighboring Muslim states and possibly even direct support for dissident Soviet Muslims. They would also undoubtedly draw direct Chinese criticism and complicate Soviet efforts to reduce Chinese influence in the Third World.

SUMMARY AND CONCLUSIONS

The Soviet Muslim population, concentrated in traditional homeland areas in Central Asia, Transcaucasia, and adjacent regions, has a long history of Russian and then Soviet domination. When compared to its prerevolutionary conditions and to most of the neighboring (and ethnically related) countries, the Soviet Muslim areas have shown impressive development in terms of agricultural production, industrialization, education, and health services, though at a cost of a loss of local political control and expression. Furthermore, by comparison with the rest of the Soviet Union, the development of Central Asia does have some significant shortcomings, specifically in its continuing position as a net supplier of raw materials. There is also a continuing and highly visible Slavic domination of both economic and political life. Increased education has brought both a growing interest in the Soviet Muslim heritage and increased pressures for a larger share in the Soviet system.

These pressures are now combining with demographic trends which project large increases in the Muslim proportion of the Soviet work force, at the same time that the demands for labor will be greatest outside the traditionally Muslim areas. This will significantly increase job competition between Slavs and Muslims in Central Asia and will face the Soviet Union with a difficult problem of how to shift population resources to areas where they are needed without alienating workers and feeding dissatisfaction, dissent and possibly even open unrest among their Muslim population. Furthermore, the growing interest in their Muslim heritage works counter to Soviet goals for the development of a single, multinational Soviet people.

Even the brief survey above of Muslim areas bordering on Central Asia shows that there is a wide variety of linkages across the Soviet border. Overt cultural and tourist linkages, including pilgrimage groups, are all carefully controlled by the Soviets and are kept to a modest level. There are also direct economic linkages, particularly in regard to Middle East energy sources. Already the Soviet bloc has felt the pinch of Iran's cutback in natural gas supplies. A worsening of Soviet ties with the Muslim world could greatly complicate the Soviet energy planning.

Additionally, there are clandestine direct linkages across the Soviet border, although there do not appear to be any significant remaining informal or spontaneous linkages between kindred Muslim groups astride the border. On the Sino-Soviet border, clandestine linkages appear to work both ways, giving each side a potential to instigate unrest among Muslim minorities and to provide active support to any dissident movements which might develop. Elsewhere along the Soviet border, such linkages appear to originate strictly in the Soviet Union and to be directed against local Muslim minorities, either across the Soviet border with Iran and Turkey, or through diplomatic missions.

Against this background, the Soviet invasion of Afghanistan is unique because it provides large scale direct inputs into Soviet Central Asia, inputs which are only partially under the control of the Soviet authorities. Central Asians in the invasion force get to see conditions in Afghanistan, speak with Afghanis in their own language and then return to Central Asia to spread their own version of events. As restricted as their experience might be, it is the first relatively large scale direct linkage into Soviet Central Asia since the Xinjiang migrations of the late 1950's. There is a potential not only for anti-Soviet Afghan rebels to draw support from Central Asians, but also for unrest to spread eventually into Central Asia, particularly if instability and fighting expand to other areas of the Soviet border.

In addition to established direct linkages, there are a number of incipient direct linkages where one side provides a direct output but there is no specific recipient. These include Soviet radio broadcasts to all the neighboring countries; broadcasts into Central Asia by China, the Voice of America, and Radio Liberty; and various cross-border appeals, such as the Iranian appeals for broader religious rights for Soviet Muslims and the Islamic Conference appeal for a Soviet withdrawal from Afghanistan. While the impact of these direct outputs is largely unmeasurable, they do act to spread a general awareness of broader indirect linkages.

These broad indirect linkages—example set by social, political and economic conditions on both sides of the border—form the

323

bulk of the linkages across the Soviet border. They have a number of implications for Soviet foreign policy, particularly in regard to the Third World.

The Soviet appeal to the Third World heavily stresses Central Asian development as a model for wide application. Any widespread dissatisfaction or unrest in this area would seriously undermine this appeal.

Islam is a major political force in South Asia and the Middle East. The Soviet Union professes that its own Muslims enjoy wide religious freedom, but unrest in Central Asia would visibly tarnish this claim. Furthermore, the growing militancy of Islam along the Soviet borders has a potential to reflect within the Soviet Muslim population and increase pressures for equality of opportunity and development of local cultural heritages.

Militant Islamic movements such as the Iranian revolution and the Afghan opposition set an example of Muslim resistance to tyranny and oppession which could encourage open unrest on the part of Soviet Muslims.

Autonomous regions which are developing in Iran could have a strong influence on their neighboring Soviet regions. While the Soviet Union has in the past supported separatist movements to help undermine unfriendly or hostile governments, separatist movements not under Soviet influence which establish autonomous regions could be disturbing sources of ideological contamination.

Although the human rights movement has to this point been largely a concern of the Western powers and has found its major international expression in the Helsinki Final Act, there is also a Third World interest in this subject. Repression in Soviet Central Asia would probably draw loud denunciations not only from the West but from China and the Third World as well.

The net result of these various linkages with Soviet Muslims is that foreign policy considerations constrain the Soviet Union's options in solving its internal political problems. Furthermore, Soviet foreign policy actions can help strengthen internal trends (such as a broad development of local culture and the growth of common ties between Muslim ethnic groups) which work against basic goals of assimilation to a common Soviet (largely Russian) culture and continued domination of the Soviet system by ethnic Russians. Therefore Soviet foreign policy, particularly toward the Muslim world, must be carefully coordinated with internal policies in Soviet Central Asia.

324

ENDNOTES

1. Richard V. Weeks, ed., *Muslim Peoples*, Westport, Connecticut: Greenwood Press, 1978, p. 527, cites a total world Muslim population of 719,721,000. Nawabzada Sher Ali Khan Pataudi, "Islam and Military Power," *Military Review,* Vol. LIX, No. 11, November 1979, p. 72, cites 800 million Muslims.

2. Weeks, pp. xxiii-xxx.

3. Flora Lewis, "Upsurge in Islam," *The New York Times*, December 28, 29, 30 and 31, 1979.

4. The theory of linkages between national and international systems is only weakly developed. The terminology and relationships used here is that proposed by James N. Rosenau, *The Scientific Study of Foreign Policy*, New York: The Free Press, 1971, pp. 307-338.

5. The 9,195,000 Uzbeks constituted the third largest ethnic group in the 1970 Soviet population of 241,720,000. Other major Muslim peoples included Tatars (5,931,000), Kazakhs (5,299,000), Azerbaidzhanis (4,380,000), Tadzhiks (2,136,000), Chuvash (1,694,000), Turkmens (1,525,000), Kirghiz (1,452,000), Dagestanis (1,365,000), Mordvinians (1,263,000) and Bashkirs (1,240,000). The total population of Muslim peoples was close to 40 million, or about one sixth of the total population. *Narodnoe khoziaistvo SSSR za 60 let (National Economy of the USSR for 60 Years)*, Moscow: Statistika Publishing House, 1977, p. 41. In this context, "Muslim" refers to ethnic and cultural origins, it does not necessarily reflect present religious orientation.

6. Murray Feshbach and Stephen Rapaway, "Soviet Population and Manpower Trends and Policies," in US Congress, Joint Economic Committee, *Soviet Economy in a New Perspective*, Washington: US Government Printing Office, 1976, pp. 127-128. In later remarks ("Population and Manpower Trends in the U.S.S.R.") delivered October 31, 1978, at the Kennan Institute (Washington, D.C.) Conference on Soviet Central Asia, Feshbach estimated that one quarter of the projected Soviet population in the year 2000 would be of Muslim origin and less than half would be Russians. His conclusions are based on tables in: US Department of Commerce, Bureau of the Census, *Population Projections by Age and Sex: For the Republics and Major Economic Regions of the U.S.S.R.—1970 to 2000*, Washington: US Government Printing Office, 1979. Unfortunately, all this analysis is based on 1970 census data; the 1979 census data is only beginning to become available (see, for example: Joint Publications Research Service No. 74505, *USSR Trade and Services*, November 1, 1979, p. 50, and *The New York Times*, February 28, 1980).

7. Gregory J. Massell, "Modernization and Nationality Policy in Soviet Central Asia" in *The Dynamics of Soviet Politics*, ed. by Paul Cocks *et al.*, Cambridge: Harvard University Press, 1976, pp. 281-285; Jeremy R. Azrael and Steven L. Burg, *Political Participation and Ethnic Conflict in Soviet Central Asia*, paper presented at the Conference on Soviet Central Asia, International Communications Agency, Washington, DC, October 31, 1978, pp. 1, 9-11.

8. Lawrence Krader, *Peoples of Central Asia*, Bloomington: Indiana University Press, 1966, pp. 118-136. This work also gives extensive data on the origins of the various ethnic groups. See also: Karl H. Menges, "People, Languages, and Migrations," in *Central Asia: A Century of Russian Rule*, ed. by Edward Allworth,

New York: Columbia University Press, 1967, pp. 92-130 and Charles Warren Hostler, *Turkism and the Soviets*, London: George Allen & Unwin, Ltd., 1957, pp. 4-83; Geoffrey Wheeler, *The Peoples of Soviet Central Asia*, Chester Springs, Pennsylvania: Dubour Editions, 1966; Weeks, pp. 210-226, 389-400, 451-469.

9. Detailed accounts of this early Russian expansion are in: Allworth, Chapters 4-7; Krader, pp. 97-109; Seymour Becker, *Russia's Protectorates in Central Asia*, Cambridge: Harvard University Press, 1968; Michael Rywkin, *Russia in Central Asia*, New York: Collier Books, 1963, pp. 15-32; Geoffrey Wheeler, *The Modern History of Soviet Central Asia*, New York: Frederick A. Praeger, Inc., 1964, pp. 48-96.

10. Establishing control and crushing independent minded local Communists were complex and lengthy tasks for the new Soviet state and involved widespread fighting among constantly shifting elements. See: Rywkin, pp. 33-62; Allworth, Chapters 8-10; Charles Warren Hostler, pp. 146-168; Alexandre Bennigsen and Chantal Lemercier-Quelquejay, *Islam in the Soviet Union*, New York: Frederick A. Praeger, Inc., 1967, pp. 65-164; William Mandel, *The Soviet Far East and Central Asia*, New York: Dial Press, Inc., 1944, pp. 105-118.

11. Donald S. Carlisle ("Modernization, Generations and the Uzbek Soviet Intelligensia," in Cocks, pp. 239-264) gives a detailed analysis of this process in Uzbekistan. For parallel actions in other Muslim areas, see: Rywkin, pp. 101-118 (general) and pp. 119-152 (also on Uzbekistan); US Congress, Senate, Committee on the Judiciary, *The Soviet Empire*, Washington: US Government Printing Office, 1965, pp. 47-61; Wheeler, pp. 117-136.

12. Elizabeth E. Bacon, *Central Asians Under Russian Rule*, Ithaca: Cornell University Press, 1966, pp. 189-201; Rwykin, pp. 85-100; Hostler, pp. 156-170.

13. Bacon, pp. 189-217; Bennigsen and Lemercier-Quelquejay, pp. 123-164; Wheeler, *The Peoples*, pp. 93-111; *The Soviet Empire*, pp. 52-65, 109-114; John H. Miller, "Cadres Policy in Nationality Areas," *Soviet Studies*, Vol. XXIX, No. 1, January 1977, pp. 3-36.

14. Alec Nove and J.A. Newth, *The Soviet Middle East*, New York: Frederick A. Praeger, Inc., 1967, pp. 39-54, 67-85.

15. Carlisle, p. 262; See also Herwig Kraus, "Leading Organs of the Communist Party of Azerbaijan," *Radio Liberty Research*, No. 49/78, February 24, 1978.

16. *Ibid.*, also John Hanselman, "Leadership and Nationality: A Comparison of Uzbekistan and Kirgizia" in *The Nationality Question in Soviet Central Asia*, ed. by Edward Allworth, New York: Praeger Publishers, 1973, pp. 100-109. Russian Second Secretaries, though, are still a consistent occurrence; see Christian Duevel, "Changing Patterns in the Top 'Watchdog' Appointments to the Union Republics," *Radio Liberty Research*, No. 365/76, July 28, 1976; Miller, p. 35.

17. *National Economy*, particularly pp. 176, 306-331, 444, 582; Leslie Symons, "Tadzhikistan: A Developing Country in the Soviet Union," *Asian Affairs*, Vol. 61, Part III, October 1974, pp. 251-252; Nove and Newth, Chapters 3-7.

18. Nove and Newth, Chapter 8.

19. *Ibid.*, pp. 115-122; Geoffrey Jukes, *The Soviet Union in Asia*, Berkeley: University of California Press, 1973, pp. 48-49.

20. Symons, p. 251; Robin and Michelle Poulton, "A Recent Visit to Bukhara and Samarkand," *Asian Affairs*, Vol. 63, Part III, October 1976, pp. 306; Ann Sheehy, "Industrial Growth Lags in Turkmenistan," *Radio Liberty Research*, No. 5/79, January 3, 1979, see also, No. 363/76, July 20, 1976; *The Soviet Empire*, pp.

51-64, 91-104; Hans-Jurgen Wagner, "The RSFSR and the Non-Russian Republics; An Economic Comparison," *Radio Liberty Dispatch*, undated (but issued in 1968); Albert Boiter, "Educational Levels of Soviet Nationalities Compared," *ibid*., June 28, 1973; Theodore Shabad, "Central Asia and the Soviet Economy: Implications for Policy," paper presented October 31, 1978, at the Kennan Institute (Washington, DC) Conference on Soviet Central Asia, pp. 2, 10.

21. Feshbach and Rapaway, pp. 127-128; Kevin Klose, "Central Asia's Population Growing," *The Washington Post*, January 2, 1979; Shabad, p. 17.

22. Massell, pp. 275-278, 287-288; there are already numerous indications of under-employment among indigenous workers, see, for example: "Squatters in Kirgizia," *Radio Liberty Research*, No. 252/78, November 14, 1978; "Reports of Unemployment in Uzbekistan," *ibid*., No. 424/76, September 29, 1976; Shabad, pp. 6-8, 17.

23. David K. Shipler, "Imbalance of Population a Key Soviet Issue," *The New York Times*, January 9, 1979; Massell, p. 288; Allen Hetmanek, "Soviet Views on Out-Migration from Central Asia," *Radio Liberty Research*, No. 70/77, March 29, 1979; Feshbach and Rapaway, pp. 124-127; Shabad, pp. 10-13.

24. Ann Sheehy, "New Measures to Improve the Teaching of Russian in the Union Republics," *Radio Liberty Research*, No. 120/79, April 17, 1979; Kestutis Girnius, "The Draft Recommendations to the Tashkent Conference: A New Wave of Russification?" *ibid*., No. 188/79, June 19, 1979.

25. Ignacy Szenfeld, "Olzhas Suleimenor Under Fire from Neoslavophile Critics," *ibid*., No. 137/76, March 15, 1976.

26. John Soper, "Uzbek Writers Look to the Past for Inspiration," *ibid*., No. 129/79, April 24, 1979; William Reese, "Soviet Literacy Policy and the Preservation of the Lyrical Arts," *ibid*., No. 78/75, February 21, 1975.

27. John Soper, "Problems in Publishing the Kirghiz Epic *Manas*," *ibid*., No. 221/78, October 10, 1978.

28. Tania Jacques, "The Central Asian Cinema: Politics and Aesthetics," *ibid*., No. 164/75, April 18, 1975.

29. Teresa Rakowska-Harmstone, "Integration and Ethnic Nationalism in the Soviet Union: Aspects, Trends and Problems," in *Nationalities and Nationalism in the USSR: A Soviet Dilemma*, ed. by Carl A. Linden and Dimitri Simes, a Joint Symposium sponsored by Georgetown University and George Washington University, Washington, October 20, 1976, pp. 34-36; see also: Tura Kamal, "Ethnolinguistic Self-Expression in the Tatar SSR," *Radio Liberty Research*, No. 523/75, December 17, 1975; Elizabeth E. Bacon, *Central Asians Under Russian Rule*, Ithaca: Cornell University Press, 1966, Chapter 8.

30. Brian Silver, "Social Mobilization and the Russification of Soviet Nationalities," *The American Political Science Review*, Vol. 68, No. 1, March 1974, p. 59.

31. "The Status of Khorezm Turks in the Uzbek National Entity," *Radio Liberty Research*, No. 61/77, March 15, 1977.

32. "An Uzbek Writer on Uzbek-Azerbaijani Cultural Ties and Common Heritage," *Radio Liberty Translation* from *Ozbekistan Madanyati* (Tashkent), June 5, 1970; Tania Jacques, "Elements of Pan-Turkism in Kazakhstan," *Radio Liberty Research*, No. 353/74, November 15, 1974; Alexandre Bennigsen, "The Nature of Ethnic Consciousness in Soviet Central Asia," paper presented October 31, 1978, at the Kennan Institute (Washington, DC) Conference on Soviet Central Asia, pp. 17-18.

33. Bennigsen and Lemercier-Quelquejay, Part IV; Kevin Klose, "Despite Soviet Teachings, Moslems Cling to Beliefs," *The Washington Post*, January 2, 1979, and 'Moslems Blunt Sharp Atheistic Thrust of Soviet Life," *ibid.*, December 31, 1978; John Soper, "Unofficial Islam Among Soviet Uigurs," *Radio Liberty Research*, No. 54/79, February 16, 1979, and "Official Attitudes Towards Islamic Customs," *ibid.*, No. 66/77, March 22, 1977; "Moslem Rituals Still Strong in Turkemenia," *The Current Digest of the Soviet Press*, Vol. XXXI, No. 47, December 1979, pp. 12-13.

34. There has been a large volume of literature on this subject in recent years. One good overview is Rudolph Tokes, *Dissent in the the USSR*, Baltimore: John Hopkins University Press, 1975.

35. US Congress. Commission on Security and Cooperation in Europe. *Basket Three: Implementation of the Helsinki Accords*, Volume II, Washington: US Government Printing Office, 1977, p. 212; Robert Conquest, *The Soviet Deportation of Nationalities*, New York: Praeger, 1960, pp. 105-107.

36. Ann Sheehy, *The Crimean Tatars and the Volga Germans*, London: The Minority Rights Group, 1971. See also the *Chronicle of Current Events*, a Moscow underground journal republished by Khronika Press, New York; issue number 31 of this journal was entirely devoted to the Crimean Tatars, other issues document numerous individual incidents, protests and arrests.

37. Ann Sheehy, "Tenth Anniversary of the Decree on the Meskhetians," *Radio Liberty Research*, No. 124/78, May 31, 1978; *Chronicle of Current Events*, No. 7 and 19.

38. "Sinkiang in the Modern World," *Royal Central Asian Journal*, Vol. 46, Part I, February 1969, pp. 42-44.

39. Wheeler, *Modern History*, pp. 176-177.

40. *Ibid.*, also J.P. Lo, "Five Years of the Sinkiang-Uighur Autonomous Region, 1955-1960," *China Quarterly*, No. 8, October-December 1961, pp. 92-105; A.R. Field, "Strategic Development in Sinkiang," *Foreign Affairs*, Vol. 39, No. 2, January 1961, pp. 312-318.

41. See, for example: *U.S. News and World Report*, January 6, 1964, pp. 53-54; *International Herald Tribune*, August 7 and 8, 1967; *The New York Times*, July 27, 1979; Joachim Glaubitz, "Soviet Politics Regarding China and Asia," *Pacific Community*, Vol. 7, No. 4, July 1976, p. 498; Michael Parks, "Rising Tensions Likely Along Sino-Soviet Border," *Baltimore Sun*, August 8, 1979.

42. Typical materials on this propaganda war are: "Ili's Ten Fruitful Years," *Peking Review*, No. 37, September 11, 1964, pp. 5, 26; Suleyman Tekiner, "Sinkiang and the Sino-Soviet Conflict," *Bulletin* (Munich), Vol. 14, No. 8, August 1967, pp. 9-16; Bukhara Ryshkanbayev, "Eto—neprikryty shovinism (This is Blatant Chauvinism),"*Lituraturnaya Gazeta,* September 26, 1963, p. 4; "War of Nerves," *Newsweek,* Vol. 59, No. 10, March 6, 1967, pp. 33-34; "Review of Sinkiang Affairs Based on Chinese Press and Radio," *The Central Asian Review*, Vol. 15, No. 1, 1967, pp. 88-92; "Soviet Broadcasts in Uygur for Sinkiang," *ibid.*, Vol. 15, No. 3, 1967, pp. 284-286; John Soper, "Is the Soviet Union Interested in Playing the Uigur Card?" *Radio Liberty Research,* No. 69/79, March 1, 1979; David R. Staats, "The Uighur Press and the Sino-Soviet Conflict, *ibid.,* No. 147/77, June 15, 1977.

43. David R. Staats, "Sinkiang and 'The China Card,'" *ibid.,* No. 171/79, July 14, 1977, p. 3; see also Tura Kamal, "Translation of Uighur Authors into Russian and the Sino-Soviet Conflict," *ibid.,* No. 214/75, May 23, 1975.

44. Kamal, pp. 2-3.

45. John Soper, "Unofficial Islam Among Soviet Uigurs," *ibid.*, No. 54/79, February 16, 1979.

46. Glaubitz, pp. 494-495.

47. Wheeler, *Modern History*, pp. 108-110.

48. Stelianos Scarlis, "Soviet Involvement in Afghanistan," *Radio Liberty Research*, No. 182/79, June 13, 1979; "The Afghans See Red," *The New York Times*, July 26, 1979; David De Voss, "Rebels, Soviet Advisers Dominate Afghan Scene," *Washington Star*, April 30, 1979; Hedrick Smith, "U.S. is Indirectly Pressing Russians to Halt Afghanistan Intervention," *The New York Times*, August 3, 1979.

49. Rosanne Klass, "The Afghans May Win," *The New York Times*, February 8, 1980.

50. Selig Harrison, "Did Moscow Fear an Afghan Tito," *ibid.*, January 13, 1980, and Robert G. Kaiser, "Soviet Afghanistan Invasion: The End of the Era of Detente," *The Washington Post*, January 17, 1980.

51. *The New York Times*, January 15, 1980.

52. *Ibid.*, January 30, 1980.

53. Peter Kruzhin, "The Ethnic Composition of the Soviet Forces in Afghanistan," *Radio Liberty Dispatch*, No. 20/80, January 11, 1980.

54. *The Washington Post*, February 8, 1980; *The New York Times*, February 3 and 7, 1980.

55. *Ibid.*, January 10, 1980.

56. "Soviet Civilians Increasingly Direct Afghan Government," *The Washington Post*, January 25, 1980; scattered reports of friction have already begun to surface, see: "Moscow Counts Its Dead," *Newsweek*, February 25, 1980.

57. For a general outline of Iranian history, see: Richard F. Nyrop, ed., *Iran: A Country Study*, Washington: The American University, 1978, pp. 45-66.

58. Mohammed Ayoob, "Two Faces of Political Islam: Iran and Pakistan Compared," *Asian Survey*, Vol. 19, No. 6, June 1979, pp. 542-543.

59. Robert Moss, "The Campaign to Destabilize Iran," *Conflict Studies* No. 101, November 1978. A summary of this document was published as: "Who's Meddling in Iran?" *New Republic*, December 2, 1978, pp. 15-18. See also: Rowland Evans and Robert Novak, "Soviet Intrigues in Iran," *The Washington Post*, April 9, 1979.

60. *Moskovskaya Pravda*, November 22, 1978, cited in *Foreign Broadcast Information Service*: USSR International Affairs, November 29, 1978, p. F-2; *Kommunist* (Yerevan), December 7, 1978, *ibid.*, December 14, 1978, p. F-7.

61. Richard Sim, "Muhammad and Marx: The Explosive Mixture," *Soviet Analyst*, Vol. 8, No. 5, March 8, 1979, pp. 4-5.

62. Ayoob, pp. 542-544.

63. Ayatollah Sadeq Rohani has called at least twice for the distribution of Islamic writings in the Soviet Union and permission for Islamic preachers to travel in the Soviet Muslim republics. "The USSR This Week," *Radio Liberty Research*, No. 181/79, June 11, 1979 and No. 190/79, June 18, 1979.

64. See, for example: "Iranian Says Soviet Aims to Split Nation," *The New York Times*, January 18, 1980. Reportedly, Ayatollah Khomeini has also complained to the Soviet Ambassador over Soviet involvement in Iran, and then broadcast the criticism over the Iranian State Radio; "The USSR This Week," *Radio Liberty Research*, No. 190/79, June 18, 1979 and *The New York Times*, June 13, 1979.

65. John Kofner, "Iran is Harried by Persistent Resistance of Its Minorities," *The New York Times*, April 11, 1979; Nyrop, p. 72; *Iran Almanac*, Tehran: Echoprint, 1975, pp. 395, 428-429.

66. Youssef M. Ibrahim, "Election in Iran: Khomeini's Victory May Prove Costly," *The New York Times*, August 8, 1979; see also December 7 and 10, 1979.

67. John Kifner, "Turkomans Battle Iranian Forces in New Outbreak of Tribal Separatism," *The New York Times*, March 28, 1979, and "Iran Promising Special Attention to Ethnic Demands," *ibid.*, March 29, 1979.

68. Ismet Vanly, a Kurdish representative, discussed several estimates (*The Revolution of Iraki Kurdistan*, Part I, Committee for the Defense of the Kurdish People's Rights, April 1965, pp. 4-5) and comes to a total of 13 million. Abdul Rahman Ghassemlou, an Iranian Kurdish leader, also examines various estimates (*Kurdistan and the Kurds*, Prague: Publishing House of the Czechoslovak Academy of Science, 1965, tr. Mirian Jelinkova, London: Collet's Holdings, Ltd., pp. 19-24) and reaches a total of 10,450,000. The *Bolshaia Sovetskaia Entisklopedia (Large Soviet Encyclopedia)*, Vol. 24, p. 90, gives a 1953 total of seven million Kurdish *speakers*. Charles Cremeans (*The Arabs and the World*, New York: Praeger Publishers, 1963, p. 76) gives under five million.

69. The short-lived Mahabad government was one early example of Soviet support for separatist Kurds in an era when Soviet relations with Iran, Iraq, and Turkey were all poor. In the 1950's, the Kurdish separatist leader Mustafa Barzini and several hundred of his followers were given asylum in the Soviet Union, (Israel T. Naamani, "Kurdish Driver for Self Determination," *The Middle East Journal*, Vol. 20, No. 3, Summer 1966, p. 288) and support for a radio and propaganda campaign including a treatise published by the Czechoslovak Academy of Science supporting an independent Kurdistan (Ghassemlou).

70. Ibrahim, p. 4, see also: William Braingin, "Kurdish Unrest Adds to Woes of Iran," *The Washington Post*, November 21, 1978; John Kofner, "Iran Promising Special Attention to Ethnic Demands," *The New York Times*, March 29, 1979, and "Iranian Troops Move Into Position to Fight Kurds' Autonomy Quest," *ibid.*, December 7, 1979.

71. Christopher S. Wren, "In New Ethnic Violence in Iran, Baluchis Battle Persians," *The New York Times*, December 21, 1979; see also: William Branigan, "Baluchi Harbor a Lure to Soviets," *The Washington Post*, February 9, 1979.

72. Ibrahim, p. 4; William Branigan, "Iranian Arabs, Khomeini Forces Clash Violently," *The Washington Post*, May 31, 1979; see also August 24, 1979.

73. Craig W. Whitney, "Moscow Gambles in Iran," *The New York Times*, January 27, 1979.

74. Tura Kamal, "Renewed Criticism of Sultan-Galievism," *Radio Liberty Research*, No. 141/76, March 17, 1976.

75. Marian Leighton, "Soviet-Turkish Friendship: Implications for the West," *Radio Liberty Research*, No. 217/77, September 20, 1977; Rowland Evans and Robert Novak, "The Confidence Game," *The Washington Post,* July 13, 1979.

76. Sam Cohen, "Turkey Watches Its Kurds," *Christian Science Monitor,* April 10, 1979.

77. Robin and Michelle Poulton, p. 304.

78. Violet Conolly, "'Jubilee Year' in Central Soviet Asia," *Asian Affairs*, Vol. 58, Part II, January 1971, p. 167; *Soviet Analyst*, Vol. 8, No. 14, July 12, 1979, p. 4; *USSR and the Third World*, Vol. 8, 1978, No. 2 and 3, p. 59.

79. Massell, pp. 281-287.

17

SOVIET POLICY TOWARD THE DEVELOPING WORLD: THE ROLE OF ECONOMIC ASSISTANCE AND TRADE

Roger E. Kanet

At the time of Stalin's death in 1953 the position of the Soviet Union in the developing world was extremely weak. Not only did the Soviets maintain virtually no diplomatic or economic relations with the countries of the Third World, but they found themselves ringed by a growing network of US-centered military alliances in Europe, as well as in the Middle East and Far East. While the Western opponents of the USSR maintained political, economic and military relations with all regions of the world—much of which still consisted of colonial appendages of the West—Soviet international contacts were restricted primarily to the countries that comprised their newly-created empire in Eastern Europe and to their Communist allies in Asia. The US policy of containment of Soviet power had resulted in the creation of a network of air and naval bases around the USSR complemented by massive nuclear deterrence. The Soviets, on the other hand, were limited in their ability to project military and political power beyond the region under the control of the Soviet army.

By the late 1970's the relative position of the two major power blocs had changed substantially. The collapse of the Western colonial empires and the ensuing rise of numerous anti-Western regimes in the developing world, Western military and political retrenchment, and other developments have resulted in the contraction of Western political and military influence throughout most of Asia and Africa. At the same time the Soviets have been able to establish a network of economic, political, and military relationships throughout much of Asia and Africa that permits them for the first time in their history to play the role of a global power with worldwide interests.[1] Beginning in the mid-1950's soon after Stalin's death the new Soviet leadership embarked upon efforts to expand contacts of all sorts with the new states of Asia and Africa, although the initial focus of that policy was on the creation of economic links as a prelude to broader political contacts. While Soviet military assistance committed during the Khrushchev era, 1955-64, averaged approximately $375 million per year, economic aid extensions during the same period averaged somewhat more than $425 million per year.[2] In addition, the decade from 1955 to 1965 witnesses a five-fold expansion of Soviet trade with the non-Communist developing countries, from $337 million (5.2 percent of total trade turnover) to $1,935 million (11.9 percent of total trade). To a substantial degree Soviet policy toward the developing countries was a response to American efforts to create an alliance system in Asia as part of the policy of containment. In the mid-1950's the Soviet leadership initiated a "policy of denial" aimed at ensuring the neutrality of those developing countries—especially Afghanistan, India, and Egypt—which professed a nonaligned approach to foreign policy and opposed the intrusion of military alliances into their regions. The Soviets sought to expand their ties with such countries, in order to prevent the uncontested growth of Western political and military influence, to ensure that gaps would remain in the US-sponsored alliance network, and to win the support of these nonaligned countries for issues that were of importance to the Soviet Union.[3]

Since the Soviets now desired to cultivate the good will of the developing countries, it was clear that their leaders could no longer be viewed as reactionaries destined to be swept away by the tide of revolution. In short, there existed a contradiction between the imperatives of Soviet policy and the USSR's ideological assessments of these countries. While the aid and political support given to countries like Egypt and India in the 1950's signalled a shift in Soviet policy, a change in doctrine at an authoritative level was made with Khrushchev's introduction of the concept of the "zone of peace" at the Twentieth Congress of the Communist Party of the Soviet Union in 1956. The nonaligned states were no longer regarded as mere outposts of Western imperialism, but as the independent proponents of peace and therefore worthy of Soviet support and assistance, although the Soviets still criticized domestic, political and economic arrangements in most of the Third World.[4]

The primary areas of Soviet involvement in the developing world during the decade of Khrushchev's leadership were those regions of special strategic concern to the Soviet leadership—the Middle East and South Asia. Measured in terms of political contacts, economic relations (including assistance), or military aid, Soviet interest in the region adjacent to the southern borders of the Soviet Union expanded extremely rapidly.[5] In addition, however, the Soviets did attempt to take advantage of a number of opportunities presented by events in other areas of the developing world, such as the civil war in Zaire (then Congo-Leopoldville) and the radicalization of the governments of Sukarno in Indonesia, Nkrumah in Ghana, and Toure in Guinea.

Although the initial Soviet push toward expanding contacts with the countries of the Third World was accompanied by optimistic statements about the prospects for the development of a revolutionary climate in these countries, the immediate Soviet goal, as we have noted, was clearly the reduction of Western influence in areas of strategic significance to the USSR. This meant that, in spite of rhetoric about support for the construction of "scientific socialism" in developing countries, the Soviets were willing to provide assistance and support to such clearly nonsocialist countries as Afghanistan and the Ethiopia of Haile Selassie in the attempt to undermine the dominant Western position. However, Khrushchev's goals far exceeded the means available to the Soviet Union. The inferior military position of the Soviet Union *vis-a-vis* the West—including the virtual absence of an ocean-going navy— made it difficult for the Soviets to provide effective support to their friends, such as Lumumba, Nkrumah, and Keita, in periods of crisis. In addition, Soviet hopes that most or at least many of the developing countries would be willing to cut their economic and political relations with the West proved to be inaccurate. Even

333

though countries such as Nasser's Egypt and Nehru's India had turned to the Soviet Union for military, economic, and political support, they continued to maintain relations with the West. The Soviet Union provided them with the possibility of lessening their dependence on the former colonial powers and represented an added source of military and economic assistance. It did not, however, provide a political-social-economic model which the majority of Third World political leaders were interested in emulating.

At the time of Khrushchev's overthrow in late 1964 Soviet policy in the developing world was in partial disarray. The optimism of the 1950's was already being questioned and replaced by a growing realism concerning prospects for political and economic developments in most of the Third World countries. Although the Soviet Union had ended its isolation from these countries, it had not succeeded in establishing significant influence relationships.[6] Where Soviet goals had been partially accomplished—for example, the reduction of the Western presence in the Middle East—success resulted far more from the initiatives of the developing countries themselves than from Soviet policy. Yet the foundations for future Soviet involvement in the Third World had been laid in many areas. In South Asia, India had already begun to depend upon the USSR for both the military assistance deemed necessary for security *vis-a-vis* China and Pakistan and for support in the development of heavy industrial projects in the state sector of the economy. In the Middle East both Egypt and Syria were now heavily indebted to the Soviets for military and economic assistance, while Turkey and Iran had begun to expand ties with their northern neighbor as a means of lessening their dependence on the United States. Throughout Asia and Africa the Soviet Union had become a force to be dealt with by Western Europe and the United States, even though the West still commanded more influence and was able to exert greater military capabilities in most areas of the developing world.

At the time of Khrushchev's dismissal the Soviets had already begun to reassess their views and policies toward the developing countries, as we have already noted. They recognized that the prospects for the introduction of their variety of socialism in the vast majority of the new states were bleak and that political and social instability often meant that leaders who were favorably disposed toward the Soviet Union might well be overthrown by "reactionary elements"—witness the fate of Ben Bella, Nkrumah, and Keita. During the first few years of Brezhnev's leadership of the CPSU the reassessment of Soviet policy continued. Confidence in the establishment of Soviet-type socialist systems and an emphasis on economic "show projects" were replaced by the effort to create firmly based relations with Third World countries that would begin to provide the Soviets with "bases of operation" from which they could expand contacts and attempt to increase their activities and build their influence. Even more than in earlier years Soviet policy focused on countries and political groupings that had inherent importance for their own purposes. First of all, they emphasized even more those countries along the southern boundaries of the Soviet Union—from India in South Asia to the Arab countries of North Africa. The importance of this area for the strategic interests of the Soviet Union is quite clear, as Soviet commentators have repeatedly noted.[7] Support for minor revolutionary groupings and for activities in Sub-Saharan Africa was downplayed in the late 1960's—to the point where some Western commentators argued that the Soviets had virtually lost interest in that continent.[8]

Even though the 1970's have witnessed a revitalization of Soviet interest in political and military opportunities offered by events in such countries as Angola and Ethiopia, there has been a growing emphasis on the value of expanding economic contacts with individual developing countries. Here the issue has not been so much the strategic location of a country as its level of development and the opportunities offered for "mutual economic benefit." At the beginning of the 1970's the Soviets were pursuing a policy aimed at producing an "international division of labor" between themselves (in conjunction with their CMEA partners) and individual Third World countries.[9] More recently there has appeared evidence of a growing Soviet awareness of the benefits of three-way cooperation among the socialist states, the capitalist West, and the non-Communist developing countries.[10] This has resulted not only in a significant expansion of Soviet assistance to projects designed to assure the Soviet economy of future sources of needed raw materials, such as bauxite and phosphates, but also in a number of joint undertakings in the developing countries that involve both Soviet and Western participation.

The present essay is concerned primarily with the economic aspect of Soviet relations with the countries of the developing world. It examines both the evolution of Soviet assistance programs and trade relations during the course of the past two decades and their importance for overall Soviet policy toward the developing world. Clearly economic relations comprise only one part of Soviet policy. A complete evaluation of that policy would also take into account military relations, including arms transfers, cultural contacts, propaganda activities, covert operations and support for revolutionary groups, and a variety of other factors.

ECONOMIC ASSISTANCE IN SOVIET POLICY TOWARD THE THIRD WORLD

Already in the 1950's Soviet commentators clarified the role of economic assistance to developing countries within the overall policy of peaceful coexistence. Soviet assistance supposedly provided the newly independent states with the possibility of developing their economies and of breaking their economic dependence on the imperialist West.[11] The primary focus of Soviet assistance was on the development of the state sector of the national economy of the recipient country. Although the Soviets have insisted that the granting of developmental credits "is not based on any political, military or other economic conditions that are unacceptable to a developing country,"[12] the major recipients have generally been countries that have been willing to follow, in part at least, Soviet guidance concerning the form of economic development of states that are strategically located in relationship to overall Soviet global interests. In recent years, however, with the modification of Soviet views concerning the expansion of economic contacts with developing countries, there has been a clear shift in the recipients of Soviet aid. In 1978, for example, 86 percent of the record $3,707 million in new Soviet aid commitments went to Morocco and Turkey, neither of which is socialist or anti-Western in orientation.

By far the greatest amount of Soviet assistance to developing countries from the very beginning of the Soviet aid program has been provided in the form of repayable credits. These credits have usually carried an interest rate of 2.5 to 3.0 percent and a repayment period of 12 years. The very small amount of Soviet assistance that has been provided as grant has usually been limited to highly visible projects that can have substantial propaganda benefits—for the construction of hospitals, schools, and other training facilities. Credits, on the other hand, have generally been allocated for the construction of major projects that will add to the overall productive capabilities of the recipient country. Approximately 75 percent of all Soviet economic assistance has gone toward the construction of an industrial base in the state sector of the economies of the recipient countries.[13]

New commitments of Soviet economic assistance for the period 1954-67 averaged $405 million per year and rose to an annual average of about $725 million for the following 10-year period. In a significant departure from their past behavior, in 1978 the Soviets pledged a total of $3.7 billion in new aid—most for projects in Morocco and Turkey (see Table 1). Deliveries, however, averaged only $182 million during the earlier period and rose to slightly less than $460 million annually during the last 11 years.[14] Although Soviet economic assistance to developing countries has been substantial over the course of the past two decades, this assistance must be viewed in perspective. First of all, given the concentration of Soviet assistance in a relatively few countries, most recipients of Soviet economic aid have received relatively small amounts of assistance. In addition Soviet aid, when compared with that of the United States and the other industrialized countries of the West, has been quite meager, until the major commitments of 1978. In 1977, for example, net Soviet aid made up only one percent of all overseas development assistance—a percentage surpassed by eleven Western developed countries, including such small countries as Denmark, Norway, Belgium and the Netherlands. In addition, Soviet developmental assistance comprised an estimated .02 percent of Soviet GNP, while it made up about .31 percent of the members of the OECD but only .22 percent for the United States.[15]

More important, however, for our present concerns—the role of economic assistance in overall Soviet policy toward the developing countries—is the fact that Soviet economic aid has been concentrated in a relatively few countries, most of which are of potential significance for Soviet strategic or economic interests. Through 1977 almost three-quarters of total Soviet credits and grants were committed to the Middle East and South Asia. (The massive 1978 credits to Morocco reduce the current percentage to slightly less than 70). (See Table 2.) Within that region aid has gone

TABLE 1

Soviet Economic Assistance To Non-Communist Developing Countries

(In Millions of current US dollars)

Total	Commitments	Deliveries
1954-78	17,088	7,595
1954-68	6,081	2,870
1969	476	355
1970	200	390
1971	1,126	420
1972	654	430
1973	714	500
1974	816	705
1975	1,934	500
1976	979	460
1977	402	540
1978	3,707	430

Source: US Central Intelligence Agency, National Foreign Assessment Center, Communist Aid Activities in Non-Communist Less Developed Countries 1978: A Research Paper, ER79-10412U, September 1979, p. 11.

primarily to a small number of countries—Afghanistan, Egypt, India, Iran, Iraq, Pakistan, Syria, and Turkey received a full 71 percent of all Soviet aid committed prior to 1978.

Soviet aid policy appears to be motivated by a number of distinct, but clearly interrelated, considerations. First of all, there has been the desire to support "progressive" or anti-Western regimes such as Egypt under Nasser, Syria, Iraq, and, most recently, South Yemen. A second but related goal has been the desire to reduce the dependence of countries such as Iran (prior to the overthrow of the Shah in early 1979), Turkey, and Pakistan on either the United States or China. Other countries, such as India, Somalia, and Egypt have attracted Soviet interest because of their strategic location and potential significance in world or regional political affairs. In addition, during the past decade Soviet aid has been tied increasingly to a concern for long-term economic benefits for the Soviet economy. The recent credit of $2 billion granted to Morocco in return for repayment in phosphates, and earlier Soviet agreements with Afghanistan, Iran, and Iraq which provide Soviet machinery and equipment in return for petrocarbons fit into this category. Finally, since virtually all Soviet assistance is provided in the form of exports of machinery and equipment, economic

assistance assures markets for Soviet industrial production which is
generally not competitive on the international market.

TABLE 2

Soviet Economic Credits And Grants Extended To
Non-Communist Developing Countries, 1954-78

(In Millions of Current US Dollars)

	1954-78		1977		1978	
	Amount	Percent	Amount	Percent	Amount	Percent
Total	$17,088	100.0%	$402	100.0%	$3,707	100.0%
Africa	3,989	23.3	31	7.7	2,010	54.2
North Africa*	2,918	17.1	0	0	2,000	54.0
Algeria	716		0			0
Mauritania	8		0			0
Morocco	2,098		0		2,000	
Tunisia	96		0		0	
Sub-Saharan Africa	1,071	6.3	31	7.7	11	.3
Angola	17		6		1	
Benin	5		0		0	
Cameroon	8		0		0	
Cape Verde	3		0		3	
Central African Empire	3		0		0	
Chad	5		0		0	
Congo	28		0		0	
Equatorial Guinea	1		0		0	
Ethiopia	105		0		negl.	
Ghana	94		1		0	
Guinea	212		1		0	
Guinea-Bissau	11		0		0	
Kenya	48		0		0	
Madagascar	20		0		6	
Mali	90		0		1	
Mauritius	5		0		0	
Mozambique	5		5		0	
Niger	2		0		0	
Nigeria	7		0		0	
Rwanda	1		0		0	
Senegal	8		0		0	
Sierra Leone	28		0		0	
Somalia	164		0		0	
Sudan	65		0		0	
Tanzania	38		18		0	
Uganda	16		0		0	
Upper Volta	6		0		0	
Zambia	9		0		0	
Other	67		0		0	
East Asia	261	1.5	0		0	0
Burma	16		0		0	
Cambodia	25		0		0	
Indonesia	214		0		0	
Laos	6		0		0	

TABLE 2 (cont'd)

	1954-78		1977		1978	
	Amount	Percent	Amount	Percent	Amount	Percent
Latin America	964	5.6	30	7.5	15	.4
Argentina	220		0		0	
Bolivia	69		0		0	
Brazil	88		0		0	
Chile	238		0		0	
Colombia	211		0		0	
Costa Rica	15		0		0	
Jamaica	30		30		0	
Peru	25		0		0	
Uruguay	52		0		0	
Middle East*	6,918	40.5	0	0	1,399	37.8
Egypt	1,440		0		0	
Iran	1,165		0		0	
Iraq	705		0		0	
Jordan	26		0		0	
North Yemen	143		0		38	
South Yemen	204		0		90	
Syria	768		0		0	
Turkey	2,380		0		1,200	
Other	79		0		71	
South Asia	4,956	29.0	341	884.8	283	7.6
Afghanistan	1,263		0		0	
Bangladesh	304		0		0	
India	2,282		340		0	
Nepal	30		1		0	
Pakistan	921		0		225	
Sri Lanka	158		0		60	

*Egypt is included in Middle East
N.B. Components may not total because of rounding.

Source: US Central Intelligence Agency, National Foreign Assessment Center,
Communist Aid to Non-Communist Less Developed Countries 1978: A
Research Paper, ER 79-10412U, September 1979, pp. 7-10.

Even though the bulk of Soviet economic assistance has gone to the countries of South Asia and the Middle East, the factors that have influenced Soviet economic assistance in Africa seem to have been similar to those in the Middle East and South Asia. In Africa the major recipients of Soviet economic assistance have generally been countries with a geographical location of some potential strategic importance, regimes that are "anti-imperialist" in their foreign policy orientation, or, more recently, countries such as Morocco that offer important economic benefits for the Soviet economy. Prior to 1978 two-thirds of all Soviet aid to Africa went to six countries—Algeria, Ghana, Guinea, Mali, Somalia, and Sudan—which were all considered "progressive" in their foreign policy orientation at the time that the major commitments were made.[16] During the 1970's, however, Sub-Saharan Africa has played a decreasing role in overall Soviet economic assistance programs. Through 1964, aid commitments to Sub-Saharan Africa represented approximately 12 percent of total Soviet aid. More recently, however, very little new assistance has been committed to this region and for the period 1954-78 aid to Sub-Saharan Africa represented only slightly more than six percent of the total.

In Latin America the bulk of Soviet economic assistance has been extended as a means of opening up markets for Soviet industrial exports. Only the $238 million in credits offered to Chile during the presidency of Allende can be viewed as motivated largely by political considerations.

As we have already observed Soviet economic assistance has consisted largely of machinery and equipment for complete projects and has focused exclusively on the state sector. The development of heavy industry and of energy and mineral resources has been the major target of Soviet aid policy in virtually all recipient countries. In recent years, for example, the Soviets have constructed, or agreed to construct, a steel mill in Turkey and an aluminum complex and a steel plant in Algeria, and they have agreed to develop phosphate production in Morocco. From the point of view of numerous developing countries Soviet project assistance has provided them with numerous benefits, in spite of various problems that have characterized some of the projects. First of all, developing countries have been able to reduce their economic dependence on the Western industrial countries, while at the same time acquiring developmental aid that often was not available elsewhere. In addition, since most of Soviet assistance can be repaid with the production of the completed enterprise, the developing country does not have to worry about acquiring convertible currency in order to repay the loans. Third, there is some evidence that the entrance of the USSR into the ranks of aid donors stimulated the West to provide additional economic assistance.[17]

Since its inception in the 1950's the Soviet assistance program has included the provision of Soviet technicians to assist recipient countries in the operation of facilities constructed with Soviet developmental aid, as well as the training of local academic students and technicians. In 1978, for example, more than 70,000 Soviet and East European technicians were working in the developing countries (more than 80 percent in the Middle East and

North Africa). (See Table 3.) Although the vast majority of these specialists are involved in constructing or operating industrial plants, many are also providing training for local cadres who will later operate the facilities constructed with Soviet assistance. In addition, large numbers of technicians from developing countries have been trained either in the Soviet Union itself or, increasingly in recent years, locally in training centers established by the Soviets. Through 1978 about 48,000 technicians had received training in the Soviet Union and Eastern Europe, although the numbers have fallen off in recent years as in-country training programs have become more efficient and less expensive (see Table 4).[18] By 1978 the Soviets and their East European allies had built and equipped 26 higher and specialized schools in the Third World and an additional one hundred technical training centers. More than 550,000 workers and technicians had been trained in these schools and an additional 600,000 locals have received training at Communist construction sites.[19] The vast majority of those trained either in the Soviet Union or Eastern Europe or locally have come from countries which have been major recipients of Soviet industrial development assistance and of the total of 600,000 who have reportedly received on-the-job training, only 25,000 have been from Sub-Saharan Africa.

TABLE 3

Soviet, East European, Cuban Economic Technicans
Working In Non-Communist Developing Countries

	1970		1975		1977		1978	
					USSR &		USSR &	
	USSR	E. Eur.	USSR	E. Eur.	E. Eur.	Cuba	E. Eur.	Cuba
Total	10,600	5,300	17,785	13,915	58,755	6,575	72,655	12,525
Africa	4,010	3,150	5,930	10,290	34,390	5,900	43,805	11,420
N. africa	-	-	-	-	21,850	15	36,165	450
Sub-Saharan Africa	-	-	-	-	12,540	5,885	7,640	8,500
East Asia	100	60	25	30	125	0	85	0
Latin America	35	140	330	225	830	335	700	190
Middle East					20,010	330	23,890	915
South Asia	6,455	1,950	8,375	3,370	3,475	0	4,145	0

Sources: US Central Intelligence Agency, National Foreign Assessment Center, Communist Aid to Less Developed Countries of the Free World, 1975, ER 76-10372U, July 1976, p. 8; Idem, for 1977, ER 78-10478U, November 1978, p. 9; Idem, Communist Aid Activities in Non-Communist Less Developed Countries, 1978, ER 79-10412U, pp. 14-15.

TABLE 4

Technical Personnel From Developing Countries
Receiving Training In The Soviet Union And Eastern Europe

	USSR	Combined	Eastern Europe
1965		2,000+	
1970	1,020		530
1971	1,310		1,435
1972	1,355		975
1973		3,715	
1974		4,380	
1975		?	
1976	4,250		?
1977		3,200	
1978		3,300	
Total 1954-78		48,000	

Sources: Annual reports published by CIA, see Table 3.

Another important aspect of long-term Soviet development assistance has been the education of substantial numbers of academic students from the Third World in Soviet institutions of higher education. The numbers of such students have risen consistently and by 1978 more than 26,000 were in the USSR with an additional 18,500 in Eastern Europe (see Table 5). An interesting aspect of this program has been the focus on Black Africa; since the early 1960's the majority of students educated in the Soviet Union has come from Africa. In 1978, for example, of a total of 26,445 students studying in the USSR, 13,635 were from Africa. Of these students more than 85 percent came from Sub-Saharan Africa. Eight years earlier, in 1970, approximately 81 percent of all African students in the Soviet Union and Eastern Europe came from Black Africa. The 21 year old academic program has been the most concessionary of all of the Soviet Union's aid programs when compared with other types of economic and technical assistance, for Soviet scholarships cover all of the expenses for the recipients, including living expenses and transportation.

Soviet academic and technical training programs in the Third World have had two major goals. First of all, they help to provide the skilled personnel needed to modernize the economies of countries receiving Soviet aid and to staff the projects and programs established with Soviet assistance. In this respect they represent an important component of the overall Soviet economic assistance program. In addition, however, the academic training

343

TABLE 5

Academic Students From Developing Countries
Being Trained In Communist Countries

	1970 All Communist Countries[1]	1975 All Communist Countries[2]	1977 All Communist Countries[3]	USSR	1978 E.Eur.	China
Total	21,415	27,275	40,345	26,445	18,560	260
Africa	10,990	14,895	20,780	13,635	9,755	160
N. Africa	2,115	2,370	2,965	2,035	1,520	20
Sub-Saharan Africa	8,875	12,525	17,815	11,600	8,235	140
East Asia	650	335	20	25	10	0
Latin America	2,425	2,940	4,445	2,760	1,890	0
Middle East	5,770	6,270	11,320	6,615	5,525	15
South Asia	1,580	2,825	3,780	3,400	1,375	80

[1]Approximately 12,500 of these students were in the Soviet Union and the remainder in Eastern Europe

[2]Approximately two-thirds of the students were in the Soviet Union and the most of the remainder in Eastern Europe

[3]More than sixty percent of the students were in the Soviet Union and most of the remainder in Eastern Europe

Sources: Same as for Table 3, pp. 11, 17-18 respectively.

program in particular is geared to prepare a future elite that, at a minimum, will be favorably disposed toward the Soviet Union.[20]

Before proceeding to a discussion of Soviet trade with the Third World and the interrelationship of their economic aid programs and trade, we should examine, albeit briefly, the relative importance of Soviet military and economic aid. Perhaps the most important development in Soviet policy toward the Third World during the past decade has been the shift from an emphasis on economic assistance to a far greater reliance on the provision of military aid as a means of expanding ties with the developing countries. Throughout the period 1955 to 1967 the Soviets delivered an average of slightly more than $300 million of military equipment per year to developing countries, while deliveries of economic aid averaged about $200 million. From 1968 through 1971 the amount of annual military deliveries rose to about $700 million, and since 1972 has increased substantially and totalled more than $3,500 million in 1977 and $3,800 million in 1978 (see Table 6). While deliveries of Soviet economic assistance averaged about $510 million annually since 1972, deliveries of military equipment and

344

TABLE 6

Soviet Military Relations With Non-Communist
Developing Countries, 1955-78

(In Millions of Current US Dollars)

	New Agreements Concluded	Deliveries
Total, 1955-78[a]	29,825	25,310
1978[a]	1,765	3,825
1977[a]	5,215	3,515
1976[a]	3,375	2,575
1975[a]	2,035	1,845
1974[a]	4,225	2,310
1973[a]	2,810	3,130
1972[a]	1,635	1,215
1971[a]	1,590	865
1970[a]	1,150	995
1969[a]	360	450
1955-68[a]	5,495	4,585
1968[b]	450	505
1967[c]	525	500
1966[c]	450	500
1965[d]	260	
1964[d]	875	
1963[d]	390	
1962[d]	415	
1961[d]	830	
1955-60[d]	1,285	
1960[e]	570	
1959[e]	40	
1958[e]	470	
1957[e]	240	
1956[e]	290	
1955[e]	110	

[a]Data from CIA publication for 1978, see below.
[b]Data from CIA publication for 1977, see below.
[c]Data from CIA publication for 1975, see below.
[d]Data from State Department publication for 1972, see below.
[e]Data from State Department publication for 1970, see below.

N.B.   Given the differing sources and the fact that all of the figures given
       are estimates, summations do not total.

Sources: US Department of State, Bureau of Intelligence and Research,
           Communist States and Developing Countries: Aid and Trade in 1970,
           Research Study, RECS-15, September 22, 1971, p. 17.
           Ibid. for 1972, RECS-10, June 15, 1973, appendix, Table 9.
           Central Intelligence Agency, Communist Aid to Less Developed Countries of
           the Free World, 1975, ER 76-10372U, July 1976, p. 1.
           Ibid., for 1977, ER 78-10478U, p. 1.
           Central Intelligence Agency, Communist Aid Activities in Non-Communist Less
           Developed Countries 1978, ER 79-10412U, September 1979, p. 2.

345

supplies were more than five times as great—$2,630 million per year. The major recipients of the recent increase in Soviet military deliveries have been Libya, which pays for weapons with hard currency earned from its oil exports, Iraq, Algeria, Ethiopia, and Angola. Until the early 1970's more than 80 percent of all Soviet arms deliveries were destined for the Middle East and South Asia. With the recent expansion of Soviet involvement in Sub-Saharan Africa—especially in Angola and Ethiopia—Africa has also become a major recipient of Soviet military equipment. (See Table 7.) Arms transfers to Third World countries have apparently provided several benefits for the Soviet Union. First of all, a number of Third World countries have become heavily dependent upon the Soviet Union for their own military security. Although this is something of a mixed blessing, the Soviets appear to see it as a means of gaining influence in the host country, for along with Soviet arms have usually come Soviet military advisors and technicians who have played an important role in training local military personnel and, in some cases, even in assisting in military operations.[21] The Soviets have, on occasion, attempted to use this dependence as a means of influencing the foreign and domestic policy orientation of the host country.[22]

TABLE 7

Soviet Military Relations With Non-Communist
Developing Countries, By Region

(In Millions of Current US Dollars)

	Total 1956–78	1956–73	1974	1975	1976	1977	1978
Agreements	29,655	13,040	4,225	2,035	3,375	5,215	1,765
North Africa	4,965	490	1,825	535	...	1,800	315
Sub-Saharan Africa	3,900	330	365	145	800	1,415	845
East Asia	890	890	...	...	...	...	...
Latin America	650	150	negl	55	335	110	...
Middle East	14,960	8,860	2,020	640	2,105	1,235	100
South Asia	4,290	2,320	15	660	135	655	505
Deliveries	25,310	11,240	2,310	1,845	2,575	3,515	3,825
North Africa	3,875	435	150	380	810	925	1,175
Sub-Saharan Africa	2,750	275	90	255	325	585	1,220
East Asia	880	880	...	...	...	...	...
Latin America	630	10	25	60	80	380	75
Middle East	13,800	7,760	1,780	975	1,065	1,125	1,095
South Asia	3,375	1,880	265	175	295	500	260

Source: US Central Intelligence Agency, Communist Aid Activities in Non-Communist Less Developed Countries 1978, ER 79-10412U, September 1979, p. 3.

A second and increasingly important benefit of arms deliveries has been the acquisition of hard currency from military sales to such countries as Libya. It has been estimated that in 1977 arms sales generated approximately $1.5 billion in hard currency for the Soviet economy. Military exports now cover large annual deficits in Soviet nonmilitary trade with the less developed countries— primarily the result of Soviet credit deliveries—and supplement significantly the USSR's hard currency earnings.[23]

SOVIET TRADE WITH THIRD WORLD COUNTRIES

Closely related to the development of Soviet economic assistance programs throughout most of the developing world has been the expansion of Soviet commercial relations. The close interrelationship is the result of the fact that growth of Soviet exports has been based in substantial part on the export of machinery and equipment for assistance projects and, in some cases, imports are beginning to come from projects originally financed by Soviet assistance. Over the period 1955 to 1978 Soviet trade, in absolute value terms, has increased by thirty-five times from $355 million in 1955 to $11,784 in 1978. As a percentage of total Soviet trade, however, trade with the developing countries has risen much more slowly during this period, from 5.2 percent to 12.2 percent. (See Table 8.) In the last 5 years virtually the entire increase in Soviet trade with developing countries has occurred on the export side. Measured in rubles Soviet imports from developing countries have actually declined from 2,999 million in 1975 to 2,831 million in 1978. As the data in Table 9 indicate, a substantial percentage of the growth in Soviet exports in recent years is unspecified in Soviet trade statistics and consists, presumably, of arms transfers to a small group of developing countries. In 1978, for example, 47 percent of total Soviet exports to developing countries was not specified. Of the remaining $3,599 million of exports most consisted of machinery, equipment, and (to certain countries) oil and oil products.[24]

During the past decade Soviet trade policy with the developing countries has undergone substantial modification. While trade with the Third World in the 1950's and 1960's was generally based on long-term intergovernmental agreements that provided for the exchange of goods at predetermined prices and the settlement of

TABLE 8
Soviet Trade With Non-Communist Developing Countries
(In Millions of Current US Dollars)

	Total Trade		Trade with Developing Countries			
	Exports	Imports	Exports	% of Total Trade	Imports	% of Total Trade
1955	3,392	3,029	141	4.2	194	6.4
1960	5,508	5,572	334	6.1	529	9.5
1965	8,093	7,978	1,111	13.7	807	10.1
1970	12,672	11,822	2,019	15.9	1,280	10.8
1975	33,166	36,805	4,569	13.8	4,138	11.2
1976	38,110	39,074	5,087	13.3	3,815	9.8
1977	45,227	40,926	7,258	16.0	4,076	10.0
1978	51,362	49,762	8,229	16.0	4,077	8.2

Exchange Rates: Through 1970, $1.11 per ruble; 1975, $1.38; 1976, $1.33; 1977, $1.36; and 1978, $1.44.

N.B. The depreciation of the dollar exaggerates the growth of Soviet trade in the 1970's.

Sources: SSSR, Ministerstvo vneshnei torgovli, Vneshniaia torgovlia SSSR: Statisticheskii Obzor, 1918-1966, Moscow: "Mezhdunarodnye otnosheniia," 1967, pp. 62-69; idem, Vneshniaia Torgovlia SSSR v . . . god: Statisticheskii Obzor for the years 1970, 1976, 1978.

payments in nonconvertible currency, in recent years approximately three-quarters of the Soviet Union's trading partners were conducting their trade or settling outstanding balances with the USSR in convertible currency and in 1977 more than 40 percent of trade was paid for in hard currency. Although, as we have already seen, Soviet economic assistance has been important in stimulating Soviet exports, the role of aid in Soviet trade has dropped in recent years.[25]

As we have already noted earlier in this discussion, Soviet aid policy—and trade policy—has been geared increasing toward the economic interests of the Soviet economy. The most important factors motivating Soviet policy appear to be the desire to expand hard-currency exports, such as military equipment and petroleum products.[26] In addition, however, exports of machinery and equipment to less developed countries are being used to cover the

348

TABLE 9

Soviet Trade With Non-Communist Developing Countries[1]

(In Millions of Current US Dollars)

	1975		1976		1977		1978	
	Exports	Imports	Exports	Imports	Exports	Imports	Exports	Imports
Total Trade with develop-ing Countries	4,567.7	4,138.3	4,960.2	3,730.9	7,227.2	4,074.3	7,707.9	4,076.6
Unspecified residual[2]	1,877.1	11.0	2,325.6	33.4	3,896.6	63.5	3,598.7	64.3
Specified total	2,690.6	4,127.3	2,634.6	3,697.5	3,330.6	4,010.8	4,109.2	4,012.3
Middle East-North Africa	1,651.5	1,824.1	1,661.4	1,617.5	1,933.3	1,698.7	2,633.7	1,740.8
Sub-Saharan Africa	184.8	324.2	182.1	284.9	317.7	388.8	403.8	428.6
Latin America	14.6	116.3	32.0	164.3	220.6	655.6	133.6	755.9
South Asia	622.8	700.1	593.2	646.2	802.7	944.9	883.8	777.0
East Asia	29.2	219.5	41.3	280.0	56.3	372.8	51.3	310.0

[1]Data from official Soviet foreign trade yearbooks. The following rates were used to convert the ruble value of Soviet trade into US dollars: for 1975, $1.38; for 1976, $1.33; for 1977, $1.36; for 1978, $1.44.

[2]Residuals are computed by subtracting the summation of trade for individual developing countries from the total for Soviet trade with developing countries listed in the foreign trade yearbooks. These amounts are believed to consist mainly of Soviet military shipments.

N.B. The devaluation of the dollar in 1978 exaggerates the amount of Soviet trade with developing countries. Calculated in rubles, Soviet exports to the developing countries rose by 7.1 percent in 1978, while imports dropped by 5.5 percent.

Source: US Central Intelligence Agency, National Foreign Assessment Center, Changing Patterns in Soviet-LDC Trade, 1976-77: A Research Paper, ER 78-10326, May 1978, pp. 8-11; based on data published in the Soviet foreign trade annual Vneshniaia torgovlia SSSR. Data for 1977 and 1978 are taken directly from Vneshniaia torgovlia SSR v 1978g: Statisticheskii Sbornik, pp. 8-14.

costs of imports of raw materials and foodstuffs and to insure future sources of these imports.[27]

Soviet imports from the less developed countries include approximately the same type of products as those of the industrialized Western states—contrary to the Soviet claims that they provide an expanding market for the industrial production of the developing countries. In 1976, for example, crude oil and natural gas comprised approximately 20 percent of total Soviet imports from developing countries; food imports, including cocoa beans, coffee, and tea made up an additional 43 percent of the imports; and most of the remainder consisted of industrial raw materials, such as

349

rubber, cotton, and metallic ores.[28] Of the Soviet Union's major trading partners in the Third World only India exported any significant amount of machinery and equipment to the USSR in 1978—approximately 7.8 percent of total exports (see Table 10). As we have already noted, Soviet imports from the developing countries have included increasing amounts of industrial raw materials.

As the figures in Table 9 make clear, the countries of South Asia, the Middle East, and North Africa have been the major Soviet trading partners, although Latin America has provided an increasing amount of Soviet agricultural imports and trade with Latin America represented approximately 11 percent of total specified trade with less developed countries in 1977 and 1978. Sub-Saharan Africa has continued to be the least important of the major regions of the Third World, outside non-Communist Southeast Asia, as a Soviet trading partner, although exports to the countries of Black Africa more than doubled between 1975 and 1978.

TABLE 10

Soviet Trade With Major Trading Partners
From The Developing World, 1978

(In Millions of US Dollars)

Country	Total Exports	EXPORTS	
		Major Export Products	Percentage of Total Exports
Iraq	970.1	Machinery, equipment and transport materials	44.8
		of which, equipment for air communications	14.0
		of which, energy equipment	9.4
Iran	623.1	Machinery, equipment and transport materials	35.6
		of which, energy equipment	12.4
		of which, equipment for food processing indus.	4.6
India	524.3	Oil and oil products	60.4
		Machinery, equipment and transport materials	15.6
		of which, equipment for iron and steel indus.	6.4
Egypt	212.4	Machinery, equipment and transport materials	48.5
		of which, trucks and truck equipment	20.6
Afghanistan	200.6	Machinery, equipment and transport materials	51.8
		of which, geological equipment	13.2
		Oil and oil products	16.8
Syria	188.9	Machinery, equipment and transport materials	54.8
		of which trucks	10.2
		of which, equipment for air communications	13.6
Turkey	127.9	Machinery, equipment and transport materials	53.1
		of which, equipment for iron and steel indus.	41.1
Algeria	127.2	Machinery, equipment and transport materials	49.9
		of which, geological equipment	37.6
Nigeria	108.6	Machinery, equipment and transport materials	74.0
		of which, trucks	58.5
Pakistan	99.2	Machinery, equipment and transport materials	86.5
		of which, equipment for iron and steel indus.	66.3

		IMPORTS	
Country	Total Imports	Major Import Products	Percentage of Total Imports
Iraq	590.8	Fuel, minerals, metals	98.1
India	596.5	Tea	14.4
		Processed and semi-processed skins	15.5
		Jute socks	8.6
Argentina	444.7	Wheat and corn (maize)	68.8
		Woolen fabrics	15.2
Iran	343.3	Cotton fiber	8.1
Egypt	285.1	Cotton thread	41.5
Brazil	187.5	Cocoa beans and cocoa butter	61.6
Malaysia	174.4	Chemical products, fertilizer, rubber	79.4
Ghana	157.4	Cocoa beans	97.7
Libya	153.8	Fuel, mineral resources, metals	100.0
Afghanistan	109.0	Gas	44.5
		Fruit, raisins, dried berries	36.1
Syria	106.3	Cotton fiber	26.5
Turkey	99.2	Hazel nuts	60.2

N.B. The Soviet trade yearbooks do not provide a complete breakdown for the composition of all trade. First of all, the summation of trade—in particular Soviet exports—with individual countries does not equal total trade with all developing countries. In recent years approximately fifty percent of total Soviet exports has not been specified and, presumably, consists of Soviet military transfers. In addition, however, a substantial percentage of trade with individual countries—beyond the presumed military exports—is not specified. In 1978, for example, approximately sixty-five percent of Soviet imports from Iran and forty-five percent of exports to that country were not broken down by category of trade. The figures for unspecified imports and exports in trade with India for 1978 are four and twelve percent respectively.

Source: Vneshniaia torgovlia SSSR v 1978 g.: Statisticheskii sbornik.

AN ASSESSMENT OF SOVIET ECONOMIC ASSISTANCE AND TRADE POLICY

It should be clear by this point that the USSR does not have a single overriding policy in the Third World that informs all of its political and economic relations. During most of the past two decades political factors have played an important role in influencing Soviet economic relations, and by far the greatest portion of Soviet economic assistance during most of this period has gone to those countries that were viewed "progressive" and following a noncapitalist path of development. This was especially true in Africa where most of the early aid went to Algeria, Guinea, Ghana, Mali, Somalia, and Sudan—all viewed by the Soviets as "progressive" at the time that major credits were extended. Closely related to the support for more radical regimes has been Soviet interest in creating ties with countries considered important for

351

Soviet strategic interests. Afghanistan, for example, has been an important recipient of Soviet economic and military aid since the mid-1950's, long before the coup which brought the present radical leadership to power. Soviet interest in Iraq, Egypt and India has also been influenced by the strategic location of these countries. In recent years military and political support have become the major instruments employed by the Soviet leadership in expanding relations with ''progressive'' regimes.

However, parallel to the shift in emphasis from economic to military assistance in the development of relations with more revolutionary governments and movements throughout the developing world has been a growing pragmatism in Soviet foreign economic policy. For the past decade, at least, economic relations with less developed countries have been based increasingly on ''mutual economic benefits.'' In practice this has meant that the Soviets have generally been willing to provide economic assistance only for projects that were likely to result in long-term economic benefits for the Soviet economy. Foodstuffs, industrial raw materials and energy continue to comprise the bulk of Soviet imports; economic aid is tied both to the export of Soviet industrial equipment and to the import of needed raw materials.

What we see, therefore, is the development of two different strands in Soviet policy toward the developing countries—a policy of political and military support for ''progressive'' regimes as part of the competition for influence with the United States and a more pragmatic economic orientation focused on long-term benefits for the Soviet economy. In some cases, such as in relations with Iraq and Algeria, the Soviets have been able to combine both strands of their policy.[29] It is highly unlikely that the Soviets will abandon either of these approaches to the developing world in the foreseeable future. The more militant approach has resulted in a number of significant ''victories'' in recent years in both Asia and Africa, as new regimes allied to the Soviet Union and dependent on continued Soviet largesse have come to power in such places as Angola, Ethiopia, Afghanistan, and Cambodia.[30] Barring a major shift in Soviet attitudes, the Soviet leadership will probably not resist the temptation to benefit from future opportunities presented by support for progressive elements throughout the Third World. At the same time, however, given the needs of the Soviet economy—and those of their East European allies—the more pragmatic developments in Soviet foreign economic policy that we have witnessed during the last decade or so are likely to become a permanent factor in overall Soviet policy toward the developing countries.

ENDNOTES

1. For a more complete discussion of Soviet policy toward the developing countries during the Khrushchev years see Roger E. Kanet, "Soviet Attitudes Toward Developing Nations Since Stalin," in *The Soviet Union and the Developing Nations*, ed. by Roger E. Kanet, Baltimore: John Hopkins University Press, 1974, pp. 27-50.

2. For data on military aid see US Central Intelligence Agency, *Communist Aid Activities in Non-Communist Less Developed Countries 1978*, ER 79-10412U, p. 1; *Ibid.*, for 1975, ER 76-1037U, p. 1; US Department of State, Bureau of Intelligence and Research, *Communist States and Developing Countries: Aid and Trade in 1972*, Research Study, RECS-10, June 15, 1973, appendix, Table 9. For data on economic assistance see US Department of State, Bureau of Intelligence and Research, *The Communist Economic Offensive Through 1964*, Research Memorandum, RSB-65, August 4, 1965, p. 6.

3. See Richard Lowenthal, *Model or Ally? The Communist Powers and the Developing Countries*, New York: Oxford University Press, 1977, pp. 185-186. Chapters 3 and 4 of Lowenthal's book provide an excellent analysis of the interaction between Soviet ideology and Soviet foreign policy objectives in the developing countries.

4. For an excellent treatment of the evolution of Soviet views concerning the developing countries see Stephen Clarkson, *The Soviet Theory of Development: India and the Third World in Marxist-Leninist Scholarship*, Toronto: Toronto University Press, 1978.

5. In 1964 more than 77 percent of Soviet exports to developing countries went to the countries of the Middle East and South Asia and almost 64 percent of imports came from this region. Of all economic credits committed during the years 1954 through 1964 more than 76 percent went to South Asia and the Middle East. *See Communist Economic Offensive Through 1964*, p. 6 and US Department of State, Bureau of Intelligence and Research, *Communist Governments and Developing Nations: Aid and Trade in 1965*, Research Memorandum, RSB-50, June 17, 1966, pp. 12-19.

6. By "influence relationship" I mean the ability to cause other countries to do something that they would otherwise not have done. Soviet military, economic and political support did, however, permit individual developing countries to pursue policies that, without Soviet assistance, they would not have been able to pursue. For a fuller discussion of influence in Soviet relations with the developing countries see Alvin Z. Rubinstein, *Red Star on the Nile: The Soviet-Egyptian Influence Relationship Since the June War*, Princeton: Princeton University Press, 1977, and M. Rajan Menon, "India and the Soviet Union: A Case Study of Inter-Nation Influence," unpublished doctoral dissertation, University of Illinois at Urbana-Champaign, 1978.

7. See, for example, the comments of Admiral S.G. Gorshkov, Commander of the Soviet Navy, in an interview printed in *Ogonek*, No. 6, February 3, 1968. For a more complete presentation of Gorshkov's views see his *Morskaia moshch' gosudarstva*, Moscow: Voenizdat, 1976.

8. See, for example, Roger E. Kanet, "The Soviet Union and the Developing Countries: Policy or Policies?" *The World Today*, Vol. XXXI, 1975, pp. 344-345; and John D. Esseks, "Soviet Economic Aid to Africa: 1959-72. An Overview," in Warren Weinstein, ed., *Chinese and Soviet Aid to Africa*, New York: Praeger, 1975, p. 114.

9. For an excellent discussion of the changes in Soviet economic policy see Elizabeth Kridl Valkenier, "New Trends in Soviet Economic Relations with the Third World," *World Politics,* Vol. XXII, 1970, pp. 415-432; and *idem*, "Soviet Economic Relations with the Developing Nations," in Kanet, ed., *The Soviet Union and the Developing Nations*, pp. 215-236.

10. The most complete discussion of the development of Soviet views on the place of the developing countries in the world economy see Elizabeth Kridl Valkenier, "The USSR, the Third World, and the Global Economy," *Problems of Communism*, Vol. XXVIII, No. 4, 1979, pp. 17-33. See, also, Richard Portes, "Est, Ouest et Sud: le role des economies centralement planifiees dans l'economie internationale," *Revue comparative des Etudes Est-Ouest*, Vol. X, No. 3, 1979, esp. pp. 63-71.

11. See V. Valil'eva, "Raspad kolonial'noi sistemy imperializma," *Voprosy ekonomiki*, No. 4, 1956, pp. 104-106.

12. V. Romanova and I. Tsviklis, "Ekonomicheskie sviazi SSSR s razvivaiushchismisia stranami," *Ekonomicheskie nauki*, No. 3, 1978.

13. See P.I. Polshikov, *Kontinent v dvizhenii*, Moscow: "Mezhdunarodnye otnosheniia," 1976; and US Central Intelligence Agency, *Communist Aid 1978*, p. 12.

14. A recent Central Intelligence Agency study of foreign aid flows estimates that, as a result of repayments, net Soviet transfers of developmental funds are now running at less than 60 percent of gross transfers. At the same time net transfers from the industrialized West make up almost 76 percent of gross transfers. US Central Intelligence Agency, National Foreign Assessment Center, *Non-OPEC LDCs: Changing Patterns of Official Economic Aid Flows: A Research Paper*, ER 78-10114, March 1978, p. 7.

15. OECD, Development Assistance Committee, Volume of Aid, September 1978.

16. The only exception to this statement for Africa is Ethiopia which was promised credits of more than $100 million in 1959, but which drew on few of these credits prior to the overthrow of the government of Haile Selassie. Presumably Soviet motives here, as in Iran and Turkey, were related to the desire to undermine the virtual monopoly position of the United States in an area of potential strategic importance for the Soviet Union.

17. For an excellent collection of recent studies of Soviet economic assistance see Deepak Nayyar, ed., *Economic Relations Between Socialist Countries and the Third World*, Montclair, New Jersey: Alanheld, Osmun and Co.; New York; Universe Books, 1977.

18. US Central Intelligence Agency, *Communist Aid Activities 1978*, pp. 15-16.

19. *Ibid.* and US Central Intelligence Agency, *Communist Aid 1977*, pp. 10-11.

20. For an examination of the early stage of the Soviet training program see Roger E. Kanet, "African Youth: The Target of Soviet African Policy," *The Russian Review*, Vol. XXVII, 1967, pp. 161-175.

21. At the end of 1978 more than 12,000 Soviet and East European military personnel were working in developing countries—supplemented by an additional 38,000 Cubans. More than 75 percent of the Soviets and East Europeans were located in six countries—Algeria, Angola, Ethiopia, Iraq, Libya, and Syria. See US Central Intelligence Agency, *Communist Aid Activities 1978*, p.4.

22. For a discussion of the generally unsuccessful efforts to use leverage in Egypt see Rubinstein, *Red Star on the Nile, passim*. See, also, Galia Golan, *Yom Kippur and After: The Soviet Union and the Middle East Crisis*, Cambridge: Cambridge University Press, 1977.

23. See US Central Intelligence Agency, *Communist Aid Activities 1978*, p. 3, and *Communist Aid 1977*, p. 1. In an interesting article on Soviet arms exports, Raymond Hutchings has argued—contrary to the assumptions of most Western specialists who have emphasized the political aspects of Soviet arms transfer policy—that the fluctuations in Soviet arms sales abroad can be understood only in the context of internal Soviet economic forces and that, therefore, the economic factor is important for an understanding of Soviet arms sales policy. See Raymond Hutchings, ''Regular Trends in Soviet Arms Exports to the Third World,'' *Osteuropa-Wirtschaft*, Vol. XXIII, No. 3, 1978, pp. 182-202.

24. In 1970 approximately 60 percent of Soviet exports consisted of industrial machinery and equipment and petroleum, while an additional 16 percent comprised other manufacture goods. In 1976 about 76 percent of total specified exports to developing countries fit these categories. See US Central Intelligence Agency, National Foreign Assessment Center, *Changing Patterns in Soviet-LDC Trade, 1976-77: A Research Paper*, ER 78-10326, May 1978, p. 3.

25. In 1965 Soviet aid deliveries and debt servicing accounted for nearly 40 percent of total trade; in 1977 the figure dropped to below 25 percent. *Ibid.*, p. 1.

26. Soviet exports of oil to Brazil, Greece, Portugal and Spain—all classified by the USSR as developing countries—are paid for in hard currency. By 1976 oil exports to less developed countries accounted for up to 15 percent of the USSR's worldwide hard currency earnings from petroleum. In 1977 sales of oil to the four countries mentioned amounted to more than $667 million. In 1978, however, sales fell to only $486 million. See *Ibid.*, p. 4 and *Vneshniaia Torgovlia SSSR v 1978 g.: Statisticheskii sbornik*, p. 61.

27. In 1977 52.2 percent of Soviet exports of machinery, equipment and transport equipment to capitalist states went to developing countries. In 1978 the percentages rose to 55.8. Of these exports to developing countries, more than 50 percent occurred as part of general economic cooperation agreements and, presumably, were covered by Soviet credits. (See table on next page.)

28. US Central Intelligence Agency, *Changing Patterns in Soviet-LDC Trade*, p. 4.

29. For differing interpretations of the significance of recent Soviet policy in the developing world see Donald S. Zagoria, ''Into the Breach: New Soviet Alliances in the Third World,'' *Foreign Affairs*, Vol. LVII, 1979, pp. 733-754 and Robert Legvold, ''The Super Rivals: Conflict in the Third World,'' *Foreign Affairs*, Vol. LVII, 1979, pp. 755-778.

30. However, these victories may prove to be ephemeral should support for client states embroil the USSR in local disputes and require the expenditure of increasing amounts of Soviet resources.

TABLE 11

SOVIET EXPORTS OF MACHINERY, EQUIPMENT AND
TRANSPORT MATERIALS TO DEVELOPING COUNTRIES

(In Rubles)

	1977	1978
Total Exports	6,246.4	6,991.4
To Socialist states*	4,438.1	4,939.4
To Capitalist states	1,808.0	2,052.0
Of which, to LDCs	944.6	1,137.0
Exports to LDCs as % of Exports to all Capitalist states	52.2%	55.4%
Exports to LDCs for projects being con- structed under coopera- tion agreements	532.6	587.0
Project Exports to LDCs as % of total exports	56.4%	51.6%

*Including Yugoslavia

Source: SSR, Ministerstvo Vneshnei Torgovli, Vneshniaia Torgovlia SSSR v 1978g.:
         Statisticheskii sbornik. Moscow: "Statistika," 1979, pp. 45-47.

18

THE SECOND WORLD, THE THIRD WORLD, AND THE NEW INTERNATIONAL ECONOMIC ORDER

Robert H. Donaldson

One of the ironies of the debate over ratification of the SALT II treaty is that it refocused congressional and media concern on the classic questions of postwar international politics—military strategy, defense budgets, the arms race, the Soviet political and ideological challenge—at a time when the attention of the American public was fixed on an entirely different (and seemingly more pedestrian) set of issues. These latter topics were economic in nature—spiralling inflation, energy supplies and prices, American industry's apparent loss of competitive advantage, threats to the environment from sources as diverse as nuclear power plants or giant ocean-borne oil spills—and they had in recent years risen high on the agenda of government and international negotiations. How well the US Government coped with these issues directly affected both its domestic and international standing; at times, the health of the Atlantic Alliance and the credibility of America's overseas commitments appeared to be more dependent on relative economic strengths and vulnerabilities than on traditional military or diplomatic indices.

What was taking place was no less than a change in the nature of international politics. There was no longer a single international system dominated by strategic concerns. Military security remained an important issue, but the ''new'' concerns of world trade, energy, food, raw materials, the world monetary system—each one with its own power hierarchy—have crowded on to the center stage. Alongside the old military alliances against well-defined enemies have arisen new fluid functional bargaining coalitions. Alongside the military rivalry traditionally arrayed on an axis of East to West has appeared a bitter economic conflict between North and South. Nor is this latter struggle necessarily less dangerous than the one it seems to be displacing. Henry Kissinger, in his 1975 speech to the Seventh Special Session of the UN General Assembly, offered a prognosis that was gloomy even for this professional pessimist:

> The division of the planet between North and South, between rich and poor, could become as grim as the darkest days of the Cold War. We could enter on an age of festering resentment, of increased resort to economic warfare, a hardening of new blocs, the undermining of cooperation, the erosion of international institutions—and failed development.[1]

As illustrated by the debate over SALT II and the encompassing issue of Soviet intentions, official and informed public perceptions of the conflicts along the two global axes seemed strangely unconnected. Observers and analysts of Soviet foreign policy, in assessing the impact on the East-West balance of Soviet behavior in the Third World, almost wholly ignored the economic dimensions of East-South relations. Conversely, discussions of the North-South dialogue and of the cluster of Third World economic demands aggregated into the platform for a New International Economic Order (NIEO) almost never considered the Soviet role in this relationship. And yet the Soviet Union's relative isolation from international economic and monetary transactions necessarily limits its capability to influence the outcome of a set of increasingly important issues. In the absence of this economic power, military power alone may not be sufficient to sustain superpower status for the USSR in the coming decades. To recall Robert Legvold's apt question: "How much of a world power is a nation without much power in the world economy?"[2]

Apart from a random comment on Moscow's deliberate nonparticipation in the North-South dialogue, there has been little effort in the expanding literature on these subjects to explore the point of intersection between the East-West and North-South competitions. By adamantly refusing to be lumped with the ''rich

North,'' Moscow thus far has in effect helped turn the latter into a West-South conflict. What effect the absence of an East-South dialogue has had and will have on both East-West and North-South relations is a question of growing importance, and it is one that this study is intended to address in a preliminary wary.

After an initial sketch of the history of the North-South dialogue and the key issues raised in the platform for a New International Economic Order, the study then explores the interests and objectives—economic, political, and ideological—that have motivated Soviet behavior in the major forums of this international dialogue. Next it analyzes the official Soviet position on particular issues in the North-South conflict. How the Soviet stand has been perceived by the Third World, and how Moscow's actual record in bilateral transactions with less-developed countries compares with its official positions is the subject of the next section. The study closes with an inquiry into the prospects for change in the Soviet position, assessing the successes and failures of the current Soviet stance and the likely costs and benefits—both for the USSR and for the future of the North-South dialogue—of alternative Soviet strategies.

THE CALL FOR A NEW INTERNATIONAL ECONOMIC ORDER

The most prominent Third World diplomatic forum, the grouping of nonaligned nations, in the first two decades of its existence virtually ignored questions of international economics. Early preoccupation with issues of war and peace and assertions of the right of the emerging Afro-Asian ''bloc'' to occupy a position of ''neutralism'' in the East-West conflict gave way in the 1960's to vigorous concern with the anticolonial struggle. A sort of Third World lobby on economic issues was institutionalized as the ''Group of 77'' at the first UN Conference on Trade and Development (UNCTAD) at Geneva in 1964, but its activities and interests received little notice until 1973, when its economic platform was in effect adopted at the Algiers summit meeting of the diplomatically more salient nonaligned movement. Having complained for a decade about discriminatory rules and institutions of the international economic and monetary systems that they had no role in creating, the Group of 77 nations (which

360

actually numbered over 120 by 1979) had found their demands largely ignored by the developed countries. But then the 1973-74 Arab oil embargo and Organization of Petroleum Exporting Countries (OPEC) price increases forcibly attracted the world's attention. The Third World enjoyed an accretion in bargaining power as a result of its unity and its alliance with OPEC, and the Algiers nonaligned summit's call for a New International Economic Order and its demand that a special session of the UN General Assembly be convened to discuss it, thereby took on new force.

With the Western states in relative disarray and the United States in particular refusing even to use the phrase "new international economic order," the UN General Assembly's Sixth Special Session in the spring of 1974 was dominated by the more radical spokesmen of the Third World, and it easily passed a Declaration on Establishment of a NIEO that called for major changes to reduce inherent inequalities in the existing international economic order. Unreconciled to the South's new-found strength and unity, the United States spent the next year seeking to encourage a split between oil-exporting and oil-importing Third World nations. The failure of this strategy, starkly evident at the April 1975 Paris energy conference, produced a shift to a more conciliatory line. Secretary Kissinger's speech to the Seventh Special Session of the UN General Assembly in September 1975 signaled Washington's new willingness to negotiate on the NIEO issues, and this session ended on a note of constructive compromise.

It was thus in a mood of optimism the 8 Northern nations and 19 Southern states convened in Paris in December 1975 for the next round in the dialogue—the Conference on International Economic Cooperation (CIEC). These talks proceeded until June 1977 and their outcome utterly betrayed the fond hopes at their inauguration. Most of the CIEC meetings were spent in feuding about the agenda, so that the substantive results were scanty indeed. The Paris "dialogue" was interrupted by the fourth UNCTAD conference—held in Nairobi in May 1976 and similarly devoid of substantive achievements—and the Colombo Nonaligned Summit of August 1976, at which the South's demands for the NIEO were stated with renewed determination.

Apart from these forums for general discussion of the North-South agenda, the past several years have brought special UN-sponsored conferences on Population (Bucharest, 1974) and Food (Rome, 1974) as well as the Third Conference on the Law of the Sea (Caracas, Geneva and New York, 1974-78). With the partial exception of the World Food Conference's decision to augment the global institutional framework for promotiong "food security," these conferences ended either in utter deadlock or by producing final documents that simply papered over continuing sharp factional disagreements.

The platform for a NIEO, on which such extensive discussions have already been held, consists of demands for greater economic self-determination, sovereignty over national resources, and equality of participation in the international economy, together with specific proposals in a number of issue areas. In the *trade* arena, the key proposal is for commodity agreements to raise and stabilize prices of exported raw materials, financially undergirded by a common fund underwritten by the developed countries. Other trade proposals include a call for expanded general (and nonreciprocal) preferences for manufactured products of the less-developed nations in the markets of the industrialized world, and other measures to expand the role of the developing countries in producing the world's industrial goods. In the realm of *aid* the NIEO platform reaffirms the target of 0.7 percent of GNP for official development assistance from North to South, and states a goal of 1 percent from private and public sources combined. It also calls for more generous financing of various emergency funds (such as that administered by the World Food Council), with the funds again to come primarily from the developed countries. Moreover, the platform demands widespread debt relief for the less-developed countries, to the point of either forgiveness or postponement of the growing external public debt of the countries of the South. In the arena of *foreign investment*, the NIEO declaration calls for elimination of certain legal restrictions on the nationalization of foreign direct investment, and for the promulgation of a set of rules to govern the behavior of multinational corporations in ways that benefit host countries. In the related area of *technology transfer*, the platform calls for a greater and less-restricted flow of technology from North to South. Finally, in the realm of the international *monetary system*, the NIEO declaration demands a larger voice for the developing countries in the reform and managment of institutions such as the International Monetary Fund and World Bank, and it proposes a method of providing automatic access to more freely created IMF reserves. In 1976 at the UNCTAD IV and Colombo conferences, a new set of demands, referring specifically to the relations between the developing countries and the countries of "the socialist commonwealth," was added to the standard NIEO list. The revised version called for an end to barter-type trade and aid practices and a switch to the use of convertible currency in Soviet and East European dealings with the developing countries.

Considering the total list of Third World demands, one must conclude that the first 5 years of bargaining on the NIEO platform have produced very little change from the practices of the "old order." Individual countries of the North, such as the Netherlands and some Scandinavian nations, have formally accepted the higher aid targets and have agreed to renegotiation or even forgiveness of Third World indebtedness. The major collective concession by the North has been the agreement (in the spring of 1979, just prior to the UNCTAD V Conference at Manila) on a common fund for commodity price stabilization. But even this did not represent a clear-cut victory for the South, since the fund's initial financing was to be at a much lower level than originally proposed by the Group of 77.

THE SOVIET POSITION

Having taken note of the history and the rather scanty fruits of the North-South dialogue, we can now proceed to consider the attitude and role of the Soviet Union in these negotiations. We should first point out, however, that in most of its pronouncements and actions relating to the NIEO, the Soviet Union has presumed to speak for (and sometimes has been formally joined by) the other members in good standing of the East European "Socialist Community." Besides Albania, this excludes Yugoslavia—one of the most active members of the nonaligned movement and thus one of the foster parents of the NIEO—and Rumania, which recently capped off 15 years of "maverick" behavior in the bloc by suggesting that it might seek formal affiliation with the nonaligned. But for Poland, Czechoslovakia, the German Democratic Republic, Hungary, and Bulgaria, the positions and behavior of the USSR with regard to these issues have generally served as guide and model.

To understand the Soviet stance toward the North-South

dialogue, one must begin with the realization that the issues involved are of relatively low priority for the current Soviet leadership. This is not surprising considering the noninvolvement of the USSR in the institutions of the international economic and monetary systems; Moscow does not belong to the World Bank, the International Monetary Fund, the Food and Agriculture Organization, and the General Agreement on Tariffs and Trade, among others. Moreover, the Soviet emergence from the Stalinist period of autarchy is relatively recent and by no means complete. Total foreign trade turnover in 1975, after 5 years of unprecedented growth, still represented only 8 percent of the Soviet GNP (compared with the US figure for the same year of 13.4 percent). Of the 1975 total, 56 percent was with the other socialist countries, 31 percent was with the West, and only 12 percent was with the developing countries. These figures and the recent trends in Soviet foreign trade suggest that the growth and management of East-West trade is far more important to Soviet planners than is the USSR's trade with the South.

But from the Soviet perspective, the entire issue of economic cooperation with the world capitalist economy—West or South—is distinctly secondary to and dependent on the outcome of Soviet policy in the "main arena" of East-West political-military rivalry. And in particular, the very ability of the developing countries to put forward the platform for a NIEO is said to be a result of progress (attributable to Soviet diplomacy) toward relaxation of international tension and the restraining of imperialist aggressiveness.

> . . . an important interdependence exists between the restructuring of international economic relations and problems of limiting the arms race, disarmament and consolidating security—further progress in political and military detente, which is of paramount significance for strengthening general peace, will at the same time contribute to the normalization of the world economic situation.[3]

Were it not for the strength and support of the socialist camp, the developing countries would not only still be prey to raw coercion by the imperialists, but would also have had no alternative markets or sources of assistance. Thus, in Moscow's view, progress toward economic self-determination in the developing countries can come only through the assistance of the socialist countries and through progress in their struggle for detente. The clear implication

364

is that the developing countries must continue to support Soviet foreign policy initiatives in the East-West competition if they are to hope for progress in the solution of their own priority issues. To the consternation of many Third World delegations at UNCTAD and UN General Assembly sessions devoted to discussing the NIEO, the Soviets have persistently sought to broaden the agenda to include discussion of their current favorite detente or disarmament proposals.

Having put it in its proper global context, the Soviets are then willing to give a very general endorsement to the NIEO program. They insist, however, that it must be understood as more than just "tinkering" with the world capitalist economy, but rather as a "vote of no confidence in the 'free enterprise' system" and in capitalism's ability to resolve Third World economic problems.[4] Thus understood, the NIEO program received the qualified official endorsement of the Soviet government in a 1976 statement:

> The program . . . for the establishment of a "new international economic order" expresses legitimate aspirations—to extend the process of the liquidation of colonialism to the economic sphere. . . . . The Soviet Union takes an understanding attitude toward the broad program of measures which reflects the vital and long-term interests of the developing countries, and it supports its fundamental thrust.[5]

In their contributions to the NIEO debate, Soviet and East European spokesmen have been at pains to direct the attention of the developing countries toward the "monopoly circles in capitalist states" as the sole cause of Third World economic backwardness and the chief obstacle to removing it. Soviet officials and analysts have warned Third World leaders not to be taken in by the seeming concessions of "so called aid" or promotion of "modernization" on the part of the "imperialist" states. Imperialist tactics are said to be more subtle and flexible but unable to change the exploitative essence of the effort to keep the developing countries in a subordinate position in the world capitalist economy. Among these tactics is the effort to buy time by agreeing to a "dialogue" with the Third World, and particularly by seeking to move the discussion to a "partial forum" (the Paris CIEC talks) where the socialist states and more radical Third World states are not present. As the Soviet government statement put it:

> The stance of monopoly circles in capitalist states has been and still is the

chief obstacle to the radical restructuring of international economic relations on a democratic basis . . . . The course of continuing and deepening the exploitation of developing countries for their part remains essentially unchanged. It is impossible to count on forcing them to abandon it with the help of all kinds of narrow group negotiations . . . .[6]

But, say the Soviets, the most objectionable imperialist trick— which unfortunately finds an echo in some of the speeches and documents of the Third World states—is the effort to lump the industrialized capitalist and socialist states together in a "rich North versus poor South" dichotomy that denies the imperialist monopoly blame and substitutes the notion of "equal responsibility." Such a tactic, which is said to be a joint imperialist and Maoist concoction, seeks to drive a wedge between the Third World and its natural ally the socialist commonwealth, and thereby doom to failure the cause of restructuring the international economic order. Foreign Minister Gromyko's denunciation of this tactic in his address to the UN General Assembly's Sixth Special Session is typical in its vehemence:

As before our country will counteract attempts to separate the national liberation movement from is natural ally—the community of socialist states. We shall never accept—either in theory or in practice—the false concept of the divison of the world into "poor" and "rich" countries which places on the same level the socialist countries and certain other states which have removed a very, very great quantity of wealth from the countries which were under their colonial yoke . . . . The responsibility of those . . . who really bear the responsibility for the economic backwardness of the developing countries is thereby seemingly removed from the agenda. We do not favor polemics for their own sake, but on this fundamental question it is necessary to call a spade a spade.[7]

Since the "monstrous falsification" of "equal responsibility" is cited as the justification for the Third World's demand that all "rich" nations share in the financial compensation of the less-developed states, there are economic as well as ideological motives in the Soviet rejection of the concept. Likewise, the Third World spokesmen who are willing to endorse the concept are characterized by Soviet writers as motivated by greed rather than by principle.

The Soviet case for discarding the concept of "rich and poor nations" rests not only on its view of the historical cause for Third World poverty but also upon the claim that the USSR is already assisting the Third World to the limits of its ability and international obligation.

366

The Soviet Union's might is based not on superprofit monopolies which have grown fat on neocolonial plundering, not on the extreme exploitation of its own working class, but on wealth created by the people's labor . . . to the extent of its capabilities it is prepared to help and does help developing countries to overcome backwardness. But the motive behind its aid does not lie in a "guilt complex;" the socialist community's aid to the developing countries expresses the new, socialist nature of international duty . . .[8]

"Bourgeois theories of interdependence" are also cited by Soviet analysts as subtle masks for the continuation of imperialist exploitation of the less developed countries. By emphasizing their mutual economic dependence with the Third World and raising the spectre of their common economic ruin, the capitalists hope to deflect the developing countries from the effort for radical reconstruction of the economic order. "True interdependence," on the other hand, is said by the Soviets to be founded on equality and mutual benefit and best exemplified in the "socialist division of labor" within the socialist community, which can also be extended, "without any element of exploitation," to the relations between socialist and developing countries.[9]

Another fashionable thesis that has been attacked by Soviet ideologists in their effort to redirect the discussion of the NIEO into a more acceptable context is the notion that international cooperation on massive global problems can unite the global community in a "single world awareness." While acknowledging the need for cooperation on such problems as food supply and protection of the environment, the Soviets insist that such cooperation cannot eliminate the social class barrier separating the capitalist and socialist systems. As two Soviet scholars wrote recently in *Pravda:*

Any attempts to represent the very existence of global problems and the necessity of jointly resolving them as a sign of the "convergence" of socialism and capitalism or as evidence of a change in the nature of one of those systems is completely invalid. Objectively these attempts can serve only one purpose: to camouflage imperialist hegemonism and the worldwide expansion of monopoly capital.[10]

This set of ideological tenets and attitudes has underlain the Soviet approach to the Third World campaign for a NIEO since the first UNCTAD meeting in 1964. At that conference the Soviet delegates sought to place blame for Third World economic woes exclusively upon the capitalist states and to deny that the USSR shared any responsibility. Although the Socialist states voted with the Third World majority on 25 of 27 principles adopted in the Final Act, this apparent bond masked two strongly opposed sets of priorities. The Soviets sought to channel Third World discontent into the broader Cold War issues, while the Southern states attempted to keep the focus on the rich-poor dichotomy.[11]

A decade later at the Sixth Special Session of the General Assembly, the Soviets were still trying to link the NIEO to broader issues of war and peace and to emphasize the need for anti-imperialist solidarity between East and South. Gromyko's opening statement urged that the economic questions on the agenda be "examined through the prism of politics,"[12] and Soviet delegates tried to include in the preamble to the final declaration a commentary on detente and peaceful coexistence. But Soviet speechmaking and lobbying on these points only tried the patience of Third World representatives, who expressed a preference for concrete proposals (absent from Gromyko's speech) over shopworn polemics.[13] On the specific issues comprising the NIEO platform, the rhetorical stance of the socialist countries was not generally more radical than that of the Third World delegations. One study of the Sixth and Seventh Special Sessions concluded that representatives of the developing countries tended to voice more extreme positions than the socialist representatives on six of nine issues at the Sixth Special Session and on four of nine issues in the Seventh.[14] The difference is explained not by a radicalization of the socialist position between 1974 and 1975, but rather by the generally more moderate and compromising tone of the Third World stance at the latter session.

At the UNCTAD IV Conference in Nairobi in May 1976, the socialist countries promulgated a 34-page joint statement which again stressed the linkage of detente and the creation of the NIEO and which gave general support to the "anti-imperialist" and "anti-monopoly" elements of the Third World stance. Soviet Minister of Foreign Trade Patolichev's speech proposed an extension of the practice of concluding long-term cooperation agreements with the developing countries and spoke of increasing "by 50 percent" Soviet technical assistance to the Third World. The Soviet press hailed the socialist states' contribution to the creation of a business-like and serious atmosphere (in contrast to the confrontationist stand of the West and the "splitting activities" of the Chinese) and claimed that many Third World delegates appreciated the Soviet stance and displayed "keen interest" in the socialist proposals.[15] In fact, however, the Soviets were rather widely criticized by Third World representatives, with particular complaints about the barter system, high-priced industrial goods, and lack of trade preferences, and a more general resentment at the socialist countries' practice of standing aloof and disclaiming any responsibility for the condition of the world economy.[16]

Standing aloof was an even easier attitude for the Soviets to assume *vis a vis* the CIEC meetings in Paris. No socialist states were invited to participate in these talks, to which the label "North-South dialogue" was frequently attached. The Soviets reportedly complained about their exclusion—a fact which may account for the statement of the host (French President Giscard d'Estaing) in his opening address that the East European socialists might possibly be involved in future work of the conference.[17] But the Soviets probably found it more comfortable to remain outside the dialogue. Had they been present, they might not have known whether to sit with the "North" or the "South." From a distance, they could easily complain about the conference's "separatist" nature ("where the stand of the developing countries is weaker and where they are deprived of the support of the socialist states"), declare that its failure was "predetermined," and urge a return to the United Nations framework.[18]

Turning briefly to consider the Soviet positions on specific issues related to the NIEO, we find first that their qualified general endorsement of the NIEO platform has not translated into firm support (in the form of positive financial commitments) for the concrete proposals embodied therein. Thus, for example, the socialist states have not endorsed or pledged to the common fund for commodity stabilization, they have expressed unwillingness to accept the 0.7 percent GNP target for official development assistance, they have not endorsed the proposal for blanket debt rescheduling, and they have withheld contributions to the special multilateral emergency fund for food assistance. In short, the Soviets have sought to "have it both ways"—acting like a great friend of the "poor South" on the rhetorical level while playing the role of the stingy "rich North" on the level of concrete measures for channeling more funds to the South.

In the arena of trade, Nikolai Patolichev's speech at UNCTAD IV gave general support to the principle of international commodity stabilization agreements. He cited as potential benefits of such agreements the maintenance of commodity prices at levels which are "economically sound, remunerative and equitable for producers and users alike," the insuring of expanded production and trade of these commodities, and the ability to "take account of changes in the costs of commodities versus manufactures."[19] As noted above, however, he did not endorse the establishment of the common fund to provide the financial umbrella for such agreements. The Soviets' commentary on commodity prices has reflected their dual role as producers and consumers. In general, however, Soviet economists have cited the "need to stabilize and balance world prices for raw material and finished articles at a definite, interdependent level within the framework of international trade agreements." They have warned that, while the "raw material boom" has brought temporary prosperity to some Third World producers, the price situation in most of the South has worsened substantially. These economists conclude that one-sided increases in commodity prices unaccompanied by "progressive socio-economic transformations" or establishment of "mutually advantageous trade agreements" cannot prove to be a successful tactic for the Third World.[20]

In the realm of aid, the Soviets have held their own program up as a model of disinterested and effective assistance, underscoring its concentration in the public sector and on industrialization projects. In explanations aimed at their own public, they stress the mutually advantageous nature of their aid agreements, noting the benefits to the Soviet economy of receiving consumer goods, agricultural products, and industrial raw materials in repayment for Soviet assistance. Soviet commentators acknowledge that the Third World nations' capacity to absorb aid is limited and that some proposed projects do not make economic sense. Moreover, in recent years they have called attention to the limited capacity of their own economy to provide aid in the volume that it might be desired by the Third World.[21] The developing countries, they say, should regard Soviet aid as a sort of bonus; they should realize that the sole obligation for restitution rests on the imperialists and that the primary contribution of the USSR lies in its capacity to restrain imperialist aggression. According to the 1976 Soviet government statement on restructuring the international economy:

The socialist states' aid to developing countries is not recompense for damage inflicted or payment for old sins: it is aid from a friend and ally in the struggle against the common enemy—imperialism. . . . It is natural, however, that the Soviet Union's potential for rendering economic assistance is not infinite. Of course, the Soviet state cannot fail to be concerned for the well-being of its own people. The Soviet Union carries a great load in ensuring peace and the people's security against the encroachments of aggressive imperialist circles. . . .[22]

The issue of the rescheduling or forgiveness of the public debts of the developing countries was another on which the Soviets assumed a generally sympathetic stance without making a specific commitment. At UNCTAD IV, Patolichev blamed the debt problem on inflation and the "excessive" transfer of profits by "foreign monopolies." Credits granted by the USSR, he implied, by virtue of the fact that they are repaid primarily through supply of the debtor's products, do not present the same sort of problem. At any rate, should a debt problem arise between the Soviet Union and a Southern debtor, "there is always a possibility for mutually acceptable solutions," taking account of particular circumstances, so that "debts could be rescheduled by mutual agreement" or in some cases "even written off."[23]

The feature of Third World economic dislocation that has attracted the greatest public attention in the West is the "world food crisis"—the precarious balance between limited food supplies and imperfect distribution mechanisms on the one hand and the rapidly expanding demand, due primarily to high rates of population growth throughout most of the developing countries, on the other. Although the food and population problems have not been directly incorporated by the Third World into the agenda for the NIEO, they have been an important backdrop for the North-South dialogue and were in fact the subject of separate conferences in 1974.

The Soviet stance at the World Food Conference in Rome was quite consistent with its general posture on NIEO issues. The Soviet delegate stressed that the main causes for the food problem were social and political rather than natural, that the essential precondition for its solution was the implementation of measures of disarmament and reduction of military budgets, and that in fact there was no ground for pessimism with regard to the world's technical capacity to produce adequate food. By his estimate, "effective use of all lands suitable for cultivation would provide enough food for 30 to 40 billion people."[24]

This sort of extravagant optimism about the supply and demand

371

balance was excised from later Soviet analyses of the problem. The noted Soviet demographer Boris Urlanis wrote in 1977 that the earth's limited resources do indeed set a definite limit to the growth of its population. Citing Soviet Central Asia as an example, he noted that radical changes in the social system will not alone guarantee a diminution of the birth rate and achievement of a stable population. Although he derided the notion of a "population bomb" and stressed that there was adequate opportunity to find an effective solution to the population problem, Urlanis was clearly advocating the adoption of family planning programs by the developing countries.[25] Although Soviet analysts now more explicitly acknowledged that population growth was a contributing factor to a world food problem of "unprecedented dimensions," they still argued that the solution could be achieved only if population policies were accompanied by radical changes in patterns of agricultural ownership and production.[26]

Moreover, the Soviets argued, the importing of food to compensate for scarcities could only be regarded as a "temporary expedient." The developing countries themselves would have to bear the primary responsibility for achieving the reforms that are necessary if food self-sufficiency is to be achieved. In the meantime, if aid is required,

> the socialist community considers it just that the developed capitalist states, which are responsible for the disastrous economic situation in most of the developing countries, should give them the necessary aid. Making claims of this kind to the socialist countries is unfounded.[27]

THE SOVIET PRACTICE

The Soviet position on the issue of food production and distribution is of particular interest because it provides one of the clearest examples of the glaring gap between Moscow's rhetoric and its own domestic and international record. The blatant hypocrisy that is evident in Soviet preachments about the unsatisfactory and expedential nature of food imports and about the miraculous results that can be achieved through socialist transformations in agriculture has not entirely escaped the notice of the Third World. At the various forums discussing the NIEO, there has been growing irritation expressed by representatives of the

South at the Soviet effort to evade all responsibility for Third World economic problems and to pretend that it is already assisting to the level of its capabilities. Encouraged perhaps by the harsh Chinese criticism of Soviet "plunder" of the Third World, developing-country delegates are less reticent to comment on the inconsistencies in Soviet rhetoric and behavior.

To return to the example of food, it is clear that the massive Soviet interventions in the world grain market in 1972 and 1975 not only helped to exhaust the world's grain reserves but also dramatically drove up the prices that had to be paid by less prosperous countries that were also seeking to buy grain at those times. As Robert Paarlberg has put it, the USSR is at one and the same time the world's largest and most irregular producer of wheat and the world's most disruptive grain trading nation. And yet the Soviet Union, by refusing to participate in international "food security" institutions or even to join in information-sharing that provides global early warning of food emergencies, has made "the smallest contribution to collective efforts to recover food security and restore price stability."[28]

In the realm of trade with the Third World, Soviet practices are in fact far from the model of good behavior that Moscow projects at the podium of international conferences. The volume of Soviet trade with the developing countries has indeed risen during the 1970's, but their relative share of total Soviet imports and exports has actually fallen. Only about 5 percent of Third World trade is with the USSR, whereas 75 percent is with the developed capitalist countries. Moreover, their trade with the Soviet Union is increasingly unbalanced, to the extent that Moscow's trade surplus with the Third World countries has been increasingly important in helping to compensate for its deficit in trade with the West. Nor by any means does the Soviet Union provide a favored market for the manufactured products of the developing countries; the capitalist West in fact imports a larger share of manufactures from the Third World total trade than does the USSR.

Soviet pricing practices have come under increasing fire from Third World sources. It is said to be common to find prices of Soviet products sold to developing countries 15 to 25 percent higher than prices of the same products sold to the West, while Third World imports into the USSR often receive 10 to 15 percent less than world prices.[29]

Asia, Africa, and Latin America have become important sources of raw materials for the Soviet Union. This includes not only foodstuffs but critical industrial raw materials as well. In 1975, 20 percent of Soviet imports from the Third World were petroleum products; Western estimates project that the Eastern bloc will be importing substantially more oil and gas by the mid-1980's. The Soviet and East European aluminum industries are increasingly reliant on foreign sources of bauxite and aluminum. Eastern bloc tin imports, principally from Southeast Asia, are increasing; the bloc is already entirely dependent on Third World supplies of natural rubber and sheet mica.[30]

In describing at international conferences the economic benefits of trade between the socialist and developing countries, Soviet spokesmen neglect to mention that weapons constitute over half of the USSR's exports to the Third World. The arms trade is an important source of hard currency for the Soviet Union, so that it proves economically as well as politically beneficial to Moscow. Nevertheless, the harsh reality of this side of Moscow's cooperative relationship with the developing countries appears to give the Soviets a vested interest in Third World turmoil and contrasts sharply with protestations in favor of detente, disarmament, and the reduction of military spending.

The Soviet Union's claims regarding its economic assistance program have been considerably scaled down since the mid-1960's; as we saw above, Moscow now stresses the limitations on its ability to provide credits but professes to be helping to the greatest extent possible. The reality is that the USSR's average annual aid contribution amounts to about .05 percent of its GNP, compared to about .33 percent for the Western countries (and .7 percent targeted by the NIEO platform). Moreover, of the $11 billion in aid pledged by the USSR in the first two decades of its assistance program, only about $6 billion was ever actually delivered. Deliveries often lag about 7 years behind commitments.[31] The Soviets contribute only tiny amounts to multilateral foreign assistance programs such as the UN Development Program, and even these amounts are often unutilized because they are provided in nonconvertible currency.

For most of the Third World nations Soviet economic assistance is virtually nonexistent, for Moscow's aid program has been highly concentrated, especially as compared to the American program. The bulk of Soviet aid has gone to countries in the Middle East and south Asia, and in fact two countries—India and Egypt—have received almost 30 percent of the total amount extended since 1955. Contrary to an impression often conveyed by Soviet propaganda, Soviet economic aid has not been in the form of grants—they actually comprise less than 5 percent of the total—but primarily in the form of long-term credits bearing varying amounts of interest. Nor is Soviet aid extended to the less-developed countries for the free purchase of needed commodities; it is strictly "tied" to Soviet goods, and then usually in the context of approved projects.

The "tying" of Soviet aid and the low rate of "draw down" of Soviet credits, though it has set limits on the usefulness of Soviet aid, has not prevented a number of Soviet aid clients from overextending themselves. A number of the most prominent early Soviet aid recipients (including Egypt, Indonesia, and Mali) had by the early 1960's greatly surpassed their abilities to borrow or absorb the aid they had accepted, and their economies were reeling under the heavy debt burdens. Contrary to the seeming generosity implicit in Patolichev's statement on debt rescheduling, the Soviets have been very reluctant to allow it, favoring only a very few close ideological allies (e.g., Cuba, South Yemen) but refusing some other heavy borrowers whose policies are judged less "progressive" (e.g., India, Egypt).

India, the largest and one of the most important of the nonaligned states, has often been cited by Soviet and non-Soviet observers as one of the examples of Moscow's ability to conduct an effective and successful economic relationship with a Third World country. But in fact, while the Soviet-Indian relationship does balance out on the positive side for both parties, the below-the-surface anomalies and strains in their economic dealings are illustrative of the defects in Moscow's record of providing support and assistance to the developing countries in the spirit of the NIEO.

Between 1950-51 and 1971-72, India's trade with the USSR and Communist East Europe rose from 0.5 percent to 20 percent of her total exports, and from a negligible amount to full 11 percent of her imports. But throughout the 1970's Soviet-Indian trade has been imbalanced, with India's exports far exceeding her imports. Part of this surplus was used by India to repay past economic assistance from Moscow, and part was utilized to purchase Soviet military equipment. Thus in recent years there has been a net transfer of resources from India to the USSR—a "negative aid flow" of $28 million in 1970-71 that climbed to $165.4 million in 1972-73 and that stood at $100 million in 1976. The total amount of Soviet economic aid to India between 1954 and 1976 was $1.943 billion in credits, of which approximately $290 million had not been drawn by the end of 1976. In recent years, in fact, the rate at which Soviet credits have been utilized has been less than $25 million annually.[32] This is largely a consequence of Moscow's reluctance to shift away from the traditional pattern of public-sector project aid to nonproject aid and the provision of raw materials, both of which are increasingly desired by the Indians as their own industrial capacity expands.

Not only are the Soviet and Indian economies noncomplementary, but the Soviets have proved to be hardheaded bargainers whose insistence on "businesslike dealings" is manifested by a reluctance to incur economic costs simply for the purpose of picking up a few additional political credits in New Delhi. The Indians have complained about an apparent Russian search for one-sided economic advantages. One incident occurred during 1975, when a visiting Soviet trade delegation, negotiating the export of fertilizer, demanded a 60-70 percent markup in price—which they later scaled down to 35-40 percent when the Indians refused to pay.[33]

An Indian complaint of broader significance concerns the effort by the USSR unilaterally to revise the rupee-ruble exchange rate. The Soviets argued that the falling price of the pound sterling—to which the rupee is linked—justified a revision of the exchange rate from 11.39 rubles per hundred rupees in 1971 to 8.66 per hundred in 1975. The Indians argued that the Soviets were creating a double standard, since the value of the ruble in terms of gold is set arbitrarily and is not subject to market forces. Since India's debt repayment to the USSR is made in rupees, the effect of the Soviet action would be to allow Moscow to purchase more Indian goods with its rupees.[34] India's acceptance of the Soviet argument would have meant an addition of $160 million to an Indian debt standing, as of mid-1976, at $450 million. The issue dragged on through many rounds of negotiation, during which both sides adhered stubbornly to their positions until compromise was finally reached in 1979.

Perhaps the most spectacular failure in Indo-Soviet commercial relations was the proposed arrangement, promised by Prime Minister Kosygin during a 1968 trip, for the Soviet Union to purchase all the rails and railway wagons that India could provide over the next 5 years (though in fact Soviet railways were built on a different scale). This pledge raised Indian hopes of boosting the production of some of their public-sector industries to a level closer to full capacity. A protocol was signed calling for 2,000 cars to be delivered in 1969, and up to 10,000 per year by 1973, with a total over the period of 26,000. But the deal fell through after prolonged haggling between the two sides. The Soviets offered a price amounting to roughly one-half of India's production costs, and then stipulated in the specifications for the wheel assemblies the use of lead and zinc alloys which were available only from the USSR at a high price. The Russians reportedly even attempted to make their purchase of Indian railway wagons conditional on India's purchase of Soviet commercial aircraft. When the deal finally collapsed, the Indians tried to convince Soviet negotiators of their obligation to buy other manufactured goods equivalent in price to the rejected railway wagons. But this argument was apparently spurned by the Soviets.[35]

PROSPECTS FOR THE FUTURE

To put in perspective the Soviet relationship with India—and indeed with the Third World in general—it is worth recalling how far Moscow has progressed in its presence and influence compared with its almost total isolation only 25 years ago. The examples and trends that we have cited are not intended to deny the fact that the USSR carries substantial weight in Asia, Africa, and even Latin America, but rather to suggest that Moscow's economic policies in particular may have reached a point of diminishing returns.

The Soviet Union's relationship with the Third World on issues relating to the NIEO appears to be increasingly frayed. As in the fairy tale of the emperor's new clothes, some voices at the edge of the crowd are beginning to shout out in anger and frustration at the nakedness that they really see in Soviet policies. Or, to cite Roger Hansen's use of a different metaphor to illustrate the same conclusion:

the Soviet Union's days as a Southern cheerleader without responsibilities would appear to be numbered. . . . Already the developing countries, viewing the Soviet Union as a 'have' power, are increasing their criticism of Soviet trade and aid policies that are negligible in their efforts to assist Southern economic development.[36]

377

What is happening to the USSR's position in the Third World is an apt illustration of the handicaps that Moscow suffers as a result of its limited international economic capabilities. The Soviets have been able to gain footholds in a number of strategic Third World locations, particularly on the periphery of the Indian Ocean, by virtue of their political and military support of leftist movements, backed up with ample supplies of Soviet arms and frequently with Cuban troops. And yet they have found it exceedingly difficult to *sustain* their influence or to prop up their client regimes through military means alone. Conversely, in areas where the USSR has *not* established a military supply relationship, it has hardly any influence at all. To put it another way, the Soviets' expanding political ambitions in the Third World, initially boosted by their military instrumentalities, are in the longer run subject to being undermined by Moscow's limited economic capabilities.

Apart from the implications that this has for the long-term success or failure of Soviet policies in the Third World, the Soviet overreliance on military instrumentalities of influence has profound consequences for both East-West and North-South relations. In the former case, the wave of initial Soviet successes in Africa and the Middle East, even prior to the invasion of Afghanistan, aroused American anxieties to the point of threatening to reverse progress in arms limitation talks and the overall detente relationship—and perhaps even to provoke American military countermeasures in the Persian Gulf-Indian Ocean area. The costs of this likely setback to East-West relationships and revival of US-Soviet zero-sum competition in the Third World are compounded by the danger that domestic stability and the prospects for progress toward development in the Third World will be even further disrupted. As the states of the South have clearly perceived, the heating up of the East-West competition may well doom the North-South dialogue and the prospects for agreement on the New International Economic Order.

One possible conclusion is that this outcome is precisely what the Soviets have sought to achieve—that by refusing to engage seriously in the North-South dialogue and by pursuing their own destabilizing bilateral relationships in the Third World, the Soviet policymakers have consciously promoted a breakdown of the North-South negotiations on the NIEO. If this is the case, the Soviets would seem to have opted for a policy that threatens them with several adverse consequences. The major spokesmen for the Group of 77 are not likely to regard the Soviets as blameless in the case of such a breakdown, and assuming that the South remains unified, it is difficult to see how Moscow could recoup sufficient prestige or display sufficient economic generosity to allow her to build a viable East-South alliance. To the extent that an embittered South (including the OPEC nations) sought to take retaliatory measures against the recalcitrant North—for example, further hikes in raw material prices, new embargoes, unilateral defaulting on debts, nationalization of joint enterprises—the Soviet Union would not likely be immune from harmful economic consequences. Even apart from the cost to its own economy that might follow from either economic warfare or economic collapse in the South, the Soviet Union is by now sufficiently dependent on the Western capitalist economies to be economically vulnerable to disruptions that might occur in the West.

These adverse consequences might well befall the Soviet Union in the event of a breakdown in the North-South dialogue, whether Moscow had stayed out of the North-South talks or had actively joined in for the purpose of disrupting them. To look at the other side of the coin, what implications might there be for the USSR in the event that some form of comprehensive accord were reached in the North-South talks? If such an agreement were concluded without the participation of the socialist bloc, it would likely result in even greater economic isolation from the international economy for Moscow and its allies. Ironically, the consequences for the USSR might be identical to those that one Soviet analyst claimed finally had forced the United States to bargain with the South: (1) US (read: USSR) dependence on trade with the South was such that "open trade and political confrontation had an extremely serious effect on the economy"; (2) from the "political standpoint it was impossible for [Moscow] to continue ignoring the NIEO program because of the obvious harm to its already low international prestige and danger of its isolation in the UN"; (3) "the developing countries began to institute some of the measures unilaterally after the [East] proved reluctant to discuss them."[37]

But if the socialist countries were to join in the North-South dialogue and contribute to a constructive compromise agreement on the NIEO issues, Moscow would by no means be immune from risks and disadvantages. On the positive side of the ledger, we might expect that the USSR would share in the benefits of expanded production and trade that would accompany the economic invigoration of the Third World, as well as enjoy the advantages that would accrue from cooperative solutions to the global problems of food supply, overpopulation, and ecological imbalances.[38]

But to the extent that a cooperative accord would mean that the Soviets would be obligated to expand greatly the level of their economic aid, to reschedule Third World debts (to the detriment of their own balance of payments), and to help underwrite commodity stabilization agreements, there would likely be—at least in the near term—a substantial direct economic cost for Moscow. Moreover, the realization of some of the goals of the NIEO could bring substantial indirect costs for Moscow as well: the USSR might well find itself paying more for raw materials and competing directly with the Third World nations for Western grain, Western credits, and Western technology. To a certain extent, then, the short-term growth in North-South trade and resource transfers might well come at the expense of East-West transactions. Added to these economic costs would be the ideological costs that might attend Moscow's greater interdependence with the world capitalist economy, including the adjustments that would necessarily flow from Soviet membership in international economic and monetary institutions.

To a believer in classical economics, with faith in the inevitability of the benefits of freer trade and comparative advantage, it would appear that any short-term economic costs to the USSR would be outweighed by the longer term expansion in general world production, trade and prosperity. Since a considerable portion of Marxian economics is founded on the principles of the British classical economists, it is not unlikely that a Marxist would share in the expectation of long-term benefits to be gained from the cooperative strategy we have outlined.

Sadly, however, there is little evidence that the present Soviet leadership is inclined to run the ideological, political, and economic risks that adoption of a cooperative strategy might entail. Equally unfortunate is the fact that the Western nations have thus far apparently made little genuine effort to invite the Soviets to assume such a role. The effort should be made, through a combination of persuasion, the promise of mutual benefit, and the implied threat of proceeding to frame constructive solutions to global problems of proceeding to frame constructive solutions to global problems even without Soviet participation. But the very magnitude of the task demands that the door be kept open, in the hope that future Soviet leaders might have the vision that would enable them to take the risks of genuine global economic cooperation.

ENDNOTES

1. Henry A. Kissinger, "Global Consensus and Economic Development," United Nations, New York, *The Secretary of State*, September 11, 1975, p. 1.

2. Robert Legvold, "The Nature of Soviet Power," *Foreign Affairs*, Vol. 56, No. 1, October 1977, p. 58.

3. Soviet Government Statement, "In the Interests of Cooperation," *Pravda*, October 5, 1976, p.4.

4. K. Ivanov, "International Trade: Methods of Restructuring," *Izvestiia*, September 1, 1977, p. 4. See also E. Obminsky, "Problems of Restructuring Economic Relations," *International Affairs*, January 1977, p. 61.

5. Soviet Government Statement, p.4.

6. *Ibid*.

7. *Pravda*, April 12, 1974, p. 4.

8. V. Sidenko, "Prospects of Nonalignment and Impasses of 'Equidistance'," *New Times*, No. 29, 1979, pp. 4-6. See also K. Brutents, "The Soviet Union and the Newly-Independent Countries," *International Affairs*, No. 4, 1979, pp. 10-11.

9. A. Sergiyev, "Bourgeois Theories of 'Interdependence' Serve Neo-colonialism," *International Affairs*, No. 11, 1976, pp. 103-111.

10. V. Zagladin and I. Frolov, "Global Problems of Our Time: The Quest for Solutions," *Pravda*, May 7, 1979, pp. 4-5.

11. Charles A. Schwartz, *UNCTAD: Soviet Politics in the North-South Conflict*, unpublished Ph.D dissertation, University of Virginia, 1973, University Microfilms edition, pp. 251-253.

12. *Pravda*, April 12, 1974, p. 4.

13. *Peking Review*, No. 17, 1974, pp. 25, 27.

14. Douglas C. Smyth, "The Global Economy and the Third World: Coalition or Cleavage," *World Politics*, Vol. XXIX, No. 4, July 1977, pp. 584-609.

15. See TASS, May 25, 1976, in Foreign Broadcast Information Service, *Daily Report: Soviet Union* (hereafter *FBIS: Soviet Union*), May 27, 1976, p. A9; TASS, May 29, 1976, in *FBIS: Soviet Union*, June 1, 1976, p. A10; TASS, May 31, 1976, in *FBIS: Soviet Union*, June 1, 1976, p. A11.

16. Congressional Research Service, Library of Congress, *The Soviet Union and the Third World: A Watershed in Great Power Policy*? Report to the Committee on International Relations, House of Representatives, May 8, 1977, pp. 111-116.

17. Jean-Marie Debouays, "L'URSS Devant le Debat sur le Nouvel Ordre Economique Internationale," *Defense Nationale*, April 1976, pp. 47-54.

18. S. Otreshko, "'North-South' Dialogue (The Results of the Conference on International Economic Cooperation)," *International Affairs*, No. 2, 1978, pp. 99-106, and B. Rachkov, "In an Atmosphere of Acute Contradictions," *Ekonomich e skaia Gazeta*, No. 25, 1977, p. 22.

19. N.S. Patolichev, "Detente and Development: Complementary Processes," *Bulletin of Peace Proposals*, No. 3, 1976, p. 241.

20. R. Andreasian, "The Raw Material Crisis and the 'Third World'," *Izvestiia*, October 8, 1974, p. 4; G. Skorov, "Imperialism and Developing Countries," *Kommunist*, No. 18, December 1974, pp. 98-108; V. Golosov, "Restructuring of International Economic Relations," *International Affairs*, January 1975, pp. 46-47.

21. *Izvestiia*, October 19, 1974, p. 4; I. Kulev, "The Soviet Union and the Developing Countries," *International Affairs*, No. 11, 1976, p. 20.

22. *Pravda*, October 5, 1976, p. 4.

23. Patolichev, p. 242.

24. TASS, November 8, 1974, in *FBIS: Soviet Union*, November 11, 1974, p. A3.

25. B. Urlanis, "Contemporary Problems of Population Growth," *International Affairs*, No. 3, 1977, pp. 106-110.

26. E. Khlebutin, "Food Resources and the 'Population Explosion'," *International Affairs*, No. 3, 1977, pp. 113-116; L. Knyazhinskaya, "The World Food Problem: Some Solutions," *International Affairs*, No. 2, 1979, pp. 65-73.

27. Statement of Socialist Countries to UN *ad hoc* committee on Food Problems and Agricultural Development, TASS, March 30, 1979, *FBIS: Soviet Union*, April 3, 1979, p. CC3.

28. Robert Paarlberg, "Shifting and Sharing Adjustment Burdens—The Role of the Industrial Food Importing Nations," *International Organization*, Vol. 32, No. 3, Summer 1978, p. 673.

29. Alexander Wolynski, "Soviet Aid to the Third World: Strategy before Economics," *Conflict Studies*, No. 90, December 1977. See also "How Soviet Revisionism Plunders the Third World Economically," *Peking Review*, No. 17, 1974, p. 23.

30. Arthur D. Little, Inc., *Dependence of the Soviet Union and Eastern Europe on Essential Imported Materials Year 2000*, Study for Navy Project 2000, September 1977, pp. 13-19.

31. Wolynski, p. 5.

32. S. S. Aiyer, "No Projects in Sight for Using Soviet Loan," *Times of India*, June 6, 1977.

33. Marcus F. Franda, *India and the Soviets: 1975*, American Universities Field Staff, Fieldstaff Reports, South Asia Series, Vol. XIX, No. 5, p. 5.

34. *Ibid*.

35. *The Statesman* (New Delhi), November 18, 1969. For additional documentation, and analysis of the Soviet-Indian economic relationship, see Robert H. Donaldson, *The Soviet-Indian Alignment: Quest for Influence*, Management Series in World Affairs, Vol. 16, Books 3 and 4, Denver, Colorado: University of Denver, 1979.

36. Roger Hansen, *Beyond the North-South Stalemate*, New York: McGraw-Hill, 1979, p. 6.

37. I. Ivanov, "SShA i 'Novyi Mezhdunarodnyi Ekonomicheskii Poriadok'," *SShA: Ekonomika, Politika, Ideologiia*, No. 9, 1978, p. 4.

38. The Soviet debate about possible costs and benefits of greater internationalization of the Soviet economy is explored in Elizabeth Kridl Valkenier, "The USSR, The Third World, and The Global Economy," *Problems of Communism*, Vol. XXVIII, No. 4, July-August 1979, pp. 17-33.

19

THE EFFECTIVENESS OF SOVIET ARMS AID
DIPLOMACY IN THE THIRD WORLD

Roger F. Pajak

The peoples of the developing "Third World" countries—i.e., most of the states of Africa, Asia, and Latin America—have traditionally been regarded by Soviet theoreticians as potential allies of the Communist world. In the immediate post-World War II period the Soviet leadership, largely preoccupied with problems of internal reconstruction and with developments in Europe, devoted only superficial attention to the governments of the newly emerging states, which Moscow regarded as lackeys of the West. Although welcoming militant action by local Communist parties to seize power in some emerging countries, the Soviet Union did little beyond formally expressing opposition to Western influence in these areas. As more developing countries attained national status and independence, however, Soviet policy became increasingly out of date. New tactics were called for, tactics which would have an appeal to the widespread desire in the developing world for national independence and economic expression.

Following the death of Stalin in 1953, Soviet policy toward the developing countries underwent a dramatic change. The new Soviet leadership, acknowledging the lack of success of the former tactics, became increasingly cognizant of the strength and potential of non-Communist nationalist movements in the emerging countries. The result was a gradual but fundamental reorientation of Soviet policy toward the newly emerging states. Instead of the hitherto traditional Soviet policy of fostering militant local Communist agitation and subversion, Moscow began to emphasize support of nationalist movements and to develop a variety of bilateral state contacts through a carefully orchestrated program of diplomacy, trade, and aid. This tactical shift apparently reflected Moscow's assessment that the most effective strategy for establishing and expanding its influence and for eroding that of the West in Third World countries lay in associating itself with the strong nationalist and anti-Western sentiment in many of these states.

One of the most consequential instruments in the transformed Soviet approach toward the developing countries was a newly-conceived program of foreign assistance, patterned somewhat after that of the West. The Soviet decision in 1955 to offer military assistance, in particular, was probably stimulated by at least three factors: the general success of the Soviet postwar recovery effort; the availability of surplus stocks of military equipment as a consequence of military manpower reductions and changes in military doctrine; and, the conspicuous lack of success of indigenous Communist elements in the developing countries.

The leaders of many Third World countries, motivated by their own political and economic aspirations, were warmly receptive to the post-Stalin changes in Moscow's policies and were generally prepared to accept Soviet foreign assistance. This receptivity was enhanced by the unwillingness of many developing states to associate their newly-won independence with the foreign policy objectives of the leading Western powers. The Soviet Union needed only to present itself as an additional source of political, economic, and military support to find a number of willing recipients.

In this milieu, foreign assistance immediately became an important policy tool for expanding Soviet influence in the Third World. Since the inception of the foreign aid program in the mid-1950's, Moscow has come to regard this instrument of policy as somewhat of an index of its power and influence in the Third World.

ORGANIZATION

Overall responsibility for implementing the arms aid and sales program is assigned to the Chief Engineering Directorate (GIU), a component of the Soviet State Committee for Foreign Economic Relations. The GIU, which acts as the "supplier" in military aid contracts, handles the negotiations with recipient governments. In addition, the GIU coordinates with the Ministry of Defense on the types and quantities of equipment and with the External Relations Directorate of the General Staff on training and technical assistance to be provided. Subsequent requests for modification of an arms agreement must be approved by the GIU. If any changes requested by a client exceed the value specified in an agreement or if they entail advanced weapon systems, the GIU apparently forwards the request to the Minister of Defense or to the Politburo. Finally, the GIU arranges for shipment of military equipment with the Ministry of Foreign Trade and the Ministry of Maritime Fleet.[1]

PRICES AND TERMS

Much of the attractiveness of Soviet military assistance to Third World countries has been due to the comparatively low prices and favorable terms offered by Moscow. The prices charged to developing countries have varied with the type and condition of the equipment, but on the whole Soviet prices have been substantially below Western prices for comparable equipment. For example, the price of the new US F-15 fighter charged Israel averaged about $12 million per aircraft, while the price of a Soviet MIG-23 fighter reportedly averaged about $6.7 million. The price for a MIG-21 fighter reportedly listed at $2 million, while that of an F-4 was $5.7 million.[2] While the types of aircraft cited are not fully comparable in terms of characteristics and capabilities, the wide variation in reported prices serves to illustrate the point.

Besides low prices, the Soviets have offered attractive financial terms to recipients. Credits generally have been made available at 2 percent interest, with repayment periods averaging 10 years, following a grace period of one to three years. Moreover, to clients hard-pressed for foreign exchange, Moscow frequently has permitted repayment in local currency or commodities. In addition, Moscow often has postponed payment when recipients have been

386

unable to meet their scheduled obligations.[3]

Discounts from list prices also have been an intrinsic feature of Soviet military assistance. Such discounts reportedly have averaged about 40 percent of the value of Soviet contracts. Although discounting probably is partly premised on Moscow's assessment of a recipient's ability to pay, political favoritism also may be discerned in the variations evident in Soviet practice.[4]

While the underlying motivation of the Soviet arms aid program remains essentially political, there has recently been an increasing emphasis on arms sales to provide hard currency revenue. For the past several years the Soviets have increasingly required payment in convertible currency, at least from oil-producing clients, such as Algeria, Libya, and Iraq. The Central Intelligence Agency estimated that the Soviet Union gained approximately $1.5 billion in hard currency earnings from arms sales in 1977 alone.[5] Sales for hard currency apparently have largely supplanted the "arms-for-commodities" trade of earlier years and will likely comprise an increasing share of total Soviet arms transactions as the program continues.[6]

COMPONENTS OF THE PROGRAM

Equipment

In the early years of the program, it was common for observers to characterize the Soviet equipment exported as antiquated materiel, much of it delivered in various states of disrepair. However, even in the first decade of the program, a careful observation of the actual items delivered indicated that probably well over half of the total types provided was still in use by Soviet or Warsaw Pact armed forces, with a substantial number of items then still in production in the USSR.[7] Although some purchases were tactically inept—a striking example was the light cruiser that Indonesia bought essentially for prestige purposes in 1960—most of the equipment provided meshed handily with the existing military framework.

An initial advantage of the program during the early years, and one which undoubtedly commended itself highly to Soviet military planners at the time, was that the Soviet Union was able to offer military aid at very little cost to itself by delivering primarily obsolescent, but still effective, weapons made available by its own modernization program. The types of equipment provided ranged from small arms to artillery, armored vehicles, destroyers, submarines, jet aircraft, helicopters, engineering and communications equipment, plus spare parts and ammunition.

The importance that the Soviet leadership attached to its arms program was shown by its willingness, since the early 1960's, to make available to certain clients modern weapons systems which were not yet possessed in quantity, if at all, by other Communist countries. During the 1960's deliveries to major recipients included TU-16 medium jet bombers, MIG-21 jet fighters, An-12 turboprop assault transports, *Komar*-class guided missile motor gunboats, and a variety of surface-to-air, air-to-air, and air-to-surface missiles. Most of these items were then in use by the USSR or were just being phased into Warsaw Pact inventories.[8]

While Soviet equipment was generally delivered in satisfactory, usable condition, problems connected with usage sometimes arose in the developing countries. One of the most blatant examples was the delivery to the Arab countries of early models of the MIG-15 fighter without the ejection seats standard in jet fighter aircraft.[9] This meant of course that, even at the MIG-15's subsonic speed, the chances for survival of a pilot of a crippled aircraft were practically nil. Given these circumstances, pilots understandably showed little enthusiasm for aerial combat in this type of aircraft.

Another perennial difficulty has concerned spare parts. The Soviets provided spares in an aid agreement supposedly sufficient for maintenance and repair for a specified period, but such stocks apparently have never been adequate to a recipient's needs. The recipients, moreover, through faulty operating and storage procedures frequently misused equipment and quickly exhausted supplies of spares,[10] with the result that a lack of spare parts has remained a characteristic of the aid program to the present day.

Another important factor influencing the flow of new equipment has been the cyclical pattern of the program, reflecting the replacement of older items in recipients' inventories. The most obvious examples have been the periodic replacement of various generations of fighter aircraft (MIG-15/17s with MIG-21s and later, MIG-23s), acquisition of the TU-16, and in some cases the TU-22, jet medium bomber after initial purchases of the IL-28 light bomber, and replacement of the T-34 tank of Korean War vintage with the T-54/55 and T-62 main battle tanks, and more recently, the first-line T-72.[11]

As the program matured, the Soviets made available an increasing proportion of late-model equipment to their clients. Especially during the 1970's, some of Moscow's Arab clients began receiving the same types of air defense equipment as the Soviet forces, again before the Warsaw Pact states in some cases. In 1970-71, Egypt—one of Moscow's most favored clients at the time—was the first non-Communist state to receive the SA-3 low-level SAM missile, the FROG tactical ground rocket, and the mobile ZSU-23-4 radar-controlled antiaircraft gun. Also noteworthy among Soviet shipments was some of the most sophisticated Soviet command and control and secure data transmission equipment intended to enhance the effectiveness of the Egyptian air defense system.[12]

Technical Assistance

The complexity of modern military equipment necessitates increasingly skilled personnel to assemble, maintain, and operate it. This has required the Soviets to provide a program—complementary to the provision of equipment—of technical assistance consisting of two parts: the training in the Soviet Union of military personnel from the developing countries and the dispatch of Soviet military technicians and instructors to countries receiving military aid. Every recipient country has received both types of technical assistance, illustrating the criticality of such assistance to the effectiveness of the program.

Trainees

In the period 1955 through 1978, an estimated 44,000 military trainees had gone to the Soviet Union for various types of training, with another 6,000 having received some military instruction in Eastern European countries.[13] About 2,000 trainees were undergoing training in Communist countries at the end of 1978. Largely reflecting the size and importance of the key aid recipients, the vast majority of the military trainees have come from eight countries: Afghanistan, Algeria, Egypt, India, Indonesia, Iraq, Syria, and Somalia. Although the arms aid program with Indonesia was discontinued in 1965, that country still accounts for the largest number of trainees, about 7,500, or 16 percent of the total.[14]

In the early years of the program, Czechoslovakia and Poland, in their role as Soviet intermediaries, played an important part in the training. Students initially received naval training in Poland, while Czechoslovakia provided flight training and instruction in elec-

389

tronics, communications, and maintenance. A wide range of courses was then established in the Soviet Union to provide all levels of instruction from motor vehicle maintenance and repair to a 3-year course for senior officers at the Moscow Military Academy.[15]

Although Soviet technicians usually arrive following the delivery of equipment, it appears that indigenous trainees frequently are sent to the Soviet Union prior to the delivery of the weaponry for which they are trained. Accordingly, more sophisticated equipment which requires a higher level of instruction can be provided at a later date, in keeping with the progress of Soviet-conducted training programs. Additional programs, as required, probably can be set up with a minimum of lead time because similar training courses are operated for Soviet military personnel.

Technicians

The continuing high level of deliveries of sophisticated Soviet weapon systems to the developing states has required increasing Soviet technical assistance in the operation and maintenance of such equipment in the recipient industries. During 1978, an estimated 10,800 Soviet and 1,300 East European military technicians and advisers were present in developing countries, about a 20 percent increase over the number present in 1977.[16] The countries with the largest Soviet military advisory contingents (over 1,000 Soviet technicians present) were Algeria, Angola, Ethiopia, Iraq, Libya, and Syria.[17]

Soviet military advisers and technicians assist essentially in three functions: the delivery, assembly, and maintenance of military equipment; the training of local personnel in the operation and maintenance of equipment; and, the instructing of indigenous military officers in staff and operational units. Training courses have been established for the entire range of armaments from small arms to jet aircraft and naval vessels. Soviet officers also serve as instructors in the staff schools and military academies of these countries. In their capacity as advisers, Soviet officers have sometimes played key roles in modernizing and reorganizing the military establishments of recipient countries.[18]

Aid to Military Industries

Another significant aspect of the Soviet program is assistance designed to develop local arms industries and maintenance facilities

390

in the developing countries. The larger recipients have received substantial aid in the establishment of new military airbases, training facilities, and naval bases, while existing facilities have been expanded and modernized. In addition, a number of small arms and ammunition plants have been constructed in countries such as Afghanistan and Egypt.[19] The largest and most sensational example of Soviet aid in this regard is the MIG-21 jet fighter production complex in India, where three large plants for series production of these aircraft and their ancillary equipment are now in operation.[20] The establishment of such sophisticated military complexes as these has necessitated substantial amounts of Soviet industrial equipment, financial aid, and technical support.

MAGNITUDE AND PATTERN OF DISTRIBUTION

It is difficult to ascertain the magnitude of the Soviet military assistance program with precision, since many facets of the program are shrouded in secrecy. Arms deals oftentimes are buried in national statistics as general commercial transactions. Western reports vary widely as to the value and types of equipment provided, so that available data must be scrutinized carefully in terms of reliability of sources, consistency with other reporting, and reasonableness.[21]

Because the Soviet program has been partly a response to available opportunities and because it is influenced by the absorptive capacity of recipients, the annual magnitude of aid and sales commitments has been highly variable, as shown in Table 1. Beginning in 1955-56, Czechoslovakia, serving as an intermediary. for the USSR, extended an estimated $200 million worth of military assistance to Afghanistan, Egypt, Syria, and Yemen.[22] The Soviet military aid program began in its own right in 1956, when Moscow concluded arms deals directly with Afghanistan and Syria and subsequently with Egypt.[23] Although neither the precise quantities of arms provided nor the prices or conditions of payment were published, by the end of 1957 about $400 million worth of Soviet arms aid was estimated to have been extended to Middle Eastern countries.[24] A dearth of reports for the next few years possibly indicates that new extensions of Soviet military aid temporarily fell off, perhaps to allow time for assimilation of previous arms deliveries.

TABLE 1

Value of Soviet Arms Transfers to
Non-Communist Developing Countries

(Million US dollars)

	Agreements	Deliveries
Cumulative		
1955-68	5,495	4,585
1969	360	450
1970	1,150	995
1971	1,590	865
1972	1,635	1,215
1973	2,810	3,130
1974	4,225	2,310
1975	2,035	1,845
1976	3,375	2,575
1977	5,215	3,515
1978	1,765	3,825
TOTAL	29,655	25,310

Source: US Central Intelligence Agency, Communist Aid Activities in Non-Communist Less Developed Countries, 1978, Washington, DC, September 1979, p. 2.

As the trade and aid offensive matured and the Soviets became embroiled in the complexities and slow fruition of economic development, the military aid program undoubtedly appeared even more attractive to supplier and recipients alike. With the open eruption of the Sino-Soviet conflict in 1960, the Soviet Union embarked on a vastly expanded wave of military aid activity,[25] evidently at least partly in an effort to demonstrate militant Soviet support for the "national liberation movement" to the rest of the Communist world and the nonaligned countries as well. The momentum of the arms program carried over into 1961, as Moscow signed additional large agreements, highlighted by one with Indonesia as its dispute with the Netherlands intensified.[26] The incidence of new military aid commitments decreased over the next several years, perhaps to allow time for assimilation of equipment previously ordered.[27] Then, due to heavy demands for equipment resupply resulting from the Indo-Pakistani War of 1965 and the Arab-Israeli War of 1967, Soviet arms exports surged dramatically upward in the late 1960's.[28] Most of the arms aid and sales activity during the 1970's reflected the continuing military buildup and modernization in India after the December 1971 conflict with

392

TABLE 2

Regional Distribution of Soviet Arms Transfers to
Non-Communist Developing Countries, Cumulative 1955-78

(Million US dollars)

	Agreements	Deliveries
North Africa	4,965	3,875
Sub-Saharan Africa	3,900	2,750
East Asia	890	880
Latin America	650	630
Middle East	14,960	13,800
South Asia	4,290	3,375
TOTAL	29,655	25,310

Source: US Central Intelligence Agency, Communist Aid Activities in Non-Communist Less Developed Countries, 1978, Washington, DC, September 1979, p. 3.

Pakistan and in the Arab countries following the 1973 war and significant commitments to Angola, Ethiopia, Iran and Libya. Table 2 indicates a regional distribution of Soviet arms transfers over the course of the program. By the end of 1978 (the latest year for which comprehensive data are available), total Soviet military aid and sales commitments to nonaligned Third World countries approximated $30 billion.[29] (For additional statistical data on the program, see the tables in the Appendix.)

EFFECTIVENESS OF THE PROGRAM
IN RELATION TO SOVIET OBJECTIVES

Of the various types of foreign assistance employed by the Soviets—military, economic, and technical—military aid has proven to be the most dramatic and consequential. Besides directly contributing to the emergence, growth, and survival of nonaligned regimes, arms aid has fostered an image of the Soviet Union as a benign but powerful anticolonialist power. It has served as the primary Soviet vehicle for acquiring influence in regions important to Western interests, often providing the Soviets with political entree into countries where their role had hitherto been limited or nonexistent. Furthermore, military aid has often provided the opening wedge for a variety of diplomatic, trade, cultural, and other contacts which would have been difficult or impossible to achieve otherwise, such as in the Arab countries in the 1950's, India and Indonesia in the 1960's, and Ethiopia more recently.

The Soviets were quick to perceive in military aid unique advantages which economic assistance or traditional methods of diplomacy did not provide. Arms agreements were easy to plan and could be implemented quickly, whereas economic aid required lengthy, detailed preparations before program implementation could begin and results seen. Arms and equipment which Moscow agreed to provide were often available from existing stocks or could be diverted from current production, and deliveries could begin relatively quickly after a deal was made.[30] Soviet military technicians could rapidly be sent to a recipient country to begin assembling equipment and initiate training programs. More sophisticated equipment which required a higher level of instruction could be provided at a later date, in keeping with the progress of training programs conducted locally and in the Soviet Union. The ability of the recipient to maintain or use the equipment was usually not an overriding consideration.

Military assistance accordingly has proven to be one of Moscow's most effective, flexible, and durable instruments for establishing a significant presence in the nonaligned countries. By furnishing such assistance, Moscow became an advocate of a recipient's national aspirations and was able to facilely exploit this position to the detriment of Western interests. Arab-Israeli tensions, the Yemeni conflict with the United Kingdom over Aden, the Indo-Pakistani dispute, and Indonesia's territorial conflicts are examples of opportunities which were initially ripe for Soviet exploitation. The developing states generally sought Soviet arms for use against their neighbors or for prestige purposes and only occasionally, as in Afghanistan since 1978, has such a state procured Soviet weapons primarily to maintain internal security.

In addition to the broader objective of undermining Western influence in recipient countries, the Soviet leadership has used military assistance and sales to affect Western strategic interests and to eliminate Western military facilities and alliances adjacent to Soviet borders. Moscow sought to neutralize the Baghdad Pact (which subsequently evolved into CENTO) and SEATO so as to disrupt the West's "northern tier" defenses against the Soviet Union. Moscow at an early date provided military equipment to

Afghanistan to ensure that Kabul remained neutral and well-disposed toward its Soviet neighbor. Soviet aid to India was intended to diminish India's reliance on the West and to extend the Soviet presence into the subcontinent. Soviet arms aid to Southeast Asian and African countries was designed to strengthen Soviet influence at the expense not only of Western, but also of Chinese Communist, interests.

While the West has viewed its own military assistance to the developing countries as an influence for national stability, Moscow has regarded arms aid, *inter alia*, as a means for creating international instability and frequently has channeled arms to areas where the West has sought to limit or control military buildups. Arms shipments to rival Arab countries, for example, have been partially intended to keep the area divided and in ferment. Soviet sensitivity toward inter-Arab rivalries has been demonstrated by the care with which advanced weapons have been introduced to different recipients at about the same time.

A LIKELY SOVIET ASSESSMENT OF THE PROGRAM

As Moscow assesses the returns from nearly 25 years of military assistance, it must conclude that, on balance, the program has served Soviet interests reasonably well. Although the Soviet Union has acquired no ideological converts directly through its arms aid (with the partial, qualified exception of the Taraki-Amin regimes in Afghanistan), it has acquired a substantial though unquantifiable degree of influence in the Third World. An arms agreement with a developing country has been the point of departure for nearly every major Soviet advance in the Third World, beginning with the first Egyptian accord in 1955. Soviet support for nationalist governments has contributed substantially to the weakening or elimination of Western influence in many countries and has facilitated an expansion of Soviet presence into a number of strategic and sensitive areas. Moreover, through the acquisition of Soviet arms, a number of developing countries—notably Afghanistan, Algeria, Iraq, Libya, and Syria—now are largely or almost totally equipped with Soviet military equipment and are heavily dependent on Moscow for logistical and technical support.

Through its military training and technical assistance program, in conjunction with economic assistance and academic training, the

Soviet Union has exposed many of the nationals of these countries to a Communist orientation—an exposure which Moscow hopes will influence institutional developments occurring in the Third World. Moreover, the Soviets have established important relationships with military leaders, as well as junior officers who may eventually hold key positions in their countries.

Moscow undoubtedly has experienced its most salient successes among the Arab countries. For nearly a quarter of a century the Soviet leadership has taken advantage of the Arab-Israeli conflict almost to the point of displacing Western political influence among its major Arab clients, again with the dramatic exception of Egypt. Although Arab recipients occasionally criticize some of Moscow's policies, they have in effect retreated from their professed policies of nonalignment and tend to cooperate with Moscow on many international issues.

On the other hand, the military aid relationship has not provided the Soviets with strong or dependable control over their Arab clients, and the fortunes of local Communists have not improved as a result of the increased Soviet presence. Moreover, as a result of the Arab-Israeli wars of 1967 and 1973 the Soviets learned that a special relationship with arms recipients can lead to risks of unwanted military involvement and possible confrontation with the United States, diplomatic and prestige losses emanating from the defeat of their clients, and the cost of replacing lost equipment and restoring a damaged relationship.

Arms aid also has produced beneficial results for Moscow in South Asia. By serving as the principal arms supplier to Afghanistan for over two decades, the Soviet Union has helped to ensure the friendly neutrality, and more recently the active friendship, of that government. Soviet military sales to India have enhanced Moscow's stature in New Delhi and circumscribed that of the West, while helping to place the Soviets on India's side in the latter's dispute with Pakistan.

In the economic sphere, the Soviet arms aid program in general has generated closer trade and economic relations with most recipients. Where aid provisions have called for repayment in commodities, this has resulted in some trade reorientation from traditional markets to the Soviet Union. Where cash terms are required by Moscow, the recipients presumably can afford these expenditures. Although no definitive figures are available, it is probable that the bulk of credits extended by Moscow remains unpaid, and the Soviets in the end probably expect to write off much of this indebtedness. (One may ask what other choice do they have?) In the meantime, Moscow can continue to win additional political returns by generous debt rescheduling. In any event, existing indebtedness has not inhibited Moscow or its clients from entering into additional arms agreements.

Despite periodic setbacks or coolness in one client country or another, the overall impact of the arms aid program appears to lie on the positive side of the Soviet foreign policy ledger. While local Communists have not appreciably advanced their causes in the developing countries, the Soviet presence and influence in these areas have grown rapidly in the past two and a half decades to a level perhaps only dreamed of by Stalin. Moscow likely has concluded that, although the policies of aid recipients frequently have failed to parallel those of its own and though periodic polemics with some recipient states recur, the program has enhanced the Soviet Union's overall international position.

SOVIET INFLUENCE: HOW DURABLE?

How much effective leverage or influence the Soviets have gained in any particular area is, of course, difficult to measure. Still more difficult to ascertain is how much of any such gain can be attributed directly to military assistance and how much to broader political considerations.

While arms aid may have increased Moscow's potential influence in many developing states, it has not enabled the Soviets to control the domestic or foreign policies of these countries. Nor have the Soviets been able to reconcile the compatibility of their own objectives with those of their clients. Realizing this, Moscow for the most part has tried not to abuse the influence it has gained, and only rarely have the Soviets attempted to directly use their aid to exact political concessions.

A number of examples may serve to illustrate the limited nature of Soviet influence. Despite receiving large amounts of aid, Iraq and Syria have not hesitated to antagonize Moscow when vital interests of these countries were at stake. Algeria has remained aloof from developing overly close ties with the Soviet Union, and Libya has not hidden its suspicions of Soviet intentions in the Middle East.

397

Moreover, Arab moves to diversify sources of military equipment are challenging the effectiveness of the arms relationship as a policy lever. While the preponderance of Soviet-origin weaponry in Arab inventories will make diversification a slow process, even a moderate degree of success in the long run will erode potential Soviet influence.

At the same time, prominent Arab Communists have not been commensurately assisted by the Soviet presence. Many of Moscow's leading supporters in various Arab countries in fact have been purged or forced into exile. In one particularly dramatic example, Soviet-Sudanese relations were seriously weakened as a result of the Sudanese Communist Party's decimation following an unsuccessful left wing coup. No doubt particularly galling to the Politburo has been the inability of leaders which it viewed with favor—such as Kassem, Ben Bella, Nkrumah, and Sukarno—to remain in power, despite large infusions of Soviet aid.

The Soviet Union's most dramatic and outstanding failures have been in Egypt and Indonesia. The Soviet eviction from Egypt resulted in Moscow's loss of influence and position in the largest and most influential Arab state. Similarly, the Soviet ouster from Indonesia after the abortive Communist coup in 1965 was a serious blow to Moscow's strategic position in Southeast Asia. The Soviets to date have not been able to fully substitute for either of these critical losses.

CONFLICTING COMMITMENTS

Moscow has skillfully exploited the political openings provided by military aid by identifying itself with a popular cause or taking sides on a current issue. This has meant alienating some states to gain the friendship of others, but for the most part this probably has been a relatively uncomplicated calculation, especially in the earlier years of the program. Enmity with Israel was a small price for friendship with the Arab states, and the resentment of Malaysia was tolerable while Indonesia was being drawn closer to Moscow.

More recently, however, Moscow has discovered that the expansion of its military assistance program and its greater involvement in the international arena have led to conflicting commitments, complicating its bilateral relations and limiting its options. A number of examples could be cited, but the most obvious recent illustration has been Soviet involvement in Somalia and Ethiopia. When the Ethiopian regime appealed to Moscow for aid in 1977, the Soviets opted to exploit this opportunity at the expense of its 14-year aid relationship with Somalia. Not only did such action naturally sour Soviet bilateral relations with Somalia and result in the loss of important Soviet naval support facilities there, but it undoubtedly sensitized Moscow's other client states to the possibility of the Soviets' choosing sides in similar situations in the future.

Moscow also has probably viewed with concern the prospect of arms recipients using their weapons for purposes not always congruent with Soviet interests, as has been the experience of other major arms suppliers. There is no evidence to suggest that the Soviet Union has prompted any major recipient to engage in open hostilities. Soviet leaders, however, obviously are aware that their equipment has been acquired for potential use against "hostile" neighbors, and the possession of sizable amounts of arms encourages countries to engage in political or military activity that they otherwise might not have undertaken. Despite its comprehensive and longstanding military aid relationship with Syria, for example, Moscow was unable to dissuade the Syrian government from intervening against the leftist/Palestinian forces in Lebanon in 1976.

BASE RIGHTS

It is unclear to what extent the Soviets have directly used their aid program in attempts to secure the establishment of formal military bases, as opposed to limited base rights arrangements. Until Egypt abrogated such arrangements in March 1976, the Soviets enjoyed the use of naval repair and fuel storage facilities at Alexandria and Port Said to support their Mediterranean Fleet operations. Similarly in 1977, as a consequence of strains resulting from the Soviet arms buildup in Ethiopia, Somalia evicted the Soviets from access to naval repair, missile-handling, communications, and other facilities at Berbera.[31] The Soviets apparently are seeking similar support arrangements elsewhere in the area, but it is doubtful that they will enjoy the use of anything approaching their former facilities in Egypt and Somalia for the foreseeable future because of Arab and African sensitivities on this score. At the same time, it is doubtful that Soviet military planners contemplate extensive reliance on foreign facilities in their normal operations. To the extent that they have military interests in a recipient country, the Soviets' intentions appear to be to prevent military cooperation with the West, to seek the use of the recipient as a proxy for various initiatives against Western interests, and to improve opportunities for limited access by Soviet forces, when desired, to ports, airfields, and other facilities.

OUTLOOK FOR THE PROGRAM

The Soviet leadership undoubtedly will continue to use military aid and sales as a primary foreign policy instrument for maintaining and expanding Soviet influence in the Third World. Such aid has a more immediate impact and creates a greater degree of dependence than other forms of assistance. The bulk of the Soviet military aid flow probably will continue to be made available to countries which have been the principal recipients in the past and which consequently have developed a dependence on Soviet arms and political support. The Soviets will likely continue to upgrade the weapons in recipients' inventories to replace obsolete equipment and to meet competition. Such modernization of necessity will concomitantly ensure a continued requirement for technical assistance. Beyond these basic trends, the magnitude of Soviet arms aid and sales will depend on the vagaries of the international arena and events, such as regional tensions and conflict, which are largely unpredictable.

It seems likely that Soviet arms will continue to flow to the Arab countries, where Soviet prestige is deeply involved and the political cost of "letting down" the recipients would impact significantly on Moscow. In South Asia, Afghanistan and India will continue to receive a high volume of equipment to maintain the large investments made and influence achieved. The tensions and uncertainties of domestic and regional politics in Africa no doubt will perpetuate prospects for the Soviets to make political and perhaps strategic gains at the expense of the West, as well as China.

In Latin America, where Moscow has established an active arms sales relationship with Peru, in addition to its longstanding connection with Cuba, ongoing tensions may offer additional opportunities for the Soviet Union. Intensifying desires for modern weaponry on the part of some Latin states, frustrated in their attempts to procure modern equipment from traditional sources, may increase their receptivity to Soviet aid blandishments.

The Soviet leaders appear confident that political and economic changes taking place in the developing countries and in the general international arena are favorable to the increase of Soviet influence and, moreover, are irreversible. Moscow appears to be relying on the cumulative effect of its diplomacy, trade, and especially its economic and military aid programs, to make at least some of the more important developing countries materially dependent and politically tractable.

ENDNOTES

1. US Arms Control and Disarmament Agency (ACDA), *The International Transfer of Conventional Arms*, Washington, DC: US Government Printing Office, April 1974, p. 37.

2. Amnon Sella, "Struggle for Air Supremacy: October 1973-December 1975," *Journal of the Royal United Service Organization* (London), December 1976, p. 34.

3. ACDA, *The International Transfer of Conventional Arms*, p. 27.

4. *Ibid.*, p. 37.

5. US Central Intelligence Agency, National Foreign Assessment Center (NFAC), *Communist Aid to Less Developed Countries of the Free World, 1977* , Washington, DC, November 1978, p. 1.

6. US Central Intelligence Agency, NFAC, *Communist Aid Activities in Non-Communist Less Developed Countries, 1978,* Washington, DC, September 1979, p. 3.

7. Leo Heiman, "Moscow's Export Arsenal: The Soviet Bloc and the Middle Eastern Arms Race," *East Europe,* May 1964, p. 3.

8. *Ibid.*, pp. 3-4.

9. *Ibid.*, p. 5.

10. *Ibid.*

11. *Philadelphia Inquirer,* August 29, 1979

12. See Roger F. Pajak, *Soviet Arms Aid in the Middle East,* Washington, DC: Georgetown Center for Strategic and International Studies, 1976, p. 4.

13. US Central Intelligence Agency, *Communist Aid Activities in Non-Communist Less Developed Countries, 1978,* p. 5.

14. *Ibid.*, pp. 3, 5.

15. "Die Sowjetische Militarhilfe—Der Ursprung Internationaler Konflikte," *Wehr und Wirtschaft,* May 1961, translated in *Military Review,* February 1962, pp. 34-35.

16. US Central Intelligence Agency, *Communist Aid Activities in Non-Communist Less Developed Countries, 1978,* p. 3.

17. *Ibid.*, p. 4.

18. Heiman, p. 5.

19. S.H. Steinberg, ed., *The Statesman's Yearbook: 1960-61,* New York: St. Martin's Press, 1960, p. 795; Arnold Rivkin, *Africa and the West,* New York: Praeger, 1962, p. 94.

20. Ian C.C. Graham, "The Indo-Soviet MIG Deal and Its International Repercussions," *Asian Survey,* May 1964, pp. 823-830.

21. For a further discussion of data sources, see US Arms Control and Disarmament Agency, *World Military Expenditures and Arms Transfers,1968-1977,* Washington, DC: US Government Printing Office, October 1979, pp. 23-24.

22. *The New York Times,* April 8, 1958.

23. Walter Z. Laqueur, *Soviet Union and the Middle East,* New York: Praeger, 1959, pp. 272-273.

24. *The New York Times,* January 15, 1958.

25. Guy Pauker, "The Soviet Challenge in Indonesia," *Foreign Affairs,* July 1962, p. 615.

26. *Ibid.*, p. 616.

27. SIPRI, *The Arms Trade with the Third World,* New York: Humanities Press, 1971, p. 190.

28. *Ibid.*, pp. 190-191.

29. US Central Intelligence Agency, NFAC, *Communist Aid Activities in Non-Communist Less Developed Countries, 1978,* p. 2.

30. In the October 1973 Middle East War, for example, equipment was taken from Soviet troop units stationed in Hungary and airlifted to Arab forces. See Roger F. Pajak, "Soviet Arms and Egypt," *Survival,* July/August 1975, p. 170.

31. US Central Intelligence Agency, NFAC, *Communist Aid to Less Developed Countries of the Free World, 1977,* p. 19.

APPENDIX

STATISTICAL TABLES

TABLE 3

Major Nonaligned Recipients of Soviet Arms Deliveries,
Cumulative 1967-76

(Million US dollars)

Rank	Country	Amount	Percent of Country's Total Arms Imports
1	Egypt	2,365	84
2	Syria	2,015	89
3	Iraq	1,795	73
4	India	1,365	81
5	Libya	1,005	55
6	Iran	611	12
7	Algeria	315	71
8	Angola	190	60
9	Somalia	181	98
10	Southern Yemen	151	92
11	Afghanistan	100	32

Source: US Arms Control and Disarmament Agency, World Military Expenditures and Arms Transfers, 1967-1976, Washington, DC: US Government Printing Office, 1978, pp. 158-159.

404

TABLE 4

Military Personnel from Nonaligned, Developing Countries
Trained in Communist Countries, Cumulative 1955-78[1]

(Number of Persons)

	Total	USSR	Eastern Europe	China
Total	52,890	43,790	5,965	3,135
AFRICA	17,525	13,420	1,400	2,705
NORTH AFRICA:	3,735	3,385	335	15
Algeria	2,260	2,045	200	15
Libya	1,330	1,265	65	...
Other	145	75	70	...
SUB-SAHARAN AFRICA:	13,790	10,035	1,065	2,690
Angola	60	55	5	...
Benin	20	20	...	...
Burundi	75	75	...	...
Cameroon	125	...	...	125
Congo	855	355	85	415
Equatorial Guinea	200	200	...	...
Ethiopia	1,640	1,190	450	...
Ghana	180	180	...	...
Guinea	1,290	870	60	360
Guinea-Bissau	100	100	...	...
Mali	415	355	10	50
Nigeria	730	695	35	...
Sierra Leone	150	...	...	150
Somalia	2,585	2,395	160	30
Sudan	550	330	20	200
Tanzania	2,855	1,820	10	1,025
Togo	55	...	...	55
Zaire	175	...	...	175
Zambia	130	85	...	45
Other	1,600	1,310	230	60
EAST ASIA:	9,300	7,590	1,710	...
Indonesia	9,270	7,560	1,710	...
Kampuchea	30	30	...	...
LATIN AMERICA:	725	725	...	...
Peru	725	725	...	...

[1]Data refers to the estimated number of persons departing for training.
Numbers are rounded to the nearest five.

405

TABLE 4 (Continued)

	Total	USSR	Eastern Europe	China
MIDDLE EAST:	18,115	15,630	2,485	...
Egypt	6,250	5,665	585	...
Iran	315	315	...	...
Iraq	4,330	3,650	680	...
North Yemen	1,180	1,180	...	...
South Yemen	1,095	1,075	20	...
Syria	4,495	3,745	1,200	...
SOUTH ASIA:	7,225	6,425	370	430
Afghanistan	4,010	3,725	285	...
Bangladesh	485	445	...	40
India	2,285	2,200	85	...
Pakistan	430	45	NA	385
Sri Lanka	15	10	...	5

Source: US Central Intelligence Agency, Communist Aid Activities in Non-Communist Less Developed Countries, 1978, Washington, DC, September 1979, pp. 4, 5.

406

TABLE 5

Soviet and East European Military Technicians
in Nonaligned, Developing Countries, 1978

(Number of Persons[1])

Total	12,070
AFRICA	6,575
NORTH AFRICA:	2,760
Algeria	1,000
Libya	1,750
Morocco	10
SUB-SAHARAN AFRICA:	3,815
Angola	1,300
Equatorial Guinea	40
Ethiopia	1,400
Guinea	100
Guinea-Bissau	65
Mali	180
Mozambique	230
Other	500
LATIN AMERICA:	150
Guyana	...
Peru	150
MIDDLE EAST:	4,495
Iraq	1,200
North Yemen	155
South Yemen	550
Syria	2,580
Other	10
SOUTH ASIA:	850
Afghanistan	700
Bangladesh	...
India	150

[1]Minimum estimates of the number of persons present for a period of one month or more. Numbers are rounded to the nearest five.

Source: US Central Intelligence Agency, Communist Aid Activities in Non-Communist Less Developed Countries, 1978, Washington, DC, September 1979, p. 4.

TABLE 6

Major Weapons Delivered to Nonaligned, Developing Countries,
By Selected Type and Primary Supplier,
Cumulative 1973-77

Equipment Type	Total	United States	Soviet Union	France	United Kingdom	China	Italy
			TOTALS				
LAND ARMAMENTS							
Tanks and Self-Propelled Guns	15,411	4,921	7,300	585	1,015	1,580	10
Artillery (Over 100 mm.)	7,506	3,546	3,140	130	30	310	350
Armored Personnel Carriers and Armored Cars	14,249	7,104	5,510	1,145	90	170	230
NAVAL CRAFT							
Major Surface Combatants	90	73	5	–	12	–	–
Minor Surface Combatants	414	134	50	45.	120	35	30
Submarines	36	18	5	–	8	4	1
Guided Missile Patrol Boats	51	–	44	7	–	–	–
AIRCRAFT							
Combat Aircraft, Supersonic	3,181	996	1,670	300	15	200	–
Combat Aircraft, Subsonic	1,248	793	325	5	50	75	–
Other Aircraft	1,640	750	200	70	270	60	290
Helicopters	2,562	1,202	410	550	40	40	320
MISSILES							
Surface-to-Air Missiles	20,219	4,459	14,870	270	620	–	–

Source: US Arms Control and Disarmament Agency, World Military Expenditures and
Arms Transfers, 1968-1977, Washington, DC, US Government Printing Office,
1979, p. 159.

20

SOVIET INVOLVEMENT IN THE THIRD WORLD:
IMPLICATIONS OF US POLICY ASSUMPTIONS

Keith A. Dunn

While the Soviet Union has been directly or indirectly involved in Third World politics for many years, the recent successes of pro-Marxist-Leninist forces in Angola, Ethiopia, Vietnam, Laos, People's Democratic Republic of Yemen, and Cambodia as well as the Soviet invasion of Afghanistan have caused a rejuvenated interest in the USSR's role in such crises. The increasing instability and violent disorder that has permeated the Third World within recent years has directly affected bilateral relations between the superpowers causing each one to question—rather vociferously at times—the motivations, involvement, and intentions of the other in a particular region. Moreover, there is a growing apprehension in some government and academic circles that the USSR is now more brazen than in the past and is willing to take more risks in its drive to expand Soviet worldwide power and influence.

Frequently, this latter apprehension has been related to the phenomenal quantitative and qualitative growth of Soviet strategic nuclear capabilities. As long as the United States had and was perceived to have strategic nuclear superiority, hardly anyone questioned America's ability to protect its basic national interests. Even though the USSR has always had a quantitative conventional superiority, the American nuclear umbrella was viewed as the great equalizer. The US nuclear force deterred the USSR from military attacks not only upon the continental United States but also upon America's closest allies in Europe and Asia. Also, America's strategic nuclear superiority combined with its refusal to adopt a no-first use of nuclear weapons position helped to discourage the USSR from undertaking adventurous actions which might bring the United States and the USSR into direct military conflict.

Currently, many analysts wonder if the former constraints upon the USSR are still operative. Neither of the superpowers can obtain nuclear superiority in the same manner as the United States did during the 1950's and 1960's; the future will be an era of strategic nuclear equality in gross terms but with asymmetries in particular means of delivery. This situation, it is feared, may encourage the USSR either by direct or proxy pressure to initiate actions which are inimical to America's long-term interests. While such activities would not necessarily be limited to the Third World, it probably would be an area of primary Soviet interest. These misgivings about future Soviet actions have caused the Chairman of the Joint Chiefs of Staff to comment:

> Although the Soviets traditionally have been very cautious in the direct use of their own military forces outside their immediate sphere of control, their present position of approximate strategic nuclear equality, with momentum toward a situation of possible overall military superiority, could create further incentives for greater risks.
>
> The greater the Soviet perception of freedom of action in the military realm, the greater the danger that they might attempt to exert the leverage of military power (threatened or used) in extending their economic, diplomatic or ideological influence.[1]

General Jones is not alone in his worries. Former Secretary of State Henry Kissinger has criticized the Carter Administration for its inability "to convey a clear perception of where it stands" on the issues. He has claimed that the Administration "sometimes conveys the impression that we are more sympathetic to elements that oppose the people who have heretofore been our friends than to our friends."[2] Senate Minority Leader Howard Baker has linked his opposition to the SALT II Treaty to the overall US-Soviet military relationship including, "the situation in Africa, the situation in Cuba, the potentially troublesome situation in the

Arabian Gulf, in Southeast Asia and the massive buildup of Soviet conventional armaments."[3]

No thoughtful observer would want to denigrate the extent of Soviet involvement in the Third World. Nor would one want to underestimate the potential damaging implications for American foreign and defense policies. Nevertheless, it is important to keep the recent Soviet "successes" in some sort of overall perspective. Undoubtedly Soviet opportunities and involvements in some areas of the world are greater than they may have ever been. But with benefits and potential successes also come costs and disadvantages. Too often, however, the latter are disregarded and the USSR is prematurely depicted as "winning" in a zero-sum game.

In an attempt to assess the implications of Soviet behavior for US foreign policy, this essay will identify and discuss some of the more often cited assumptions concerning Soviet behavior in the Third World.[4] The list is far from exhaustive, and the assumptions are listed in no particular order. These assumptions are just some of the more important and common ones that have permeated some American policymaking and academic circles. The analysis of them may help to sharpen "American perspectives regarding Soviet opportunities and capabilities."[5]

Assumption One: Somehow the Soviets are Primarily Responsible for Events Which are Adverse to American Interests.

As John Kenneth Galbraith has argued, two overriding fears have pervaded all aspects of American political life: "one is the fear of Communism; the other is the fear of being soft on Communism."[6] Those preoccupations have made it difficult—if not impossible—to develop a coherent, consistent policy toward the USSR. Nevertheless, almost all major US foreign policy initiatives in the post-World War II era have been related to American policymakers' perceptions of the USSR. Even the recent normalization of relations with China has been widely characterized as an attempt "to play the China card" in the poker game with Moscow. Moreover, American force posturing, planning, and programming is predicated upon the intelligence community's assessment of Soviet capabilities and the policymakers' evaluation of Soviet intentions.

Given the military strength of the USSR, no prudent policy could belittle its significance for American foreign or defense policy. The

USSR is America's main political, ideological, and military adversary and is currently the only nation which is militarily capable of inflicting significant damage upon US territory. However, the obsession with the USSR and communism has often desensitized Americans and caused them to seek simple solutions— the Russians "must be" involved—for complex international events. In particular, the United States has continually underestimated the importance of nationalism and its powerful motivating appeal for the Third World.

A contemporary example is the ongoing Iranian Revolution. Since the autumn of 1978, there have been numerous reports implying that the USSR contributed to the events which exacerbated that crisis; the first question usually asked of American policymakers was, "what is the extent of Soviet involvement?" While the official American position was, as President Carter explained in February 1979, that the "revolution in Iran is the product of deep social, political, religious, and economic factors growing out of the history of Iran itself," many analysts—both inside and outside government—believed that Moscow could not be absolved of all responsibility.[7] Former Secretary of State Henry Kissinger struck a responsive chord in many peoples' minds when he told an *Economist* reporter: "No one can claim that a Soviet decision started the upheavals that led to the departure of the Shah. But somebody who starts a rockslide nonetheless must be held responsible for the impact of stones that he himself did not throw."[8] In other words, whether the USSR was or was not directly involved in the crisis it must share in the blame.

While Moscow disliked the Shah's close ties with the United States and probably would have preferred a more sympathetic government in Teheran, one should not mix desire with results. While neither nation completely trusted the other, it appears that, by 1978, they had agreed to coexist as peaceful neighbors, particularly as long as Iran, Saudi Arabia, and the Gulf Sheikhdoms did not form a hostile coalition against Moscow's friends in the Middle East. If negotiated long-term agreements are any indication of the Kremlin's perception of the Shah's longevity, it would appear that Moscow believed there was no imminent crisis in store for Iran. Prior to the Shah's departure, Moscow and Teheran signed a new trade and economic agreement and discussed expanding their joint economic relations with several major new projects.[9]

Moreover, it appears that the USSR, like the United States, was surprised that Ayatollah Rouhallah Khomeini was able to organize such an effective anti-Shah movement in such a short period of time. Moscow's Marxist-Leninist perspective, which emphasizes the economic class nature of conflicts, inhibited the USSR from properly evaluating the religious motivations underpinning the anti-Shah movement. Throughout the fall and winter of 1978 commentators continually downplayed the importance of the Islamic element in the crisis. *Kommunist* claimed that "the religious factor has been of only secondary importance ...."[10] *Izvestiia* argued that the apparent growing Moslem involvement in the crisis was a "religious guise"; the real motivations of the Iranian people were socioeconomic and a concern for who would determine Iran's destiny—the imperialists or Iranians.[11] It was not until the end of January 1979, after the Shah had departed Teheran and the interim government of Shahpour Bakhtiar was disintegrating, that Moscow stopped describing Khomeini as one of the religious opposition leaders and began to refer to him as "the main figure in the popular anti-Shah movement" and "the recognized leader of the Iranian people ...."[12]

Even though the indications are strong that Moscow was just as surprised as was Washington at the way Iranian events developed, initial American reactions appear to contradict the stated Administration position that the Iranian Revolution was wholly a domestic phenomenon. For instance, the January F-15 shuttle to Saudi Arabia was primarily intended to show that the United States could militarily support an ally in the area if the need should ever rise. In February, Secretary of Defense Brown visited Riyahd apparently carrying with him a long shopping list of military equipment which the United States was willing to sell the Saudis. He even discussed establishing a base in the area—an idea which the Saudis rejected.[13] The main purpose of the Brown visit was, as the Secretary stated at a state dinner in Riyahd, to demonstrate that the "American government is even more determined to provide the strength to meet *external threats* to the kingdom."[14] The Department of Defense began contingency planning to create a new 100,000 personnel corps which would include 40,000 combat troops to use in defense of American interests in sensitive areas. Also, the Departments of Defense and Navy advocated an increased naval presence in the Indian Ocean, probably at Diego Garcia. This

413

increased presence on a permanent basis would include an aircraft carrier, destroyers, amphibious assault ships with helicopters and armed P-3's in order to assure friendly states in the area "that we need them and will protect them," as one Navy official said.[15]

The question is, however, to protect them from whom or what? The overt American responses to the Iranian Revolution were primarily actions to protect American friends in the region from external threats. But the most significant problems that confront Iran and many of the other Persian Gulf/Arabian Peninsula states, as well as other Third World nations, cannot be solved or ameliorated by F-15's, aircraft carriers, or lists of available military equipment hardware. They are internal problems of modernization: growing unemployment, unfulfilled expectations, disparity of wealth, destruction of traditional values, corruption, a gap between economic reality and expectations, and restricted participation in the process of government in societies which are often monarchical and authoritarian.

Clearly, not all upheavals which occur in the world can be reduced, as Raymond Garthoff has said, "to fit the procrustean level of Soviet-American politico-military confrontation."[16] To do so is not only to fail to learn from experience but also to misunderstand the complexities of international events.

Assumption Two: The USSR has no Legitimate "Interests" Necessitating its Involvement in the Third World.

This assumption is founded upon the belief that the USSR is virtually self-sufficient in natural resources; its historical interests have been continental, rather than global like America's; it is not dependent upon overseas trade for its economic survival; and it does not "need" flexible military forces deployable outside the European continent to protect its closest allies or core interests. Therefore, the USSR must be involved for disruptive rather than constructive purposes in the Third World.

There are several obvious flaws in this assumption. First, it depends upon a definition of "interests" which is American and not Soviet; it is a reverse mirror image of justifications for US global involvement. From a Soviet perspective, however, it is not only a legitimate interest but a Soviet duty to support "progressive" anticolonial factions which are fighting wars of national liberation. Second, it essentially postulates an overarching

414

reason for Soviet interest in all Third World countries. In fact, as Roger Kanet has concluded, Soviet Third World policy is characterized chiefly by its diversity "rather than developing a single unified policy towards the Third World."[17]

But the most important flaw is that the USSR has never accepted that its interests in the Third World are any less legitimate than those of the West. In fact, Moscow believes that it is one of the rights of a global power to participate in events and decisions which shape the events that occur in other parts of the world. Historically, all other world powers have played such a role, and, since World War II, Moscow has increasingly emphasized that it sees this as its legitimate right. This is why, as early as 1945, Soviet representatives asked for a trusteeship in Tripolitana in order to establish a naval base so that USSR could "take her share" in the inevitable world trade which would develop in the postwar period. As Foreign Minister V.M. Molotov told the American Secretary of State in September 1945, because of "the part she has played in the war," Moscow "had a [moral]right to play a more active part in the fate of the Italian Colonies than any rank and file member of the United Nations ...."[18] Also, Moscow's perception of itself as a major world power explains in part why the Russians angrily chafed when they were eliminated from effective participation in the Allied Control Commissions in Italy and Japan. As Stalin once told W. Averell Harriman, the USSR "had its self-respect as a sovereign state" and it was distasteful to be treated as a "piece of furniture" in the Far East. Since the Soviet Union was one of the strongest postwar powers, Stalin objected that General Douglas MacArthur simply told the Russian representatives what he and the American government intended to do in Japan rather than consulting and soliciting Soviet advice. Harriman captured the essence of Stalin's 1945 concerns when he cabled the State Department: "Being new rich with a lingering inferiority complex and feeling gauche uncertainty in international society, Russia is inordinately sensitive re appearance as well as substance of prestige."[19]

Much of the concern about being treated as one of the world's major powers is still present today. Andrei Gromyko has regularly stated that the USSR is now so powerful and important that "no major international issue can, as a matter of fact, be decided now without the USSR's participation."[20] This helps to explain the Kremlin's generally dim view of Sadat's peace initiative and the

Camp David accords, since those moves circumvented the Soviet-American joint declaration of October 1977 and left Moscow with virtually no participation in that peace process. One of many reasons the Soviets rejected the Carter Administration's radical March 1977 SALT II proposal was a belief that the United States had unilaterally rejected previous commitments and refused to negotiate with the USSR "on the basis of equality." Instead, the Carter Administration publicly announced its SALT proposal and sent its Secretary of State to Moscow not to negotiate but to get the Soviet signature on the American proposals.[21] Likewise, much of Moscow's vehement reaction to the human rights issue is a result of its hurt "ideological-national pride." As Adam Ulam has argued: "How could the Soviet Union, at the pinnacle of its power, give even an appearance of tolerating such interference in its internal affairs ...?"[22] Finally, Admiral Sergei Gorshkov has with great frequency commented that one of the primary reasons and motivating factors for the growth of the Soviet Navy is that all influential world powers have had strong navies:

> Navies have always played a great role in strengthening the independence of states whose territories are washed by seas and oceans, since they were an important instrument of policy. Naval might has been one of the factors which has enabled individual states to advance into the ranks of the great powers. Moreover, history shows that those states which do not have naval forces at their disposal have not been able to hold the status of a great power for very long.[23]

In other words, the USSR perceives that it does have justified reasons for involvement in Third World politics. Moscow would like to reduce American presence and influence in the Third World and increase that of the Soviet Union. Because it is a global power, Moscow's political, economic, and military engagement in the developing world is, at least from a Soviet perspective, no more illegitimate than America's. It is worthwhile to keep this distinction in mind because to assume the USSR has no right to participate directly or indirectly in the decisions which determine Third World outcomes makes it difficult to affect future Soviet actions in the direction of peaceful solutions to international problems.

Assumption Three: The Soviet Union now has a Major Capability to Project Military Force Far From its Homeland.
There is a growing concern in the American defense community that the USSR has significantly improved its "power projection"

and "global reach" capabilities. With these enhanced capabilities it is feared that the USSR "has the potential to interfere with US interest around the globe ..." and "given the Soviet propensity to fish in troubled waters, could precipitate a confrontation which neither side wants."[24]

No responsible observer believes that Moscow's enormous military investment for the last 10-15 years has resulted in a "Potemkin Village" force. As the invasion of Afghanistan indicates, the Soviet military is large, powerful, and useable in particular scenarios. However, much of the discussion about growing Soviet capabilities has been characterized by a failure to define the basic terminology.

Although most American strategists realize that "power projection" is a broad term that includes the ability to influence, they most often use it in a much narrower fashion: the capability to insert military forces into an area when opposed by a hostile adversary. This is the sense in which it will be used here.

The ability to convert theoretical military capabilities to actual military power is more difficult than some observers have suggested. A nation's military force structure, its geopolitical situation, the threats for which the military force was primarily designed to counter, and the types of military units which exist present all nations with particular opportunities but also constraints. For example, Soviet armored divisions and their tactics have been optimized for a European land battle which has a high potential to become nuclear. Soviet emphasis upon speed, mobility, preemption, unit replacement, limited organic logistical support, large mobilizable reserves to augment understrength divisions, and a preponderance of armored/mechanized units are military attributes tailored for Euope and thus make ground divisions inherently less "projectible."

Most of the discussions about Soviet enhanced force projection capabilities, however, have not focused on the Red Army but rather the Soviet Navy and its overseas "bases" and new "blue-water" capabilities. Again much of the cause of the debate is a failure to define what is being discussed. Specifically, in too many instances, the term naval "base" is used in a vague and improper fashion. As the case of "power projection," the term naval "base" has a rather definite meaning to most American strategists. As defined by the Joint Chiefs of Staff, it includes the activities and facilities for which the US Navy "has operating responsibilities, together with interior lines of communication and the minimum surrounding area necessary for local security."[25] Moreover, normally it is considered that American forces have either permanent or negotiated long-term access to a "base." Places like Subic Bay, Diego Garcia, and even Guantanamo are naval bases. The USSR has no such similar overseas ports anywhere in the world.

It does have access to land facilities for docking rights, port calls, repairs, and replenishment of depleted stocks at places like Vishakhapatnam, Um Qasr, most recently Cam Ranh Bay, and until 2 years ago Berbera. However, there is apparently no negotiated permanence to the Soviet presence. Also, the Soviets have used anchorages in sheltered international waters as floating logistic and supply facilities. While these accommodations have been helpful, in a conflict they would not be able to support the long-term needs of the navy, and, more importantly, they could be readily destroyed.[26]

But even if we hypothesize the worst case from a Western perspective and assume that in the future the Soviet Union does obtain true overseas bases, this would ameliorate some problems but would exacerbate others. Much of the Soviet Union's naval strategy is determined by its geographical location which has forced Moscow to maintain four separate fleets. None of those fleets have uninhibited access to the open seas. Each one of the fleets must bypass chokepoints that unfriendly nations control. However, it is often argued that if the USSR could obtain real overseas bases its warships could be forwardly deployed and thus avoid the problem of bypassing the chokepoints during a conflict. This is a spurious argument. Since resupply vessels would still have to traverse those chokepoints, the Soviet Navy would remain in a vulnerable position.[27]

Moreover, acquisition of true overseas bases would necessitate a significant change in the Soviet Union's naval posture. Currently the Soviet Navy's most credible capabilities occur at the ends of a continuum. At one extreme the USSR can display its naval power, carry out demonstration deployments (*Okean* '70 and '75 are good examples), react to localized shooting incidents, or engage in a brief "war at sea." At the other extreme, the Soviet Navy has the capability to participate in a strategic nuclear war. However, between these two extremes there is a large "gray area" which includes the ability to oppose naval intervention, participate in a prolonged theater conflict, engage in an extended "war at sea," or fight an all-out conventional war.[28]

If the USSR intended to alter its current Navy posture in a way to handle those "gray area" missions and to move away from its sea denial role toward sea control mission, analysts would observe new trends in ship construction rates. Since navies are high cost items and require long construction lead-times, one would expect to see some major changes in Soviet naval construction rates. However, no alterations are now apparent. Soviet ship designers and builders still tend to concentrate their efforts in two traditional non-"force projection" areas: strategic nuclear submarines and antisubmarine warfare.[29]

Although Soviet military forces are primarily oriented toward a European contingency which constrains its ability to "project" Soviet power, Moscow does have the capability to use its military to influence the outcome of events in Third World nations. In an emergency the USSR has the proven capability to provide equipment and supplies to its allies, friends, and proxies, when unopposed by hostile forces. During the 1973 Middle East War, Moscow flew 930 sorties in order to supply its Egyptian ally with 15 million tons of supplies.[30] More recently, over a 3-month period in 1977-78, the USSR airlifted 600 armored vehicles, numerous tanks, and over 400 artillery pieces to Ethiopia.[31] During the Angolan crisis, the more than 25,000 Cubans, which Aeroflot airlifted to Launda, played a determining role in the outcome of that conflict.

This relatively new Soviet capability is quite important because in many contingencies a limited input of force can greatly affect the military situation. Tanks and aircraft, which are antiquated by American and Soviet standards, can provide quantum technological advantages to one contender when the other adversary has no tanks or aircraft. Moreover, the mere appearance of power can have an impact upon the perceptions of developing nations. Although the differences between the Soviet *Kiev* vertical takeoff and landing (VTOL) ship and the USS *Nimitz* or *Enterprise* strike carriers are so immense as to make them nearly incomparable, quite frequently "in a world of unsophisticated propaganda targets, a carrier is a carrier is a carrier ...."[32]

Kenneth Booth has made a powerful case that analysts should

not dismiss the importance of Soviet naval deployments in particular regions of the world just because they are not significant threats to Western navies. Limited deployments of small naval forces may have significant political and diplomatic results.[33] Nevertheless, policymakers must keep in mind to what they are responding. The appropriate response to Soviet actions that have a military character but are primarily focused on influencing events should be much different than the response to a Soviet attempt to inject its military forces into a situation. The current analysis on Soviet "power projection" capabilities needs to be refined and sharpened.

Assumption Four: Change/Instability is Always Good for the USSR and Bad for the United States.

Of all the assumptions discussed here, this is one which probably most closely approximates reality. It should not be so but unfortunately the United States has generally aligned itself with the status quo and opposed major changes in the sociopolitical structure of developing nations fearing that radical change would bring anti-American governments to power. As a result, American actions have had an element of the self-fulfilling prophecy in them. Washington's past supportive arrangements with colonial powers have made many developing nations suspicious of its intentions and interests.

From the Kremlin's perspective there is also a great deal of truth to this assumption. Economic, political, and military disorder in the developing world inevitably must hurt US and Western interests from a Soviet view because the West has been the "imperialist colonizer" of the world. Indeed, the USSR believes that the capitalist and socialist worlds are locked in a constant struggle for survival—a struggle which socialism will ultimately win. As Boris Ponomarev, candidate member of the CPSU Politburo, has commented, "if the influence of socialism on the course of events grows, this means that the resources of the imperialist and reactionary forces will diminish correspondingly, and the resources of peace, national independence, and social progress will increase."[34] Individual relapses may temporarily occur but the "general crisis of capitalism" will inevitably cause Western capitalism to fall apart. Thus, a capitalist setback is a socialist success by its very nature. And, from a Soviet perspective, progress in the struggle against colonialism has improved dramatically during the last 10 to 15 years. By one calculation the ratio of victories to defeats has improved from 60:62 from 1956-60 to 33:12 in the first half of the 1970's "in favor of the forces of progress and national liberation."[35]

A long abiding Soviet problem, however, has been how to balance its national interests with the struggle against capitalism. When national interests clash with revolutionary interests which one should predominate? China asked Moscow the question nearly two decades ago and the Soviet response contributed to the Sino-Soviet split. Since historically Moscow has been quite willing to sacrifice local Communists and their interests for good relations with national regimes,[36] it would appear that Moscow does differentiate and does not see all destabilizing trends as leading to positive benefits for the USSR.

Assumption Five: Soviet Presence and Influence Has Significantly Expanded.

The first part of this assumption is quite obvious. The other part, however, is less clear but is often accepted due to the Soviet Union's increased presence. There is no question that Soviet involvement and presence in the Third World has increased dramatically over the last two decades. Although Soviet economic aid to developing nations has declined in recent years, its arms sales programs have remained at near-record highs. In 1977 alone, Moscow signed agreements for $4.2 billion and delivered $3.2 billion in arms to the Third World. Only in 1974 were sales higher and that was because Moscow had to restock badly depleted Middle East stocks in the aftermath of the Middle East War.[37]

Moreover, a significant number of Soviet and East European military personnel, not to mention Cuban, have been sent to Third World nations to train local forces in combat techniques and to assemble, operate, and maintain the influx of new military equipment. In 1977, there were more than 10,000 Soviet and East European military technicians in the Third World; over half of the military technicians were in Africa. Between 1976 and 1977, Soviet and East European advisers increased in the Third World by more than 10 percent.[38]

As a result of this increased Soviet presence, it is becoming more common to hear assertions like "the importance of American friendship" or "American influence" is on the decline in the post-Vietnam era. On the other hand, Soviet "power and influence" is seen to be expanding, at the expense of the West in general and the United States in particular. Moreover, as one former member of Kissinger's National Security Council has recently argued, the increased Soviet presence and arms deliveries to the Third World—Africa particularly—is intended "to cement dependency relationships," directly influence the course of armed struggles, and "obtain leverage over states hosting guerrillas."[39]

As was noted earlier, increased Soviet presence and involvement in the Third World is an indisputable fact. However, the level and extent of Soviet influence upon the events and nations of the developing world is less obvious.

As K.G. Holsti and others have argued, influence is not something that one nation holds over another like a club. Rather influence is an ongoing process by which one nation tries to convince another to take or not to take particular actions. It is not a one-sided relationship but a mutually interactive process. Thus, it is not necessarily true that the nation which has the most obvious and visible economic, military, or political capabilities will automatically have the most "influence" in this dynamic relationship. If influence were one-sided, the United States would have been able to convince the Shah to participate in holding down oil prices in the aftermath of the 1973-74 oil embargo.[40]

Two recent works, one by Alvin Z. Rubinstein and the other by Robert H. Donaldson, quite clearly illustrate that an extensive presence is no assurance of Soviet influence.[41] Rubinstein has concluded that between 1967 and 1972 Moscow adjusted more than did Cairo to the demands of their relationship, that the USSR had limited influence upon any important Egyptian foreign or domestic decisions, and that Moscow was unable "to mobilize or strengthen the position of Egyptian officials or interest groups disposed to accommodate to Soviet desires."[42] Likewise, Donaldson has concluded that, since 1967, there were only two very minor instances where the Soviet Union caused India to take actions which it otherwise would not have taken.

The history of Soviet (and American) involvement in the Third World is replete with other examples of the Kremlin's inability, despite extensive economic and military investment in a country, to curb actions which are antithetical to its long-term interests.

Moscow's expulsion from Indonesia, Somalia, Sudan, Egypt, and Ghana, the Iraqi government's recent execution of 21 Communists for trying to reestablish party cells in the military, and China's total break with the USSR in the 1960's are other examples of the USSR's lack of influence over its erstwhile allies.

To define American interests in various areas of the world in terms of Soviet presence or nonpresence is to misunderstand the dynamics of the influence relationship. It makes US policy reactive rather than deliberate. Worst of all, it can put American policymakers in the uncomfortable position of supporting less popular and narrow-based movements, as in Angola in 1975, primarily because they are anti-Communist and oppose the USSR, and not because they meet any other standards compatible with American national interests.

Assumption Six: Some Grand Design Lies Behind all Soviet Actions.

A major and influential school of thought still exists which works from an assumption—most often implied but occasionally stated overtly—that the best way to understand Soviet behavior is to view it as motivated by deep-rooted imperialist impulses combined with Communist ideology. Particularly in the post-SALT II period, people like Paul Nitze, Richard Pipes, Leon Goure, Admiral Elmo Zumwalt, Major General George J. Keegan, Jr., and other members of the Committee on the Present Danger have warned American policymakers that the USSR marches to a different drummer than does the United States. The Soviet Union, according to this school of thought, is committed to an expansion of its influence as well as its military power. As Colin Gray has put it, the Kremlin's "commitment to world domination is nonnegotiable. Moreover, its intentions are written indelibly in the course of Russian/Soviet history," because "expansionism is the Russian/Soviet 'way': The Pacific Ocean has been reached but not (yet) the Atlantic."[43]

The adherents of this school of thought implicitly assume that a consensus concerning the direction and scope of Soviet foreign and defense policy objectives exists within the Soviet bureaucracy. Such an assumption can and has been criticized in numerous works which have identified perceptual differences within the Soviet elites and demonstrated how different interest groups interact to affect Soviet policy.[44]

It is important, however, to point out that this assumption can have significant impact upon American policymakers. By overestimating the consensus within Soviet elites we may encourage US officials to react to events as if Soviet actions were always the intended result of some evil blueprint rather than occasionally being the result of bureaucratic politics or simple inertia.

For instance, one quite plausible explanation for the large number of items of equipment in the Soviet arms inventory is the Soviet decisionmakers' need to protect the vested interests of design bureau managers.[45] One example of this problem is the production of the *Foxbat* aircraft. It is generally accepted that the *Foxbat* was originally designed to counter the planned production of the American B-70 bomber. However, rather than stop production of their aircraft when the United States failed to build the B-70, the Soviet Mikoyan factories continued to produce *Foxbats* into the 1970's. The production of the Yak-25 is another example of an attempt to satisfy bureaucratic interest group needs rather than military requirements. In the 1950's, when the Mikoyan design bureau rather than the Yakovlev received Stalin's approval to produce a new combat aircraft (the MIG-15), Yakovlev personally appealed to Stalin to revise his decision because, as Yakovlev recounts, "I was very worried about the situation developing in our design bureau. You see, behind me stood 100 people who might lose faith in me as the leader of the design collective." The net result was that Stalin also approved production of the Yak-25 in order to satisfy Yakovlev.[46]

Thus, the outputs of the Soviet decisionmaking process need to be examined on an issue-by-issue basis. Bureaucratic and interest group analyses can never totally explain Soviet behavior in the Third World. But, if American policymakers are interested in obtaining a complete picture of the Soviet political process, it is another tool to further expand their knowledge. Moreover, it can help US decisionmakers to react in more rational methods to Soviet actions and thus to avoid interpreting every Soviet action "in a totally offensive, threatening light."[47]

Assumption Seven: The Soviet Union is Attempting to Put Itself in a Position Where it Can Deny Vital Raw Materials to the Developed World.

It is sometimes argued that one objective of the Soviet Union is to establish a Third World alliance system in order to enable the

USSR to exert pressure or even to sever in times of crisis the industrialized world's vital trade and natural resource supply lines. Most discussions based on this assumption focus upon Middle Eastern oil and particularly the vulnerability of supertankers and the sea routes which carry more than 80 percent of Western Europe's and Japan's essential oil resources. If the Kremlin could assist pro-Soviet governments to come to power in areas near to the Gulf of Aden, Gulf of Oman, Mozambique Channel, Straits of Malacca, the African Cape, and the West African littoral and those governments would either refuse the United States port-call rights or would allow Soviet naval vessels to obtain port facilities, it is argued that Moscow could not only pressure the industrialized nations' commerce and oil routes, but also limit Western access to other valuable natural resources such as chromium, cobalt, platinum, and manganese. Alvin J. Cottrell and Walter F. Hahn in a recent work captured the essence of this assumption and voiced the concerns of a significant group of American analysts:

> The Soviet pattern of naval expansion, in short, seems to be following the trajectory of Western tanker routes from the Persian Gulf around the Cape of Good Hope to Europe .... One clear objective is the achievement of a position from which leverage could be applied over the Cape sea route around Africa—with all the implications that this could have in the event of a conflict or crisis.[48]

When considering and evaluating this assumption, it may be helpful to keep some caveats in mind which might sharpen the speculation on this issue. First, this assumption is primarily based upon a belief that there is a great amount of coherence to Soviet actions. While some of the fallacies of this view were discussed in relation to Assumption Six, it is worthwhile to reiterate that such consistency is not always as apparent as some analysts have hypothesized. For instance, if the USSR is primarily interested in putting itself, or its friends, in positions to sever Middle Eastern oil lines, one would have expected that it would have refrained from taking actions which threatened its access to Berbera. In fact, by supporting the Ethiopian cause, it did exactly the opposite. While the USSR followed a course which it could easily justify ideologically and morally, its actions quite clearly have damaged its geopolitical situation on the Horn of Africa and caused it to lose access to the best port facilities in the area.

Second, a putative Soviet aim to coerce the United States and its allies by pressuring the oil supplies during peacetime or in a crisis situation is a risky policy option and would seem to run counter to Moscow's historical inhibitions against taking actions which might cause a direct confrontation with the United States. During the Iranian crisis, America policymakers publicly announced that the steady flow of oil was considered a vital US security interest. President Carter reconfirmed this interest in his 1980 State of the Union Address. Thus, any direct or indirect Soviet attempt to impede the flow of oil could very well turn a crisis situation into a conflict.

The increased American interest in forming a rapid deployment force is just one of many options apparently being considered as a means to protect the flow of Middle Eastern oil to the industrialized nations. The implicit message which Washington has recently attempted to convey to Moscow is that it would be willing to use military force to protect its vital interest in the Middle Eastern oilfields. In other words, if the USSR or its allies want to somehow attempt to restrict the flow of oil, they must be willing to face the risk of escalating a crisis situation to the point where the United States may commit military forces to defend its vital interests. This the USSR has not historically been willing to do, primarily because it fears that a direct confrontation between the superpowers has a great potential to escalate to a nuclear confrontation.[49]

Third, if Soviet military leaders are seen as cautious planners interested in maximizing their options in order to economize military forces and insure success, for them to dedicate a significant portion of their navy in war to sever the industrialized world's oil supply sealine would be a less than optimum use of their sea denial forces. By far the easiest and most efficient method to stop the flow of oil would be to stop it at its source. Minimal military actions, even sabotage, could easily destroy Middle Eastern oilfields, drilling equipment, pipelines, and storage areas from which the supertankers are refueled. This would be less difficult than destroying convoys of tankers at sea.

Those analysts who assert a major Soviet threat to the Cape sea route conveniently disregard the Soviet Union's naval geographic situation and resupply problems. If one takes a map, as Kenneth Booth has suggested, and inverts it so the African Cape is on the top and Murmansk is on the bottom, it is possible to see the problems of interdicting the sea line from a Soviet perspective.[50] To sever the sea line, the USSR would have to accomplish more than individual acts of terrorism against tankers. It would require a coordinated, systematic campaign which would necessitate secure ports—most likely bases—in order to resupply ships and exchange crews on a rotating basis. Since the USSR not only lacks the bases but also employs ship construction rates and designs that do not appear able for the foreseeable future to support such an ambitious program, the most rational choice open to Moscow would remain disruption of oil at the source.

Finally, if the past is any indicator of the future, possible restrictions upon US access to Third World raw materials are less likely to result from Soviet actions than from actions taken by new nationalistic governments in response to American policies. It is important to remember that, in the case of access to vital raw materials, OPEC actions since 1973 have done more to damage US security interests than have any Soviet actions. The 1979 oil crisis was in part the result of a conservative reaction in Iran to the Shah's pro-Western policies and to the extensive American/Western impact upon the Iranian traditional society. Moreover, it is quite possible that some African nations may attempt to increase prices or deny American access to their natural resources as a means of punishing the United States for its former support of all-white African governments.

Assumption Eight: Moscow's Use of Proxies is a Low Risk and High Benefit Approach.

There is an increasingly popular perception that the Soviet Union has been able to employ proxies to achieve a variety of successes from Africa to Southeast Asia at very minimal cost to Moscow. Indeed pro-Marxist-Leninist factions have come to power in a number of states with outside military assistance but without the USSR suffering military casualties. For a variety of reasons, most of which relate to Cuban motivations rather than to Soviet directions, Havana has been willing to commit its men and blood, at least in Africa, and Cuban soldiers have become, in a sense, the Soviet Union's "cannon fodder."

The surrogate/proxy is not necessarily a one-way street of benefits for the USSR. Accomplishments beget commitments; commitments quite often lead to entangling responsibilities;

427

successes create some risks; and benefits sometimes must be balanced by costs.

On the issue of costs, Colin Legum has pointed out a potential liability facing the USSR as a direct consequence of the Cuban-Soviet connection in Angola and Ethiopia. In the past, a majority of African leaders saw the USSR as neither a reliable friend nor a major threat, but as a valuable counterweight to continuing domination by the West. However, Soviet activities have contributed to a debate about Moscow's overall ambitions and have given credence to a former minority view that the Soviet Union does present a serious threat to the non-Communist African governments. Now, as Legum has argued, African leaders are reading with great interest the writings of Soviet military personnel in an attempt to evaluate the Kremlin's Third World military activities.[51] If this evaluation should gain increasing prominence as Soviet activities increase, Moscow's short-term successes could actually work against Soviet long-term abilities to affect the policies of black African nations.

Moscow is learning that efforts to become more politically, economically, and militarily involved in world events beget commitments and, as the United States has learned over time, those commitments sometimes create unwanted responsibilities. When the Cubans sent thousands of troops to Angola in 1975 and the Soviets provided military arms and assistance to the Popular Movement for the Liberation of Angola (MPLA), was this because the Kremlin dictated that the Cubans should act as its proxies? Or did the Cubans act independently, as Fidel Castro has continually claimed, without Moscow requesting intervention? Probably the truth lies somewhere in the middle, as Soviet and Cuban interests coincided but for different reasons.[52]

Moscow did not start flying Cuban troops to Angola until after January 1976. This was after the United States had successfully pressured various countries to deny landing rights to Cuban planes, so that Cuban commercial aircraft could no longer support Havana's committed military forces. Moreover, Soviet IL-62 flights began only after South African and Cuban forces clashed in early December 1975, resulting in a resounding defeat for the Cubans. Thus, the sequence of events can suggest that Moscow was forced to come to the assistance of a valuable ally to bail it out of a very dangerous situation.

In addition, Moscow's growing propensity to sign treaties of friendship that call for consultation, collaboration, and in some instances coordination of foreign policies between the signatories may create special problems for the USSR. As Legvold has pointed out, "the rather casual or ill-considered decision to grant a special relationship to parties like the Vietnamese who want protection for their own aggressive purposes is fraught with dangers," and carries with it the risk of drawing "the Soviet Union into local instabilities far more than it may now intend."[53]

As the USSR becomes more involved in its attempt to fulfill the global role to which it aspires, the more it will face complicated and entangling situations. With greater frequency its Third World friends and allies will initiate actions that Moscow may prefer they not take. Nevertheless, because of formal and informal commitments, the Kremlin will be forced to respond in some manner. The decision to support an ally might endanger Soviet relations with other regional powers or global East-West relations. But failure to support a Third World friend might perpetuate a common belief within some developing nations that the USSR is opportunistic and contradictory—too often willing to sacrifice friends, even Communists, in order to further Russian state aims.

While not all the cards have yet been played in the China-Vietnam game, it could be one of those entangling situations that Moscow would have preferred to avoid. This may suggest why the USSR took no major diplomatic or military actions against China during the crisis.

Suffice it to say, the problems of a global power are many and great. If Moscow's opportunities are greater than ever before, the complexity of the situations are also greater. To argue because of the absence of Soviet casualties that Moscow has followed a course of maximum benefits with little costs is to miss the complexity of the problem. With benefits come costs, and the Kremlin will—if it has not already done so—learn this as did the United States and all the world's other imperial powers of the past.

Assumption Nine: Force is the Best Way to Respond to Soviet Actions.

Finally, there is a belief among a small but influential group of observers that military force is the best way to respond to Soviet opportunistic action. No one is really advocating a military shoot-out with the USSR, because the possibility of escalation to strategic nuclear weapons is too great when the two superpowers confront

429

each other directly in an international game of chicken. But it has been suggested that force or threat of force are the only actions which Moscow understands. As Helmut Sonnenfeldt has recently argued, "random punitive responses" are unlikely to halt Soviet military actions once they are underway because "substantial risk on the ground" is what deters Soviet leaders.[54] In his first military posture statement to Congress, the Chairman of the Joint Chiefs of Staff has also implied that the force or the threat of force is the primary instrument which will cause the USSR to desist from its adventurous and mischievious activities:

> We should not regress to the tensions and confrontation of the Cold War, but neither should we permit present trends in Soviet capability and behavior to achieve by default in the 1980s what they could not accomplish by force or threat in the 1950s. I see little cause for optimism in the future unless the United States maintains both the power and the will to deter encroachment, defend our interests, and steer Soviet policy away from adventurism.[55]

Colin Gray has probably more succinctly captured the essence of this school of thought when he wrote: "The Soviet Union, as Russia before it, is an expansionist power that can be contained only by the threat of force and by a manifest, credible (in the Soviet eyes) determination to exercise that force."[56]

The fact that military is an important element of the Soviet notion of the "international correlation of forces" provides some credence to this belief. However, it is often overlooked that the "correlation of forces" is not predicated upon physical force alone. It is only part of the equation, and economic, political, social, and psychological factors are given equal consideration. In the long run, American policymakers need to shape US foreign and defense policy so that Third World nations do not regard military actions—supported and sometimes sponsored by the USSR—as the only option available to them.

America should not seek to obtain more popular and successful surrogates to fight and defeat Soviet surrogates. This is a response to symptoms and not to causes. Rather it should be an American objective when possible to work to eliminate the causes of intra and interstate Third World conflict. This could make the resort to force in some instances a less attractive Third World option and thus reduce the number of situations which Moscow can support for its own interests.

This brings us back nearly full circle to where we started in Assumption One. The inability to see that Mohammad Reza Shah Pahlavi's dynasty was not in touch with its traditional Muslim society and thus was inherently more unstable than a series of American administrations believed was a classic foreign policy failure. The United States was quite willing to provide the Shah with nearly unlimited military assistance because he supported American objectives and goals in the area. However, until it was too late, we were relatively unconcerned with the Shah's domestic policies. The United States and most of the industrial world is now reaping the results of that myopic policy. In hindsight, it would have been more in America's interests to have had a less pro-Western but more stable Iranian government than the situation we now face.

The United States must become more sensitive to the internal dynamics of Third World nations and less obsessed with the Soviet Union. The reality of the situation is that most threats to US prestige and security or economic, political and military interests cannot be solved by military foce. The use of American military force could not have altered the fate of the Shah of Iran, deterred OPEC oil price rises which threaten world economic chaos, bolstered confidence in the dollar, protected American markets, or developed a comprehensive peace settlement in the Middle East. Such matters can, however, be affected by sophisticated reassessment of American "long term interests, and a more skeptical look at what military power can do."[57]

CONCLUSION

Robert Jervis has written that if a person or nation is to act intelligently it must predict how others will behave. The better policymakers know and understand their adversaries the more aware they should be to their own policy alternatives and options.[58] This essay suggests a complementary adaptation of the Jervis argument: it is equally important to know and understand the assumptions about an adversary's behavior which are prevalent in one's own policymaking circles. In some instances those assumptions are valid while in other instances they are not. Nevertheless, what policymakers expect or are predisposed to believe about Soviet actions can significantly influence how they

431

interpret Soviet behavior, and thus how they fashion responses.

In the future, if the United States wishes to formulate a rational and developed approach to Soviet involvement in the Third World, it must begin with a more refined analysis of Soviet opportunities, capabilities, advantages, and disadvantages. To do this it will be important to keep in mind some caveats about recent Soviet experiences. First, in recent years, pro-Marxist-Leninist factions have come to power in Afghanistan, Angola, Ethiopia, Vietnam, Laos, People's Democratic Republic of Yemen, and Cambodia. In many of these instances, Moscow has seized the opportunity to enhance its influence by supporting various pro-Soviet factions. The USSR has also been willing to provide military support—or in the case of Afghanistan unilateral invasion—in order to bolster pro-Soviet factions. However, in the final analysis, the Kremlin has resorted to the use of military force only when it apparently believed it could do so cheaply and with minimum risk to the Soviet Union and its interests. If there are threads which tie such disparate events and movements as Angola, Ethiopia, and Afghanistan, the answer probably cannot be found in some Soviet master plan theory. Rather, Stanley Hoffman is probably correct when he said that recent Soviet successes are tied by two threads: "low risks, and opportunities provided by previous Western mistakes, defeats, or (as in Afghanistan) indifference."[9] Second, most Western nations made few attempts—other than declaratory—to inhibit Soviet activities in any of those recent crisis areas. Thus, it is difficult to conclude, as some observers have, that Soviet activities in Angola, Ethiopia, or even Afghanistan were great accomplishments of "force projection." Third, while Soviet presence in an area such as Afghanistan may show sudden growth, such situations are not immutable and can become heavy burdens for the USSR rather than net additions to enhance its politico-military capabilities. If the United States absorbs these and other "lessons," its approach to the Third World may produce more understanding and success in the future.

ENDNOTES

1. Organization of the Joint Chiefs of Staff (JCS), *United States Military Posture for FY 1980,* Washington, DC: US Government Printing Office, 1979, p. vii.

2. "An Interview With Kissinger," *Time,* January 13, 1979, pp. 29-30. See also "Kissinger's Critique," *The Economist,* February 3 and 10, 1979, pp. 17-22 and 31-35.

3. John Robinson, "Baker to Tell Soviets of Hill Doubts on SALT Ratification," *The Washington Post,* January 7, 1979, p. A20.

4. The technique used in this essay is one that Raymond L. Garthoff used in "On Estimating and Imputing Intentions," *International Security,* Vol. 2, No. 3, Winter 1978, pp. 22-32, when he identified the ten most common fallacies used to estimate Soviet military and foreign policy intentions.

5. Robert Legvold, "The Super Rivals: Conflict in the Third World," *Foreign Affairs,* Vol. 57, No. 4, Spring 1979, p. 761.

6. Quoted in J. William Fulbright "The Soundness of U.S. Policy-Making Procedure," in US Senate Committee on Foreign Relations, *Perceptions: Relations Between the United States and the Soviet Union,* Washington, DC: US Government Printing Office, 1979, p. 441.

7. *The New York Times,* February 21, 1979, p. A4. While there were few overt dissenters from the Administration position on Iran, private conversations with individuals would indicate much less consensus. Moreover, on the larger issue of Soviet involvement, there are some indications that highranking Presidential advisers were sharply divided. Secretary of State Cyrus Vance and Marshall D. Shulman, the State Department's top ranking Soviet expert, had a greater tendency to emphasize Soviet limitations and Moscow's need for closer relations with the United States. Zbigniew Brzezinski and James R. Schlesinger were much less optimistic and focused on Soviet challenges to American security interests. See Bernard Gwertzman, "Issues for US: Soviet's Intent," *The New York Times,* December 7, 1978, p. A12.

8. "Kissinger's Critique," *The Economist,* February 10, 1979, p. 31.

9. US Central Intelligence Agency (CIA), *Communist Aid to Less Developed Countries of the Free World, 1977,* ER 78-10478U, Washington, DC: Central Intelligence Agency, November 1978, p. 31.

10. J. Bereznikovskiy, "What is Happening in Iran," *Kommunist,* December 7, 1978, in Foreign Broadcast Information Service, *Daily Report: Soviet Union,* December 14, 1979, p. F7 (hereafter cited as *FBIS: Soviet Union).*

11. U. Kudryavtsev, "Iran: Sources of the Crisis," *Izvestiia,* December 7, 1978, in *FBIS: Soviet Union,* December 11, 1978, p. F7-8.

12. *FBIS:Soviet Union,* January 23, 1979, p. F6 and January 31, 1979, p. F1.

13. Richard Burt, "Saudis Reject Idea of a U.S. Base," *The New York Times,* February 27, 1979, p. A2.

14. John K. Cooley, "Brown Reconfirms US Defense of Mideast Allies," *Christian Science Monitor,* February 12, 1979, p. 4. Emphasis added.

15. Drew Middleton, "U.S. Earmarks Force for Fast Deployment in Middle East," *The New York Times,* April 20, 1979, p. A12 and Bernard Weinraub, "Pentagon is Urging Indian Ocean Fleet," *The New York Times,* March 1, 1979, p. A14.

16. Garthoff, "On Estimating and Imputing Intentions," p. 27.

17. Roger E. Kanet, "The Soviet Union and the Developing Countries: Policy or Policies," *The World Today,* August 1975, p. 338.

18. Department of State, *Foreign Relations of the United States; Diplomatic Papers, 1945: Volume II General; Political and Economic Matters,* Washington, DC: US Government Printing Office, 1967, pp. 173 and 192 (hereafter cited as *Foreign Relations* with appropriate year and volume). Secretary of State James F. Brynes recounted the conversation more bluntly and wrote in his memoirs that Molotov had said: "The Soviet Union should take the place that is due it...and therefore should have bases in the Mediterranean for its merchant fleet." See James F. Brynes, *Speaking Frankly,* New York: Harper and Brothers Publishers, 1947, p. 16.

19. *Foreign Relations, 1945,* Vol. VI, pp. 789, 790 and 809.

20. *FBIS: Soviet Union,* Supplement, Part IV, March 20, 1979, p. 55.

21. *FBIS: Soviet Union,* April 1, 1977, pp. B1-10.

22. Adam Ulam, "U.S.-Soviet Relations: Unhappy Coexistence," *Foreign Affairs: America and the World 1978,* Vol. 57, No. 3, 1979, p. 559.

23. Sergei G. Gorshkov, "Navies in War and Peace," *US Naval Institute Proceedings,* Vol. 100, January 1974, pp. 21-22.

24. JCS, *United States Military Posture for FY 1980,* pp. 17 and vii.

25. Department of Defense, Joint Chiefs of Staff, *Dictionary of Military and Associated Terms,* JCS Pub. 1, Washington, DC: US Government Printing Office, p. 223.

26. C.J. Jacobsen, *Soviet Strategy—Soviet Foreign Policy,* 2nd ed., Glasgow, Great Britain: Robert MacLehose and Co. LTD, 1974, p. 143; and F.M. Murphy, "The Soviet Navy in the Mediterranean," *US Naval Institute Proceedings,* Vol. 93, No. 3, March 1967, pp. 42-43.

27. Too many people underestimate the importance of geography and logistics in determining a nation's strategy. As Theodore Ropp has written, "Geography is the bones of strategy; the terrain and lines of communication have governed the course of many campaigns and battles." While it may be personally exhilarating to discuss and analyze grand strategy, the actions most nations take or fail to take are determined by other factors. World War II is a good example. Geography and logistics were two of the prime determining factors in America's decision to fight in Europe, not the Pacific, first. Rather than some abstract gamesmanship strategy guiding the US decision, it was a recognition that because of America's geographic position and logistics constraints it could not prosecute both campaigns with equal vigor. Choices were made and policy determined on the basis of those factors. See Theodore Ropp, *War in the Modern Age,* New, Revised Edition, New York: Collier Books, 1973, p. 6, and K. Booth, *Navies and Foreign Policy,* London: Croom Helm, LTD: 1977, pp. 175-176.

28. Steve F. Kime, "Soviet Naval Strategy for the Eighties," *National Security Affairs Monograph 78-3,* Washington, DC: National Defense University, June 1978, pp. 5-9.

29. Alva M. Bowen, *Comparison of U.S. and U.S.S.R. Naval Shipbuilding,* Washington, DC: Library of Congress, Congressional Research Service, March 5, 1976; Michael MccGwire, "Western and Soviet Naval Building Progammes 1965-1976," *Survival,* Vol. VIII, No. 5, September/October 1976, pp. 204-209; and Gary Chairbonneau, "The Soviet Navy and Forward Deployment," *US Naval Institute Proceedings,* Vol. 105, March 1979, p. 37.

30. To put these numbers in some sort of perspective the United States flew 567 sorties and supplied its ally Israel with more than 22.4 million tons. In other words, the United States flew nearly half as many missions and provided 50 percent more supplies over a distance which was four times greater than the Soviet effort. Also, the US effort was severely hampered because most US allies—except Portugal—refused landing rights to American planes. See Robert P. Berman, *Soviet Air Power in Transition,* Washington, DC: The Brookings Institution, 1978, p. 65.

31. Daniel S. Papp, "The Soviet Union and Cuba in Ethiopia," *Current History,* Vol. 76, March 1979, p. 113.

32. K. Booth, *Navies and Foreign Policy,* p. 71.

33. *Ibid.,* pp. 29-47

34. Quoted in Michael J. Deane, *The Soviet Concept of the "Correlation of Forces,"* Arlington, Virginia: Stanford Research Institute, Strategic Studies Center, May 1976, pp. 28-29.

35. General I. Shavrov, "Problems of Theory of the Postwar Period: Local Wars and Their Place in the Global Strategy of Imperialism," *Voyenno—Istoricheskiy Zhurnal,* No. 3, March 1975, translated in *Joint Publications Research Service* 64649, p. 38.

36. For just a few examples, see John C. Campbell, "The Soviet Union and the Middle East: In the General Direction of the Persian Gulf," Part II, *Russian Review,* July 1970, pp. 248-253; and Walter Laqueur, *The Struggle for the Middle East: The Soviet Union and the Middle East 1958-68,* Baltimore: Pelican Books, 1972, pp. 192-212.

37. US CIA, *Communist Aid to Less Developed Countries of the Free World, 1977,* p. 1.

38. *Ibid.,* pp. 2-3.

39. Chester A. Crocker, "The Quest for an African Policy," *The Washington Review of Strategic and International Studies,* Vol. 1, No. 2, April 1978, p. 72.

40. See K.J. Holsti, *International Politics: A Framework for Analysis,* 2nd ed., Englewood Cliffs, New Jersey: Prentice-Hall, Inc., 1972, pp. 154-173; and Alvin Z. Rubinstein, "Assessing Influence as a Problem in Foreign Policy Analyses," in *Soviet and Chinese Influence in the Third World,* edited by Alvin Z. Rubinstein, New York: Praeger Publishers, 1975, pp. 1-22 for more conceptional analysis of the influence relationship.

41. Alvin Z. Rubinstein, *Red Star on the Nile: The Soviet-Egyptian Influence Relationship Since the June War,* Princeton, New Jersey: Princeton University Press, 1977; Robert H. Donaldson, *The Soviet-Indian Alignment: Quest for Influence,* Monograph Series in World Affairs, Vol. 16, No. 3-4, Denver, Colorado: University of Denver, 1979.

42. Rubinstein, *Red Star on the Nile,* p. 334.

43. Colin Gray, *The Geopolitics of the Nuclear Era: Heartland, Rimlands, and the Technological Revolution,* New York: Crane, Russak, and Company, Inc., 1977, pp. 38 and 67. See also, Committee on the Present Danger, *Is America Becoming Number 2? Current Trends in the U.S.-Soviet Military Balance,* Washington: The Committee on the Present Danger, 1978, p. 1. On announcing the formulation of the Committee on Present Danger Paul Nitze claimed that the Soviets continue to "cling to their goal of worldwide domination." Cited in Dennis Ross, "Rethinking Soviet Strategic Policy: Inputs and Implications," *The Journal of Strategic Studies,* Vol. 1, No. 1, May 1978, p. 3.

435

44. For some examples, see Samuel B. Payne, Jr., "The Soviet Debate on Strategic Arms Limitation: 1968-1972," *Soviet Studies,* Vol. 27, No. 1, January 1975; H. Gordon Skilling, "Interest Groups and Communist Politics," *World Politics,* Vol. 17, No. 2, April 1966, pp. 435-451. Edward L. Warner, *The Military in Contemporary Soviet Politics: An Institutional Analysis,* New York: Praeger, 1977; and Arthur J. Alexander, *Decision-Making in Soviet Weapons Procurement,* Adelphi Papers, No. 148, London: The International Institute for Strategic Studies, Winter 1978/79.

45. The author recognizes that other reasons to include threat analysis, geopolitical considerations, and arms transfer policies, are major inputs into determining Soviet force posture and equipment inventories. The point is that there are factors other than some grand politico-military plan which affect Soviet decisionmakers' perceptions.

46. Alexander, *Decision-Making in Soviet Weapons Procurement,* pp. 24 and 34.

47. Ross, "Rethinking Soviet Strategic Policy: Inputs and Implications," p. 2. Although Ross was primarily interested in Soviet strategic weapons, doctrine, and policy, the quote is equally applicable to a macroview of Soviet foreign and defense policies.

48. Alvin J. Cottrell and Walter F. Hahn, *Naval Race or Arms Control in the Indian Ocean? (Some Problems in Negotiation, Naval Limitations.)* Agenda Paper No. 8. New York: National Strategy Information Center, 1978, pp. 34-35. See also Patrick Wull, ed., *The Southern Oceans and the Security of the Free World: New Studies in Global Strategy,* London: Stacey International, 1977.

49. Afghanistan notwithstanding, this still seems to be a valid judgment. A recent Brookings Institution study, *Mailed Fist, Velvet Glove,* indicates that the Soviet Union has not rashly resorted to the use of military force to achieve its objectives in the Third World and to challenge the United States. The study concludes that the Kremlin has used military force pragmatically and turned to its use only when Moscow believed that it could do so cheaply and with minimum risk to the Soviet Union and its interests. Moscow has been willing to support the use of military force in Third World countries like Angola but not necessarily to signal, "an increased Kremlin aggressiveness or acceptance of risk in the use of military power....What Moscow did was take decisive advantage of extremely easy pickings." Likewise, Soviet involvement in the Ethiopia-Somalia conflict was a low risk military operation because if the United States had chosen to intervene in opposition to the USSR, Washington would have had to support Somalia which had started the conflict and who had been condemned by the Organization of African Unity. Given America's historic lack of interest in South Asia and past diplomatic failures in the region, one can present a good case that from a Soviet perspective the invasion of Afghanistan was also a low risk venture. See Stephen S. Kaplan, ed. *Mailed Fist, Velvet Glove: Soviet Armed Forces as a Political Instrument,* Washington, DC: The Brookings Institution, 1979. The study was originally done under contract for the Defense Advanced Research Projects Agency. In 1980, it should be published as a Brookings study under the same title.

50. Booth, *Navies and Foreign Policy,* p. 173.

51. Colin Legum, "The African Environment," *Problems of Communism,* Vol. XXVIII, January-February 1978, p. 11.

52. For a few examples of Soviet and Cuban objectives in Angola, see William J. Durch, *The Cuban Military in Africa and the Middle East: From Algeria to Angola,* Professional Paper no. 201, Arlington, Virginia: Center for Naval Analyses,

September 1977; Gabriel Marcella and Daniel S. Papp, *The Future of Soviet-Cuban Relations*, Military Issues Research Memorandum, Carlisle Barracks, Pennsylvania: Strategic Studies Institute, February 1, 1979; and William M. Leo Grande, "Cuban-Soviet Relations and Cuban Policy in Africa," paper presented at the annual meeting of the International Studies Association, Toronto, Canada, March 22-26, 1979.

53. Legvold, "The Super Rivals," p. 769.

54. Helmut Sonnenfeldt, "Linkage: A Strategy for Tempering Soviet Antagonism," *NATO review*, No. 1, February 1979, p. 4.

55. JCS, *United States Military Posture for FY 80*, p. viii.

56. Gray, *The Geopolitics of the Nuclear Era*, p. 67.

57. Richard J. Barnet, "U.S.-Soviet Relations: The Need for a Comprehensive Approach," *Foreign Affairs*, Vol. 57, No. 4, Spring 1979, p. 792.

58. Robert Jervis, *Perception and Misperception in International Politics*, Princeton, New Jersey: Princeton University Press, 1976.

59. Stanley Hoffman, "Muscle and Brains," *Foreign Policy*, No. 37, Winter, 1979-80, p. 5.

PART 5
SUMMARY AND CONCLUSIONS

21

THE SOVIET UNION IN THE THIRD WORLD:
SUCCESSES AND FAILURES

Joseph L. Nogee

As the title of the 1979 Military Policy Symposium indicates, Soviet policy in the Third World has produced both successes and failures. What can we in conclusion say of Soviet efforts in the Third World? Have they on balance been more or less successful? Does the answer to this question depend upon region? Can we identify success with proximity to the Soviet Union, cultural environment, type of instruments used or degree of commitment made by Moscow? What have been the important instruments of Soviet policy in the Third World? Antecedent to all of these questions, of course, is the more fundamental question: What are Soviet objectives in the Third World? One cannot measure success unless one can identify the goal or purpose behind a particular effort. Finally, there is the issue of the implications of these findings for US policy. This essay, based upon the contents of the papers from the symposium, will address itself explicitly to these questions. It will summarize the findings of the contributing authors in order to identify those conclusions upon which there is a consensus and to note those where significant differences exist.

438

Before we consider those generalizations which might broadly apply to the Third World, we will first summarize the findings described above as they apply more specifically to the four geographical regions we have examined: Latin America, Africa, the Middle East and Asia.

For Moscow, Latin America has held consistently the lowest priority among all the regions of the Third World. This neglect stems in part from the fact that the region is not in the Soviet Union's vital military and economic zone. It supplies the Soviet Union with no critical materials or important markets. Furthermore, Moscow appears to recognize the primacy of American interests and power in Latin America. American radio, cinema and literature negate Soviet influence culturally just as Western capital and technology undermine it economically.

Moscow's objectives in Latin America as summarized by Raymond Duncan are:
- To sharpen the economic conflict between Latin America and the United States;
- To deny strategic raw materials and markets to the United States while acquiring them for itself;
- To strengthen Latin American Communist parties; and
- To check Chinese influence in Latin America.

Another current objective is to maintain the USSR's special relationship with Cuba. Indeed, Cuba is the only Latin American country where all of the above objectives largely have been achieved already. But as Paul Sigmund notes, the Cuban experience may well have stimulated a reaction making unlikely any more "Cubas" in Latin America. For one thing, the existence of a Communist state in the Caribbean has stimulated the United States to resist the spread of communism. For another, Castro has been sufficiently expensive for Moscow to avoid taking on a similar burden elsewhere.

Is Cuba an example of Soviet success or failure? The two authors who directly assess this question agree that Cuba has been a Soviet success. Sigmund agrees that "the Cuban intervention in Africa which clearly turned the tide in Angola, and probably in Ethiopia as well, makes the Soviet expenditures of the last twenty years worthwhile." Gabriel Marcella and Daniel Papp point to the importance of Cuba as "the most successful indication to which the Kremlin may point as proof that Soviet Marxism-Leninism. . .has

439

relevance to the economic and social growth of developing nations." Regarding Cuba's role in Africa, the authors agree that Castro is not simply a surrogate or proxy for the Kremlin. Cuban involvement in Angola, for example, originated independently of Moscow. If there sometimes appears to be a puppet relationship, it is largely because Soviet and Cuban interests essentially converge. It is Marcella's and Papp's expectation that for the foreseeble future, Soviet-Cuban relations will remain close.

What about Chile? The overthrow of Allende notwithstanding, Sigmund does not consider Soviet policy there to have been a failure. The basic fact is that Moscow never had high expectations for Allende to begin with, and the Kremlin certainly made no solid commitment to him in terms of economic or any other kind of assistance. In Chile, Moscow was cautious. Indeed until now, the overall pattern of Soviet involvement in Latin America, says Sigmund, "is one of conservatism, caution and preference for gradual change."

By contrast, Soviet involvement in Africa, particularly following the collapse of Portuguese colonialism, has been activist if not adventurous. Before the Soviet invasion of Afghanistan, no single issue so undermined the carefully nurtured Soviet-American detente as the presence of Soviet and Cuban forces in Angola and the Horn of Africa. Direct Soviet military involvement in Africa is unprecedented, raising the question: Why is the Kremlin taking new risks in Africa? Arthur Klinghoffer, Daniel Papp and Richard Remnek describe a combination of offensive and defensive objectives of Soviet policy. They include:

• Reducing both Western and Chinese influence on the continent;

• Undermining the remaining white-dominated regimes in Southern Africa and, in particular, disrupting the dialogue South Africa was attempting to cultivate with some black African states;

• Obtaining leverage over the liberation movements in the region, notably the Southwest African People's Organization (SWAPO), the Zimbabwe African People's Union (ZAPU), and the African National Congress (ANC);

• Enhancing Soviet relations with all the countries of Africa, particularly the "front-line" states of Angola, Botswana, Mozambique, Tanzania and Zambia.

• Denying the United States strategic rights in Angola, including

440

access to ports, aircraft overflights and landing privileges; while seeking to obtain these privileges for the Soviet Union;

• Countering not only American but South African, Zairian and Zambian influence in Southern Africa and the support given by these pro-Western regimes to the front for the National Liberation of Angola (FNLA). For this, Klinghoffer contends that part of the Kremlin's motivation to support the Movement for the Popular Liberation of Angola (MPLA) with troops and arms was defensive;

• Denying the West the mineral resources of South Africa which include gold, diamonds, chromite, copper, antimony, platinum, cobalt and uranium; and,

• Gaining for the Soviet Union facilities in Africa to support their naval forces. Opinions differ regarding the purposes which these naval forces would serve. Papp hypothesizes that Moscow may wish to use facilities in Africa in order to threaten US and European oil supply lines. Remnek contends that the Soviet naval presence in the Indian Ocean is best explained by a peacetime mission. Because the shortest sea route open year round between the Soviet European and Pacific ports runs through these waters, Moscow has a vital interest in keeping these sea lanes open.

The motives impelling the Soviet Union to intervene on behalf of Ethiopia against Somalia in the Ogaden War (1977-78) were both offensive and defensive. Mengistu's coup brought to power a Marxist regime in one of Africa's most populous countries. In ideological terms, the Soviets saw the struggle between the Dergue and its enemies as a confrontation between the forces of progress and reaction. By late 1976 or early 1977 when Moscow made its military commitment to Ethiopia, the country was threatened with disintegration and anarchy. Domestically, nationalization and land reform had created widespread instability. Ethiopia's failure to crush the Eritrean secessionists raised the specter of a breakup of the Ethiopian state and the possibility that, under Saudi leadership, an Arab coalition of Saudia Arabia, Eritrea and the Sudan might turn the Red Sea into an Arab anti-Soviet lake. To counter this potential coalition, Moscow proposed a federation of Marxist states which would have included Ethiopia, Somalia, South Yemen and Djibouti.

Clearly among all these objectives, considerations of national interest and Soviet power predominate. Nevertheless, Klinghoffer, Papp and Remnek are in agreement that, in both Angola and Ethiopia, ideological factors also played an important role. The

441

Marxist identification of the Neto and Mengistu regimes was significant. In the latter case even more important were the policies of the Dergue which were designed to uproot Ethiopia's feudal system. Moscow had suffered too many setbacks in Africa after giving extensive aid to non-Communist governments, and apparently it wanted the assurance that would come from an alliance based upon a common ideological perspective.

The assessments of Soviet success in Africa differ markedly from the popular view that recent Soviet activism has resulted in a substantial gain for the Soviet Union at the expense of the West. At best, the authors view Moscow's accomplishments as mixed. In no case has the Kremlin gained anything without paying a substantial cost. On balance, Papp says that "it cannot be argued that Soviet policy has been overly successful in achieving its objectives in Southern Africa." Relations between Moscow and the "front-line" states are "friendly and cordial," but not intimate. Clearly they are not subservient to the Kremlin. Nor is Angola, for all the Soviet investment there. Angola has chosen not to enmesh its economy with that of the Communist bloc nor to terminate its economic ties with the West. Perhaps most significant of all, not a single African country has permitted the Soviet Union to use its territory for a permanent military base. Klinghoffer describes some internal political developments in Angola after the MPLA victory which suggest that there existed elements in Neto's government opposed to strong ties with the Soviet Union. In 1977 there was an attempted coup against Neto which may have had the support of the Soviet Union.

Somalia was an obvious, though not necessarily irretrievable, Soviet loss. Moscow's support for Ethiopia led Mogadiscio on November 13, 1977, to abrogate its Friendship Treaty with Moscow and terminate Soviet access to extensive naval support facilities in Somalia. Remnek contends that the Soviet leadership miscalculated Mogadiscio's behavior because it assumed that common sense and state interest would keep Somalia from invading the Ogaden. However, he believes that even more serious than Moscow's losses in Somalia was the collapse of the Indian Ocean Naval Arms Limitation Talks which might have curbed naval activity of the nonlittoral states in the Indian Ocean.

To cite Moscow's frustrations in Africa is not to deny obvious gains. In the Horn of Africa the net Soviet position today is stronger than before. The loss of Berbera has been "more or less"

442

made up with access to support facilities in Ethiopia and South Yemen. Soviet assistance has to some extent stabilized Ethiopia. And, although the Russians have failed to bring about a federation of Marxist states, they have been able to frustrate the ambitions of the pro-Western Arab states to mobilize a bloc of conservative Arab states in the Horn. Finally, it should be noted that the Soviet Union has virtually displaced Chinese influence in Southern Africa.

The authors of the studies on the Middle East agree that the Soviet Union has pursued in recent years an offensive (rather than a defensive) policy. The overall goal of that policy has been to increase Soviet influence in the Middle East at the expense of the United States and other western powers. A concerted effort has been made to unite the Arab states of the Middle East into an "anti-imperialist" bloc of pro-Soviet states. To date this goal has eluded the Kremlin, in part, as Robert Freedman explains, because of the opposition of Iraq, ostensibly a Soviet ally. Iraqi xenophobia is as much a barrier to close relations with its Communist benefactor as with the so-called imperialist enemies. The Ba'athist regime has been no more tolerant of the Communist party than it has of any other oppositon party. Notwithstanding the large quantity of military and economic aid given by the Soviet Union, Moscow has been unable to persuade Baghdad to accept the Iraqi Communist Party as a viable component of a "national front" government. Indeed, Iraqi persecution of its domestic Communists has been among the most viscious in the Middle East, resulting in the 1978 execution of a number of party members. Soviet-Iraqi relations appear to fluctuate with the degree of Iraqi dependence upon the Soviet Union. In 1973-74 that dependence was rather substantial; since then it has lessened and Soviet influence has waned. "All in all," says Freedman, "the course of Iraqi-Soviet relations in the 1968-79 period indicates the low level of Soviet influence over its client state which has given relatively little in the way of political obedience in return for a large amount of Soviet economic and military assistance."

Before the Islamic revolution, Iran was as pro-Western as Iraq was anti-Western. That did not prevent Moscow from maintaining surprisingly good relations with the Shah. As Robert Irani points out, if it could not incorporate Iran into its orbit, Moscow was determined at least to neutralize the country. During the 1960's and 1970's Soviet relations, if not close, were at least correct. Moscow pursued a "reasonable, pragmatic, nonideological" policy toward Iran. Indeed, from the mid-1960's to the mid-1970's the Soviet Union became one of Iran's principal trading partners.

However satisfactory Soviet-Irani relations may have been in the 1970's, there is no doubt that the rise to power of the Ayatollah Khomeini in January 1979 was a major victory for the Soviet Union, if for no other reason than it was a colossal defeat for the United States. Edward Corcoran and Irani both agree that Moscow is the beneficiary of events in Tehran that were not its doing. Although there is some evidence of Soviet instigation during the upheavel leading to Khomeini's return in 1979, and Soviet propaganda has consistently supported the revolution, Moscow certainly did not engineer the overthrow of the Shah. It is possible that the espousal of Islamic fundamentalism in a neighboring country might even stimulate Muslims in the Soviet Union to demand greater religious freedoms for themselves.

The Moslem peoples of Soviet Central Asia offer the Soviet Union some leverage in its relations with Moslem countries throughout the world. Moscow has sought to use the peoples of Central Asia as a source of identification with the Moslem peoples as well as a developmental model for the entire Third World. In this endeavor, even before the invasion of Afghanistan, the Kremlin had only limited success. Corcoran points out that the influence relationship between Moslem communities flows in more than one direction. Because of its relations with the Third World, Moscow has been restrained in its handling of some of its internal problems of Moslem assertiveness. Indeed, the use of Soviet Moslem troops in Afghanistan creates unique linkages between Moslems on both sides of the Soviet border which may well have unpredictable and unsettling consequences for Soviet control in Central Asia.

One of the probable objectives of the Soviet invasion of Afghanistan in December 1979 was to keep that country from establishing the kind of fundamentalist Islamic (in Soviet eyes "reactionary") republic that Iran and Pakistan have. Another may have been to move closer to a port on the Indian Ocean. As Corcoran points out, only Pakistani Baluchistan now separates the Soviet Union from its long sought after warm water port.

There were other factors behind the Soviet invasion. According to Shirin Tahir-Kheli, the Soviet Union, perceiving the United States to be weak and preoccupied with Iran, took advantage of an opportunity that could in time give Moscow its long desired warm water port on the Indian Ocean. Apparently Soviet action was necessary, too, in order to reinvigorate Afghanistan's "faltering socialist experiment." Both Nur Muhammad Taraki and Hafizullah Amin had attempted ruthlessly to implement radical land and educational reforms which stimulated large-scale popular opposition to their regimes.

On balance Tahir-Kheli considers Soviet policy in Afghanistan to be successful. The principal advantage to Moscow is that Afghanistan remains outside of the Western orbit and is available as a base to exert pressure against Pakistan. Still, the costs to the Kremlin have been substantial. Moscow is now under pressure to endorse a very unpopular regime; detente has been (at least temporarily) destroyed; and the Soviet Union has suffered severe propaganda defeats in the Third World and among Moslem nations in particular. And, finally, as Corcoran notes, a worsening of Soviet ties with the Moslem world could significantly complicate its future energy planning.

In Asia, Soviet objectives are described as follows:
• Establishing stable relationships with the countries in the region;
• Obtaining support for its policies generally and in particular to win Indian and the Association of Southeast Asian Nations (ASEAN) endorsement of its China policies;
• Containing China and complicating China's security requirements;
• Reducing the influence in Asia of China, Japan and the United States; and,
• Bringing Vietnam into the Soviet economic and strategic orbit.

India is a particularly interesting case because it is the only democracy to have established a close relationship with the Soviet Union. Rajan Menon explains this relationship in terms of the mutuality of their national interests, a condition that continued even after the fall of the pro-Soviet Indira Gandhi in 1977. Since 1965, India has relied upon the Soviet Union for its military arms to meet a potential threat from either China or Pakistan. That dependence has produced a responsiveness to Soviet foreign policy interests, but only insofar as there is no contradiction with basic Indian national interests. Thus, for example, India refrained from openly criticizing Moscow's invasion of Czechoslovakia in 1968, but it refused to endorse the Kremlin's support for an Asian collective security system or the Nonproliferation Treaty. Because a rapprochement with China is important to India, the Indian Government refused to endorse the Vietnamese position in the 1979 Sino-Vietnamese war or to back the enemies of China in Cambodia. In sum, says Menon, "the Soviet Union's success in utilizing arms supplies and security dependence to influence Indian behavior has, on the whole, been rather modest."

Douglas Pike's assessment of Soviet accomplishments in Asia is negative. He notes: "Nothing seems to work very well for the USSR in Asia and despite considerable input and energy over the years it has surprisingly little to show for its efforts. Vietnam at the moment is the promising exception. . . ." Vietnam's responsiveness is linked closely with its virtual total dependence upon the Soviet Union for both military and nonmilitary supplies. Today approximately 20 percent (possible 30 percent) of the rice consumption in Vietnam is supplied by the USSR. Even with this dependence, Vietnamese compliance comes grudgingly. Pike's analysis of Vietnamese national stereotypes of the Russians explains the basis for considerable animosity between both peoples. The Vietnamese see the Russians as alien, racist, barbarian and chauvinistic. They feel both suspicious of and superior to the Russians. Thus, during the Vietnam war, in spite of Hanoi's virtual dependence upon the Soviet Union for its war machine, Moscow had little influence upon Hanoi's war policies. Vietnam was able to exploit the Sino-Soviet conflict to its advantage, causing some Soviet leaders to look upon the Vietnamese as ingrates. Moscow's cause was not aided by its tendency to use heavy handed tactics toward an ostensible ally.

Until fairly recently the ASEAN countries (Indonesia, Malaysia, Philippines, Singapore, and Thailand) ranked low on Moscow's priorities. When ASEAN was founded in 1967, Moscow had diplomatic relations only with Indonesia and Thailand. The Soviets now not only have diplomatic relations with each country but relatively extensive economic and cultural ties as well. The importance of the region to Moscow increased as a result of the 1979 Vietnamese invasion of Cambodia and the open conflicts between China and Vietnam. Thomas Wilborn concludes, however, "that there is no evidence of success" in current Soviet policy towards ASEAN. It may be true that US influence in recent years has declined, but that is not the result of Soviet activities. Nor has a decline of Western influence meant a corresponding increase in

Soviet influence. The Kremlin has sought in vain to win ASEAN over to its position in the political struggle with China. It has been particularly dissatisfied with ASEAN support for Pol Pot rather than Heng Samrin in Cambodia. Moscow was hurt by its sponsorship of Vietnam's invasion of Cambodia in 1979 and its failure to do anything to stem the flow of refugees from Vietnam, many of whom ended up in ASEAN countries.

The instruments of Soviet policy in the Third World are the traditional ones used by great powers in their relations with lesser powers: economic and military aid, technical assistance, trade, diplomacy, propaganda and, in a few rare instances, the use of military force. Of these, economic and military assistance have been particularly important. Soviet use of aid programs to influence the Third World began in the post-Stalin period. The construction of large, showy (and sometimes economically useless) projects in the underdeveloped countries was a hallmark of Khrushchev's foreign policy. Brezhnev brought more economic rationality to Soviet aid programs, replacing the show projects with ones better designed to bring economic benefits to the Soviet Union as well as to the recipients.

"Mutual economic benefit," notes Roger Kanet, became one of the central purposes behind Moscow's program of economic assistance during the 1970's. Other objectives of the Soviet program of economic assistance are: to support "progressive" or anti-Western regimes; to reduce the dependence of Third World countries on the United States; and to obtain influence in countries that are strategically located. Kanet stresses the interrelationship between Soviet economic aid and trade. A substantial portion of Soviet exports now consists of machinery and equipment for projects which have been developed with Soviet aid, and some imports come from projects originally financed by Soviet assistance. Third World trade is also important as a source of hard currency for Moscow. Soviet sales of manufactured goods, military equipment and petroleum are an important source of income for the purchase of needed raw materials such as bauxite and phosphates. In the future one can expect, according to Kanet, "pragmatic developments in Soviet foreign economic policy . . . to become a permanent factor in overall Soviet policy toward the developing countries."

During the past decade there has been an important shift in

emphasis away from economic assistance to a far greater reliance upon military aid as a means of ties with the Third World. The objectives of Soviet military aid are to undermine and supplant Western influence, to contain Chinese influence, to establish military bases to project Soviet power, and to gain economically. With regard to the last mentioned goal—economic gain—the transfer of arms has been an important source of hard currency for the Kremlin. In 1977 for example, the Soviet Union reportedly acquired an estimated $1.5 billion in hard currency through arms sales alone. On the negative side, however, it needs to be noted that a substantial portion of Soviet military aid is simply never repaid.

How successful has the Soviet military program been? Roger Pajak describes a mixture of successes and failures, though on balance his assessment is, from the Soviet perspective, more positive than negative. "Military assistance," notes Pajak, "... has proven to be one of Moscow's most effective, flexible, and enduring instruments for establishing a position of influence in the nonaligned countries." Today several strategically located countries—notably Afghanistan, Algeria, Iraq, Libya and Syria— have military forces largely equipped with Soviet arms and are thus dependent upon Moscow for parts, supplies and servicing.

Still, there is a serious question of how extensive or durable the influence achieved by the military connection really is. Robert Donaldson argues that the Soviets have found it very difficult to sustain their influence or to prop up client regimes exclusively by military means. The Kremlin's greatest success to date has been in the Arab world, and this was a consequence of the Arab-Israeli conflict, a situation it did not create. Moscow cannot determine the domestic or foreign policy of any of its clients, and, as Pajak points out, many of the largest recipients of Soviet arms have in recent years opposed Moscow on very important issues.

With all of its limitations, military arms still constitute the single best instrument for influence available to the Kremlin. Certainly nothing else has been shown to be more effective. As a possible model for development for the Third World the Soviet Union has been a conspicuous failure. By its own choice, the Soviet Union is not a major factor in the economic development of the Third World, and as Donaldson comments, its "limited international economic capabilities" undermine its "expanding political ambitions in the Third World." Soviet trade is a marginal part of the total international trade of the Third World, comprising only about 1/15 of the amount of trade conducted between the developed capitalist countries and the developing nations. Nor is Soviet economic aid any more substantial. The USSR's average annual aid contribution amounts to about .05 percent of its GNP compared to about .33 percent for the Western countries.

During the 1970's the Third World pressed vigorously for the creation of what they call a New International Economic Order (NIEO) which was intended to lead to a new distribution of resources and wealth between the developing and the developed economies of the world. Though itself a developed economy, the USSR has refused to participate in the dialogue leading to the NIEO. Moscow has attempted to harness the economic plight of the world's poorer countries onto its political contest with the West. The Soviet Union's argument is that the West, not the East, is responsible for Third World poverty and that its responsibility is limited to restraining "imperialism." That stance, plus the generally hard bargains driven by Moscow in its trade relations, encounters increasing resentment among Third World leaders. As Donaldson concludes: "Moscow's economic policies. . .may have reached a point of diminishing returns."

Finally, what are the implications of Soviet involvement in the Third World for US foreign defense policies? Among the authors represented here, only Keith Dunn addressed himself directly to this question, though the findings of all of them are relevant to American foreign policy.

To begin with, it is clear that Soviet involvement in the Third World is antagonistic to Western interests in general and to US interests in particular. There is a consensus represented here that an underlying purpose of Soviet activity in Asia, Africa, and Middle East and Latin America is to undermine US influence in favor of the Soviet Union. Thus, in this arena the cold war continues. Agreement breaks down, however, over the question as to how effective an adversary the Soviet Union has been.

Part of the problem lies in the elusiveness of the concept of influence. The authors represented here generally use the concept in a manner similar to that developed by Alvin Rubinstein: "influence is manifested when A (the Soviet leadership) affects, through non-military means, directly or indirectly, the behavior of B. . . .so that it rebounds to the policy advantages of A."[1] As Rubinstein demonstrates in his classic study of Soviet-Egyptian relations, the concept of influence is difficult to operationalize or measure. Thus while one can easily demonstrate a greater Soviet presence in the Third World at the beginning of the 1980's than a decade ago, one cannot equate that presence with influence.

The evidence adduced in these studies is that Soviet influence in the Third World remains limited. Where a country heavily mortgages its military establishment to the Soviet Union as Cuba and Vietnam have done, the fact of Soviet influence is undeniable. But otherwise Moscow has rarely been able to compel a Third World government to adopt a policy that it was not inclined to pursue anyway. In those instances where one did—the issue was marginal to the complying party. On an important issue, such as admitting Communists into Third World governments, the Soviet Union has been notably unsuccessful. Even governments heavily indebted to Moscow have been able to maintain a wide margin for maneuver by balancing other major power influence against that of the Soviet Union. Iraq, for example, was able to balance French power against that of the USSR, and Vietnam balanced China against the Soviet Union during the period of the Vietnam War.

Many of Moscow's biggest victories have resulted from events over which it had no control. The collapse of Portuguese rule in Africa led to the formation of anti-Western regimes which automatically looked to the Soviet Union for support. The Islamic revolution in Iran led to the downfall of one of the staunchest pro-American governments in the Middle East. Even some US policies calculated to stabilize Third World politics such as the Camp David agreement between Egypt and Israel produced side effects beneficial to the Kremlin. There is a tendency, which Dunn cautions against, to assume that every defeat suffered by the United States in the Third World is the result of Soviet cunning and planning. In fact, like the West, the Soviet Union sometimes comes out looking good in spite of what it did.

The prescriptions for American policy of these findings are largely implicit and, of necessity, general. They suggest that the focus of American policy should be more on the internal conditions of the Third World and less on the Soviet connection. There are serious limits on the ability of either side to influence, let alone control, what happens in these countries. The United States might learn from Soviet failures the limits of great power capabilities.

Short of outright military intervention, which can be undertaken only under very limited circumstances, the use of military instruments is less effective than the use of economic measures. Though it is a powerful nation, the United States is subject to more political restraints on the use of force than is the Soviet Union. It should, therefore, give priority to the use of economic instruments over military measures in the Third World. However unlikely the prospects, particularly since the Soviet invasion of Afghanistan, the United States should make an effort to enlist the cooperation of the Soviet Union to promote the economic development of the developing countries. If performance counts for more than rhetoric, in the long run the United States is in a better position than the Soviet Union to influence the outcome of events in the Third World.

ENDNOTE

1. Alvin Z. Rubinstein, *Red Star on the Nile: The Soviet-Egyptian Influence Relationship Since the June War,* Princeton: Princeton University Press, 1977, p. xiv.

CONTRIBUTORS

DR. ROBERT H. DONALDSON is Professor of Political Science and Associate Dean of the College of Arts and Sciences at Vanderbilt University. Dr. Donaldson holds a PhD from Harvard University and has been a Consultant to the Bureau of Intelligence and Research at the Department of State under the auspices of the Council on Foreign Relations Fellowship Program. He was a visiting professor with the Strategic Studies Institute from 1978 to 1979.. He has contributed numerous articles and chapters on Soviet and American foreign policies to scholarly publications and is author of *Soviet Policy Toward India: Ideology and Strategy* (1974).

DR. DAVID E. ALBRIGHT is Senior Text Editor of the journal, *Problems of Communism*. Previously he was a research associate at the Council on Foreign Relations. Dr. Albright holds a bachelor's and master's degree from Indiana University in journalism. He earned a certificate from the Russian Institute at Columbia University as well as a doctorate in international relations from that institution. He is editor of and contributor to *Communism in Africa* (1980), *Communism and Political Systems in Western Europe* (1979), and co-editor of and contributor to *The Communist State and Africa* (forthcoming in 1981).

LIEUTENANT COLONEL EDWARD A. CORCORAN joined the Strategic Studies Institute in 1978 after a tour as materiel officer at an ammunition depot in Korea. An ordnance officer with a background in missiles and special weapons, he holds a doctorate in political science from Columbia University and is a member of the Foreign Area Officers Program specializing in the Soviet Union. Past assignments have included service in the Office of the Deputy Chief of Staff for Intelligence in Headquarters, US Army Europe, and as a liaison officer to the Soviet Commander-in-Chief in East Germany.

DR. W. RAYMOND DUNCAN is Distinguished Teaching Professor of Political Science and International Affairs and Director of the Global Studies Program at the State University of New York at Brockport. He holds a bachelor's degree in political science from the University of California at Riverside, masters degrees in international affairs and law and diplomacy from the Fletcher School of Law and Diplomacy, and a doctorate in international affairs from the same institution. Dr. Duncan is the author of *Latin American Politics: A Developmental Approach* (1976), the editor of *Soviet Policy in Developing Countries* (1970) and of *Soviet Policy in the Third World* (1980), and the co-editor of *The Quest for Change in Latin America* (1970).

DR. KEITH A. DUNN joined the Strategic Studies Institute as a civilian in the summer of 1977. Prior to that time he was an Army intelligence officer. Dr. Dunn earned a master's degree and doctorate from the University of Missouri in American diplomatic relations, and has written and published articles on the interrelationships between detente and deterrence, the origins of the Cold War, and the Soviet military.

453

DR. ROBERT O. FREEDMAN is Dean of the Peggy Meyerhoff Pearlstone School of Graduate Studies and Professor of Political Science at the Baltimore Hebrew College. Dr. Freedman received a bachelor's degree in diplomatic history from the University of Pennsylvania. He is a graduate of Columbia University's Russian Institute, and he also earned his master's and doctorate from Columbia University. He has written two books, *Economic Warfare in the Communist Bloc: A Study of Soviet Economic Pressure Against Yugoslavia, Albania, and Communist China* (1970) and *Soviet Policy Toward the Middle East Since 1970* (1975); the latter book appeared in a revised and expanded edition in December 1978. In addition, he is editor of the book, *World Politics and the Arab-Israeli Conflict* (1979). Prior to coming to Baltimore, Dr. Freedman served as Associate Professor of Political Science and Russian and Middle East Area Specialist at Marquette University and, until completion of his Army service in July 1970, he was Assistant Professor of Russian History and Government at the US Military Academy at West Point.

DR. ROBERT G. IRANI joined the Strategic Studies Institute in 1975. He graduated from Glenville State College with a bachelor's degree in history and social sciences, earned a master's degree in international relations from the American University, and a second master's degree and a doctorate in government and politics and international relations from the Univerity of Maryland. Dr. Irani's research abroad includes trips to both sides of the Persian Gulf and one year of field research as a Research-Associate at the Institute for International Political and Economic Studies, Tehran, Iran. His published works include, *American Diplomacy: An Option Analysis of the Azerbaijan Crisis, 1945-1946, (1978); Iran's Foreign Policy, 1941-1974: A Selective Bibliography, (1976);* and several articles in English and Farsi for professional journals.

DR. ROGER E. KANET is Professor of Political Science at the University of Illinois at Urbana-Champaign. He received a Ph.B. from Berchmanskolleg (Pullach-bei-Munchen, Germany), a bachelor's degree from Xavier University, master's degrees from Lehigh University and Princeton University in international relations and political science respectively, and a doctorate in political science from Princeton University. He has held research grants from the American Council of Learned Societies, the NATO Faculty Fellowship Program, the US Department of State, the International Research and Exchanges Board, and the US Information Agency. His published works include numerous articles on Soviet and East European foreign policy and the following edited or co-edited books: *The Behavioral Revolution and Communist Studies* (1971); *On the Road to Communism*, with Ivan Volgyes (1972); *The Soviet Union and the Developing Nations* (1974); *Soviet and East European Foreign Policy: a Bibliography . . . .* (1974); *Soviet Economic and Political Relations with the Developing World*, with Donna Bahry (1975); and *Policy and Politics in Gierek's Poland*, with Maurice D. Simon (1980).

454

DR. ARTHUR JAY KLINGHOFFER is a Professor of Political Science at Rutgers University. He received his bachelor's degree from the University of Michigan and his master's and doctoral degrees from Columbia University. He also received a certificate from the Russian Institute of Columbia University. Dr. Klinghoffer is the author of *Soviet Perspectives on African Socialism* (1969), *Soviet Oil Politics in the Middle East and Soviet-American Relations* (1976), *The Soviet Union and International Oil Politics* (1977), and *The Soviet Union and the Angolan War* forthcoming. He contributed to two collections edited by Roger Kanet, *On the Road to Communism* (1972) and *The Soviet Union and the Developing Nations* (1974), and one by Della Sheldon, *Dimensions of Detente* (1978). His articles have appeared in *Africa Report*, *Mizan*, *African Affairs*, *Journal of Modern African Studies*, *The World Today*, *International Relations*, *Asian Survey*, and the *Journal of the Institute for Socioeconomic Studies*.

DR. GABRIEL MARCELLA joined the Strategic Studies Institute in 1974. A graduate of St. Joseph's University, he holds a master's degree in history from Syracuse University and a doctorate in Latin American history from the University of Notre Dame. He was awarded a Fulbright-Hayes fellowship for postgraduate study in Ecuador, 1964-65, and taught at Temple, Notre Dame, and Indiana Universities. Dr. Marcella has written on a broad range of topics relating to Latin American history and politics, international affairs, and Italian communism.

DR. M. RAJAN MENON joined Vanderbilt University as an Assistant Professor of Political Science in 1978. He graduated from St. Stephen's College, Delhi, with a bachelor's degree in history, earned a master's degree in international relations from Lehigh University, and a doctorate in political science from the University of Illinois at Urbana-Champaign. He has contributed to *Asian Survey, Current History,* and *Osteuropa*.

DR. JOSEPH L. NOGEE is Professor of Political Science and Director of the Russian Studies Program at the University of Houston. He is currently a visiting research professor with the Strategic Studies Institute, US Army War College. Previously he taught at New York University and Vanderbilt University. Dr. Nogee earned a bachelor's degree in foreign service from the Georgetown School of Foreign Service, a master's degree in history from the University of Chicago, and a doctorate in international relations from Yale University. He is the author of *Soviet Policy Toward International Control of Atomic Energy* (1961); co-author of *The Politics of Disarmament* (1962) and of *Soviet Foreign Policy Since World War II* (forthcoming); and editor of *Man, the State and Society in the Soviet Union* (1972). Dr. Nogee has served on the Council of the American Political Science Association and is currently on the Editorial Board of *The American Political Science Review*.

DR. ROGER F. PAJAK, Senior Foreign Affairs Advisor with the US Arms Control and Disarmament Agency, has been with ACDA since 1971. He received his bachelor's degree in international relations from Michigan State University, his master's degree in Soviet area studies from Harvard University, and his doctorate in international relations and Soviet studies from American University. He spent two years in the US Army as a military intelligence officer from 1961-63, and has been with the US Government as a Soviet foreign affairs specialist since that time. Besides speaking overseas on behalf of the US International Communication Agency, Dr. Pajak has lectured at the National War College, the Foreign Service Institute, the Army Russian Institute, the Council on Foreign Relations, and at various universities. He is the author of *Soviet Arms Aid in the Middle East* (1976), as well as a number of studies on Soviet Middle East policy and the international arms trade.

DR. DANIEL S. PAPP is an Associate Professor of International Affairs at Georgia Institute of Technology. From 1977 to 1978, he served as a research professor with the Strategic Studies Institute. A graduate of Dartmouth College, he received his doctorate in international affairs at the University of Miami's Center for Advanced International Studies. He has published articles in *International Journal, Social Science Quarterly, Soviet Union, Resources Policy, Parameters, US Naval War College Review, Air University Review,* and *Current History.* He is the author of *Vietnam: The View from Moscow, Peking and Washington* (1980).

MR. DOUGLAS PIKE is a US Foreign Service Information Officer who has served most of his adult life in Asia. He was educated at the University of California, Berkeley, American University, and the Massachusetts Institute of Technology. For the past 18 years he has been professionally concerned with the Communist movements in Indochina, serving in posts in Saigon, Tokyo, Hong Kong and Taipei. He was a member of the State Department Policy Planning Council 1974-77 and currently is on detail to the International Security Agency at the Pentagon. Mr. Pike is the author of *Viet Cong: The Organization and Techniques of the National Liberation Front of South Vietnam* (1964), *War, Peace and the Vietcong* (1970), and *History of Vietnamese Communism* (1978). Currently he is working on a book on the present leadership in Hanoi.

DR. RICHARD B. REMNEK is a member of the professional staff of the Center for Naval Analyses, Alexandria, Virginia. He received a bachelor's degree from Brandeis University, a master's degree in Russian area studies from the City University of New York, and a doctorate in political science from Duke University. From 1970 to 1977 he was Assistant Professor of Political Science at Memphis State University. Dr. Remnek is the author of *Soviet Scholars and Soviet Foreign Policy: A Case Study of Soviet Policy Towards India* (1975), and editor of *Social Scientists and Policy Making in the USSR* (1977). He has also authored a number of articles on Soviet political and military affairs.

DR. THOMAS W. ROBINSON is Professor of International Relations at the National War College, National Defense University. He previously taught at the University of Washington, was Visiting Fellow at the Council on Foreign Relations, and was a member of the Research Staff of the Rand Corporation Social Science Department. Additionally, he has taught at Dartmouth, Columbia, Princeton, and UCLA. Dr. Robinson received his bachelor's degree in physics and mathematics from Carleton College and the master's and doctorate in international relations and Soviet studies from Columbia University. He has published two books and numerous articles in the fields of Chinese and Soviet policies, Asian international relations, and international relations theory.

DR. ALVIN Z. RUBINSTEIN is Professor of Political Science at the University of Pennsylvania. He earned his bachelor's degree in government from the City College of New York and his master's degree and doctorate in political science from the University of Pennsylvania. His published works include: *Red Star on the Nile: The Soviet-Egyptian Influence Relationship Since the June War* (1977), *The Foreign Policy of the Soviet Union*, 3rd ed. (1972), *Yugoslavia and the Nonaligned World* (1970), and, *The Soviets in International Organizations* (1964). He is also editor of *Soviet and Chinese Influence in the Third World* (1975).

DR. PAUL E. SIGMUND is Professor of Politics and Research Associate of the Center of International Studies at Princeton University. He received his bachelor's degree from Georgetown University and his master's and doctrate from Harvard where he was instructor and senior tutor in government before coming to Princeton. He has also taught as a Visiting Professor at Bryn Mawr and at universities in Ghana and Chile. Professor Sigmund is the author of numerous articles on political theory and Latin American politics and his most recent books include *Natural Law in Political Thought* (1971), *The Ideologies of the Developing Nations* (2nd rev. ed., 1972), *The Overthrow of Allende and the Politics of Chile* (1977), and *The Multinational Corporation in Latin America: Beyond Nationalization* (forthcoming).

DR. SHIRIN TAHIR-KHELI has been an Assistant Professor of Political Science at Temple University since 1973 and a Research Fellow at the Foreign Policy Research Institute since 1978. A graduate of Ohio Wesleyan University, she received her master's degree and doctorate in international relations from the University of Pennsylvania. Her publications include a book on *Soviet Moves in Asia* (1976), a study on "Nuclear Decision-Making in Pakistan" in James Katz and Onkar Marwah, eds., *Nuclear Decision-Making in Developing Countries* (forthcoming), and several articles on South and Southwest Asia in such journals as *Naval War College Review, Orbis, Asian Survey,* and *World Affairs.* She is currently engaged in a study of *The United States-Pakistan Influence Relationship After 1971* (1980).

457

DR. THOMAS L. WILBORN has been with the Strategic Studies Institute since 1974. He earned a bachelor's degree in journalism and a master's degree and doctorate in political science from the University of Kentucky. In addition to teaching political science and international relations at Madison College and Central Missouri State University, his professional background includes a position with the University of Kentucky educational assistance program at Bandung, Indonesia. Dr. Wilborn is the author of several research memoranda on nuclear strategy and Southeast Asia and has written book reviews published in professional journals.